Society and Economy i
1700–1850

For both c_____ _aries and later historians the 'industrial revolution' is viewed as a _____ng point' in modern British history. There is no doubt that change occurred, but what was the nature of that change and how did it affect rural and urban society?

Beginning with an examination of the nature of History and of Britain in 1700, this volume focuses on the economic and social aspects of the Industrial Revolution. Unlike many previous textbooks on the same period this emphasizes British history, and deals with developments in Wales, Scotland and Ireland in their own right. It is the emphasis on the diversity not the uniformity of experience, on continuities as well as change in this crucial period of development which makes this volume distinctive.

In a companion title Richard Brown completes his examination of the period and looks at the changes that took place in Britain's political system and in its religious affiliations.

Church and State in Modern Britain completes Richard Brown's two-part study of British history 1700–1850.

Richard Brown, co-editor of *Teaching History*, is currently SCIL co-ordinator at Manshead School, Bedfordshire.

Society and Economy in Modern Britain 1700–1850

Richard Brown

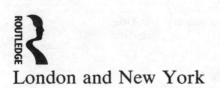

London and New York

First published 1991 by Routledge
11 New Fetter Lane, London EC4P 4EE

Simultaneously published in the USA and Canada
by Routledge
a division of Routledge, Chapman and Hall, Inc.
29 West 35th Street, New York, NY 10001

Phototypeset in 10/12 pt Times Linotron 300
by Input Typesetting Ltd, London
Printed in England by Clays Ltd, St Ives plc.

British Library Cataloguing in Publication Data
Brown, Richard
  Society and Economy in Modern Britain 1700–1850
  I. Great Britain. 1714–1837
  I. Title
  941.07

Library of Congress Cataloging-in-Publication Data
Brown, Richard
    Society and economy in modern Britain 1700–1850
    Richard Brown.
      p. cm.
    Includes bibliographical references.
      1. Great Britain—Economic conditions—18th century.
    2. Great Britain—Economic conditions—19th century.
    3. Great Britain—Social conditions—18th century.
    4. Great Britain—Social conditions—19th century. I. Title.
    HC254.5.B92 1991   91–8163
    330.942′009′034—dc20   CIP

ISBN 0–415 01120–5
      0–415 01121–3 (pbk)

To Margaret, without whose constant support
I could not have written these volumes

Contents

Figures

Tables

Preface

'What is history?', asked Robert Lowell in his *Notebooks 1967–68*,[1] and with the wisdom of the poet he responded: 'What you cannot touch.' Into the fabric of our own existence we incorporate the records and the multifarious expressions of thought and action of past peoples and social groups. They put us in touch with human history and yet they do not enable us to touch that history alive. They compel us to listen and yet their sound alone cannot bring us fully within hearing presence of the word of history. Intangible and inaudible though it is, this historical reality, this sense of 'pastness' is nevertheless formatively present in our lives and reflections. Lowell's question remains to incite us to improve our understanding of that past and his answer also stands as a caution against any belief that we can fully discover what happened and why.

People study history for many reasons but all have in common a need to explain and understand past societies. We ask questions, many of which have their origins in our own present-day experience, like how did individuals react to rapid change, why did society change so slowly, what was it like to live then, have people's needs changed, what was the nature of belief or power and how did people register their protest against the action or inaction of those in government? In attempting to answer questions like these it seems to me perfectly legitimate to use ideas and methodologies from disciplines other than history. We may begin to understand people in the past by examining, for example, the social sciences, geography, technology, science and philosophy. We may develop 'models' which can be applied to past events and people. But they must always be grounded in the available sources of information, the raw data from which historians draw their conclusions.

Society and Economy in Modern Britain is the first of two volumes which consider the economic, social and political history of Britain from the beginning of the eighteenth century until 1850. Two further volumes will bring the story up to date. It is aimed at students studying A or AS Level examinations and first-year students at university or college. This book covers the history of Britain from the beginning of the eighteenth century through to the mid-nineteenth century. It provides an explanation of what actually happened and why, since narrative and description form the basis for historical studies at all levels. It examines how historians have interpreted the past and provides a conceptual framework through which the past can be illuminated. Each chapter has references to both contemporary and secondary sources. Volume I divides into two parts, corresponding to the economic and social dimensions of past experience. Chapters 1 and 2 set the scene, outlining the nature of history and what Britain was like around 1700. Chapters 3 to 12 cover the major economic themes of the period, in particular the issue of the economic revolutions. Chapters 13 to 19 cover the main social questions. Any division of the past is bound to be arbitrary to a certain extent. Religion, and popular politics are left to the second volume.

It is a history of Britain in which the histories of Wales, Scotland and Ireland are given an emphasis in their own right not simply mentioned when their experience had some impact on England. Recent trends in historical writing have led to a growing awareness of the role of women in the past and particularly their marginalization in a male-dominated and male-focused society. Historians have also become aware of the place of ethnic minorities within the dominant cultural hegemony. Both these issues receive particular emphasis. The past was, like the present, lived and if we are to understand that fully it is fundamental that we should aim to achieve some 'totality' of past experience.

My debt to others in writing this volume will be obvious from the references to each chapter. I hope I have not misrepresented their views. I am particularly grateful to Bedfordshire County Council for giving me two years secondment to do research in education at Cambridge University between 1985 and 1987. This gave me time to think out my ideas in a less hectic atmosphere than that of a school. I have been fortunate to teach in an authority and at two schools, Houghton Regis Upper School and Manshead School, Dunstable, in which students have been both stimulating and unwilling to accept my views as 'tablets from Sinai'. My thanks to Anna Fedden who originated the project, Nancy Marten who kept me going over the writing period, and Claire L'Enfant, Julia Hall and Antonia Pledger who saw it to its conclusion. Above all I must thank my wife and children whose forbearance, patience and willingness to leave me in peace created the right atmosphere in which to write. This book is dedicated to them.

Richard Brown
1 January 1990

Note

1 R. Lowell *Notebooks 1967–68*, Farrar, Strauss and Giroux, 1967.

1 The nature of history

'A SOCIAL NECESSITY'

Much has been written about the uses of history.[1] Understanding of the present and the potential of the future is impossible without a temporal perspective. History is to society what remembered experience is to an individual. Marwick sees it as 'a social necessity'. There are three practical advantages to society from the study of the past. First, it alerts people to the sheer variety of human mentality and achievement and thus to the range of possibilities people have now. History provides imaginative range but is also an inventory of assets whose value may only be realized by later generations. Secondly, it is a source of precedent and prediction. Though this is primarily a justification for contemporary history, the drawing of historical analogies, often half-consciously, is a habitual and unavoidable dimension of human reasoning. Comparisons across time can illuminate the present by highlighting both what is recurrent and what is new, what is durable, transient and contingent on our present conditions. Finally history provides a critique of the myths that pervade society. It has a crucial corrective function in that by removing myths, it can act as the conscience of society.

HISTORY – A DEFINITION

History is about people in society, their actions and interactions, their beliefs and prejudices, their pasts and presents. 'People in society' means people as individuals, communities, groups, institutions, states and nations. Individuals can be simultaneously members of a community (the village where they live), an institution (the church they attend), a group (the occupational group they belong to), a nation (Wales, Scotland, Ireland or England) as well as a member of the United Kingdom. 'Actions and interactions' mean the ways in which people behave as individuals and communities and the ways they react to each other. 'Beliefs and prejudices' mean the ways in which individuals and communities perceive(d) 'their worlds', the values upon which 'their worlds' are based and the consequences of this in terms of their own perceptions of others and others' perceptions of them. 'Pasts and presents' provide people in society with an individual and collective memory, a storehouse of experience through which to develop their sense of social identity, to judge present actions and assess future prospects.

HISTORIANS ON HISTORY – DIFFERING METHODOLOGIES

History is also about how historians examine and interpret the past.[2] Although there are more than 'two kinds of history' the recent debate between Fogel and Elton brings out some of the different ways in which historians approach their study. Fogel sees 'traditional historians' as aspiring

> to portray the entire range of human experience, to capture all of the essential features of the civilizations they were studying, and to do so in a way that would clearly have relevance to the present. They were continually searching for 'synthesising principles' that would allow them to relate in a meaningful way the myriad of facts that they were uncovering.[3]

In their analysis, he maintains, historians turn to the social sciences for insights into behaviour. But they recoil from its analytical methods because these threaten history's intrinsic qualities: 'its literary art, its personal voice and its concern with the countless subtle questions that are involved in the notion of individuality'.[4]

Fogel believes that this is the result of the way 'traditional' historians evaluate evidence. They use a 'legal model' which is well suited to examining specific events and individuals but which is suspicious of statistical evidence and scientific method.

So how do 'cliometricians' like Fogel approach their study of the past? First, they want it to be based on explicit models of human behaviour. Secondly, they believe that all historians use behavioural models in relating the facts of history to each other. The difference is that for traditional historians these are implicit, vague and incomplete whereas for the cliometrician they are explicit, specific and complete. They allow historians to cut through the diversity of experience and behaviour that characterize human activity and to make judgements as to why people are likely to have behaved as they did. Thirdly, this approach often leads cliometricians to represent behaviour in mathematical equations which are then verified or refuted with quantitative evidence. However, quantification is not the universal characteristic of this approach. The crux of the difference between these two methods is that

> many traditional historians tend to be highly focused on specific individuals, on particular institutions, on particular ideas, and on nonrepetitive

occurrences . . . they make only limited use of explicit behavioural models and usually rely on literary models. Cliometricians tend to be highly focused on collections of individuals, on categories of institutions and on repetitive occurrences. . . . These involve explicit behavioural models and . . . quantitative evidence.[5]

The traditional historian may want to explain why Thomas Edwards of Risby, Suffolk stole four hen's eggs in 1864 whereas the cliometrician would wish to understand why egg-stealing expanded in the nineteenth century. Both types of history are concerned with explaining the past. Both search for meaning using evidence that is often incomplete, inconsistent and ambiguous. Historians can and should use any method, concept, or model which help them to do this.

HISTORY AND ITS CONCEPTS

Historians examine the past through a number of methodological concepts. First, historians need to have an understanding of historical context, a sense of time and chronology. Secondly, the nature of events, their causation and consequences needs to be made clear. Piecing together what happened in the past will, thirdly, result in narrative, analysis and synthesis. Fourthly, historians examine the past in terms of change and continuity, progression, regression, evolution or revolution and discrete phenomena as 'agents' or 'inhibitors' of change. It is now fashionable to emphasize the continuities in historical experience and to play down the importance and effects of change and discontinuities in the past.[6] Finally, history is less about truth than about possible and tentative interpretations on the basis of the available evidence.

What concepts can historians use to examine people in the past? These can be divided into –

  (i) understanding people in the past as individuals and social groups.
 (ii) understanding the role of specific individuals and social groups.
(iii) understanding the actions, values, beliefs, attitudes and decisions of individuals.
 (iv) understanding people in their local, regional, national and global context.
  (v) understanding the various choices open to individuals and groups at particular times and why they opted for one direction rather than another.
 (vi) understanding the different dimensions of life which people in the past have experienced and the relationship between them – I will highlight economic, social, political, cultural (including religious), technological and scientific and environmental experiences.
(vii) understanding that people live different lives within the same time-scales – the diversity of contemporary experience.

(viii) understanding that the historical process is one of development, that, despite appearances, it is not static and that development may be resisted.

(ix) understanding the relationships, tensions and conflicts that exist between individuals and social groups.

Through the use of these concepts, and the available evidence historians can attempt to explain what happened in the past.

PEOPLE IN HISTORY

Individuals in the eighteenth and nineteenth centuries lived in various types of association. There were quite definite forms of the family, marriage, religious worship, property and inheritance, economic organization, governmental procedures and so on and these formed something more than the individuals who lived and behaved within their contexts.

These associational forms were interconnected. Together they made up a total social system and it is important that they are examined as part of that system. Three points make this clear. First, a social system came into being and regulated the activities and experiences of people who shared the same collective conditions of life – who worked out a particular pattern of life in relation to the same ecological constraints, economic resources and historical experiences. In eighteenth-century Britain this was evident not just in the collective conditions of Ireland, Wales, Scotland and England but in different regional experiences and expectations. Secondly, associational forms were essentially forms of regulation. Each association had its own set of rules – some implicit, others formalized – by which some individuals exercised authority which others were obliged to obey; by which different tasks were defined; through which satisfactory work or behaviour was rewarded and the unsatisfactory punished. Finally, the place of a particular association within the social system was made even more clear by the existence of institutions which actually linked and inter-penetrated them all. 'Marriage', for example, was not just a familial one but was also a religious, legal, political and economic institution.

Associations and social systems are essentially characterized by meanings and values. Every social institution contains a set of values at its core: it forbids certain things and requires, upholds and encourages others. Although not all individuals agreed or abided by all the values embodied within social institutions, the network of regulation was a moral condition.

Individuals born within a particular social system with particular associational forms have a multi-dimensional private experience from birth to death quite different from those born within another. The experience of a Welsh farmer was different from a Scottish one. These different private experiences are articulated, understood and expressed in terms of the language with which they are familiar. The collective conditions and social systems shared by individuals have played a large part in making private experience and in shaping the nature of individuals. This view does not negate the role of individuals in the past but places them in a context that did influence, though did not determine, their responses to particular circumstances. For example, in periods of high food prices those whose standard of living was directly affected were likely to riot for the restoration of the 'moral economy'. But similar circumstances did not always bring about the same individual response.

Associations and the social system will be inherited by generation after generation. Although certain aspects will be sustained and continued, others will be gradually, or in some cases radically, altered. This 'heritage' plays an important part in the way that individuals perceive their presents. It establishes systems of culture based upon inherited symbols, meanings, sentiments, values, ideologies and sanctions. Through cultural hegemony, control over values and beliefs, the governing association in eighteenth- and early nineteenth-century Britain was able to maintain its dominant economic and political position. Inherited experience underpins existing cultural values.

HISTORY AND CHANGE

This can help historians understand features of importance in a society at a particular point in time. But it does not explain the dynamics of change within that society. There is a surprising amount of agreement between social theorists about how societies change. First, the contemporary social experience (at any point in history) was, they maintain, the result of social evolution. Secondly, they agree on the central importance of the transition from a predominantly 'traditional' to a predominantly 'rational and contractual' social order. Thirdly, the promise and threat of this transformation is recognized, as is the necessity for the deliberate reconstruction of associations and institutions. These theories have a direct relevance in explaining the development from a pre-industrial society (though whether it was a 'traditional' society is a separate question) to an industrial society in Britain. The development of industrial and particularly urban society led to existing forms of association and institutions being brought into question. Parliamentary reform, in 1832 and particularly in 1867 and 1885, was the result of the increasing difficulty in defending a demonstrably irrational system of suffrage. Developments in women's rights were part of the same process. Resistance to logical change, the defence of the indefensible, however, also played an important part in the chronology of these developments.

Richard Wilkinson

These sociological theories identify progress as the driving force behind change. Marx, for example, saw the creation of a more humane, non-exploiting society as the end of social development. But this is not the only possible explanation. Richard Wilkinson[7] argues that development is the result of a society outgrowing its resources and productive system. As the established economic system proved inadequate and subsistence problems became more severe, he maintains, a society is driven to change its methods

> Development comes out of poverty, not out of plenty as many economic theories would lead one to suppose. Poverty stimulates the search for additional sources of income and makes people willing to do things they may previously have avoided.[8]

He identifies the ending of constraints upon population growth as the major cause of change.[9] This led to growing resource scarcities. In England and Wales rising cost of living, falling real wages and population growth coincided before 1800: 'In English history there can be no mistaking the intimate connection between the periodic appearance of population pressure and economic development.'[10]

Wilkinson then goes on to analyse the English industrial revolution:

> The ecological roots of the English industrial revolution are not difficult to find. The initial stimulus to change came directly from resource shortages and other ecological effects of an economic system expanding to meet the needs of a population growing within a limited area.[11]

Population growth from the 1740s put pressure on land resources and Britain changed from the 1760s from being a net exporter of wheat to a net importer. Initially, change in industry did not involve the establishment of new industries but technical innovation in existing industries. Stimulus came from the limitations which land shortage imposed on the supply of industrial raw materials. Three examples illustrate his argument. First, the substitution of coal for wood. From the early sixteenth century there was a consistent increase in firewood prices. By the 1630s it was about two and a half times as expensive in relation to other prices as it had been in 1500. Rising cost and growing scarcity put pressure upon both industrial and domestic consumers with the result that during the seventeenth century there was a shift from wood to coal. Iron-smelting was the only major industry not to make this change by 1700. It took ironmasters longer to work out a solution because of the complexity of smelting iron with coal. The move to coal, Wilkinson argues, was followed by other innovations: 'The invention of the steam-engine was a direct result of the new technical problems posed by deep mines.'[12]

Using coal meant that woodlands could be converted to arable farming and the pressure of feeding a growing population eased. Second, the introduction of canals and then railways had the same effect. They released land which had previously been used to provide horse feed. In 1800 a canal engineer wrote that

> as one horse on an average consumes the produce of four acres of land, and there are 1,350,000 in this island that pay the horse-tax, of course there must be 5,400,000 acres of land occupied in providing provender for them. How desirable any improvement that will lessen the keep of horses. . . . [13]

Wilkinson states that

> Undoubtedly one of the most important reasons for the commercial success of canals was the high price of horse feed. Only when competition for land had forced the price of horse feed sufficiently high was it worth expending labour on the construction of canals which allowed larger loads to be drawn by fewer horses.

Finally the growth of the cotton industry meant that the manufacture of clothing could be expanded without threatening the production of food.

Wilkinson admits that his analysis is based upon the cultural imperative of 'survival' and that it is neutral towards the place of progress in development.[14] But his ecological model is, he believes, based on the reality of living people not on some idealized form. Development is the response to actual and perceived 'needs' and 'wants' rather than some notion of human perfectibility.

Other models

There are alternative models: W. W. Rostow put forward his 'stages of economic growth' in 1960 and E. E. Hagen his 'theory of social change' in 1962. In 1965 the historian R. M. Hartwell proposed an approach to the industrial revolution based upon the techniques of developmental economics and as early as 1955 W. A. Lewis had recognized the social influences on economic development. Historians specialize in both time and place. This is the result of their need to reduce the volume of primary evidence to manageable proportions. This often leads them to ignore the interaction between the various themes.

Interactions

In attempting to explain or understand any problem historians are struggling with a number of interactions. It is possible to see one element as a 'prime mover', in the sense of being something from which all others follow. This is an attractive approach but it imposes an order on the past which was not obvious to contemporaries. At its extreme the 'prime mover' attitude can become Whiggish history, an approach which examines the past in relation to the present. A second approach is one that sees a particular factor as the stimulus to change – for example population growth stimulated agricultural change. This too is inadequate. It is clear that, important as the connection between population and agriculture was, their relationship must be explained in a wider context, of interaction between a number of social, economic and intellectual variables. It is in the mutual interaction of the various elements that make up a particular past that the best means of understanding that past is to be found.

CONCLUSIONS

To understand fully the development of Britain between 1700 and 1850 it is important that the mutual interaction between the main themes is established. One of the reasons why social and economic change appeals to many historians is that it allows them to get to grips with the historical experience of whole societies rather than with restricted elites or parliamentary sessions. This has led to a move towards 'total' history or *histoire intégrale*, examining the life of a total society in an integrated way. This has proved immensely difficult for a single country and has resulted in the geographical limits of the enquiry being narrowed down to a particular locality. 'Total' history may therefore mean local history. W. G. Hoskins maintains that 'The local historian is in a way like the old-fashioned G. P. of English medical history, now a fading memory confined to the more elderly among us, who treated Man as a whole.'[15]

History concerns both events and structures, individuals and groups, ideas and perceptions, reality and myth. Historians need to combine narrative with analytical skills. They need to re-create and give meaning as well as provide valid explanations and interpretations based on an objective analysis of primary and secondary evidence. But as Antonio Gramsci wrote, though he neglects the role of women, it is more than that

> I think you must like history, as I liked it when I was your age, because it deals with living men, and everything that concerns men, as many men as possible, all the men in the world in so far as they united together in society, and work and struggle and make a bid for a better life, all that can't fail to please you more than anything else. Isn't that right?[16]

NOTES

1 The most convenient recent statements are to be found in J. Tosh *The Pursuit of History*, Longman, 1984, pp. 1–26 and A. Marwick *The Nature of History*, 3rd edn, Macmillan, 1989.

2 On the question of historical method and writing see J. Cannon (ed.) *The Historian at Work*, Allen & Unwin, 1980; G. Kitson Clark *The Critical*

Historian, Heinemann, 1967 and R. W. Fogel and G. R. Elton *Which Road to the Past?*, Yale, 1983. P. Veyne *Writing History*, Wesleyan University Press, 1984 provides a valuable theoretical perspective. D. N. McCloskey *Econometric History*, Macmillan, 1987, summarizes the issues. C. Parker, *English Historical Tradition since 1850*, John Donald, 1990 is a critical account of the empiricist approach.

3 Fogel and Elton op. cit. p. 19.
4 ibid. p. 21.
5 ibid. p. 29.
6 D. Cannadine 'Change and Continuity in British History', *History Today*, April 1985, pp. 4–5 is a straightforward examination of the issues involved.
7 The following discussion is based upon R. Wilkinson *Poverty and Plenty – an Ecological Model of Economic Development*, Methuen, 1973.
8 ibid. p. 5.
9 ibid. pp. 57–89.
10 ibid. p. 81.
11 ibid. p. 112.
12 ibid. pp. 123–4.
13 ibid. p. 124.
14 ibid. pp. 217–18.
15 W. G. Hoskins *English Local History: the Past and the Future*, Leicester University Press, 1966, p. 21.
16 From a letter to his son written shortly before Gramsci's death in 1937, quoted in H. J. Kaye *The British Marxist Historians*, Polity Press, 1984, p. 222.

2 Britain in the early eighteenth century

In 1749 the philosopher Montesquieu made the distinction in his *The Spirit of the Laws* between the internal (social and psychological) and external (physical or environmental) aspects of human life suggesting that the link between them was to be found in legal structures which institutionalized a society's relationship with its environment.[1] He explained that different physical environments gave rise to different needs which in turn produced different modes of life. This chapter is concerned with outlining the contrasting experiences that existed in the early eighteenth century in the four parts which made up the British Isles.

GEOGRAPHY – STRUCTURE AND CLIMATE

Although the geological structure of the British Isles is extremely complex when looked at in detail, in broad outline it is quite simple.[2] The basic division is between the Highland zone of the west and north and the Lowland zone of the south and east and Ireland. The Highland zone consists of very old rocks eroded and shaped by glaciation in some areas leaving nothing but a thin covering of soil. But the glaciers also dumped heavy boulder clays and finely sifted sands and gravels. The human response to these differences in soil type, drainage and structure in the early eighteenth century was diversity of meadow, heath, pasture, arable field and bog. Oats were the main corn crop. Hunting and fishing took on a central importance in supplying basic needs. Defoe wrote in the 1720s of north-west Scotland that

> the people [live] dispersed among the hills without any settled towns. Their employment is chiefly hunting, which is, as we may say, their food; though they do also breed large quantities of black cattle, with which they pay their lairds or leaders for the rent of the lands . . . these cattle . . . are driven annually to England to be sold, and are even brought up to London. . . . [3]

The prevailing western winds bring high rainfall. Annual rainfall is rarely below 40 inches and in some areas of Wales, the Lake District, the

Western Isles and north-west Scotland it exceeds 100 inches. This too has influenced what people could do. Drainage is poor, the rain has washed out many of the nutrients leaving a soil capable of sustaining only poor vegetation. Altitude has the greatest impact on human activity. In the 1760s the Duke of Hamilton determined rent for his farms by height above sea-level – the higher the farm, the lower the rent. There was variation of human response to these different conditions. In Scotland, for example, there were differences in farming techniques between the wetter West Highlands and the East Highlands. In parts of Wales and Cornwall animals were driven up to the summer pastures and brought down to the shelter of their byres at the beginning of winter. In or around the Highland zone lie most of Britain's mineral resources: coal in Wales, Lancashire, Yorkshire, Durham and Scotland; tin, copper and kaolin in Cornwall; lead in the Mendips and Derbyshire; iron in the Forest of Dean, the Cleveland Hills and central Scotland.

Lowland Britain and Ireland contains as much diversity as the Highland zone (see Figure 2.1). The underlying rocks are softer and have weathered more quickly than those in the Highland zone to produce deeper and more fertile soils. There is less rain and the climate is generally less harsh. In Lowland Britain the type of soil also determines what sort of farming is possible. In the early eighteenth century the heavy clay soils were difficult to drain and plough. Lighter sandy soils were easier to till. In Ireland, for example, woodland was strongest below 500 feet and had been largely cleared so that the rich alluvial valleys could be used for pastoral or arable use. Flooding was a problem in the river valleys after heavy rain. The coastal area between the Humber estuary and the mid-east coast was turned to swampy fens by the sluggish estuarine rivers. Some advance had been made in the Fens proper in the seventeenth century as the result of the imported Dutch drainage methods associated with Cornelius Vermuyden.

PEOPLE AND PLACES

In 1700 there were about 4.9 million people living in England, 406,000 in Wales, about a million in Scotland and about 2.5 million in Ireland. In Ireland there were concentrations of population on the coastal plain from Belfast to Dublin and around Limerick and Cork in the west. In Scotland there were three sharp regional divisions: the greatest concentration was in the Central Lowlands with Edinburgh containing about 40,000 people and Glasgow 12,000. The Southern Uplands, with their better soils and climate, were more densely populated than the Highlands with its settled population concentrated on the coasts and islands. The population of Wales was evenly distributed though some concentration had already begun in the Vale of Glamorgan. Towns were small. Wrexham was the largest, with only about 3,000 people. In England there was a marked

Figure 2.1 Physical divisions and resources in Britain

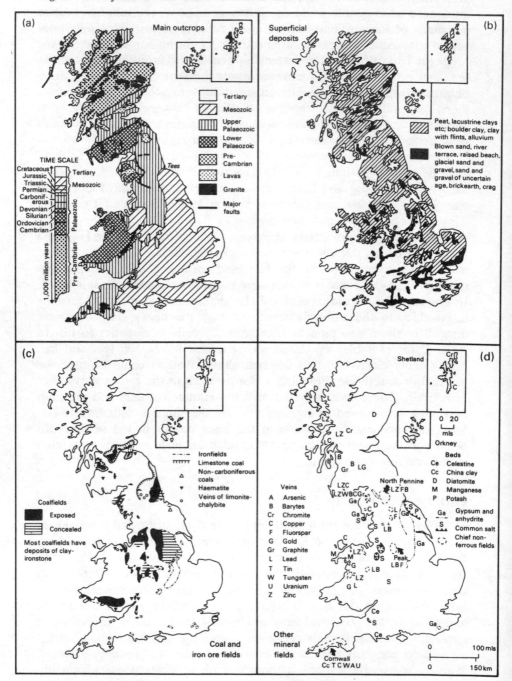

(a) Main outcrops

Tertiary
Mesozoic
Upper Palaeozoic
Lower Palaeozoic
Pre-Cambrian
Lavas
Granite
Major faults

TIME SCALE

Cretaceous — Tertiary
Jurassic
Triassic — Mesozoic
Permian
Carboniferous
Devonian — Palaeozoic
Silurian
Ordovician
Cambrian
Pre-Cambrian

1,000 million years

Tees
Exe

(b) Superficial deposits

Peat, lacustrine clays etc; boulder clay, clay with flints, alluvium
Blown sand, river terrace, raised beach, glacial sand and gravel, sand and gravel of uncertain age, brickearth, crag

(c)

Ironfields
Limestone coal
Non-carboniferous coals
Haematite
Veins of limonite-chalybite

Coalfields
Exposed
Concealed

Most coalfields have deposits of clay-ironstone

Coal and iron ore fields

(d) Shetland

Orkney

0 20
mls

Beds
Ce Celestine
Cc China clay
D   Diatomite
M   Manganese
P   Potash

Ga Gypsum and anhydrite
S   Common salt
     Chief non-ferrous fields

Veins
A   Arsenic
B   Barytes
Cr Chromite
C   Copper
F   Fluorspar
G   Gold
Gr Graphite
L   Lead
T   Tin
W   Tungsten
U   Uranium
Z   Zinc

North Pennine
Peak

Other mineral fields

Cornwall
Cc T C W A U

0   100 mls
0   150 km

Source: J. Langton and R. J. Morris (eds) *Atlas of Industrializing Britain 1780–1914*, Methuen, 1986, p. 3

contrast between the heavily populated areas of south and eastern England, the mining areas of Northumberland and Durham and the textile manufacturing West Riding of Yorkshire and the rest of the west and north, where people were thinly scattered. London and its suburbs, containing about 600,000 people, was the densest concentration of people in Europe. Its influence on almost every aspect of national life is difficult to exaggerate at this time. This dominance can be seen by comparing it with the other major cities: Norwich, the second city, had just 30,000 people, as did Bristol, but Birmingham had only 12,000, Newcastle 15,000 and Manchester and Leeds 10,000 each.

IRELAND

In 1700 Britain had a largely rural economy and society. Ireland was separate from mainland Britain physically and was not constitutionally assimilated until the Act of Union in 1800. During the seventeenth century it emerged from a woodland economy with hides as the only major export to a substantial agricultural country based on exporting cattle, beef, sheep and dairy produce.[4] Much of this went either to the continually growing London or to the expanding textile areas of North Wales and England. Growing trade led to concentration of traffic in Cork, Belfast and particularly Dublin, which had a population of about 60,000 in 1700. This marked the beginning of the distinction between a 'maritime' economy based on a cash economy which looked outwards and a 'subsistence' peasant economy.

In 1700 the Anglo-Irish Protestant landowners, who ruled through their control of 80 per cent of the land, were a beleaguered minority. They accounted for about a quarter of the Irish population, were often absentees and were bitterly resented by the Catholic tenant majority on religious and national grounds. This position was worsened by the nature of their settlement. Theirs was a gentry plantation without the buffer of yeomanry and small freeholders which characterized England. Landlord control was limited by the terms of the lease. Roman Catholics, who were excluded from public office, could not hold a lease for longer than thirty-one years as a result of an act of 1704. But it was in the landlord's interest to give Protestants life-leases. This effectively made the tenant a freeholder with the right to vote in parliamentary elections and the landlords' influence depended on how many votes they could muster. Leaseholders were reasonably secure and many were well off by 1700. But other sections of society were less comfortable. Some leaseholders sub-let all or part of their land at a substantially higher rent than they themselves paid. Worse off still was the large body of labourers or 'cottiers' which made up about half of Ireland's population and lived on or below subsistence level. This was largely the result of underemployment since Irish farming did not require high levels of labour. Wages were low, about 4d. per day, and were inadequate even though prices were lower than those in England. An agrarian economy cannot easily absorb an expanding population and it was the cottiers who suffered most and came to depend most heavily on the potato by 1800. By comparison with England they may have appeared backward but, compared to much of the rest of Europe, their conditions were perhaps less wretched. Domestic production of woollen cloth provided both additional employment and the basis for expanding woollen exports after 1660. Low land prices in Ulster led to an influx of Scottish and English immigrants in the 1680s, whose Presbyterianism was as suspect to the Anglo-Irish as was Catholicism. Ulster was transformed from being the most backward of Ireland's four provinces to being the centre of linen production, with Belfast as the fourth port in the country.

The relationship between the Anglo-Irish and England was based upon survival for the former and security for the latter. The Anglo-Irish could not survive in Ireland's hostile environment without England's permanent military presence and they provided a secure base through which the country was governed. In England the relationship between landlord and tenant was based on a shared religious tradition. In Ireland the landlords were almost all Protestant while most of their tenants, with the exception of those in Ulster, were Catholic. Little wonder that contemporaries and later historians have seen Ireland as a 'colonial possession'. For the Catholic Irish majority the memory of war, conquest and dispossession survived and was maintained through Gaelic, the everyday language of the peasantry, which kept alive a sense of cultural distinctiveness. This 'colonial' status was reflected in the constitutional machinery through which Ireland was ruled.[5] Power was exercised in theory from Dublin Castle by the Lord Lieutenant or, in his absence, a commission of Lords Justices. The Lord Lieutenant was appointed from England and was responsible to English ministers. The English Crown enjoyed substantial 'hereditary revenues' and the Irish Parliament was only called to vote for additional supplies to top them up. Right to prepare legislation lay with the Irish Privy Council, but approval had to be obtained from England. The Irish Parliament could either accept or reject these bills but could not amend them and, if necessary, the Westminster Parliament had the power to legislate directly for Ireland.

In practice the situation was somewhat different. The early eighteenth century saw the Irish Parliament develop a power of the purse and its Commons began to question legislation presented to it. These constitutional debates coincided with the increase in restrictive English economic legislation, especially the Woollen Act of 1699, and came to a head in the 1720s. The 1720 Declaratory Act reasserted Westminster's authority 'to make laws and statutes of sufficient force and validity to bind the kingdom and people of Ireland'.

The prolonged struggle over 'Wood's Halfpence', between 1723 and 1725 raised greater issues than that of copper coinage. William Wood, a

Figure 2.2 Counties of Ireland

COUNTIES OF IRELAND

1 – Antrim
2 – Armagh
3 – Carlow
4 – Cavon
5 – Clare
6 – Cork
7 – Donegal
8 – Down
9 – Dublin
10 – Fermanagh
11 – Galway
12 – Kerry
13 – Kildare
14 – Kilkenny
15 – Laoighis
16 – Leitrim
17 – Limerick
18 – Londonderry
19 – Longford
20 – Louth
21 – Mayo
22 – Meath
23 – Monaghan
24 – Offaly
25 – Roscommon
26 – Sligo
27 – Tipperary
28 – Tyrone
29 – Waterford
30 – Westmeath
31 – Wexford
32 – Wicklow

Source: Based on R. K. Webb, *Modern England*, Allen and Unwin, 1969, pp. 4–5.

Wolverhampton ironmaster, obtained a patent in July 1722 to mint copper coins for Ireland. This project was viewed in Ireland both as a symbol of English oppression and as a real threat to the Irish economy. It roused Irish patriotism against what was seen as a government-inspired financial scheme and Walpole proved incapable of dampening opposition both in England and Ireland. In 1725 he recalled the patent. Walpole had yet to develop an effective system of managing government. During the next decade he built up a more effective way of managing the Irish Commons through several leading MPs known as the 'undertakers' who guaranteed to put through government business in return for a considerable share of Crown patronage. This reinforced the strength of the Protestant minority.

Mainland Britain had been brought under the control of the Westminster Parliament by 1710. Wales was assimilated into England by two acts of Parliament: the 1536 Act divided it up into counties on the English model and gave it representation in the English Parliament and in 1543 an act provided for the appointment of justices of the peace and the replacement of Welsh land law with English common law. Although the crowns of England and Scotland were united on the death of Elizabeth I in 1603 a more tangible union between the two countries was delayed until the Act of Union of 1707. In the early eighteenth century the kingdom of Great Britain was of recent origin.

SCOTLAND

Scotland retained much of its own character after 1707 particularly in the legal system, in the kirk and in education.[6] The Act of Union abolished the Scottish Parliament. It added 45 new members to the English Commons, made up of thirty county representatives and fifteen from royal 'burghs' and added sixteen 'representative peers' to the House of Lords. The twenty-seven largest counties received one member while the remaining six (Nairn and Cromerty, Clackmannanshire and Kinross, Bute and Caithness) were paired with one seat each. The county electorate was confined to 'freeholders of the old extent' or to owners of land rated at £400 Scots (£35 sterling), one that was much smaller than in England and open to fraud. The burghs[7] were arranged into fourteen groups each of which had one seat, with Edinburgh taking the fifteenth. Each burgh council elected a representative which met with the other representatives in its group and these individuals then proceeded to choose the MP.

The abolition of the Scottish Privy Council in 1708 effectively removed central government in Scotland. There was a Secretary of State between 1708 and 1725 and again from 1742 to 1746 but Scotland was 'managed' by London-appointed Scottish Whigs – Jacobites being excluded because they did not acknowledge the Hanoverian succession. Scotland was largely governed from local level for much of the century and the Scottish aristocracy totally dominated political and social life. Administration lay in the hands of the burghs and the parishes. The burghs fell into two types: royal burghs established by the Crown and burghs of barony established by the aristocracy. In both cases they were completely dominated by the landed interest. Theoretically the sixty-six royal burghs had a monopoly of trade, domestic or foreign, and their Convention, an annual assembly of delegates, did attempt to maintain this monopoly. But burghs in general were essential to rural society as markets or market-places and it was impossible to enforce this against growing burghs of barony like Kilmarnock, Greenock and Hawick.

The parishes

The 938 Scottish parishes were governed by kirk sessions, the Scottish equivalent of the English vestry, which used money raised by church-door collections and fines to finance poor relief. In Scotland levying a poor rate

Figure 2.3 Counties of Scotland

COUNTIES OF SCOTLAND

1 – Aberdeen
2 – Angus
3 – Argyll
4 – Ayr
5 – Banff
6 – Berwick
7 – Bute
8 – Caithness
9 – Clackmannan
10 – Dumfries
11 – Dumbartonshire
12 – East Lothian
13 – Fife
14 – Inverness
15 – Kincardine
16 – Kinross
17 – Kircudbright
18 – Lanark
19 – Midlothian
20 – Moray
21 – Nairn
22 – Orkney
23 – Peebles
24 – Perth
25 – Renfrew
26 – Ross & Cromarty
27 – Roxburgh
28 – Selkirk
29 – Shetland
30 – Stirling
31 – Sutherland
32 – West Lothian
33 – Wigtown

Source: Based on R. K. Webb, *Modern England*, Allen and Unwin, 1969, pp. 4–5.

was discretionary rather than mandatory, with the result that less than one in ten parishes chose to do so. But since Acts of 1616 and 1633 each parish was required to establish a school, provide a schoolhouse and pay for a schoolmaster. In the 1696 Act for Settling Schools landowners were rated for this system, though they could and did pass half of the burden on to their tenantry. By 1700 most Lowland parishes had a school but in the Highlands their establishment came more slowly, particularly because of the difficulty in getting Gaelic-speaking teachers.

The parish was also a system of ecclesiastical administration. In 1690 episcopal church government was replaced by Presbyterianism ruled by a General Assembly. The parish minister had considerable power over his congregation on moral, education, religious and other issues. Ministers received a regular stipend which in 1633 was laid down as a minimum 800 Scottish merks or just over £44 sterling. Tithes were less of an issue in Scotland than in England. In 1633 they became a fixed charge or 'teind' paid in cash or meal by each estate in the parish. Provision was made for commutation of teinds at nine years' purchase. Glebe land was of little importance.

Legal systems

The most radical difference between Scotland and England lay in their respective legal systems. England had a unified and centralized jurisdiction under the Crown but in Scotland heritable jurisdiction and offices, notably the sheriffs, were widespread. The baron courts were the basic units of rural society dealing with petty crimes and community rules. The Act of Union guaranteed the survival of the Courts of Session, Justiciary and Admiralty in their existing form and in article 20

> That all heritable Offices, Superiorities, heritable Jurisdictions, Offices for life and Jurisdictions for life, be reserved to the Owners thereof, as Rights of Property, in the same manner as they are now enjoyed by the Laws of Scotland, notwithstanding of this Treaty and an independent legal profession was to become the 'bearers and defenders of nationality'.

Justices of the Peace had been introduced by legislation in 1587 and 1609 though they were never as important as in England. Their role was complemented by the commissioners of supply who were responsible for collecting the land tax introduced in 1667. The difficulty in collecting this led to the commissioners becoming more involved in parish affairs and helping the justices keep Scotland's roads in working order. In the eighteenth century their work was made easier, for two reasons. First, in 1748 heritable jurisdiction was abolished. Secondly, commissioner and justice were often the same person and also a local landlord with much wider and more clearly defined powers over tenants than in England.

Scotland – an agrarian society

Scotland was a largely agrarian society. There were three main farming regions, with many smaller sub-regions further complicating the picture. Good soils were largely concentrated in the Central Lowlands, the corridor sandwiched between the poorer soils of the Highlands and the Southern Uplands. Both these areas were better suited to pastoral than arable farming. By 1700 the Border region was geared to rearing sheep for marketing both wool and meat, usually in England. In Galloway, in the south-west, the rise of large-scale cattle production for the English market produced large enclosed cattle parks of up to 2,000 acres. Arable farming was based on common grazing with an infield and outfield round the settlement. The settlement was a cluster of houses known as a 'ferm toun' in the Lowlands and a 'clachan' in the Highlands. The infield, the land under continuous cultivation, was divided into 'breaks'. The land of individual farmers was distributed 'runrig' and lay dispersed throughout the infield in strips (rigs). Each 'break' was sown with oats and barley and, sometimes in the Lothians, with wheat. Sometimes a break was allowed to lie fallow for a year but generally the only time it was not under cultivation was in the winter:

> In place of a chequerboard of separate fields one must imagine the ground everywhere lying as open as moorland . . . seldom divided in any way by hedge, wall or dyke . . . The pastoral land . . . was all more or less rough brown waste: there was no question of grass being cultivated as a crop. The ploughed land within was in a series of undulating strips or rigs.[8]

In 1700 there were about 10,000 landowners in Scotland. Eighty per cent of these were the 'bonnet lairds', who owned small farms and were more akin to English yeoman than landowners living on rents. But there were still 1,500 more substantial landowners. In the Highlands power and authority lay with the clan chiefs and society was organized for war. Extensive areas were leased by the clan chief to 'tacksmen' who in turn sub-leased, generally on an annual verbal basis, to as many tenants as possible. Payment was often in terms of goods and particularly military service. The nature of rural society in the Lowlands and Southern Uplands, with some 'middling groups', in many areas holding direct from the Crown or by virtual ownership known as 'feuing', was rather more complex. By 1700 most tenant farmers in the Lowlands had written leases for up to twenty years'. The older system of joint leases, where tenants held a specific fraction of a farm, gave way to single tenancies starting in the Lowlands. Tenants sub-let to people variously called acremen, crofters (who held infield but not outfield), cottars (who held small amounts of land to supplement their main works as hired labourers), grassmen (who had rights of pasture on the outfields but no arable land), mailers and pendiclers.

Urban society

The small burghs were completely dominated by the landed interest and were not cut off from agriculture. They used their common grazing, took peat from the hills and had arable lands to which their own labour force was restricted in harvest time. Towns were important centres of specialist services, craft activity and mercantile capital. But they were generally small because the centres of industrial activity – soap and salt production, the linen industry and the cattle trade – did not need towns to process their products. The larger cities gained support from international trade – Glasgow, for example, was growing as a centre of the tobacco trade – and also made specialized goods for the aristocracy.[9]

The Scottish economy at the beginning of the eighteenth century had a dual nature. There was a basic agricultural sector which was weak in its market aspects though capable of producing a surplus to sustain an aristocratic elite. There was also a more sophisticated sector supplying that elite with imported luxury goods though increasing amounts were home-made. But Scotland was an insecure society. It was split culturally between the Gaelic-speaking world and the Scots speech of the Lowlanders. It was split politically between those who had Jacobite sympathies and those who looked to the Hanoverians. The Highland society was based on clan kinship and personal loyalty whereas in the Lowlands a commercial relationship between landlord and tenant was beginning to develop. The reality of 1707 was that England absorbed Scotland. The 45 Scottish MPs only just exceeded the 44 returned by the county of Cornwall.

WALES[10]

Wales returned MPs from twenty-seven constituencies to the House of Commons. Wales only had half the representation given to England – one county member (except for Monmouthsire) and one borough member. In 1700 between 1.8 and 4 per cent of the county population could vote. The voting qualification for the twelve county MPs was the 40-shilling freehold, and the size of the county electorate reflected the restricted number of freeholders, which was a result of the smallness of the farming units. The term 'freeholder' was interpreted flexibly and, as in Ireland, often admitted people with long leases or copyholds to the vote. Borough MPs were elected by a group of boroughs consisting of the county borough and a number of 'out-boroughs'. In the case of Glamorgan seven out-boroughs shared with Cardiff, the county borough, the right of election. In some boroughs, like Beaumaris, the franchise was vested in the corporation. In others, like Brecon, only resident freemen could vote, while non-resident freemen could vote in Cardigan. More people voted in Welsh boroughs than in the counties. In England there was a growing number of people who converted wealth into land but they were not sufficiently numerous in Wales to affect the political monopoly of established landed interest.

Physically Wales can be divided into three regions: the highland areas; the coastal areas around these and the areas adjacent to England. Pastoral farming was the dominant feature in the first two regions, with some elements of it apparent in the third. In the highland areas farms consisted mainly of rough grazing with some meadowland around the farmhouse. In the second area upland farms with little arable land were common in 1700 though in the lowlands arable land made up about a third of the land used and mixed farming dominated. Cattle rearing, for consumption in the massive English market, was still more important than sheep rearing and was dominated by the 'porthmon' or cattle dealer. By 1700 much of the lowland was already gathered into compact farms but strip farming existed in the Vale of Glamorgan, Vale of Clwyd and Pembrokeshire. However, the traditional Welsh pattern was more diffuse with dispersed small farming units together with an occasional hamlet. Even in lowland Wales the response to farming was intensely local, reflecting differences in soil, slope, altitude and drainage.

Welsh society and economy

Welsh society was traditionally divided into *bonedd a gwreng* which broadly represented an upper and lower class. *Bonedd* related to lineage which was accepted as the basis for authority and lay with the gentry. The aristocratic element was not prominent though some Welsh land formed part of English aristocratic estates. Social and economic changes in the seventeenth century depressed the conditions of the lesser gentry, who lost their traditional position in the Inns of Court and the universities, in politics and Parliament. Just as in England it was those people with larger estates who capitalized on new techniques and sources of income who prospered. There were between thirty and forty families in Wales with incomes in excess of £3,000 a year: families like the Bulkeleys in Anglesey, the Mostyns in Flint, the Vaughans of Transcoed in Cardiganshire, the Vaughans of Golden Grove in Carmarthanshire and the Morgans of Monmouthshire monopolized Commons seats and the patronage which went with them. Each county contained between twenty-five and fifty families with incomes between £500 and £1,000 a year, who served as JPs and ran their counties through the quarter sessions. Recent work on Glamorgan[11] has spotlighted the diverse nature of this broad description. In 1700 there were ten families with incomes over £1,500 per year and forty-seven men owned 80 per cent of the county. But in the next fifty years many of the older families died out and their heiresses were married off. Glamorgan's ruling elite became Anglicized, creating a language barrier with those they ruled. By the late eighteenth century such names as Corbet, Pennant, Assheton-Smith, Cawdor and Bute testified to the extent of English and Scottish penetration. They were increasingly marked off from the community by a growing gulf of language and religious and political affiliation. Smaller landowners switched their enterprise into fields which brought them into contact with the growing 'middling order'. This process of modernization can also be detected in Denbighshire and Flintshire under the pervasive influence of Watkin William Wynn of Wynnstay in the north-east and in Monmouthshire. These men rented their land out to tenant farmers who in turn employed farm labourers, hired for the year or half year. Single labourers usually lived in as did women servants on the larger farms. Though workers were hired for a specific job there was no strict division of labour and in the winter hired men often did the weaving.

The woollen industry was next in importance to the cattle trade in the Welsh rural economy. The cloth trade had been moved to North and mid-Wales in the sixteenth century and was subjected to the Drapers' Company of Shrewsbury. Its farm-based production was concentrated in the area running from Machynlleth on the west coast through Merioneth, Montgomery and Denbigh to the borderlands. Output was small in comparison with England: the four counties of Merioneth, Montgomery, Monmouth and Pembroke in 1747 was estimated at £100,000 compared to Yorkshire's £2,371,940. The whole of the south and north had a scattering of industries. Copper, tinplate and related industries had existed in Swansea-Neath and Pontypool since the sixteenth century. By 1700 most British production was concentrated there and was yoked to the mines of Anglesey. By 1720 a sixth of British pig-iron production was from the scattered charcoal furnaces of South Wales. Slate production in north-west Wales was already a major exporting industry to England and Ireland – a million slates were exported in 1688.

The economies of Wales and England were closely linked. The cattle industry was based on English needs. North Wales was under the control of Shrewsbury and this was to pass to Liverpool after 1770. South Wales was enmeshed by Bristol. It has been argued that

> Generally, this core of the British imperial economy was itself colonial. . . . Many of the Welsh, on their upland farms and at their treadmill of loom and spinning wheel and domestic drudgery, were trapped in a back-breaking poverty and an unremitting colonial dependence which sent great droves of skinny cattle and skinny people seasonally tramping into England to be fattened.[12]

POLITICAL, SOCIAL AND ECONOMIC STRUCTURES

Who could vote

The economies, societies and politics of Ireland, Scotland and Wales were dominated by England. In Ireland, a dual system of administration between Westminster and Dublin testified to the separate role of Ireland in public policy. In Wales, the Home Office and Court of Chancery made no distinction between Welsh and English problems. No Welsh-speaking bishop was consecrated in the eighteenth century after 1714. But in Scotland, the Presbyterian kirk remained a representative assembly of a Scots community. Parliament at Westminster legislated for all four countries

Figure 2.4 Counties of England and Wales

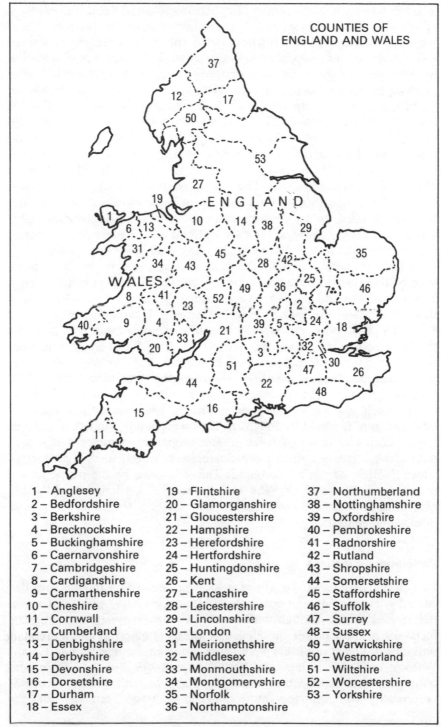

COUNTIES OF
ENGLAND AND WALES

1 – Anglesey	19 – Flintshire	37 – Northumberland
2 – Bedfordshire	20 – Glamorganshire	38 – Nottinghamshire
3 – Berkshire	21 – Gloucestershire	39 – Oxfordshire
4 – Brecknockshire	22 – Hampshire	40 – Pembrokeshire
5 – Buckinghamshire	23 – Herefordshire	41 – Radnorshire
6 – Caernarvonshire	24 – Hertfordshire	42 – Rutland
7 – Cambridgeshire	25 – Huntingdonshire	43 – Shropshire
8 – Cardiganshire	26 – Kent	44 – Somersetshire
9 – Carmarthenshire	27 – Lancashire	45 – Staffordshire
10 – Cheshire	28 – Leicestershire	46 – Suffolk
11 – Cornwall	29 – Lincolnshire	47 – Surrey
12 – Cumberland	30 – London	48 – Sussex
13 – Denbighshire	31 – Meirionethshire	49 – Warwickshire
14 – Derbyshire	32 – Middlesex	50 – Westmorland
15 – Devonshire	33 – Monmouthshire	51 – Wiltshire
16 – Dorsetshire	34 – Montgomeryshire	52 – Worcestershire
17 – Durham	35 – Norfolk	53 – Yorkshire
18 – Essex	36 – Northamptonshire	

Source: Based on R. K. Webb, *Modern England*, Allen and Unwin, 1969, pp. 4–5

and after 1707 only Ireland had its own legislative assembly. The House of Lords was composed of some 220 peers in the early eighteenth century, of whom 26 were bishops and 16 'representative' Scottish peers. These were the wealthy landowners whose vast territorial possessions gave them social standing and political influence through their control of nomination to many seats in the House of Commons. They were a relatively homogeneous group united by interest, blood and marriage. The House of Commons was made up of 489 English members: 80 county MPs, 405 borough members and 2 MPs each for the universities of Oxford and Cambridge. The county MPs were elected by the 40-shilling freeholders. There were about 200,000 of these in 1700 but, if there was an election, they could generally be influenced to vote, in accordance with the wishes of the dominant landowners. The cost of county elections meant that it was usual practice to try to get agreement between the rival groupings without the need for an electoral contest. Of the 203 English boroughs, 196 returned two members, the City of London and Weymouth returned four members each, and five boroughs one member. Voting qualifications were far more varied. In 1700 the total electorate was probably no more than 85,000. In the 12 'potwalloper' boroughs all residents who had a house or hearth and did not receive poor relief could vote – in Preston this meant a large electorate but in St Germans, Devon only twenty. The 37 'scot and lot' boroughs saw the franchise given to those who paid this medieval poor rate – again the size varied, from 9,000 for Westminster down to two for Gatton. There were 27 'corporation' boroughs where the mayor and members of the corporation had the right of election and 92 'freeman' boroughs. In some boroughs the right to vote was attached to certain freeholds – in 29 'burgage' boroughs it was vested in tenancy of land and in 6 'freehold' in the ownership of land. The scale of the borough electorate gave far greater scope for influence and intimidation. Well over a hundred constituencies belonged to the category of 'close', 'rotten' or pocket boroughs. This was aided by the public nature of voting on the 'hustings'. The 1716 Septennial Act lengthened the life of a parliament from three to seven years, cutting down on the expense of electoral contests.

Parliament – functions

Parliament made laws, largely of a local nature, voted monies and discussed grievances. It was dominated by ministers who, with the Crown, determined policy. Though the House of Commons was increasingly the focus for political power the House of Lords retained its importance, if only because most ministers were peers. Successful ministers like Robert Walpole were able to 'manage' both the Commons and the Crown, and political success depended on being acceptable to both. Government was very much a co-operative venture between Commons, ministers and the

Crown, and was concerned with external security, promoting and protecting commercial interests, and maintaining law and order at home. Government gave ministers access to Crown patronage and offices, many of which
were sinecures carrying a good salary without involving duties, through
which they could 'manage' affairs.[13] This was an administrative conception
of government, concerned with maintaining the existing system rather
than changing it.

Local administration – county and parish

At local level power was wielded by institutions working within the fixed
and known boundaries of the county, parish and borough. At the head
of the county stood the Lord Lieutenant, a royal appointment. Below him
were the JPs, usually from among the gentry and were required by acts
of 1732 and 1744 to possess land worth at least £100 per year, who
exercised their judicial and administrative powers through the quarter
sessions but also had increasing powers of summary justice. The only real
check on their actions was that they had to act within the law though
there was some supervision in Wales through the Courts of Great Session,
for which Wales was divided into four circuits, each of three counties.

There were some 9,000 parishes in England and Wales in 1700 which
were governed by the vestry, composed of the most important inhabitants
often with an Anglican clergyman as chairman. It dealt with nearly all
aspects of parish life: it appointed churchwardens and received the
accounts of the surveyors of highways and overseers of the poor though
these were appointed by the JPs. The vestry was the only institution in
the country other than Parliament that could levy taxes or rates. Parishes
were also ecclesiastical units of the Established Church. Parishes were
arranged into dioceses controlled by bishops and the dioceses in turn were
grouped into two provinces under the control of the archbishops of York
and Canterbury. The close proximity of manor house and church reflected
the lay patronage in the church. The right of appointment or advowson
to a benefice generally lay with the landed gentry – this applied in Scotland
as well. The parson drew his income from fees, from his glebe land and
from tithes. Tithes were paid by all, whether members of the Anglican
Church or not and were bitterly resented.

Local administration – town and city

Urban local government was less uniform. There were about 800 towns
in England and Wales. About 200 were boroughs and were governed by
a corporation composed of mayor, aldermen and burgesses. Corporations
had extensive powers – the right to have civil courts of law and their own
Sessions of the Peace, to have markets and make their own by-laws for
the regulation of trade and manufacture. The Corporation Act of 1661

and the Test Act of 1678 excluded Nonconformists and Catholics from public office locally as well as nationally, though Nonconformists could get round this by annually attending the Anglican church. The position of the non-corporate towns, including some of the most rapidly growing areas like Manchester and Birmingham, was different: these relied on increasingly ineffective parish and manorial organizations for their government.

A rural society

English economy and society too was largely rural. What marked England off from continental Europe, except for Holland, was that during the eighteenth century it became increasingly less rural in outlook. The open field system of farming was widespread in much of central, midland and southern England at the beginning of the eighteenth century. Although there had already been substantial enclosure since the sixteenth century much of this had been piecemeal, affecting some parishes completely, others partially whilst some were unaffected. In spite of the basic unity of practice the operation of the common field system varied considerably. Farming on the heavy clay soil was different from that on chalklands and lighter soils. It is a gross oversimplification to imply that northern and western England were given over entirely to animal farming. In these areas there were small areas of intensely farmed arable land and large expanses of unenclosed pastures.

England was both diverse and remarkably united. It was a close-knit country partly because, despite regional differences, its economy was interlocking. London lay at the centre of this economy and one in eight people in England lived there. Defoe commented in the 1720s that 'The neighbourhood of London sucks the vitals of trade in this trade to itself.'

British farming fed London: cattle from Wales and from the Scottish Borders; vegetables from the market gardens that grew up in Kent and Berkshire; fish from East Anglia, Sussex and Devon. Yet England had a market economy with each region specializing in particular commodities. It is possible to identify certain regional differences which were profoundly important.[14] There was the divide between the south-east and the north-west, broadly the contrast between the richer and poorer counties, and the greater and lesser urbanized parts of the country. The area south of the Bristol–Humber line was both heavily industrialized and heavily farmed. Iron-founding was still concentrated in the Weald and the Forest of Dean. Textile production was largely in the West Country and East Anglia, though the West Riding was fast gaining in importance. Luxury trades were concentrated in London. A second divide was between coastal and inland areas or, more importantly, between those places which had access to navigable water and those which did not. Sea and river transport was the cheapest and safest way of carrying people and goods before the development of canals. The most important English towns were either ports or had easy access to the sea. A third contrast was between 'lowland' and 'upland', which usually meant the difference between open and wooded country, arable and pasture, nucleated villages and dispersed settlement and between densely and thinly populated areas.

Town and country

The close interrelationship of country and town and of farming and manufacturing meant that there was considerable social understanding within this segregated economy. The aristocratic elite's authority and power was based on their possession of land. The flexible way in which they exploited their industrial as well as their agrarian advantages contrasts with the myopic attitude of some continental nobilities towards their economic role. The Court never took on the same symbolic importance to the English aristocracy as it did to the French. Despite the differences in religion, occupation, gender role and status there was a remarkable unity in English society. At the top of the social hierarchy stood a numerically small aristocratic elite whose control of both the economic and political systems made it into a 'ruling class'. Aristocratic status came from owning property. From a peer like the Duke of Newcastle, whose income in 1710 was over £30,000, down to the poorest yeoman with an income of £100 there was a community of interest based on the ownership of land. They may have done other things – held government or local office, engaged in trade, commerce or manufacture – but rank in society was a consequence of land. At a local level it was the gentry who were the real rulers of the countryside monopolizing political and economic power through their ownership of land, position as MPs and as employers of labour. Many people rented land as tenant farmers and large-scale farmers could outrank smaller owner-occupiers. Below them were the labourers who worked the land and who received wages in either cash or kind. In 1700 up to three-quarters of the English population was directly dependent on the land. Its social fabric was intricate and this complexity was mirrored in a deep-rooted division of labour and by the moral force of custom and tradition. The remaining quarter of the population looked to other sources of income. But no rigid distinction can be made, since landowners invested in industry and commerce and many smaller farmers and tenants relied on their rural industry for survival. The successful merchant or financier used his profits to buy land to give him the status which money alone did not provide.

BRITAIN – A DEVELOPED COUNTRY?

In 1700 Britain was not, in the modern sense of the term, an underdeveloped country.[15] However, there were marked variations in the level of development of its constituent parts. Much of England was productive farmland with regional economies served by a web of market towns with London exerting a powerful economic influence. There were loose concentrations of industrial activity. Wales, Scotland and Ireland were considerably different. Urban development was less advanced than in England though Edinburgh, Dublin, Glasgow and Belfast were beginning to advance. Agriculture in all three areas was largely geared to subsistence in grain and capitalism in animals which could be exported to England. But even if Britain had achieved a fair level of development by 1700 it still showed many of the characteristics of underdevelopment. Its economy was relatively unspecialized, based upon agriculture and the production of very basic goods. Economic activity was dominated by London with no provincial towns to rival it in size or influence. Fortunately London was a wealthy market and source of enterprise and a future focus for economic changes. Finally, people were still subject to the vagaries of nature. Famine and disease were still widespread. Scotland, for example, was hit by famines in the 1690s. The death rate was high and life expectancy low. Demographically Britain was an insecure society. In 1700 therefore the British economy was quite advanced in some respects and relatively underdeveloped in others. It was only its market economy, in which a high proportion of the population participated, that prevents Britain in 1700 from being labelled as an underdeveloped country in a Third World sense.

NOTES

1 For a fuller discussion of Montesquieu see D. Thomson (ed.) *Political Ideas*, Penguin, 1978, chapter 6. J. N. Shklar *Montesquieu*, Oxford, 1987 is a recent, brief study.
2 For landscape history the seminal work is W. G. Hoskins *The Making of the English Landscape*, Penguin, 1964. Hodder & Stoughton have published a series of books dealing with the making of the English landscape covering counties while Longman has adopted a regional approach. On Wales see M. Williams *The Making of the South Wales Landscape*, Hodder & Stoughton, 1975 and on Scotland M. L. Parry and T. R. Slater (eds) *The Making of the Scottish Landscape*, 1980. M. Reed *The Georgian Triumph 1700–1830*, Methuen, 1983 is an excellent brief synopsis.
3 D. Defoe *A Tour Through the Whole Island of Great Britain*, ed. P. Rogers, Penguin, 1971, p. 664.
4 On the state of the Irish economy and society in 1700 see L. M. Cullen *An Economic History of Ireland since 1660*, Batsford, 1972, chapters 1 and 2, E. M. Johnston *Ireland in the Eighteenth Century*, Gill & Macmillan, 1974.
5 A convenient summary of the problems of early eighteenth-century Irish politics can be found in D. Hayton 'Walpole and Ireland', in J. Black (ed.) *Britain in the Age of Walpole*, Macmillan, 1985, pp. 95–119, and R. Foster *Modern Ireland 1600–1972*, Allen Lane, 1988.
6 On Scotland R. Mitchison *Lordship to Patronage: Scotland 1603–1745*, Edward Arnold, 1983 and T. C. Smout *A History of the Scottish People 1560–1830*, Collins, 1969 provide excellent background while B. P. Lenman 'A Client Society: Scotland between the '15 and the '45', in J. Black (ed.) op. cit., pp.

69–93 is the most recent account. Two recent collections are essential: T. M. Devine and R. K. Mitchison (eds) *People and Society in Scotland*, vol. 1, 1760–1830, John Donald, 1988, and R. A. Houston and I. D. Whyte (eds) *Scottish Society 1500–1800*, Cambridge University Press, 1989.

7 See M. Lynch 'The Scottish Early Modern Burgh', *History Today*, February 1985, pp. 10–15.

8 T. C. Smout, op. cit. p. 120.

9 On trade see A. J. G. Cummings 'Scotland's Links with Europe 1600–1800', *History Today*, April, 1985, pp. 45–9.

10 For Wales convenient starting points are D. Williams *A History of Modern Wales*, John Murray, 1977, E. D. Evans *A History of Wales 1660–1815*, University of Wales Press, 1976 and the infuriating and eminently readable G. A. Williams *When Was Wales?*, Penguin, 1985.

11 P. Jenkins, *The Making of a Ruling Class: the Glamorgan Gentry 1640–1790*, Cambridge University Press, 1983.

12 G. A. Williams op. cit. p. 145.

13 W. A. Speck *Stability and Strife: England 1714–1760*, Edward Arnold, 1977, chapter 1 and D. Marshall *Eighteenth Century England*, Longman, 1974, chapter 2 are good starting points.

14 R. Porter *English Society in the Eighteenth Century*, Penguin, 1982, rev. edn 1990, pp. 56–61 discusses this more fully.

15 E. Pawson *The Early Industrial Revolution*, Batsford, 1979, pp. 13–22 examines these issues.

3 The revolution in numbers –
demographic change 1700–1850

In his diary for late 1782 Cornelius Ashworth wrote:

> I saw 10 graves open in Halifax Churchyard, 9 of them for children,
> and was informed that 110 children had been interred in the above
> yard in four weeks which had died of the small pox.

By modern standards eighteenth-century mortality rates were high, particularly for young children. The vicar of Cardington in Bedfordshire said,
in 1782, that 'near 47 per cent die under the age of two'. Yet there was
a population explosion in Great Britain during the second half of the
century. By the early nineteenth century population was growing at an
unprecedented rate and the economy was able to absorb the expanding
labour force with little change in living standards.

POPULATION SOURCES

Why did population grow? What happened to birth and death rates and
why? How did internal and external migration affect total population?
Although there are simple answers to these questions – population went
up because of fluctuations in the death and birth rates – the causes of
these movements, their chronology and relative importance are far more
difficult to resolve because of problems with the available evidence. At
one extreme it has been argued that the acceleration was mainly due to
increased mortality while at the other the sole cause of increasing population growth lay in falling mortality. In general the 'pro-mortality' arguments have held the field. It is necessary, therefore, to review the four
main sources and see how historians can approach them.[1]

Listings

First, there are various listings of people compiled by either institutions
or individuals for different purposes. These are, however, of value less
for their demographic information than for their analysis of social structures. The most famous for England and Wales are Gregory King's esti-

mate for 1696[2] based upon hearth-tax returns as well as his own sample surveys, Joseph Massie's in 1759 and Patrick Colquhoun's complex calculations from income-tax, census and poor-relief records in 1803.[3] Alexander Webster surveyed Scotland in 1755 as part of his work on a pension scheme for the widows of Scottish clergy. He circularized ministers in every parish in Scotland asking them the population of their parishes. For Ireland historians rely upon the Irish hearth-tax returns, the 1766 census of Catholics and Protestants, the estate maps of 1756–62 and the borough surveys of 1798–1800 which returned the number of occupied houses. Although King, Webster, Massie and Colquhoun were careful in their calculations their conclusions have all been questioned. D. V. Glass has suggested that there are valid reasons for reducing King's final estimate by up to 5 per cent. M. W. Flinn regarded the Webster's Highland figures as suspect and K. H. Connell believed that the Irish hearth-tax returns understated the number of households by up to 50 per cent in all returns up to 1785. Local listings provide much more detail on the age, sex, marital, household and family structures of the eighteenth-century population. The Cardington survey for 1782 compares favourably with the census enumeration books from 1841. The 1771 listing for Rothesay in Scotland records people family by family and the 1795 census of Tullow in Ireland contained the number of houses and inhabitants as well as their occupations and religion. But valuable as these listings may be they are biased towards small rural communities.

Parish registers

The most abundant source for the eighteenth century and also the most difficult to interpret is the parish register. Registration was introduced in England, Wales and Ireland in 1538 but printed registers were not used until after Rose's Act in 1813. Throughout the eighteenth century the quality of registers varied. In Wales registers existed for only one in three parishes for much of the century. Few Irish registers have survived because they have been lost or destroyed or, more likely, they were never compiled. In Scotland only ninety-nine parishes had regular registration of baptisms and burials and these favour east coast communities. It is difficult to draw general conclusions from this sample. For England the registers are far more complete and allow historians to reach more definite conclusions. Their most serious disadvantage as a source is the problem of under-registration. Rapid population growth, the rise of Nonconformity, the focal point of demographic growth moving from rural to urban settings, where the influence of the church was often less than in the countryside, all resulted in every uncertain and imperfect registration. In a sample of forty-five small rural parishes between 1760 and 1834 only two out of every three births were registered. In urban parishes this was probably higher. Under-registration of burials was lower than baptisms for much of the eighteenth century but rose to about the same level after 1800. Hardwicke's Act of 1753, which was extended to Scotland in 1784, recognized as legally valid only those marriages conducted by a clergyman in an Anglican church. By 1820 the number of marriages omitted from the registers was as low as 2 per cent.

The range of data which can be extracted from the register entries of baptisms, burials and marriages is large. One approach is family reconstitution which depends on being able to link together a family's nuptiality, fertility and mortality history. A second approach which guarantees a rapid and substantial return of information is the aggregative technique. This entails counting the numbers of baptisms, marriages and burials month by month which can then be converted into crude birth, marriage and death rates. Aggregate back projection, a third technique, has been used by Wrigley and Schofield and provides estimates of population at five-yearly intervals from 1541. They start in 1871, when the size and age structure of the population are known. The aggregate population in each age group in 1866 is calculated by estimating the number of people who died between 1866 and 1871 and adjusting the figure to take account of the balance between in- and out-migration. Having calculated figures for 1866, the procedure is repeated for 1861 and so on back to 1541. There are difficulties with these techniques. In family reconstitution the accurate identification of individuals and families can be difficult and is feasible only where unambiguous data are available. Back projection depends on the validity of assumptions about the age structure of mortality. Conclusions are often reached using very small samples. Wrigley and Schofield use a sample of 400 parish registers covering the whole period from 1538 to the introduction of civil registration in 1837. This has led some historians to question their representativeness. Most existing studies are of small, rural communities while the larger, urban parishes, where population was less stable and parish registers less reliable, have been neglected. Aggregative techniques suffer from the twin problems of under-registration and ambiguous interpretation. It is difficult to extrapolate reliable birth and death rates from baptisms and burials.

Censuses and civil registration

In the nineteenth century the accuracy of demographic data was improved by the introduction of civil registration and the national census. Civil registration of births, marriages and deaths began in England and Wales in 1837 but this reform was delayed in Scotland until 1855, and in Ireland until 1864. During the 1840s registration of births in England and Wales was 93 per cent accurate and continued to fall until the 1880s when it was practically perfect.

Nationwide decennial censuses conducted by the civil authorities were introduced in England, Wales and Scotland in 1801 and in Ireland in

1813–15, though the first effective Irish census was really in 1821.[4] Before 1841 collection of census information was left in the hands of largely unsupervised enumerators – in England and Wales poor-law officials, in Scotland schoolmasters or 'other fit persons' and in Ireland for 1821 and 1831 tax-collectors – who visited each home and transcribed oral information into special notebooks from which the data were extracted and processed centrally. In 1841 the procedures of census-taking were improved and, in England and Wales, placed under the control of the Registrar-General of Births, Marriages and Deaths. This improvement was continued in the 1851 census. The census enumerators' books into which the schedules for each household were copied are an invaluable source for mainland Britain, though few have survived for Ireland. Today the mechanical extraction of information from enumerators' books has been replaced by the widespread application of microcomputers by historians.

POPULATION GROWTH

The rate of population growth since the beginning of the eighteenth century is shown in Table 3.1.

Table 3.1 Population growth (in millions)

Date	England and Wales	Scotland	Ireland	England (less Monmouth): Wrigley and Schofield	Compound annual rate of growth over preceding decade: Wrigley and Schofield
1701	5.30	1.04	2.54	5.058	–
1751	6.50	1.25	3.12	5.772	–
1761	6.70			6.147	0.6
1771	7.20			6.448	0.5
1781	7.50			7.042	0.9
1791	8.25	1.50	4.75	7.740	0.9
1801	9.20	1.60	5.22	8.664	1.1
1811	10.20	1.80	6.00	9.886	1.3
1821	12.00	2.10	6.80	11.492	1.5
1831	13.90	2.40	7.80		
1841	15.90	2.60	8.20		
1851	17.90	2.90	6.50		

Sources: P. Deane and W. A. Cole *British Economic Growth 1688–1959*, Cambridge University Press, 2nd edn, 1969, p. 6 for eighteenth-century figures and B. R. Mitchell and P. Deane *Abstract of British Historical Statistics*, Cambridge University Press, 1962, pp. 6–7 for census figures between 1801 and 1851. The figures from G. A. Wrigley and R. S. Schofield, *The Population History of England 1541–1871: A Reconstruction*, Edward Arnold, London, 1981 (revised edition, Cambridge University Press, 1989) pp. 528–9 are included separately.

Between 1711 and 1740 total population grew very slowly. From the 1740s
to the 1770s the pace of demographic increase accelerated. Between 1780
and 1800 this growth was twice as high. Throughout the first half of the
nineteenth century population increased by about 1.5 per cent, over twice
that achieved between 1740 and 1780. Between 1680 and 1820, the 'long'
eighteenth century, England's population rose by 133 per cent, far above
the growth rate for other European countries. But there were differences
between the growth rates of England and Wales, Scotland and Ireland
(see Table 3.2).

Table 3.2 Population growth rates (as percentages)

Country	1700–50	1750–1800	1800–50
England and Wales	0.3	0.8	1.8
Scotland	0.6	0.5	1.6
Ireland	0.6	1.1	0.6

Source: N. Tranter *Population since the Industrial Revolution*, Croom Helm, 1973, p. 43,
Wrigley and Schofield *op. cit.* pp. 528–9.

Variations in England

In England and Wales the pace of population growth was greatest in
manufacturing and trading areas and slowest in the purely agricultural
areas. In the first half of the eighteenth century, when the population of
England grew by about 14 per cent, rural counties grew hardly at all but
relatively high rates of increase were already evident in certain industrializing regions – the populations of Lancashire, Warwickshire and the West
Riding of Yorkshire increased by 33 per cent, 28 per cent and 26 per cent
respectively. Evidence of abnormally high rates of growth in manufacturing areas is provided by various local and regional analyses – for example
in twelve parishes round Bromsgrove (Worcestershire), which were partially industrialized, population increased by about a quarter between 1700
and 1750; in the seventeen parishes centred on Coalbrookdale in

Figure 3.1 Population growth in England, Wales, Scotland and Ireland,
1741–1926

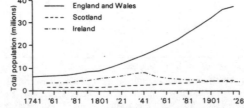

Source: J. Langton and R. J. Morris (eds) *Atlas of Industrializing Britain 1780–1914*,
Methuen, 1986, p. 11.

Shropshire there was an annual growth rate of 1.3 per cent in the same period. In these areas growth predated that of the 1780s. During the second half of the eighteenth and early nineteenth centuries population growth was greatest in the industrial areas of the north-west, Yorkshire and the Midlands and in the industrial and commercial complex of the south-east centred on London. Between 1750 and 1850 the rate of growth in rural England and Wales, though higher than it had been between 1700 and 1750, continued to lag behind industrial and commercial regions. Deane and Cole have calculated that between 1750 and 1850 the population of the industrial and commercial counties rose by 129 per cent whereas the rural counties rose by only 88 per cent.

The effects of these regional variations in the rate of population growth were twofold. First, they resulted in major changes in the geographical distribution of English and Welsh populations. Secondly, they led to a dramatic shift in the numbers living in urban and rural settings. The proportion of people living in urban settings rose from perhaps one in four in 1700 to one in two by 1850.

Variations in Scotland and Ireland

In Scotland the 'population revolution' did not begin until the early nineteenth century. Most of this increase was concentrated in the relatively narrow area of the Western and, to a lesser extent, Eastern Lowlands, which were the main centres of industrial and commercial expansion. In Ireland, by contrast, population expansion came in the second half of the eighteenth century when rates of growth were three times those of Scotland. In the early decades of the nineteenth century the rate of population growth declined and this was exacerbated by the Great Famine between 1845 and 1851. Ireland remained an agricultural country throughout this period and its distribution of population changed little – industrial and commercial developments were gradual with the result that movement to industrializing areas occurred slowly and without major disruption. Unlike the situation on the mainland, rates of population increase were higher in poorer than wealthier areas – growth in the economically backward areas of the west and south was greater than in the more diversified economies of Ulster and Leinster.

BIRTHS AND DEATHS

Population growth during the eighteenth and first half of the nineteenth century was largely the result of changes in the relative numbers of births and deaths. Migration played a secondary role.

Figure 3.2 Changes in the distribution of population, 1801 and 1851

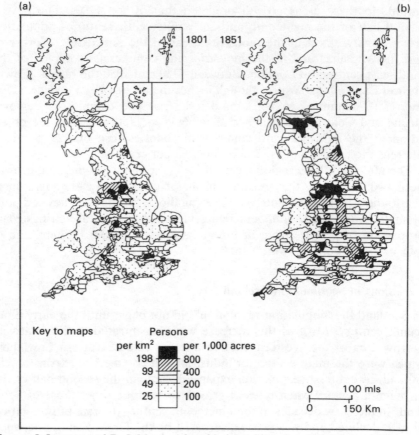

Source: J. Langton and R. J. Morris *Atlas of Industrializing Britain*, Methuen, 1986, p. 11.

Death rates

During the eighteenth century life expectancy rose from about 32 years to 39 years, an increase of a little over 20 per cent, except for a drop to 30 in the 1720s. After 1800 it rose to the low 40s where it remained until the late nineteenth century. This gradual increase hides the great variations that occurred in mortality. Pre-industrial populations were afflicted by 'demographic crises', sharp rises in mortality and falls in conceptions and marriages. Such crises were often connected with harvest failure – this was clearly the case in Ireland in the 1840s and Scotland in the 1690s – but during the eighteenth century they were more usually the result of epidemics and thus largely independent of the state of the economy.

Figure 3.3 Birth and death rates for (a) England and Wales, 1761–1931 and (b) Scotland, 1861–1931

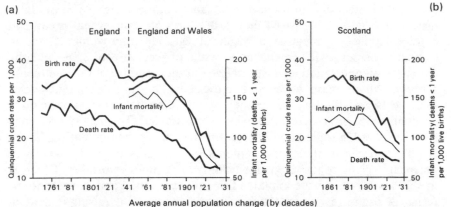

Source: J. Langton and R. J. Morris *Atlas of Industrializing Britain*, Methuen, 1986, p. 19.

England experienced two such 'crises' in the first half of the eighteenth century: from 1727 to 1730 with mortality 80 per cent above normal in 1729 with a second in 1740 to 1742 with deaths peaking 40 per cent above normal in 1742. Grain prices were not strikingly high and these 'crises' were caused, as contemporary medical observers reported, by a wide variety of epidemics. Later industrial and urban growth also led to an increase in mortality caused by a deterioration in environmental conditions. In Carlisle death rates were 25 per thousand in the 1780s but 27 per thousand in the 1840s. There was variation within towns and cities. Areas where the labouring population lived had higher levels of mortality than areas where the more wealthy lived.

Despite this, English death rates fell from 25–6 per thousand in 1750 to 22 per thousand a century later, with much of that decline taking place after 1810. In Scotland, too, mortality fell even more rapidly than in England during the second half of the eighteenth and early nineteenth centuries. Scottish death rates fell from 37–8 to 29 per thousand, infant mortality from 236–8 to 163–4 per thousand live births between 1750 and 1820. In Ireland absence of direct statistical evidence has led to differing views on the behaviour of mortality rates. K. H. Connell argued that death rates did not decline. He based this conclusion on the continued severity of epidemics, lack of improvements in sanitation and the inadequacy of medical advance. On the other hand Drake and Razzell have argued that death rates did decline in the late eighteenth and early nineteenth centuries. There are few local studies to test these competing claims. But those that have been carried out favour the view that in Ireland, too, death rates did fall.

In the 1920s historians suggested that the fall in mortality was caused by the beneficial effects of mid-century legislation restricting the manufacture and consumption of gin, improvements in the health of towns up to the early nineteenth century and to advances in medicine. To these, later historians added an improved diet in the form of better wheat bread and ampler supplies of meat as a result of agrarian improvements, raised standards of personal hygiene as a result of freer use of soap and the extension of inoculation against smallpox in the last third of the eighteenth century. All of these have been criticized. The 'gin' argument seems to have lapsed though the impact of this essentially urban vice on a predominantly rural society has been overestimated. Town conditions may have improved in some areas but not for the bulk of the population. There is little to indicate that improvements in standards of public health or personal hygiene contributed significantly to declining mortality. Changes in the death rate can be explained in both economic and non-economic terms. A rise in real income may reduce death rates by raising individual food consumption, or by increasing the funds available to public authorities for public health services or better housing. Changes in dietary patterns or land tenure can produce similar results without changing real income. The introduction of the potato, especially into Ireland and Highland Scotland, may have had this effect. Rising standards of nutrition have been seen as the single most significant cause of declining mortality rates since the mid-eighteenth century. Falling Irish death rates have been seen as due, wholly or partially, to the introduction of the potato. In Scotland rising real wages enabled people to eat better, a situation assisted by improvements in marketing food supplies. In England, too, rising standards of nutrition have been given considerable credit for the decline in mortality. But the evidence for changes in diet is notoriously difficult to interpret.

The most important reason for the varying decline in mortality – the reduction in deaths from infectious diseases both endemic and epidemic – has also been criticized. In 1955 two medical historians, McKeown and Brown, challenged the prevailing views on the demographic impact of medical improvements. But Michael Flinn stated that 'It may be that epidemiology rather than economics may explain some of the fluctuations in mortality . . .'.[5]

Tranter suggests that the reduction in mortality was the result, first, of forces which were independent of improvements made by people to their own condition and environment and, secondly, of influences over which people did have control.[6] Human resistance to disease as well as the replacement of the black by the brown rat led to plague ceasing to influence mortality. The natural virulence of the large number of infectious diseases seems to have been reduced between the mid-eighteenth and mid-nineteenth centuries, though urban expansion saw a resurgence of water-borne diseases, especially cholera, 'the new plague'.

There may well have been pathological reasons for this but falling death rates were primarily the result of individuals' efforts to improve their conditions. In the eighteenth and early nineteenth centuries there was an impressive increase in facilities for medical assistance. The number of voluntary general and specialist hospitals and dispensaries funded by private charity and providing free treatment and medicine was expanded. In Ireland seven voluntary hospitals were opened in Dublin between 1718 and 1773. By 1804 there was at least one general infirmary in each county and, by 1845, 632 dispensaries. In Scotland a similar process was evident. In England 33 voluntary hospitals were founded between 1720 and 1800 and dispensaries were treating over 50,000 patients a year in the London area by 1800. The extent to which the new medical services contributed to the decline in death rates depended on whether they treated illnesses prominent among the main causes of death and whether the treatments were effective. Medical advance was as much the result of guesswork as scientific knowledge and surgical techniques were conservative. It was the introduction of inoculation and vaccination against smallpox and the increasing practice of isolating victims of infectious diseases that made the greatest contribution to declining death rates. Immunization against smallpox was introduced into England in the early eighteenth century, but became common only after the 1760s as a result of safer methods of inoculation pioneered by the Sutton family. By the early nineteenth century inoculation, together with Edward Jenner's new technique of vaccination, provided effective methods for combating the major killer disease of the eighteenth century. Even before vaccination was made compulsory in 1852 – it was not legally enforceable until 1871 – there had been a considerable reduction in the risk of smallpox as a cause of death. In 1750 smallpox accounted for about 16 per cent of all deaths but only 1–2 per cent by the mid-nineteenth century.

There is little consensus on the causes of falling death rates.[7] In 1970 M. W. Flinn wrote that 'The problem of explaining the decline of mortality . . . remains largely unsolved.' Fifteen years later N. Tranter said that 'The only safe conclusion that can be reached about the rise in life expectancy . . . is that its causes were diverse. . . . For the period between the mid-eighteenth and mid-nineteenth centuries the degree of uncertainty is still greater.'

Birth rates

The birth rate measures the number of births per thousand of the population over a given period of time (usually a year). Such a rate is the function of three main variables: the ratio of births to women of child-bearing age; the ratio of women of child-bearing age to the total population; and the proportion of women of child-bearing age who marry. Fertility, by contrast, is defined as the physiological ability of men to impregnate and of women to conceive and bear healthy children. Until the 1950s the view that population expanded in the eighteenth century as a result of the reduction of the death rate was not seriously challenged. Recently, the belief that rising fertility was the major element in Britain's demographic growth has found persuasive support.

Fertility in pre-industrial societies was overwhelmingly marital. Changes in the age of marriage therefore had an important impact on the birth rate. Connell suggested that falling age of marriage and thus rising fertility was chiefly responsible for the accelerated rates of population growth from the 1780s though to the Irish Famine and that rising ages of marriage led to population deceleration in the decades after 1850. Though his ideas provoked intense controversy, recent work has given some support to his thesis.

In England there is considerable evidence of a substantial decline in the mean age of marriage between the late seventeenth and early eighteenth centuries, a decline that was especially pronounced after 1750. In general the average age at which women married fell by 2.7 years between the early eighteenth and early nineteenth centuries. There was also a significant decline in women who did not marry. Wrigley and Schofield estimate that this fell from 15 per cent of each age group in 1700 to only 7 per cent by 1800. Changes in marriage patterns were one of the major reasons why population began to grow.

Table 3.3 Mean age at first marriage

Period	Male	Female
1700–49	28.1	27.0
1750–99	27.1	25.4
1800–49	26.5	24.3

Source: E. A. Wrigley 'Age of Marriage in Early Modern England', unpublished paper quoted in R. Floud and D. McCloskey (eds) *The Economic History of Britain since 1700*, vol. I, Cambridge University Press, 1981, p. 27.

Illegitimacy

Long-term trends in illegitimacy, bridal pregnancy and legitimate bridal fertility moved roughly in unison. The rates of premarital conception and illegitimacy increased from about 10 per cent of all first births in 1700 to 25 per cent in 1800 and a further quarter of all births were prenuptially conceived: 2 per cent of all births to 6 per cent. These rates were markedly lower in Ireland than in England and Wales and highest in Scotland. Legitimate fertility was higher in the industrializing north-west than elsewhere and consistently higher in industrial than agricultural villages.

Table 3.4 Births per thousand population: England 1750–1850

Year	Birth rate
1751	34.2
1761	34.8
1771	35.2
1781	35.5
1791	38.4
1801	33.9
1811	40.0
1821	40.9
1831	35.2
1841	36.0
1851	36.4

Source: E. A. Wrigley and R. S. Schofield *The Population History of England, 1541–1871, a Reconstruction*, Edward Arnold, 1981, rev. edn Cambridge University Press, 1989, pp. 528–9.

Birth rates gradually grew in the seventy years before 1750, increased sharply in the late eighteenth century to a peak in the 1810s, declined between 1820 and 1845 and then rose moderately until the mid–1860s (see Table 3.4).

The causes of the rise in levels of illegitimate and legitimate fertility are a matter of considerable dispute. The only issue on which historians appear to agree is that birth rates were determined by people exercising choice about whether to marry or not, when to marry and how many children to have inside and outside marriage. Increase in illegitimacy occurred against the background of falling, not rising, ages of marriage and increasing marriage rates. This has been explained in various ways. The Hardwicke Marriage Act of 1753 drew a distinction between church marriages which were considered legally valid and clandestine or 'irregular' ones. It removed the situation that existed before 1753 where children from either type of union were generally considered 'legitimate'. The general validity of this thesis, put forward by B. Meteyard in 1980 and 1981, has been questioned on several counts but especially because it overlooks the fact that most illegitimate births in the late eighteenth and early nineteenth centuries were the result of casual liaisons which were not followed by regular unions.

A second viewpoint, expressed by E. Shorter,[8] sees increased rates of illegitimacy as the result of a revolution in sexual morality, from the sexual chastity of the seventeenth century to one of sexual licence. Shorter sees this as the result of urban industrialization and the growth of employment opportunities for women outside the home. This growing independence was translated into a sexual rebellion against parental constraints on pre-marital sexual relationships. Sex became an expression of personal choice and pleasure rather than a procreative necessity. The Shorter thesis is flawed on several grounds. First, illegitimacy rates in the late eighteenth century were not so much greater than those in the seventeenth century so the notion of sexual revolution may be exaggerated. Secondly, urban industrialization did not immediately lead to more than a moderate increase in employment out of the home, a situation that anyway existed before the industrial revolution with large numbers of young women working in domestic service. In Scotland, for example, there were lower levels of bastardy in urban rather than rural settings, which owed much to the attitude displayed in those communities to premarital sex. The third explanation sees illegitimacy, not in terms of legal change or sexual revolutions, but as a response to the forces of economic change. Economic growth led to increased social mobility among the 'sexually vulnerable' – unskilled and propertyless men and women – which removed them from the protection traditionally afforded by kin and family, which generally led to marriage if premarital sex led to pregnancy.

Legitimacy

Rising legitimate fertility can be explained in terms of the falling age of marriage. E. A. Wrigley places marriage as 'holding the centre of the stage' accounting 'almost entirely' for the great increase in fertility, and holds the view that timing of marriage was closely related to long-term trends in economic conditions. But it is possible to identify other factors which influenced the rising tide of fertility in this period. One explanation sees it as a 'delayed response' to an earlier period of rising fertility. This thesis, put forward by Wrigley and Schofield, argues that children born and brought up in the relative prosperity of the 1725–50 period, when employment opportunities and real wages were high, were inclined to marry young in the third quarter of the century, despite the less conducive economic conditions. The reduction of real wages in the 1770s and 1780s led to declining fertility between the 1810s and the 1830s, while the higher real wages of the first decade of the 1800s led to higher fertility after 1835. This assumed that the 'remembered past' of childhood will influence the timing and extent of marriage.

Economic growth and births

Other explanations involve the effects of economic growth in stimulating birth rates. Running through most of these arguments is the Malthusian proposition that, for the mass of the population, there is a positive correlation between income and births. Adam Smith wrote in *The Wealth of Nations* in 1776, that 'The reward of labour must necessarily encourage in such manner the marriage and multiplication of labourers, as may enable them to supply that continually increasing demand by a continually increasing population.' Arthur Young said in *Political Arithmetic* in 1774: 'Is it not evident that demand for hands, that is employment, must regulate the number of the people?', and Malthus in his *Essay on Population*: 'What is essentially necessary to a rapid increase of population is a great and continued demand for labour.'

There is some evidence to suggest that their judgements were correct. In Ireland, for example, rising levels of fertility after 1750 may be partly explained by the shift from livestock to arable farming caused by an increased English demand for grain. Similarly, falling levels of Irish fertility after 1815 can be seen as a result of a move back to tillage brought about by falling grain prices and the repeal of the Cattle Acts which had smothered cattle production. Agricultural areas generally had more 'traditional' attitudes to marriage than the newly emerging industrial communities, with the result that the birth rate was higher in the latter than the former. Arthur Young again: 'Why have the inhabitants of Birmingham increased from 23,000 in 1750 to 30,000 in 1770? . . . where employment increases, the people increase: and where employment does not increase . . . the people do not increase . . .'.

Contemporaries were in no doubt that the effects of economic growth on child labour may have been to encourage earlier marriages and larger families. Deane and Cole argued in 1962 that 'the expansion of population in those districts which felt the direct influence of industrial growth was much more clearly due to an increased birth rate . . .'.[9] The modern view that birth rates rose in response to rises in income, real or actual, or increased opportunities for child labour or even, as Malthus believed, as a result of the system of poor relief which after 1795 incorporated family allowances is attractive.

Mortality or fertility?

Birth and death rates are fairly crude and fallible ways of determining reasons for population change. Wrigley and Schofield believe that it is necessary to use more refined measures. They have calculated the gross reproduction rate (the number of female babies which would be born to the average woman at prevailing fertility rates assuming she survived to the end of the child-bearing period) and expectation of life at birth (the number of years a newborn child will live at prevailing age-specific mortality rates). They have concluded that since (a) the gross reproduction rate rose by almost half from slightly over 2.0 to almost 3.0 between 1681 and 1821; and (b) expectation of life rose by about 20 per cent from 32 to 39 years, that (1) two-thirds or more of the acceleration in population was due to a rise in fertility; and (2) one-third or less was due to improved mortality.

For mortality alone to have accounted for population growth it would have had to improve far more dramatically. Growth was therefore a combination of both fertility and mortality, but with an emphasis on the former.

MIGRATION

Emigration

The increase in fertility and the decline in mortality were certainly largely responsible for the rise in the total population of Great Britain between 1700 and 1850. But from the late eighteenth century emigration had a marked, though secondary, impact on national trends in population growth.[10] There were important regional differentials. Between 1780 and 1840 1.8 million left Ireland for either mainland Britain or North America and Australasia. The famine years between 1845 and 1851 exacerbated that trend. Outmigration, especially from the Highlands, had an important effect on Scotland's demographic growth. In England and Wales the effect of emigration on population increase was less dramatic. In fact there was widespread opposition to emigration well into the late nineteenth century and until after 1815 the cause of emigration attracted little sympathy. But in 1826 the Select Committee on Emigration advocated voluntary emigration as a solution to the problems of excess labour at home and the needs of the colonies for labour and security from attack. Many contemporaries saw emigration as the only real means of combating over-population. It was encouraged by a variety of public and private schemes. Large Highland landowners provided assistance for their tenants to emigrate. Between 1815 and 1826 there were six ventures in state-aided emigration and the Poor Law Amendment Act of 1834 assisted some 25,000 paupers, chiefly agricultural labourers from the south-east of England, to emigrate by 1860. Emigration could be a way of escaping from poverty but the poor could not leave without assistance. In Ireland low rates of emigration from County Cork before 1840 can be explained by the large number of landless labourers unable to meet the costs of movement. Only after 1846, when conditions improved, did emigration rates increase. Regional and socio-occupational patterns of emigration show that the worst extremes of poverty prevented as often as they promoted movement abroad.

Internal migration

The most striking features of internal migration in the pre-industrial period were its frequency and its usually restricted geographical range. In eighteenth-century England most people changed their permanent residence at least once in their lives though few moved more than ten miles from their place of birth. Deane and Cole identified several features that characterized internal migration during the eighteenth and early nineteenth centuries.[11] First, the level of migration between counties increased two-fold between 1700 and 1800. Secondly, the bulk of the migrant population went to the four counties in the London area, Middlesex, Essex, Kent and Surrey. Thirdly, migration appears to have played a small role in the expansion of newer industrial areas during the eighteenth century. Between 1700 and 1750 about 40 per cent of the migrants attracted to areas outside London went, not to the North or the Midlands, but to Gloucestershire and Hampshire, Bedfordshire, Buckinghamshire and Hertfordshire. Population growth in the industrial centres of Lancashire, Staffordshire, Warwickshire, the West Riding, Cheshire and Monmouth in the eighteenth century was the result of natural increase and not until after 1800 did internal migration play a more important role.

Migratory patterns altered little during the eighteenth centuries for the following reasons. First, there were many traditional barriers to mobility. Poor standards of education, low incomes, family loyalties, difficulties in transport were all factors that limited movement. Secondly, employment opportunities increased in many rural areas, particularly where textile industries continued to expand. As a result there was less need to look for employment elsewhere. Most of the early industrial centres relied on nearby populations for their labour supply. Thirdly, the old poor laws restricted mobility in two important ways. Many parishes dispensed relief liberally and this was a disincentive to movement. In 1836 a contemporary claimed that

> the chief cause which has prevented English in distant counties from availing themselves of the vast demand for labour in such thriving . . . towns as Birmingham, Liverpool . . . is the operation of the poor laws, by which the unemployed poor has been chained to the soil. . . . Where the parish is bound to maintain a man at home it is natural that he should not go abroad to seek for work . . . he will prefer the certainty of a scanty maintenance on idleness among his own friends.[12]

The other poor law restraint was the settlement laws which forcibly removed paupers to their own parish if they needed assistance. Though the impact of these laws upon mobility is debatable they certainly reinforced the identification of the parish with security and may well have given potential migrants reasons to stay.

Internal migration, however, did play an important part in determining regional differentials in the rate of population growth within each of the countries of the United Kingdom. In mainland Britain the number of people who temporarily deserted their homes and became seasonal migrants grew rapidly between 1750 and 1850. This was particularly the case for the Irish[13] and, to a lesser extent, Scottish Highlanders who migrated because of overpopulation and poverty and lack of employment opportunities outside farming in their own countries. The great increase in migration from the Highlands in the half-century after 1810 owed much to the decline of kelp fishing and illicit whisky distilling industries and the disappearance of military employment after 1815 as well as the 'clearances' of tenants by landlords converting arable land to pasture. Much of the seasonal work done by the Irish on the mainland fell into the semi-skilled and unskilled categories. In farming they provided the manual labour needed for harvesting – by 1794 open field farmers in Bedfordshire relied on the wandering Irish for harvesting crops; in the building trade, for labourers; navvies for road building, canal digging and railway construction. Those who turned seasonal migration into permanent settlement were largely involved in work English people found dirty, disreputable or otherwise disagreeable – jobs like petty trading, keeping lodging-houses and beerhouses. In 1840 three-quarters of the stall-holders in Manchester were Irish. Only in Scotland did the Irish get higher-paid jobs and this was due to their willingness to use new machinery in place of the more conservative Scottish cotton spinners and weavers. The Famine led to an enormous increase in the influx of Irish into Britain especially to Liverpool, Glasgow and the South Wales ports. In 1846 over 280,000 Irish immigrants arrived in Liverpool, of whom no more than 123,000 eventually went to other countries. In fact the Famine marked the high point of Irish migration to Britain.

POPULATION GROWTH AND ECONOMIC CHANGE

Population growth had a positive influence on British economic growth in the eighteenth and early nineteenth centuries. It is the precise nature of that relationship about which historians disagree. Economic expansion and population growth tend to be closely associated. But the history of Ireland in this period demonstrates that rapid economic growth is far from being a necessary or inevitable result of demographic growth.

If population growth did exert a decisive influence upon economic growth then it would have been evident chiefly through a growth in demand. Deane and Cole[14] discuss its effects upon demand and the labour supply, upon transport improvements and upon the search for inventions and their commercial application. They argue that movements in demand coincided with population movements. The expansion of the economy in the first half of the century was limited by restricted demand and this restriction was lifted by population growth after 1750. This argument holds good if economic and population growth did coincide. But they did not. Accelerated economic growth was concentrated in the last quarter of the eighteenth century whereas the maximum rate of population growth on mainland Britain was not achieved until after 1810. Population began to expand after 1750, and some historians argue that this provided the final ingredient necessary to trigger off industrialization. Deane and Cole have shown that the origins of higher growth rates in most eighteenth-century industries went back as far as the 1740s but recent estimates have pushed growth back to the early decades of the century. A. H. John[15] argues that rising demand for commercially produced products came from the bulk of the population as food costs fell in the early part of the eighteenth century. This demand stimulated industrial expansion, which calls into question the existence of an economic upturn in the 1740s and smoothes the upturn after 1780. The symbiotic relationship between population and economic growth should not be overstated.

There are, however, many possible ways in which population growth may have had favourable effects on the rate of economic development. In 1963 H. J. Habakkuk saw three possible consequences

> an abundant supply of labour at the going wage was favourable to accumulation . . . and a high rate of natural increase was a necessary condition of an abundant supply of labour. Population growth was therefore favourable to the widening of capital. . . . [16]

> a growing population might stimulate investment by its effects on the demand side . . .

> a growing population is likely to spend a higher proportion of its income on housing and transport facilities.

This third tendency is encouraged, he argued, by urban concentration which made it profitable to create or improve services. For example, the building of the canal from the Bridgewater coal-mines at Worsley to Manchester took advantage of the growing demand for domestic coal.

The role of demographic change in the genesis of the British 'industrial revolution' was not a straightforward one. More people in England, Scotland and Wales stimulated demands which the growing economy was largely able to satisfy. But in Ireland population growth in the eighteenth century was followed by stagnation and immiseration in the first half of the nineteenth century.

NOTES

1 N. Tranter *Population since the Industrial Revolution: the Case of England and Wales*, Croom Helm, 1973, pp. 13–42 and his broader *Population and Society 1750–1940: Contrasts in Population Growth*, Longman, 1985 provide the most straightforward discussion of the problems. E. A. Wrigley and R. S. Schofield *The Population of England 1541–1871, A Reconstruction*, Cambridge University Press, 1989, first published 1981, is contentious, combative but ultimately convincing.

2 Useful analyses of Gregory King can be found in P. Mathias *The First Industrial Nation*, Methuen, 2nd edn, 1983 pp. 23–30 and G. S. Holmes 'Gregory King and the Social Structure of Pre-industrial England', *Transactions of the Royal Historical Society*, 1977.

3 A convenient discussion of Massie which includes a comparison with King and Colquhoun can be found in P. Mathias 'The Social Structure in the Eighteenth

Century: a Calculation by Joseph Massie', first published 1957 and reprinted in his *The Transformation of England*, Methuen, 1977, pp. 171–89.

4 On the nature of nineteenth-century censuses and how to approach them see R. Lawton (ed.) *The Census and Social Structure*, Cass, 1978 especially pp. 1–27 and E. A. Wrigley (ed.) *Nineteenth Century Society: Essays in the Use of Quantitative Methods for the Study of Social Data*, Cambridge University Press, 1972. W. A. Armstrong *Stability and Change in an English County Town: A Social Study of York 1801–1851*, Cambridge University Press, 1974 shows what can be produced.

5 M. W. Flinn *Origins of the Industrial Revolution*, Longman, 1966, p. 22.

6 N. Tranter, op. cit. 1985, pp. 64–91, M. W. Flinn *British Population Growth 1700–1850*, Macmillan, 1970, pp. 37–50 and E. A. Wrigley 'The Growth of Population in Eighteenth Century England: A Conundrum Resolved' *Past and Present*, vol. 98, 1983. R. Porter *Disease, Medicine and Society in England 1550–1860*, Macmillan, 1987, especially pp. 23–48, is a convenient summary of the impact of disease and society's response to it.

7 M. W. Flinn 1970, p. 45, N. Tranter 1985, pp. 87–8.

8 E. Shorter *The Making of the Modern Family*, Oxford University Press, Glasgow, 1977. J. R. Gillis *For Better, for Worse: British Marriages 1600 to the Present*, Oxford University Press, 1985 is excellent and A. Macfarlane *Marriage and Love in England 1300–1840*, Blackwell, 1986 is contentious.

9 P. Deane and W. A. Cole *British Economic Growth*, 2nd edn, Cambridge University Press, 1967, pp. 133–4.

10 A good analysis of nineteenth-century migration trends can be found in E. H. Hunt *British Labour History 1815–1914*, Weidenfield & Nicolson 1981, pp. 144–87, especially pp. 158–76 on the Irish impact. See also A. Redford *Labour Migration in England 1800–1850*, Manchester University Press, 1964.

11 P. Deane and W. A. Cole op. cit. pp. 111–14.

12 Quoted in E. H. Hunt op. cit. p. 149.

13 R. Swift and S. Gilley (eds) *The Irish in Britain, 1815–1939*, Pinter 1989 is a useful study on this subject and should be used in conjunction with E. H. Hunt op. cit.

14 P. Deane and W. A. Cole op. cit. pp. 88–97.

15 A. H. John 'Agricultural Productivity and Economic Growth in England 1700–1760', in E. L. Jones (ed.) *Agricultural and Economic Growth in England 1650–1815*, Methuen 1967.

16 H. J. Habakkuk 'Population Problems and European Economic Development in the Late Eighteenth and Nineteenth Centuries', *American Economic Review*, vol. 53, 1963.

4 Change on the land

In 1700 agriculture was the mainstay of both British economy and society. Little was to change until after 1800 and even by 1850 farming was the largest single employer of labour. 'The most opulent nations, indeed, generally excel all their neighbours in agriculture as well as in manufactures.'[1]

Adam Smith believed that agriculture was the foundation of economic development, and historians have been eager to point to the connections between industry and agriculture. But they have generally treated agriculture as the 'sleeping partner'. This anti-agrarian prejudice was conveyed clearly by John Stuart Mill:

> The improvements which have been introduced into agriculture are so extremely limited, when compared with those of which some branches of manufactures have been found susceptible, and they are, besides, so very slow in making their way against those old habits and prejudices, which are perhaps more deeply rooted among farmers than among any other class of producers. . . .[2]

Agriculture, in fact, played a dynamic role in the wider economy. Without a responsive farming sector the expanding population could not have been properly fed and important areas of manufacture might have grown less rapidly. In 1700 Britain was more or less self-sufficient in food supplies and was a net exporter of wheat until the 1760s. Nearly 400,000 quarters of wheat went abroad each year between 1740 and 1750. Yet despite the increase in population British farmers still met 80 per cent of home needs in 1850. This revolution in output was the result of the widespread introduction of new methods of farming – new crops, better rotation systems and, particularly in the nineteenth century, new machines – and new modes of organization – enclosure of some open fields and waste, and better farm management.

AGRICULTURE – A DIVERSE REGIONAL FRAMEWORK

In 1700, with the exception of parts of upland Wales and Scotland, Britain was not characterized by self-supporting rural communities.[3] Agriculture existed in a diverse market-oriented regional framework. Regions tended to specialize in the production of those goods for which they were best suited. Highland Scotland and Wales raised cattle and sheep which were driven to the fattening pastures of the Midlands and East Anglia before sale in the growing urban markets, especially London. The southern English counties and much of Ireland were notable granaries. The western counties were mainly under grass. Market towns were in a denser network in the wealthier southern part of England, except on the downland zones. In northern England, Wales, Scotland and Ireland the market areas were more extensive. This reflected not only the different types of farming but different market specializations. Cattle markets on the uplands and the sheep markets on the heathlands had much wider limits than the corn, fruit and dairy markets of south-west, south and eastern England. There were, however, some markets which had a significance outside their own area: large wheat markets at Ipswich, Farnham, Basingstoke, High Wycombe and Bedford with Haddington and Dalkeith in Scotland; barley markets at Ware, Royston and Abingdon; Falkirk was the main centre for Highland cattle sales, Shrewsbury, Wolverhampton and Birmingham had trade in Welsh cattle; the annual sheep fairs at Weyhill, near Andover and Market Weighton in the north saw over 100,000 animals change hands; specialist fairs were held at Norwich for fish, Banbury and Dunkeld for horses and Dorking for poultry.

BRITISH FARMING – MARKETS AND 'MODERNITY'

British farming was modern in two important respects. It was both market-oriented and regionally specialized. But it would be wrong to overestimate its sophistication. Eric Pawson[4] identified three features which put this 'modernity' in context: the amount of land that lay waste, the organization of farming and the techniques used in cultivation.

'Waste land'

'Waste land' consists of all land not used either for permanent farming or for extensive grazing. In 1696 Gregory King estimated that about a quarter of the total area of England, Wales and Ireland was 'waste'. The figure was considerably higher in Scotland, perhaps as much as a half. Some waste was brought into use during the eighteenth century – some 2.8 million acres – and even more in the nineteenth. In Wales, for example, between 1801 and 1815 there were seventy-six enclosure awards involving some 200,000 acres, most of which was waste land lying between 700 and

1,000 feet on the upland fringes. Despite Vermuyden's drainage schemes of the mid-seventeenth century much of the Fens was still unusable because of flooding. The relative distribution of waste lands in 1850 was very similar to that in 1700.

Organization of farming

Much of England's arable area – perhaps as much as half – and most of Scotland's was organized on the traditional common or open field system. Lands were held by farmers throughout the large open fields in strips or, in Scotland, 'rigs'. The regional pattern of remaining open fields was very distinctive: outside Scotland, it was largely limited to the English clay vales. By 1700 substantial areas of England and especially the lowlands of Wales had already been enclosed. Large parts of the Weald, the Chilterns, East Anglia, the south-west and northern England had never been subject to communal organization, the result either of the type of farming practised there or because they had gradually been reclaimed by individual farmers.

Both the English and Scottish open field systems[5] were based on the interdependence of arable and pasture, though the English system was more developed. In Scotland the 'infield', the best cropped area, amounted to about a fifth of the arable acreage and was kept in permanent tillage through applications of manure. The 'outfield' was cropped by shifting cultivation with an area tilled until exhausted. In England, by contrast, the equivalent of the infield had evolved into common fields. These were used in rotation, with one field left fallow or sown with a grass ley for common grazing. This supplemented the common and waste and explained the grazing of animals on the stubble after the harvest. The remaining fields had spring and winter sown grains. In Scotland climatic conditions led to all grains being spring sown. The systems did overlap. Parts of lowland Scotland, especially in the Lothians, operated a common system similar to that of England. On the other hand, the use of the infield–outfield system operated south of the Border, especially in the Yorkshire and Lincolnshire Wolds, in Derbyshire and the Brecklands in Norfolk.

Contemporaries were quick to condemn the open field system, none more so than Arthur Young. He wrote in 1809:

> When I passed from the conversation of the farmers I was recommended to call on, to that of men whom chance threw in my way, I seemed to have lost a century in time, or to have moved a thousand miles in a day. Liberal communication, the result of enlarged ideas, was contrasted with a dark ignorance under the cover of wise suspicion. . . . The old open-field school must die off before new ideas can become generally rooted.[6]

Communal farming could be conservative and wasteful but the open field system was both adaptable and efficient,[7] and much of the increase in output up to the 1780s in fact occurred through its use. But Eric Pawson is probably correct when he writes that 'Nevertheless, the open-field system of England and Wales was not the most suitable means of organizing eighteenth century agricultural production.'[8]

Farming techniques

Techniques used on both open and enclosed land were generally crude in 1700. Tools were very simple and mainly made of wood. This remained the case throughout the eighteenth century. Iron ploughs were not widely used until the 1780s, later in Wales and Scotland. Wooden ploughs pulled by oxen were still used in Sussex in the 1850s. In some upland areas farmers moved their produce on wooden sledges while their more innovative neighbours were using steam engines and waggons on railway tracks. Farming was labour-intensive. Harvesting was by scythe or sickle; threshing by flail and winnowing by the wind.

The relatively primitive state of farming was reflected in the quality of output. Grain yields per acre, though they varied, were low and increased by only 10 per cent during the next century. Increased output was to be achieved by bringing more land under arable cultivation. Animal size was also low because of the quality and quantity of feed. Cattle and sheep frequently died or lost weight in the winter months because of lack of fodder.

'Modernity'

British agriculture in 1700 possessed features which were strikingly modern – it was based on markets and was regionally specialized – but was still backward in other areas – the existence of large areas of wasteland, communal organization and primitive practice. The process of change in farming during the eighteenth century was slow and its origins lay in the sixteenth and especially the seventeenth centuries. Eric Jones has recently commented that 'The agricultural growth of the eighteenth century was, as it were, a part of the history of an expanding universe not something that began with a "big bang".'[9]

A REVOLUTION 'IN SLOW MOTION'

Historians have reinterpreted their traditional view that the agricultural and industrial revolutions ran parallel from the mid-eighteenth to mid-nineteenth centuries. Some have even questioned whether there was a unique growth in agriculture which can be referred to as the 'agricultural revolution'. The fundamental change in eighteenth-century agriculture was in its scale of production. Overall output rose by almost a half, with all branches of farming participating to a lesser or greater extent. But what form did these changes take and what was the chronology of growth? Chambers and Mingay[10] maintain that the difference between the changes after 1750 and those of the preceding period was one of scale, adding that the advances after 1650 were 'of supreme importance; but it was a condition rather than a fulfilment of the promise of agricultural revolution'. This view of slow growth in the first half of the eighteenth century with more concentrated growth after 1750 is confirmed in Table 4.1.[11]

Table 4.1 Real output in agriculture (1700=100)

1700	100
1720	105
1740	104
1760	113
1780	126
1800	143

Source: M. Berg *The Age of Manufacture 1700–1820*, Fontana, 1984, p. 27

These figures are well below growth for industry and commerce and for total overall growth (see Table 4.2).

Table 4.2 Total real output and real output for industry and commerce (1700=100)

	Industry and commerce	Real output
1700	100	100
1720	105	108
1740	131	115
1760	179	147
1780	197	167
1800	387	251

Source: M. Berg op. cit., p. 27

Deane and Cole[12] suggest that wheat output per acre increased by about 10 per cent during the eighteenth century to about 22 bushels and that by 1850 output was about 25 bushels per acre. Between 1700 and 1850 yields of wheat increased by about a quarter, and grain yields as a whole by rather less. But the most significant advance was not in yield per acre but in the extension of land under grain by about half. Total corn output rose from about 13 million quarters in 1700 to 15 million in 1750, 19 million by 1800 and 25 million in 1820. Livestock estimates are even less certain than those for grain. The number of sheep probably doubled in the eighteenth century to about 26 million but declined subsequently. Cattle numbers in Britain were more constant at about 4 million but increased after 1800. There were, however, imports of cattle from Ireland and the Continent and the total supply of meat was affected by the increase in the average size and weight of animals. The achievement appears even more moderate when it is remembered that the major part of the increase in grain output was the result of the expansion of cultivated land and that the average increase in the size of livestock accounted for perhaps only a third of the total increase. G. E. Mingay sums up the difficulties in the following way

> The agricultural revolution of this period, then, consisted in the adoption over the larger part of the farmland, in the course of a century and a half, of methods of production significantly more efficient than those which formerly prevailed. This is an unsatisfactorily vague definition, but it is perhaps as good a one as can be formulated in the existing state of knowledge.[13]

New methods of farming were introduced gradually – advance in agriculture was not simply a post-1750 phenomenon. The foundations for expansion, in the spread of new methods and the shift in emphasis away from the heavy to the lighter arable soils, were laid then.

CHANGES IN FARMING

New crops

The most important change in agriculture lay in improved techniques of farming: the introduction of new crops, greater attention to soil fertility, and improved livestock breeding. The impact of new fodder crops – leguminous grasses (clover, rye-grass, lucerne and sainfoin) and roots, especially turnips, swedes and potatoes was widely felt. They were first introduced from the Low Countries in the mid-seventeenth century, popularized by 'Turnip' Townshend and other improving landowners and were widespread by the 1750s. Their impact was of major importance. First, they allowed large waste areas to be brought into cultivation. These included extensive areas of light soil on scarpland England which had previously been used only as sheep runs but also the areas which had previously been 'bare' fallow. New rotations were introduced. There was a Kentish system and a Hertford system but the most famous was the four courses of wheat, turnips, barley and clover introduced in Norfolk in the late seventeenth century. This 'Norfolk rotation' and other variants spread throughout the eighteenth century. Roots and grasses were used in the Scottish counties of East Lothian and Berwick by the 1730s. Clover had spread as far as the Hebrides by 1760. Turnips spread outside England more slowly, accounting for only 5 per cent of arable acreage in Wales by 1800 and not reaching the Highlands until the early nineteenth century. Potatoes were the only root crop widespread outside England during the eighteenth century and then primarily as a major item in people's diet. A second consequence of the new crops was that they underlay the increase in livestock production in the eighteenth and early nineteenth centuries by providing winter feed. For this reason they were also introduced slowly on the heavier lands.

New crops cannot be examined entirely in terms of clover and turnips. By the 1770s difficulties arising from clover-sick soils and diseased turnips were already matters of concern. The turnip crop could be unreliable and was restricted to areas of free-draining soil. The result was a diversification of rotations using sainfoin, lucerne or other alternatives to clover and the introduction of the hardier Swedish turnip and mangel-wurzel in place of turnips.

Improving soil fertility

In addition to the new crops a variety of methods were used to improve soil fertility. The supply of manure remained of critical importance in maintaining the fertility of the soil. Until after 1850 the main source of manure was, and remained, the dung of animals – hence the importance of new root crops and legumes which made it possible to keep more animals. Dung was also brought in from outside and farmers within easy reach relied heavily on 'town muck'. Farmers also made use of industrial waste materials – coal ashes, soot, waste bark from tanneries, bones, pulverized slag from ironworks. Seaweed was widely used in Scotland and coastal areas and pilchards in Cornwall. More widespread was the use of marl and lime. 'Marl' was a term applied to calcareous clays that were quarried and then spread on sandy and clay soils to improve their structure and to neutralize acidity. It was widely used, despite its high cost, throughout East Anglia, on the Chilterns and the Weald. Eighteenth-century leases often laid down how many acres were to be marled each year. Increasingly marling gave way to liming, which was used in many areas before 1700, and by 1800 most villages, even many farms, had their own lime-kiln. Liming was an essential part of the reclamation process on the moorlands of Devon and Somerset, where turf was cut, burnt and the ashes spread on the ground, before ploughing and liming. Guano, the dried droppings of seabirds, began to be imported in 1835 but quantities remained small till the 1840s. 'Artificial' fertilizers were introduced on a commercial scale in the 1840s largely as a result of the work of Sir John Bennet Lawes.

Water meadows were widely used on areas adjacent to rivers to stimulate early pasture. This filled the 'hungry gap' in the early spring and enabled more stock to be kept over winter. The practice spread from the West Country in the seventeenth century into the West Midlands and the southern downland counties. In due course the adoption of roots in rotation provided a more convenient and cheaper alternative, though water meadows were still in use in 1850.

Drainage was not a new problem in 1700. Although some surface drainage was achieved by the ridges and furrows created during ploughing, the importance of effective under-drainage was not recognized until the mid-eighteenth century. Joseph Elkington had proposed the making of borings to enable water to pass through the impervious stratum to a porous one in 1764 and James Smith used shallow drains in the 1820s. But it was not until the appearance of a tile-making machine invented by Thomas Scraggs and mole or drainage ploughs in the 1840s that the claylands were brought into more productive farming.

Improved livestock breeding

Livestock breeding improved considerably during the eighteenth and early nineteenth centuries. Before then the general standard of animals, often grazed on the commons, where they bred indiscriminately, remained low. Each area had its own local varieties of livestock, often well suited to the purposes required – wool, manure, meat or milk – and through natural adaption acclimatized to the local environment. In order to improve livestock cattle were brought in from the Low Countries, the Channel Islands and Denmark, and merino sheep from Spain. Robert Bakewell emerged as Britain's foremost livestock expert by the 1770s but his work was an extension of the work of earlier breeders and was complemented and improved by contemporaries and successors like the Culleys, the Collings, Jonas Webb, Thomas Johnes who introduced the merino sheep into Wales, Thomas Bates and Edward Corbet, the foremost cattle-breeder in North Wales. Bakewell's pre-eminence rested with his improved longhorn cattle and the 'Dishley' or 'New Leicester' sheep. Though both his sheep and cattle had defects – his longhorns were deficient in milk and fecundity, and his sheep fattened quickly – he did succeed in his main object of producing animals that were ready for the market quickly. Local breeds were improved by cross-breeding with Dishley sheep or Colling's shorthorns. This led to improvements in the Hereford beef breed, while experiments in Scotland by Barcley of Urry, the Booths and Cruikshank of Sittyton improved on shorthorn cattle, Guernseys were brought into the south-west and crossed with Devons, and the Aberdeen Angus became famous as a great beef animal.

Better machinery

Advances in stock, drainage, fertilizers and crops emphasized the need for improved farm tools and machinery. Before 1800 changes in implements, other than ploughs, proceeded slowly. The Rotherham plough, patented in 1730, only came into favour at the end of the century and then only in the north and east. In the 1780s Robert Ransome of Ipswich introduced the self-sharpening plough. This marked the beginning of mass-produced tools but in 1840 Ransomes too were producing as many as eighty-six different designs of ploughs to suit local needs. Jethro Tull invented the seed drill in the 1720s but it was not widely adopted until after 1800. From 1786 Andrew Meikle's threshing machine began to be adopted and horse-drawn reapers appeared in the early decades of the nineteenth century.

Mechanization in farming was primarily a mid-nineteenth-century development. The threshing machine was first adopted in Scotland and by 1815 was common both there and in north-east England. But it was not general in the south or in Wales until after 1850. Mention of drills rose rapidly after 1820 in Oxfordshire newspaper advertisements. Reapers and mowing machines did not appear until the 1850s and became common only after 1870. In 1850 most of the British corn crop was still cut and threshed by hand. The unreliability of some of the early machines partly accounted for this. But far more important was the cost of labour. In the north, where labour costs were higher because of competition from non-agricultural employment, the early adoption of powered threshing had economic justification. Adoption was more sluggish in the south where male labour was cheap and plentiful. Some farmers kept the old methods to provide a major source of winter employment in order to prevent throwing their regular men on to the parish.

The general effect of the spread of new farming techniques was to alter radically the pattern of eighteenth- and early nineteenth-century agriculture. Until the 1820s arable prosperity shifted away from the heavy clay vales to the lighter chalkland and heath soils. Many of these areas were close enough to the London market to profit from the overall rise in grain prices after 1750. The expansion of farming on to the lighter soils increased the overall farmed acreage in Britain by about a quarter. Some of this had been waste in 1700 but nevertheless the area of waste in England and Wales still exceeded one fifth of the total in 1800. The key counties were Northumberland, Lincolnshire, Leicestershire, Northamptonshire, Suffolk, the east counties of Scotland and above all Norfolk. Change occurred more quickly on the lighter soils, more slowly on the heavy clay soils which suffered from a shorter growing season, least flexibility in cropping and a higher risk of harvest failure. But important though these changes were their impact would have been lessened, especially after 1780, without the changes in the organization of farming – the gradual evolution of estates and farms through enclosure.

LANDOWNERSHIP

Although contemporaries placed considerable emphasis on the consolidation of estates during the eighteenth and early nineteenth centuries there was no rapid change in estate and farm size. Most farming was on a small scale. In 1851 62 per cent of farm occupiers in Britain held land between five and a hundred acres. There were only 7,771 farms in England of over 1,000 acres while some 142,358 farms were under 100 acres. The experience of Buckinghamshire was representative of southern counties: in 1851 1,810 farms can be identified of which 872 were between 100 and 300 acres and only 229 over 300 acres; the average size was 179 acres. In Yorkshire, by contrast, 70 per cent of farms were under 100 acres and in Lancashire and Cheshire the figure approached 90 per cent. Despite the relative importance of large estates, most farms of over 20 acres were tenanted and of sufficient size to be economically viable. Only in Ireland and parts of Scotland was Britain a nation of peasant occupiers where the cultivation of potatoes was intensive and allowed the increase in viable market units – by 1845 25 per cent of all holdings were between one and five acres and a further 40 per cent between five and fifteen acres.

There were three main categories of landownership in England.[14] The large landowners had estates of several thousand acres and gradually increased their share of the total area from 15–20 per cent in 1700 to between 20 and 25 per cent by 1800. The gentry,[15] with estates between 300 and 2,000 acres, remained relatively stable with about half of the total. But freeholders, with less than 400 acres, saw their position decline particularly at the expense of the large landowners.[16] Landowners leased their land to tenants, allowing them to consolidate their farms and to remove the inefficient farmer more easily. Below the tenantry were landless labourers who were employed either on a daily or annual basis. By the mid-eighteenth century this three-tier structure was characteristic of England and eastern Scotland. In these areas universal access to the land no longer existed because landowners did not subdivide their land to accommodate the rising population. The farm workforce grew by only 8.5 per cent compared to a rise of 81 per cent in the population of England and Wales between 1700 and 1800. By contrast in many parts of Ireland, central Wales and the rest of Scotland rural society was composed of landlords and rent-paying family cultivators whose potatoes allowed subdivision of holdings. Farming in England and eastern Scotland had evolved into a capitalist mode with underemployed marginal labour being absorbed in the expanding industrial sector. Elsewhere farming remained a subsistence pursuit without the profits which could be ploughed back into the land to improve it.

Technological progress and organizational forms cannot really be separated, as the function of the landed estate in promoting innovation showed. Organizational changes too had their origin in the seventeenth century. Farm book-keeping, textbooks, land surveying methods, the specialist development of land law and estate management, the development of the farm steward, societies with an interest in scientific agriculture, and the development of two legal devices, strict settlement and new legal terms for raising a mortgage, were all in being before 1700. These developments aided the dissemination of agricultural knowledge after 1700. It led to the formation of many local societies – the Dublin Society founded in 1731, the Society of Improvers in the Knowledge of Agriculture in Scotland 1723, the Breconshire Society in Wales 1755, the Smithfield Club 1798 – which published journals, held annual shows where prizes were offered for improvements in crops, livestock, implements and buildings, and some maintained fields for experiments. By 1810 there were seventy societies throughout the country. In Scotland they were concentrated in the Lowlands and in England around the new industrial towns. These evolved into national societies: the Highland and Agricultural Society of Scotland in 1785 and the Royal Agricultural Society of England in 1838. Most of the early societies probably had very little direct impact on improvement. The Board of Agriculture, formed in 1793, also proved ineffective as a means of accelerating agricultural progress. It lacked official status, was inadequately financed and poorly managed by Arthur Young, its secretary. With few exceptions its county reports were badly prepared and failed to attract a wide audience. The efforts of these societies became more effective after the 1810s because of the necessity of efficient farming if profits were to be made and were supplemented in the 1840s by the work of other private institutions like the Rothamsted farm of J. B. Lawes, the founding of the Royal College of Veterinary Surgeons in 1844 and the Royal Agricultural College at Cirencester the following year.

ENCLOSURE

Enclosure did more than any other development to alter the face of the countryside. But it is important to appreciate that in 1700 about half of the cultivated areas in Britain had already been enclosed or had never known open field cultivation. Enclosure was therefore an irrelevant measure of improvement for much farming in what has been regarded as the vital period. It is also true that British historians have tended to be far more interested in the controversial issue of the effects of enclosure on rural society than in its economic advantages, though these were of more permanent consequence.

Through enclosure the dispersed and fragmented holdings in common fields were replaced by holdings that were individually controlled, highly consolidated, much easier to work and more flexible in their use of soil.

It was important in improving the efficiency and flexibility of the open fields and in bringing into fuller use wastelands, marshes, heaths and hill grazings. It also provided the opportunity to rationalize the earlier piece-meal enclosures. Tithes were often abolished as part of the arrangements with the titheholder, who was compensated either with land or, less often, by a corn-rent. Enclosure allowed villages to improve their road system, dig drainage channels, rebuild farmhouses, barns and byres, and plant new hedgerows to provide windbreaks and shelter for stock.[17]

Chronology

Enclosure between 1750 and 1850 was largely as the result of parliamen-tary acts and fell into two phases (see Figures 4.1–4.3). Thirty-eight per cent of all acts were concentrated between 1750 and 1780, with 630 acts in the 1770s. The second phase of activity occurred between 1790 and the mid-1830s, though 43 per cent of all acts were passed during the French Revolutionary and Napoleonic wars.

The first phase was concentrated on the heavier-soiled counties of Mid-land clay belts, the lighter clays of much of Lincolnshire and over 60 per cent of East Riding acts. The second phase completed this process but included the lighter soils of East Anglia, Lincolnshire and the East Riding, marginal soils of the Pennine uplands and heaths of Surrey, Berkshire and Middlesex.

Historians who have examined the amount of arable and the marginal land enclosed have probably overestimated the former at the expense of the latter. M. E. Turner has provided the current summary of enclosure statistics shown in Table 4.3.

Table 4.3 Enclosure statistics

	Open field Arable	Common and waste	Total
Acts	3,093	2,172	5,265
Acres (millions)	4.5	2.3	6.8
Percentage of England	13.8	7.1	20.9

Source: M. E. Turner op. cit., p. 62.

Regional variations

There were considerable county and regional variations. In the Fens drain-age was the equivalent of enclosure elsewhere. In the seventeenth century the draining of fens and marshes had been met with considerable oppo-sition because each scheme gave the monarch one-third of the recovered

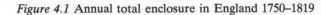

Figure 4.1 Annual total enclosure in England 1750–1819

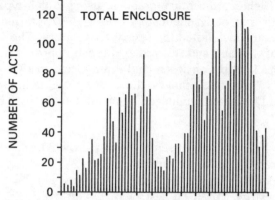

Figure 4.2 Annual open field arable enclosure in England, 1750–1819

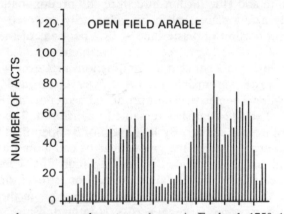

Figure 4.3 Annual common and waste enclosure in England, 1750–1819

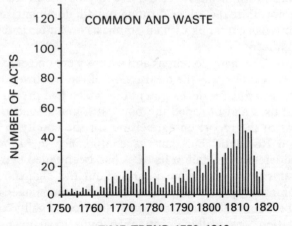

Source: M. E. Turner *English Parliamentary Enclosure*, Dawson, 1980, p. 70.

land, the drainers another third leaving only one-third for those with rights of common. Eighteenth-century drainage using Dutch-type tower mills, beginning with that of Haddenham Level in 1727, started a process of piecemeal action which lasted the rest of the century. The Crown did not take a third of the land and this reduced much opposition. By 1820 over 200 windpumps kept the enclosed land drained and in 1821 steam engines were first used.[18] An inscription on the existing engine house built for the Littleport and Downham Drainage Commissioners in 1830 records this in verse:

These fens have oft times been by Water drown'd.
Science a remedy in Water found.
The Powers of Steam she said shall be employ'd
And the Destroyer by Itself destroy'd.

Bedfordshire and Huntingdonshire were still predominantly open fields in 1750; only a few places had been voluntarily enclosed. Bedfordshire had a high proportion of waste land – 38.7 per cent of the total county area compared to 7.1 per cent in Northampton, 1.3 per cent in Buckinghamshire and 9 per cent in Huntingdonshire, even with its fenland tracts. This waste was mainly on the Lower Greensand and was still unenclosed when Thomas Bachelor produced his report in 1808. He found that only 43 of the 124 parishes remained unenclosed. The proportion in Huntingdonshire was similar. By 1820 most of its open-field parishes were enclosed and even some of the great areas of common grazing, whether heath or fen, had been divided up among individual commoners. The disappearance of fields brought about an economic revolution that was as important as the new hedged landscape. Tithe maps in the 1840s reveal the spread of pastoral farming across Huntingdonshire and much of Bedfordshire north of the River Ouse. Only on the Lower Greensand of central Bedfordshire did arable farming remain dominant, and in southern Bedfordshire dairy farming with an emphasis on butter and cheese for the London market.[19]

In Staffordshire many commons and wastes were enclosed before 1850.[20] The largest operation was the destruction of the Needwood Plateau, seen by improvers as ripe for development but which had previously had many agricultural uses and provided the poor with much-needed fuel. William Pitt, author of the report on agriculture for the county in 1796, thought it 'wild and Romantic' but that 'its continuance in its present state is certainly indefensible'. Half of its trees had been felled between 1697 and 1701 and this process continued throughout the eighteenth century. In 1801 all common rights were extinguished, the remaining 9,400 acres were enclosed between 1801 and 1811 and the trees finally cut down. This disafforestation was scathingly attacked by a local magistrate, Francis Mundy, in his poem 'the Fall of Needwood' (1808).

Alas, no gentle sprite remains!
But foul fiends scour th' affrighted plains,
Rob of their honour hills and lawn,
Trace the mean ditch that greedy yawns,
And teach the reptile hedge to crawl;
Twin pests, confederates, seizing all!

Wales

By 1700 much of lowland Wales had already been gathered into compact farms and enclosure reinforced this tendency.[21] But only thirteen acts were passed before 1795 involving some 28,596 acres mostly in the border areas. The great enclosures in Wales occurred between 1801 and 1815, when 76 acts were introduced affecting some 200,000 acres mainly on the highland commons and wastes. These were due to the great rise in the price of corn which led to attempts at cultivation at a higher altitude than ever before. The 1845 General Enclosure Act resulted in extensive enclosure in the 1850s and 1860s when 89 acts were passed. Enclosure and the spread of English land law had important social consequences leading to the virtual extinction of leaseholders in favour of tenancies-at-will, often renewed annually. By the 1830s a network of small farms of less than 100 acres had been created. Although the initial stimulus to enclosure in the wartime period may have been corn prices, most acts were motivated by pastoral considerations providing the low-lying farms with much-needed pasture. The enclosure of the hill slopes, coastal wastes and low-lying marshes led to improvements in cattle-breeding with the Castlemartin blacks and Glamorgan reds dating from this time.

Scotland

Enclosure in Scotland took a different form, although the result in the Lowlands was very similar to England.[22] Despite the passage of several acts by the Scottish Parliament after 1661 to facilitate enclosure, especially the acts of 1695, the major transformation of the agricultural economy was apparently a very rapid one and also, by English standards, a late one. There was some enclosure before 1750 but the peaks of activity were between 1750 and 1780, especially in the 1760s with lesser peaks in the 1810s and 1830s. The Lothians and Berwickshire were largely enclosed by 1770 but in Ayrshire and Perthshire the process was only just beginning. Nearly half a million acres were dealt with between 1720 and 1850.

Before 1750 the broad Highland straths were enclosed in the same way as the Lowland areas. But increasingly after the 1745 Rebellion, and particularly after 1780, large parts of the Highlands were cleared by the lairds and ordinary people swept off their traditional lands and replaced by the new commercial sheep breeds developed in England.[23] Farms were amalgamated and leased, at higher rents, to sheep graziers from the Lowlands. By 1800 large parts of the Central Highlands, southern Inverness and Perthshire had been cleared and this process continued in the first half of the nineteenth century throughout the north-west Highlands and Islands. Only in parts of the Western Highlands, the Outer Hebrides and Shetland did the old crofting framework persist and then largely because of the interdependence of fishing and farming. The social consequence of this was the progressive depopulation of the Highlands with the emigration of many people to North America and Australasia or movement to join the growing factory workforce of southern Scotland or England.

Historians have often seen this process as an unmitigated disaster for the Highlands, in which evictions were perpetrated by landowners who turned over their ancestral lands to capitalist sheep farmers who rejected the values of the old Highland clan system. At a general level this may well be accurate but it neglects the fact that migration from the Highlands pre-and postdated the clearances, that many people left the Highlands willingly, attracted by the better prospects of life in the southern towns, and that many of the sheep farmers were Highlanders. The clearances are better understood as 'the consequence of seemingly inexorable demographic and economic forces, operating upon a dependent and insecure society, and beyond the influence of local agency.'[24]

The pressures upon Highland landlords to rationalize their land use was far more severe than in England. Agricultural resources were narrow – the Highland economy was essentially a subsistence one – the levels of technology utilized were low and there were severe limits on industrial production. The economy was unable to accommodate an expanding population in contrast to the English or even southern Scottish experience. The Highlands could not follow the English example and expand the area under arable production – these had already been set by geographical constraints – and 'improvements' would have led to little increase in productivity. There was a reallocation of land within the pastoral sector of the Highland economy with an expansion initially in cattle production and a later switch of emphasis towards sheep production after 1760. The landlord, who controlled the resources of the Highlands, stood between the old society and the sheep farmers and was faced with a difficult moral and economic dilemma. The clearances were far more 'revolutionary' than any other part of Britain's agricultural transformation.

Ireland

The trend towards larger farms on mainland Britain did not occur in Ireland. Only on prime grassland did large farms remain intact as production units. In upland districts, on poorer soils and in areas away from centres of demand, small-scale farming increased, subdivisions of land occurred and supplementary income was obtained from spinning and weaving. By 1800 the most important change was the emergence of medium-sized, independent farming families. But generally in Ireland the pattern of land ownership emerged in the 1690s and remained intact throughout this period. There were some 2,000 large private farms. A few were compact but most were broken up into non-contiguous parcels of land. Landowners rarely adopted an active development of their estates as a whole and management of their properties was devolved to their tenants. Tenants tended to be the 'improvers' of land while landlords were more heavily involved in infrastructure improvements to road systems, canals and village planning. Improvement tended to be technical rather than structural: new crops rather than enclosure.

Of the general extent of enclosure there is little doubt but the details of its chronology and regional nature changes as research advances. It was a highly varied process whose role in change is questionable and the significance of which, relative to earlier enclosures, is still not fully understood. Recent work has placed more emphasis on enclosure by agreement in the seventeenth and early eighteenth centuries.

Why enclosure?

What motivated people to invest in enclosure after 1700? For investment to occur farmers must have believed or have observed that enclosure would result in significant economic gains. Although some historians have noted the problematic nature of efficiency gains many contemporaries were certain about the increased productivity achieved in terms of both improved output and rent. Gains of about 10 per cent on the yield of grain have been identified in Oxfordshire, Warwickshire and Northamptonshire when enclosed fields were compared with open ones. But improvements of 25 per cent may well have been possible. Arthur Young wrote of enclosure in Buckinghamshire in his *General Report on Enclosures*, in 1808, that 'the rents before were fourteen shillings but now arable lands let to twenty eight shillings per acre; none under a guinea; and grass from forty shillings to three pounds, all tithe free.'

For the landlord enclosure was an advantageous investment. Substantial rent increases meant that net profits of between 15 and 20 per cent could be made. Rental revaluation was thus both a cause and a consequence of enclosure. From the mid-eighteenth century until the end of the Napoleonic Wars prices rose. This too stimulated landowners, who often relied on fixed rents for income, to enclose and renegotiate leases with tenants who had previously gained from the rise in prices.

Figure 4.4(a) Wheat prices index 1731–1819

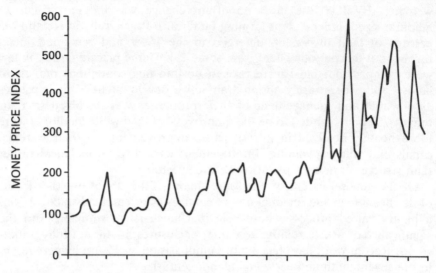

(b) 'Real' wheat prices index 1731–1819

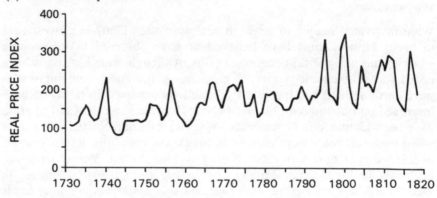

Source: M. E. Turner *English Parliamentary Enclosure*, Dawson, 1980, p. 107.

Interest rates?

Were interest rates or prices the more important factor in the decision to enclose? Figures 4.4a and b show the wheat price index from 1731 to 1819.

Between 1700 and the early 1790s growth was between 1 and 2 per cent per annum. Prices were relatively stable between 1730 and 1750 with the significant rise beginning from the 1750s culminating in the inflationary prices during the French Wars. The coincidence of this with the growth of parliamentary enclosure is obvious. Rising wheat prices and the inevitable effect of market forces are attractive in explaining motivation behind the additional enclosure of commons and waste after 1793 even though much of this was poor in quality and capable of only low yields.

Ashton emphasized the importance of money supply as a determinant of enclosure investment.[25] Relatively stable interest rates in the 1760s and 1770s coincided with the growth of enclosure while the higher rates during the American War of the late 1770s and early 1780s saw a significant decline. However, during the French Wars high interest rates and large numbers of enclosures coexisted. But the level of inflation was higher than the interest rates and in real terms money was 'cheaper'.

Population growth?

After 1740 population growth increased the demand for agricultural products. Price levels moved ahead more rapidly than those in industry, turning the market in the farmer's favour. Market orientation and regional specialization intensified as demand grew and this was reflected in the nature of change. Although British farming was largely capitalized by 1800, high-intensity farming was situated near the main centres of population in the band from Lancashire to London and in the Scottish Lowlands and in Ireland while lower levels of intensity were to be found on the upland fringes where stock breeding dominated.

Rising population increased the supply of labour. In 1700 between 60 and 70 per cent of Britain's population was occupied wholly or partially in farming. The number of mixed occupations was, however, very large and farming was often a valuable supplement to working in rural manufactures. By 1801 3.301 million people or 36 per cent of the population of England and Wales were involved in agriculture, forestry and fishing. This was a per capita increase of about 8 per cent over the century compared to a 81 per cent increase in total population. Although there were only slightly more people working in farming they were feeding more people:[26] one person in 1700 fed 1.7 persons whereas in 1800 one person fed 2.5 people. Although the percentage of the total population employed in farming continued to fall relative to other industries after 1800 in absolute terms people employed continued to rise until 1850 and no English county declined in population between 1750 and 1850. Farming remained a labour-intensive industry with no dramatic breakthrough in mechanization. Wages fell after 1800 only in those areas where there was little competition from alternative employers or where, as in the Highlands, change led to less labour being needed. Here the social impact of change was at its most devastating.[27]

Change in farming, particularly the willingness or ability of landowners to invest and labourers to introduce improved techniques and enclosure, related closely to growing demand, high food prices and interest rates. Abundant harvests and low prices were beneficial to everyone except farmers and landowners. This is reflected in the broad chronology of developments in agriculture between 1700 and 1850. Although there were regional variations five main stages can be identified: 1700–50, 1750–90, 1790–1815, 1815–35 and 1835–50. The first half of the eighteenth century, when total grain output rose from 13 to 15 million quarters, saw a growing agricultural surplus – the result largely of better use of available resources occasioned by the spread of new rotations and crops – when total population was not growing rapidly. From 1713 to the 1740s agricultural prices were either stable or falling slightly and considerable wheat surpluses were exported. This was encouraged by bounties imposed by statute in 1689 while import duties protected British farming when prices were low. Only between 1710 and 1719 and to a lesser extent between 1740 and 1749 did corn imports make any impact on the British market. G. E. Mingay[28] considers the period 1730 to 1750 one of 'depression'. W. Allen wrote in 1736 that

> the interest of our British landholders has been declining several Years last past. It has been a general Observation, that Rents have been sinking and tenants as unable to make as good Payments as formerly . . . great Men's Estates are commonly cheaply rented . . .

and three years later S. Trowell stated that 'farmers are at present as much depressed, though they labour a whole Year round; and too many are reduced to the utmost Necessity . . .'

The extent and intensity of depression remains uncertain. Mingay bases his case on the estates of the Duke of Kingston which spread over six counties. He shows that wheat prices fluctuated more than meat prices and that rents remained stable. The same general features were evident on other estates. The main reason for this 'depression' was a series of good harvests, particularly in the 1740s, which forced prices down and benefited the consumer. There is the paradox of landowners undertaking significant 'improvements' during a period of 'depression'. Real output in agriculture rose by about 5 per cent and this cannot be construed as revolutionary in quantitative terms. It is therefore in qualitative terms that historians must seek the 'agricultural revolution' before 1750.

An end of famine? enclosure and food prices

Rising population, more favourable interest rates and a rise in food prices led to a quantitative revolution after 1750. Adam Smith observed in *The Wealth of Nations* in 1776 that

> not only grain but many other things from which the industrious poor derive an agreeable and wholesome variety of food, have become a great deal cheaper. Potatoes . . . turnips, carrots, cabbages; things which were formerly never raised but by the spade, but which are now

commonly raised by the plough. All sorts of garden stuff, too, has become cheaper.

Between 1750 and 1790 there was a gradual but consistent increase in all food prices paralleled by gradual but accelerating enclosure. Wheat increasingly became the staple grain food – 89 per cent of Londoners were on a wheat diet by 1764 – and barley and rye continued to be important in northern Britain, Scotland, Wales and Ireland. Potatoes took on an increasing importance and help to explain demographic growth in Ireland and parts of Scotland. A rough balance between population and food supplies lasted until about 1780 but after that substantial and mounting imports were necessary. Corn prices began to rise faster than other prices and faster than wages. This stimulated further agricultural change.

Years of shortage, amounting between 1795 and 1800 and 1808 and 1812 to 'famine', became more frequent and local shortages and disturbances were often caused by the inability of the market structure to distribute supplies effectively. Increased demand was met largely primarily by the increased output of domestic farmers. Domestic production of grain rose at the same rate as total population – 14 per cent between 1793 and 1815. This increase was achieved by a widespread extension of the area under cultivation and the use of new crops and new breeds of livestock. The short-term response of farmers may have taken the form of temporary alterations in their grain acreage but their long-term response was a sustained effort to obtain a relative increase in their animal products. On the heavier clay soils, for example, unsuited for low-cost arable production, land was enclosed for grazing and dairy production at the expense of grain. The surviving records for a Wiltshire farm show that between 1793 and 1815 grain production fell by 20 per cent while that of livestock and dairy products rose between 20 and 25 per cent. The major problem facing farmers in this period was labour costs. The extent to which enclosure and new techniques required more labour has been challenged by Snell but in some areas labour shortages pushed up costs further. Many areas were forced to rely heavily on temporary inflows of casual workers. Yet, with the exception of a few areas, this did not result in the adoption of alternative hand tools or machines. In south Lincolnshire turnips and beans were widely grown for fodder, but their potential benefit was lost since they were not hoed and the sheep not allowed to feed on them, thus depriving the land of manure. Between 1790 and 1815 British agriculture increased its productivity by only 0.2 per cent per annun. This compares unfavourably with the 0.3 per cent per annum between 1816 and 1846, a period generally regarded as one of 'depression'.

Prices fell dramatically after 1814 and thousands were demobilized or released from war industries. This caused problems throughout agriculture[29] but the severity of distress was greatest on the clayland arable farms and least in dairy and stock-rearing districts or in areas like Kent and

Hereford where hops and fruit were important crops. Depression was therefore closely related to the adaptability of the land under cultivation. Clayland farmers could not compete with the more advanced farms of the light lands since they were unable to reduce their costs. Initially farmers sought legislative support in the form of protection or reductions in taxes. The Corn Law of 1815 was the result. This delayed the necessary adjustment of British farming since many clayland farmers clung on to their arable acreage in the persistent but vain hope that wartime prices would eventually return. They provided vociferous testimony before various parliamentary inquiries which took place between 1813 and 1843 into the causes of 'distress'. But by the 1830s many of them were making cost adjustments to lower prices or moving across to mixed farming. The social cost of 'depression' were most severe in areas with falling agricultural wages.[30] Tarrifs did little to protect arable farmers and provoked a violent reaction which the Anti-Corn Law League built on the 1830s and 1840s. Byron expressed the public wrath at the rapacity of the landlords in 'The Age of Bronze'

> Safe in their barns, these Sabine tillers sent
> Their bretheren out to battle – why? for rent! . . .
> The peace has made one general malcontent
> Of these high market patriots; war was rent!
> Their love of country, millions all misspent,
> How reconcile? by reconciling rent!
> And will they now repay the treasures lent?
> No! down with everything, and up with rent!
> Their good, ill, health, wealth, joy or discontent,
> Being, end, aim, religion – rent, rent rent!

TOWARDS A 'GOLDEN AGE OF FARMING'

By the mid-1830s British farming had surmounted its 'depression'. The introduction of inexpensive drainage techniques liberated the claylands from high production costs. Farming generally became more 'scientific', producing higher output at lower unit cost. From the mid-1840s till the 1870s agricultural production rose at 0.5 per cent per annum. There was a more intensive application of the techniques of mixed farming on the light soils of southern and eastern England and on the Lothian area of south-east Scotland. There was some shift on the clay soils, especially those in the north and west of England, to beef and dairy production. Distance from alternative markets protected arable farming after 1846 far more effectively and much less contentiously. Cheap food had become both an economic and a political necessity. R. S. Surtees caricatured this move to *High Farming* in 1845

'. . . you take your tenants in hand, Mr Jorrocks – make them drain.'

'Drainin's a great diskivery, your Grace. It's the foundation of all agricultural improvement. . . .'

'Guano, nitrate o' sober manure,' continued Mr Jorrocks. 'We'll have such a Hagricultural 'Sociation. . . . We'll make the grass grow, the grass grow. . . .'

There is no doubt that British farming was more productive than it had been in 1700.[31] But this development was neither as linear nor as progressive as the conventional view of agricultural change would have us believe. The point at which radical change began has been pushed back into the sixteenth and particularly the seventeenth centuries. The role of Tull, Townshend, Bakewell and their like has been reassessed. The chronology and regional experiences of farming changes were complex and the notion of an 'agrarian revolution' unhelpful unless qualified by reference to particular aspects of those changes. As Mark Overton commented:

If the meaning of a phrase is determined by its consistency of use, then the phrase 'agricultural revolution' has no meaning. . . . During the last twenty years at least four claims have been made for the existence of an 'agricultural revolution' at some time during the period 1560–1880, yet all differ in chronology and all emphasise different facets of agricultural change.[32]

NOTES

1 A. Smith *The Wealth of Nations*, ed. A. Skinner, Penguin, 1970, p. 111.
2 J. S. Mill 'The Nature, Origins and Progress of Rents' (1828) in *Collected Works*, Toronto, 1967, p. 177, quoted in M. Berg *The Age of Manufactures 1700–1820*, Fontana, 1985, p. 93.
3 For the state of farming in 1700 and the role of topography reference should be made to chapter 2. J. Thirsk *England's Agricultural Regions and Agrarian History 1500–1750*, Macmillan, 1987 provides a brief statement. More detail can be found in J. Thirsk (ed.) *The Agrarian History of England and Wales*, Vol. 5, Cambridge University Press, 1985. J. C. Beckett *The Agricultural Revolution*, Basil Blackwell, 1990 is a short and concisely argued book which provides the best starting point for a discussion.
4 E. Pawson *The Early Industrial Revolution* Batsford, 1978, pp. 45–52.
5 On the Scottish system see chapter 2 pp. 16–18.
6 A. Young *General View of the Agriculture of Oxfordshire*, 1809, pp. 35–6.
7 A detailed discussion of this can be found in J. D. Chambers and G. E. Mingay *The Agricultural Revolution 1750–1880*, Batsford, 1966, pp. 50–3.
8 E. Pawson op. cit. p. 50.
9 E. L. Jones 'Agriculture 1700–1780' in R. Floud and D. McCloskey (eds) *The Economic History of Britain since 1700*, Vol. I Cambridge University Press, 1981, p. 66.
10 J. D. Chambers and G. E. Mingay op. cit. pp. 12–13.
11 M. Berg op. cit. p. 27.
12 P. Deane and W. A. Cole *British Economic Growth 1688–1959*, Cambridge University Press, 1967, pp. 67–75.
13 G. E. Mingay *The Agricultural Revolution*, A & C Black, 1977, p. 6.

14 The best discussion is to be found in G. E. Mingay *English Landed Society in the 18th Century*, Routledge & Kegan Paul, 1963.
15 Mingay again is useful here in *The Gentry*, Longman, 1976, especially pp. 80–164.
16 On this issue see G. E. Mingay *Enclosure and the Small Farmer in the Age of the Industrial Revolution*, Macmillan, 1968.
17 The literature on enclosure is extensive but the most recent brief study is M. E. Turner *Enclosure in Britain 1750–1830*, Macmillan 1984. More detailed studies are M. E. Turner *English Parliamentary Enclosure*, Dawson, 1980, J. A. Yelling *Common Field and Enclosure in England 1450–1850*, Longman, 1977 and W. E. Tate *The English Village Community and the Enclosure Movement*, Gollancz, 1967. K. D. M. Snell *Annals of the Labouring Poor: Social Change and Agrarian England 1600–1900*, Cambridge University Press, 1985, pp. 138–227 is essential.
18 On the Fens see C. Taylor *The Cambridge Landscape*, Hodder & Stoughton 1972 and H. C. Darby *The Draining of the Fens*, Oxford University Press, 1940.
19 See P. Bigmore *The Bedfordshire and Huntingdonshire Landscape*, Hodder & Stoughton, 1979 and J. Godber *History of Bedfordshire*, Bedfordshire County Council, 1976.
20 See D. M. Palliser *The Staffordshire Landscape*, Hodder & Stoughton, 1976, pp. 119–32.
21 D. Williams *A History of Modern Wales*, John Murray, 1977, pp. 177–96 and E. D. Evans *A History of Wales 1660–1815*, University of Wales Press, 1976, pp. 124–36 provide a general overview. D. Thomas *Agriculture in Wales during the Napoleonic Wars*, University of Wales Press, 1963 is a more detailed study.
22 See J. E. Handley *The Agricultural Revolution in Scotland* 1963 and M. L. Parry and T. R. Slater (eds) *The Making of the Scottish Landscape*, 1980.
23 E. Richards *A History of the Highland Clearances*, Croom Helm, 1982.
24 ibid. p. 7.
25 T. S. Ashton *An Economic History of England: the Eighteenth Century*, Methuen, 1955, pp. 40–1.
26 Quoted in E. L. Jones 'Agriculture 1700–1780' op. cit. p. 71.
27 On the social impact of agricultural change, particularly the impact of enclosure, see chapter 17.
28 G. E. Mingay 'The Agricultural Depression 1730–50', *Economic History Review*, 2nd Series, 8 (3), 1956.
29 E. L. Jones *The Development of English Agriculture 1815–1873*, Macmillan, 1968 provides a brief analysis of the nature of 'distress' and 'depression'.
30 For a detailed discussion of the fortunes of agricultural labourers see chapter 17.
31 G. E. Mingay (ed.) *The Agrarian History of England and Wales*, Vol. 6, Cambridge University Press, 1989 must now be regarded as *the* major work on agricultural change.
32 Quoted in R. Butlin 'Agrarian Changes in the 18th and 19th Centuries – the Experiences of the East Midlands', *The Historian*, 6, (1985). p. 11.

5 The revolution in technologies – industrial change

Our engineers may be regarded as the makers of modern civilization. . . . Are not the men who have made the motive power of the country, and immensely increased its productive strength, the men above all others who have tended to make this country what it is.[1]

To England alone the whole world is indebted to these inventions, and as her just reward, she has reaped, beyond all comparison, the largest share of the golden results which have flowed from them.[2]

The technological and scientific achievement of the period between 1700 and 1850 was substantial. The immense force of that achievement in revolutionizing industrial production and organization, rapidly expanding trade and transport, stimulating vast amounts of capital investment and altering the whole structure of the labour force in particular and society in general has conventionally been examined in relation to the great inventions and inventors. This chapter will examine the relationship between technology, science and industrial growth, particularly in textiles, iron, coal and the diffusion of steam power.

Industrial production throughout the eighteenth century was tailored largely towards satisfying the basic needs of the population. It was not, by later standards, a sophisticated structure requiring widespread capital investment. There were regional clusters of manufacturing activity, particularly around the ports, the provincial textile and metal-working centres and in London. But these were loosely organized, dispersed and generally small-scale, often based round family groupings in a rural setting. Throughout the eighteenth century and to a lesser extent in the first half of the nineteenth century, there was a symbiotic relationship between the manufacturing and agricultural sectors. Employment was often 'mixed' and labour moved freely from one sector to the other, often depending on the season.

ELEMENTS OF PRODUCTION

Raw materials

The four elements of production that combine in the manufacturing process are: raw materials, capital, labour and entrepreneurship. Raw materials are important in two respects: as the source of production material and as a means of power. In 1700 most industrial raw materials were of organic origin: farm products like wool, leather and flax; timber; water. Power was either provided directly by labour or through machines powered by waterwheel, horse-gin or windmill. These sources of materials and power were dispersed throughout the country and, as a result, so were many branches of industry. Coal, as a source of raw material and power was, however, growing in importance. Brewing, glass and pottery manufacture had already replaced wood with coal for fuel. Non-ferrous smelting and the iron industry were to make this transition during the eighteenth century. By 1850 the raw material function in industry had changed. This was in response to the increased scale of output and the widening range of products demanded by the growing market. The shift was from natural to steam power and from timber and stone to iron and coal. But this was a process which occurred more gradually than has conventionally been admitted.

Capital

Capital requirements also changed slowly.[3] Throughout the first half of the eighteenth century investment in capital stock was low. Increased output was achieved not by increasing the scale or sophistication of production but by increasing the size of the labour force. This was a capital-widening rather than a capital-deepening process. Advances in spinning technology could only be fully utilized by increasing the number of hand-loom weavers until new technology became available in weaving. Capital widening did not require intensive investment. However, the main thrust of investment after 1750 was capital deepening especially where the adoption of improved or new technology involved intensive investment in fixed capital stock. This was evident in cotton textile spinning with the costs induced by technological improvements and the application of steam power after 1790. But this process must be kept in perspective as large-scale factory mechanization was by no means typical of the industry in 1800 or even 1850. Larger-scale investment was most notable in the iron industry, particularly with re-organization into large-scale integrated concerns. Most eighteenth-century enterprises were either partnerships or family firms – joint-stock companies had been virtually outlawed after the Bubble Act of 1720 following the collapse of the speculative South Sea

Company the previous year. Money could be borrowed by established firms but it was ploughed-back profits that provided much of the money for fixed capital. However, the major part of capital was held not in fixed plant but in working capital until after 1750. This was essential in outworking manufacture.

Labour

Labour requirements[4] were generally not large in 1700 though they too were to alter slowly in the next century. Rural industry, usually controlled from the towns, was often used to supplement inadequate agricultural earnings. These cheap supplies of labour enabled merchants to meet rising demands for goods. As manufacturing became more capitalized and as new technology was developed, the nature of labour changed. Factories, mills and large mines required a more rigorous regime than rural industries.

Entrepreneurship

The remaining factor of production was entrepreneurship.[5] The most successful regions, industries and firms were those in which people saw the potential of new markets or of new products, then organized a means of exploiting them and raised the capital necessary to finance both production and distribution. They were rarely inventors but seized the opportunities afforded by the new technologies. They were the risk-takers of manufacturing industry and have been described as fulfilling 'in one person the functions of capitalist, financier, works manager, merchant and salesman'.[6]

The eighteenth-century entrepreneur often made innovations in order to increase output and to earn windfall profits. A critical part of the entrepreneurial function lay in seizing a market opportunity. But the nineteenth-century counterpart was often forced to adopt new methods in order to maintain profits threatened by falling price levels and by increased competition.

The British economy that developed during the eighteenth century at once looked backward and forward. It was an economy in which artisan skills and traditions mingled with new products, demands, markets, labour forces and above all new technologies. David Landes has produced a bold description of sweeping technological change centred on the cotton industry, reinforced by the development of steam power and the expansion of the metal industries.[7] His apocalyptic vision needs to be set against those historians like Sir John Clapham and more recently N. F. R. Crafts[8] who emphasize the continuities of the period and see an industrial revolution 'in slow motion'.

BRITAIN'S INDUSTRIAL EXPERIENCE IN 1700

England

The industrial experience of Britain in 1700 was complex. The weight of industry is partially discernible in the demographic geography of the country. Certain areas were able to sustain a population in excess of local agricultural capacity through employment in manufacturing or extractive industries. Central Devon supported woollen manufacture. The West Riding of Yorkshire was not only sustained by textiles but also by coal mining and, in the Sheffield area, by metal-working. South Lancashire leant heavily on linen, fustian and woollen products. The north-east lived off coal and associated industries, especially glass and salt. Less obvious, because they were situated in good agricultural areas, were the woollen manufactures of Wiltshire, Somerset, Gloucestershire, Norfolk, Suffolk and Essex. Silk was important in London. The hardware trade, supplemented by coal mining, was the economic base of parts of Worcestershire, Staffordshire and Warwickshire centred on Birmingham. Leicestershire, Derbyshire and Nottinghamshire maintained many thousands of people in framework knitting for the hosiery industry. These main English regions apart there were numerous local industrial pockets, sometimes dominating the locality, sometimes an adjunct to farming: iron, lead, tin and copper mining and processing; shipbuilding; glass-making and salt production; paper-making; lace and rope-making. Brick-kilns were dotted throughout lowland England. Industry was overwhelmingly rural in its location. With the exception of London only three large towns could be called industrial centres in 1700: Norwich making worsteds; Birmingham, hardware and Manchester assorted textile goods, and even these were not just production centres but marketing and distribution points for rural manufactures. Gregory King's estimate of those employed in commerce and industry was 110,000 people in England at the close of the seventeenth century. This survey has recently come under scrutiny, which has led to upward revision. P. H. Lindert has estimated a figure over 400,000 people excluding labourers.[9] England probably had a much more industrialized economy than historians previously assumed. But it was not, in any useful sense of the term, an industrial country.

Wales, Scotland and Ireland

The situation in Wales, Scotland and Ireland was very different. In all three areas industry was an adjunct to the predominant agrarian economy. The woollen industry figured next in importance to the cattle trade in the Welsh rural economy but its output was, in comparison to England, small. In South Wales its early development had been in the boroughs – there are many records of it in Cardiff and Caerffili – but by 1700 it was declining as a town-based industry. In North Wales it was a rural craft from the beginning though firmly under the control of the Shrewsbury clothiers and dependent on the English market. Metal industries, notably iron, lead, copper and tin, coal and slate expanded largely because landlords were quick to exploit the resources of their estates. Welsh industry in 1700 was diffuse and expansion limited by the lack of substantial domestic demand and poor communications, both of which adversely affected the market. In Scotland too industry was overwhelmingly rural, though Elgin, Ayr, Dumfries, Falkirk, Paisley and especially Edinburgh catered for a fairly large luxury market. Salt, soap, woollens and linen were the major manufacturing industries with significant coal mining in the Ayrshire and Forth coalfields. Ireland lacked the same natural mineral resources as Wales and Scotland and had little heavy industry. But it did possess a growing textile industry, particularly in Ulster, based on wool and linen.

Realigning industrial activity

The eighteenth century witnessed a realignment of industrial activity (Figure 5.1). In some cases, this meant the expansion of industries that existed in 1700, such as woollen manufacture in the West Riding, iron in the Midlands, Lancashire cotton, linen in eastern Scotland and northern Ireland. In others, it meant the rapid emergence of new activities like the South Wales iron industry and the Glasgow and Irish cotton industries. Change also brought industrial decline as with the framework knitters of London, the spinners and weavers of the West Country and East Anglia and the ironmasters of the Weald and Forest of Dean. W. W. Rostow argues that 'these rates tend to be related to the time of the last major technological breakthrough which granted them a phase of increasing returns'.[10]

M. Flinn echoed this view ten years earlier:

> In the last resort, the decisive factor both in increasing the scale and in changing the methods and location of production was technology . . . the industrial revolution stemmed from the adoption of new techniques of production.[11]

Historians have emphasized inventors and their inventions without fully examining the rate of technological change or diffusion.[12] The following questions need to be considered fully: what is technological change and what was its relationship to science? What caused technological change? What was the rate of technological change and what were its effects?

CHANGING TECHNOLOGY

Technological change has been seen by Simon Kuznets as the process of transforming innovations into productive use in relation to capital invest-

Figure 5.1 England before the Industrial Revolution

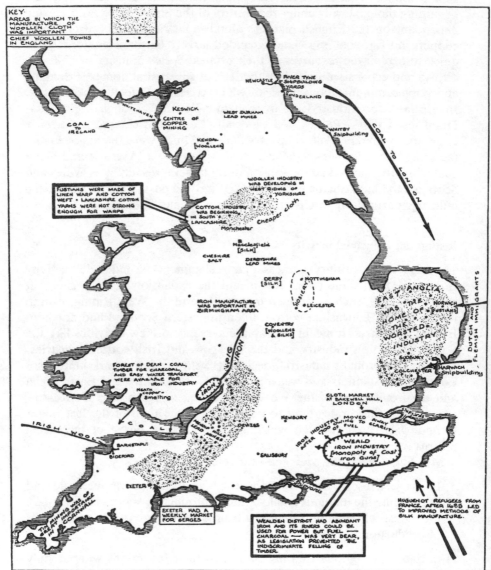

Source: J. L. Gayler, I. Richards, J. A. Morris *A Sketch-Map Economic History of Britain*, George Harrap, 1966, p. 72.

ment, entrepreneurial talents and market demand.[13] It is the practical application of a new machine or technique – which may not have labour-saving effects – to the productive economy. Kuznets distinguished between (a) a scientific discovery, an addition to knowledge; (b) an invention, the application of existing knowledge to a useful end; (c) an innovation, the first industrial use of an invention; (d) an improvement, an adjustment to the existing innovation; and finally, (e) diffusion, the spread of an innovation usually with additional improvements.

Relationship between science and technology

Just what was the relationship between science and technology in the economic changes that occurred between 1700 and 1850? W. W. Rostow is not alone in thinking that 'The scientific revolution also related, some-how, to the coming of the first industrial revolution at the end of the eighteenth century.'[14] There is little doubt of the importance of the tentative steps which were taken in the seventeenth century. They put people in a position to understand, predict and consequently to manipulate nature and the environment. Alexander Pope accurately satirized this reality when he wrote

Nature and Nature's law lay hid in night;
God said, Let Newton be! and all was light.

The scientific revolution preceded the major industrial changes whether it is dated from the foundation of the Royal Society in 1662 or earlier in the century. But to what extent was there a direct link between advances in scientific understanding and technological change? The traditional claim by historians of science that it was the 'mother of invention' and that there was practically no interchange between scientists and industrialists has been vigorously denied, for example by T. S. Ashton:

The sciences were not . . . as yet so specialised as to be out of contact with the language, thought and practice of ordinary men. . . . Physicists and chemists, such as Franklin, Black, Priestley, Dalton and Davy, were in intimate contact with the leading figures in British industry: there was much coming and going between the laboratory and the workshop . . . [15]

His view has been confirmed by more recent studies.[16] There were significant meeting places for scientists and industrialists in the Royal Society and there was a similar community of interest in local societies like the Birmingham Lunar Society and the Manchester Literary and Philosophical Society. Some leading industrialists, particularly Nonconformists, were educated in either Scottish universities or Dissenting Academies where the practical application of knowledge was given a high priority. This has led some historians to see Nonconformity as an important training ground in 'achievement motivation' leading to entrepreneurial enterprise and technological innovation. A. E. Musson argues: 'There is now plentiful evidence of fruitful collaboration between industrialists and scientists, and of applications of science in various fields.'[17]

John Smeaton improved on waterwheels as a result of practical-scientific experiments and Richard Trevithick was aided in the development of the high-pressure engine by Davies Gilbert. The list of people who made significant scientific contributions or used experimental methods and were either educated in Scotland or who were born there is impressive – for example, James Watt, Alexander Chisholm the chemist who assisted Josiah Wedgwood, Charles Macintosh, John Rennie and David Mushet. The machinery which revolutionized textile production owed nothing to science. But textile production was broader than spinning and weaving and in the finishing processes, particularly bleaching, advances in industrial chemistry did play an important part. Natural bleaching meant exposing cloth that had been 'soured' – soaked for about 48 hours in a weak acid, usually buttermilk – to the sun for many days. Rising output increased the need for a faster technique. Although sulphuric acid was used for 'souring' from the 1750s it did not remove the need for sun-bleaching. In 1774 a Swedish chemist, Karl Scheele, discovered the gas we now call chlorine and C. L. Berthollet experimented with its use in bleaching cloth in France between 1785 and 1786. By 1787–8 the process was being used by two firms in Scotland and one in Nottingham and soon spread to Lancashire. Chlorine was both difficult and dangerous to use and in 1798–9 Charles Tennant and Charles Macintosh invented bleaching powder (from the action of chlorine on slaked lime) which finally solved the problem. This shattered the bleaching bottleneck and, it has been argued, was as much responsible for the expansion of textiles in the nineteenth century as new machines. Science played an important role in the chemical industries and in other industries like pottery, glass and paper-making, which relied heavily on chemical transformations.

There are, however, good reasons for retaining the conventional view. Although contemporary science could and did introduce inventors to the properties of the physical world and to methods and perceptions they might otherwise not have commanded, it could scarcely be described as a technological goldmine. In most areas science was disarticulated and its insights had not been brought together into a coherent framework. Some theory was frankly wrong. Although this did not prevent Jethro Tull, who believed mistakenly that air was the best manure, from developing the horse-drawn hoe and seed-drill, it could retard developments. The caloric theory of heat which envisaged heat as a substance certainly obstructed study of the theory of the steam engine. Up to 1800 most scientific achievements occurred in areas like astronomy, magnetism and analytical mechanics which, although undoubtedly important when applied to technology, were well removed from the major industrial advances. The oblique relationship between science and technology was summed up by James Watt:

> Although Dr. Black's theory of latent heat did not suggest my improvements on the steam-engine, yet the knowledge upon various subjects which he was pleased to communicate to me, and the correct modes of reasoning and of making experiments of which he set me the example, certainly conduced very much to facilitate the progress of my inventions . . . [18]

David Landes concluded that before 1850 instances of connection between science and technology were 'exceptional' and that 'such stimulus and inspiration as did cross the gap went from technology towards science rather than the other way'.[19]

For example, in the nineteenth century Cornish pumping engines were performing more efficiently than contemporary physics said was theoretically possible. Carnot's work in the 1820s and 1830s on heat-engine theory was partly inspired by reports of these high-pressure engines. Landes went on to argue that technical change was 'anonymous', 'essentially empirical and on the job training' and that the innovators were 'a line of tinkerers'.

The direct links between science and technology may have been greater than historians originally thought but questions have been raised as to how representative they were and there is little evidence to suggest that these links played a major part in inducing economic growth. Science did not initiate industrial trends, it merely solved some problems which the general direction of industry had created. But the indirect influence of science upon technological change was crucial, creating a social and cultural milieu in which scientific questioning and particularly method became widespread. During the course of the nineteenth century, particularly after 1850, when technology took on more fully the mantle of initiator of economic change, it was a technology that was based on science.

Why did innovation occur?

But why did innovation occur? Marxist historians link technological change with profit. E. J. Hobsbawm wrote that

> It has often been assumed that an economy of private enterprise has an automatic bias towards innovation, but this is not so. It has a bias only towards profit. It will revolutionize manufactures only if greater profits are to be made in this way than otherwise.[20]

Demand

Greater profits will occur when they are a response to growing economic demands. Samuel Lilley maintained that this was the primary reason for inventions: 'Inventors did not act, nor did the social environment encourage them to act, unless the need was already clear – indeed, pressing.'[21] And Phyllis Deane said that innovation occurred 'only when the potential market was large enough and demand elastic enough to justify a substantial increase in output'.[22]

Technological innovation, in these cases, was an effect not a cause of market demand. Growing population, rising standards of living, at least until the 1790s, and growing commercialization combined to produce a steady expansion of the domestic market. In fact there is no necessary conflict between profit and demand as explanations for technological change. New products, as T. S. Ashton pointed out,[23] did not come into being by accident.

The argument that innovation was the result of increasing demand can be seen in the use of charcoal v. coke for smelting iron. Pig-iron smelted from coke was inferior to charcoal-smelted iron in the first half of the eighteenth century. The shift to the former from the latter was justifiable on cost grounds only after 1760. What caused the change in relative fuel prices? The use of charcoal may have been almost sufficient to satisfy existing demand but new demands led to an increase in the scale of operations and this raised charcoal prices. But it is equally possible to use a supply explanation to explain the move from charcoal to coke.[24]

Challenge and response

Technological innovation can also be seen in terms of challenge and response. Changes in one sector of an industry caused demand pressures on another sector. There was, for example, interaction between the various branches of the iron industry. Innovation in the furnace was matched by innovation at the forge. But the most famous example was in the textile industry, where innovation in weaving led to a demand for improvements in spinning to keep up with handloom output. This situation was then reversed. The output of powered spinning could only be used by increasing the number of handloom weavers until efficient powered weaving was developed. This too is capable of alternative explanation. Rising demand for spinners quickly exhausted the potential of a family-based labour force of a textile-producing community. Traditionally women did the spinning but at lower wages than men and the speed-up of weaving quickly exhausted local supplies. Additional male labour could have been drafted in but this would have pushed up labour costs and consequently the cost of yarn. The imbalance caused by the diffusion of the flying shuttle and the need for spinning machines lay as much in inadequate labour supplies as increasing demand. Patent records provide only a rough guide to the English inventiveness because being granted a patent did not mean that it was of either industrial or productive value (Table 5.1). What is clear from the patents granted is that from the 1760s there was a sharply rising trend which after

1780 coincided with W. W. Rostow's notion of 'take-off' in the British economy.

Table 5.1 English patents granted 1700–1809

1700–09	22
1710–19	38
1720–29	89
1730–39	56
1740–49	82
1750–59	92
1760–69	205
1770–79	294
1780–89	477
1790–99	647
1800–09	924

Source: B. R. Mitchell with P. Deane *Abstract of British Historical Statistics*, Cambridge University Press, 1962, p. 268.

TEXTILES

In textiles, ironmaking, coal mining and the development of an efficient steam engine innovation has been seen as a response to clear-cut economic incentives. Increased demands meant that reducing costs, particularly those associated with labour or increasing productivity, could lead to financial gain. Attractive though the demand explanation for innovation is, as G. N. Von Tunzelmann argues, 'the a priori case that technical change stemmed from changes in demand is disquietingly slim . . .'.[25]

Technological change

The major developments in textile spinning and weaving[26] were: Kay's flying shuttle, first introduced in the 1730s and widely adopted by weavers in the 1740s and 1750s, which roughly doubled output and furthered the incentive to increase productivity in spinning; Hargreaves' spinning jenny, perfected in 1768, which increased the output to be spun by a single operator; Arkwright's water frame, patented in 1769, which permitted the production of a yarn strong enough for cotton warp as well as weft; Crompton's mule of 1779 which combined the principles of the jenny and water frame, and was made 'self-acting' by Richard Roberts between 1820 and 1825; powered weaving, which was pioneered by Cartwright in the 1780s but not perfected until the 1820s by William Horrocks and particularly Richard Roberts. Parallel to the developments after 1780 were changes in preparation and finishing, particularly Whitney's cotton gin in the 1790s, rotary printing and chlorine bleaching. This chronology of technological change opens up a range of issues – How was technology diffused? Is technology itself sufficient to explain increasing productivity? What resistance was there to change?

Early inventions were technically so simple that they can be seen as responses to social and economic conditions that offered widening opportunities for self-advancement through innovation. The achievement of Richard Arkwright illustrates this. He used, some would say pirated, the work of others particularly the roller technique of Lewis Paul. Apart from the use of power drive, Samuel Lilley states that 'it was essentially the late medieval spinning wheel (with flyer this time) . . .'.[27]

Arkwright's genius lay in marketing the invention, over which he had patent control, until 1785. Adapting later machines to productive use required engineering not 'tinkering' skills. From 1790 attempts were made to adapt the mule for power. By 1800 this had occurred though the services of a skilled operator were still needed to control it. But it was Richard Roberts, a professional machine-builder, who developed a self-acting mule between 1820 and 1825 and a final version was perfected by Henry Maudsley, rightly called the 'king of mechanics'. Diffusion therefore had two stages. In the first 'simple' stage inventions were developed which required no special qualifications or training, as Lilley says:

> apart from the one really novel idea of drawing out by rollers, the cotton-spinning inventions up to about 1800 were essentially a matter of connecting together in new combinations the parts of the spinning wheel which had been familiar for centuries.[28]

It was in the second stage, when the technical difficulties became more severe, that engineering skills were required. Not until after the self-acting mule and the powerloom had been perfected can it really be said that the revolutions in textile production take place. Arguably, the revolutionary developments occurred in preparation and finishing.

Cotton – chronology of growth

Cotton production fell into three stages during the eighteenth century, in each of which production increased at a remarkably constant rate (Figure 5.2). From 1700 to the 1740s the rate of growth was about 1.4 per cent per annum. This was largely because of legislation forbidding the import of brightly coloured Indian calicoes from 1700 which was reinforced in 1721 by forbidding their wearing. Though this legislation was largely ineffective it enabled home producers to penetrate the domestic market. The incentive for growth came from changing market potential not new technology. From the 1740s until the 1770s the growth rate doubled. In the third period, after 1780, the annual rate leaped to 8.5 per cent per annum and this was maintained into the nineteenth century.

Technological change allowed expansion to occur, particularly in the

Figure 5.2 The growth of the cotton industry 1710–1800

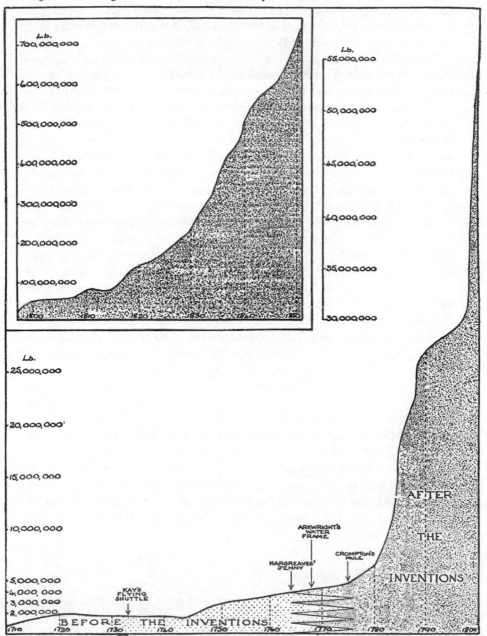

Source: J. L. Gayler, I. Richards and J. A. Morris *A Sketch-Map Economic History of Britain*, George Harrap, 1966, p. 94.

third period. But technology did not initiate cotton's explosive expansion. Mass home demand was the foundation of the industry's success though by 1800 two-thirds of the output went abroad. It was quantity rather than quality that was the basis of Britain's cotton success.

Technological change laid the foundations of the nineteenth-century success of the cotton industry, seen in the adoption of mechanical power and the consequent increase in productivity.[29] Until 1820 waterwheels provided most of the power for the industry. Early textile production had modest power requirements which enabled mill-owners, particularly in the Pennines, to keep costs low. Only in lowland areas and in urban centres was Watt's rotary steam engine a necessity. By 1835, however, steam was responsible for three-quarters of the power used. This was particularly evident in Lancashire, Cheshire, Derbyshire and the West Riding. Only in Scotland and the Midlands was water power still widely used. This steam-power concentration was paralleled by productivity concentration. In 1790 Lancashire and the surrounding counties accounted for 70 per cent of output but by 1835 this had reached 90 per cent. Steam-powered spinning had two main advantages. It allowed finer-quality yarn to be produced and it reduced labour costs by reducing the time taken to spin: in 1795 it took 300 spinner-hours to process 100 lb of cotton using power-assisted mules but by 1830 the self-acting mule had reduced this to about 135 hours. Mule-spinning soon superseded the older 'roller' spinning techniques pioneered by Arkwright. It was not until the investment booms of 1823–5 and 1832–4 that powered weaving was widely adopted. Weaving and knitting were technically more difficult to subject to either water or steam power. There were two major reasons for this. No commercial machine has been produced that was sufficiently reliable. The poor wages of the handloom weavers and framework knitters, which kept production costs down, inhibited its adoption. From the 1820s powered spinning and weaving became increasingly widespread. In 1833 there was estimated to be 100,000 power looms in Britain compared with 250,000 handloom weavers. This led to larger industrial units and a process of integrating spinning and weaving under one roof. Machines and production had become standardized.

Locating the cotton industry

Important cotton-producing regions emerged after 1770. Lancashire was of primary importance, but some production occurred in Derbyshire and Nottinghamshire, and Norwich retained a minor interest in cotton with fifteen cotton firms in 1810. There were a few scattered mills in North Wales and cotton replaced linen as Belfast's major textile between 1780 and 1830. The Scottish industry round Glasgow also experienced a rapid rise to success but was a poor second to Lancashire.

Table 5.2 Cotton production and exports 1750–1849

	Raw cotton (000 lbs)	Exports of piece goods (million yards)
1750–9	2,820	–
1760–9	3,531	–
1770–9	4,797	–
1780–9	14,824	–
1790–9	28,645	–
1800–9	59,554	–
1810–9	96,339	227
1820–9	173,000	320
1830–9	302,000	553
1840–9	550,000	978

Source: B. R. Mitchell and P. Deane *Abstract of British Historical Statistics*, Cambridge University Press, pp. 177–81.

There is little doubt that the 1780s witnessed a spectacular growth in cotton output and that between 1790 and 1831 its annual growth rate did not fall below 4 per cent (Tables 5.2 and 5.3).

Table 5.3 Real output in cotton – percentage per year

1700–60	1.37
1760–70	4.59
1770–80	6.20
1780–90	12.76
1790–1801	6.73
1801–11	4.49
1811–21	5.59
1821–31	6.82

Source: As Table 5.2.

This was well above any other industry and in that sense cotton development was atypical.

Wool

The woollen industry expanded by 0.8 per cent per annum between 1700 and 1740, and by 1.3 to 1.4 per cent for the next thirty years, falling to 0.6 per cent for the years before the end of the century. From the 1780s the position of the industry relative to cotton declined even though its output grew in absolute terms. By 1800 it accounted for about one-tenth of industrial production, about the same as cotton, and its exports were valued at a quarter of the British total. There were also major changes in its geographical distribution: the West Riding of Yorkshire grew in importance while the industry of Suffolk, Essex and the West Country declined.[30]

Table 5.4 Woollen output

Year	UK wool clip (000 lb)	Wool imports (000 lb)	Exports Yarn (000 lb)	By the yard (000 yd)
1775–9	80,000	1,566*	–	–
1780–9	90,000	2,535	–	–
1790–9	90,000	3,747	–	–
1800–9	100,000	7,451	–	–
1810–19	100,000	13,181	14**	8,277†
1820–9	113,000	22,300	159	6,635
1830–9	120,000	42,800	2,270	6,953
1840–9	128,000	57,700	7,865	93,316††

* 1772–9; **1819 only; † 1815–19; †† including carpet.
Source: As Table 5.2 pp. 190–7.

The woollen industry lagged behind cotton in applying new technologies. The conservatism of production with its ancient regulated organization may have had some influence but other factors were probably more important. There were greater technical problems in applying power-driven machinery to wool fibre. Markets did not expand as rapidly as in cotton and the labour supply was more plentiful, preventing the same yarn bottleneck as in cotton.

Power-driven mechanization was initially confined to the preparatory stage. Spinning and weaving remained manual until well into the nineteenth century. The jenny was introduced into Yorkshire in the 1770s but did not become widespread until the later 1780s. Mules were introduced much more slowly and made little headway before 1830. Though initially used in a domestic setting, by 1800 there were eighteen worsted spinning mills in Yorkshire and by 1830 little worsted yarn was hand-spun any more. Powerloom weaving made very slow progress: by 1850 there were only 9,500 powerlooms in the whole woollen industry compared to 100,000 in cotton. Handloom weaving was still dominant, though weavers were commonly brought together in 'loomshops'.

Reaction to new technologies was variable. In Essex weavers revolted against the factory system but accepted the flying shuttle. In Yorkshire the jenny and carding machines were introduced by domestic spinners in times of expanding employment but the hand-combers struck, unsuccessfully, in 1825 against mechanization which was finally achieved in the 1840s. Spinning machines were widely but again unsuccessfully resisted in the West Country. Differences in the reception of new technology have been attributed to regional social structures. In the south there was a sharper polarity between master and man compared to the more uniform small weaver communities of the north. In reality explaining why an area took up, resisted or ignored technical change necessitates examining power sources, product choice as well as employment structures and community relations. Resistance to machinery was not always a consequence of the technology itself. The framework-knitters were provoked to direct action, not by the machine as such, but by the malpractice of employers regarding apprenticeship and quality.

Yorkshire never achieved as complete a dominance in wool as cotton did in Lancashire. Nevertheless, by 1850 the West Riding contained 87 per cent of all worsted spindles and 95 per cent of the looms. Only in the Tweed valley was there a dynamism and momentum in wool comparable to that of the West Riding. How did this happen? Proximity to Lancashire and easy access to the whole series of innovations in technology played a major part. There is ample evidence of diffusion across the Pennines. Worsted manufacture took to cotton-derived technology more easily and speedily than woollens and soon became concentrated on the coalfields. Bradford ousted Halifax as the main worsted town because of its better supply of coal. By 1850 it possessed half the county's worsted spindles and more than half the power looms. Coal became important only at a later stage in woollens. The Leeds–Huddersfield area concentrated on the cheaper and coarser end of the market and thus in the nineteenth century had a larger and more readily expandable market. The shoddy trade was set up in 1813 and by 1858 Batley alone had at least fifty rag-shredding machines.

Tweedside, particularly Galashiels, also expanded. A remote low-quality industry whose production was valued at £26,000 in 1830, was transformed to a £200,000 a year industry by 1860. It moved into the 'quality' end of the market based on discoveries in the design of woollen cloth, shrewd market sense and the exploitation of the nineteenth-century mania for things Scottish. The Welsh industry failed to follow its northern rivals' success, despite mechanization and concentration into factories. The most successful Welsh mills were in the south-west, supplying blankets and flannels via the new railways to the coalfield. But elsewhere the isolation of mills, their primitive technology and dependence on local raw materials meant that their market applications were small.

Linen

Linen was the most important manufactured import in 1700. But in the early eighteenth century a domestic industry developed making coarse-quality cloth used largely for sacking, canvas and sailcloth. Linen cloth worn in public still tended to be imported from Holland, Germany and France. By the 1770s the English linen industry accounted for 6 per cent of the total value of exports and ranked second only to woollens. Between 1740 and 1780 English linen production expanded rapidly, based upon flax imports from Russia and Germany but with an increasing input from home-grown crops. This growth occurred largely because, until Arkwright's invention, it provided the warp thread that was mixed with cotton weft to make fustian. During the technological revolution of the late eighteenth century the industry declined in relative importance. But linen remained an important cloth for furnishing, sackcloth, thread and fine clothing with Knaresborough and Darlington as important centres. An initial breakthrough in flax spinning was made in Darlington in 1787. But it was Leeds that became the major centre of production largely because of the factory of John Marshall.

The English industry was also hit by growing competition from the Scottish and Irish industries. Although there had been a long tradition of linen production in Ireland, especially in Ulster, during the late eighteenth century technological change led to cotton production superseding linen. However, the Irish cotton industry was unable to compete with Lancashire and from the 1820s the trend was reversed. Belfast became the centre of production which quickly mechanized after 1829 when John Mulholland set up the first steam mill exploiting the 'wet-spinning' process. The Scottish industry was the major industry of the central lowlands in the first half of the eighteenth century. The application of scrutching and heckling machines to the preparation stage led to a rapid increase in 'lint' mills – there were 4 in 1732 and 317 in 1782. Spinning machinery was gradually introduced from the 1790s. There was some regional specialization with the eastern counties of Fife, Forfar and Perth, centred on Dundee producing coarser, cheap cloth spun from flax, tow and hemp and after 1830 jute, while the western counties of Renfrew and Lanark, centred on Glasgow, produced finer cambrics, gauzes and mixtures. Fine linen fabrics lost out in competition to fine Glasgow cottons and the balance of production swung increasingly to the east.

New technology may have been applied to preparation and spinning but power-weaving had made little headway by 1850. Throughout the United Kingdom in 1850 there were 965,000 spindles but only 1,200 power-looms. Weaving remained the province of the linen handloom workers.

Silk

In 1700 the focal point of silk production was at Spitalfields in London but during the following century production grew in Norwich and especially in Cheshire and Derbyshire. Production was about 1.6 per cent of industrial production in 1812 compared to 4.2 per cent in linens, 11 per cent in wool and 12 per cent in cottons. Its technological revolution was earlier than in other textile industries. Silk-throwing machines were introduced from Italy in the early eighteenth century. Weaving was still largely manual by 1850 though machines like the Dutch 'engine looms' were introduced in the late eighteenth century for weaving ribbons, especially, in Coventry, and the Jacquard looms for patterned weaving in the first half of the nineteenth century. The comparative progress of mechanization in United Kingdom textiles can be seen in Table 5.5.

Table 5.5 The impact of mechanization in textiles

Textile	Factories	Spindles	Powerlooms	Horsepower steam	water
Cotton	1,932	20,977,017	249,627	71,005	11,550
Wool	1,497	1,595,278	9,439	13,455	8,689
Worsted	501	875,830	32,617	9,890	1,625
Linen	393	965,031	1,141	10,905	3,387
Silk	277	1,225,560	6,092	2,858	853

Source: Factory Inspectors' Returns, 1850, quoted in A. E. Musson *The Growth of British Industry*, Batsford, 1981, p. 93.

Knitwear and hosiery

New technologies were applied very slowly to some branches of textiles. The geographical localization of knitwear and hosiery owed much to the invention, in 1589, of a stocking frame by William Lee, near Nottingham. By the 1840s 90 per cent of the industry was in Leicestershire, Nottinghamshire or Derbyshire with a dispersed domestic structure within defined areas around central warehouses. There were major technical problems in applying power to knitting machines and that plus the superabundance of cheap labour meant that employers had little incentive to innovate. Steam was first used at Loughborough in 1839 but did not spread to Nottingham until 1851 and it was not until the 1860s that high-quality factory goods could be made. There were secondary centres of framework knitting at Tewkesbury, Hawick, Dumfries and in Devon. Framework knitters were even more depressed than handloom weavers and in the 1851 Census 65,000 people were employed in the industry: 35,000 men and 30,000 women.

Lace-making

Hand lace-making was a staple industry for women and children in Bedford, Buckingham, Northampton, Devon, Dorset, Somerset, Wiltshire, Hampshire, Derby and Yorkshire. By the end of the century it was concentrated in the first three of these counties and employed 140,000 people.

The late eighteenth century saw the development of point-net and warp-lace using modified framework knitting machines in Nottinghamshire. In 1808–9 John Heathcoat patented a bobbin-net machine but he moved to Tiverton in Devon after his frames were smashed in 1816 and was employing 1,500 people by the mid-1820s. Hand-made lace was faced with competition from two sources after 1815: the machine-produced lace of Devon and Nottingham, and cheaper foreign imports. Demand for hand-made lace revived in the 1840s and the industry gained a new lease of life.

About half of the lace and a sixth of the hosiery was exported. This led to both industries experiencing sharp trade fluctuations. Changing fashions could, as in the case of hand-made lace between 1815 and 1840, have an impact on growth. This was also evident in glove-making which was centred in the late eighteenth century in London and Woodstock, Yeovil and Worcester, where it was overwhelmingly domestic in organization. It too, was an industry of fashion and there was a great decline after Huskisson removed the prohibition on French imports in 1830. The response of the clothing trade was also not technological. Increased demand was satisfied by a simple increase in the number of tailors, needlewomen, seamstresses and dressmakers. The sewing-machine was not widely used before the mid-nineteenth century and even then it was hand or treadle-operated at home.

Conclusions

In textiles from 1700 to 1850 the contrast was between those industries which used new technology in one or more stages of production and those which retained the older methods of production. John Dyer wrote of an early spinning machine in 1757 in his poem 'The Fleece':

> A circular machine of new design
> In conic shape; it draws and spins a thread
> Without the tedious task of needless hands.

Important though advances were to contemporaries in spinning and, ultimately, weaving the technologies of preparation and finishing have recently received their just credit. Cotton-spinning machines could not have functioned as effectively as they did without the cotton-gin of Eli Whitney or the new bleaching processes. Historians have emphasized the achievement of cotton, its revolutionary growth and the impact of its technological innovations but they are also beginning to reappraise the continuities of the textile industry as a whole and in that appraisal, technological change plays a far less important role.

IRON

Charcoal to coal

No other industry underwent the explosive development of cotton. But in two cases – iron and coal – a long, slow, even hesitant, evolution throughout the years between 1700 and 1850 produced changes that were, in the long run, to be perhaps more significant. For almost a century before 1720 the British iron industry had been in decline.[31] The reason was the rising cost of timber and charcoal which were used as fuel for smelting. In principle the solution was easy: substitute coal for wood. But there were major technical problems and it was not until 50 years after Abraham Darby developed his coking process at Coalbrookdale in 1709 that coke-smelted pig-iron posed a major threat to charcoal-smelted iron. It was of lower quality and although it was widely used for casting goods, it was considered inferior to charcoal-smelted pig for making wrought iron at the forge, as well as being more expensive. C. K. Hyde has shown that capital and fuel costs remained higher than those of charcoal furnaces and this, not Quaker secrecy, accounted for the slow spread of coke smelting beyond Shropshire. Not until the demand for iron began to rise rapidly did charcoal pig lose its price advantage. The move from charcoal to coke led to a change in the location of the industry.

The decline in the number of charcoal furnaces is shown in Table 5.6.

Table 5.6 Charcoal furnaces 1717 and 1790

	1717	1790
Hampshire	1	0
Weald	14	3
S. W. England	16	11
S. Wales } Midlands }	13	2
Cheshire, North Wales	5	1
Sheffield, North-East	9	2
North-West	3	5
Scotland	0	0

Source: H. R. Schubert *History of the British Iron and Steel Industry from B.C. 450 to A.D. 1957*, London 1957 p. 175.

The Weald dominated ironmaking in the sixteenth and early seventeenth centuries. It had the necessary resources – ironstone, coppice woodland for charcoal, streams to drive waterwheels that powered the furnace bellows – and had, in the fifteenth century, taken the continental idea of the blast furnace which it monopolized for the next hundred years. It was also close to the main markets: the naval dockyards and arsenals on the Thames and Medway and at Portsmouth which took the region's major output of guns and cannon balls. Its decline dated from about 1650 with the development of the Forest of Dean, which had as many furnaces as the Weald by 1717. It was a major exporting region sending high-quality pig up the Severn to Birmingham and the Midlands. In the eighteenth century both regions declined in relative importance to the growing coke-iron producers. The coalfields were readily accessible to expanding industrial markets but could also provide an elastic supply of fuel and coal measures ironstone. Demand for pig-iron grew at about 50 per cent per decade between 1750 and 1820 and the price advantage of charcoal pig disappeared. In 1806 there were 162 coke furnaces but only 11 charcoal ones had survived. The pattern of change was not quite as straightforward as a decline in charcoal furnaces and an increase in coke furnaces. Dean pig was of a higher quality than that from the Weald and its value to the Birmingham trades helped to sustain an industry there. For ordinary cast-iron goods the Weald was soon outclassed by Dean and Midland producers. It also lost its monopoly of gun-making contracts from government after 1756 and in 1775 the Board of Ordnance made the final decision to transfer all its contracts to lower-cost producers.

Scotland benefits

It was Scotland that benefited from this decline. In 1759 the Carron Company was established as a partnership at Falkirk. Between half and two-thirds of its sales came from government contracts for cannon and shot which were made in an integrated concern with four coke furnaces using a skilled workforce, many of whom came from the Weald. Until the 1780s it remained the only sizeable Scottish works largely because the domestic market was too small to support much more capacity and its pig was of too poor quality to sell outside Scotland. In 1806 its production of over 7,000 tons made up one-third of the Scottish total. Not until the 1830s did the Scottish iron industry undergo a transformation with the application of James Neilson's 'hot-blast' process – whereby pre-heated air was blasted into the molten iron reducing fuel costs and permitting raw coal to be used – combined with the use of the rich blackband ores that had been found in central Scotland in 1801. Hyde argues however that this was not a major factor in Scotland's success.[32] It was adopted less quickly in England and Wales where qualities of coal were different. By the late 1840s Scotland was producing a quarter of total British pig-iron output.

Slowness of diffusion

The slowness of the diffusion of the coking process before 1760 – there were only seventeen coke furnaces in that year in Britain – was not just the result of difficulties in applying Darby's original technique. The production of castings was much less important than the conversion of pig into wrought iron whose malleability and tensile strength made it the leading useful metal until the coming of cheap steel in the mid-nineteenth century. Darby II (1711–63) who, like his father was based at Coalbrookdale, started producing a metal that was much better adapted for conversion. But forge-masters were reluctant to use the new material despite the patents taken out in the 1760s for refining and reverberatory furnaces by the Woods brothers, the Cranages and others. The breakthrough came in 1784, when Henry Cort perfected his puddling and rolling process. This substituted coal for wood in a reverberatory furnace and this, coupled with some agreement to accept a rather lower quality in return for a much reduced price, led to the rapid adoption of coke-smelted pig particularly in South Wales as the starting point for conversion for wrought iron.

South Wales benefits

It was South Wales that benefited from the puddling and rolling or 'Welsh' process but there had been a long tradition of ironmaking in this area. Charles Lloyd of Dolobran attempted, unsuccessfully, to improve on Darby's coking process in the 1710s. English ironmasters took over some existing forges: Thomas Pratt acquired the works at Tredegar and Machan in 1732 and Thomas Maybery the Brecon furnace in 1753. From the late 1750s demand was stimulated by the Seven Years War, which broadened the market perspectives of the industry. Entreprencurs were attracted from the Midlands and large-scale development occurred particularly on the north-eastern rim of the coalfield where iron ore was found along with coal and limestone for lining the furnaces. The Hirwaun furnace was extended in 1757, Dowlais founded in 1759 and the Cyfarthfa and Plymouth furnaces in 1765. Merthyr was the nucleus of this development and by 1765 was surrounded by new coke-fired furnaces. By 1800 South Wales produced one-third of all British pig (Figure 5.3). South Wales ironmasters did improve on the puddling process: Samuel Homfray of Penydarren inserted an iron floor to the furnace instead of sand and improved blast potential and in the 1830s Joseph Hall used furnace cinders to assist oxidation, the 'wet-puddling' or 'pig-boiling' process. James Nasmyth invented his 'steam-hammer' in 1839 which soon replaced the old steam or water-powered tilt-hammers (Table 5.7).

Figure 5.3 Ironworks in South Wales in 1811

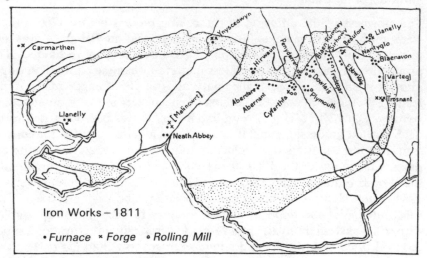

Source: W. Rees *An Historical Atlas of Wales*, Faber, 1951, plate 66.

Table 5.7 The growth of the South Wales iron industry

	Furnaces	Output in tons
1788	8	8,200
1796	23	33,593
1811	53	182,325
1823	72	277,643
1830	113	354,919
1840	134	505,000
1848	192	631,280

Source: A. H. John *The Industrial Development of South Wales 1750–1850*, Cardiff, 1950, p. 192.

Growth

In 1700 pig-iron production was about 20,000 tons and until the 1760s iron output rose slowly by about 0.6 per cent per year. 144,000 tons of iron was imported between 1700 and 1759 and domestic production came mainly from areas that had been important in 1700: the Weald, Forest of Dean, the Birmingham area, north Staffordshire, Nottingham and south Yorkshire. After this growth was more rapid.

War stimulated growth in the late 1770s and early 1780s and between 1793 and 1815. Ninety-two per cent of production was concentrated in Shropshire, Staffordshire, Yorkshire, South Wales and Scotland in 1806. Even so, in 1812 iron and steel comprised only 9.2 per cent of total industrial output compared to the 29 per cent of cotton, wool, linen and

Table 5.8 British pig-iron output 1760–1850

	000 tons
1760	30
1785	50
1796	125
1806	244
1823	455
1830	677
1840	1,400
1850	2,200

Source: P. Riden 'The Output of the British Iron Industry before 1870', *Economic History Review*, Second Series, 30, pp. 443, 448 and 455.

Table 5.9 Growth in real output in iron – percentage per year

1760–70	1.65
1770–80	4.47
1780–90	3.79
1790–1801	6.48
1801–11	7.45
1811–21	−0.28
1821–31	6.47

Source: As Table 5.8.

silk. Negative growth between 1811 and 1821 can be accounted for by the fall in demand after 1815.

Iron in use

Iron became the basic constructional material for machinery, replacing wood; for example John Smeaton specified it in 1754 for the main shaft of a windmill and Abraham Darby III (1750–89), who continued the Coalbrookdale dynasty, demonstrated its structural possibilities with his iron bridge in 1779. This applied to agricultural as well as industrial machinery. Iron rails were first used at Coalbrookdale in 1767. John Wilkinson built an iron boat in the 1780s, used iron pipes for water in Paris and was buried in an iron coffin. Lord Liverpool even suggested iron pavements to stimulate demand at slack times. The railway 'manias' of the 1830s and 1840s increased demand for building lines, stations, bridges and locomotives. An American commentator wrote in 1835 of the puddled iron of the English and Welsh furnaces that

All countries throughout the world must get their railway iron from

England where it is manufactured so rapidly and so perfectly that it is useless to pretend to compete with this branch of industry . . .

The bulk of increased output went into the domestic market before 1830. From the 1830s exports of heavy iron rails went to Germany, France, Belgium, America, Russia, India and Australasia where British contractors and engineers played a leading role in developing railways. Iron and steel were exported as finished goods ranging from pins, nails, chains, cutlery and hardware of all kinds to machinery.

Steel

Sheffield was the centre of British steel production between 1700 and 1850, though there were secondary centres round Newcastle. Until 1740 'blister' steel was produced using the cementation process in which bar iron was heated with charcoal in closed clay pots in a coal-fired furnace. To produce fine-edged tools it was reheated and hammered to form shear steel. This failed to produce steel of reliable quality. In about 1740 Benjamin Huntsman developed the 'crucible' process, which produced a better-quality steel but was very slow. Both blister and crucible steel continued to be produced throughout the eighteenth century and its cost ensured that it was only used for small articles requiring a high degree of hardness or sharpness. Cheap steel was a development of the second half of the nineteenth century.

Historians have placed their emphasis upon iron and this obscures the importance of non-ferrous metals. By 1850 Britain was producing 75 per cent of the world's copper, 60 per cent of the tin and half the world's lead. Many of the technological changes later used in ironmaking had their origins in the mining and smelting of these metals. The use of coal in reverberatory furnaces was pioneered in the non-ferrous metals. Savery and Newcomen developed their pumping engines to drain the tin and copper mines of Devon and Cornwall. High-pressure engines were pioneered in Cornwall by Trevithick and Woolf.

COAL

In 1837 J. R. McCulloch wrote in his *History of Commerce* that

The mineral riches of Great Britain, if not superior, are at least equal to those of any other country. We cannot, it is true, boast of gold or silver, but we possess that which is of still more importance to a manufacturing nation, an all but inexhaustible supply of the most excellent coal.

Coal production[33] had been growing throughout the eighteenth century as it replaced charcoal in a range of activities – salt and sugar refining, brewing, brick, tile and pottery manufacture, soap and glass-making and in the non-ferrous trades as well as for domestic heating. British coal output was about 2.5 million tons and in 1700 was produced in several areas of Britain in generally small mines. Around Bristol there were only 123 colliery workers, including carriers, in more than 70 pits at Kingswood in 1684. The largest mines were found in north-east England and the dominance of this area is reflected in its shipping of 800,000 tons of coal in 1690, much of it to London.

Technology and growth

During the eighteenth and early nineteenth centuries coal output increased. From under 3 million tons in 1700 output rose to 10 million tons in 1800 and to over 50 million by 1850. This increase reflected increased demand from industry, particularly after 1760, when canals cut transportation costs and of the resolution of important technical difficulties. Large-scale mining created problems, particularly with drainage. The Newcomen pumping engine was quickly adopted by mine-owners and, despite its high fuel consumption which was not a major problem on coalfields, it remained the major steam engine used throughout Britain until well into the nineteenth century. Only in the bigger collieries were the more reliable Boulton and Watt engines purchased.

The greater depth of shafts increased the problems of ventilation, lighting, underground transport and of maintaining tunnels. Accumulations of 'chokedamp' and 'firedamp' were major problems for miners. Crude furnace ventilation, used to course fresh air through the workings, was still commonly used until the 1840s. Experiments had been made with air-pumps and fans like that developed by John Buddle in the first decade of the century but costs limited their use to the larger mines. Candles were generally used for lighting and often ignited the explosive 'firedamp'. They continued to be used despite the invention of 'safety-lamps' in the mid-1810s by Sir Humphrey Davy, George Stephenson and George Clanny. Maintaining tunnels was expensive and it was often cheaper to dig a new shaft than to extend old ones. But the chief cost for colliery owners was moving coal from the coal face to its markets. Horse-gins for winding coal to the surface remained common though Watt's rotative engine began to be used from the 1790s. But by 1850 coal was still being raised in most areas either in free-swinging baskets or on the backs of men and boys – the use of women and children underground had been made illegal by the Mines Act of 1842. The coal industry was never technically distinguished apart from its limited use of the steam engine. Coal remained a labour-intensive 'pick and shovel' industry where growing demand was satisfied by increasing the size of the labour force. The number of miners in Great Britain increased from 118,000 to 219,000 between 1841 and 1851 to allow

Figure 5.4 The eighteenth-century coal industry

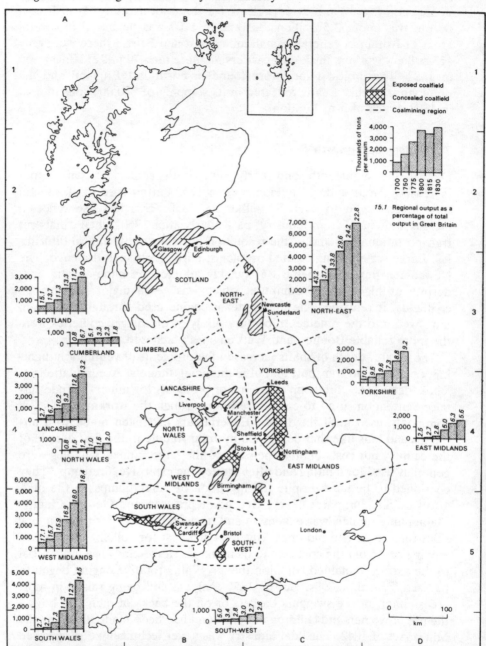

Source: R. Pope (ed.) *Atlas of British Social and Economic History since c. 1700,* Routledge, 1989, p. 69.

output to rise from 33.7 to 49.4 million tons – a fall in output from 285 to 225 tons per person per year.

Reducing costs

It was the construction of canals on a nationwide scale that enabled the coal industry to meet growing market demand after 1760. Between 1758 and 1801 Parliament sanctioned 165 canal schemes of which 90 were primarily intended for the movement of coal. Transport costs were reduced to as little as 0.25 pence per ton per mile[34]. The use of all coalfields was extended. In central Scotland, the growth of Glasgow led to the construction of the Monksland canal to the Lanarkshire coalfield in 1793. Large-scale mining in South Wales came with the opening of four great canals into the valleys between 1794 and 1799.

Canals liberated the economy from dependence on water for power since industry could now be built on or adjacent to coalfields. Arthur Young wrote in 1791 that 'all the activity and industry of this kingdom is fast concentrating where there are coal pits'.

Growth and demand

The growth of the coal industry up to 1800 should not be exaggerated. Coal output may have increased fourfold between 1700 and 1800 but it was to multiply twenty times in the next century (Table 5.10).

Table 5.10 Growth in real output in coal – percentage per year

1700–60	0.64
1760–70	2.19
1770–80	2.48
1780–90	2.36
1790–1801	3.21
1801–11	2.53
1811–21	2.76
1821–31	3.68

Source: N. Crafts *British Economic Growth during the Industrial Revolution*, Oxford University Press, 1985, p. 23.

The early nineteenth-century industry was still largely concerned with traditional domestic and industrial markets. South Wales provided coal for its ironmasters and Durham and Northumberland still provided coal for London. Despite the development of canals, accessibility was of prime importance and until the mid-nineteenth century the coastal coalfields maintained their advantage over those inland. Railways opened up these inland areas and brought a measure of unity to an industry which had previously been distinguished by its diversity.

Demand for coal from domestic users increased after 1800. The iron industry was a large customer but it was the expansion of the railway network that provided a new and enormous market for steam coal. The continuing growth of the industrial economy, driven by steam, also extended markets and such enterprises as Bute Dock, built in Cardiff in 1839, opened up the export trade. The north-east coast gradually lost pre-eminence to South Wales, at first in the more accessible Aberdare valleys and later in the Rhondda. Increasingly the export trade came to dominate production. In 1830, 500,000 tons, about 2 per cent of output, was exported. This had risen to 4 million tons in 1855, and by 1860 10 per cent of coal output was exported: the basis of Britain's mid-century growth and dominance.

POWER – WIND, WATER AND STEAM

The stationary steam engine has often been regarded as the single most important invention underlying British industrialization. Technically the steam engine was seen as 'prime mover'; that is, it supplied the energy to work the machines which in turn produced the consumer goods. An exhaustible energy resource, it could be argued, would hamper industrialization across many sectors. Historically the concentration by historians like Rostow on the late eighteenth century has implied a concentration on the steam engine of James Watt which improved on the earlier engines of Thomas Savery and Thomas Newcomen. This view does, however, neglect the importance of developments in steam before 1780 and technical improvements to existing power sources.[35]

The steam engine was developed when it was no longer possible to cope with expanding needs by traditional means. Deeper mining led to an enormous increase in the power needed to keep them dry. In 1702 one Warwickshire colliery was using 500 horses for this purpose. The response was the first commercially successful steam-atmospheric engine developed by Thomas Newcomen between 1708 and 1712. It was quickly adopted by collieries and was too inefficient and too costly in fuel to be used widely elsewhere though the high value of tin and lead meant it was used in Cornwall and Derbyshire. By the 1750s demand for power was again seriously straining available resources. This was clearly reflected in the strong interest which arose at that time in the improvement of prime movers. John Smeaton applied scale-model techniques to improve the design of both waterwheels and windmills. This marked the beginning of a long series of advances in design and construction that brought the waterwheel to virtual perfection by 1830. The windmill was improved by the addition of a fantail mechanism in 1745, the increased use of cast-iron working parts and the development of adjustable sails. Smeaton also brought the Newcomen engine to about the limit of its potential (75 horsepower in the 1770s). But it was not adaptable to drive machinery directly but was frequently installed to pump water to supply a water-wheel for that purpose. James Watt improved on the Newcomen engine in two important respects. In the mid-1760s he developed a 'separate condensor' which reduced the fuel consumption of the pumping engine. Secondly, he designed the first effective rotative engine in which the motion of the engine could be communicated directly to machinery – he took out a patent on the 'sun and planet gear' in 1781, a double-acting engine in 1782, centrifugal governor in 1788 and steam engine indicator in 1796.

Just how dramatic was the impact of the steam engine and how did this compare with other forms of power? The speed of diffusion of the Boulton and Watt engines was not as great as historians originally believed. In Lancashire and Cornwall, where steam power was being most rapidly introduced, Boulton and Watt engines accounted for no more than 35 per cent of the total in 1800. It is possible to explain this in the following ways. First, the Newcomen engine remained the most important if not most cost-efficient pumping machine on many coalfields until the 1840s. Secondly, the Watt engine was applied to machines that already existed and which had been driven by water. Mill-owners or ironmasters had to consider whether the cost of installing a steam engine or replacing their existing Newcomen machine was economically justifiable. Thirdly, most workshops were small concerns where installing steam could also prove too expensive given Watt's control of the market through his patents until 1800. Watt's engine had made striking advances in powered mule-spinning and also to carding, printing and bleaching but its impact elsewhere was more limited. Steam engines were vastly outnumbered by waterwheels and the great majority of manufactures were still handicrafts.

It was only in the long term that industry was freed from its dependence on water power. J. P. Harris has estimated conservatively that there were about 1,200 steam engines of all kinds in operation in 1800.[36] These produced less than 20,000 horsepower of which Watt's engines may have contributed 12,500 hp. After 1800 the application of steam engines to textiles, particularly spinning, accounted for their rapid diffusion. By 1924 there were about 5,000 engines generating 100,000 hp in industry and mining and by 1850 300,000 hp was generated in industry alone. Factory inspectors' returns can be used cautiously to indicate the balance between steam and water power in cotton and woollen and worsted industries. Water power provided 36 per cent of all power used in the textile industry in 1838 and it was still 19 per cent in 1850.

The quantity of steam power therefore increased after 1800 though as von Tunzelmann argues

Table 5.11 Horsepower used in textile factories

| Year | Cotton | | Woollen and Worsted | |
	Steam	Water	Steam	Water
1838	46,826	17,389	17,389	10,405
1850	71,005	11,500	23,345	10,314

Source: A. E. Musson *The Growth of British Industry*, Batsford, 1978, p. 112.

Apart from the application of the steam engine to locomotive and shipping purposes . . . the most important 'spin-off' of the steam engine so far as manufacturing industry was concerned did not come until forty to sixty years into the nineteenth century.[37]

Concentration on diffusion in cotton has led historians to overestimate the extent to which steam was applied to other industries. It was not until the diffusion of high-pressure stationary engines after 1840 that there was a substantial reduction in fuel costs and an increase in the speed at which machines could be run. This was not possible until accurate and reliably engineered machines had been developed. The fullest application of steam power had to wait until an engineering industry had evolved. The view that Watt revolutionized industrial production after 1780 is broadly correct but the point at which that revolution occurred is much later than the classic period of 'take-off'.

CONCLUSIONS

The traditional emphasis by historians upon technological advances in textiles, iron, coal and the application of steam power was based upon the contemporary perceptions of where the important changes occurred. Important though they undoubtedly were, the typical British worker in 1850 was not a machine operator in a factory but still a traditional craftsman or labourer or domestic servant. Technological innovation and diffusion was concentrated in some sectors of the economy more than others. The reason for this lay initially in domestic demand. But as W. W. Rostow says,

Invention and innovation at any period of time are marginal activities in society. They engage small numbers of human beings relative to the population as a whole. Life goes on in familiar ways, with familiar technologies, while the creative few dream their dreams and struggle. . . . Only looking backwards, after innovation has led on to large new sectors in the economy, are the achievements of the inventors and innovators generally understood, appreciated and accorded a grand place in history.[38]

NOTES

1 S. Smiles *Lives of the Engineers: Early Engineering*, 1904 ed, p. xxiii.
2 J. James *History of the Worsted Manufacture in England*, 1857, p. 333.
3 See chapter 9.
4 See chapter 15.
5 See chapter 10.
6 Quoted in E. Pawson *The Early Industrial Revolution*, Batsford, 1979, p. 97.
7 D. Landes *The Unbound Prometheus*, Cambridge University Press, 1969.
8 N. F. R. Crafts, *British Economic Growth during the Industrial Revolution*, Oxford University Press, 1985.
9 P. H. Lindert 'English Occupations 1670–1811', *Journal of Economic History* 40 (4), 1980 and 'Revising England's Social Tables', *Explorations in Economic History* Vol. 1. XIX, 1982.
10 W. W. Rostow *How It All Began, Origins of the Modern Economy*, Methuen, 1975, p. 143.
11 M. W. Flinn *Origins of the Industrial Revolution*, Longman, 1966, p. 102.
12 A notable exception is A. E. Musson and E. Robinson *Science and Technology in the Industrial Revolution*, Manchester University Press, 1969 extracts of which are printed in A. E. Musson (ed.) *Science, Technology and Economic Growth in the Eighteenth Century*, Methuen, 1972.
13 S. Kuznets *Economic Growth and Structure*, Oxford University Press, 1965 and *Modern Economic Growth*, Oxford University Press, 1966 contain references to his earlier work and provide the best statment of his views.
14 W. W. Rostow op. cit. pp. 133 and 144–57.
15 T. S. Ashton *The Industrial Revolution*, Oxford University Press, 1948, p. 16.
16 The introduction in A. E. Musson (ed.) op. cit. especially pp. 56–68 gives a full, well-referenced discussion of this specific issue.
17 ibid. p. 62
18 Quoted in W. W. Rostow op. cit. p. 156
19 David Landes op. cit. quoted in P. Mathias 'Science and Technology during the Industrial Revolution', in P. Mathias *The Transformation of England*, Methuen, 1979, p. 77.
20 E. J. Hobsbawm *Industry and Empire*, Penguin, 1968, p. 25.
21 S. Lilley 'Technology Progress and the Industrial Revolution' in C. Cipolla (ed.) *The Industrial Revolution*, Fontana, 1973, p. 213.
22 P. Deane *The First Industrial Revolution*, Cambridge University Press, 1965, p. 129.
23 T. S. Ashton op. cit. pp. 13–16.
24 The ecological case put forward in R. Wilkinson *Poverty and Progress*, Methuen, 1973, pp. 115–18 exemplifies this view.
25 G. N. von Tunzelmann 'Technical Progress during the Industrial Revolution' in R. Floud and D. McCloskey (eds) *The Economic History of Britain since 1700*, Vol. I, Cambridge University Press, 1981, p. 146.
26 A detailed discussion of changing technology in textiles can be found in M. Berg *The Age of Manufactures*, Fontana, 1985, pp. 234–63.
27 S. Lilley op. cit. p. 193.
28 ibid. p. 194.
29 A brief discussion of this and other issues can be found in S. D. Chapman *The Cotton Industry in the Industrial Revolution*, Macmillan, 1972, 2nd edn, 1988.
30 M. Berg op. cit. pp. 108–28.
31 For the iron industry see T. S. Ashton *Iron and Steel in the Industrial Revolution*, Manchester University Press, 1963 and A. Birch *The Economic History of the British Iron and Steel Industry 1784–1879*, 1967. An important reassess-

ment can be found in the work of C. K. Hyde 'The Adoption of Coke-Smelting by the British Iron Industry 1709–1790', *Explorations in Economic History* Vol. X, 1972–3, 'Technological Change in the British Wrought Iron Industry 1750–1815: A Reinterpretation', *Economic History Review,* 2nd Series, Vol. XXVII (1974) and *Technological Change and the British Iron Industry*, Princeton, 1977. J. R. Harris *The British Iron Industry 1700–1880*, Macmillan, 1988 is an up-to-date synthesis.

32 C. K. Hyde 'The Adoption of the Hot-blast by the British Iron Industry – a Reinterpretation', *Explorations in Economic History* Vol. X, 1973.

33 The definitive work on coal is now M. W. Flinn *The History of the British Coal Industry Vol. II 1700–1830: The Industrial Revolution*, Oxford University Press, 1984 but see the short summary by B. Lewis *Coal Mining in the Eighteenth and Nineteenth Centuries*, Longman, 1971.

34 For a more detailed discussion of canals see chapter 7.

35 On pre-industrial sources of energy see the series of papers, especially on wind and water power, in *History Today*, March 1980. R. L. Hills *Power in the Industrial Revolution*, Manchester University Press, 1970 is a useful introduction to the subject but needs to be considered in relation to G. N. von Tunzelmann *Steam Power and British Industrialization to 1860*, Oxford University Press, 1978.

36 J. R. Harris 'The Employment of Steam Power in the Eighteenth Century' *History*, 52 (1967).

37 G. N. von Tunzelmann 'Technical Progress during the Industrial Revolution' op. cit. pp. 157–8.

38 W. W. Rostow op. cit. p. 184.

6 The revolution in industrial organization

Much, probably most, of the country's work was carried on in family units: apprentices became part of a family; the family home – the cottage of the poor weaver; the house-cum-shop of the urban craftsman or retailer, even the country mansion of the landed gentleman – was also the place of work . . . for most people the modern distinction between dwelling-places and work-places was unknown.[1]

Time went on in Coketown like its own machinery: so much material wrought up, so much fuel consumed, so many powers worn out, so much money made . . . the piston of the steam-engine worked monotonously up and down like the head of an elephant in a state of melancholy madness . . . (the complement to the machines were the workers – human beings reduced to Hands) a race who would have found more favour with some people, if Providence had seen fit to make them only hands or, like the lower creatures of the seashore, only hands and stomachs. . . . A special contrast, as every man was in the forest of looms where Stephen worked, to the crashing, smashing, tearing piece of mechanism at which he laboured. . . . So many hundred Hands to this Mill; so many hundred horse Steam Power.[2]

Central to many people's image of Britain's industrial revolution stands the dark, satanic mill and its the antithesis, the domestic method of production. The pace of work changed from being determined by the choice of the worker to the monotonous movement of the steam-piston. The ceaseless clanking of machines replaced the quieter movements of the hand machines. Men, women and children were exploited, paid starvation wages, dehumanized. The tyrannical, licentious, grasping factory master was caricatured by Charles Dickens in the hypocritical and loud-mouthed Mr Bounderby. This image, crude and exaggerated as it clearly is, depicts the main features of the pattern of production which became widespread in Britain by the end of the nineteenth century. It highlights the emergence of the factory, stresses the importance of new technology in production and emphasizes that ownership of the means of production rests with the capitalist who paid wages to his propertyless workers. Just how accurate is this picture of industrial organization in the eighteenth and early nine-teenth centuries? This chapter will first examine the nature of industrial organization, particularly the notion of 'proto-industrialization', and sec-ondly, through a number of case-studies, show how key industries were organized and how their organization changed.

A STEREOTYPED VIEW

Why and how has this stereotype emerged?[3] Peoples' perceptions of the industrial revolution – themselves the result of how historians and others have presented it – tend to see a stark contrast between the domestic and factory system. There is an assumption that, in the undisciplined, fulfilling and relatively classless world of cottage industry, ordinary people were happier and probably better off. Robert Southey wrote about 'content-ment spinning at the cottage door' and William Radcliffe, writing in 1828, was even more emphatic about a 'golden age'.[4]

> they [the weavers] might be truly said to be placed in a higher state of 'wealth, peace and godliness' by the great demand for, and high price of their labour than they had ever before experienced. Their dwellings and small gardens clean and neat – all the family well clad . . . every house well furnished. . . .

Peter Gaskell, in *The Manufacturing Population of England* (1833), con-trasted the horrors of working in the mills with the alleged idyllic con-ditions of an earlier age. His views were later taken up uncritically by Friedrich Engels in *The Condition of the Working Class in England* (1845) and used as historical justification for a radical critique of proletarian conditions and capitalist exploitation.[5] This view of a 'golden age' just before the industrial revolution was and is a myth. Domestic spinners and weavers had been exploited by clothiers as ruthlessly as the factory operatives were by manufacturers in the 1840s. People worked long hours for low wages under the domestic system, as under the factory system. The Children's Employment Commission of 1842 showed that those employed in small workshops – the sewing girls and shirt-makers in the East End of London or the apprentice nail-makers in the Willenhall – were treated far more cruelly than factory piecers in Lancashire. It was because factories brought many people together under one roof that it became possible to identify bad conditions which had formerly been hidden in isolated cottages and workshops. But the realities of employ-ment for the handloom weavers by the 1830s, caught in the vice of chang-ing technology and fashions leading to falling wages, gave the picture painted by Engels, John Fielden, J. P. Kay and others credence. Investi-gations concentrated on textile production, particularly cotton. Factory legislation up to 1850 was, with the exception of the 1842 Mines Act, exclusively concerned with conditions in the textile trades. Select Parlia-

mentary Committees investigated the weavers but they provided no remedies for their plight. They were doomed, as Malcolm Thomis says:

> The handworkers would eventually have to go, at different speeds in
> different places, but they would all in time have to go. But the process
> of their going was a painful one, and the pain was so widespread
> because of the enormous buildup of the hand trades immediately prior
> to their collapse.[6]

The image developed in the 1820s and 1830s was of the contrast, conflict
and competition between old and new systems. Closer examination reveals
that this stark contrast is questionable and that there was important continuity between the factory and pre-factory stages of development and that
handworking continued to play a major role in the British economy until
after 1850. Thomis again: 'the factory operative was not the typical industrial worker in 1850, still heavily outnumbered by the millions of domestic
outworkers who were surviving the technological revolution'.[7]

'PROTO-INDUSTRIALIZATION'

Some historians have recently suggested that the existence of domestic
systems of production in textile and other industries distinguished the pre-
industrial economies of Europe from the Third World countries of today.
They have developed the concept of 'proto-industrialization'[8] arguing that
industrial revolutions could not have taken place without the prior development of a form of production which provided key changes in the use
of land, labour, capital and entrepreneurship which made industrialization
possible. This concept needs close examination since revisionists emphasize that, as late as the 1840s, over 75 per cent of British manufacturing
was in diverse, dispersed and unspectacular industries – neither cotton
nor iron and decidedly not steam-powered.

Characteristics

Proto-industries were marked by four features. First, they produced goods
for markets outside the region where the craftsmen lived. Sometimes these
markets were overseas. An example of an export-led expansion of a rurally
located textile industry occurred in Ireland during the eighteenth century.
Poor-quality linen for domestic consumption expanded from the late seventeenth century with the influx of English and continental expertise into
Ulster coupled with the opening of the English market to Irish producers.
In 1770 there were perhaps 42,000 weavers in Ulster. In the West Midlands
a considerable proportion of the rural population manufactured nails,
knives, scythes, locks etc much of which was destined for the American
market.

Secondly, industrial products were made by workers who combined manufacturing and farming. For example, in 1839 Scottish weavers round Largs derived a small income from fishing and letting out boats in the season and the beneficial effects of seasonal employment in the fields, a practice common among women, of whom a considerable number put aside their 'needles and other implements of manufacture' in summer and autumn and 'hire themselves to the farmers in the neighbourhood at potato-planting, hay-making, hoeing and weaving, and latterly, at reaping, digging potatoes and raising turnips'. Labour employed in this way was cheap and made minimal demands on fixed capital since no special industrial premises were required and the machinery used was usually small and inexpensive.

Thirdly, rural manufacturing stimulated commercial farming by creating a market for food. Proto-industrial workers did not grow enough food for their own needs and were obliged to buy supplies from other producers. In Ulster cultivation was, according to Arthur Young, often neglected in favour of linen weaving. It has been suggested that rural industry in the seventeenth century developed in those areas not well suited to grain production.

Finally, towns located in a region were principally centres of trade and commerce. The merchants who provided the raw materials to producers lived in the towns and some finishing processes were carried out there by skilled workers. The functions of towns are well illustrated by the example of Ulster where, in the late eighteenth century, there were about sixty places scattered through the province which acted as weekly linen markets. Most were small and the bulk of trade was concentrated in the three towns of Armagh, Lisburn and Lurgan. Proto-industrialization draws a clear distinction between countryside and towns: manufacturing was done principally in the former, with the latter as market centres. This distinction should not be pushed too far since some towns were manufacturing centres as well. Lisburn was a centre for skilled damask weaving on complex looms too large and expensive for rural cottages.

Mass production: domestic and factory goods

The putting-out system was a method of increasing production. But it was, in a whole variety of ways 'less' of a method than the factory. It already showed a clear distinction between the capitalists, who controlled and financed it, and the wage-earners, who depended on it for their living. The merchant-manufacturers bought the appropriate raw materials – though not in a few minor rural trades like straw-plaiting – and hired the wage-labour to convert them into finished products. The workers generally owned their own tools, though in the case of more elaborate pieces of machinery like knitting-frames they were often rented. Most workers worked on their own premises but it was not uncommon for the individual knitter or nail-maker to rent space in another person's shop. They then dispatched the finished products, not only in textile fabrics but ready-made clothes, hosiery, boots and shoes and hardware, to domestic and foreign markets. This level of production required considerable sophistication. The capitalists sometimes deployed considerable numbers of workers: in the 1830s cotton manufactures in Carlisle employed 3,500 weavers scattered over the Border counties of England and Scotland and in Ulster; Wards of Belper provided work for some 4,000 knitting-frames in Derbyshire, Nottinghamshire and Leicestershire. Considerable logistical skills in co-ordinating were needed for such large and scattered workforces. Day-to-day management was often delegated to agents – variously known as 'foggers', 'putters-out' and 'bagmen'. What existed before industrialization was a three-tier system: capitalists who provided the raw materials and access to widespread markets; 'middle managers' who, in large enterprises, dealt with the labour-force; and wage-earners, who happened to own some of the tools of their trade.

Continuity between systems

Is it possible to show that the firms which set up as the first modern factories were already active on a putting-out basis and whether the last generation of domestic workers transformed themselves into factory hands? The continuity was not direct or complete in every single industry or region where the transition from domestic to factory systems occurred. In some regions, like East Anglia or the Cotswolds, the change-over simply did not take place and once-important industries gradually declined. Why did deindustrialization take place? The cloth industry of Essex died out between 1700 and 1800. Rural weaving declined first in the villages and then in the towns. Spinning continued and in the 1740s employed the majority of women. Coggleshall was in decay by 1720 and in 1733 it unsuccessfully petitioned Parliament for help but had collapsed by 1760. Was this decline a result of the comparative advantage of the new agricultural techniques to the light arable soils of Essex which made farming a more profitable activity than manufacturing, as E. L. Jones has argued?[9] Certainly both the profitability and social standing of agriculture improved after 1700 and this may have been sufficient to induce some clothiers to strengthen their links with farming. Local industrial investment was no longer rewarding enough. There is evidence in the West Country for the transfer of capital into land by clothiers whose assets were no longer liquid enough to tide them over trade depressions. Mechanization reinforced this process of decline. Enterprise was inhibited by extensive workers' opposition to technical change. In Essex conflict was often acute: in 1757 there was a big strike at Colchester; weavers in Barking fought against the wool mill in 1759; there was also some resistance to the flying shuttle in the 1750s and the use of jennies was delayed until 1794. In Ireland,[10] with the exception of factory-based linen production in eastern

Ulster and the short-lived cotton industry from the 1780s to the 1830s traditional domestic industries declined in the nineteenth century. Three interrelated reasons have been put forward to explain this deindustrialization. From a socio-political point of view Irish industry was exposed to competition from the technologically superior industries of mainland Britain, especially after the Act of Union in 1801. Secondly, markets for Irish goods were generally small, restricting the possibility of more efficient organizational patterns despite low labour costs. Finally Irish industry lacked capital, itself a result of poor profits from low productivity. One common feature of all areas that underwent deindustrialization was that they experienced competition from other areas to which they could not respond and which caused them to lose markets. Norfolk, for example, suffered from Yorkshire competition. It produced higher-quality cloth, demand for which fluctuated with changing fashions, the disruptions of foreign wars and the removal of tariff duties in 1826, which allowed cheaper French worsteds to undercut the market. East Anglia could have responded by following Yorkshire into the cheaper textile market using new technology but it lacked coal supplies. Competition was a necessary explanation of decline but it was not a sufficient one.

'Modernization'

Where 'modernization' did occur in traditional outworking industries in the late eighteenth and nineteenth centuries it was existing firms which played a leading role. In both Yorkshire and the West Country the majority of new factory entrepreneurs had previous connections with the industry through its domestic organization. The marketing and management skills which they had applied were important in enabling the new system to develop. A recent study of the 150 Arkwright-type cotton mills operating in 1787 emphasizes the continuity of investment between the two systems.[11] For example, John Ashworth (1696–1767) was by 1720 already employing spinners and fustian weavers in the area between Bolton and Blackburn. This was continued by his son Henry (1728–90). He carried on an extensive business 'in the manufacture of a coarse durable fabric called Thick Sets Fustians and Jeans', purchasing his raw materials in Manchester. The family business was continued by John (1772–1855), who built the New Eagley mill in 1793 for power-spinning.[12] But the same study showed that a quarter of mill-owners did not emerge from the textile industry.

Continuity of workers?

There is less agreement as to how far existing handworkers in any particular industry really did 'shift over' to the factory. The theory of 'proto-industry' suggests that the domestic system created a landless proletariat in many ways at odds with the traditional economic values and practice of the rural society around them. They only had a limited involvement in the rural economy and their manual skills were largely irrelevant in farming. They had to be responsive to the opportunities and pressures of a market economy, and were well equipped to form the first generation of the modern labour force.

Is the theory correct? There were distinct labour advantages, from the capitalists' point of view, for locating industry in the countryside. Population growth created labour surplus to the requirements of agriculture in some parts of Britain. In other areas this growth resulted in surplus labour being absorbed by changing farming. Underemployment was endemic in eighteenth-century Britain and there were large numbers of landless labourers for whom supplementing farming wages by industrial work was a necessity. There were demographic effects which were both a consequence and cause of proto-industries. David Levine draws the contrast between the villages of Shepshed and Bottesford in Leicestershire.[13] Shepshed was a community of smallholdings and low incomes until, in the late seventeenth century, it became involved increasingly with framework knitting organized by London capitalists. By 1800 it was highly industrialized. The mean age of marriage fell by about five years – twice the national fall – and this had a direct impact on marital fertility, which rose significantly. Bottesford remained a landlord-dominated community of tenant farmers which turned from arable to pastoral farming. Employment opportunities contracted and, with no rural industry to provide alternative employment, the age of marriage rose and fertility fell.

Hostility to 'new' technology

The traditional picture suggested that there was a stubborn hostility and refusal to accept new technology, albeit unsuccessfully, and this view was reinforced in peoples' minds by references to the Luddite movement of 1811–16 but some people 'stuck to their trade'. The nailers of Worcestershire and the Black Country continued to put their children into it when only the hope and never the reality of a decent living remained. Andrew Ure believed that women were willing to sacrifice their health in lace-embroidery at home rather than enter the higher-paid factory, since to do so implied a loss of caste or gentility. But the continuities were many. Much factory industrialization took place in small village communities. Mill-owners like the Ashworths used the skills of labourers who had previously been outworkers. Factories took men and women out of the home, but few married women with small children were amongst them. Evidence from Lancashire suggests that many urban textile workers seemed to have some experience in rural textile industries and that younger married men were more willing to work in the new powerloom sheds than the elderly who remained on their handlooms. Trades disappeared either when they were no longer necessary or when people were no longer willing to do the work for the wages provided. Children did not follow in their parents' footsteps but at least they probably sought a similar industry even if that meant working in a factory.

'Proto-industrialization' – some conclusions

The proto-industrial model highlights the division between capital and labour which characterized parts of the domestic no less than the factory system, and it considers the continuity between the two systems. In doing so it has pinpointed certain misconceptions about cottage industry. First the model makes quite clear what the domestic system entailed. It was one of several methods of production that existed in the eighteenth and nineteenth centuries. In the urban context there were artisan structures and small commodity production developed. Artisan manufacture, especially in London, made many of the consumer goods. Some industries were organized round a central plant but, particularly in iron production, this was combined with putting out. In the villages there were self-employed craftsmen – the shoe-maker or tailor or blacksmith – who produced and sold goods directly to the order of their local customers.

Secondly, proto-industries were mass producers and, in many ways, this did not require 'skill' or 'craft' in the same way as artisan trades did. Cottage industry involved the making of plain, simple, inexpensive goods by hand or with simple tools. This did not require much initial training and was largely done within the family unit. Some processes, like weaving heavy woollens and hammering nails and chains, required considerable strength. But others, like sewing buttons on shirts, plaiting straw, sticking matchboxes with glue, spinning yarn, called for neither brain nor brawn. Apprenticeship to learn 'skills' was unnecessary because the work was simple, monotonous and undemanding – particularly suitable for women and children, contemporaries believed. The domestic system involved as much drudgery as working in factories: the major difference was that it was the wage-earner not the steam engine that determined the pace.

Thirdly, just as historians need to abandon the notion that the domestic system was all about skilled craftsmen, so the notion that it was predominantly about 'men' needs to be abandoned as well.[14] Women and children became an attractive pool of cheap labour for merchant manufacturers. Spinning was the archetype of the female domestic craft. In the 1790s the majority of women in Essex were employed in spinning wool in town as well as countryside. The second most important women's industry was lace-making. Handknitting occupied women and children in many parts of the country. The significant economic position of women and a sexual division of labour were demonstrated in linen manufacture. In pre-famine Ireland the male weavers may have formed the linchpin of the manufacturing process but the viability of the industry depended on the reliable source of yarn produced by women. Despite the constraints imposed on the expansion of textiles by the supply of yarn and the almost entirely female nature of spinning, women were among the lowest paid workers. They were an unorganized mass of sweated labour. Mechanization forced women's wages down still further and their dominance over hand and jenny spinning was eroded with the development of male control over mule-spinning. Men struggled to maintain their skilled priority in the labour force against machinery and against the encroachment of unskilled women and this explains why gender segregation occurred in the economy. Deliberately ignored by their better-organized menfolk and incapable of effective collective self-defence, before the 1870s women were accustomed to regarding any earnings, however minute, as a worthwhile contribution to the family income. Women's work was often part-time or casual. This suited many employers and husbands or fathers. Domestic service reinforced the low status and value of women's work. It was in the 'sweated trades' like needlework that female outworking remained particularly important and gender exploitation occurred.[15]

Finally, the contrast is often made between the corporate and highly organized culture of urban workers and the dispersed and totally disorganized rural manufactures. Although resistance was easier in towns there is ample evidence of a high degree of organization among rural workers. The decline of industry in southern England can be partly explained by the more forceful workers' resistance to machinery. Wiltshire and Somerset were extremely hostile to machinery. There were riots against the flying shuttle in Trowbridge in 1785–7 and 1810–13 which postponed its introduction there and in west Wiltshire until after 1815. Weavers were still rioting against the shuttle in Frome in 1822. By contrast the clothworkers of Gloucestershire had long adopted the gig mill. The degree of labour activity and resistance depended on local conditions and customs and the relationship between employers and their workers. Strikes in centres of handloom weaving like Manchester, Coventry, Barnsley and Norwich, in the major centres of framework knitting in Nottinghamshire and Leicester or among the nail-makers of the Black Country were not just anti-technological in character but were motivated by what was perceived as an attack on a 'moral economy' in which fair wages and prices were central.

It should now be easier to see the similarities and points of continuity between the domestic and factory systems. Both were systems for mass production – though the domestic system was labour-intensive while factories were capital-intensive in terms of plant – which overlapped in time and complemented rather than competed with each other. The emphasis placed on the complete triumph of the factory system in cotton textiles with the consequent demise of handworkers has diverted attention from the expansion of outwork methods in the ready-made clothing trade and in the boot and shoe industries. By the 1850s outwork had more or less disappeared from the staple textile industries but it was more firmly entrenched than ever in and around the industrial towns of the Midlands and south of England and above all in London, where there was a reservoir of cheap, unskilled and underemployed labour.

TEXTILE PRODUCTION

The textile industries are frequently viewed as the epitome of the whole story from proto-industry to factory production. In fact there was considerable variety of organization in textiles. In 1700 the wool and worsted industries of both the West Country and Yorkshire were dominated by small clothiers. Their labour force was largely determined by the minimum number of people it took to make a piece of cloth: in the case of kersey it took six – often the family – sorting, carding, spinning, weaving and shearing for one week to produce one finished but undyed piece. During the eighteenth century a division arose in Yorkshire between woollen and worsted branches. Woollen continued to be produced by the small clothiers who often combined manufacture with farming. By the 1720s Defoe found that the worsted industry, especially round Halifax, was organized in a highly sophisticated combination of domestic and workshop manufacture. Worsteds had never been produced by small independent clothiers and the Yorkshire worsted manufacturers ran extensive putting-out networks commonly distributing wool within a radius of 20–30 miles. Capitalistic structures were not, by contrast, a feature of worsted manufacture in Norfolk where the independent weaver, who brought yarn from independent spinners and who marketed his own product, was the pivot of the industrial structure.

Framework knitting

In framework knitting capitalist relations were an eighteenth-century development. It started out as a skilled occupation practised by people of some substance and master knitters operated an apprentice-journeyman system. The main centre of the industry, originally in London and controlled by the London Chartered Framework Knitters' Company, quickly spread to the Midlands after 1680 and by 1750 was focused on Leicester and Nottingham. The Midland hosiers expanded quickly and responded to changing market fashions. They ignored the old guild controls laid down by the London Company and increasingly formed a capitalist elite. Population growth and agrarian change led to regional poverty and a cheap workforce and reinforced the hold of the large hosiers.

Silk

Silk was a luxury industry in which capitalist and artisan confronted each other across the throwing and weaving branches of the trade. After the introduction of Lombe's silk-throwing machinery in 1719, mills sprang up in many areas and by 1800 the industry was scattered over twenty counties and fifty towns employing proportionally far more children than other textile mills. Tightly capitalist, from the outset it supplied the traditionally organized and skilled weaving branch. In Spitalfields, London, the industry was artisan in structure and in the early eighteenth century manufactured elaborate brocades, velvets and other rich fabrics. Weaving in other areas grew after the Spitalfields Act of 1773, which provided a procedure for fixing weavers' wages. It was extended to include silk mixtures in 1792 and in 1811 covered women as well as men. This tended to depress the metropolitan industry and prompted many manufacturers to move their trade elsewhere. Silk weaving spread into Essex, Suffolk and Norfolk. The silk-button trade moved to Macclesfield. Silk-ribbon weaving became important in Coventry and a number of surrounding villages. A distinction between the town and villages soon arose. Urban weavers succeeded in preventing an influx of cheap labour and kept wages low in the villages by banning rural workers from the more efficient looms.

Linens

Linen production was a home occupation even after it was commercialized. Never defined as a skilled occupation, it was largely assumed to be a woman's preserve. Linen fostered the growth of the cotton industry through its close association with fustian manufacture. Fustian producers were more caught up in capitalist relations than either linen workers or many wool producers. By the mid-eighteenth century there was systematic intervention by middlemen and a developed putting-out system.

'Mixed' firms

After 1770 technological change affected the organization of production.[16] Increasingly some processes took place in a central mill or workshop around which the outworkers were ranged. At first, perhaps, only one process was mechanized while others remained manual but as mechanization continued the industries were increasingly concentrated in factories until eventually the whole industry was transformed. 'Mixed' industries or 'mixed' firms continued to exist until after 1850. In the silk industry mixed production by a single large firm was common from the mid-eighteenth century. By 1818 Henry Critchley had 50 of his 150 looms inside his Macclesfield factory and John Heathcote's factory in Tiverton employed 850 'in' and 1,500 'out'. In cotton major inventions in spinning, carding and other subsidiary processes were followed only after a generation by parallel changes in weaving. In 1788 there were 108,000 outworker hand weavers and this increased to 240,000 by 1820. In 1786 Samuel Oldknow employed some 800 outworker spinners and weavers in Stockport and

Anderton. But he concentrated the finishing in his own warehouse, where he had twenty warping mills and fifty girls hand-finishing the muslin, and he controlled his own bleach and print works at Heaton. Among textiles, it was, however, the woollen industry which kept its 'mixed' character longest. The spinning process remained manual for longer, owing to the greater difficulty of dealing with the woollen than the cotton fibres. The real breakthrough came with the adaptation of machine spinning to worsted and woollen yarns from the early 1790s onwards. Until the 1830s the typical 'mixed' works was a central mill, steam- or water-driven, containing preparatory, spinning and finishing processes together with domestic weavers.

Cotton mills – phases of factory development

Cotton mills were among the earliest and most numerous of industrial concerns. The pioneer firms were built along the swift streams of Nottinghamshire, Derbyshire, North Wales and some of the less accessible parts of Scotland, but the industry quickly became localized around Manchester and Glasgow. The minor centres, such as the West Riding, the Furness district, North and South Wales, the Belfast and Dublin areas and the older centres of calico printing round London, declined after 1800. Although regional and local differences provided diversity in response to factory development and 'staggered' the adoption of powered technology, it is possible to identify three main stages in the adoption of factory production in cotton. Richard Arkwright and his partners pioneered the first stage of spinning mills in the 1770s and their number multiplied, especially after Arkwright's patent was declared void in 1785. By 1788 there were at least 142 water-driven mills in Great Britain, including 49 in Lancashire and Cheshire, 39 in Derbyshire and Nottinghamshire and 19 in Scotland. By 1796 Glasgow had 39 water-mills and 30 large calico-printing works. Even in this early water-powered spinning phase there were some large concerns, particularly in Scotland. New Lanark had 1,300 indoor and 300 outdoor workers while other mills including Catrine, Deanston, Stanley and Blantyre employed up to 1,000. In England mills at Mellor and Styal or the works developed by the Peels in Bury reached a similar size.

The second phase of factory development was based on steam power for the spinning mule and eventually the powerloom. After 1815 firms increasingly combined spinning and weaving in the factory. A Lancashire witness before a House of Commons Select Committee in 1833 observed that at that date all new spinning mills had weaving sheds attached. New Lanark was employing 1,600 inworkers and the 41 Glasgow mills averaged 244 workers each. The Strutts at Belper and Milford employed 1,494 in 1815 and 1,613 three years later. The increase in the size of cotton mills during the first half of the nineteenth century appeared to be a classic case of capitalist concentration, a point made by Engels in 1844. But this is too simplified a picture. Up to 1850 capital and credit were available to small as well as large producers. In the 1840s the average firm in Manchester employed 260 hands and a quarter employed fewer than 100. The impression that all cotton production was factory-based is also too simplistic. The handloom survived as the dominant machine in parts of Lancashire for almost a generation after it had given way to the powerloom in others: in large centres like Stockport, Blackburn and Oldham factory production in spinning was widespread by the 1820s but it made little progress in the smaller villages of north-east Lancashire, like Colne and Haggate, before the 1840s.

The geographical separation of cotton spinning and weaving in Lancashire, the third phase of factory development, began in the 1840s. New weaving factories were set up in northern towns like Blackburn and Burnley. This was partly the result of the economics of increased specialization in a growing industry, but also reflected the differences in commercial needs and attitudes of each branch of the industry. Weaving was the more risky, and successful management seems primarily to have been a matter of matching order book and output. This tended to keep firms small and combination with a spinning mill ceased to be advantageous. What attracted weaving to the north from the 1840s was cheaper labour, coal and improved rail access. Spinning was far more certain and straightforward, allowing for considerable economies in scale and the early development of large joint-stock companies. There was no reason for such firms to leave established spinning districts with their reservoir of skills and contacts. While combined firms remained common, certainly in 1859, by 1884 62 per cent of looms were in the north and 78 per cent of spindles in the south.

Up to 1850 factory textile production, like its proto-industrial predecessor, operated not so much by directly subordinating large bodies of workers to employers, but by subcontracting exploitation and management. This can be seen in mule-spinning. Each pair of mules had a team of three workers. The 'minder' was in charge and was paid by the owner according to the output of his mules. He had two assistants: a 'big piecer', who was usually a young adult, and a 'little piecer', usually a youth or child. The piecers were essentially employees of the minder rather than the owner and the division of proceeds from a given output was determined by the workers themselves. The minder was, in effect, a subcontractor. The burden of labour management was passed on to the workforce and both recruitment and supervision were the responsibility of the minder. He had a vested interest in increasing the output of his mules and a swifter pace of work could be enforced on the piecers by payment on a time rate. The craft status of the minders rested less on their technical expertise than on their ability to keep the piecers in a subordinate position. The minder-piecer system proved to be an effective method of labour management and shows that skill and craft status could be socially constructed rather than technologically determined.

METALLURGICAL AND ENGINEERING INDUSTRIES

Ironworking

The second major group of industries to develop large-scale enterprises in this period consisted of the metallurgical and associated engineering concerns. A distinction may be drawn broadly between those industries which smelted and refined the ore and those which made a product with the refined metal. Two main groups of ironworks can be distinguished in the eighteenth century. The first consisted of survivals from the charcoal age which adapted themselves, and by the process of vertical integration, acquired both the rolling mills, wiremills and other later stages of production, as well as, in some cases their own ore-fields and coal-mines. The other works were, from the outset, based on coke-smelting and were greatly furthered by Cort's puddling process in the 1780s. The typical organization for charcoal smelting was a combine of works in associated ownership which were often physically and geographically separate and separately managed. Despite this they rarely employed more than a hundred workers, many of whom were scattered as charcoal burners or carters. The proximity of iron and coal allowed concentration of production in one works complex though it was not until after 1750 that works were consciously planned as a unit. The 'typical' labour force increased during the first half of the eighteenth century from below 100 to nearly 200. The real increase in size came in the 1790s with an average of 250 workers but some ironworks were much larger. This was particularly the case in South Wales, developed by the commercial genius of Anthony Bacon and the technical ability of Isaac Wilkinson in the 1760s which quickly exploited the puddling process to become the major centre of wrought ironmaking. By 1830 the actual output of South Wales, 277,600 tons, represented 42 per cent of British output. In the early eighteenth century labour was organized on a subcontracting method whereby a subcontractor undertook part or all of a process, hired and paid his own men in return for an agreed sum for the tonnage produced. This was a transitional stage in industrial management but it served the purpose of the ironmasters who were merchants rather than industrialists. The ironworks of Merthyr Tydfil – the Cyfartha works of the Crawshays, Penydaren of the Homfrays, Dowlais of the Guests and Plymouth of the Hills – exemplified large-scale organization. They employed labour on an extensive scale: the workforce of Cyfartha reached 1,500 by 1810. Skilled labour – smelters, puddlers and forge-men – constituted between 30 and 40 per cent of the workforce, had served a long apprenticeship and were often on long contracts. A piece-work or a time plus bonus system generally operated for unskilled labour.

Mining and smelting

Lead-smelting also had some very large units, though these were either associated with mines, as in the case of the Quaker Lead Company, or with lead warehouses, as with Walker, Parker & Co. It was in the copper-smelting industry and the related brassworks that some of the largest firms and some of the most innovative managerial experiences were developed. There were several reasons for the early development of large capitalist enterprises in the copper industry. Capital equipment was expensive and there were sound economic reasons for combining copper-smelting, brass-making and some final goods manufacture. At the same time, the geo-graphical concentration of copper and zinc mining and the major markets in London and Birmingham, allowed these firms to assume a mercantile role and carry heavy stock, to bring these two markets into contact with each other. Growth began in the 1690s and was partly a result of the development of a new reverberatory smelting furnace. For most of the eighteenth century large companies were concentrated in the two main existing regions: the Bristol area and the North Wales–Cheshire and Lan-cashire belt. The Warmley Company of Gloucestershire, set up by William Campion in 1746, employed 2,000 people, including outworkers, in 1767. In general, however, employment at a typical smelting mill was not large, 100 in 1750 rising to 200 by 1830, but most companies had several plants. The largest combine was headed by Thomas Williams who had smeltworks at the Mona and Parys mines at Amlwch, the Ravenhead works, the Holywell works, Upper Banks works in Swansea and the Penclawdd works as well as the Mona Mine Company, the Stanley works at St Helens, the Middle Bank works in Swansea and the Greenfield works. In the nine-teenth century the weight of the industry increasingly shifted to Swansea, to the coal, where 80 per cent of British smelting capacity was sited by 1830. Control also increasingly came to be exercised by mercantile and coal-owning interests, particularly the Vivian family, who took over Pen-clawdd in 1800 and the Hafod works in 1810, Grenfell and Williams, arising out of the Anglesey combine and Nevill & Co at Swansea in 1794 and Llanelly ten years later.

In 1786 a foreign visitor, Sophie von la Roche, admired the English for 'their skill in working metal – the great advantage it gives them as regards the motion, lastingness and accuracy of machinery. . . .' Metal processing spawned a whole series of relatively small-scale industries using iron, steel, brass, copper and various alloys. These relied on skilled workers, diversity of output, innovative practices and handtools and were organized within the artisan and putting-out systems. Many of these industries remained small-scale even if they adopted steam power and factory premises.

Engineering

The development of the engineering industry was closely associated with iron processing. Coalbrookdale, Carron and Bersham were also builders of machine tools. Millwrights and blacksmiths played a significant part in this development and from being concerned with the mechanical and power needs of industry soon turned to the manufacture of machinery itself. The creation of a skilled engineering labour force involved a division of labour and specialization of function. In 1824 Galloway, a London engineer, had between 75 and 115 employees who were divided into a number of different trades – pattern makers, iron and brass founders, hammermen, filers, wood turners etc. Firms tended to be small: in 1825 there were up to 500 engineering firms in the London area employing no more than 10,000 men. Henry Maudslay, who introduced the first mass-production engineering in Britain, only employed about 80 men. It was not until the 1830s that there was a significant increase in size among engineering firms and the industry was transformed from a labour- to a capital-intensive one. The Forth Street works of Robert Stephenson & Co. at Newcastle employed 100 workers making steam locomotives in 1830 but by 1838 this had increased to 400.

Skilled labour and regional differentiation in terms of levels of skills emerged in the late seventeenth century in the hardware and cutlery trades of the Black Country, Birmingham and Sheffield. The unit of production was small and there was an extensive division of labour. This division occurred both within specific industries and between products. By 1700 the Sheffield industry had divided into three trades: culters, scissor-makers and those making scythes, and the skills of forging and grinding. Large-scale centralized enterprises like the Birmingham Soho works of Matthew Boulton were exceptional. Boulton used the larger scale of production to divide and subdivide tasks which were then mechanized and he employed skilled artists and designers to develop products which were uneconomic for smaller concerns. He was able to reduce labour costs because skilled labour was no longer necessary, and in 1762 a large proportion of his workers were women and children. It is likely that other large industrialists in Birmingham, like John Taylor, who employed 500 in 1755, and Henry Clay with 300 workers, were controlling domestic workshops only and this was certainly so outside the Birmingham area. William Whitehouse, a West Bromwich ironmonger employed his 1,200–1,500 nailers largely as outworkers as did the Carron ironworks. The different forms of industrial organization that developed through the eighteenth and part of the nine-teenth centuries reflected the traditional artisan independence in the metal trades. The distinction between outworker, manufacturer and artisan was ill-defined but friendly and trade societies attempted to enforce customary demarcation lines on wages, prices and employment policy and exerted some degree of workplace control.

MINING

Mining became capitalized very early and, in some respects, was the model for other industries. Pits were large even by 1700 with sixty pits in nineteen collieries on the Tyne producing up to a million tons per year. The north-east monopolized large-scale coal production because of its grip on the London and export trades. This made it a profitable, progressive and booming industry which responded to growing demand by deepening its pits and increasing its labour force. The typical northern mine was the property of either an active landowner or of a large capitalist partnership employing skilled managers or 'viewers'. There was a clear division of labour between the various types of coal miners throughout Britain. For example, in 1828 Lord Wandesford's Leinster collieries employed 1,870 workers to get the coal out (1,000 colliers, 200 hurriers, 300 thrusters, 300 pullers at pit top and 70 scavengers) plus 115 proprietors' staff (18 agents and clerks, 2 weighman, 80 rangers and watchmen and 15 roadmen and labourers). In smaller pits the 'banksmen' dominated production, employing up to twenty men with their families but, although they were found in several other areas in 1800, they had disappeared in the north by 1720. Elsewhere large-scale mining came later and largely depended on proximity to growing markets. The pits in the Yorks–Nottingham–Derby coalfield expanded after 1780. The expansion of coal in South Wales paralleled the development of iron. Staffordshire remained a county of small mines, though expansion in iron production led to large mining enterprises after 1770.

Large units also developed among metal mines also in this period. The tin mines of Cornwall were owned by groups of 'adventurers' on the 'cost-book' system (shares which meant that an investor could limit losses in risky businesses) who contracted groups of workers to do the mining. There were two main types of workers, the 'tributers' who acted as independent contractors at their own risk and paid the adventurers a percentage of the proceeds of ore sales; and the 'tut-workers' who contracted to do certain tasks for specific sums. These contracts ran for a few months and could then be renewed. This system was also adopted in copper mines which very quickly outdistanced the tin mines in size and economic importance in the second half of the eighteenth century. This group contract system greatly reduced the load of management of large numbers of workers in difficult conditions: in 1786 Dolcoath mines had 23 groups of tut-workers and Cook's Kitchen had 17 gangs of tut-workers and 11 sets of tributers. Lead-mining was not affected by sudden large increases in demand in the eighteenth century and the Derbyshire workings were relatively small though the Leadhills deposits under the Earl of Hope-toun's land in Scotland employed up to a thousand workers in 1800. Mining as a whole showed certain common features. Rising demand during the eighteenth century gave ample opportunity for expansion. This was achieved by more extensive and, above all, deeper working, made possible initially by the Newcomen steam engine. Production was largely based on a system of group 'bargains' which relieved managers of some of their most difficult problems up to the 1820s. Direct control of labour by managers developed after 1830.

CONCLUSIONS

Between 1700 and 1850 British industry was a complex web of improvement and decline, large- and small-scale production, machine and hand processes. Some industries began to grow in size well before 1750. An important group of industries passed through this threshold in the 1780s, including cotton spinning, bar-iron making and engineering. Others, like gas-plants, did not develop until the early nineteenth century while others like linen and woollen weaving had not really undergone substantial organizational change by 1850. The widespread use of internal contracts between employer and workers and their use to ensure differentiation between the higher-paid skilled workers and the poorly-paid manual workers was part of a social process rather than a technological imperative. In 1850 much industrial production was characterized by the internal contract rather than hierarchical or bureaucratic control and differentiated production by hand technology rather than standardized production by machines.[17] Consumer preference in Britain was for differentiated hand-produced goods and the artisan trades suited this heterogeneity with its short production runs of unique items. The industrial revolution was marked by considerable continuity in the organization of work, with the early factories tending to use the managerial practices of the outworking and workshop modes of production which continued to exist. The extension of factories to the bulk of the economy, the development of a domestic consumer market based on machine-produced standardized goods and the creation of new managerial techniques was a product of the late not the early nineteenth century.

NOTES

1 D. C. Coleman *The Economy of England 1450–1750*, Oxford University Press, 1977, p. 8.
2 Charles Dickens *Hard Times*, 1854, edited by D. Craig, Penguin, 1971, pp. 24–5.
3 What follows uses M. Thomis *The Town Labourer and the Industrial Revolution*, Batsford, 1974 and *Responses to Industrialisation*, David & Charles, 1976 and, more briefly, D. Bythell 'Cottage Industry and the Factory System', *History Today*, April 1983. Documentary material can be found in M. Berg *Technology and Toil in Nineteenth Century Britain*, Cambridge University Press, 1979 and R. Brown *Change and Continuity in British Society 1800–1850*, Cambridge University Press, 1987.
4 W. Radcliffe *Origins of Power-Loom Weaving*, Stockport, 1828, pp. 59–61.

5 F. Engels *The Condition of the Working Class in England*, edited by W. O. Henderson and W. H. Chaloner, Blackwell, 1971 is the best edition. The introduction, especially pp. xiii–xxiv, is valuable for its discussion of Engels' sources and the unhistorical way in which he used them.

6 M. I. Thomis op. cit., 1974, p. 92.

7 ibid. p. 89.

8 L. A. Clarkson *Proto-Industrialization: The First Phase of Industrialization?*, Macmillan, 1985 examines the literature but see also M. Berg *The Age of Manufactures 1700–1820*, Fontana, 1985, pp. 69–91.

9 E. L. Jones 'Environment, Agriculture and Industrialisation', *Agricultural History*, 51 (1977).

10 J. Mokyr *Why Ireland Starved*, Allen & Unwin, 1985 especially chapters 6 and 7.

11 K. Honeyman *Origins of Enterprise: Business Leadership in the Industrial Revolution*, Cambridge University Press, 1982 and F. Crouzet *The First Industrialists*, Cambridge University Press, 1985.

12 R. Boyson *The Ashworth Cotton Enterprises*, Oxford University Press, 1970 chapters 1 and 2 is seminal.

13 D. Levine *Family Formation in an Age of Nascent Capitalism*, Academic Press, New York, 1977 especially pp. 58–87 and 'Industrialisation and the Proletarian Family in England', *Past and Present*, 107 (May 1985).

14 On the role of women in the domestic system see M. Berg op. cit., 129–77, I. Pinchbeck *Women Workers and the Industrial Revolution*, London, 1930 (Virago edn, 1981) is still of major value but can be supplemented by N. McKendrick 'Home Demand and Economic Growth: a New View of Women and Children in the Industrial Revolution', in McKendrick (ed.) *Historical Perspectives, Studies in English Thought and Society*, Cambridge University Press, 1974, E. Richards 'Women in the British Economy', *History*, 53 (1974) and B. Taylor *Eve and the New Jerusalem*, Virago, 1983. L. Davidoff and C. Hall *Family Fortunes: Men and Women of the English Middle Class, 1780–1850*, Hutchinson, 1987, pp. 272–316 is essential.

15 D. Bythell *The Sweated Trades*, Batsford, 1978.

16 On the development of management and the factory S. Pollard *The Genesis of Modern Management*, Penguin, 1965 is a good starting point.

17 M. Dauton 'Toil and Technology in Britain & America', *History Today*, April 1983 provides a valuable comparative perspective.

7 The revolution in communications – land and water

Our servant came up and said, 'Sir, there is no travelling today. Such a quantity of snow has fallen in the night that the roads are quite filled up.' I told him, 'At least we can walk twenty miles a day, with our horses in our hands.' So in the name of God we set out. We kept on, on foot or on horseback, till we came to the White Lion at Grantham.[1]

John Wesley was an inveterate traveller who, as this entry from his *Journal* shows, was not put off by the weather. Between 1739 and 1791 he rode a quarter of a million miles to found his 356 chapels and preach 40,000 sermons. But he was the exception. For most people travel was an unfortunate necessity leading, as Laurence Sterne noted, to people simply staying at home

Nature has set up by her own unquestionable authority certain boundaries and fences to circumscribe the discontent of man: she has effected her purpose in the quietest and easiest manner, by laying him under almost insuperable obligations to work out his ease, and to sustain his suffering at home. . . . [2]

Growth and redistribution of population and developments in farming and industry led to the steady expansion of internal trade. This was achieved by improvement and innovation in the transport system and in transport services. Turnpike roads with their stage-coaches, canals and new harbours were symbols of progress as much as factories and enclosed fields. Alexander Pope reflected contemporary attitudes when he wrote, in 1731:

Bid Harbours open, public ways extend,
Bid Temples, worthier of the God, ascend.
Bid the broad Arch the dang'rous Flood contain,
The Mole projected break the roaring Main;
Back to his bounds their subject sea command,
And roll obedient Rivers thro' the Land;
These Honours, Peace to Happy Britain brings,
These are Imperial Works and worthy Kings.[3]

IMPROVING COMMUNICATIONS

Widespread improvement in a communications system requires a larger and different capital outlay from that involved in industrial or agricultural investment. The notion of 'social overhead capital' has been used to explain this difference. It must be provided before an underdeveloped economy can expand its output of goods and services at a rate which will lead to appreciable increases in per capita incomes. A. O. Hirschman[4] defined 'social overhead capital' as: firstly, capital formation in an area that is 'basic' to a range of public activities, which provides the necessary infrastructure for growth elsewhere in the economy; secondly, it is usually carried out by public authorities and is often regulated by governmental agencies; thirdly, it is non-importable; and finally, there are high capital–output ratios. Hirschman suggests that a 'wide' notion of social overhead capital is defined by the first three characteristics while the addition of the fourth 'narrows' the concept, focusing on transport facilities and away from expenditure on social amenities like health, education and social security. It is capital used by society as a whole rather than by particular enterprises and without which the economy will remain underdeveloped and natural resources inaccessible. Social overhead capital investment has the following characteristics. Firstly, it requires much greater outlays of capital than individual entrepreneurs can get access to. Secondly, the longer time necessary for construction means that it takes an even longer time to yield substantial profits. Thirdly, the gross return on investment comes indirectly to the community as a whole rather than directly to the initiating entrepreneurs though the initial willingness to invest is usually occasioned, as in the case of the Duke of Bridgewater, by personal motives. This means that investment is often collective and public rather than individual and private and is therefore better mobilized through foreign borrowing or taxation by governmental or financial agencies. The first two characteristics were certainly applicable to the British experience between 1700 and 1850 but the third was not. The initiative and capital for laying down the British system of communication came almost entirely from native private enterprise, though in the collective form of the trust or company.

ROADS AND WATERWAYS

Situation in the early eighteenth century

Roads had always been provided collectively, largely because they were associated with questions of military security. Despite the volume of internal trade they were generally in a poor state in the first half of the eighteenth century. Roads were at their best in and around London though in late 1736 the Court at Kensington Palace was cut off from the City by 'a great impassable gulf of mud'. Over the rest of the country the state of roads depended on the soil and the season. On the Wealden clays of Sussex, Surrey and Kent travel was difficult even in the summer and wheeled transport came to a standstill in the winter. Arthur Young commented that the Oxfordshire roads in the 1760s 'were in a condition formidable to the bones of all who travelled on wheels.'[5]

In the Midlands roads were so bad that most of the trade of the Potteries went by packhorse in the 1750s. In the north-west there were no roads for wheeled transport out of Liverpool until 1760. In Northumberland, according to a traveller in 1749, there were no carts. In Scotland wheeled traffic was so unfamiliar that when a cartload of coal was brought from East Kilbride to near Glasgow in 1723 crowds of people came out to see it. The first coach did not run from Edinburgh to Glasgow until 1749 and even in the 1780s the Chester Guide, though it advertised waggon and coach services to a number of English towns, mentioned only packhorse services to North Wales. It was not until the late eighteenth century that this vicious circle was broken. The necessity for passable roads reflected the distribution of population and the nature of economic activity. In both Scotland and Wales the dominant economic activities were for markets in England. Meat walked itself to market along the drovers' ways from Wales, the Borders and the Scottish Highlands to the fattening pastures of the Midlands, East Anglia and Essex. Some 40,000 Scots cattle were sold annually at St Faith's cattle fair just north of Norwich in the early eighteenth century. The state of land communication in Scotland and Wales was both a reflection and a cause of the undeveloped nature of their economies. Had there been more goods to move, there would have been an incentive to improve the roads. By contrast inter-regional and local communications enabled goods, often perishable, to be taken to the many markets of south-east England and, in particular, to London. Defoe calculated that 150,000 Norfolk turkeys were driven in 300 droves down the Ipswich road to London each year. Poultry was taken in special four-tiered waggons, pulled by teams of twelve horses, from Peterborough to London twice a week. Live fish were carried in water butts on waggons from the Lincolnshire and Cambridgeshire Fens to London. The quality and quantity of roads declined, the further they were from London.

Administration of roads: parishes and turnpikes

The poor quality of roads reflected the inadequacy of engineering skills and the localized nature of their administration (Figure 7.1). The Highways Act of 1555 was the first legislation passed applying to roads in general in England and Wales. The parish was made responsible for road repair and two people were appointed annually to act as surveyors with powers to supervise four days' work which parishioners were obliged to render annually on the parish roads. This 'statute labour' was extended to six days in 1562 and was not abolished formally until 1835. The status of the Surveyor was raised in 1575 and in 1691 appointment was transferred to the quarter sessions. After 1662 parishes could levy a rate to cover the cost of repair and employ hired labour to do the work. The interests of local communities seldom went beyond their parish boundaries and, though this system may have been adequate for dealing with local roads, the trunk roads were usually repaired in a perfunctory manner. Local inhabitants thought that the people who used these roads should pay for their upkeep. This was recognized in 1663 with the passage of the first Turnpike Act, which gave authority to local Justices and allowed them to charge tolls, though its ineffectiveness outside Hertfordshire resulted in no further legislation until 1695–6. The private turnpike trust did not develop until after 1706. In so far as central government interfered at all, it was mainly to fit the traffic to the roads rather than roads to the traffic. The inadequacies of the statute labour system was recognized by Parliament in a long series of ad hoc measures. After 1691 JPs could levy road rates on parishes for a limited time. In Marylebone parish, then on London's outskirts, thirteen rates were levied between 1705 and 1723 to help repair the Edgware and Great West Roads, taxing local people more heavily as through traffic grew. Legislation to restrict the weight of waggons, the width of wheels and the number of horses began in the 1620s. The amount of additional legislation – in 1629, 1662, 1670, 1696, 1718, 1741, 1751, 1753 and 1773 – demonstrated the inadequacy of this approach but until the late eighteenth century it was one of the few known ways of saving the road system from complete collapse.

In these conditions travel was both slow and expensive. Most people, who had to travel to work or who wanted to travel cheaply, simply walked. People who could afford to travelled by horse. The person on horseback was the symbol of travel in eighteenth-century Britain and was more typical than the stage-coach or private carriage. Goods were carried slowly by packhorse or mule or in big carriers' waggons. The costs were high and it was impossible to carry cheap and bulky commodities like grain or coal very far and still sell them at a profit.

Travel by water

Apart from the roads the water carriage system of navigable waterways and the sea played a vital role. Andrew Yarranton wrote in 1698 that

> Of necessity we must always be Sailing round about the Island, carrying and recarrying such heavy Commodities from Port to Port, to be taken into the more Inward parts of the Kingdom, otherwise the charge of carrying such goods by Land, would rise to a very vast charge, the High-ways of our Island being very uneven, and the ways therein in Wintertime very bad.[6]

Figure 7.1 Major road networks in 1700

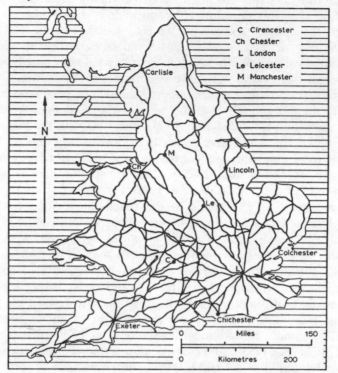

Source: H. J. Dyos and P. H. Aldcroft *British Transport,* Leicester University Press, 1971, p. 32.

Few areas in England were more than 15 miles from navigable water and those areas that were were, with the exception of the area round Birmingham, were not economically important – the moors and mountains of the Pennines, Salisbury Plain, Dartmoor and parts of the Downs. For the transport of bulk goods water transport was considerably cheaper than land carriage. Adam Smith pointed out that:

> Six or eight men . . . by the help of water-carriage, can carry and bring back in the same time the same quantity of goods between London and Edinburgh, as fifty broad-wheeled waggons, attended by a hundred men, and drawn by four hundred horses.[7]

Cambridge undergraduates sent their trunks by sea and river from London rather than the 51 miles by road. Timber brought out of the Weald to the coast cost about one shilling per ton per mile to transport by road in the 1670s while iron cost between 5d. and 7d. But timber from the Forest of Dean, via Bristol to Chatham, cost as little as 1d. per ton per mile. The river basins were extremely important arteries of trade in the early eighteenth century, particularly if they crossed major agricultural and

Figure 7.2 Major river and coastal communication systems in 1700

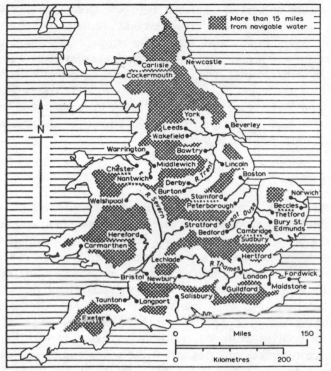

Source: H. J. Dyos and D. H. Aldcroft *British Transport*, Leicester University Press, 1971, p. 84.

industrial regions: the Severn, the Humber (fed by the Yorkshire Ouse, Aire, Calder and Trent), the Cambridgeshire Ouse and the Thames. The Severn, for example, carried Shropshire coal, Droitwich salt, and corn, fruit and cheese downstream and Dean iron for the Staffordshire metal-workers, timber, brass and groceries from Bristol upstream. The coastal trade was similarly important and, as late as 1841, accounted for three times the tonnage of that of shipping from destinations overseas. It was concentrated on the east coast. Of the 97,000 tons of coastal shipping in 1709, nearly 50,000 belonged to the ports of Scarborough, Whitby, Newcastle, Yarmouth and King's Lynn, variously engaged in the fishing, coal and corn trades. The coal trade was of particular importance, with the major shipment of Newcastle coal down the east coast to London, though smaller flows went to many other major or minor ports as far west as Exeter (Figure 7.2).

The water transport system did not overshadow land communications, even for bulk goods. The cost advantage of water was often reduced by the longer distances taken by river or sea. Many areas were too far from navigable water to make full use of it. Water transport had certain disadvantages. It was often slow and easily disrupted by war and weather. The Newcastle colliers did not sail between December and February. Convoys could not always be organized and groceries had to be diverted overland. Rivers froze, were subject to drought and flood and were obstructed by weirs, mills and dams. But the two systems were interdependent. Water transport, where easily available, coped with the cheap, long-distance movement of bulky and non-perishable goods. Road transport acted both as a feeder and distributor for this system and was important in its own right for the transfer of small goods, perishables, passengers and information, but at a higher cost.

TURNPIKES

Expenditure on maintaining and improving roads was not a new activity in the eighteenth century. Just under £1 million was spent on parish roads by mid-century. This was, however, insufficient to maintain the road system necessary to growing commerce and manufactures.[8] The development of turnpike roads was one way out of this transport bottleneck. There had been several schemes in the second half of the seventeenth century but these had been managed by local JPs. After 1706 it was normal for Parliament, by special Act, to give authority to an independent and private body of trustees to raise the necessary capital, improve the roads, place turnpikes or gates across the roads and charge users a toll within the limits prescribed in the Act. Merchants and landowners were enthusiastic supporters of the new roads, which enabled them to get their goods to market more quickly and so more cheaply and to cut the cost of highway repair for themselves. The West Riding routes were turnpiked in the 1740s largely because of the actions of merchants in Leeds and Wakefield, who joined with the tradesmen and merchants of the Lancashire towns to get the trans-Pennine roads improved. Wedgwood took an active interest in turnpike schemes round the Potteries. Abraham Darby III and John Wilkinson were active trustees in Shropshire. The number of trusts grew only slowly in the first half of the eighteenth century: on average eight acts were passed each year. From 1750 to 1770 the annual average rose to about 40, a result of growing economic confidence and low interest rates. Between 1770 and 1790 there was a slight fall in activity but from 1790 the annual average increased again to about 55. Over 1,600 trusts were formed between 1750 and 1800. During the first 30 years of the nineteenth century 2,450 turnpike acts were passed, some creating new trusts, some re-establishing old ones (powers were generally granted for twenty-one years only) and there was some consolidation of smaller trusts into larger units. By the mid–1830s there were 1,116 turnpike trusts in England and Wales managing some 22,000 miles of road – averaging just over 19.7 miles of road per trust. At the same time there were 104,770 miles of parish highways so turnpikes accounted for slightly more than a sixth of all roads.

In 1838 the trusts in England and Wales spent £1.75 million or £51 per mile of road, whereas only £11 3s. was spent on each mile of parish road. Trusts had considerable flexibility over how much money they spent and it was not until the Turnpike Act of 1822 that they had to keep proper audited accounts. Management was often notoriously inept and fraudulent. For example the Kensington trust had an income of almost £10,000 for the three years between 1749 and 1751. Its 15 miles of road were being maintained for no more than £100 per mile and yet the trust was in debt in 1752 by £3,300. However, in Scotland and Wales trusts controlled networks covering a whole county, though they were usually split into 'divisions' to facilitate management. The great drawback of the turnpike system was that it was not really a system at all but a response to limited local and sometimes individual needs. With the exception of the London–Holyhead road, on which £750,000 was spent by government between 1810 and 1835, and the establishment of the Commission for the Highland Roads in 1803, which brought the military roads begun by General Wade up to coaching standards, there was no overall national scheme. The result was a 'patchwork' of improved and unimproved roads. Road engineers like Macadam were fully aware of the disadvantages of the piecemeal method of improvement and pointed out the advantage of trust consolidation. His views were partially adopted by the turnpikes of north London in 1826 but an attempt to consolidate trusts on the Great North Road was frustrated in 1830 by the marshalling of local vested interests against his plan. Turnpikes did improve transport despite their maladministration and piecemeal development. There is little doubt that something more closely resembling a national system of roads was emerging in Britain by the 1820s. But whether these roads served national rather than predominantly local purposes is open to question. Turnpikes linked the major centres of population but they made up only a small proportion of all roads (Figure 7.3).

The turnpike trusts allowed the road improvers the opportunity needed to test their theories. Road-making was in a poor state in the mid-eighteenth century. Repairing, by filling in holes with rubble was considered more important. A critic, writing in the *Gentleman's Magazine* in 1751, rightly commented on the inability 'to lay a foundation nor make the proper slopes and drains . . . .'.

The engineers: Metcalfe and Telford

John Metcalfe (1717–1810) dealt with each of these criticisms in the 180 miles of roads, mostly in Yorkshire and Lancashire, which he supervised between 1765 and 1797. He used a firm foundation of large rocks, covered these with loose stone chippings which were rammed down into the cracks

Figure 7.3 The turnpike road network in England and Wales in 1700

Source: R. Pope (ed.) *Atlas of British Social and Economic History since c. 1700*, Routledge 1989, p. 100.

and formed into a convex camber which drained water off into the ditches dug below the level of the road. Thomas Telford (1727–1834) was the first roadbuilder to gain employment by turnpike trusts and was a genius in construction. He built canals, bridges, aqueducts and docks as well as roads and bridges. Robert Southey nicknamed him the 'Colossus of Roads'.[9] His roads were expensive and of a very high standard. He laid a flat foundation of larger stones which, in the middle 18 feet of the road, were covered with closely packed stones of no more than 2.5 inches. Once these stones has been compacted together by the weight of traffic passing over them a final 1.5 inches of gravel was added. He applied these principles to the London–Holyhead road but, despite the criticisms of unnecessary expense on the foundations and the disintegrating effects of frost and water on the gravel surface, his roads were an enormous improvement on those of his predecessors. Like Brunel's work later with railways, Telford's approach to road and bridge-building was aesthetic as well as functional.

Macadam

John Loudon Macadam (1756–1836) ultimately had more influence on road engineering than any of his predecessors. Like Telford, he came from Scotland and he built on the work of Scottish engineers which he became familiar with as a road commissioner from 1783. He took great pains to ensure good drainage and did not pay as much attention to the road foundations themselves, arguing that foundations were less important than an impervious and indestructible surface. He raised the level of the road above the level of the ground on which it was built and provided a camber of no more than three inches. This significantly reduced the costs of building. The impervious surface was to be achieved by the compacting of stones of no more than 2 inches' diameter. His technique was both simple and effective. Macadam repaired more roads than he built and it was his administrative efficiency as much as his engineering skills which led to his appointment as surveyor to the Bristol Trust in 1816. By February 1818 his methods had been adopted by eleven other trusts, managing over 700 miles of road in fifteen counties. All three of his sons followed their father's profession and by 1823 the Macadam family supervised over 2,000 miles of road for 107 trusts. His influence was felt throughout the 1820s in his evidence before parliamentary select committees in 1819, 1820, 1823 and 1825 and in the advice he gave to other public bodies. Macadam's vision of an efficient road system capable of being developed on a national scale was thwarted by the intervention of the railways.

The geography of turnpikes

In England lines of turnpike roads radiated from London to the north and east and particularly into the Midlands. The line of trusts on the Great North Road was almost unbroken to the Scottish Borders. The West Midlands and the area round Bristol had a large number of turnpikes serving expanding industry and agriculture. Many roads in Wales were so bad that wheeled carts could not move along them. In 1769 Arthur Young found the roads between Chepstow and Cardiff 'mere rocky lanes, full of hugeous stones as big as one's horse, abominable holes. . . .' Indeed the poor state of roads here, as in Scotland, was partly due to the lack of wheeled traffic. The steady growth of industry after 1770 was the greatest spur to road-building in Wales. Industrialists joined with the gentry and innkeepers in this movement to improve the very poor state of Welsh roads. Much of the activity was in the borderlands, along the main routes to Ireland through North and South Wales, to Holyhead and Fishguard, and in the newly developing industrial areas. In the north quarry owners like Lord Penrhyn and Assheton Smith built roads from Bethesda to Bangor and Llanberis to Port Dinorwic in 1782 and 1809 respectively. The needs of the woollen trade led to turnpiking the roads between Welshpool and Shrewsbury and Oswestry after 1752. Similar activity followed in Flintshire after 1756 and Caernarfonshire after 1759. By 1800 North Wales had about 1,000 miles of turnpike roads organized on a county basis. In South Wales Anthony Bacon was the first industrialist to build a road between his ironworks at Merthyr and Cardiff in 1767. In 1755 and 1758 two Acts were passed in Parliament permitting the construction of turnpikes in Monmouthshire, and these were soon extended throughout South Wales (Figure 7.4). The old landscape of road communication was modified at the hands of twelve trusts in Carmarthenshire, four in Pembrokeshire, two in Cardiganshire, two in Radnorshire, one in Breconshire and twelve in Glamorgan. It was in this area that opposition to the turnpikes was at its most intense, leading to the Rebecca Riots in the early 1840s.

Scotland

The statutory basis for the upkeep of Scottish roads was laid down in a series of acts, chiefly in the seventeenth century. In 1719 Scotland was brought into line with England when JPs and Commissioners of Supply were authorized to appoint overseers to ensure that roads were properly maintained with six days' annual labour from tenants and others and money provided by a tax on heritors not exceeding 10s. in the £100 Scots of value rent. As in England, the effectiveness of the provision varied. Roads were not considered of major economic importance in eighteenth-century Scotland and improvements were thus limited. The first turnpike trust act was passed in 1713, the next in 1751. The only co-ordinated

Figure 7.4 Early roads, including drovers' roads and early turnpike roads, in Wales

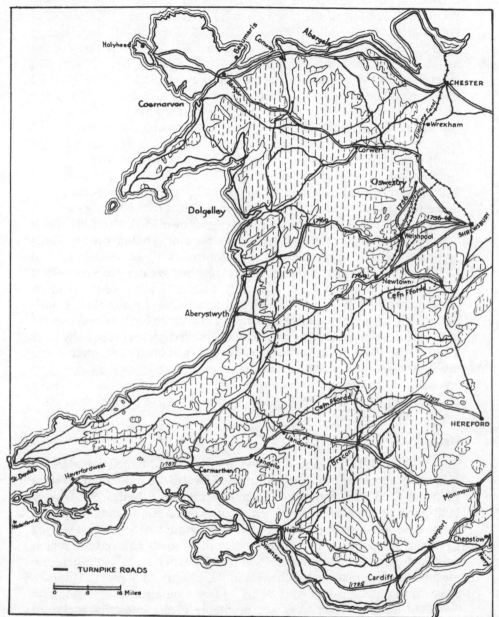

Holyhead

Beaumaris

Conway

Abergele

CHESTER

Caernarvon

Bangor

Wrexham

Corwen

Oswestry

Dolgelley

1769

Welshpool

SHREWSBURY

1756-6

Montgomery Road

Ellesmere Canal

1756

Newtown

1769

Cefn Ffordd

Aberystwyth

Cefn Ffordd

1771

HEREFORD

Llandovery

Llandeilo

Brecon

St. David's

Haverfordwest

1787

Carmarthen

Monmouth

Haverford W.

Newport

Chepstow

Neath

Swansea

Cardiff

1788

— TURNPIKE ROADS

0   8   16 Miles

Source: W. Rees *An Historical Atlas of Wales*, Faber, 1951, plate 67.

group of road improvements, some 1,050 miles and over 1,000 bridges carried out at public expense for military rather than economic purposes, occurred in the Highlands under General Wade between 1725 and 1737 and after the '45 by Major William Caulfield. These roads were funded from annexed Jacobite estates and when, in 1784, these were restored the maintenance of the roads was transferred to local funds. By 1800 they had fallen into disuse because of the insufficiency of local funding. Telford was commissioned to survey these roads in 1801 and again in 1802. His reports were not just concerned with Highland roads but with the changed conditions of Highland life. He believed that crofting and fishing should be encouraged rather than sheep farming and that a network of good roads was essential for this purpose. The result was the setting up of the Commissioners for Highland Roads and Bridges in 1803. The state paid half the cost of road maintenance and building and landowners raised the remainder, either voluntarily or by assessment. Over 900 miles of new roads and 1,117 bridges were built at a cost of over £500,000, £267,000 of which came from government. In 1813 the remaining military roads – only 300 miles by then – came under their control, with an annual grant of £5,000 for maintenance. Road improvements had greater economic effect south of the Highland Line, especially as canals were never of much consequence in many parts of Scotland and railways made their contribution only later in the nineteenth century. Turnpike construction and the industrial development of central Scotland moved parallel especially after 1790. By the 1840s the major network of roads had been built, often under the supervision of Telford, in many parts of Scotland. Statute labour was compulsorily commuted to money payments in 1845 but was not finally abolished until an Act of 1878, which became effective no later than 1883.

Ireland

The 1730s and 1740s were a period of rapid road-building in Ireland coinciding with an upturn in inland traffic. Many of the roads built between 1730 and 1760 were turnpiked. From Coleraine and Belfast roads were built south to Dublin to carry linen. From Dublin itself roads were built to the west as far as Roscommon and to the south and south-east serving Cork and Limerick. A fairly dense network of roads covered the region from Dublin to the Shannon and south to Limerick and Cork where the most intensive agricultural exchanges in the country took place. Turnpike trusts had limitations and their utility as financing agencies depended on projected income. They were not profitable in economically backward areas. From the 1760s, however, most Irish road-building was financed by other means. The Grand Jury in each county had always had the power to build roads. This was extended to levying a county rate to support road-building by statutes in 1759 and 1765. The great bulk of road-building after the 1760s was financed in this way. This made possible the development of a road network without relating it directly to the income that traffic might generate, itself a limiting constraint in much of rural Ireland. Further advance came in the first half of the nineteenth century. First, there was an increase in coach routes which improved surfaces and had an impact on commodity carriage as well. Secondly, roads were built in the more remote areas where they had been few or non-existent, as in Connemara and West Mayo. From 1822 parliamentary grants were available to help road-building and in 1831 the Board of Works was established which took over from various bodies the management of canals, roads and public works. In both Ireland and Wales the degree of centralized control over turnpikes was significantly greater than in England, where private enterprise dominated.

Effects of turnpikes – opposition

Turnpikes were a mixed blessing. Toll charges could prove inconvenient and expensive. Some contemporaries argued that turnpike development would lead to produce being sent to more distant markets, while others believed it would put up the cost of bringing produce into an area. Arthur Young commented in 1769 in his *Tour Through the North of England* that

> all the sensible people attributed the dearness of their country to the turnpike roads; and reason speaks the truth of their opinion . . . make but a turnpike road through their country and all the cheapness vanishes at once.

By 1800 opposition was spasmodic, and generally localized.[10] Protests occurred in five main areas. In 1727, 1731, 1735 and 1793 there were riots in and around Bristol with the destruction of toll-gates. Opposition seems to have been centred on the Kingswood colliers, who were concerned that no toll should be imposed upon the provisions necessary to supply a growing manufacturing area. Between 1735 and 1738 there were riots to the north of Bristol led by the 'country people', small farmers. The area round Bristol, Gloucester and Ledbury had seen a multiplication of turnpikes in a small area in the 1720s. Similar motives may have been present in attacks on turnpikes in the West Riding of Yorkshire in 1752 and 1753. The major objection, however, was the high toll on the coal essential to cloth production. This explains the location of the protests and the lead taken by small independent clothiers in the disturbances. The fourth area affected was the southern part of Scotland between 1792 and 1815 with the consolidation of the turnpike system.

Why were turnpike riots relatively few in number? Turnpikes were generally promoted by the large landowner, the capitalist farmer or industrialist who benefited from lower transport costs, fewer delays and access to newer markets. Disturbances did not occur in areas of advanced industrial and agrarian capitalism but in communities of small farmers and

Figure 7.5 The Rebecca Riots
Figure 7.5a Turnpike gates 1839–44

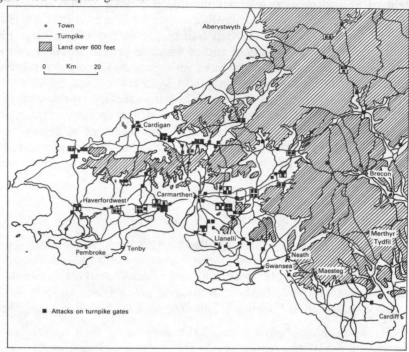

○ Town
— Turnpike
▨ Land over 600 feet

0   Km   20

Aberystwyth

Cardigan

Haverfordwest

Carmarthen

Brecon

Pembroke   Tenby

Llanelli

Neath

Merthyr Tydfil

Swansea

Maesteg

Cardiff

■ Attacks on turnpike gates

Figure 7.5b Mass meetings 1843–4

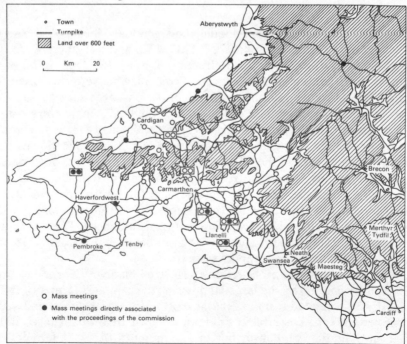

○ Town
— Turnpike
▨ Land over 600 feet

0   Km   20

Aberystwyth

Cardigan

Haverfordwest

Carmarthen

Brecon

Pembroke   Tenby

Llanelli

Neath

Merthyr Tydfil

Swansea

Maesteg

Cardiff

○ Mass meetings
● Mass meetings directly associated
   with the proceedings of the commission

independent workers. To these people turnpikes were simply an unjustifiable tax on their already small incomes. This was not, however, in itself sufficient to cause riots. The density of turnpikes has to be taken into account. In the areas examined above and in South Wales there was a multiplication of trusts, which meant that even short journeys were liable to encounter a significant number of toll-gates.

The Rebecca Riots between 1839 and 1844 grew out of a rural community undergoing rapid social change and growing economic pressure. The name Rebecca was taken from the scriptural reference in Genesis 24:60: 'And they blessed Rebecca and said unto her, Thou art our sister, be thou the mother of thousands of millions, and let your seed possess the gate of

Figure 7.5c Other collective protests 1842–4

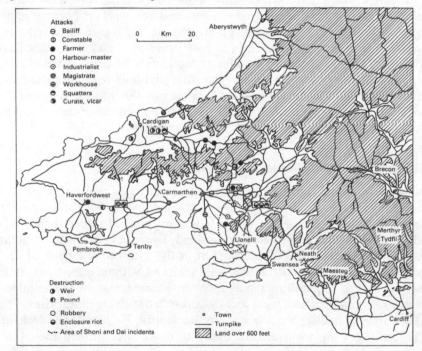

Source: A. Charlesworth (ed.) *An Atlas of Rural Protest in Britain 1548–1900*, Croom Helm, 1983, pp. 166–7.

those which hate them.' Men dressed in women's clothing, often white gowns with their faces blackened or wearing masks – though only some rioters would wear women's clothing – attacking toll-gates at night to the accompaniment of much noise and, in the early stages, a mock trial before the work of destruction began. Although the outward expression of unrest was the destruction of the turnpike trusts, the grievances of the Rebeccaites were many: church-rates, tithes, high rents, the poor law, clerical magistrates and the actions of insensitive agents. The extension of toll-gates on country roads, the poor harvests of 1839–41 and the collapse of prices in 1842–3 translated unrest into direct action. The main attacks were concentrated in January 1839 along the Carmarthen–Pembrokeshire border and from the winter of 1842 to 1844 in Carmarthen, Pembrokeshire and south Cardiganshire. Small farmers played a leading role in the earlier attacks though when unemployed workers and iron-workers became active in west Wales farmers, fearful of attacks on their own property, co-operated with government. The toll-gate problem evaporated after 1844 with the Turnpike Act of 1844 which consolidated the trusts. County road boards took over all the trusts in each shire and tolls were simplified and made more uniform. David Williams argues that this was the result of the removal of remaining tensions in the isolated communities occasioned by the coming of the railways.

Effects of turnpikes – impact on communications

What contribution did the turnpike and parish roads make to improved communication in Britain in the eighteenth and first half of the nineteenth century? Expenditure on parish roads was maintained rather than markedly increased after 1750. There was a steady increase in turnpike spending rising from under £100,000 per annum in the 1750s to the peak of £1.5 million in the 1820s. All of this was achieved without significant state intervention in England and Wales. With the exception of the London–Holyhead road the trusts were locally controlled, private enterprises. The major areas of public spending were in the Scottish Highlands and Ireland. The local and private nature of many turnpikes determined their limitations and, despite Defoe's eulogy in the 1720s,[11] many roads were still in poor repair in 1800. Arthur Young found in 1769 that, of the 930 miles of turnpike he used in his 1,460-mile tour of the Midlands, Yorkshire, Northumberland and Cumberland, half were good and the rest were equally divided between middling and bad. By 1813, however, he found that there had been substantial improvements. Carl Moritz spoke of firm, smooth roads in his tour of England in 1782. The road system was, and remained until after 1850, patchy, and arguably this was its greatest defect.

Not everyone saw these developments in a positive way. William Cobbett deplored the improvements which were, for him, a wicked way of stealing the fruits of the earth from honest country-folk in order to sustain the 'vermin' living in the 'Wens' as he called the burgeoning towns and cities. Moralists deplored the vast amount of unnecessary travel. The restlessness of the English was proverbial – contemporaries believed that this was to do with their propensity for melancholy and suicide. But rhetoric aside, Henry Homer summed up the impact of improvements in 1767:

> There never was a more astonishing revolution accomplished in the internal system of any country. The carriage of grain, coals, merchandize, etc. is in general conducted with little more than half the horses which it formerly was. . . . Everything wears the face of dispatch and the hinge which has guided all these movements, and upon which they turn, is the reformation which has been made in our public roads.[12]

The coaching industry

The reduction in journey times between main centres of population was one clear measure of the reality of the revolution on the roads (see Figure 7.6). Times were reduced by up to 80 per cent between 1750 and 1830. In the mid-1750s it took between 10 and 12 days to travel from London to Edinburgh; by the 1830s it took 45.5 hours. In 1751 it took two days to reach Oxford, in 1828 six hours. On average coaches maintained a speed of about 8 m.p.h. but faster performances were possible. It was not just speed but the amount of travelling that increased dramatically, especially in the period after 1780. The number of stage-coach services increased eightfold between 1790 and 1836. In 1740 there was one coach per week between London and Birmingham, 30 in 1783 but 34 a day by 1829. P. S. Bagwell maintains that

> It would not be wide of the mark to claim that 15 times as many people were travelling by stage coach in the mid-1830s as were doing so 40 years earlier. . . . Assuming an average of eight passengers per trip (though many coaches could carry up to 16 persons) and 2,500 trips per week, the number of individual coach journeys made in the course of that year (1835) must have been over 10 million. . . . [13]

Public mail continued to be carried on horseback or by chaise between 1720 and 1762 when Ralph Allen had the monopoly. His system was increasingly inadequate compared to the speed of ordinary stage-coaches. Newspapers were widely circulated using coach, post or carrier from towns where they were printed to many others where agents distributed them to townsfolk and through the countryside. After 1784 the Post Office was a powerful influence on the speed and reliability of road transport, largely through the efforts of John Palmer. His scheme for carrying mail by stage-coach from Bristol to London via Bath quickly spread to the rest of the country. One outcome of this was that the Postmaster-General had a

Figure 7.6 The decline in journey times using the fastest coaches 1660–1840

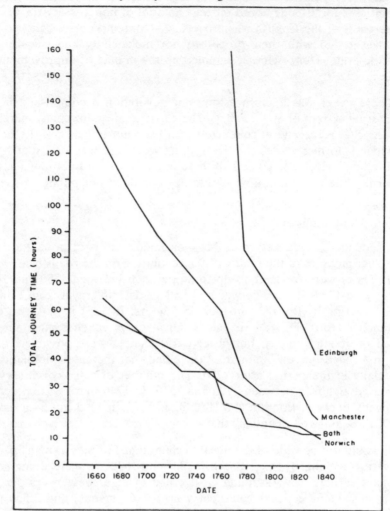

Source: E. Pawson *The Early Industrial Revolution*, Batsford, 1979, p. 144.

keener interest in the state of the roads. More travel meant better coaches and those made for the Royal Mail were of very high standards. John Vidler of Millbank was awarded the contract for constructing these coaches according to the patent of John Bezant in 1787. These coaches were heavy and cumbersome and passengers were subjected at times to severe pendulum-like jolting – in the 1790s being 'coached' meant getting used to the nausea which these vehicles induced. By the early nineteenth century the Post Office was losing revenue from passengers partly because of competition and partly because of the public controversy over its construction of coaches. The result was the development of lighter coaches and the use of the elliptical spring (patented by Obadiah Elliot in 1805) which both reduced the cost of construction and led to greater comfort for passengers. Bagwell argues:

> Elliot's elliptical spring and the redesigning of road vehicles which it made possible was as important in the history of stage-coaching as the introduction of the multi-tubular boiler was in the history of the steam locomotive.[14]

The combined effects of better road engineering and improved coach design made possible a dramatic growth in passenger travel in the early nineteenth century. By 1820 it was quicker to travel by fast coach than on horseback.

The growth of coaching generated a considerable industry. Most industry was organized on a small scale but there were a significant number of large coaching firms. Almost 20 per cent of all the daily coaches leaving London were controlled by William Chaplin, Benjamin Horne and Edward Sherman. This concentration in large firms was paralleled, though not in such a large way, in provincial centres. A third of the coaches from Bristol were controlled by R. Coupland, J. Weeks and C. Bessell. A similar situation existed in Birmingham, Derby and Leeds. Most coaching firms, which had the contract for certain routes, were based on an inn from which they frequently gained their principal income. Chaplin's headquarters was at the 'Swan with two Necks' in Lad Lane but he also owned four other inns in London and two large stables. In 1838 his coaching business, inns and hotels employed over 2,000 people and 1,800 horses and had an annual turnover of some £500,000. Most proprietors hired their coaches and horses. In addition they had to pay for coachmen, guards and ostlers, turnpike tolls, the costs of maintenance and advertising and a stage-coach levy charged by the Stamp Office (in 1776 it stood at £5 per coach and 0.5d. a mile; by 1804 this was raised to 2d. a mile for a coach with four inside seats – these charges had to be paid whatever the actual load and were not abated until 1838). Despite this, profits of 100 per cent on journeys were not uncommon and generally they were over 30 per cent. These were shared between a number of contractors and sub-contractors who were responsible for maintaining the service on different stretches of the road, and could be maintained by adjusting fares because there was no official ceiling on charges.

Coaching stimulated the breeding of horses, the provision of hay and fodder and led to the rapid expansion of inns and hotels. But it was not without its problems. Travelling by stage-coach could be dangerous. Accidents were common, highway robbery a continuous threat. Hotels and inns could be less than hygienic. In 1781 John Byng decided, after a tour of the West Country, that innkeepers were insolent, ostlers sulky, chambermaids pert and waiters impertinent; the meat was tough, wine foul, beer hard, the sheets wet, linen dirty and the knives never cleaned.

The expansion of goods carriage after 1750 was not so spectacular as the growth of passenger traffic because a well developed traffic already existed. However, there can be little doubt that the road system as a whole performed an indispensable function, bearing the considerable traffic in all kinds of industrial material and products. The number of carrier firms increased after 1750. In London in 1680 there were 322 distinct carrier services. This had only increased to 353 by 1790 but had more than doubled to 735 by 1823. Exeter had three times as many firms in 1831 than in 1792. The most dramatic growth was in the Birmingham area, where there was a fivefold increase between 1790 and 1830. The significance of this increase – some 131 per cent in the ten largest cities – has to be placed against the 800 per cent increase in coaching traffic between 1790 and 1830 and the 120 per cent growth in population. The number of carriers barely kept up with the increase in population, a situation exacerbated by the increase in canal and coastal traffic with which they were unable to compete. Unlike stage-coaching, road goods haulage was dominated by small family businesses, particularly in the provincial centres, and it was often unable to compete with coastal or canal transport. In 1822 the Leeds directory lists 163 haulage firms of which 131 were small businesses operating between Leeds and the surrounding villages. Only 32 concerns, including Pickfords, provided a long-distance service. Hull, by contrast, was completely dominated by small firms. JPs could, between 1692 and 1827, fix haulage rates in their counties. In practice, however, the absence or presence of alternative carriers determined freight charges.

The challenge of railways

Roads and road traffic were ill-equipped to meet the challenge of the railways. Turnpike trusts operated on a scale too small to be run economically. Amalgamation, an effective remedy, came very slowly. From 1806 there were numerous parliamentary inquiries into turnpikes and in 1844 Parliament endorsed the findings of a Royal Commission which recommended consolidation under county authorities. By 1850, however, only the six counties of South Wales (1844) and the Metropolitan Turnpike Trust (1826) had achieved this. The decline in long-distance stage-coaching, which contributed more than anything else to the revenue of turnpike trusts, led to a fall in total revenue between 1837 and 1850 of a third. The 29 coaches that plied between Liverpool and Manchester had been reduced to four within five months of the opening of the railway in September 1830. Within three months of the opening of the London to Birmingham railway the 22 coaches that operated this route had been reduced to four. Coaching remained – long-distance in parts of Wales, Scotland and Ireland – but it was relegated to filling the gaps where the railways did not run or providing haulage to the railway stations. The triumph of the railways took longer in haulage than with passengers. The demand for sheer horsepower increased in the constructional stages of the railways. Pickfords and Chaplin & Horne deliberately dovetailed their operations with railways – Chaplin so well that he became chairman of the London & South Western Railway. By 1850 roads had generally given way to rail.

Well before 1700 a variety of efforts had been made to break through the constraints imposed by poor road communications by turning to water transport particularly for the movement of heavy, bulky goods. Improving rivers to make them more navigable and the use of coastal transport were two ways of achieving this as were canals from the second half of the eighteenth century.

CANALS

Improvements to rivers

Improving Britain's rivers was a continuous process dating back to the second half of the sixteenth century.[15] The state's role was limited to approving schemes and protecting the interests of the various parties affected. England's rivers were chiefly maintained by Commissioners of Sewers who could compel riparian owners to clear their stretches of a river or could levy a rate to do this. The legal powers of the Commissioners did not stretch to improvements like locks, dredging, new cuts and the regulation of weirs, and responsibility for this was given to separate bodies or individuals by letters patent or more usually by Parliament. Change was promoted and finance provided by local efforts. There were spurts of state approval for river improvements throughout the seventeenth and early eighteenth centuries – 1634–8 (by letters patent for the Great Ouse, Lark, Tone, Stour and Soar); 1662–5 (more than a dozen were authorized – most important on smaller rivers in the Severn basin and for the Welland and Great Ouse into the Wash); 1670s (the Fal, Wey, Witham, Waveney and Bedfordshire Ouse); 1697–1700 (schemes for rivers further north, the Aire and Calder, Trent and Dee and in the south the Yar, Tone, Lark and Bristol Avon); 1719–21 (in the north, the Douglas, Derwent, Idle, Irwell, Mersey, Weaver, Dane and Eden). By 1720 over a thousand miles of improvements had been sanctioned and even though some important work took place after 1720 the scope for further advance was limited and providing more navigable water meant canals.

Improvements such as these were often piecemeal when seen from a national perspective. Sums invested were small and the burst of legislation between 1697 and 1700 and 1719 and 1721 can partly be explained by low interest rates. Unlike turnpikes the money was on the whole well spent. Like turnpikes, promoters were often motivated by local considerations.

The main reason for the promotion of navigations, especially the later ones, was to secure or to distribute supplies of coal, wool, lead, timber, iron and cloth. The Aire and Calder, the Don, Weaver and Mersey were made navigable primarily in the interests of industries in which coal was a crucial factor. Dyos and Aldcroft recently commented that 'It is generally true to say that coal was the dominant influence on the development of the whole programme of inland waterways, of rivers as well as canals.'[16]

River improvements and later canals sought, however, indirectly, an outlet to the sea. Coastal shipping, working through small ships in and out of dozens of ports and harbours that lined the coasts of Britain and Ireland, provided an outlet for local products, together with the means by which foreign goods could be distributed from the larger ports. In 1768 Baldwin's London Directory named 580 places in England and Wales to which goods could be sent by water. The transport of coal dominated coastal shipping. Between 1670 and 1750 40 million tons of coal was brought to London. Coal from South Wales found a sale from Cardigan in the north to Plymouth and Exeter in the south, where it came into competition with Newcastle coal. There was also a small market for Pembrokeshire anthracite coal in the larger London breweries and in the hop-drying kilns of Kent and Herefordshire. Shipments of Welsh coal increased from about 300,000 tons in the 1790s to 1.29 million tons by 1840. In the eighteenth century corn was the second most important commodity carried by coastal traffic. Most of this was carried to the growing cities, especially London. The development of steam navigation on the Irish Sea made it possible for Ireland to contribute food for these cities. The tonnage employed in the coastal trade between Britain and Ireland increased by 250 per cent between 1801 and 1849, with the bulk of that increase after 1827 when steam power took on its predominant role. If tonnage of shipping entering British ports is taken as a measure of comparison then coastal shipping had a far higher profile than shipping involved in trade with the colonies and foreign countries throughout the eighteenth and nineteenth centuries. In 1841 coastal shipping entries were over 12.5 million tons excluding ballast while the tonnage from the foreign and colonial trade was 4.65 million tons including ballast.

Coastal shipping

Coastal shipping provided an important means of transporting passengers, though storms restricted this to the period between April and October. William Lovett came to London from Penzance in 1821, to seek employment as a rope-maker, by sea. Passenger traffic achieved its greatest importance in the early 1840s when there were over 1400 miles of regular sailings linking 90 ports and harbours. The gradual development of steam-powered ships aided this process. William Symington successfully experimented with a steamship in 1788 but it was not until 1812 that Henry

Bell's *Comet* became the first commercially successful steamboat. In 1821 the Post Office decided to maintain a continuous service on the Holyhead–Howth route and between Liverpool and Dublin in 1826. This stimulated steamship companies and by 1830 there were continuous steam-packet services all round the British coast and between Britain and Ireland. The popularity of passenger steamship services in the 1830s and 1840s is explained by their greater speed and reliability compared to the sailing ship and by their cheapness compared to coach travel.

Port improvements

Ports for much of the eighteenth century were 'open': open to the rise and fall of the tides which left ships beached on the mud when the tide was out and open on the landward side to thieves. The increase in coastal and overseas trade, however, led to continuous improvement in harbour facilities from the 1690s. The first wet dock was built at Rotherhithe on the Thames in 1700, a second at Liverpool between 1710 and 1715 and a third at Bristol after 1717. Harbour commissions built or improved harbours at Bridlington in 1697, Whitby in 1701 for fishing, and Whitehaven 1708, Sunderland 1717 and Maryport (Cumberland) 1747 for coal. New harbours were built on the south coast at Newhaven, Littlehampton, Shoreham and Ramsgate. The most extensive and sustained programme of harbour and port improvements occurred in Scotland. Improvements were made at Leith in the 1750s with a wet dock added in the 1790s, at Greenock, Ayr, Banff and Aberdeen and along the River Clyde. Thomas Telford made a substantial contribution and at Ullapool and Tobermoray he planned and built entirely new towns for the British Fisheries Society which had been founded in 1786 to encourage fishing from the coasts of Highland Scotland as a possible answer to falling population and emigration.

The real spate of port improvements came from the 1790s and was closely linked to the growth in foreign trade, though the requirements of the coastal trade were a significant and, sometimes decisive, influence on the side of modernization and extension of berthing facilities. London acquired several new docks in the early nineteenth century – London Docks completed in 1803, West and East India Docks in 1806, Surrey and East Country Docks in 1807 and Commercial Docks in 1815 – largely because the Committee of West Indian Merchants threatened to transfer their trade elsewhere in 1793. The expansion of the South Wales coal trade led to deepening river mouths and new wet docks at Llanelly in 1828, Cardiff in 1839, Newport in 1844 and Swansea in 1852.

The emergence of canals

There were limitations to river improvements. Cuts had already been made to bypass some of the more tortuous bends and, with the example of the Continent, it was not long before there was a move from natural to entirely artificial waterways.[18] Apart from the Exeter Canal, built between 1564 and 1566, the earliest canal in the British Isles was the 18-mile canal linking Lough Neagh and Newry built in the 1730s so that coal could be more easily carried from the Tyrone coalfield to Dublin. From 1736 to 1742 the work was directed by Thomas Steers, who had engineered the Liverpool dock in the 1710s. The cradle of the canal age proper was in south-west Lancashire. Liverpool's salt trade with Ireland and Europe depended on cheap transport from the Cheshire salt-fields and coal from the Lancashire coalfields. The Mersey was improved as far as Warrington after 1694 and the Weaver out of Cheshire by 1733. The transport of coal was still a problem and this stimulated the Liverpool Corporation to commission the construction of the Sankey Brook Navigation. It was built between 1755 and 1757 under the supervision of Henry Berry. It was an outstanding success and provided the crucial stimulus to the industrial development of the South Lancashire coalfield and the rise of St Helens. Its success has, however, been overshadowed in popular imagination by James Brindley and the Duke of Bridgewater (Figure 7.7).

The cost of moving coal from the Bridgewater mines at Worsley was high and cutting this would, undoubtedly, lead to a corresponding increase in sales for which demand was elastic. Using the engineering experience of his agent, John Gilbert, and the energies of James Brindley, Bridgewater planned to link his mines to the rapidly growing markets of Manchester and Liverpool. The first phase was completed between 1759 and 1761. Brindley used an aqueduct to carry the canal over the River Irwell, drained the mine by taking the canal into the workings and used 'puddled' clay to prevent seepage. The economic potential of canals was clearly demonstrated by the reduction of the price of coal in Manchester from 7d. to 3.5d. per hundredweight. The construction of the main trunk routes followed in quick succession with a meteoric burst of promotions between 1766 and the crisis of 1772. The Staffordshire and Worcestershire canal linked the Mersey and Severn at Stourport in 1772 and the Grand Trunk canal linked the Mersey and Trent in 1777. The Birmingham canal linked that town to the Staffordshire and Worcestershire canal via Wolverhampton. All three were engineered by Brindley. By 1776 Birmingham had two further links, the Stourbridge and Dudley canals. Between them they brought cheap water carriage into the Birmingham–south Staffordshire area. Midlands coalowners promoted the Coventry and Oxford canals in 1768 and 1769 but financial problems led to delays and it was not until 1790 that there was a direct link between the Thames and the Grand Trunk. Work started on the Leeds and Liverpool canal in 1770.

Figure 7.7 Lancashire canals

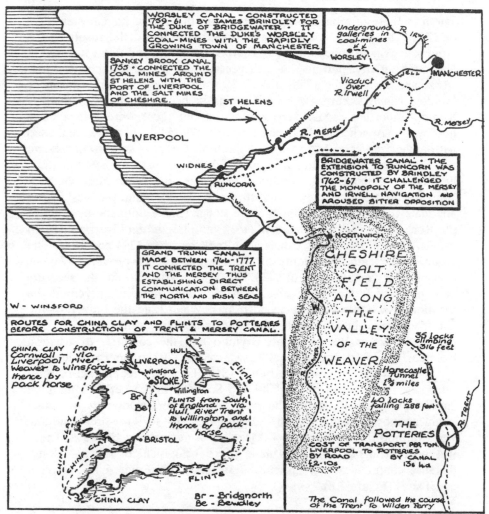

Source: J. L. Gayler, I. Richards, J. A. Morris *A Sketch-Map Economic History of Britain*, George Harrap, 1966, p. 98.

Work was suspended in 1777 and did not resume until 1790 and it was not completed until 1815. In Scotland the Forth and Clyde canal was begun in 1768 but it too was delayed and not finished until 1790. The Monkland canal, which brought coal from the Lanarkshire field to Glasgow, was started in 1770 and also took some years to complete.

Later canal developments

The first phase of canal building ended with the act for the Chester canal in 1772. This was followed by a period of inactivity, the result of the American War of Independence. The peace of 1783 led to an upsurge in economic activity, putting renewed pressure on the communication network, and early in the 1790s a period of almost feverish enthusiasm for building canals occurred which has rightly been called 'canal mania'. Several important canals were completed but there were also a large number of new schemes. Between 1791 and 1796 51 canal acts were passed with authorized capital of over £7.5 million. The most important scheme was the Grand Junction Canal, authorized in 1793 and completed in 1805, linking the Midlands with London. The Kennet and Avon canal, built by John Rennie between 1794 and 1810, linked London and the west. More adequate trans-Pennine facilities were not available until the opening of the Rochdale (1804), Huddersfield (1811) and Leeds and Liverpool (1816) canals. Most of the Welsh canals were built between 1794 and 1814. The Glamorgan, Neath, Monmouthshire and Swansea canals provided 77 miles of canal at a capital outlay of £420,000. They carried iron to the seaports and food and fodder in reverse. Existing canal interests prevented the creation of a viable network in north-east Wales, and the branch of the Ellesmere canal built by Telford to the quarries beyond Llangollen left the ironworks at Bersham and Brymbo and the collieries of Ruabon isolated. The Montgomery canal was started in 1797 to join the Ellesmere system but it was not completed until 1816 and served mainly agricultural purposes. In the north of England and Scotland in the period after 1790 canals were generally small. The exception was the Caledonian ship canal engineered by Telford between 1803 and 1822. By 1830 the great building was over and there were over 4,000 miles of navigable waterways. There was no central plan and this made the development of through, long-distance communications difficult, a situation exacerbated by different canal sizes (Figure 7.8).

Canals in Ireland and Scotland

With the notable exceptions of Ireland, the Caledonian and Crinan canals in Scotland and the Royal Military canal in Kent and Sussex, all canals were funded from private sources.[19] Canal navigation had been in mind as early as 1715 in Ireland when a statute envisaged the construction of a canal network. Since 1730 the income from certain duties had been earmarked for this purpose but the only substantial work undertaken was the Newry canal. In 1751 these funds were entrusted to a national body called The Corporation for Promoting and Carrying on an Inland Navigation in Ireland. It began constructing the Grand Canal in 1756 and undertook navigation work on the Shannon, Boyne and Barrow. From 1772 it was

Figure 7.8 The canal network *c.* 1830

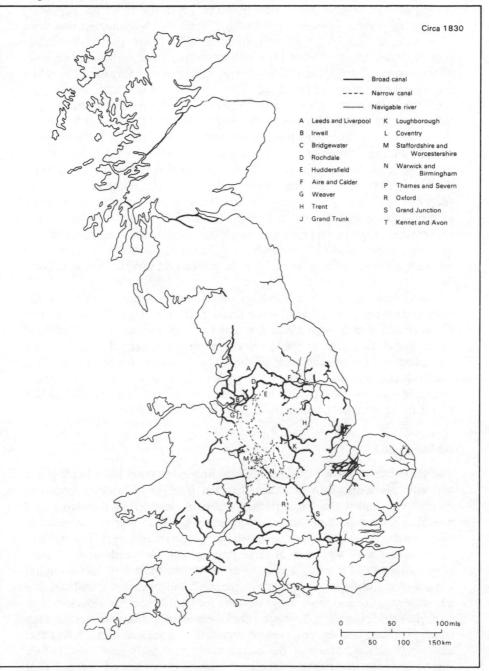

Circa 1830

—————— Broad canal

- - - - - - Narrow canal

————— Navigable river

A Leeds and Liverpool
B Irwell
C Bridgewater
D Rochdale
E Huddersfield
F Aire and Calder
G Weaver
H Trent
J Grand Trunk

K Loughborough
L Coventry
M Staffordshire and
   Worcestershire
N Warwick and
   Birmingham
P Thames and Severn
R Oxford
S Grand Junction
T Kennet and Avon

| 0 | | 50 | | 100 mls |

| 0 | 50 | 100 | | 150 km |

Source: J. Langton and R. J. Morris *Atlas of Industrializing Britain 1780–1914,* Methuen, 1986, p. 85.

allowed to make grants to private companies which undertook the administration of existing schemes or new projects. From the 1770s an increasing amount of private money supplemented state funds either in the form of private companies or by way of local investment in the bodies of commissioners charged after 1787 with executing navigation work on individual rivers. The incentive for several canals and navigations was the movement of coal on the mainland. The Newry canal was built to transport coal from the Lough Neagh region to Dublin. The Barrow Navigation was influenced by the Leinster coalfield and in the early nineteenth century the Grand Canal Company became owner of a mine on the Leinster field. Canal building continued into the nineteenth century – the Grand Canal was completed to the Shannon, the Royal Canal was completed in 1817, the Ulster canal from the Blackwater to the Erne was completed between 1825 and 1842 and the Ballinamore and Ballyconnell canal from the Erne to the Shannon in 1860. From 1800 a Board of Directors of Inland Navigation was charged with promoting work not transferred to separate bodies and after 1831 it was taken over by the Board of Works. The Irish canal network was the result of work by both public and private bodies (Figure 7.9).

The Caledonian canal in Scotland was financed almost entirely by the state and cost over £1 million, three times Telford's original estimate. The Crinan canal, which provided an alternative to the journey round Pentland Firth, began as a private concern but was only completed with state aid and passed to the management of the Commissioners for the Caledonian Canal. It is ironic that, as its cost of construction increased, so the contribution of the Caledonian canal to the economic life of Scotland diminished and it never became a commercial success (Figure 7.10).

Building costs

The initiative for most private canal building came from local landowners and entrepreneurs, who had most to gain from local internal improvements, who called the promotional meetings, employed surveyors and provided a large part of the necessary capital. There were exceptions to this, like the Forth and Clyde canal which was financed largely in England. Canal shares were generally of large denominations – units of £200 were very common and it was rare for units to be less than £50. Initial capital tended to come from the locality concerned, but once the canal became a commercial success, ownership became more diffused. By 1822 less than a third of shares in the Ellesmere canal were held in the counties through which it passed and the rest were diffused throughout almost all England and North Wales. Many of the canals were extremely profitable before the 1830s, with many industrial canals paying dividends of 5–6 per cent within a few years of starting operations. Others were complete failures either because the route was not economically viable or because of escalat-

Figure 7.9 Canals in Ireland

Figure 7.10 Canals in Scotland

Source: C. Cook and J. Stevenson *Longman Atlas of Modern British History*, 1978, p. 53.

ing construction costs. Most canals cost more to build than had been expected, though the Caledonian canal was an extreme case.

The construction of canals was by navvies using a combination of simple manual techniques and horsepower. Aqueducts became common – though few were as aesthetically pleasing as those of Telford at Chirk and Pontcysyllte on the Ellesmere canal – tunnels a standard alternative to expensive and time-consuming flights of locks and a variety of technical devices like inclined planes and lifts were developed to meet particular problems. It brought civil engineering into being and when the Institution of Civil Engineers was chartered in 1818 it was fitting that Telford should have been elected its president. Brindley and Telford apart, the leading canal builders were John Smeaton (1724–92), his protégé William Jessop (1745–1814) who worked with Telford on the Ellesmere canal, John Rennie (1761–1821) who built the Crinan and Kennet and Avon canals and James Green (1781–1829), trained by Rennie, who built canals in the south-west. Brindley spawned disciples – Hugh Henshall, his brother-in-law, and Robert Whitworth and Thomas Dadford, both of whom had been Brindley's assistants and whose sons learnt from them. Such personal connections were vital in transmitting skills from one generation to another. The creation of the canal network was the first opportunity people had to grapple with large-scale engineering problems, an experience that 'stood them in excellent stead for the construction of the solid infrastructure of the Industrial revolution: docks, harbours, railways, factories and warehouses'.[20]

Economic benefits

It is difficult to exaggerate the contribution of canals to the economic development of Britain between 1760 and 1830. Their effects touched almost every aspect of national life and very few parts of the British Isles could have escaped their influence entirely. Dyos and Aldcroft[21] identified three major economic effects. First, canals dramatically enhanced the efficiency of the whole economy by making a cheap system of transport available for both freight and passengers. The price of raw materials like coal, timber, iron, wood and cotton tumbled dramatically. Building materials, whether bricks, sand or slate, became cheap and accessible. It was the beginning of the end of the vernacular tradition in building. The needs of agriculture, whether for manure or lime or for access to markets for grain, cheese and butter, were more easily satisfied wherever the canal penetrated. By the early 1840s estimates for the total tonnage on British canals vary from 30 to 35 million tons: 75 per cent of this was carried by canals in the area bounded by the Tweed, Thames, Severn and North Sea; 7 per cent was carried by both the Welsh and Scottish canals. South and south-east England carried little more than 6 per cent and the south-west less than 5 per cent of the national total. Secondly, canals were a means of overcoming a fuel crisis which threatened to limit industrial growth by making cheap, abundant coal supplies available. Bridgewater was convinced that 'a good canal should have coals at the heels of it'. Thirdly, the building of canals created massive employment and spending power at a time of strategic importance for the growth of industries looking for mass markets.

The advent of the railways soon put canals under pressure though their goods traffic reached its greatest volume after the arrival of the railway in a district. Until 1845 canal companies were not legally entitled to act as carriers since Parliament feared the creation of a transport monopoly. The work of transporting goods and passengers was undertaken by firms of national reputation like Pickfords or Sutton. From 1845 Parliament allowed all canal companies to act as carriers in the belief that they would then be better able to compete with railways. But almost none of the canals were suited to the successful application of steam power. Boats could only go uphill by using the expensive and time-consuming pound-locks. England was too hilly for canals to provide a long-term solution. Birmingham was the canal capital of England and the canal was at its best in the flat lands bounded by Birmingham, Liverpool and Manchester. Topography was perhaps the main reason for the essentially provincial character of the canals and hence their ultimate uncompetitiveness. The proliferation of companies should have meant that there was healthy competition but in practice the canal user lost rather than gained. This can be seen in the case of the Bridgewater Trustees who ran the canal after the Duke's death. They followed a policy of maximizing income regardless of long-term considerations and neglected maintenance work while increasing tolls. The attitude of Manchester merchants changed from enthusiasm for the canal to anger. Warehouses were inadequate, pilfering common and consignments often took months to get from Liverpool to Manchester and were ruined. In 1825 plans were drawn up for a railway between Liverpool and Manchester:

> it is not altogether on account of the exorbitant charges of the water-carriers that a railroad is desirable. The present canal establishments are inadequate to . . . the regular and punctual conveyance of goods at all periods and seasons. . . . [22]

It is ironic that discontent with the first major canal should have produced the first major railway.

CONCLUSIONS

Through the period between 1700 and 1850 Britain remained a horse-drawn society. Stage-coaches, stage-waggons and canal barges were hauled by horses. Freight was carried on packhorses. People, particularly the wealthy, rode horses. Power was symbolized by the people on horseback.

Steam alone was a threat – and even it was measured in terms of horse-power. In 1830 the threat of steam, on land if not at sea, seemed very remote. Short colliery railways were operated by horses and a few unreliable and cumbersome engines were used in the north-east. Most people regarded railways as frightening and dangerous, no more than a curious novelty. Few saw, as Bridgewater did, the potential of tramways plus steam locomotion. Thomas Creevey wrote to his step-daughter on 14 November 1829:

> Today we have had a lark of a very high order. Lady Wilton sent over yesterday from Knowsley to say that the Loco Motive machine was to be upon the railway at such a place at 12 o'clock for the Knowsley party to ride in if they liked. I had the satisfaction, for I can't call it pleasure of taking a trip of five miles on it, which we did in just a quarter of an hour – that is 20 miles per hour. But the quickest motion is to me frightful: it is really flying, and it is impossible to divest yourself of the notion of instant death to all upon the least accident happening. It gave me a headache which has not left me yet. Sefton is convinced that some damnable thing must come of it.[23]

NOTES

1 John Wesley *Journal*, 18 February 1747.
2 Laurence Sterne *A Sentimental Journey*, 1768, quoted in A. Briggs *How People Lived*, Vol. III, *1700–1815*, Blackwell, 1969, p. 81.
3 Quoted in E. Pawson *The Early Industrial Revolution*, Batsford, 1979, p. 133.
4 A. O. Hirschman *The Strategy of Economic Development*, Oxford University Press, 1958, p. 133.
5 A. Young *View of the Agriculture of Oxfordshire*, London, 1809, p. 324.
6 A. Yarranton *England's Improvement by Sea and Land*, London, 1698, Vol. II, p. 92.
7 A. Smith *The Wealth of Nations*, Dent, 1905 edn, Vol. I, p. 19.
8 On road developments in general see P. S. Bagwell *The Transport Revolution from 1770*, Batsford, 1974, chapter 2 and H. J. Dyos and D. H. Aldcroft *British Transport – an Economic Survey from the Seventeenth Century to the Twentieth*, Leicester University Press, 1969, pp. 19–36, 62–80. W. Albert *The Turnpike Road System of England 1663–1844*, Cambridge University Press, 1972 is the central work and E. Pawson *Transport and Economy: The Turnpike Roads of Eighteenth Century Britain*, 1977 is more analytical.
9 L. T. C. Rolt *Thomas Telford*, 1958 is the standard and very readable biography.
10 A brief discussion of turnpike disturbances can be found in J. Stevenson *Popular Disturbances in England 1700–1870*, Longman, 1979, pp. 43–5, 94–5. The disturbances in South Wales in the 1840s are best approached through D. Williams *The Rebecca Riots*, Cardiff, 1955, P. Molloy *And They Blessed Rebecca*, Gomer, 1985, and D. J. P. Jones *Rebecca's Children*, Oxford University Press, 1989.
11 D. Defoe *A Tour Through the Whole Island of Great Britain, 1724–6*, Penguin edn, pp. 429–432 lists the turnpikes built by the 1720s.

12 H. Homer *Enquiry into the Means of Preserving and Improving the Publick Roads*, 1767, quoted in Dyos and Aldcroft op. cit. p. 70.
13 P. S. Bagwell op. cit. p. 43.
14 ibid. p. 49.
15 T. S. Willan *River Navigation in England 1600–1750*, 1936 is still the best study though the 1970 reprint of J. Phillips *General History of Inland Navigation*, 1792 is worth dipping into.
16 Dyos and Aldcroft op. cit. p. 41.
17 T. S. Willan *The English Coasting Trade 1600–1750*, 1938 gives the fullest treatment of the subject.
18 On canals see P. S. Bagwell op. cit. chapters 1 and 6 and Dyos and Aldcroft op. cit. chapter 3. More detailed studies can be found in E. C. Hadfield *British Canals*, 1969 and his series of regional histories. J. Lindsay *The Canals of Scotland*, 1968 is essential. L. T. C. Rolt's biography of Telford op. cit. is a reliable account of his work.
19 The definitive study of this is J. R. Ward *The Finance of Canal Building*, Oxford University Press, 1974.
20 E. Pawson *The Early Industrial Revolution*, Batsford, 1979, p. 151.
21 Dyos and Aldcroft op. cit. pp. 102–3.
22 The prospectus of the Liverpool and Manchester Railroad Company is printed in T. Baines *History of Liverpool*, London, 1852, pp. 601–3.
23 Sir Herbert Maxwell (ed.) *The Creevey Paper*, 1903, Vol. II, p. 204.

8 The revolution in overseas trade

All States and Kingdoms have flourished, and made a Figure in Proportion to the Extent of their Commerce. . . . [1]

Historians like being able to identify primary causes. Nowhere is this more
evident than in explanations for the upturn in Britain's economic growth
during the eighteenth century. Overseas trade has been highlighted by
several historians for different reasons. Many of the external features of
economic growth, particularly the growth of export industries at a faster
rate than other industries, were associated closely with foreign trade.
There are reasonably reliable annual statistics of foreign trade – from 1696
for English trade, 1755 for Scotland and 1772 for Great Britain – the only
annual series available for the whole century. It is tempting to attribute
a causal rather than a dependent role to so well-documented an area.
H. J. Habakkuk and P. Dean[2], R. Davis[3] and W. W. Rostow[4] have
adopted the notion of commercial pre-eminence whereas this has been
disputed by W. A. Cole,[5] R. Hartwell,[6] A. Thompson[7] and N. F. R.
Crafts.[8] This chapter is concerned with examining the changing character
of trade between 1700 and 1850, the policy of government towards trade
and the overall impact of trade on the growth of the British economy.

SITUATION IN THE EARLY EIGHTEENTH CENTURY

The sixteenth century had seen a spirit of trading enterprise which led to
the establishment of the Muscovy Company in 1555, the Spanish Company
in 1577, the Eastland Company in 1579 and the Senegal Adventurers in
1588. The East India Company was founded in 1600 and set up its first
trading base at Surat in 1609. The settlement of North America began at
Jamestown in 1607 and a position was staked out in the West Indies in
Barbados in 1605. Formally organized trade in Africa began in 1618 and
from the 1670s the Hudson's Bay Company contested the French position
in Canada. But until 1660 both the scale and character of English foreign
trade was modest. Woollens acounted for between 80 and 90 per cent
of exports and the major dynamic element in the export trade was the

development of lighter woollen cloths for sale in southern Europe. Imports and re-exports of products from the growing American colonies and from the footholds in the West Indies and India expanded. Tobacco was London's major import by 1640. Sugar surged forward in the 1650s and accounted for 28 per cent of English exports by 1660. Between 1600 and 1640 English exports grew at an annual average rate of 1.5 per cent and this accelerated with an increase in re-exports after 1650. The merchant fleet probably doubled between 1610 and 1660 linking not just home, colonial and foreign markets but carrying goods directly between foreign ports. The Navigation Acts of 1650 and 1651 consolidated this position by restricting the carrying trade, including the re-export of colonial products, to English merchants and vessels.

Between 1660 and 1713 England was involved in conflicts, first with the Dutch (1665–7 and 1672–4) and then with France (1689–98 and 1701–13), which were as much concerned with commercial and colonial considerations as with dynastic issues. Britain came into direct competition with the Dutch in the early seventeenth century over their control of the Baltic trade, their entrepôt trade and policies in the East and West Indies. The wars fought between England and Holland in the 1650s as well as in the 1660s and early 1670s were far from conclusive. In France Colbert adopted a commercial policy in the 1660s with three strands. First, he built up the mercantile marine and a navy to protect it. Secondly, he introduced tariffs to encourage French exports and finally, he founded trading companies which pushed French interests in the Mediterranean as well as into the Baltic, America, Africa and India. This proved a direct threat to England's position and made France England's greatest adversary in the late seventeenth and eighteenth centuries. Between 1660 and 1700, though largely by 1689, there were major changes in English overseas trade. By 1700 woollen cloth had fallen to less than half of the total exports despite its continued growth. The reason for this change was the great expansion in the re-export trade to almost £2 million. Sugar and tobacco made up about 40 per cent of the total in 1700. The re-export of goods brought in by the East India Company, particularly Indian and Chinese textiles, accounted for a similar proportion. Calico imports were insignificant until the 1650s but increased from 240,000 pieces in 1663–9 to 861,000 in 1699–1701. A third branch of the re-export trade was in European manufactures sent to the expanding colonial market. Parallel to this was expansion in the slave trade with Africa to supply labour to West Indian Plantations (Table 8.1).

The bulk of the export and re-export trade was with Europe, 82 per cent and 77.3 per cent of the respective totals; 61.3 per cent of imports came from the same area. The impact of commercial expansion before 1700 on the overall growth in the English economy was limited. Much of the growth was concerned with the import and re-export of goods which did not directly stimulate English manufacturing growth. It did, however,

Table 8.1 English foreign trade in the late seventeenth century (£000)

	1663–69	*1699–1701*	Percentage increase
Exports	3,239	4,433	37
Re-exports	900	1,986	121
Total exports	4,139	6,419	55
Total imports	4,400	5,849	33

Source: R. Davis 'English Foreign Trade 1660–1700' in W. E. Minchinton (ed.) *The Growth of English Overseas Trade in the Seventeenth and Eighteenth Centuries*, Methuen, 1969, p. 92.

lead to increased capital investment in trade itself and in its ancillaries such as shipbuilding and repairing.

CHANGING FOCUSES FOR TRADE

Before 1750

In the 1680s the expansion of overseas trade slowed and the outbreak of the French wars in 1689 exacerbated this new situation. Several causes for this stagnation can be identified. First, there were market changes. Woollen exports encountered competition from East Indian cottons and silks which both extended the European market for textiles and shifted demand away from English cloths and, contemporaries maintained, had an adverse effect on the English industry. The re-export trade also encountered competition. After 1707 Glasgow came to dominate the tobacco trade, to the benefit of Scottish merchants who had few links with England. The French encouraged sugar production in Hispaniola, acquired from Spain in 1697, severely reducing sales of English sugar in Europe, especially after 1713. The growth of tariff systems by many European countries[9] and the transformation of the English protective system after 1689[10] tended to hamper commerce. The monopolistic commercial pretensions of the state partially explain why merchants sought greater freedom to carry on their business and reduce the power of the trading companies. The monopoly of the Royal African Company was breached in 1698 and the Newfoundland and Russian trades were thrown open the following year. Only the Hudson's Bay, East India and Russia companies were able to ward off these attacks. Finally, war disrupted trade, together with accompanying strain upon the financial and banking systems. Between 1690 and the late 1740s England was involved in a series of costly wars.[11] The war of the Spanish Succession (1702–13) caused trade to fall to a low level between 1704 and 1708. War could, however, have trade bonuses. The Methuen treaty with Portugal in 1703 stimulated trade and helped to establish London as a major market in bullion. England expanded her American possessions at the expense of France by the treaty of Utrecht. The growing American population stimulated expanding trade after 1720. From Spain England took Gibraltar and the 'Asiento' which gave English and colonial slave traders a thirty year legal monopoly of the supply of slaves to the Spanish American colonies though this brought little gain to English trading companies. The South Sea Company made a loss on the only two significant slave ships it sent to the Spanish colonies but the prospect of profit was one of the reasons which helped to build up the 'stock' of the Company in the 'Bubble' of 1720. Trade revived after 1713 but the dispute with the Baltic Powers in 1717–19, the wars with Spain in 1718 and 1727–8 and the threat of war in 1734 all prevented consistent growth. The War of Jenkin's Ear, which began in 1739 and merged into the broader European conflict of 1740–8, made trade difficult, particularly between 1744 and 1748. Trade slowed down markedly because the dynamic factors in it – the woollen cloth trade and re-exports – lost their vigour. Between 1690 and 1750 years of active trade were limited and short – 1699–1701 aided by the removal of export duties in woollens and grain, 1711 when woollen exports reached a new peak, 1714, the mid-1720s following Walpole's abolition of customs duties on English manufactures and some imports, 1735–8 when export of manufactured goods to the colonies first began to expand, and in 1743. In general the English overseas trade grew at only about 1 per cent per annum between 1690 and 1750 (Table 8.2).

Table 8.2 English trade 1700–49 (£m)

	Imports	Exports	Re-exports	Exports and re-exports
1700–9	4.7	4.5	1.7	6.1
1710–19	5.5	4.8	2.1	6.9
1720–9	6.8	4.9	2.8	7.7
1730–9	7.5	5.8	3.2	9.0
1740–9	7.3	6.5	3.6	10.1

Source: E. B. Schumpeter *English Overseas Trade Statistics 1697–1808*, Oxford University Press, 1960, pp. 15–16.

After 1750

After 1750 both the amount of trade and the rate of growth showed dramatic increases. Between 1750 and 1770 the average rate of growth was 1.7 per cent per annum and between 1770 and 1800 2.6 per cent annually. The impetus for growth in the 1750s came from an expansion of domestic manufactured goods for export, particularly to the American colonies. In the 1760s and early 1770s the swelling volume of re-exports was made possible by the continued expansion of imports. Between 1700 and 1800 imports expanded by 523 per cent and the exports and re-exports used to pay for them by 568 and 906 per cent respectively. In the same time population grew by about 250 per cent. It is clear that foreign trade became a more important component of national income during the eighteenth century (Table 8.3).

Table 8.3 English trade 1750–99 (£m)

	Imports	Exports	Re-exports	Exports and re-exports
1750–9	8.4	8.7	3.5	12.2
1760–9	10.8	10.0	4.4	14.4
1770–9	12.1	9.3	5.1	14.4
1780–9	13.8	10.2	4.3	14.5
1790–9	21.8	17.5	9.4	26.9

Source: B. R. Mitchell and P. Deane *Abstract of British Historical Statistics*, Cambridge University Press, 1962, pp. 279–83.

Throughout the second half of the eighteenth century a series of wars with France, Spain and the American colonies interrupted the development of foreign trade while stimulating the development of domestic manufacturing. Trade expanded steadily in the 1750s and was initially unaffected by the outbreak of the Seven Years War in 1756. There was a slight check in 1759 but in 1760 English exports reached a new peak. It was not until 1761–2 that the war adversely affected trade and mercantile pressure on Parliament as much as military and naval victory accounted for the Treaty of Paris in 1763. England made significant territorial gains. French power in America and India was broken and Spain lost ground in the West Indies. The English merchant fleet grew from 421,000 tons in 1751 to 594,000 tons in 1770. Trade revived in 1764 and 1765 but the potential of the American markets has to be viewed against growing colonial unrest and shrinking trade with the German states, Portugal and Spain after 1764. Although new trading peaks were reached in 1770 and 1771 the worsening situation in America and more difficult trading conditions in Europe saw a decline in both exports and re-exports. Exports did not exceed the 1771 peak until peace was restored in 1783 and re-exports took longer to recover not regaining the peak figures of 1773 until 1794.

The American war between 1775 and 1783 marked a watershed in the nature of English trade. When expansion resumed in the mid-1780s it took place on the basis of the new British manufactures. This marks the end of the commercial revolution for many historians. In what ways did the balance of trade shift between 1700 and the 1780s and did the

expansion of foreign trade during the century induce the English economy to become more specialized in manufacturing and less dependent on agriculture, beginning a process that was to continue until the late nineteenth century?[12]

Between 1700 and 1780 there was a significant growth in the import of non-European products (Table 8.4).

Table 8.4 English and Welsh imports in 1699–1701 and 1772–4 (£m)

	1699–1701	1772–4
Raw materials		
Silk, raw and thrown	346	751
Flax and hemp	194	581
Wool	200	102
Cotton	44	137
Textile yarns	232	424
Dyes	226	506
Iron and steel	182	481
Timber	138	319
Oil	141	162
Tallow	85	131
Miscellaneous	248	607
TOTAL	2,036	4,201
Foodstuffs		
Wine	536	411
Spirits	10	205
Sugar	630	2,364
Tobacco	249	519
Fruit	174	159
Pepper	103	33
Drugs	53	203
Tea	8	848
Coffee	27	436
Rice	5	340
Corn		398
Miscellaneous	174	561
TOTAL	1,969	6,477
Manufactures		
Linens	903	1,274
Calicoes	367	697
Silks and mixed fabrics	208	82
Metalwares	72	7
Thread	79	14
Miscellaneous	215	111
TOTAL	1,844	2,185
TOTAL IMPORTS	5,849	12,863

Source: As Table 8.1, pp. 119–20.

Of particular importance among textiles were linen yarn and linen cloth imported from the German states and the Baltic countries. Raw silk imports grew to a peak of 697,529 lb in 1769 and raw cotton imports paralleled the growth of the British cotton industry. Despite the acts of 1700 and 1721, which prohibited the import of printed calicoes and cottons for domestic consumption though not for re-export, imports of Indian calicoes continued to grow. Colonial imports increased rapidly after 1700 with growing demand for coffee, sugar, tea and tobacco. This led to some reduction in prices and further expanded potential demand. The price of tea fell from £1 a pound in 1700 to 5s. in 1750. Other significant imports were rice, timber, port and, after 1765, increasing amount of corn. The expanding domestic market acted as an important stimulus to colonial economic expansion particularly after 1750.

Table 8.5 English and Welsh exports and re-exports in 1699–1701 and 1772–4 (£m)

	1699–1701	1772–4
EXPORTS		
Raw materials		
Lead	128	182
Tin	97	116
Coal	35	333
Miscellaneous	102	163
TOTAL	362	794
Foodstuffs		
Grain	147	37
Fish	190	70
Hops	9	136
Miscellaneous	102	329
TOTAL	448	572
Manufactures		
Woollens	3,045	4,186
Linens		740
Silks	80	189
Cottons etc.	20	221
Metalware	114	1,198
Hats	45	110
Miscellaneous	279	1,843
TOTAL	3,583	8,487
TOTAL EXPORTS	4,393	9,853

Table 8.5 Continued

	1699–1701	*1772–4*
RE-EXPORTS		
Raw materials		
Dyestuffs	85	211
Silk	63	125
Miscellaneous	151	378
TOTAL	299	714
Foodstuffs		
Tobacco	421	904
Sugar	287	429
Pepper	93	110
Tea	2	295
Coffee	2	873
Rice	4	363
Rum		199
Drugs	48	132
Miscellaneous	84	237
TOTAL	941	3,542
Manufactures		
Calicoes	340	701
Silks etc.	150	501
Linens	182	322
Miscellaneous	74	38
TOTAL	746	1,562
TOTAL RE-EXPORTS	1,986	5,818
TOTAL EXPORTS AND RE-EXPORTS	6,379	15,671

Source: As Table 8.1.

The most notable trends demonstrated in Table 8.5 are the declining contribution of woollens to English manufactured exports and the rapid expansion of re-exports. The total amount of woollen cloth exported grew with the opening of the American market and in the slave trade but European demand was stifled by the expansion of protected domestic industries. In 1700 woollens accounted for 57.3 per cent of English exports and this had fallen to 42.2 per cent by 1772. Among other exports iron set the pace, particularly to the American colonies from 1740. Overseas sales of coal, cotton goods, linen and refined sugar grew even before the dramatic increases in productivity from the later part of the eighteenth century. The removal of export duties or prohibitions on manufactures aided this process. Corn exports expanded in the first half of the century but declined sharply after the mid-1760s when Britain became a net importer. Fishing entered a more prolonged period of decline. Re-exports accounted for over 37 per cent of all exports in the 1770s, an increase of about 7 per cent over the previous century. They were dominatd by East Indian and colonial products. Grocery re-exports accounted for nearly 40 per cent of the total, tobacco about 16 per cent and textiles 26 per cent. North-west Europe, Ireland and the colonial markets developed a strong re-export market for coffee, rice and particularly tea. Generally exports and re-exports moved in the same direction though in 1728–9, 1762–3, 1768 and 1773 depression in exports was partly offset by a rise in re-exports.[13]

Changing patterns of overseas trade

Between 1700 and 1780 there was a major change in the geographical pattern of overseas trade.[14]

Table 8.6 Geographical distribution of English and Welsh trade (as percentages)

	1700–1	1750–1	1772–3
Imports from:			
Europe	66	55	45
North America	6	11	12
West Indies	14	19	25
East Indies and Africa	14	15	18
Re-exports to:			
Europe	85	79	82
North America	5	11	9
West Indies	6	4	3
East Indies and Africa	4	5	6
Domestic exports to			
Europe	85	77	49
North America	6	11	25
West Indies	5	5	12
East Indies and Africa	4	7	14

Source: P. Deane *The First Industrial Revolution*, Cambridge University Press, 1965, p. 56.

Europe and Ireland remained major destinations for both exports and re-exports between 1700 and 1780. Two main trends can be identified in England's trading relations with Europe. First was the changed position of England within the European agricultural system. From 1700 up to the 1760s grain exports rose, peaking at over 6 million tons in the 1740s and 1750s. In 1772 only 0.7 per cent of imports were grain but by 1800 the figure reached 8.7 per cent. The second major change was the shift away from the Netherlands as a major source of both exports and imports.

Dutch imports fell from 15 per cent to 3.6 per cent between 1696 and 1772 while her share of English exports fell from 41.5 per cent to 12.7 per cent. Trade with the German states rose slowly in the first half of the century, rapidly in the early 1760s but declined steeply after. Imports from the Baltic states increased without any major change in English exports. In southern Europe trade was affected by the series of wars, though trade with Portugal expanded until the early 1760s.

Trade with Ireland

Ireland was treated like any other colony and its trade was restricted by legislation.[15] The import of Irish sheep and cattle into England was prohibited in 1667, butter and cheese in 1681 and wool and cloth, except to England, in 1698. Some changes were made in the eighteenth century – exempted from duties in England from 1696, Irish linens also benefited from the bounties on re-exports from 1743 and the restriction on animal and dairy produce was removed after 1758–9 – which gave Irish products easier access to mainland markets than to high tariffs of European markets. Trade between England and Ireland expanded quickly after 1750 and Ireland's share of total English imports increased from 3.9 per cent in 1700 to almost 10 per cent in 1771. Linen replaced wool as the major Irish export to England. Growth in imports was paralleled by an increase in English exports to Ireland, 4.2 per cent to 14.9 per cent in 1700 and 1771 respectively. The once shattered Irish market became one of the chief outlets for the products of English industries.

Trade with America

The main development in English trade in the eighteenth century was the expansion of the import and export trade with America. In 1700 the American colonies had only 300,000 inhabitants, by 1776 nearly three million. Colonial purchasing power – as measured by the goods sent across the Atlantic – increased fivefold and American purchases from England grew even faster. Trade with the West Indian colonies grew similarly. Colonial imports were of immense variety and served almost all the needs of the colonial population. The American market for iron and brassware increased on a large scale and contributed significantly to eighteenth-century development of those industries in England. Woollen cloth found a big colonial market after mid-century, so that total English woollen exports began to rise again after remaining stationary for over sixty years. The colonies had no difficulty in selling to England, especially as the Navigation Acts prevented direct export to European markets. This trade depended on the production of a few staples in the warm southern colonies – above all rice, tobacco, sugar and coffee. The northern colonies, from Pennsylvania to Maine, acquired much of their purchasing power in

England from supplying timber to the West Indian planters. Trade between England and America was mutually beneficial and, despite the American Revolution, continued to expand after the 1780s.

Finally there were the African and Asian trades. Direct trade with Africa was small though the expansion of the slave trade after 1750 led to a growth of exports to expedite that trade. Imports from the East Indies increased from about £500,000 in 1700 to £1.85 million by the mid-1760s while exports increased even more dramatically from about £100,000 to £1.1 million in the same period. The southern colonies of America and the British West Indies were good trading partners throughout the eighteenth century. They were well populated with a wealthy planter class with a taste for luxury goods and, with a climate different from Britain, capable of growing a variety of crops. The West Indies provided sugar but also rum, coffee and mahogany. In addition to raw cotton the southern colonies produced rice, tobacco and hardwoods. Britain was eager for tropical goods, and provided people in return for crops. Orphans were sent in the seventeenth century to be 'servants' of tobacco and sugar planters. Criminals were also used. But the most valuable human commodity was the negro slave. Trade with America led to trade with West Africa. Between 1680 and 1786 some two million slaves were taken to the colonies. In 1700 slaves fetched on average £15, but by 1750 up to £40 a head. Slave-trading was big business. Manufactured goods were taken to Africa and exchanged for slaves. The slaves were then taken to the Atlantic colonies and sugar and tobacco brought back to Britain.

The slave trade stimulated Britain's economic growth. Britain enriched the American South and the West Indies by buying their products, while they in turn bought British goods. The growth of the British economy was in part financed by the profits from slavery. Marx suggested that profits from foreign trade were an essential source of investment capital for industrialization. He argued that the sugar industry and slave trade and riches looted from India provided higher levels of profit than from other activities and thus provided the capital needed for industry. The major weakness of his argument is that notorious as the slave trade was, it was only a minor part of the British economy as a whole. It has been suggested that even if profits were high and even if a high proportion had been invested, the maximum total investment which the slave trade and extra-European trade could have contributed to the British economy was 15 per cent. It was the immorality of the slave trade that made a real contribution to British development.

A 'commercial revolution'

The commercial revolution between 1700 and the 1780s extended markets and diversified the commodities in which England traded. It was the classic type of market-widening that Adam Smith believed would encourage specialization in manufacture and increase efficiency. It is important to distinguish between the effects of expanded trade on real income and on the process of invention and technological innovation. The two processes are not identical – output, income and population can expand without substantial change in technology. First, a wide range of activities associated with trade widened expanding real income – banking, insurance, ship and port construction and the scale of internal trade to distribute imports. Secondly, the expansion of trade had many positive direct effects on real income. It reduced the cost of sugar, tobacco, tea and other items of popular consumption, and provided increased employment in manufactures. Finally, enlarged trade brought with it some increase in manufacturing and processing activities. W. W. Rostow has argued that:

> The commercial revolution set in motion demands that made it increasingly profitable to solve these problems on the supply side with new technology. . . . .(but) more than the commercial revolution is required to explain the industrial revolution, a Smithian widening of the market was not enough. . . .[16]

SCOTLAND'S TRADE

Wales and Ireland were already integrated into the English trading system by the beginning of the eighteenth century but Scotland was not. The pattern of Scottish foreign trade in the seventeenth century reflected deficiencies in its domestic economy. Imports fell into three categories. First, raw materials, often from the Baltic, which could not be produced in sufficient quality or quantity – iron, copper, timber, pitch, tar and flax. Secondly, manufactured goods such as fine-quality linens and woollens and metalware reflecting an inability to compete in superior finished goods usually from England and Holland. Thirdly, luxury goods like wines came from France, sugar and tobacco from the West Indies and the English colonies in America. Exports were largely raw materials and manufactured goods of poor quality. Re-exports played little part in this commercial system. In the mid-seventeenth century both exports and the markets to which they were sent changed. Grain exports increased, particularly to Norway. Baltic markets attracted herring and coal exports expanded dramatically. In the 1680s almost half the ships leaving Scottish ports were freighted with coal destined for Holland, Ireland and even London. Scottish trade encountered some difficulties after 1660 – the English Navigation Act applied to Scotland, a source of potential damage given the growing importance of trade with England notably in cattle and linen; imports of salted herring to France were prohibited in 1689; surplus grain became more difficult to sell in Norway because of competition from Baltic producers. The growing importance of trade with England predated union. A surplus trade with England could be used to offset imports from areas with which Scotland had a trading deficit. The Act of Union of 1707 was not completely responsible for the growth of Scottish trade, as has sometimes been assumed. It did make trade between England and Scotland easier and gave Scotland access to England's overseas markets. But the impact of the Navigation Acts on Scotland before 1707 can be overstated. An illicit trade developed with English colonies leading to the emergence of Glasgow as a trading centre though there was a time lag of over thirty years before it reached a dominant position in the tobacco trade. Union confirmed directions evident in the late seventeenth century. Trade with Europe was becoming more difficult and commercial success was better achieved through England's continually growing foreign markets.

It is difficult to estimate the effect of trade on the development of the Scottish economy since the trade which grew up most successfully was in re-exporting goods – in 1771 47.25 million lb of tobacco was imported of which 45.5 million lb was re-exported. Until the 1750s Scottish linen manufacturers had difficulties in competing in colonial markets with German and Austrian cloth re-exported through London. By the 1770s perhaps a third of Scottish production was for the overseas trade direct or through England. But Scottish overseas trade still provided a continuing demand for Scottish goods which, though not absorbing a large part of industrial production, did play an important role in the linen industry and the Carron ironworks. Merchants with their interests rooted primarily in the domestic linen industry rather than the re-exporting merchants made the most direct contribution to the new industry that appeared after 1780. It is this contribution to trade that should be stressed.

GROWTH IN TRADE AFTER 1800

Growth of foreign trade averaged 1.5 per cent over the period 1737 and 1771, peaking at 3 per cent in the 1750s. From the 1780s there was a dramatic increase in growth to nearly 5 per cent per annum. Significant in this increase were changes in the composition of domestic exports. There was a shift from primary products to manufactured goods and from the products of the domestic type of industry to the products of capitalist industry. By 1800 England was an importer of grain. Woollens fell from 46 per cent of exports in 1750 to 28.4 per cent in 1800, while cottons had increased from 0.8 per cent to almost a quarter of all exports in the same period (Table 8.7).

Cotton production depended on international trade and was responsible for half the increase in value of all exports between 1780 and 1830. It quickly eclipsed the woollen and worsted trades reaching just over half of all exports in 1830. By the 1830s barely three-quarters of all British exports were from the textile and dress industries. The diversification of exports that characterized developments between 1700 and 1780 was replaced by

Table 8.7 The structure of the domestic export trade 1750–1850 (as percentage of total exports)

	1750	1770	1800	1830	1850
Coal, coke etc.	1.6	2.7	2.0	0.5	1.8
Grain	19.6	–	–	–	–
Fish	1.0	1.0	1.0	1.1	1.0
Iron/steel goods	5.2	7.0	5.8	10.2	12.3
Cotton	0.2	2.0	24.1	50.8	39.6
Wool/Worsted	45.6	43.3	28.4	12.7	14.1
Linen	2.4	4.5	3.3	5.4	6.8
Silk	1.2	1.4	1.2	1.4	1.5

Textile figures include both yarn and manufactures. Figures for 1770 and after are for England, Wales and Scotland. The 1750 figures are for England and Wales only.
Sources: P. Deane and W. A. Cole *British Economic Growth 1688–1959*, 2nd edn, Cambridge University Press, 1967, p. 31; E. Pawson, op. cit p. 220.

a swift but unbalanced growth and an increasingly narrowing trading base. From the 1830s a new form of diversification emerged. Cotton began to decline in relative importance before 1850 and although woollens and linen made slight advances textiles as a whole were falling back. This was due in part to the more rapid increase in other categories of export and the saturation of some markets, particularly those in Europe in the 1830s and early 1840s. Metal-making and manufacturing industries made progress – from 6 per cent of all exports in 1814–16 to 12 per cent by the 1830s and rising to 20 per cent by 1850. The steadily increasing share of coal is also important after 1830, particularly the 'steam' coal from South Wales.

Table 8.8 Structure of British imports 1770–1830 (percentage of total value)

	1770	1800	1810	1820	1830
Corn	3	5	5	5	3
Other foods	32	35	42	41	35
Textile raw materials	16	15	19	26	33
Other raw materials	6	4	6	8	10
Miscellaneous	43	41	28	20	19

Source: B. R. Mitchell and P. Deane op. cit. pp. 285–9.

During the first half of the nineteenth century the largest share of imports consisted of either food or raw materials for industry (Table 8.8). Textiles, either raw materials or manufactured goods, dominated the import trade almost as much as the export trade.

The focal point of British trade continued to move away from Europe and to the American markets. This American focus for British trade was confirmed during the French Wars, a process aided but not initiated by Napoleon's Continental System and reinforced by the opening of Latin American markets after 1808. The economy of the United States was subject to sharp cyclical fluctuations causing Anglo–American trade to vary widely. In the face of these problems after 1820 British trade sought new, more stable markets. India was found to be a huge market for cotton goods after the abolition of the East India Company's monopoly. Similar possibilities existed in the Middle East and South America, though the expectations of exporters on the winning of independence by South America were too high and ultimately they were greatly disappointed. But the outlets were far from negligible and these new markets helped Britain to overcome the crisis in exports after 1815 and were responsible for the bulk of the increase in exports between 1820 and the 1840s. Britain was partly shifting trade towards less developed economies which provided increasing imports of tropical products to Britain and other industrially advanced countries (Table 8.9).

Table 8.9 Geographical distribution of British export trade by continent (as percentage of total value)

	1816–18	*1836–8*	*1849–51*
Europe	44.2	41.1	38.0
Africa	1.0	3.6	3.8
Asia	8.3	11.3	14.8
North America	37.3	21.2	24.5
South America	9.3	20.7	16.0
Australasia	–	2.2	3.6

Source: W. Schlote *British Overseas Trade from 1700 to the 1930s*, Oxford University Press, 1952, pp. 156–8.

The evolving pattern of overseas trade reflected the changes in Britain's industrializing economy. Europe and North America remained important markets but exports were able to rise quickly by supplying young primary-producer economies that sent raw materials in return.

THE NATURE OF BRITISH FOREIGN TRADE

Problems with sources

Conclusions about the nature of British foreign trade that depend entirely on imports and exports of goods, whether raw materials, food or manufactured goods, have been altered by recent re-examination of the statistical evidence on which assumptions were based and by an examination of the role of trade in services. Records from 1696 give an annual evaluation of English imports, exports and re-exports. The quantities traded were entered annually, but they were valued at fixed prices selected at the beginning of the century. Such entries approximate to a quantity index of the physical volume of trade rather than a value index. These figures show fairly accurately the course of England's trade but not the actual prices paid for imports and exports which are relevant when examining the balance of trade. Before 1854 no record of the actual cost of imports based on current prices exists and details of current costs of exports were only collected by customs men after 1798. During the eighteenth century this was not important since the pattern of prices between imports and exports, except for re-export commodities like sugar and tobacco, did not vary much. However, in the first half of the nineteenth century the 'official' figures misrepresent the balance of trade position and conceal important trends in the values of foreign trade.

A 'balance of trade'

The official values give an optimistic picture, with the flood of cotton goods creating a mounting surplus in the balance of trade. Exports, not re-exports, of British products were under £40 million in 1816–20 but almost £120 million thirty years later. Imports rose at a much slower pace and fell more and more behind exports resulting, when re-exports were taken into account, in the rising balance of trade: £17 million in 1816–20 to £70 million in 1846–50. This explanation ignores the steep fall in the price of exports between 1800 and 1850 compared to the price of imports. Britain had to sell twice as much by quantity to earn the same amount of imports in 1860 as in 1800. The balance of trade shows that British industrialization did not produce an accumulating surplus but a mounting deficit. The surplus balance of trade was created entirely from the earnings from 'invisible' exports – services of various kinds – rather than goods (Table 8.10).

From 1800 until 1843 foreign trade had not grown faster than the growth in national income. If anything domestic exports, though increasing greatly in volume, had declined from their original ratio of about 14 per cent of the national product of Great Britain while import values had remained at about 16 per cent. After 1843 this situation changed and by the mid-1850s these percentages had almost doubled to 22 per cent for exports and 33 per cent for imports of the national product. During the 1840s Britain became an 'export economy' in a new sense, with most of the momentum coming from foreign trade. The industrial crises of 1815 to 1820 and 1837 to 1842 were symptomatic of the saturation of the domestic market and the need to find alternative markets abroad.

Table 8.10 Balance of trade 1800–50

	(a)	(b)	(c)	(d)	(e)	(f)
1801–05	47.9	39.9	−8.0			
1806–10	54.0	42.9	−11.8			
1811–15	50.4	42.9	−7.5			
1816–20	49.3	40.3	−9.0	14.5	1.7	7.2
1821–25	45.4	37.3	−8.1	14.2	4.2	10.3
1826–30	48.7	35.9	−12.8	10.6	4.6	2.6
1831–35	53.6	40.5	−13.1	14.1	5.4	6.4
1836–40	73.8	49.8	−24.0	18.6	8.0	2.6
1841–45	71.0	54.0	−17.0	15.4	7.5	5.9
1846–50	87.7	60.9	−26.8	22.0	9.5	4.7

(a) annual average of net imports in £m at current prices.
(b) annual average of net exports of UK products in £m at current prices.
(c) balance of commodity trade; (c)=(b)−(a).
(d) net income from services including shipping credits, insurance, banking, emigrant funds, tourist spending, profits from foreign trade etc. in £m.
(e) net income from interest and dividends in £m.
(f) balance of trade in £m; (f)=(c)+(d)+(e).
Source: A. H. Imlah Economic Elements in the Pax Britannica, 1958, pp. 37–8, 70–5, 94–8, in P. Mathias The First Industrial Nation, Methuen, 2nd edn, 1983, p. 279.

'Invisible' exports

Invisible exports reversed the growing deficit in the balance of trade. These invisible exports fell into two main categories: income from services and interest and dividends from capital invested abroad. Income from services received little attention from contemporaries and much less attention from economic historians than the issue of the export performance of British industries. These services fell into two categories: servicing international trade, and industrial expansion. A large amount of Britain's foreign imports and exports were shipped, serviced and financed from Britain. A high proportion of the difference between the manufacturer's price for exports and the price paid by the foreign importing merchants went to Britain from shipping, insurance and international banking. In the new markets created by British merchants between 1800 and 1850 – in Asia, Australasia and South America – there were no long-distance shipping fleets, no local discount markets and few native merchant houses. The result was that British merchants organized the cargoes, insured them in London and banked in branches of British banks that grew up in those markets. The same process was evident in some of the older markets. By 1815 London was firmly established as the major European discount and insurance market. Only in two foreign markets was British hegemony in shipping broken and even then financing and insurance was on sterling account. Norwegians and Swedes still carried more than twice the tonnage of British ships in the Scandinavian timber trade. But the main field lost to British ships up to 1850 was the American market where three-quarters of the Anglo–American trade was carried on by American ships. Until the 1840s at least American ships could carry more, cost less to provision and build and were faster than British ships. Britain shook off the American challenge during the transition from sail to steamship.

The export of ideas, skills and technology played a less important role in the balance of trade, though its contribution should not be under-estimated.[17] Britain contributed much to the industrialization of the Continent especially France and Belgium, and of America. During the eighteenth century legislation, which was not repealed till 1843, prohibited the export of British machinery, parts or plans and the Acts of 1719 and 1780, not repealed until 1825, forbade the emigration of skilled workers. They reflected the attitude of many manufacturers, who in the absence of effective international patent laws, sought secrecy to maintain their profits and competitive edge. In practice this legislation was largely ineffective and both plans and skilled workers were smuggled out of the country. James Nasmyth summed up the situation as follows:

> restrictions in the communication of new ideas on mechanical subjects to foreigners of intelligence and enterprising spirit serves no practical purpose. . . . It is better to derive the advantage of supplying them with the machines they were in quest of, than to wait until the demand was supplied by the foreigners themselves.

British skilled workers installed new machines and instructed foreign workers in their use. In the late eighteenth century this applied to the flying shuttle, water frame and jenny. At the same time British engineers fitted steam pumps. Some British were also important as managers and entrepreneurs helping European industries to modernize and improve their communication systems. Aaron Manby aided the development of the French engineering industry and in the 1830s Thomas Ainsworth exercised the same influence in the Twente textile district of Holland. Thomas Brassey not only built the Paris–Rouen railway but played a central role in the development of continental railway construction. More important in terms of balance of trade was direct British investment in continental and American industrial enterprises.

Exporting capital

The export of capital during the first half of the nineteenth century was relatively low.[18] With the exception of 1821–5, it was under £8 million per annum. Only just over £200 million had been invested by 1850 and the annual interest from this, some £11.7 million, was not of major significance when compared to income from trade or from services. London became the world's financial centre as a result of the disruption caused both to maritime trade and to the commercial and financial centres of Europe.

The demands of war finance from the 1790s extended the experience of the London mercantile community in the flotation of debt and payment of subsidies to Pitt's continental allies. Some foreign bankers came to England – the Rothschilds in 1798 and the Huths in 1809. After 1815 the Barings and the Rothschilds acted as brokers for the legitimist regimes of Europe. The Barings, who had been customers of the French since they handled the 'Louisiana purchase' for Napoleon, broked the £10 million loan which solved the problem of French war indemnity between 1817 and 1819. They lent Russia £2 million while the Rothschilds broked £5 million for Prussia and £1 million for Austria. It was their success which led directly to increased capital investment abroad. Between 1815 and 1850 this fluctuated in seven- to ten-year cycles with peaks of speculation in 1824, 1835, 1844 and 1850 and troughs in 1827, 1840 and 1847. Foreign lending was catholic in scope but tended to be concentrated both geographically and in forms of debt at any particular point in time. Between 1815 and 1820 Europe was the focal point of attention. During the 1820s the centre of interest shifted to Latin America and Greece, in the first case a response to rising trade and in the second to the dominant classical education and romantic aspirations for Greek independence. Some £24 million was actually paid to these governments, most of it for mining schemes. Almost all these investments proved worthless and in late 1825 the speculative bubble collapsed. By the end of 1827 all the Latin and South American republics had defaulted on their debts. This collapse dried up the flow of funds abroad for several years and when they resumed in the 1830s their direction had switched north to the United States. The same process of boom and crash was, however, evident. The main openings for loans in America were state bonds, covering transport investments and banks. The boom in trade in 1836 was mirrored by the boom in loans. By 1837 American state borrowing amounted to $172.3 million of which a quarter had been issued to aid railway development. The financial crisis of 1837 in Britain had little effect on the market and borrowing reached a peak in 1838. Falling trade values in 1839, however, set off a general financial panic in the United States and by 1841 nine states were defaulting on loans. It was not until 1847 that capital again began to flow to the United States with the success of the Mexican war, the discovery of gold in California and the collapse of the British railway mania. With the American loan market dead in 1841 the flow of capital switched back to Europe and to the development of the continental railway network. This continued into the 1850s except for the British financial crisis of 1847 and the European revolutions of 1848–9. The 1840s also saw the beginning of investment in colonial amenities – a Jamaican railway company was established by members of the sugar trade and some railways were built in India. Between 1815 and 1850 capital investment and trade were closely linked. Any shift in the direction of trade was paralleled by a switch in the direction of investment.

'MERCANTILISM' TO 'FREE TRADE'

'Mercantilism'

In 1700 the commercial policy that historians have called 'mercantilism'[19] was barely established in England. Charles Wilson has written that

> The mercantile system was composed of all the devices, legislative, administrative and regulatory, by which societies still predominantly agrarian sought to transform themselves into trading and industrial societies, to equip themselves not only to be rich but to be strong, and to remain so. . . . [20]

The justification for this has been questioned, particularly by the classical economists and found absurd, illogical, even immoral. But in the context of the eighteenth century the system of protecting domestic interests made sense. Underlying some of the legislation lay the fear of unemployment with its attendant social upheavals. Protecting textile industries maintained local levels of employment and so, at least in the minds of contemporaries, reduced social tension. This meant a favourable balance of trade and the maintenance of a manufacturing advantage over competitors – hence the legislation preventing the export of machinery and skilled labourers. Associated with the protection of the domestic economy was the control of colonial economies and the maintenance of complementarity between them. There was an attempt to ban the woollen industry in the colonies in 1699, to limit the export of Irish wool textiles only to Britain and to outlaw any inter-colony trade in woollens. This implies a considerable degree of strategic planning which neglects the fact that the rise of protection was essentially accidental.

In 1689 England was not wedded to protection of domestic interests. Some imports were prohibited, but this was a small number compared with later practice. The tax on most goods was 5 per cent on the 'official' value of both imports and exports found in a book of unalterable rates that did not reflect actual costs. Wines, spirits and tobacco had higher duties as luxury items. Colonial goods were, in return, given a monopoly of the home market, which aided colonial capital accumulation. The search for new revenue led to the average level of duties on imports quadrupling between 1690 and 1704. These higher duties exposed certain industries to hardship and the government to constant pressure from the merchants involved. The result of this was a series of modifications and exemptions which established the precedent of future manipulation of tariffs in aid of special interests. The result in the eighteenth century was a tariff list of great complexity with duties, exemptions, prohibitions, drawbacks and bounties. There was also an upsurge in smuggling with peaks in the 1730s and 1740s and the 1770s. William Pitt's reform of the customs in the 1780s marked the end of the heyday of smuggling though it continued well into the nineteenth century and only finally ended when free-trading policies triumphed.

The tying by the Navigation Acts of the British empire to the economy of England was also arguably the result of changing circumstances, not of strategic planning. The Navigation Acts dated from the mid-seventeenth century and it was not until 1763 that the first British empire reached its zenith. The Navigation Acts consisted of four types of regulation. First, they determined the nationality of the crews and the ownership of vessels in which foreign trade could be carried. This was a response to the more efficient Dutch operation of the carrying trade in the first half of the seventeenth century. It ensured that Englishmen as a whole held an unbreakable monopoly of the carrying trade and allowed the other features of the Acts to be enforced. Secondly, the Acts laid down the destinations to which certain colonial goods could be shipped. Thirdly, they laid down the system of duties etc. which aided particular domestic industries and finally, they prohibited the manufacture of certain goods in the colonies. Though these laws and regulations may have benefited the English economy they were extremely restrictive for the colonies. Inter-colonial trade was illegal, though as in England smuggling was widespread, and all British and non-British goods had to be exported or re-exported through the mother country. Despite the restrictive nature of this policy it is probable that 'The first British empire, bound by the laws of trade, was a self-sufficient and expanding economy enriching its centre, surely, but also its periphery.'[21]

Whether this trading policy actually contributed to the economic growth of Britain and whether it imposed a significant hardship on the colonies has been a matter for historical debate, particularly among American historians concerned with the causes of the American Revolution. Adam Smith thought that the Atlantic colonies were 'mere loss instead of profit'. His extreme view is not borne out by the evidence. But the colonies were not as profitable and the imposition of the strictly economic aspects of the trading policies on the American colonies less restrictive than once thought. The policies were not a consistent national strategy designed to maximize the wealth of Britain as a whole. Mercantilism was the economic equivalent of political and social interests. There was, however, a considerable difference between the interests of a Scottish tobacco importer or a Liverpool slave trader or a sugar planter and the interest of the British economy as a whole.

A challenge to 'mercantilism'

Between 1780 and 1850 the mercantile system became less justifiable in political and social as well as economic terms. The theoretical challenge began before Adam Smith but was formalized by him, Ricardo, Bentham and the Mills and popularized by J. R. McCulloch and many others. Smith

believed that the sacrifice of the interests of the consumer to those of
the producer, those of the nation to those of particular individuals was
indefensible. He believed that a system of freely-operated market prices,
under naturally competitive conditions, would ensure the lowest possible
prices for the consumer and, by the impact of comparative costs, produce
a more efficient allocation of resources between different branches of
economic activity, nationally and globally. There should be free trade
within an international market economy.

Up to 1820 free-trade arguments were not received well by the business
interests. Pitt's proposal for freeing trade to some extent with France and
Ireland in 1785–6 had been met with considerable opposition and some
scepticism. The French Wars delayed the dismantling of state-created
regulations and the 1815 Corn Laws for many symbolized the iniquities
of the 'economics of interests'. It was not until 1820 that the London
merchants petitioned Parliament for free-trade policies. The monopoly of
the East India Company with India was abolished in 1813 and with China
in 1833. William Huskisson removed obsolete duties in 1822 and in the
Reciprocity Duties Act of 1823 made possible a wider range of treaties
with most of Europe, together with Latin America and the United States.
In 1840 the protectionist system still remained largely intact with 1,146
articles paying duties, though only a handful of them provided the bulk
of the customs revenue. The 1840s saw the system dismantled partly
because of pressure from the Anti-Corn Law League and partly because of
the initiative of Sir Robert Peel. His budgets of 1842 and 1845 completely
abolished duties on more than 700 articles, largely raw materials, as well
as prohibiting exports and imports that persisted, and he reduced tariffs
on many other goods, including many manufactured articles. The Corn
Laws were repealed in 1846, the Navigation Acts in 1849 and the last
traces of protectionism, notably 'imperial preferences' in favour of sugar,
timber and coffee coming from British possessions, were eliminated in the
1850s. The Anglo–French treaty of 1860 is often seen by historians as the
symbol of a free-trading nation.

It has been argued that protectionism slowed down the growth of British
exports and industrial production during the first decades of the nineteenth
century. The Corn Laws prevented the widening of the domestic market
for manufactured goods by keeping food prices inflated. They also reduced
the purchasing power of foreign countries which were unable to import
grain freely and regularly to Britain and so reduced their ability to buy
British exports. Customs duties on many raw materials were a charge on
industries and influenced the extent to which exports could expand. This
negative impact of protectionism should not be overestimated – the
volume of British exports rose by 4.3 per cent per annum between 1814
and 1846 compared to 4.7 per cent between 1846 and 1873. Nonetheless
there was a phenomenal growth after 1845 – the exact turning-point was
1848 – in the value of exports, a rise from 1.1 per cent per annum between

1814 and 1846 to 5.7 per cent from 1846 to 1873. Free trade reflected the nature of an economy which was open and specialized, which had pushed far the international division of labour, had abandoned primary production (except in coal) to concentrate on industry (with special emphasis on a few staple industries), services and international trade. Changes in tariff policy had only limited direct effects on this growth.

TRADE AND ECONOMIC GROWTH

To what extent was growth in trade between 1700 and 1850 central to Britain's economic development? Did trade precipitate the industrial revolution? P. Deane[22] argues that foreign trade had this central role in six major ways. First, it stimulated an internal demand for the products of British industry. Secondly, international trade gave access to raw materials which both widened the range and cheapened the products of domestic industries. Thirdly, it provided purchasing power for countries to buy British goods since trade is a two-way process. Fourthly, profits from trade were used to finance industrial expansion and agricultural improvement. Fifthly, it created an institutional structure and a business ethic and finally it was a major cause of the growth of large towns and industrial centres. The supremacy of British trade must, however, be put into perspective. Changes between the mid-eighteenth and mid-nineteenth centuries in terms of the basic pattern of British trade – the export or re-export of manufactures in return for imports of raw materials and foodstuffs – were relatively minor and the industrial changes from the 1780s consolidated existing tendencies. Exports were concentrated in a few commodities, especially textiles and iron, which were major users of steam power and cheap low-grade labour, and did not come to any great extent from the unmodernized traditional manufacturing sectors that still constituted much of the economy in 1850. The expansion of trade for the export-oriented cotton industry is central only to a 'factory-steam' definition of the industrial revolution which figures so much in the historiography of British development.

NOTES

1 R. Campbell *The London Tradesman*, London, 1747, p. 286.
2 H. J. Habakkuk and P. Deane 'The Take-off in Britain', in W. W. Rostow (ed.) *The Economics of Take-Off into Sustained Growth*, Oxford University Press, 1963, pp. 63–82.
3 There are several important studies by R. Davis 'English Foreign Trade 1660–1700', 1954 and 'English Foreign Trade 1700–1774', 1962 both reprinted in W. E. Minchinton (ed.) *The Growth of English Overseas Trade in the Seventeenth and Eighteenth Centuries*, Methuen, 1969; *The Rise of the English Shipping Industry in the Seventeenth and Eighteenth Centuries*, David & Charles 1962, *A Commercial Revolution*, The Historical Association, 1967 and *The*

Industrial Revolution and British Overseas Trade, Leicester University Press, 1979.

4 W. W. Rostow *How It All Began, Origins of the Modern Economy*, Methuen, 1975, pp. 107–31.

5 P. Deane and W. A. Cole *British Economic Growth 1688–1959*, 2nd edn, Cambridge University Press, 1967.

6 R. M. Hartwell 'The Causes of the Industrial Revolution: an Essay in Methodology', 1965 in his *The Industrial Revolution and Economic Growth*, Methuen, 1971.

7 A. Thompson *The Dynamics of the Industrial Revolution*, Edward Arnold, 1973, pp. 93–103.

8 N. F. R. Crafts *British Economic Growth during the Industrial Revolution*, Oxford University Press, 1985, pp. 141–54.

9 The issue of continental tariff systems is examined in G. Treasure *The Making of Modern Europe 1649–1789*, Methuen, 1985, pp. 78–86.

10 See below, pp. 179–80.

11 A broad picture of foreign policy during this period can be obtained from P. Langford *The Eighteenth Century 1688–1815*, A. & C. Black, 1976 and J. R. Jones *Britain and the World 1649–1815*, Fontana, 1980.

12 R. P. Thomas and D. N. McCloskey 'Overseas Trade and Empire 1700–1860' in R. Floud and D. N. McCloskey (eds) *The Economic History of Britain since 1700*, Vol. I, Cambridge University Press, 1981, p. 90.

13 The discussion by T. S. Ashton *Economic Fluctuations in England 1700–1800*, 1959 especially chapters 3 and 6, provides a detailed analysis of trade and should be used as a corrective to E. B. Schumpeter *English Overseas Trade Statistics 1697–1808*, 1960.

14 R. Davis *The Rise of English Shipping*, op. cit. gives an interesting discussion of the location of trade.

15 The work of L. M. Cullen especially *Anglo-Irish Trade 1660–1800*, Manchester University Press, 1968 and *An Economic History of Ireland since 1660*, Batsford, 1972, especially chapters 2, 3 and 5, is fundamental.

16 W. W. Rostow op. cit. p. 131.

17 On Britain and the exchange of technology and ideas see W. O. Henderson *Britain and Industrial Europe 1750–1870*, Leicester University Press, 1972 edn, especially pp. 1–9, 211–18.

18 On capital investment abroad the simplest starting point is P. L. Cottrell *British Overseas Investment in the Nineteenth Century*, Macmillan, 1975.

19 On British trading policies in the eighteenth century see C. H. Wilson *Mercantilism*, Historical Association, 1958 and D. C. Coleman (ed.) *Revisions in Mercantilism*, Methuen, 1969. J. B. Williams *British Commercial Policy and Trade Expansion 1750–1850*, Oxford University Press, 1972 charts the transition to free trade and A. G. L. Shaw (ed.) *Great Britain and the Colonies 1815–1865*, Methuen, 1970 examines the debates over the imperialism of free trade.

20 C. H. Wilson op. cit. p. 26.

21 R. P. Thomas and D. N. McCloskey op. cit. p. 95.

22 P. Deane *The First Industrial Revolution*, Cambridge University Press, 1965, pp. 66–8.

9 Capital and banking

By the beginning of the eighteenth century there were enough rich people in the country to finance an economic effort far in excess of the modest activities of the leaders of the Industrial Revolution . . . what was inadequate was not the quantity of stored-up wealth but its behaviour. The reservoirs of savings were full enough, but conduits to connect them to the wheels of industry were few and meagre.[1]

The accumulation of capital has been of major concern to economists since Adam Smith and to economic historians since the mid-nineteenth century. To Smith, Malthus, Ricardo and Marx capital accumulation was the crucial regulator of economic growth. For writers after 1880 Britain's industrialization was seen to have depended, almost entirely, upon it. Recently more scepticism about the central role of capital formation in the process of economic development has entered the writings of both economists and historians. This chapter is concerned with the examination of the financial structure and attitudes that underlay capital and credit between 1700 and 1850.

CAPITAL – SOME ISSUES

It was not until the 1840s that the notion of capitalism emerged as a way of describing an entire social structure dominated by systems of economic acquisition by private interests possessing capital. The general characterization of 'capitalism' is one of strenuous debate – is it to be regarded as a system of production relations or a system of exchange relation? what role does capital play within capitalism? is capital accumulation the result of the mentality and voluntarily preferred actions of individuals or the result of structural features of society generally? Two broad options can be discussed when examining the nature of 'capital' within capitalism. One view defines capital as a stock of resources or factor of production which the individual combines with other factors like labour, thereby exercising 'entrepreneurship'. In this model the unit of action within capitalism is the individual. Success as a capitalist is explained either in relation to increased market demands to which the individual responded or by the notion of self-help expressed through industry, energy and uprightness. The second model, owing its genesis to Marx, sees capital as grounded in the social relationship between the capitalists, who control the means of production, and the wage-labourers, who have nothing but their labour to sell in the market. Capital is not, in this approach, a 'factor of production' but a key component in determining the structure, relations and reproduction of society.[2]

The ability of any society to accumulate usable capital depends on the capacity of that society to create wealth, either through production or through the process of savings. It has been suggested that a significant difference between an underdeveloped country and a developed one is that the former normally saves about 6 per cent of its national income while the latter saves 12 per cent or more. W. W. Rostow maintains that an increase in savings to 10 per cent of national income is a sufficient condition for 'take-off into sustained growth'.

It is important to distinguish between 'fixed' and 'working' capital. 'Fixed' capital is the finance needed to set up a business (buy the equipment, buildings etc.) against which has to be set the cost of capital depreciation (machines and buildings need replacing after a certain number of years). Capital for fixed plant can come from several sources: it can be profits from one business used to set up another or maintain an existing one; it can come through selling shares in a business from which investors receive a dividend or establishing partnerships though in this period, apart from specific authorization by act of parliament for canals, raising capital by share issue was made illegal by the 'Bubble Act' of 1720; it can be borrowed from financial institutions, like banks, and interest paid on it. In the last two cases the anticipated level of dividend and the interest rate can influence the extent to which people are willing to invest or entrepreneurs borrow. The low rate of interest in the eighteenth century has been seen as a cause of industrial and agricultural expansion.

'Working' or 'variable' capital is the finance necessary for the day-to-day running of a business (the costs of management and labour, transport, insurance, raw materials etc.). This capital comes from profits ploughed back into running the business, advances from contracts and sometimes from short-term 'bridging' loans from banks. The extent to which a particular business can keep down running costs will determine the initial profit that will be made. Once dividends, bank loans etc. are paid off a business is left with its 'surplus' capital which can either be ploughed back to improve product, plant or wages, saved or spent outside the business. The extent to which capital is accumulated is important in any developing society since it is a fund upon which society as a whole can draw. Two types of use to which capital can be put have already been discussed – 'social overhead' capital[3] and 'export' capital.[4]

CAPITAL TO SPARE?

Given that capital investment is seen as central to the transition from an underdeveloped to a developed economy, was there any capital shortage in the eighteenth and early nineteenth centuries? There is general agreement that this was not the case though the implication of this conclusion was not always appreciated. Because the economy grew historians have assumed that there was no shortage of capital. Peter Mathias, for example, wrote that 'In aggregate it seems clear that no absolute shortage of savings relative to the demand for productive investment threatened to constrain the process of growth in eighteenth-century Britain.'[5]

The contemporary statistician Gregory King calculated the value of the stock of capital at various points in the seventeenth century and for 1688 suggested an investment of £2.4 millions, representing about 6 per cent of a national capital stock of about £112 million. As 1688 was a prosperous year, 6 per cent may be too high for an average figure and Deane and Cole suggested, in the 1960s, a figure of between 3 and 6 per cent as being 'an intelligent contemporary guess'. Estimates for the nineteenth century indicate that domestic investment had risen to about 10 per cent. Between 1700 and 1750 growth in levels of capital formation occurred largely because of the steady increase in the rate of urbanization and the continued expansion of overseas trade, particularly after 1730. In the middle years of the century there was a rising rate of capital accumulation in roads, canals, buildings and enclosures. This wave of investment lasted from the 1750s to the late 1770s. By 1780 it appears that the nation's capital stock had grown appreciably. From the 1780s through to 1850, with the exception of the first two decades of the nineteenth century, an upward shift in capital accumulation occurred with continued enclosure and canal building, textile and iron expansion and, after 1830, speculative booms in railways. The annual rate of domestic capital investment rose from about £10 million in the 1770s to £20 million by the 1820s (Table 9.1).

Recent work has concentrated on the speed at which capital accumulated. Charles Feinstein[6] has created a data base to investigate the quantitative aspects of capital formation. This allows historians to test two hypotheses which have dominated writing on the subject – the Lewis-Rostow claim that the investment ratio doubled during the industrial revolution and the Hicks thesis that the fundamental change was a shift from predominantly circulating to fixed capital. Feinstein's data shows that the Rostow hypothesis was generally valid. The ratio of gross investment as a ratio of gross national product rose from 8 per cent in the 1760s to 14 per cent by the 1790s at which level it remained, except for a temporary setback in the early nineteenth century, until 1850. Crafts[7] has recently revised Feinstein's figures downwards but he also found that the investment ratio doubled from 5.7 per cent in the 1760s to 11.7 per cent by 1830, though more gradually than Rostow thought. The second

Table 9.1 Gross domestic investment and gross national product 1761–1850 (£m per annum)

	Domestic investment	GNP	Investment as % GNP
1761–70	7.5	93	8.06
1771–80	9.0	98	9.18
1781–90	13.0	111	11.70
1791–1800	17.5	134	13.05
1801–10	17.5	161	10.06
1811–20	22.5	203	11.08
1821–30	32.5	278	11.70
1831–40	42.0	372	11.29
1841–50	54.5	460	11.84

Source: P. Deane and W. A. Cole *British Economic Growth 1688–1959*, Cambridge University Press, 2nd edn 1967, pp. 161 and 282.

hypothesis is also supported by the Feinstein data. Fixed capital rose from 30 per cent of national wealth to 50 per cent between 1760 and 1860, while the corresponding ratio of circulating capital fell slightly, from 11 to below 10 per cent. The absolute amount of circulating capital increased during the industrial revolution but its growth is dwarfed by the rise of fixed capital.

The capital structure of eighteenth-century businesses is relevant to the developing nature of capital investment. In the outworking systems almost all capital was 'working' or 'circulating' with a very small amount in fixed assets, such as buildings and machines. Even the most capitalized industries like iron, textiles and brewing, typically had less than 20 per cent of their total assets in buildings and plant. The Truman, Hanbury and Buxton brewery at Spitalfield was exceptional in having just under a quarter of its assets fixed. Widespread capital investment was largely confined in the years between 1700 and 1850 to a small, though undoubtedly important, part of the economy. Capital investment rose in farming, communications and textiles, especially cotton and iron and coal. The other parts of the economy often remained undercapitalized relative to these industries. Even in the progressive areas of the economy fixed capital did not rise dramatically – at the Ashworth's New Eagley Mill in 1802 it accounted for less than 30 per cent of the total assets (£3,100 out of £9,800) and other firms generally had a lower percentage.

CHANGES IN NATIONAL CAPITAL

Tables 9.2 and 9.3 give a broad picture of the changes in national capital between 1760 and 1860. They show a striking transformation, with national

Table 9.2 National capital of Great Britain by sector in 1760 and 1860

	1760		1860	
	£m	%	£m	%
Residential and social capital	130	16	860	18
Agriculture, industry and	600	74	1,710	36
commerce	60	7	1,120	24
Transport	20	3	590	12
Overseas assets	–	–	470	10
TOTAL	810	100	4,750	100

Source: C. H. Feinstein 'Capital Accumulation and the Industrial Revolution', in R. Floud and D. McCloskey (eds) *The Economic History of Britain since 1700*, Cambridge University Press, Vol. I, p. 129.

Table 9.3 National capital of Great Britain by type of asset in 1760 and 1860

	1760		1860	
	£m	%	£m	%
Land – farm	380	47	1,020	21
Land – non farm	30	4	420	9
Fixed capital – farm	110	14	440	9
Fixed capital – non-farm	150	18	1,930	41
Stocks – farm	110	13	250	5
Stocks – non-farm	30	4	220	5
Total domestic capital	810	100	4,280	90
Overseas assets	–	–	470	10
TOTAL	810	100	4,750	100

Source: As Table 9.2.
Note: 'Stocks' refers to stocks of raw materials, semi-manufactured products and finished goods held by producers and to work in progress.

capital increasing almost sixfold during the century. Most of this growth, about 60 per cent, was a result of the real increase in the quantity of capital, the rest the outcome of prices roughly doubling in the century. There were also major changes in the composition of the total. Agriculture's share of the total fell from 74 per cent to 36 per cent. Within this sector the contribution of unimproved land fell from 47 to 21 per cent and crops and livestock from 15 to 6 per cent. This relative decline was paralleled by increases in industry, transport and commerce from 10 to 36 per cent, with the greater part in fixed capital.

Fixed capital expenditure in agriculture, a contribution by both landowners and tenants, was largely on enclosures, drainage and buildings. Landowners seem to have ploughed back about 6 per cent of their total incomes into the land. This figure rose to about 16 per cent during the French Wars when high prices encouraged enclosure. It fell back after 1815 and did not rise until the 1840s, with landlords spending liberally on drainage, steam engines, covered yards and other improvements. Table 9.4 shows that in 1760 agriculture was the largest of the five sectors, accounting for about a third of all investment, yet by the 1850s it was the smallest. In marked contrast the industrial and commercial sector saw a rapid expansion of fixed capital. Annual capital spending rose from about £2 million per annum in the late eighteenth century to £17 million by the 1850s. Outlay on machines has been seen as symbolizing industrialization. Relative to national investment and even to capital building costs in industry and trade technological outlay was in fact quite small – 25 per cent of total capital spending in industry and trade between 1761 and 1790, rising to about a third by the 1850s. Machines were cheap relative to their housing costs. Outlay on transport accounted for about a fifth of the total until 1840. In the next two decades massive railway investment raised this share to just over a third. Improvements in water and road communications in the eighteenth and early nineteenth century resulted in annual investment of about £1.5 million between 1760 and 1850 with canals accounting for two-thirds of investment up to 1800 and roads after 1800. Other transport included the merchant navy, docks and harbours. Capital spending rose from £1 million per annum between 1760 and 1820 to £4 million per annum in the 1840s and 1850s, reflecting the expansion of overseas trade and the costs of iron and steel ships. These figures are dwarfed by the outlay on railways, which peaked at an average £15 million in the mid-1840s and then dropped back to £9 million per annum in the 1850s – in the 1840s this accounted for some 28 per cent of the total capital outlay. This dramatic increase was almost entirely offset by the drop in the proportion used for residential and social capital – it is conjectural whether there was capital diversion from building to railway construction.

CAPITAL FORMATION OUTSIDE ENGLAND

Wales

Capital formation certainly had a major impact on the development of the British economy as a whole but just how great was its effect on Wales, Scotland and Ireland? Finance for economic growth was a serious problem for Wales in the first half of the eighteenth century because of its distance from financial centres and inability to generate sufficient internal capital. As the Welsh economy grew after 1750 and the labour force expanded, so the necessity grew for more investment and money in circulation. Cattle dealers often borrowed money to have capital to trade and in Denbighshire and Radnorshire the Receiver of the King's Taxes lent money from the

Table 9.4 Gross domestic fixed capital formation by sector 1761–1860 (£m at 1851–60 prices, and as a percentage)

	1761–90	*1791–1820*	*1821–40*	*1841–60*
£million				
Agriculture	2.5	4.0	4.5	6.5
Industry and trade	2.0	4.5	11.5	17.5
Railways			2.0	11.5
Other transport	2.0	3.5	4.5	7.5
Residential and social	2.0	5.0	11.0	11.0
TOTAL	8.5	17.0	33.5	54.0
Percentage				
Agriculture	33	25	13	12
Industry and trade	22	26	35	33
Railways			6	21
Other transport	23	20	14	14
Residential and social	22	29	32	20
TOTAL	100	100	100	100

Source: C. H. Feinstein op. cit. p. 133.

revenue and pocketed the profits. Loans were usually short-term and procured on the security of bonds, the dealer paying his debt to the Bank of England or some other London house which was a safeguard against robbery on his travels. Several dealers used their financial expertise to open banks in the late eighteenth century – the Black Ox Bank at Llandovery, the Black Sheep Bank at Aberystwyth and Tregaron – in centres of the cattle and sheep trade. Although the role of native entrepreneurs was not inconspicuous the development of Welsh industry was financed largely from England by entrepreneurs who brought both capital and technology. Undercapitalization was a recurrent problem. In the lead industry, for example, technical difficulties and unstable prices during the eighteenth century meant that landlords could not maximize potential. The result of this was the leasing of mineral rights to mining companies in return for royalties. Most of these mining companies came from northern England. The Quaker Company, for example, operating in Flintshire, invested in long-term development and even in research. It had its own smeltworks and profits were often put into mining elsewhere. Copper production reached its zenith during the mid-nineteenth century. It was dominated by master-smelters from Bristol and South Wales but in the 1770s Thomas Williams upset the equilibrium of the industry and broke the domination of the mining companies by undercutting prices and exploiting the advantage of cheaper production in the newer mines in Anglesey. Williams' 'reign' was shortlived as the easily worked ores were quickly exhausted. Although Welsh gentry played a prominent role in the pre-1750 development of the iron industry, the amount of capital which could be deployed from land was inadequate for post-1750 developments and landowners were relegated to the role of lessors of mineral rights. Entrepreneurs after 1750 were almost invariably English and, although some formed partnerships with Welsh landowners, the role of the capitalist grew while that of the landed interest declined. The units of iron production in Wales were larger than those in the Midlands and required more capital. Little of the capital invested in Welsh iron came from the Midlands. Most was supplied by Bristol iron merchants and linen drapers and from London. High profits were earned and much of them were ploughed back to increase productive capacity. Capitalization increased dramatically – at Cyfarthfa fixed capital rose from £14,370 to reach £104,000 by 1798 and £160,000 by 1813; at Blaenafon capital was £250,000 in 1816 and at Tredegar £100,000 in 1818. The personal nature of the capital market was a notable feature of the iron industry; much capital raised was from relatives and friends, with the gentry giving short-term loans which met temporary needs before banking was developed. By contrast much of the capital for developing the slate industry was found within Wales. In general, however, there was a lack of both capital and reserves in Wales and arguably too narrow a concentration of investment and lack of liquid reserves. It was insufficient to generate the same momentum within the Welsh economy before 1750 that was evident in England. After 1750 expansion owed much to English capital.

Scotland

Unlike Wales, Scotland developed a framework of banking early in the eighteenth century.[8] The Bank of Scotland was founded in 1695 and had a monopoly on public banking until the foundation of the Royal Bank of Scotland in 1727. This was in marked contrast to England, which is discussed later, where the Bank of England long and actively maintained its exclusive privileges. Up to 1849 these two banks provided public chartered banking. A second identifiable group of banking institutions was the private or merchant banks which provided most of the bills of exchange necessary for successful economic development. The origins of such bankers were diverse and many entered banking after success in other areas of economic activity. For example, John Coutts based his fortune on the corn trade, William Alexander on tobacco, William Cumming on textiles. The third group of banking institutions existed in the provinces and by 1772 accounted for 25 per cent of the total liabilities of the banking system. The financial crises of the eighteenth century were usually linked to problems with Scotland's balance of payments. Deficits required the transfer of bullion or other reserves out of the country and so reduced the banks' liquid assets. The limited credit available to entrepreneurs impeded industrial and agricultural growth. This strain was reduced by agricultural improvements which cut the need for certain imports and industrial expansion which increased exports. The general expansion of the Scottish economy after the 1770s protected the financial institutions against some of the pressures that had characterized the earlier years of the century.

Union should have given readier access to the capital of England. Little moved north until political stability had been achieved after the defeat of the Jacobite rebellions. Until 1750 economic growth and capital formation was generated largely from within Scotland. From 1727 a steady income from any surplus of the malt tax was given to the Board of Trustees for Fisheries and Manufactures for economic development. The Board was particularly active in the development of the linen, herring and woollen industries. The clear emphasis was on linens – in 1727, of the £6,000 available, the Board spent £2,600 on linen and only £700 on woollens. Money was spent on research into the problems of linen and representatives were sent abroad to learn from foreign example. Official help for linen, dynamic entrepreneurship as in the case of the Cannon Company and agrarian improvement were inadequate to ensure prosperity. There was an intense suspicion within Scotland of risk and speculation among those with capital, and intense poverty which meant that internal demand – a major reason for investment in England – was depressed.

Foreign trade was the key to capital accumulation and industrial expansion. Scottish enterprise overseas widened in the nineteenth century. This investment was necessary to obtain the raw materials for the industrial economy but in other instances it was an extension of activities for which there was only limited potential at home. Growing trade led to the appearance of more efficient trading agencies and services. Of direct importance was capital investment on increasing port facilities, notably on the Clyde, government expenditure to fund some improvements of roads and canals and finally the railway boom of the 1840s. Entrepreneurs in the cotton industry generally obtained their capital in linen production though often in partnership with merchants. David Dale, for example, became Glasgow's leading importer of foreign yarn for linen workers particularly in the west of Scotland. When new technology provided the opportunity Dale was able to move easily to cotton spinning. His partnerships and associations show how he was able to draw upon different sources of capital and innovation. Richard Arkwright was associated with him at New Lanark and at Blantyre he combined with James Monteith, a pioneer in muslin production. At Catrine his partner was Claud Alexander of Ballochmyle, who had made money from trade, had become a laird with land near a good supply of water and had capital to spare. The Buchanan family built the Deanston works in Perthshire in partnership with Robert Dunmore who had made his money in the tobacco trade. Smaller mills were, however, more representative of the development of the cotton industry. Even then the conversion of buildings to cotton production was expensive – one estimate showed that between £3,000 and £4,000 was necessary to convert an old sugar mill of seven stories to house 9,360 spindles. Recent estimates of the amount of capital invested in cotton differ, but, being a new demand on limited resources, the expansion of the industry could only be sustained by the support of landowners and others with capital to spare. Compared with England, the Scottish industry was undercapitalized, slower in adopting newer mechanized methods (which often came from Lancashire) and after the mid-1830s found it very difficult to compete with Lancashire. Expansion in the iron industry was particularly evident after 1830 with the reduction of fuel costs achieved by James Neilson with the 'hot-blast'. This stimulated further capital investment which almost doubled from 1836 to over £6 million in 1840 on 'fixed' capital alone as over twenty new furnaces were brought into blast – and this was during a period of a fall in prices and a gradual decline into depression between 1837 and 1843. By 1850 the Scottish economy mirrored its English counterpart.

Ireland

The Irish economy was very vulnerable in the 1680s because of its dependence on foreign markets. The 1690s saw some revival explained, in part, by an inflow of capital. Some of this can be accounted for by the very cheap land in the north and by abnormally poor harvests and economic conditions in Scotland, which stimulated emigration during that decade. However, much of this capital inflow financed consumption rather than investment. There were high levels of tobacco imports in 1692, 1694 and 1695 – good harvests, particularly in 1694, increased the real income of ordinary people who had a high propensity to spend rather than save. Consumption use of capital rather than saving or investment is a common theme throughout this period. As in Scotland, the linen industry received government assistance with the establishment of the Linen Board in 1711. The degree to which the Board's activities stimulated the growth of the industry is debatable. It certainly regulated the industry, subsidized various projects and disseminated information, but vital to the expansion of the industry was the provision of working capital. Short-term loans, on the security of the cloth or of bills of exchange, were borrowed in Dublin and without the constant stream of working capital supplied by Dublin merchants the industry could not have expanded as rapidly. This was recognized by the Board, which in 1728 opened a White Linen Hall for selling bleached cloth in Dublin, confirming its position as both a financing and marketing centre. In the eighteenth century there was little shortage of capital to finance industrial and communications developments. Merchants' profits were spread across a range of industrial activities. Landowners too, invested in industry particularly in the linen industry in southern Ireland. They provided much of the capital of turnpike trusts, canal companies and other large-scale social overhead capital projects. There was also an inflow of capital from England attracted by belief in Ireland's economic potential and by slightly higher interest rates. Some of this capital was long-term but much short-term working capital was provided for the linen industry. The state contributed throughout the eighteenth century, particularly after 1750, to financing public works and economic development. Parliament established the Linen Board in 1711, financed the Newry Canal and some colliery development. This sense of prosperity masked major structural weaknesses which the dramatic expansion of population after 1750 exacerbated. There had been insufficient investment in agriculture and a serious lack of fertilizer (lime, seaweed or kelp, turf ash or animal dung) which was one of the main stumbling-blocks on the path towards modernization of farming:

> want of manure is the cause always assigned by the poor man for the portion of his land which is annually allowed to remain untilled . . . the tenant of ten acres gets more value from his holding than the tenant of one acre because he is more likely to have manure or the money to purchase it.[9]

Potatoes consumed most of the manure, limiting both total acreage and the potential of other crops in the crop rotation. William Blacker, writing in 1834, believed that Irish landlords would lend money to their tenants to allow them to change to a more capital-intensive cultivation based on green crops. This proved too optimistic but his view that one could measure the degree of improvement in agriculture by the size of manure heaps summarized an important truth about pre-Famine farming. Where improvement did occur it proved very profitable. Arthur Young remarked in the 1770s that while capital invested in English trade and manufactures yielded a return of 5–10 per cent, Irish agriculture promised rates of between 15 and 20 per cent. The Devon Commission of 1845 estimated a return of 15 per cent on investment in drainage and subsoiling. The potential for improvement, both in investment and productivity, was appreciated by contemporaries so why was there no substantial shift to the new techniques? Small-scale farming, lack of knowledge and the high degree of self-sufficiency contributed to this situation as well as lack of agricultural capital. In some parts of Ireland climate and soil conditions were unfavourable to an unmodified adoption of new rotations and crops. Some soils would not take the mangel-wurzel, others were not suitable for turnips and vetches. The 'new husbandry' was seen by some as the vanguard of the capitalistic local gentry and their agents – one result of this was that turnips were stolen from fields as an expression of social protest, while potatoes were not. Important though these were, the major block to agricultural progress was lack of capital. Moving to a new system of rotation – something that could not be done gradually – required investment in soil fertility, drainage and buildings. Lack of capital investment was reflected in the 6.3 million acres or 30 per cent of the total surface area uncultivated, according to the 1841 Census. The Devon Commission estimated that of this 3.75 million acres could be improved and that about 1.5 million acres were suitable for tillage. What kept most of the Irish poor was, however, not the amount of land available to each farmer but the way in which the land was farmed and the scarcity of planned investment.

Many aspects of Ireland's stunted industrialization can be traced back to inadequate capital formation.[10] The major weakness of the Ulster cotton industry was that entrepreneurs were unable or unwilling to plough back profits into the equipment necessary to convert the industry from a domestic to a factory-based activity. The result was a transfer of capital from cottons to linen after 1830. Why then did linen take over the assets from cotton rather than accumulate its own? There was no reason why both industries could not have coexisted. Ulster had sufficient water power, cheap labour and good sites for both industries to prosper. There is little strong evidence that cotton spinning was unprofitable though it did have to compete with the more highly mechanized and capitalized Lancashire industry. Lack of capital meant that the Irish industry was more vulnerable to downturns in the economy in 1816, 1825 and 1837. Lack of fixed capital led to a more expensive and inferior product while lack of working capital deprived firms of resilience during economic slump. Failure to accumulate capital meant that successful and consistent industrialization was made more difficult.

The one exception to the general slowness with which capital accumulated in Ireland was social overhead capital. By the 1840s Ireland was widely reported to have one of the best networks of roads in Europe. This compared incongruously with the poverty of its people, as J. E. Bicheno wrote in 1830: 'the traveller witnesses on every side the appearance of beggary and filth, he feels he is rolling over roads as well-formed and made as he may have passed over in more fortunate countries'.

The same was true, though to a lesser extent, of the Irish canals. However, in both cases, the direct economic effects were limited and arguably some of the capital used on roads and canals could have been used better elsewhere in the economy. Investment in the schooling system represented a large investment in overhead capital particularly after the creation of a National Board of Education in 1831. It was in charge of the formation of a centralized and non-denominational uniform education system to improve on the privately funded education. By the mid-1840s its budget was almost £100,000 per annum and it employed the majority of Ireland's 12,000 teachers. By 1849 the Board controlled 4,321 schools with almost half a million pupils. The overhead capital invested in Ireland between 1700 and 1850 was not insubstantial but it did little to help the economy. It can perhaps best be explained in terms of political and security considerations.

Why was there such a scarcity of capital in Ireland during the eighteenth, and particularly the first half of the nineteenth, centuries? It cannot be attributed to the failure of financial institutions to provide long-term funds. There was a growth in the number of banks in Ireland after 1820 though they were very cautious about large-scale investment in enterprises less certain than government securities. The Agriculture and Commercial Bank ventured into more hazardous projects and promptly failed in the crisis of 1836. In general terms the emphasis throughout the Irish economy was upon working, not fixed, capital. The Devon Commission found that 'the tenant willingly expends any capital he may possess in obtaining the possession of the land and thus leaves himself without the means of tilling it effectually afterwards'. Robert Kanes wrote in 1845 in his *The Industrial Resources of Ireland* that

> England has capital, Ireland has not; therefore England is rich and industrious, and Ireland is poor and idle. But where was the capital when England began to grow rich? It was the industry that made the capital, not the capital the industry . . . when money is made in England it is re-invested in the same or in a similar branch . . . until the amount of capital attains the vast dimensions which we now see.

Low savings led to the low rate of accumulation in the Irish economy.

INVESTMENT DEMANDS

Undercapitalization, particularly in fixed assets, played a major role in the development, or rather, underdevelopment of much of Scotland and Wales during most of the eighteenth century and of Ireland through to 1850. England does not appear to have suffered from this problem between 1700 and 1850. How can this difference be accounted for? In simple terms there was no shortage of savings relative to the demands for productive investment which constrained the process of economic growth in other parts of Britain. There was also a developed system of money and banking before England entered on widespread modernization.

Investment demands in the eighteenth century – given the nature of technology and modest rates of growth – were more modest than for underdeveloped economies today with the massive cost of modern technology. The problem was not lack of savings but establishing the channels through which capital could flow to those groups or individuals who needed credit to support innovation.[11] It is easy to exaggerate the need for capital in industry in the eighteenth century, though this is less true of the mid-nineteenth century. Fixed capital tended to be met by long-term loans, while working capital was usually short-term in character. The former was, as has been noted, a relatively small proportion of the total capital requirement of industry in the eighteenth century. It was the working capital, investment of which was simultaneous with fixed capital, which expanded potential productive capacity to keep pace with increasing demographic demands. It was the lack of working capital that slowed growth in other areas of Great Britain. What raised capital formation to the forefront of the economic problems associated with modernization was that the relatively small industrial demand was only one of a range of demands being made on the national supply of capital at the same time. Competing demands came from improvements in communications, housing and other social overheads and in agriculture. In 1825 eighty canal companies had paid-up capital of £13.2 million and in 1836 the total accumulated capital on English turnpike roads amounted to £32 million. Enclosure became increasingly expensive in the second half of the eighteenth century. Between 1761 and 1801 a conservative estimate of investment in this field was £7 million. Government was also a borrower in the capital market, particularly in long-term borrowing, which continued throughout the period, but an important new feature in the eighteenth-century capital market was the growth of a permanent national debt (Table 9.5).

Table 9.5 National debt and debt charges 1700–1849

Year	National debt (£m) (cumulative)	Debt charges (£m)
1700–9	19.1	1.3
1710–19	41.6	2.7
1720–9	52.1	2.8
1730–9	46.9	2.1
1740–9	77.8	2.4
1750–9	91.3	2.9
1760–9	130.3	4.5
1770–9	153.4	4.8
1780–9	244.3	8.4
1790–9	426.6	11.6
1802–9	599.0	20.0
1810–19	844.3	28.5
1820–9	801.3	30.4
1830–9	788.2	28.9
1840–9	794.3	29.2

Source: P. Mathias *The First Industrial Nation*, Methuen, 2nd edn, 1983, p. 429.

Unlike private investment, government borrowing was largely unproductive. Some went into fixed assets in naval dockyards but overwhelmingly it simply met current expenditure in wartime, much of it overseas. The increase in the national debt and the debt repayments represented drainage of capital from more productive investment. It was, from the point of view of economic growth, capital lost.

The historian T. S. Ashton insisted that the rate of interest was a major influence on the demand for capital and in the eighteenth century there was a gradual but substantial reduction in levels of interest on most sorts of loan. In 1700 rates stood at between 7 and 8 per cent. The rates on government loans were progressively reduced: 5 per cent in 1717, 4 per cent in 1727 and 3 per cent in 1757. Heavier government borrowing after 1760, to finance increasingly frequent wars, tended to push the rates abnormally high more frequently than in the first half of the century. The most favourable period for borrowing in the eighteenth century was in the 1730s and 1740s rather than after 1770 when the most rapid period of economic growth took place. These fluctuations in interest rates affected economic developments in two ways. First, the long-term decline up to 1750 brought certain public works and the more expensive types of enclosure within the limits of feasibility. Secondly, short-term fluctuations may have determined the exact timing of some economic activities, especially after 1770. Ashton's emphasis on the centrality of low interest rates to investment and industrial expansion has not gone without criticism. Massive injections of capital are no guarantee that industries will be productive. Factory owners in the early nineteenth century increased output simply by increasing hours. Reorganizing existing resources can have the same result. Increased agricultural output could be achieved without more land or new machinery by introducing a new rotation of crops.

INSTITUTIONALIZING INVESTMENT – TOWARDS A BANKING SYSTEM

The Bank of England

The eighteenth century saw an increase in the institutionalizing of capital accumulation and investment. The most important of the new institutions that opened channels for the flow of capital were the banks. Three main groups emerged in the English banking system in the eighteenth century: the Bank of England, the London private banks and the country bankers.[12] The Bank of England was founded in 1694 by charter, with a capital of £1.2 million (of which £0.5 million was in paper notes issued on their credit), with raising money to finance William III's wars as its main objective. By 1695 it was transferring foreign exchange and from 1700 storing imported gold against which it made loans. In 1708 it was given the monopoly of joint-stock banking which restricted other English banking to partnerships (of not more than six partners) and family concerns. This position lasted until 1826. The Bank played a key role in reducing the national debt in the 1720s and 1730s and by the 1750s its relationship with the Treasury had become formalized. P. Deane says that 'Beginning as a 'speculation' with an uncertain future, it had become a national institution, though not yet a central bank with control over the money supply.'[13]

Until 1793 £10 was the lowest denomination of note the Bank could issue and until 1797 and after 1821 notes were convertible on demand into cash. This threat of convertibility and consequent 'runs' on the Bank acted as a check against over-issue. Notes were largely confined to London, though they became popular in Lancashire after 1770. Technically the eighteenth-century pound was based on silver but gradually relative short- age of silver throughout continental Europe led to merchants obtaining coins which were sold abroad for gold (foreign silver prices were higher than English Mint prices). This debased English sterling and increasingly England was on a gold standard, though this was not legitimated until 1816. Other kinds of money were in common use by 1750. Cheques date from the seventeenth century but did not become common until after 1800. Trade tokens were used by several manufacturing firms to get round the shortage of silver and copper coins. More important were banknotes, which were issued by private London and country banks as well as by the Bank of England. The note issue by London private banks never formed an important part of their business and had died out almost completely by 1770.

The amount of money in circulation is of major importance to economic development. If the supply of money does not expand in line with the growth in trade then prices will tend to stagnate or fall. Producers will be discouraged from expanding their business and entrepreneurs prevented from obtaining resources necessary to innovate. Yet, if money is too freely available inflation will occur as prices rise and speculative investment is drawn into businesses that benefit most from price increases. In the eight- eenth and early nineteenth century the volume of specie in circulation depended largely on the supply of gold at the Bank of England and this in turn depended on the world price of gold and England's balance of trade. The essence of trading policy was to prevent an outflow of gold by keeping exports and re-exports higher than imports.

Table 9.6 Money stock in circulation and means of payment (£m)

	1688	1750	1775	1800	1811	1821	1831	1844
Specie	10	15	16	20	15	18	30	36
Bank notes	2	5	10	25	45	32	29	28.5
Deposits	*	*	*	5	15	25	40	80.5
Total money (M1)	12	20	26	50	75	75	99	145
Other	8	20	37	115	140	76	67	75
Means of payment (M2)	20	40	63	165	215	151	166	220

* – no data available

Source: R. E. Cameron *Banking in the Early Stages of Industrialization*, Oxford University Press, 1967, p. 42.

During the eighteenth century limits on the extent that credit could be given were dependent on the volume of deposits and the state of confidence in the banks (Table 9.6). The limit to expansion of credit was set by the amount of gold in the country. In 1797 cash payments were suddenly suspended and the Bank of England was freed from its obligation to convert its notes to gold. The country banks had no option but to follow suit. Contemporaries blamed the Bank for over-expanding credit and for the inflationary price rise that had occurred since 1794. Certainly the poor harvest of 1795 increased imports of grain which was paid for by an outflow of gold. The market price of gold rose above Mint prices. Government military and naval spending as well as subsidies for foreign allies all pushed up the balance of payment problems. The abortive French landing at Fishguard in 1797 – itself of no military importance – was sufficient to turn a growing lack of confidence into a panic run on the country banks, which in turn presented their Bank of England notes for repayment. It was not until 1821 that the gap between Mint and market prices of gold came close enough together to allow the resumption of cash payments.

London's private banks

The London private banks were not, after 1770, engaged in the creation of currency, in contrast to both the Bank of England and the country banks. The number of London banks rose during the second half of the eighteenth century from under 30 in 1750 to 50 in 1770 and 70 by 1800. Their main business came from discounting bills of exchange for merchants and industrialists and making short-term loans. After 1770 they acted as agencies for the country bankers, sending down supplies of gold and silver and Bank of England notes from London. This agency business was the main institutional link between London and the financial structure of the provinces after 1770. It exposed London bankers to the risk of involvement in a provincial panic if too heavily committed – in 1825 the London bank of Pole, Thornton & Co went bankrupt largely because it had 43 correspondent banks.

Country banks

There were only 12 country banks in 1750 but their number outside London increased dramatically in the second half of the century: 120 in 1784, 290 in 1797, 370 by 1800 and between 650 and 780 in 1810. Numbers expanded particularly during periods of easy credit conditions: in the 1750s, between 1789 and 1793 and then more generally during the French Wars when the Bank went off gold. This certainly fed the surges of economic activity experienced at these times. Many merchants, manufacturers and successful farmers simply added dealing in money and credit to their other successful activities – Fosters in Cambridge were millers and corn merchants, Lloyds in Birmingham traded in iron, the Gurneys in Norwich were worsted manufacturers. They offered a link between a locality – very few had branches outside their region – and the credit potential of London. Initially they were note-issuers but gradually many grew into deposit bankers. Confidence by the communities they served was essential for the country banks but they were vulnerable to economic conditions. Between 1809 and 1830 there were 311 bankruptcies of which 179 took place in two crisis periods – 1814–16 and 1824–6.

A weakened credit structure

The essential weakness of the credit structure of the country banks was brought home when the speculative boom of 1823 deteriorated into financial collapse in 1825. There was a burst of company promotions, heavy foreign lending on dubious South American mining projects and many unpaid-for exports. The boom burst with disastrous consequences for many country banks, seventy-three of which suspended payment in England and Wales, and the country was almost forced off the gold standard. The result was legislation in 1826 which reduced the influence of the country banks, prohibited the issue of notes under £5, permitted the establishment of joint-stock banks with more than six partners (except within a 65-mile radius of London) and authorized the Bank of England to set up its own branches throughout the country. Joint-stock banks were allowed, after 1833, within the area round and in London as long as they did not issue notes. This legislation, though it broke the Bank's monopoly, paradoxically strengthened its position by giving it the virtual monopoly of note issue in and around London and allowing it to establish branches. The bank rate was kept at 4 per cent though the Bank still occasionally altered it temporarily, as in 1836, 1839 and 1847.

The 1839 crisis was caused by the flow of gold from the Bank to pay for grain imports, aided by a continental panic which led to short-term loans to London being repatriated. Confidence was only restored by putting up the bank rate and mobilizing a £2 million credit with the Bank of France. The role of foreign exchange as the vulnerable part of the system and an important source of financial crisis was increasingly recognized in the first few decades of the nineteenth century. 'Bullionists' or the currency school argued that it was only when money was lent out on speculative ventures that danger of over-issue arose. It was necessary, they believed, to control note issue and reduce domestic credit. The banking school, by contrast, maintained that adverse exchange rates generally arose from independent sources like bad harvests or abnormal foreign demand for gold. Contracting domestic credit did not solve these problems and it was necessary for banks to have sufficient reserves to allow market conditions to return to normal. It was when banks reduced credit without reference to domestic considerations that financial crises occurred.

The Bank Charter Act of 1844 saw the triumph of the currency school, though they had already won the argument within the Bank. After 1839 the Directors of the Bank had themselves proposed to limit note issue and accepted the connection between issue, prices and exchange rates. Provincial note issuing had already begun to decline and the proportion of Bank of England notes in circulation had been growing before 1844. The issue of notes by country banks was now restrained by preventing any bank – existing or new – that had not issued notes from doing so. This amounted to a statement that note issue would eventually become the monopoly of the Bank. The Act restricted the Bank by allowing it to issue only £14 million of notes uncovered by gold (fiduciary), above which all notes had to be covered pound for pound by gold. The issue and banking departments were separated and gold reserves covering note issue were not allowed to be used to help the banking department when it was under strain. Ironically the 1844 Act was so strict that some of its provisions had soon to be disregarded. During the crisis of 1847 the Directors paid out almost all of their reserves in the banking department while the vaults were stacked with gold covering their notes. The Treasury gave permission for the Bank to draw on these, though it ultimately proved unnecessary. But in 1857 permission was again granted and on this occasion used. The controversy between the currency and banking schools concentrated on note issue without realizing that its importance to the economy was declining. They took no account of the great increase in bank deposits, overdrafts and the use of cheques which caused banknotes to be used less. The 1844 Act said nothing about deposits and the Bank soon realized how much influence it could wield over the money supply and on other banks through their management. The 1844 Act remained the statutory basis of British banking until 1914 but in practice its basic principle became a dead letter.

Banking and industrial development

It is important to stress the contribution of banks in financing industrial development in this period and few historians now agree with the minimalist view of their role. Discounting bills of exchange by banks certainly released mercantile and industrial capital for fixed investment. It was, however, in the area of short-term loans that banks played a major role. London bankers were generally more cautious than provincial banks with regard to long-term loans, as the number of bankruptcies indicated. Most fixed capital was contributed by working partners supplemented often by relatives and friends. Loans on mortgages from wealthy merchants with whom the new firm would trade were also an important factor. Expansion was largely self-financed by ploughing back the major part of the profits. Removal of the parliamentary sanction for joint-stock companies – established by the Bubble Act of 1720 – and subsequent legislation in 1856 and

1862 ended the restrictions on limited liability companies and opened up financial opportunities. Railway expansion, generally funded by local people, brought capital in from all over Britain and during the 1840s the City played a prominent role in developments. Despite this, self-financing remained the major way of raising capital throughout this period. Banks, certainly until the 1820s, were arguably the product of economic expansion, rather than the reverse.

The increase in the availability of capital permitted growth to occur. It was not in itself a cause of growth unless it can be shown that a shortage of capital had previously inhibited growth. There is little evidence for this in 1700. The fall in interest rates in the late seventeenth and early eighteenth centuries was possibly the result of a growing surplus in the supply of capital over demand for it. The low rates of interest through to 1850 indicate that, although there was increased accumulation of capital because of the widening of markets for consumer goods, there was still ample capital available. In these circumstances increased availability and use of previously underemployed capital was little more than the removal of constraint upon growth. It was a necessary precondition of accelerated growth, not a cause of this acceleration.

NOTES

1 M. M. Poston 'Recent Trends in the Accumulation of Capital', 1935, in F. Crouzet (ed.) *Capital Formation in the Industrial Revolution*, Methuen, 1972, p. 72.

2 On the capitalistic aspects of capital see R. J. Holton *The Transition from Feudalism to Capitalism*, Macmillan, 1985.

3 On 'social overhead' capital in communications see the discussion in chapters 7 and 11.

4 On 'export' capital see the discussion in chapter 8.

5 P. Mathias *The First Industrial Nation*, Methuen, 2nd edn, 1983, pp. 130–1.

6 C. H. Feinstein 'Capital Formation in Great Britain', in P. Mathias and M. M. Postan (eds) *Cambridge Economic History of Europe* Vol. VII (1), Cambridge University Press, 1978, pp. 28–96.

7 N. Crafts 'British Economic Growth 1700–1831: A Review of the Evidence', *Economic History Review* 2nd Series, (2).

8 On the development of Scottish banking see S. G. Checkland *Scottish Banking. A History 1695–1973*, Collins, 1975.

9 *Parliamentary Papers* Vol. xxx–xvxiv 'Reports of the Commissioners of Inquiry into the Condition of the Poorer Classes in Ireland', Vol. xxxiii, p. 84.

10 The question of capital scarcity in Ireland is best approached in J. Mokyr's emotively titled *Why Ireland Starved*, Allen & Unwin, 1985, chapter 6, especially pp. 159–94.

11 On the issue of capital and credit see P. Mathias 'Capital, Credit and Enterprise in the Industrial Revolution', in his *The Transformation of England*, Methuen, 1979, pp. 88–115, M. W. Flinn *Origins of the Industrial Revolution*, Longman, 1966 and F. Crouzet (ed.) op. cit.

12 The central works on banking are R. F. Cameron *Banking in the Early Stages*

of *Industrialisation*, Oxford University Press, 1967 and L. S. Presnell *Country Banking in the Industrial Revolution*, Oxford University Press, 1956.

13 P. Deane *The First Industrial Revolution*, Cambridge University Press, 1965, p. 168.

10 The social and institutional bases for economic change

> In most other countries, society presents hardly anything but a void between an ignorant labouring population, and a needy and and profligate nobility . . . but with us the space between the ploughman and the peer, is crammed with circle after circle, fitted in the most admirable manner for sitting upon each other, for connecting the former with the latter, and for rendering the whole perfect in cohesion, strength and beauty.[1]

This nostalgic Tory view of a fast disappearing society was written in the 1820s. The unity of the 'celestial spheres' had their earthly counterpart in the social notion of 'chain of being'. If history is more than narrative then historians have to explain how a society with views like this could generate an 'industrial revolution'. How could an institutional structure create wealth on a scale not seen before the eighteenth century? The openness of British eighteenth-century society, the freedom of business association and capital accumulation and the wide diffusion of Newtonian views of events 'obeying' natural laws have all entered into the discussion on the 'causes' of the industrial revolution. Putting these three generalizations into juxtaposition suggests that there is some empirical and logical link between them. This quest can lead historians to conclude that all causes are connected with each other and that the more causes which can be identified the better the explanation. This chapter is concerned with examining the social and institutional bases for economic changes and with assessing how far they enabled those changes to occur.

EXPLANATIONS OF CHANGE

People do not live in isolation. They live with others with whom they act and react. Changes on the scale of an industrial revolution consisted of modifications in the ways in which a large mass of individuals behaved and were initiated by a smaller number of other individuals with business and technical acumen.[2] But why did people accept changes that had such a dramatic effect on their lives? It is important not to exaggerate the extent to which any one generation experienced change in this dramatic sense between 1700 and 1820, though between 1820 and 1850 the sense of change was much more apparent. Change 'in slow motion' and the persistence of many older industries calls into question some of the more extreme notions of social and economic discontinuity. The sense of continuity with a past, variously mythologized, was, throughout much of this period, a major influence on how individuals perceived their 'worlds'. And their 'worlds' were different even though contemporary. The response of one community to change differed radically from a second. In some areas new technology was welcomed but in others it was smashed. How can historians explain this? Explanations vary but there is always the danger that

> snatching from the enormous and complex mass of facts called reality a few, simple, easily manageable key points . . . when put together in some cunning way, becomes for certain purposes a substitute for the reality itself.[3]

British society

What was there about British society in the eighteenth and early nineteenth centuries which enabled it to underpin an economic revolution? Not everyone would go as far as Harold Perkin:

> No one today would deny that the Industrial Revolution, that 'vast increase of natural resources, labour, capital and enterprise' which began in Britain in the late eighteenth century . . . was a social revolution, at least in its effects.[4]

Social revolution 'in its effects' it may well have been but not in its origins. What was there about British society which enabled it to undergo an economic revolution?[5] By 1700 English society was remarkably capitalist in character and organization. An aristocracy, Perkin calls it 'open', dominated the landed economy and, through its control of this, monopolized political power. They were not 'seigneurs' living off custumal dues and labour services as many of their continental contemporaries did. They owned their land and at least in the south-east were able to exploit it as they pleased – farming it commercially, renting it to large tenants on long or short leases, developing it for building purposes or mining it for minerals which elsewhere were reserved to the Crown. Customary rights were not so easily extinguished as this implies and in the north and west customary tenure was much more resilient. This economy was serviced, not by a repressed peasantry with few rights and many duties, but by landless labourers earning wages for work on other people's land or materials. Wales, Scotland and Ireland were, to a lesser or greater extent, continental in structure. Between the aristocracy and the landless labourers lay a long and carefully graduated hierarchy, layer upon layer of status and occupational group. It was an unequal society but one in which deference and patronage ensured that reciprocal responsibilities existed, were acted upon and gave a sense of mutual social responsibility. Status was dependent on property and an individual's position in the hierarchy. This is not to say that there were no social tensions, and spontaneous riot against high bread prices, machinery or unpopular employers were endemic. But these occurred within the framework of a 'moral economy', the ideological basis of paternalism.

English society was a fluid one. The price of absolute ownership of land meant that anyone with sufficient wealth could purchase an estate and join the landowning ranks with the same rights, responsibilities and status. There was not just upward mobility but mobility from within the aristocracy, with younger sons being sent into the world to earn their living in trade or the professions. The result was a two-way flow of people and wealth – an important distinction from the Continent. The most successful merchants, professional and businessmen in each generation were funnelled off into the landed gentry – success brought wealth, which was necessary for a higher place on the social ladder, though this was generally insufficient to ensure social acceptance immediately, such was the snobbery of 'old money'. This openness and freedom of social mobility and lack of legal constraints gave English society the paradoxical character of dynamic stability. Harold Perkin comments speculatively that

> It syphoned off in every generation the newly rich and talented of the middle ranks, who might otherwise have been socially frustrated and politically discontented. France, where social climbing was frustrated, had a political revolution. Britain, where it was not, had an industrial one.[6]

It was this society which created the circumstances which made economic change easier. Compare, for example, the problem of improving agriculture in Ireland with its fragmented system of tenure with the larger and more easily amalgamated units of land in England. Is this sufficient to explain why change occurred more quickly in England than Ireland? Certainly, without the active co-operation of the owners of land, in Parliament and the land market, the preconditions of industrialization in farming, mining, transport and town development would not have been present.

During the eighteenth century and at least until 1830 the key to economic growth was elastic home demand for consumer goods. Perkin argues that the key to that demand lay in 'social emulation' or 'keeping up with the Joneses'.[7] The *British Magazine* in 1763 stated that 'The present rage of imitating the manners of high-life hath spread itself so far among the gentlefolks of lower-life, that in a few years we shall probably have no common people at all.'[8] The nature of British society enabled this emulation to occur in a way that continental societies did not.

Individuals respond

Accepting that economic change was a drama enacted on a crowded stage and that success was a result of collective effort it is necessary to examine why certain individuals became involved in improving the potential of the economy. What motivated individuals to invest or invent or modify existing practices in the eighteenth and early nineteenth centuries? In simple terms individuals change either because they are compelled to (by circumstances or some coercive power) or because they can see some benefit (profits, fame, altruism) in changing for themselves. Central to change were the entrepreneurs. There is some difference between historians over defining entrepreneurs, but few would broadly disagree with the following criteria developed by Michael Flinn:

(a) entrepreneurs organized production;
(b) entrepreneurs brought together capital (their own or others') and labour;
(c) entrepreneurs selected the geographical site for operations, the technologies to be used, bargained for raw materials and found outlets for products;

while Charles Wilson maintains that entrepreneurs were often financiers, capitalists, work managers, merchants and salesmen. Three main explanations for the role of the individual, particularly the entrepreneur, have been identified. The first examines the social environment in which people operated. It sees increases in entrepreneurial activity as resulting either from changes in the level of tolerance accorded to deviance from the traditional norms of entrepreneurial behaviour or from changing attitudes to economic tasks in a broad social context. The second recognizes that, though of vital importance, entrepreneurship has to be seen in relation to the conditioning of the labour force into the discipline of modern industrial organization with its high degree of division of labour. The third considers the capacity of a society to increase the number of energetic and innovative entrepreneurs and inventors in its total population.

The social environment

The first of these directions rests on theoretical foundations laid down by the American sociologist Talcott Parsons in the early 1950s. His work has led to the development of two ways of examining entrepreneurship in the context of economic developments. First, there was a change in the way in which people viewed status from one where it was ascribed to one where it was achieved – status had to do with what you did and achieved not who you were and had much to do with the openness of social mobility. Secondly there was a shift in the distribution of economically productive tasks. Workers became more specialized and there was an increased division of labour. Parsons also considered the importance of the changing relationship between entrepreneurs and the society in which they operated, where particular social roles were limited by a particular traditional set of sanctions. These sanctions existed to discourage deviance from the established norms and fell into two categories. Formal sanctions were prescribed legally or institutionally and were part of the whole process of legitimating social structures. Early eighteenth-century attitudes, for example, on usury and apprenticeship were legally enforceable and part of a system which maintained a moral fairness in social relationships. Is it possible to explain the rapid expansion of the cotton industry in Lancashire after 1750 in terms of the lack of formal sanctions, in the form of textile guilds, in this area? Informal sanctions were enforced by social opinions and attitudes. They are *de facto* rather than *de jure* in that they do not have the force of law. In the eighteenth century the Quakers would cut off from membership a Friend who had deviated to the extent of going bankrupt, a form of sanction experienced by Charles Lloyd, uncle of the founder of the bank, in the 1720s. The major problem with this approach lies in its limitation to certain situations since these particular social changes did not occur in every major economic advance. Michael Flinn concluded, perhaps rather harshly, that

> The gradual nature of the British development would have allowed these social changes to have occurred in a period remote from the take-off. They may, in other words, have occurred, say, as an aspect of the transition from Rostow's traditional society to his pre-industrial stage, rather than of the transition from the pre-industrial conditions to the take-off.[9]

Entrepreneurs and workers

The second approach maintains that a society, however vigorously led by entrepreneurs, will not advance economically unless it can persuade or compel its labour force to fall easily and unprotestingly into the discipline and rigidity of large-scale industrial production. It has been argued that educational development in the form of the Charity and Sunday schools, was the most significant and influential force being focused on the social attitudes of large sections of the working population during the eighteenth and early nineteenth centuries and that the introduction of the monitorial system after 1810 continued this process. Through education, it is maintained, social control was exerted over the aims and ideologies of the industrial labour force.[10] In 1786 Beilby Porteus, Bishop of London, said that

> a well-informed and intelligent people, more particularly a people well acquainted with the sacred writings, will always be more orderly, more

decent, more humane, more virtuous, more religious, more obedient
to their superiors, than a people totally devoid of all instruction and
all education.[11]

Charity, Sunday and monitorial schools were intended clearly to strengthen the educational barriers between social groups. Education was viewed
in static terms of inculcating a sense of social obedience, humility and
conformity – a sense of one's proper place in the social order with an
absence of social or economic climbing – functional in a collective manner.

There was a sharp contrast between these aspirations and those of the
Mechanics' Institute movement from the 1820s and the notion of 'self-
help', popularized by Samuel Smiles in the middle of the century which
were individualist in an aggressively upward-looking sense. Just how far
this succeeded is contentious, though it must be said that a suitable, if not
always compliant, labour force patently was created to service Britain's
industrial growth.

Quality and quantity

The third explanation centres on the quantity and quality of entrepreneurs
and innovators. In the early 1900s Max Weber suggested a causal link
between the 'Protestant ethic' and the 'spirit of capitalism', that there was
a direct connection between the economic development of the Protestant
world and the doctrinal attitudes of its churches.[12] Though Weber was
concerned primarily with the Reformation, in the 1920s R. H. Tawney
moved the debate nearer the industrial revolution in his *Religion and the
Rise of Capitalism*. For Tawney the crucial point in the spread of capitalism
was not the Reformation itself but the emergence of Puritan sects in the
late sixteenth and particularly seventeenth centuries. After 1660 members
of these sects – Presbyterians, Congregationalists, Baptists, Unitarians
and Quakers – began to occupy a disproportionately large place in the
ranks of the entrepreneurs. Everett Hagen has shown that, of a random
selection of principal entrepreneurs, 49 per cent of those whose religious
affiliations could be ascertained were Dissenters. Tawney argued that they
saw work as an end in itself, as a moral duty; that labour and enterprise
were identified with service to God and that, in the eighteenth century,
this sense of aggressive capitalist activity was inculcated through the broad
and more practical and relevant curriculums of Dissenting Academies and
the Scottish universities. Tawney's arguments have undergone considerable criticism – for example, that the Protestant sects had an extremely
cautious approach to money-making and that the ideas of thrift and dili-
gence applied to personal consumption not to an aggressive work ethic –
and the direct causal link put forward by Weber has been called into
question for the eighteenth century.

So how can the increase in the proportionate number of effective innovators in society be explained and why did Dissenters form such a significant number? David McClelland in *The Achieving Society*, Princeton University Press, 1961, sees human actions as resulting from the pursuit and the satisfaction of a range of psychological needs. But why do certain individuals pursue their needs with more intensity and drive than others? Individual motivation is determined by various things: the need for affiliation, a sense of 'belonging', for recognition, approval, friendship; the need for autonomy achieved through the application of the mastery of knowledge to specific problems; the need for order; and the need for achievement. It is the need for achievement which seems to have most relevance for economic history. McClelland is able to establish that a high need for achievement is closely correlated with the principal 'entrepreneurial' attitudes – special attitudes towards risk-taking, willingness to expend energies and innovate and a readiness to accept responsibilities and make decisions. This may not result in wealth or status but it does lead to the satisfaction of success. Achievement motivation, as part of an individual's personality, is the result largely of an upbringing in which there was conscious training in self-reliance and mastery and avoidance of the extremes of allowing the children to make their own way (leading to neglect or indifference) or excessive authoritarianism. The optimal conditions for this were, McClelland argues, found among Protestants. He believes that these conditions were found particularly among the Wesleyan Methodists. There are, however, major problems with this in that Methodists were authoritarian in their attitude to the young and McClelland's index of need for achievement upturns around 1700 while Methodism did not take off until the 1740s. On the other hand there is some evidence that the numerically smaller Quakers, Congregationalists and Unitarians, who did adopt a liberated child-rearing approach, produced a disproportionate share of entrepreneurs.[13]

Everett Hagen examines the issue of individuals through the reaction of minority or 'subordinate groups' to the 'withdrawal of status'. This removal of status respect involves, he argues, the banning of some activity vital to the sense of status for the minority group. This is followed by two stages of reaction. First, there is 'retreatism' by which the normalized standards of behaviour and action are abandoned. This leads, Hagen maintains, to children denying the importance of their parents' traditional values. This is followed by 'the emergence of innovational personality', a reaction usually by the mother to the erratic and 'retreatist' attitude of the father. The mother substitutes the son for her husband or father in her own pattern of values and aspirations and requires from him the promise of achievement she sought in vain. This, says Hagen, will lead to the development early in life of the personality traits of the entrepreneur or inventor. Hagen can be criticized in two major ways. First, he makes assertions about what will happen without any real evidence to back them up. Secondly, the chronology of the move from 'retreatism' to 'innovative creativity' is unclear. There is a gap in chronology between the beginnings of 'retreatism' brought about by the ecclesiastical settlement after the Restoration in 1660 and the traditional starting point for the industrial revolution in the 1760s or 1780s. However, if the point at which change 'in slow motion' began is pushed back to the early eighteenth century the causal connections are somewhat clearer.

Weber, McClelland and Hagen show both the benefits and dangers of applying models based on sociological and psychological concepts to a specific historical problem. These models can inform historians about why people may have acted as they did but have to be tested against the available evidence. So who were these individuals? They were the people who saw economic opportunities and grasped them, who realized the potential of some resources that had lain latent or who used their own wit and resource. Most entrepreneurs were not pioneers of major innovations or inventions but realized how best to utilize them and, more importantly, how to market the goods produced. They often bypassed local merchants and public markets by buying raw materials to their own specifications direct from importers.

Fieldens, the Todmorden cotton spinners, had their own buying agent in America in the early nineteenth century. These entrepreneurs also had control over the marketing of finished goods through their awareness of the changing demands of the consumer. Their control was often from raw material to market or construction. Thomas Cubitt, for example, was in 1817 the organizer and permanent employer of over 1,000 skilled and unskilled building labourers. He had centralized stores and workshops and his efficiency could be seen in the steady flow of large contracts for building barracks during the Napoleonic War and city building after 1815. This he achieved without any major technical innovation. Despite what Weber, McClelland and Hagen have written, it is difficult to make any real generalization about the social origins of entrepreneurs. François Crouzet's study, *The Early Industrialists: The Problem of Origins*, Cambridge University Press, 1985, is the most recent and comprehensive analysis of the issue. He found that most entrepreneurs came from the middle ranks of society, often from a mercantile background, and that movement was within the middle classes rather than across classes. The Cokes of Holkham, later the earls of Leicester, Jethro Tull, Robert Bakewell were all entrepreneurs in farming. The bishops of Durham and the duke of Bridgewater were entrepreneurs in coal mining; Roebuck, Bolton and Walker in iron.

The capital for entrepreneurial innovation came from oneself, one's family and friends. Kinship was the organizational principle of most business in the eighteenth century. In religious terms the notion of kinship can be applied more readily to the Dissenting sects than to the Anglican church. It was this that explains the scale of Dissenting intrusion into the ranks of the entrepreneurs. Success for these Dissenting entrepreneurs contained the seeds of potential decay. Success brought wealth and attention and, perhaps most importantly, acceptance into the establishment through the buying of landed property as a resassertion of status. This sometimes led to a change in values and the potential loss of achievement motivation. Samuel Whitbread, for example, committed suicide in 1815 as a near-bankrupt after letting the family brewing business slide while he pursued a career as a Whig parliamentarian. The importance of British society to entrepreneurs was that it did not prevent them from using or misusing their talents and motivation.

SERVICING THE ECONOMY

By 1801 perhaps one in three people in Britain was involved in servicing the economy and society in some way or other.[14] Some services like the law, medicine and the Church, domestic service and transport and distribution existed well before 1700, though they did not make up a particularly large part of the economy. Their productivity was low and cost to the consumer high. Professional services were generally available only to the rich, though their necessity for other sections of society, who could not afford them, was increasingly recognized after 1750. In some cases the cost of services, as in the case of transport, was a constraint on growth. Most service needs were self-provided in a rural setting. Much education was provided at home. For medicine herbal remedies and potions often sufficed. Simple goods could be obtained from pedlars and hawkers or at the periodic fairs and markets or by arrangement with local craftsmen. Services were concentrated in urban settings and only in the largest towns did a wide range of professional and specialist basic services exist. This situation changed in the eighteenth century when services became more numerous, accessible and specialized.[15] Services which had formerly been carried out within the framework of existing enterprises developed as separate entities. This was fostered by the increased scale and regularity of business operations. The economy became more complicated, raising demands for lawyers, accountants, engineers and surveyors as well as for better educational provision. Demographic growth and increased urbanization meant that the traditional means of law enforcement, public health provision, street maintenance and institutional entertainment were called into question and alternative services considered. It is important to ask whether these were a response to the demands of expanding industries and agriculture or whether their development enabled economic change to occur more easily. These two perspectives are quite compatible. The initial development of an industry, say pottery, resulted in demands for better managerial control of all aspects of the industry, the employment of salesmen to travel the country obtaining orders, insurance to protect the pottery factory and financial services through banking. As a result of this initial response industries were able to expand more effectively and efficiently.

The role of services

R. M. Hartwell has analysed the role of services during the industrial revolution under four broad headings:

> as part of the necessary *social overhead capital* without which industrialisation would not have occurred, or would have occurred more slowly; as part of those *intermediate services* between producer and producer, and producer and consumer . . . and as part of those *cultural services* which expanded with the increasing wealth of society, and with its enlarged demand for culture and entertainment.[16]

He also identifies personal or domestic services. He divides the service sector along functional lines in the following way:

I Social Overhead Services:
   (i) Transport and Communications.
   (ii) Government and Public Utilities
   (iii) Learned Professions.
II Intermediate Services:
   (i) Retail and Wholesale Trade.
   (ii) Finance (Banking, Insurance, Brokerage, etc.)
   (iii) Land Agents, Auctioneers, etc.
III Cultural and Entertainment Services
   (i) Entertainment and Sport.
   (ii) Cultural Services (Music, Art, Libraries, etc.)
IV Domestic Services.[17]

The role of transport and communications and finance have already been touched upon.[18] Three aspects of the service sector will now be considered: education, the law and the development of a consumer society.

Economic growth and education

Education – both in schools and as technical training in firms – is a vital process of 'human capital formation'. It was, and is, in many ways more than just a service. Sociologists link education with levels of social mobility, political theorists with democracy and economists with economic growth. There are, as R. M. Hartwell stated, two problems:

> to determine the character and quantity of education before the industrial revolution and whether or not changes in that education were important in bringing about the industrial revolution; to determine,

once the industrial revolution had begun, how, and how much, education was necessary to sustain growth.[19]

Historians have differed on the extent to which they have perceived education as playing a role in economic growth. It may contribute directly to economic performance by improving the technical quality of the workforce. Indirectly it may induce a sense of discipline and order in which change can occur and thrive. Christopher Hill and Peter Laslett[20] maintain that better education was a necessary prerequisite for the industrial revolution in two senses. First it provided the literacy essential for an industrializing society and secondly, it reinforced the duties of humility and submission to superiors. Hill does, however, suggest that education could be a subversive activity. This essential paradox between 'control' and potential 'liberation' underlay much of the contemporary debate on education. Eric Hobsbawm, by contrast, argues for its unimportance to Britain's needs during the industrial revolution.[21] N. Smelser maintains that education lagged behind or deteriorated in comparison with economic growth or the growth of population and that

> education was justly a subject of concern in the early nineteenth century, because it had lagged so noticeably behind other institutions in the English industrial revolution. The Sunday Schools had surged, as had the National Schools of Bell and Lancaster, but both contemporaries and historians agree that educational standards for the young were extremely low in these years.[22]

Improving literacy

The general levels of literacy in the period between 1700 and 1850 were relatively high. The major problem for historians lies in what 'literacy' actually means. If it is taken to mean the ability to write one's name – the lowest level of literacy – then, according to W. L. Sargant's work in 1867, 51 per cent of couples in England and Wales marrying between 1754 and 1762 were literate and 54 per cent between 1799 and 1804. His figures have been confirmed by several local studies. This upward trend in literacy continued until 1850. Laurence Sterne saw this upsurge in literacy as underlying the process of industrialization and believed that it was partly due to the demands for a literate workforce for an industrializing society. So during the period of economic change levels of literacy did continue to increase in general terms. There are, however, grounds for questioning this optimistic view of literacy for England as a whole. There was significant regional variation. Levels were highest in the market towns and old regional centres with their commercial trades dependent upon numeracy and writing abilities. They were lower in the expanding industrial centres, falling in the late eighteenth and early decades of the nineteenth centuries as growing population swamped the available provision of schools. It was into this vacuum that the Sunday schools were able to fit. There were important differences in literacy among different occupations. It was universal among the gentry, the professions and retailers and lower among servants, miners and labourers. Literacy among *all* social groups was not a prerequisite for economic change.

Improvements in literacy were largely the result of an increase in elementary education. In England and Wales Charity schools were established after 1698 by the Society for Promoting Christian Knowledge largely run by Anglican clergymen and until the 1760s were a dynamic area of growth in education. They were reinforced after 1780 by the Sunday schools. The movement began in Gloucester but expanded rapidly. By 1851 there were 23,135 schools with over 2 million enrolled children. Thomas Lacquer argues, in his *Religious Respectability: Sunday Schools and Working Class Culture 1780–1850*, that three-quarters of all working-class children aged 5–15 were attending these schools by 1851. The extent to which Sunday schools sustained the literacy rate has, however, been questioned. After 1800 many schools ceased teaching writing and Lacquer's view that they created a working-class culture of respectability and self-reliance has been criticized by those who see them as middle-class conservative institutions for the reform of working-class children from above.

This voluntary principle was continued into the nineteenth century with the establishment of the National and British School Societies. There was some continuum in elementary education for the poor in many areas of the country though this could easily break down in the areas of dynamic demographic adjustments. In Wales Griffith Jones began the circulating schools movement after 1730. In order to win souls he believed that people should be taught to read the Bible. This meant short-term schooling in a given area. Itinerant schoolmasters, often teaching in Welsh, taught both children and adults – to read using the Bible and Anglican Book of Common Prayer as readers. This movement certainly provided an intellectual stimulus to the Welsh language and laid the foundations for adult education. It created an interest in education which Thomas Charles could build on after 1779 with Welsh Sunday schools. In Scotland, by contrast to England and Wales where education was based on voluntary principles, there had been vigorous attempts in the 1690s by the Scots Parliament to establish universal schooling and this led to higher literacy figures.

How precisely literacy was translated into economic change is difficult to say. The demands made upon an individual's education in many occupations did not change between 1700 and 1850. But what did change was the amount of reading material available – between 1700 and 1760 the provincial newspaper became an important medium for education and politics among all levels of society and printed materials generally were more available. People became more informed and, from the 1770s, more critical through the medium of literacy. This liberating impulse was paralleled by the force of social control exerted by Griffith Jones, the Wesleys and others through determining the type of literature people read.

There was an important distinction between the voluntary schools, which were largely concerned with inculcating basic skills and proper social attitudes, and institutions concerned with training in particular occupational skills. In many outworking occupations this training took place in the home. Straw-plaiting and lace-making were both taught in this way in Bedfordshire, Buckinghamshire and parts of Oxfordshire until well into the nineteenth century. Apprenticeship was in the same category, though it fell into disrepute in some trades after the 1750s. It generally applied to a more 'skilled' occupation and was a process that lasted several years.

This crudely instrumental attitude to education among the bulk of society can be contrasted with the broader curricular objectives of education for the male minority. Girls from the middle and upper levels of society by contrast often received little more than basic educational skills and what education they had was to prepare them for the running of the home. For girls education was certainly concerned with social control and, literally, with social reproduction. There were about 500 endowed grammar schools in England and Wales, and every large Scottish burgh had its own. The strict idea of a classical education had been under increasing attack for its lack of relevance since the 1690s and some grammar schools did respond to contemporary educational needs. This was not limited to Scotland as has often been assumed and was, if anything, motivated by a wish for profit. Increased competition between private schools and academies meant that modernizing the curriculum could bring in more pupils. Two new streams of subjects were introduced: the 'scientific' (mathematics, chemistry, physics, astronomy) and the 'commercial' (modern languages, accountancy, commercial law, navigation, geography). The modernized curriculum was particularly evident in the academy where classical education was supplemented by courses in scientific and practical subjects. Some were specialized like the naval academies at Chelsea (1777) and Gosport (1791) but many were for Dissenters barred from official study at Oxbridge (though they could attend Scottish universities).

Evidence from the eighteenth and early nineteenth centuries points to a general increase in education affecting all levels of society and that this increase dated from the early eighteenth century. Its relationship with economic change is somewhat more problematic. Education imparts skills and attitudes. But to what extent did the expanding economy require a greater stream of 'educated' people? Industrial and commercial developments after 1700 led to an increased need for a better-educated managerial and workforce: artisans and clerks who could make calculations and read plans, write letters and keep accounts. Education could also 'tame' or 'civilize' the working population, educating them into the discipline of an industrial and urban society. This notion presumes that workers before

1700 were resigned and contented, that the congregation of large numbers of workers in an urban environment was politically dangerous and that industrial life required a different sort of worker from rural life. It also sees education as something being imposed on the labouring population whereas in the eighteenth and early nineteenth centuries much education was demanded and paid for by the poor. At the same time charity schools were increasingly funded by those who employed labour and who saw the advantages of a better-educated labour force. Education was a necessary but not sufficient explanation for economic growth.

Economic growth and the law

The relationship between economic growth and the law is more difficult to establish and has been neglected by economic historians.[23] The relationship is generally seen in terms of law responding to changes in the economy. M. W. Flinn wrote of government regulation that 'Certainly there was no material change in effective policy growth which could have any bearing on the pace of economic growth before the early nineteenth century.' His view is paralleled by Peter Mathias.[24] Their argument, for the relatively unimportant nature of law, depends much on the withering away of legal restrictions from the 1660s and that, as a result, very little legislative change or action was necessary for economic change to occur. Both, however, qualify their generalizations in the cases of patent law and joint-stock enterprises. Generally, to both Flinn and Mathias, the importance of law was a negative one barring change rather than promoting it. Discussion centred on the role of government in the dismantling of the mercantile system and the establishment of *laissez-faire* as the appropriate medium for economic growth.

This view denies a positive role to law in hindering or encouraging growth and of an interaction between law and economic change with causation flowing both ways. In Britain by the early eighteenth century the concept of property – political, social and legal – was not confined to the ownership of 'real things' like land or coalmines but also to the ownership of 'non-tangible' claims to property like mortgages, debts, copyrights and company shares. It was well established before widespread economic change occurred that loans, patents or dividends were part of a person's property. These rights to property were generally settled through the common law courts which were practical, useful, capable of wide application and were quick to respond to social pressures and economic incentives. As R. M. Hartwell says: 'Where there was conflict in eighteenth-century England between law and economy, it was generally because of Statute Law imposed, rather than because of Common Law interpreted.'[25]

Law was also closely linked with the social structure. The rise in the social and political importance of merchants in the seventeenth century saw the growing incorporation of mercantile law into the common law. The eighteenth century saw commercial law replace land law as the increasingly important part of the common law. Hartwell argues that

> This mutually beneficial combination of ascendant merchant, independent legal profession and flexible Common Law was a powerful lever for economic change, either unhindered by legal restriction or positively aided by legal encouragement. Changes in law were obviously important . . . to the legal needs of a manufacturing society.[26]

The view that changes in the economy were followed by changes in the law conforms largely to the one-way causal relationship between economy and law put forward by Marxist writers. But was it as simple as that? Changes in economic behaviour, either by producers or consumers, leads to changes in the efficiency of the market. If the industrial revolution was really about establishing an increasingly efficient market then conditions for that to occur must have existed. Economic change necessitated investment and capital mobility. In particular there needed to be mobility of short-term capital which depended on two things: the general acceptance of a price for money in the form of interest and of means for transmitting money in the form of bills of exchange. This meant the rejection of the doctrine of usury, removing legal restrictions on interest and the legal protection of negotiable bills. The distinction between interest that was usurious and that which was not had been established in the sixteenth century and was extended in the early eighteenth century to apply to loans over 5 per cent. Certain transactions were exempted but, supplemented by the rules of Equity, the Elizabethan statute remained the basis of the laws of usury until its repeal in 1854. This meant that lenders in the eighteenth century knew that they acting legally if they lent at 5 per cent or below and that their lending would be backed by law in case of default. Courts had recognized the use of bills of exchange by the seventeenth century and by the early eighteenth century they had become a flexible paper currency of great convenience. Without the establishment of certain legal positions by the early to mid-eighteenth century the creation of a market economy would have been much more difficult. The view expressed by Lord Mansfield that 'the law should exist to assist and not to frustrate the needs of the mercantile community' was widely accepted by contemporaries.

TOWARDS A 'CONSUMER SOCIETY'

In 1688 Gregory King estimated that there were 2,000 'eminent merchants and traders', 8,000 'lesser merchants and traders' and 50,000 'shopkeepers and tradesmen' in England and Wales. They were the core of the system of distribution, wholesaling and retailing which expanded with economic growth after 1700. Manufacturing became more specialized and localized commodity production was separated from consumers. This same separation existed between manufacturer and the producer of raw materials. In 1700 most retailing and wholesaling functions were not generally concentrated in fixed shops and warehouses but were performed by low-cost forms of organization – most internal trade was carried on at fairs and markets and by itinerant pedlars and hawkers. Fixed forms of organization became more common during the eighteenth century as communications improved, production increased, the market became more affluent and consumer demand was stimulated.

Distribution

The system of distribution changed as the market expanded and production increased since sales all the year round could produce significant economies of scale in manufacturing industries. Agriculture responded to the growing needs of urban markets and a rather different system of distribution emerged. Some manufacturers developed their own systems of distribution with showrooms and warehouses. This was particularly the case with Josiah Wedgwood. Others, like Boulton and Watt, used their own agents or engaged the services of a general agent. Many firms established direct links with the consumer, negating the role of the middlemen. The 'Manchester men', used by Lancashire cotton firms, were early commercial travellers. They carried their patterns with them from which the consumer could order. Matthew Boulton used a similar system and his outriders carried a pattern book containing over 1,400 designs. Widespread opposition from manufacturers in many areas, including Liverpool, Manchester, Halifax, Wakefield, Wigan and Paisley, led to the withdrawal of a bill in 1785 which aimed to protect the interests of shopkeepers by outlawing the activities of itinerants.

The distribution of agricultural products changed during the eighteenth century. Livestock fairs retained their importance until well into the nineteenth century. These periodic fairs were well suited for disposing of cattle and sheep but generally the fair lost ground to regular markets. The food requirements of London and the expanding cities meant more regular and frequent markets. Wholesale buying was often dominated by a few merchants. Corn sent direct to London was sold at the markets of Bear Key and Queenhithe. From the 1750s the Corn Exchange supplemented these by displaying samples which were sold as lots. The trade was concentrated since the Exchange was a private enterprise, divided into 80 shares held by corn factors, Kentish hoymen and buyers. By 1800 this meant that fourteen factors controlled almost all the trade. The result of this concentration was that prices in London, Birmingham in the Midlands, Newcastle and Edinburgh in the north and Cardiff and Chester for Wales determined prices in their surrounding areas.

Patterns of retailing

Changing patterns of wholesaling were paralleled by changing patterns in retailing. Fairs lost their importance here while, particularly in the urban market, the number of fixed shops grew and itinerant dealers increased their trade. Basic needs for most of society could be satisfied in the market-place but in larger towns permanent shops developed in trades with large volumes of sales: groceries, clothing, textiles and luxury goods. In 1774 Edinburgh had 169 grocers, 45 milliners, 52 tailors, 21 booksellers and jewellers, 20 ironmongers, 12 tobacconists, 8 confectioners, 4 stationers and 2 music shops. In London a distinction emerged in the mid-eighteenth century between the late-night shops of the well-lit and paved West End catering for the rich and the muddled shops of the City which traded with the capital's ordinary inhabitants. The gaps in this network were filled by street traders: in 1850 there were about 41,000 in London selling fish, fruit, vegetables and milk.

Did these changes in distribution and retailing constitute a consumer revolution? R. M. Hartwell, writing in the late 1960s, thought not

> As D. Davis writes: 'Until at least halfway through the nineteenth century the size of shops, the kind of people who ran them and their methods of buying and selling were all much the same as they had been a hundred years before.' There was no revolution in retail trade until after 1850.[27]

This view seems to neglect the dramatic increase in internal trade necessary to satisfy the needs of the growing population and the changes that did occur in the pattern of both distribution and retailing goods. The emphasis of internal trade changed, as did its techniques. The process of modernization applied to selling and buying goods. In that sense it was a revolutionary change. Like education and law, changes in satisfying consumer demands were an essential part of the process of economic growth. They created an environment that allowed manufacturers to base their growth upon known and growing demand and enabled change to occur.

THE STATE AND ECONOMIC GROWTH

The state can, through its control of legislation and coercion, take action to prevent something occurring, slow down the process or encourage it. It can do nothing and allow individuals within society to take action. But the ability of any state to contain pressures or to coerce is always limited. Also, the state embodies in its politicians and bureaucrats, what Sidney Checkland calls, 'a supervising intelligence' which considers the options that confront it in order to make choices between them. There is also the shifting dynamic of power between different groups in society which leads to their constant redefinition, generating new opportunities for some and resentment and frustration for others. Ideologies alter in response to pressures and changes. What role did the state play in the economic changes that occurred between 1700 and 1850?[28]

Throughout this period the state and its government were dominated by the land. It was the major source of economic, social and political power through which control of the economy in general was mediated. P. Deane characterizes the generally accepted position as follows:

> One of the myths that has grown up about the industrial revolution in England is that it happened in the absence of rather than because of government intervention, that government's role in the process was to efface itself as rapidly as possible in order to allow private enterprise to pursue its beneficent part in generating sustained economic growth.[29]

This myth owed its origins to some misunderstanding of Adam Smith's 'doctrine of the invisible hand' as stated in *The Wealth of Nations*:

> [an individual] generally, indeed, neither intends to promote the public interest nor knows how much he is promoting it . . . he intends only his own gain, and he is in this, as in many other cases, led by an invisible hand to promote an end which was no part of his intention.

If the economic changes that occurred after 1700 were a response to market pressures in what ways did the public policy of the state help these changes to take place?

Laissez-faire and an interventionist state – a paradox resolved?

It is generally agreed that between 1780, but particularly after 1815, and 1850 there was a change in the ideology of the state away from direct intervention towards an idea of *laissez-faire*. There is no doubt that between 1760 and 1850 a mass of restrictions and rules concerning economic activity were swept away. Much of the paternalistic legislation controlling apprenticeship, wages, usury, the formation of joint-stock companies and trade were either repealed or fell into disuse. This has been seen as part of the triumph of *laissez-faire*, which supposed that these restrictions had been effective in hampering economic activity. In practice, however, by the early eighteenth century many regulations were simply evaded or ignored. Widespread smuggling, for example, got round trading restrictions. The extent of evasion can be seen from the reduction of import duties on tea from 119 per cent to 12.5 per cent in 1784, which was followed by a rise in the amount of tea entering Britain legally from under 5 million lb to nearly 16.5 million lb. Smuggling had become unprofitable. Some of the circumstances responsible for state restrictions on different aspects of the economy lay in the political development of Britain. The Navigation Acts were an attempt to maintain the Atlantic trading system against commercial enemies. Trading monopolies, like that of the East India Company, provided means for administering an informal empire. Corn Laws represented protection for the landed interest. Regulation of the labour market was a compromise between fear of the outcome if labour was permitted to bargain too strongly or move too easily and the need for a reliable and responsive labour supply. Their rationale lay in perceived needs or fears and was perpetuated by continuing power positions. There was no economic strategy integrated in thought or action.

Despite the emergence of *laissez-faire* as a counter-ideology, the state continued to play a major role in regulating the economy throughout this period. This was clearly evident in control over the monetary and banking systems, over debt and taxation and over change in agriculture. Control of the labour supply and its behaviour was strengthened through legislation over combinations and the ending of wage regulation. The state could use market control in order to sponsor improvement in the infrastructure though the extent to which it did so varied. Parliament was the great authorizer of canal companies, turnpike trusts and railway companies. In 1834 local weights and measures were finally abolished and the state then imposed a set standard. The legal system enforced business contracts and by its maintenance of civil order and its protection of property provided the necessary conditions for business confidence. It could mobilize the economic resources necessary for war. The role of the state was more interventionist in Wales, Scotland and Ireland than in England, though development in communication were often motivated more by fears for security than by economic advantage. Despite the emergence of *laissez-faire* as the ideology of non-intervention in economic affairs, the state created the necessary framework within which change could occur. It is paradoxical that *laissez-faire* spawned by political economy, should be seen by contemporaries and later historians as epitomizing an economic system which was, by its increasingly complex nature, to become far more regulated than mercantilism.

CONCLUSIONS

When examining the social and institutional bases for economic change it is important to distinguish between intentional and unintentional consequences of actions. There was no blueprint for economic change produced by the state. Neither developments in education nor the law were motivated entirely by economic considerations. Services industries grew in response to the initial changes in the economy. The social structure was adaptable and flexible but it could also be reactionary and traditional in attitude. Not one of the areas considered in this chapter caused economic changes on its own. All each did was to create an environment within which change could occur, if that was what individuals wanted.

NOTES

1 'Y.Y.Y.' (David Robinson) 'The Church of England and the Dissenters', *Blackwood's Edinburgh Magazine*, 16 (1824), p. 397.
2 On the issue of change see M. Argyle 'The Social Psychology of Social Change', in M. Argyle et al. *Social Theory and Economic Change*, Tavistock, 1967, pp. 87–102.
3 E. D. Domar *Essays on the Theory of Economic Growth*, Oxford University Press, 1957, p. 22.
4 H. Perkin, 'The Social Causes of the Industrial Revolution' (1968), in his *The Structured Crowd*, Harvester Press, 1981, p. 28. This question of 'social revolution' is examined in more detail in his *The Origins of Modern English Society 1780–1880*, Routledge & Kegan Paul, 1970.
5 The nature of British society and the ways in which it changed is examined in chapters 13–16 where several points raised here are examined in more detail.
6 H. Perkin op. cit. 1981, p. 38.
7 ibid. pp. 40–2.
8 Quoted ibid. p. 41.
9 M. W. Flinn 'Social Theory and the Industrial Revolution', in M. Argyle et al. op. cit. p. 14.
10 The question of education is examined as an enabling factor in more detail on pp. 214–18.
11 B. Porteus *Charges to the Clergy*, London, 1786.
12 M. Weber *The Protestant Ethic and the Spirit of Capitalism*, Allen & Unwin, 1930. A useful discussion of writings on religion and the social environment can be found in D. Thompson *The Dynamics of the Industrial Revolution*, Edward Arnold, 1973, pp. 122–40.
13 M. W. Flinn op. cit. pp. 22–31 examines the Dissenting connection in more detail.
14 A brief discussion of services can be found in E. Pawson *The Early Industrial Revolution*, Batsford, 1979, pp. 160–91.
15 On the development of the professions in the early eighteenth century see G. Holmes *Augustan England: Professions, State and Society*, Allen & Unwin, 1982.
16 R. M. Hartwell 'The Neglected Variable: the Service Sector', in his *The Industrial Revolution and Economic Growth*, Methuen, 1971, p. 209.
17 ibid. pp. 213–4.
18 Canals and roads are examined in chapter 7, finance and banking in chapter 9 and railways in chapter 11.
19 R. M. Hartwell 'Two Services: Education and Law', in R. M. Hartwell op. cit. p. 229. M. Sanderson *Education, Economic Change and Society, 1780–1850*, Macmillan, 1982, is a useful summary of views.
20 C. Hill *Reformation to Industrial Revolution*, Penguin, 1979; P. Laslett *The World We Have Lost*, Cambridge University Press, 1965.
21 E. Hobsbawm *Industry and Empire*, Penguin, 1968.
22 N. J. Smelser *Social Change in the Industrial Revolution*, Routledge & Kegan Paul, 1959, p. 286.
23 R. M. Hartwell op. cit. provides a useful starting point on the issue of law and economic growth.
24 M. W. Flinn *The Origins of the Industrial Revolution*, Longman, 1966, p. 93; P. Mathias *The First Industrial Nation*, Methuen, 2nd edn, 1983, pp. 31–3.
25 R. M. Hartwell op. cit. p. 253.
26 ibid. p. 254.
27 ibid. p. 219. See also N. McKendrick et al. *The Birth of a Consumer Society*,

Hutchinson, 1983 and H. and L. H. Mui *Shops and Shopkeeping in Eighteenth Century England*, Routledge, 1989.

28 On the role of the state in economic change between 1700 and 1850 the most straightforward accounts can be found in P. Deane *The First Industrial Revolution*, Cambridge University Press, 1965 and P. Lane *The Industrial Revolution*, Weidenfeld & Nicolson, 1978. S. Checkland *British Public Policy 1776–1939*, Cambridge University Press, 1983 provides a more detailed analysis and P. Corrigan and D. Sayer *The Great Arch*, Blackwell, 1985 gives a more radical critique.

29 P. Deane op. cit. p. 202.

11 Railways – the great connectors

It burst rather than stole or crept upon the world. Its advent was in the highest degree dramatic. It was even more so than the discovery of America. . . . [1]

Canals will last my lifetime, but what I fear are those damned tramways. [2]

The British railway system may have come into being to meet the needs of rapidly expanding mining and textile industries but it had a dramatic impact on both the British economy and society in general. It symbolized the 'spirit of the age' in a way that no other development did, with the possible exception of the factory or mill. It made possible the development of an integrated and national economic system where canals and turnpike roads had not. Railways brought people closer together by cutting down the time spent travelling, broke down parochialism and regionalism and made the products of economic change more readily available. It was 'the great connector'. John Ruskin wrote that

all along the iron veins that traverse the frame of our country, beat and flow the fiery pulses of its exertions, hotter and faster every hour. All vitality is concentrated throughout those throbing arteries into the central cities; the country is passed over like a green sea by narrow bridges, and we are thrown back in continually closer crowds upon the city gates. [3]

The inscription in the porch of the south door of Ely cathedral for William Pickering and Richard Edger, who were killed in a railway accident, best expressed Victorian attitudes to the railway. Religion and technology were fused.

The Spiritual Railway

The line to heaven by Christ was made
With heavenly truth the rails were laid
From Earth to Heaven the line extends
To Life Eternal where it ends.

Repentance is the Station then
Where passengers are taken in
No Fee for them is there to pay
For Jesus is himself the way
God's Word is the first Engineer
It points the way to Heaven so clear
Through tunnels dark and dreary here
It does the way to Glory steer
God's Love the Fire, his Truth the Steam,
Which drives the Engine and the Train.
All you who would to Glory ride
Must come to Christ, in him abide
In First and Second and Third Class,
Repentence, Faith and Holiness
You must the way to Glory gain
Or you with Christ will not remain
Come the poor Sinners, now's the time
At any Station of the Line
If you'll repent and turn from Sin
The train will stop and take you in.

After 1830 the four distinctive features that define a modern railway as a means of transport – a specialized track, mechanical traction, the accommodation of public traffic and the conveyance of passengers – came together. By 1850 the basis of a railway network had been established throughout Britain.

TWO TECHNOLOGICAL DEVELOPMENTS

Tramways

The development of the railway network after 1830 was the result of two technological developments coming together – the tramway and the steam locomotive. Tramways can be traced back to the sixteenth century and were used to ease the passage of horse-drawn or man-drawn waggons carrying heavy goods over muddy roads. By the early seventeenth century they were being used in Nottinghamshire and Durham to transport coal from the pits to wharves on rivers. By 1660 they were in widespread use round coalfields in Shropshire, the north-east, the Severn valley and in Scotland. Waggons with brakes and metal wheels were used by Ralph Allen on a tramway he built in 1728 to supply stone for the building of Bath. Advances in iron production led to cast iron being used to cover wooden rails at Coalbrookdale in 1767 and by the 1790s rails made entirely of cast iron appeared. More durable wrought iron rails began to be produced in 1808, by which time the wooden rails had virtually disappeared.

By 1810 there were some 300 miles of railways in the British Isles though, despite Bridgewater's fears, they were chiefly short-distance feeders to water transport, but some, like the Surrey Iron Railway and Oystermouth Railway near Swansea, carried passengers. Before the advent of steam locomotion railways were well known and well developed but they remained a local phenomenon.[4]

Application of steam power

The adaptation of the steam engine to these railways was a relatively slow process. Steam locomotion was an idea much in people's minds before it actually happened. The power of steam was well appreciated, just as people today are aware of the potential of atomic power.[5] James Watt developed rotary motion in 1781 and this had aroused widespread interest in the possibility of steam-powered transport. It could be adapted to rail haulage as a stationary engine hauling waggons on a cable. By 1800 it was being used in the northern coalfields and until 1830 it was looked upon as a practicable alternative to the locomotive.

Watt to Trevithick

Watt was suspicious of the use of high-pressure steam, which he considered dangerous. Whether this explains why he took out a patent for a high-pressure engine in 1785 is debatable but by 1800, when it expired, engineers were aware of the pressing need to improve methods of mechanical haulage and were free to adapt the steam engine to locomotive motion. Watt had developed a condensing engine using steam at pressures of up to 10 lb per square inch. Expansion engines, necessary for locomotion, used steam at higher pressures, at least 25 lb per square inch. It was Richard Trevithick (1771–1833) who showed that Watt's fears about boilers exploding were groundless. He was a Cornish mining engineer and manager and took out a patent for a high-pressure engine using steam at 50 and then a 100 lb per square inch. He had already built and used two steam carriages in 1801 and 1803. Although he had shown the feasibility of the idea he had difficulty in following it up. Samuel Homfray, the South Wales ironmaster, was attracted by his experiments and invited him to build a locomotive for the railway from Penydaren to Abercynon. Problems with breaking the cast-iron tramway occurred for both this engine and Trevithick's second locomotive constructed for Christopher Blackett, owner of the Wylam colliery near Newcastle. His third engine, 'Catch-me-who-Can', built in 1808 was a venture into blatant publicity and operated on a circular track near the present Euston station in London. It aroused public interest but no commercial prospect came from it. These disappointments led Trevithick to give up locomotives but he was certainly the pioneer, the person with the necessary imagination. In 1868 the leading technical journal *Engineering* said of him that

> Trevithick was the real inventor of the locomotive. He was the first to prove the sufficiency of the adhesion of the wheels to the rails for all purposes of traction on lines of ordinary gradient, the first to make the return flue boiler, the first to use the steam jet in the chimney and the first to couple all the wheels to the engine.

Trevithick to Stephenson

The major problems which Trevithick left to be solved were how to strengthen the rails and to increase the power of the locomotive in relation to weight so that it could outclass the best horses in speed. These were the problems which occupied a handful of people, mainly in the north, for the next twenty years. The increasing use of wrought-iron rails after 1810 resolved the first difficulty. The second problem took longer. John Blenkinsop used a 'rack and pinion' system on his locomotives as a way of increasing pulling power. It proved to be an evolutionary dead-end as far as England was concerned though it did find a later use in railways built in mountainous areas. William Hedley and Christopher Blackett were responsible for the next group of locomotives. Hedley distributed the weight of his locomotives over eight driving wheels to prevent breaking the rails. George Stephenson (1781–1848) brought locomotives and the potential of railways to public prominence. He was a self-taught man who worked at the Killingworth colliery in Northumberland from 1795. By 1812 he already had a solid record of achievement as an enginewright and mechanic behind him. In 1814 his employer, Lord Ravensworth, provided the finance for his first engine, the 'Blucher'. It was based largely on Blenkinsop's ideas without the central cog-wheel and with steam-springs to make travelling less rough. The basic design laid down in the Blucher was not altered in the next seven years and he built sixteen 'Killingworth' engines. 'Locomotion', built for the Stockton–Darlington line was essentially of this type. They could haul up to 70 tons at 5 miles per hour but the use of the open-flue boiler meant that if the load was too great they simply ran out of steam. Unlike Blenkinsop and Hedley, Stephenson built his engines for several rather than one line. Between 1800 and 1823 only 28 locomotives had, however, been built and none of them were decisively superior to horse traction. The seal of the Newcastle and Carlisle Railway, opened in 1835, showed a horse-drawn waggon. Even ten years after the opening of the Stockton–Darlington railway steam locomotion had not entirely triumphed.

The 1820s – 'take off'

It was the 1820s that the 'take-off' for railways occurred.[6] In that decade
the Stephensons engineered three railways. The Hetton Railway, built for
the Marquis of Londonderry, showed how efficiently the combination of
locomotive, stationary engines and self-acting inclines could be. It was
opened in 1822, was 8 miles long and rose over 800 feet from the River
Wear to the collieries. In 1821 Edward Pearce offered Stephenson the job
of engineering the new Stockton–Darlington public railway, a distance of
27 miles. Pearce originally intended to use horses to pull waggons but
Stephenson persuaded him of the power of steam. It was finally opened
in September 1825, and carried both coal and passengers. The building of
this railway coincided with the first sustained propaganda on behalf of the
railway as a nationwide carrier. Some of the most important developments
of the 1830s like the London to Birmingham Railway, were mooted at
the same time but were suspended in the financial crisis during late 1825
and were not revived during the economic recession of the late 1820s.
The potential of the 'coming railway' age was expressed in 1825 in the
following way by Henry Booth, treasurer of the Liverpool and Manchester
railway:

> When the steam-coach is brought fully into use, practice will teach us
> many things respecting it, of which theory leaves us ignorant. With the
> facilities for rapid motion . . . there is nothing extravagant in expecting
> to see the present extreme rate of travelling [10 miles per hour] doubled.
> We shall then enjoy being carried at a rate of 400 miles per day. . . .
> Commodities, inventions, discoveries, opinions, would circulate with a
> rapidity hitherto unknown, and above all, the intercourse of man and
> man, nation and nation, province and province, would be prodigiously
> increased.

The Manchester–Liverpool railway

The Stockton–Darlington Railway was still only a local railway, but it did
stimulate the patent interest of the commercial classes in Manchester and
Liverpool. They argued that canals were too slow and too expensive and
in the Prospectus of 1824 for the railway maintained that

> It is not that the water companies have not been able to carry goods
> on more reasonable terms, but that, strong in their enjoyment of their
> monopoly, they have not thought it proper to do so. . . . IT IS COMPE-
> TITION THAT IS WANTED. . . .

Though Stephenson and his son Robert (1803–59) were not originally
chosen as its builders, by 1826 they had taken on the task. There was
initially opposition from the Trustees of the Bridgewater Canal and from

the earls of Derby and Sefton across whose estates the railway would run. The opposition of vested interests to change continued after 1830 as did the conservatism of ordinary people:

> What is to be done with all those who have advanced money in making and repairing turnpike trust roads? What was to become of the coach-makers and harness-makers, coach-masters, coachmen, inn-keepers, horse-breeders and horse-dealers? The beauty and comfort of country gentlemen's estates would be destroyed by it. . . . It would be the greatest nuisance, the most complete disturbance of quiet and comfort in all parts of the kingdom, that the ingenuity of man could invent. . . .

There were also important technical problems: the boggy area of Chat Moss near Manchester, the deep cutting at Mount Olive, the tunnel under Liverpool from Edgehill to the docks and the viaduct to carry the railway over the Sankey canal. Despite these obstacles, the railway was completed in four years. The Rainhill Trials in 1829 settled the disputed question of the mode of traction to be employed on the line. The directors offered a prize of £500 to the designers of a locomotive, not exceeding 6 tons in weight, which could pull a load at least three times its weight at not less than 10 m.p.h. Stephenson's Rocket was the only engine to comply with these conditions, through the use of the multi-tubular boiler, reaching speeds of 30 m.p.h. The track was opened on 15 September 1830 not without incident (William Huskisson, an MP for Liverpool, was run down and killed). What marked off the Liverpool–Manchester Railway from earlier undertakings was that it combined all the essential features of a railway: there was a clear emphasis on passenger traffic, from which it drew half its revenue from the start; it carried freight and was run entirely by mechanical traction. The Railway Age had arrived.

A 'RAILWAY REVOLUTION'

In the two decades after 1830 the 'railway revolution' took place. There was no attempt to plan a proper railway network, resulting in a haphazard system with frequent duplication. Yet during the 1830s the foundations of the main lines were laid in Britain and by 1840 some 1,500 miles of track were in use. Britain's economic growth was at its maximum rate during the 1820s and 1830s and there were ample funds available for investment.[7] Between 1825 and 1835 54 Acts were passed authorizing the construction of railways, of which the most important was the London and Birmingham Railway opened in 1838. The characteristics of expansion between 1833 and 1840 are summarized in Table 11.1.

Trade recession in 1837 and the poor harvests from 1838 to 1841 pushed up the bank rate and reduced the availability of credit, undermining business confidence. Railway expansion continued when the more important lines, sanctioned earlier, were completed. London was linked by

Table 11.1 Railway Acts 1833–40 and what they sanctioned

Year	Companies	Mileage	Capital (£m)	Railway share index (June 1840=100)
1833	4	218	5.5	69.3
1834	5	131	2.3	67.8
1835	8	201	4.8	71.1
1836	29	955	22.9	111.1
1837	15	543	13.5	81.4
1838	2	49	2.1	91.1
1839	2	54	6.5	79.9
1840	–	–	2.5	86.4

Source: R. C. O. Matthews *A Study in Trade Cycle History*, London, 1954, p. 107.

railway to Birmingham in 1838, with Bristol and Southampton in 1840, Brighton in 1841 and Dover in 1843. In Wales Merthyr Tydfil was linked to Cardiff in 1841 and in Scotland a railway was built across the Lowlands linking Ayr, Glasgow and Edinburgh in 1842. East Anglia lagged behind in both canal and railway development. Railways were chiefly concerned with passengers, who were more profitable than freight, and until the early 1840s canals were still the chief carrier of bulky goods and were still making good profits. From the 1840s the shift in freight was away from canals and towards railways. The importance of canals and of turnpike trusts, which often ran parallel to the railways, was eclipsed.

The revival of the economy from 1843 led to a revival in railway promotion.[8] Better harvests in 1842 and 1843, Peel's reduction of tariff duties and the low interest rate of 2.5 per cent underlay the 'railway mania' of 1844–7. The extent of this can be seen in Table 11.2.

Table 11.2 Railway Acts 1841–50 and what they sanctioned

Year	Companies	Mileage	Capital(£m)	Railway share index (June 1840=100)
1841	1	14	3.4	83.8
1842	5	55	5.3	89.4
1843	3	90	3.9	98.2
1844	50	805	20.5	121.3
1845	120	2,896	59.5	149.0
1846	272	4,540	132.6	139.4
1847	184	1,295	39.5	117.1
1848	82	373	15.3	95.5
1849	35	16.5	3.9	77.1
1850	3	6.75	4.1	70.4

Source: Railway Returns quoted in P. S. Bagwell *The Transport Revolution from 1770*, Batsford, 1974, p. 94.

Figure 11.1 The railway system in 1845

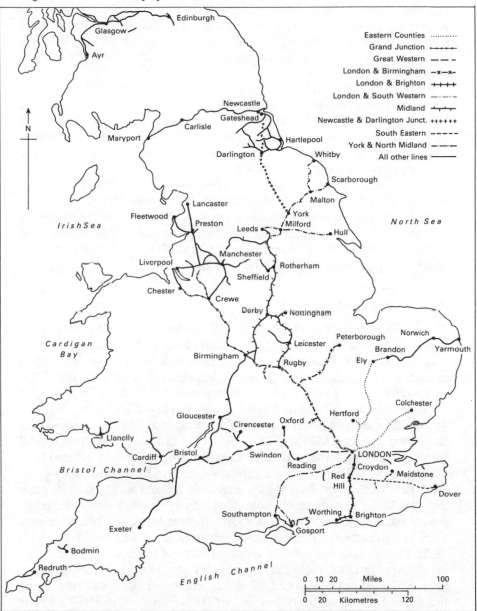

Source: H. J. Dyos and D. H. Aldcroft *British Transport*, Leicester University Press, 1971, pp. 120–1.

Impressive though these figures are, they do not take into account the 600 schemes which never reached their first reading. A substantial proportion of the schemes which actually got through Parliament were never carried out. However, the lines that were laid down as a result of projects passed during these years brought the total mileage open to just under 7,500 mile by 1852.[9]

By the early 1850s there were two through routes to Scotland, a tight network in the Midlands, Yorkshire and Lancashire, East Anglia had been opened up with a line to Norwich and Yarmouth via Colchester and there were lines through to the coasts of both South and North Wales. The major gaps that remained were in the south and south-west, the Scottish Highlands and in mid-Wales. By 1852, though a great deal still remained to be done, the railway system in England, Wales and, to a lesser extent Scotland, was in all essentials already complete, with London at its heart. The system had reached physical maturity and the formative influences of its youth and adolescence had left indelible marks. The problems of the railways in the twentieth century had their origins in the genesis of the system between 1830 and 1860.

Railways in Ireland

The development of railways in Ireland followed a similar pattern to mainland Britain. The first line, the 6-mile long Dublin–Kingstown line, was opened in 1834 but ten years later only two further lines were open to traffic: the 32-mile Dublin–Drogheda line opened in 1844 and the 17.75-mile stretch of the Ulster Railway which reached Portadown in 1842. The boom in railway building in Ireland began in 1844–5 and coincided with the second wave of railway speculation in England. The major reason for the lacuna between 1834 and 1844 lay in the inadequacy of Irish capital formation and the consequent need to attract English investment into Irish schemes. By 1850 half of private capital subscribed for Irish railways came from English sources. By 1847 the mania in Ireland had passed its peak and, unlike on the mainland, some government capital was essential to sustain the confidence of investors. Government loans accounted for only £1.5 million out of the total capital investment of £12.5 million up to 1852. Though this was only a small part of total investment government involvement was an important element in attracting cautious investors after the investment boom of 1844–6 was exhausted and only three out of the nineteen Irish railways opened by 1853 were constructed without government loans. The increase in opened railway track in Ireland in the 1840s was dramatic: in 1845 only 65 miles of track were opened but by 1849 there were 428 miles opened and 183 under construction. This rose to 865 miles in 1854. By the early 1850s lines were in operation to five major urban centres: Belfast, Cork, Galway, Limerick and Waterford. The railways were remunerative, partly because of the halving of English

Figure 11.2 The railway system in 1852

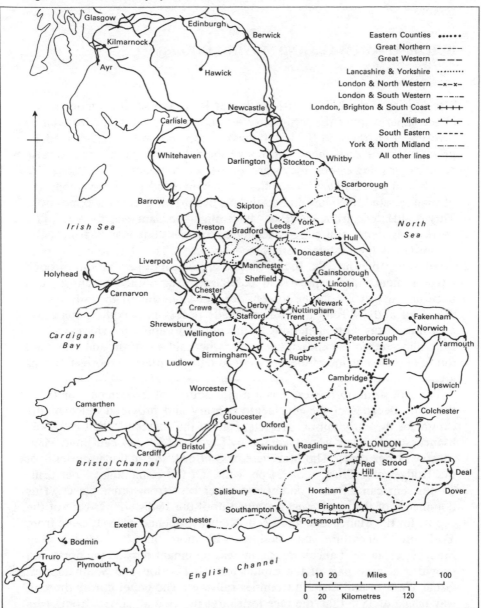

Eastern Counties	••••••
Great Northern	-----
Great Western	— — —
Lancashire & Yorkshire	··········
London & North Western	–×–×–
London & South Western	–··–··–
London, Brighton & South Coast	+++++
Midland	+–+–+
South Eastern	–·–·–
York & North Midland	–··–··–
All other lines	———

Source: H. J. Dyos and D. H. Aldcroft *British Transport*, Leicester University Press, 1971, pp. 136–7.

construction costs and partly because the companies avoided the poorer regions.

BUILDING RAILWAYS AND MOVING GOODS

Investment

The success of the Liverpool–Manchester Railway and the demonstration of the superiority of the locomotive led to a major change in attitudes to investment in railways.[10] Most railway companies were inaugurated by private Acts of Parliament which gave their directors permission to raise money by issuing shares: they were joint-stock companies. The procedure for obtaining parliamentary sanction, which involved an ad hoc committee of inquiry, could be slow and costly, particularly if there was opposition. This could come from interests which might be damaged by a railway, particularly canal and stage-coaching companies, but mainly from large landowners whose estates were to be transected. They had to be compensated, sometimes heavily. In the 1820s a great deal of persuasion, through advertisements in the press and publicized promotional meetings, was necessary to get the public to consider, let alone invest in, railways. In the 1830s and 1840s all that was normally necessary was the publication of a prospectus with invitations to the public to apply for shares. These were allocated to the chosen investors, who paid a deposit and only paid the full nominal value of the shares once parliamentary authorization was given.

The industrial north-west was a major source of investment capital in the early decades of the nineteenth century and provided much of the capital for the early railway projects. Half of the shares for the Liverpool–Manchester Railway were taken up by Liverpool (47 per cent) and Manchester (3 per cent). The Marquess of Stafford, the major proprietor of the Bridgewater Trust, took 24 per cent. Of the remaining 26 per cent, 20 per cent came from London and 6 per cent from other places. This dominance of the north-west remained until the 1840s. 78 per cent of the capital for the Manchester and Leeds Railway, opened in 1841, came from Yorkshire, Lancashire and Cheshire, with more than half coming from Manchester alone. Lancashire capital was dominant outside the north and provided a large part of the capital for the London and Southampton, Great Western and Eastern Counties railways. The belief during the railway mania of 1845 that 'the rage for shares infected all classes from peers to peasant'[11] is not based upon any real analysis of the available evidence. There is little to suggest that wage-earners held any significant proportion of railway capital. In England and Wales most capital came from industrial and commercial sources, with the landed interest playing a far less significant role than in canal and turnpike trust promotions. This was paralleled in Scotland where the promotion of the early railways was undertaken chiefly by merchants and coalmasters, some of whom were also leading figures in the iron industry.

Railway shares in the 1830s paid dividends of up to 9 per cent. The mania of the 1840s resulted in the promotion of many uneconomic schemes and excessive competition between companies. This led to a sharp fall in the return on investments. The average dividend on share capital fell from 5.48 per cent in 1845 to 3.31 per cent in 1850. The result of this was a slackening of eagerness to subscribe to ordinary shares and a move to the greater security offered by preference shares and debentures. The expansion of the rail network led to a trend toward concentration and amalgamation through mergers and takeovers (Table 11.3). Early companies had been formed to build single lines from one place to another, which led to a multiplicity of companies, usually small. There were about 200 in 1843. To the investor amalgamation offered the prospect of more economic use of capital and the potential of higher profits. 1846 saw twenty amalgamations and there were nine the following year. For example, in 1846 the Manchester & Leeds Railway and five smaller companies came together adopting, in 1847, the name of the Lancashire & Yorkshire Railway. The most important figure in this process was George Hudson, 'the railway king'. In 1836 he launched the York and North Midland Railway and then in 1844, from the merger of three lines, created the Midland Railway which radiated from Derby. With this as his base Hudson aimed at controlling the traffic from London to the north-east, also pushing a line to the south-west as far as Gloucester and Bristol, moving north into Scotland and into East Anglia. By the mid-1840s he controlled 1,500 miles of line and capital of £30 million. In doing this he over-extended himself and went bankrupt in 1849.

The pattern of railway investment can be taken from three separate series:[12] Kenwood's series of British gross investment, excluding land purchase, legal and parliamentary costs, but including spending on repairs and renewals; Mitchell's estimate of gross capital formation by United Kingdom railways and Hawke and Reed's raised capital data (paid-up capital and loans).

Table 11.3 Railway investment 1825–55 (annual averages, £m)

	Kenwood	Mitchell (i)	Mitchell (ii)	Hawke & Reed
1825–9	0.25	–	–	0.28
1830–4	0.55	0.63*	0.53*	0.79
1835–9	4.69	6.52	5.62	6.44
1840–4	5.76	6.22	5.58	7.27
1845–9	20.03	29.02	25.18	31.02
1850–4	9.58	11.12	9.06	11.26

Mitchell (i) includes the cost of land purchase, while Mitchell (ii) does not. * covers 1831–4.

The extent to which railway investment played a part in the overall process of economic growth is an issue of some importance. Mitchell has shown the speed with which the railways became a significant element in domestic investment, with gross capital formation consuming 2 per cent of national income by the late 1830s. It was, however, in the 1840s that the dramatic shift occurred, with investment not far short of 7 per cent of national income in 1847 and an average of 4.5 per cent between 1845 and 1849. Railway investment was sizeable but what part did it actually play in the growth process? Did railway promotions lead economic growth or were they the product of favourable economic conditions? There is general agreement that while railway promotion was an undoubted influence on general economic activity from the 1830s, its role was supportive rather than leading. Railway investment, up to the early 1850s, tended to be concentrated in the upswing of the trade cycle and the lag between promotion and construction meant that the contra-cyclical influence of railway-building was central in providing employment when the economy generally was depressed.

How far did factors endogenous to the railway industry influence patterns of investment? Speculation has to be stimulated by something. The developments in railway technology and the success of the Liverpool–Manchester Railway encouraged promotional activity in the early 1830s before the speculative boom of 1835–6. The schemes after 1844 are usually attributed to a revival in business confidence. But endogenous factors were also important. Alterations in parliamentary standing orders made promotion more difficult after 1838 and easier after 1842. Gladstone's Act of 1844 referred to the possibility of a state purchase after 21 years of new companies earning 10 per cent or more and this helped to encourage over-optimism. The timing of railway investment and the business cycle before 1850 suggests that boom conditions encouraged company promotions and that, while the importance of speculative investment must be admitted, the presence of endogenous factors indicates that promotion was not only influenced by itself but influenced the prevailing economic climate.

British railways were built by private enterprise and with private capital, unlike those of continental Europe where governments intervened in route-planning and contributed to the costs of construction. Whether this was alone responsible for the high costs of constructing the British railway system is open to question but the average cost per mile was over £40,000 compared to £36,000 in Belgium, £27,000 in France and only £11,000 in the United States. It is important to take into account the high price of land, the nature of the terrain, especially in the north, Wales and Scotland and the perfectionism on the part of the engineers. One has only to look at the routes, stations, bridges etc. designed by Brunel to understand the spiralling nature of costs. Despite all their over-capitalization and heavy fixed charges, most British companies remained profitable throughout the nineteenth century.

Construction

The achievement of the railways is even greater when the method of their construction is examined. Until the 1850s, when some steam-driven equipment was introduced, railways were built by hand and dynamite by the railway navvies.[13] In the 1880s a railway chaplain, D. W. Barrett, wrote that

The term navvy is simply an abridgement of the longer and less poetical word navigator, which savours too much of the sound of alligator to be pleasant. And in fact some people have a rough idea that the navvy is a sort of human alligator who feeds on helpless women and timid men and frightens children into fits.

In 1851 J. R. Francis, the contemporary historian of the early railways, wrote of navvies in his *A History of the English Railway* as

Rough alike in morals and manners, collected from the wild hills of Yorkshire and Lancashire, coming in troops from the fens of Lincolnshire, and afterwards pouring in masses from every country in the empire; displaying an unbending vigour and an independent bearing; mostly dwelling apart from the villagers near whom they worked; with all the propensities of an untaught, undisciplined nature; unable to read and unwilling to be taught; impetuous, impulsive and brute-like, regarded as the pariahs of private life, herding together like beasts of the field, owning no moral law and feeling no social tie, they increased with an increased demand, and from thousands grew hundreds of thousands. They lived but for the present; they cared not for the past; they were indifferent to the future.

Not all agreed with this pessimistic picture. Brunel, for example, thought that navvies were very manageable 'if well treated'.

In *Dombey and Son* Charles Dickens described the digging of a cutting at Camden Hill:

Houses were knocked down; streets broken through and stopped; deep pits and trenches dug in the ground; enormous heaps of earth and clay thrown up; buildings that were undermined and shaking, propped by great beams of wood. Here, a chaos of carts, overthrown and jumbled together . . . there confused treasures of iron soaked and rusted in something that had accidentally become a pond. Everywhere were bridges that led nowhere; thoroughfares that were wholly impassable; Babel towers of chimneys, wanting half their height; temporary wooden houses and enclosures in the most unlikely situations; carcasses of ragged tenements and fragments of unfinished walls and arches and piles of scaffolding and wilderness of bricks and giant forms of cranes and tripods straddling above nothing. There were a hundred thousand shapes and substances of incompleteness, wildly mingled out of their places, upside down, burrowing in the earth, aspiring in the air, mouldering in the water. . . . In short, the yet unfinished and unopened Railway was in progress; and, from the very core of all this dire disorder, tailed smoothly away, upon its mighty course of civilisation and improvement. . . .

In the 1840s and 1850s with the exception of those employed in agriculture and textiles, navvies made up the largest occupational group in Britain. An average of 60,000 men were engaged annually in railway construction between 1831 and 1870 or about 1 per cent of the occupied male labour force. Construction booms led to sudden surges in demands for labour, and especially for unskilled labourers, who made up over 80 per cent of those recruited. During 1847 some 6,455 miles of line were being built by over 256,000 men, 4 per cent of the male workforce. The annual wages in 1845–9 were about £11 million, or 2 per cent of the national product. It is little wonder that to the communities upon which they descended, they were an army.

The construction of a railway line was subject to an elaborate division of labour. In charge was a consulting engineer responsible to a board of directors for the progress and successful completion of the line. He in turn contracted out to various people parts of the route, though the more important sections tended to be given to the leading firms like those of Samuel Morton Peto, who in 1850 was employing 15,000 people, or Thomas Brassey. For example, in the case of the London–Southampton line Joseph Locke, the engineer, employed Brassey to build the key stretch between Basingstoke and Winchester and used lesser men for other sections of the route. Contractors then subcontracted the work and at the base of the managerial structure was the 'butty man' or 'ganger' who did limited tasks like removing an agreed amount of waggon loads of earth from a cutting. Some butty men were specialists in particular things like drainage, bricklaying or cutting. The workforce itself fell into two types: skilled men, like bricklayers or carpenters, who were paid about 5s. a day, and unskilled workers who were paid half that rate. Among the unskilled the Irish predominated, especially in the north of England and Scotland. In southern England and Wales redundant agricultural labourers were more frequently employed. For the navvies life was unruly and violent in both their work and ordinary lives. Shortcuts were taken in building since time was often too short to fulfil contracts. Earth was often undermined too far. The construction of the Woodhead tunnel in Cheshire between 1839 and 1845 brought the issue to public attention. Thirty-two men were killed and there were twenty-three cases of compound fractures, seventy-four of simple fracture and 140 cases of serious burns and blast wounds.

> William Jackson, miner, No. 5 shaft. He was looking over John Webb's shoulder, while he was stemming a hole charged with powder, when the blast went off, blowing the stemmer through Jackson's head and killed him on the spot.

Edwin Chadwick wrote of this tunnel that

> The losses in this one work may be stated as more than three per cent killed and fourteen per cent wounded. The deaths in the four battles of Talavera, Salamanca, Vittoria and Waterloo were only 2.11 per cent of privates; and in the last forty-one months of the Peninsula War the mortality of privates was 4.2 per cent in battle, 11.9 per cent of disease. . . .

The Woodhead scandal did result in a Select Committee on Railway Labourers being set up in 1846, but it did not act upon Chadwick's suggestion that contractors should be liable to pay compensation to employees or their next of kin for accidents and deaths even when it was the worker who was at fault. Chadwick reminded the committee that in France, where it was the law, the accident rate had been significantly reduced. Sympathy was expressed for his proposals but government was unwilling to intervene and before long the number of navvies decreased rapidly.

Increasing traffic

Railway traffic – both passenger and freight – grew steadily from 1830, though reasonably reliable evidence was only collected from the early 1840s (see Table 11.4).

Table 11.4 United Kingdom railway traffic 1842–50.

Year	Passengers		Freight		Total revenue (£m)
	Numbers	£m	Tons	£m	
1842	24.5	3.1	5.4	1.6	4.8
1846	43.8	4.7	17.0	7.6	7.6
1850	72.9	6.8	38.0	6.4	13.2

Source: Railway Returns (Mail, parcels etc. were counted as freight).

Initially the aim of most railway companies was to supply improved transport facilities for existing customers. The trunk-line railways, which eventually dominated the system, established by specializing in high-tariff business, taking passengers from stage-coaches and high-value goods from the road carriers but, not until the 1840s from canals and coastal shipping. Both in price and in reliable, round-the-year service railways were unmatched by their rivals. Between 1830 and 1845 railways undercut stage-coaches by up to 20 per cent and canals by about 40 per cent. During the 1840s as the system expanded, there were two significant changes in the type of business railways handled. From the mid-1840s an increasing emphasis was placed on heavy freight. Between 1835 and 1845 companies had derived 75 per cent of their gross revenue from passengers but by 1850 this had fallen to below 50 per cent. The market-widening effects of railway freight operations were limited before 1850. It was not until the early 1840s that locomotives were equal to hauling heavy goods trains. Amalgamations and the administration of the Railway Clearing House certainly facilitated long-distance freight traffic, but until the 1850s this was generally limited to short distances. The second change was the shift in passenger traffic to third class. In 1845–6 third-class passengers made up half of the total numbers and produced only a fifth of the total revenue. By 1870 the proportions had risen to 65 and 44 per cent respectively. This change was largely the result of intensified competition between companies, encouraged by government policy which led to companies pursuing a larger-volume–lower-margin business.

The search for larger traffic volumes after 1845 had the effect of lowering the average rates of railway companies. Between 1845 and 1858 passenger fares fell by as much as 30–40 per cent. There was a similar trend in freight where the low-tariff mineral trade, especially coal, became an increasingly dominant element. New trades were encouraged in perishable goods – fish, meat, fresh milk and vegetables and led to a vast improvement in urban diets. The fish trade of the Great Eastern Railway was the envy of other companies. The London & South-Western Railway and Great Western Railway even invested their rivalry in steam vessels to intercept fish at sea. Railways helped to open up a number of new industrial sites: iron and anthracite in south Wales, coal in the north-east and Yorkshire and iron ore in Northamptonshire. The extension of services was accompanied by an improvement in communications at all levels – postal services, newspaper and telegraph – all closely dependent on rail facilities. Railways reduced the cost and greatly improved the quality and volume of Britain's transport.

The state and the railways

Railways may have been developed by private enterprise but government could not entirely escape involvement in railway matters from the very outset.[14] Railway companies needed parliamentary approval, not merely for sanctioning the company, but for authority to purchase land, if necessary by compulsory purchase. Parliament also laid down maximum charges for particular goods in the same way that it had regulated the tolls charged by canal companies. It was, however, not long before Parliament recognized the futility of endeavouring to maintain the same competition between railway companies as existed between road-carriers and canals. Select Committees of either Lords or Commons were established in every year between 1835 and 1840 and in 1843, 1844, 1846 and 1849, while a Royal Commission reported in 1846. These investigations often led to fresh legislation which either attempted to circumscribe the powers or limit the freedom of the railway companies. Parliament's major concern, from the outset, was to protect the interests of the railway user from the monopolistic tendencies on the part of the railway companies.

By the early 1840s with company promotions, amalgamations, manipulations and speculation the issue of the monopolistic pretension of companies came to a head. The Railway Act of 1840 set up a Railway Department at the Board of Trade to collect information from the companies, to promote public safety and, where necessary, to initiate prosecutions. The 1842 Act extended state control over issues of rail safety. The 1844 Act went further. The Department became the Railway Board. In the case of new lines, railway profits could not exceed 10 per cent on capital and Parliament gave the Board of Trade powers to force the rate of carriage down or compulsorily purchase companies which did so. In addition all companies were compelled to run a daily passenger service each way, stopping at all stations with a maximum charge of one penny a mile – the 'Parliamentary Train'. An inspectorate was set up to enforce minimum standards of safety, signalling and braking and telegraph systems. In 1846 Parliament intervened in the 'Battle of the Gauges' – between the 'standard' gauge used by Stephenson and others in the north and Midlands and the 'broad' gauge used by Brunel in the south – in favour of the 'standard'. This meant that, in the long term, lines were at least compatible in terms of engines and rolling stock. In 1846 a Railway Department, called the Commissioners of Railways, was set up, separate from the Board of Trade, to control directly the rates charged, but it was suspended in 1851. Despite the control of profits through pricing policy and enforcement of basic services and safety railway companies made substantial profits throughout the 1840s and Henry Booth wrote that:

> The effects of this extraordinary improvement in the means of travelling, especially since the introduction of railways, have been as striking on the manners as on the industry of all classes. . . . During the spring London is crowded with visitors of all ranks and orders from the remotest provinces, and during the summer and autumn vast numbers of the citizens are spread over the country. . . .

MOVING PEOPLE

'The great connector'

The *Illustrated London News* in September 1850 noted that

> 'the people', popularly so called, have been enabled, thanks to railways and to the organisation of cheap pleasure-trips, to indulge in travels to distances which their forefathers had neither time nor money to undertake. . . . Now travelling bids fair to become not only the necessity of the rich, but the luxury of the poor. The great lines of railways in England, by granting facilities for 'monster' or excursion trains at cheaper rates, have conferred a boom upon the public.

Railways were the great connectors but also the great liberators.[15] The Great Exhibition of 1851 would not have been as successful without the 'monster' trains and this confirmed their importance in increasing population mobility. Examination of census returns in Suffolk for 1851 and 1861 showed that movement was up and down the lines. Alexander Somerville, in his autobiography published in 1848, summed up the wonder of the railway

> All sights which I had seen in London and elsewhere . . . shrank into comparative nothingness when, after reaching Liverpool, I went into the country for a week, in the neighbourhood of Prescot and saw (each day I sought to see it, each hour of the day I could have seen it again) the white steam shooting throughout the landscape of trees, meadows and villages, and the long train, loaded with merchandise, men and women and human enterprise, rolling along under the steam. I had seen no sight like that; I have seen nothing to excel it since. In beauty and grandeur, the world has nothing beyond it.

Railways allowed people to move 'out of town' to the burgeoning suburbs or to go away for holidays. Though slow to develop because of the economic conditions of the 1830s and 1840s, the seaside trip, either for a day or for longer, had become part of the cultures of the growing working and middle classes by the 1860s. New towns developed and expanded in close proximity to urban centres as holiday resorts: Blackpool for the Lancashire area, Scarborough for Yorkshire and Southend for London. Charles Dickens described the new railway hotel – the Grand at Folkestone – as follows

> If you are for public life at our Great Pavilionstone Hotel, you walk into that establishment as if it were your club; and find ready for you, your news-room, dining-room, smoking room, billiard room, music-room, public breakfast, public dinner, twice-a-day (one plain, one gorgeous), hot baths and cold baths. . . . If you want to be bored, there are plenty of bores always ready for you and from Saturday to Monday,

in particular, you can be bored (if you like) through and through. . . . You shall find all nations of the earth and all styles of shaving and not shaving, hair cutting and hair letting alone, for ever flowing through our hotel. Couriers you shall see by hundreds; fat leather bags for five-franc pieces, closing with violent snaps, like discharge of fire-arms, by thousands; more luggage in a morning than, fifty years ago, all Europe saw in a week.

The hotels, of which this is one example, multiplied as travel became more common on the Continent as in Britain. They were the passenger equivalents of the freight depot, palaces from which, with the aid of Thomas Cook's travel agency and Murray's, Bradshaw's and Baedeker's guides, people set out to explore the culture of their own and foreign countries.

Railways as 'social levellers'?

Were railways 'the great levellers' as some contemporaries believed? If by this was meant that railways led to British society becoming less class oriented then probably not, but if they meant that there was an increase in awareness about people and in communication, in all senses of that word, then certainly yes. Railways were feared by some people in the 1820s and 1830s since they would, in Wellington's words, 'allow the lower orders to move around', as a potential threat to aristocratic control. This conservatism was quickly abated, yet in *Sybil* (1845) Benjamin Disraeli's Lord de Mowbray upholds the traditional view:

'I rather counted on him', said Lord de Mowbray, 'to assist me in resisting this joint branch line here; but I was surprised to learn that he had consented.'

'Not until the compensation was settled', innocently remarked Lady Marney: 'George never opposes them after that. He gave up his opposition to the Marham line when they agreed to his terms.'

'And yet,' said Lord de Mowbray, 'I think if Lord Marney would take a different view of the case and look to the moral consequences, he would hesitate. Equality, Lady Marney, equality is not our metier. If we nobles do not make a stand against the levelling spirit of the age, I am at a loss to know who will fight the battle. You may depend that these railways are very dangerous things.'

Good business, as demonstrated by Lord Marney in fiction and the Marquess of Stafford in fact, soon overcame this conservatism and railways became the progressive spirit of the age. A survey of the Essex economy in 1907 stated that 'It was not easy to lay rails in the soft Essex soil and a good deal of the country is still untouched by railroads and therefore quietly unprogressive in spirit.' It is the 'and therefore' which is significant here. Railways ended the isolation of different areas of the country; parochialism died out. In 1839, the *Quarterly Review*, optimistically and prematurely, maintained that railways had ended barbarism in manners and social customs: 'by the power of steam every nation is enabled to see, without flattery, its own faults clearly reflected in his neighbour's mirrors'.

Yet railways started the standardization of language and speech which was carried more speedily forward in the twentieth century by the influence of radio and television. The Cambrian, Taff Vale, Chester and Holyhead and other railways in Wales were powerful agencies in the decline of the speaking of Welsh.

Railways and economic demand

There was an increased demand for coal, both for steam power and for use in the iron industry on which the railway depended. Wrought-iron rails were the major product purchased, but there was also a demand for locomotives, rolling stock and bridges. Though this may have been significant in the development of the iron industry in the late 1840s, railway's share of total iron output and home demand fluctuated. G. R. Hawke's conclusion is nothing if not direct. Railways, he asserts, 'were not essential to the existence of an iron industry . . . nor were they responsible for technical advances and external economies in the finishing processes and rolling mills'.[16]

The diffusion of the 'hot-blast' process in the 1830s and the surge of export demand in the 1840s are now stressed as the decisive influences on the expansion of the industry as a whole. However, railway demand did stimulate growth of iron production in particular areas. This was evident in South Wales. Industries in Cleveland and south Staffordshire also appeared to have received a welcome stimulus from railway demand but in Scotland they were not dependent on the orders of Scottish railways. It is possible to conclude that domestic railways alone took under 10 per cent of pig-iron output between 1835 and 1869 and were dominant for only a short time in the 1840s.

Railway construction stimulated demand for other products, notably coal, timber and building materials and engineering products. In terms of total production, railway's impact on the coal industry was small. In the peak years of 1844–51 between 6 and 10 per cent of coal output went into making iron for railway uses. The rail network required locomotives, rolling stock and signalling equipment. In the late 1830s and 1840s about 20 per cent of the industry's output was in the form of railway rolling stock. Towns grew up round the established engineering centres at Swindon, Crewe, Rugby and Doncaster. The brick-making industry expanded as the result of the numerous bridges, stations, aqueducts, viaducts and embankments being built. By 1845 some 740 million bricks had been used in the fifteen years since the opening of the Liverpool–Manchester Railway and in the 1840s between 25 and 30 per cent of brick production went into railways.

How much did the railways really contribute to British economic growth after 1830? Contemporaries did not hesitate in assuming a direct relationship between the growth of the railway network and economic growth, but historians today are more cautious. The notion that railways rescued Britain from a serious investment crisis in the 1830s and 1840s – a 'crisis of capitalism' – is seen as an exaggeration. G. R. Hawke concluded, on slim evidence, that in 1865 railway services represented a social saving of between 7 and 11 per cent of the net national income of England and Wales. His conclusions have not been accepted uncritically and there is a need for further research into the impact of railways on engineering and retail trading, general communications and business skills and technological change and industrial location in what Sir John Clapham[17] termed 'The Early Railway Age'. His certainty is not as acceptable today. Railways did not occupy the central place in Britain's industrialization of the mid-nineteenth century and were not indispensable to economic growth. But their impact was greater than that of any other single innovation in the period and they were seen by contemporaries as tangible proof of the spirit of 'progress'. Railways represented the confidence of industrialization.

NOTES

1 An American writing, in 1870, on the impact of the Liverpool–Manchester Railway.
2 Francis Egerton, Duke of Bridgewater made this statement around 1800.
3 John Ruskin *Seven Lamps of Architecture*, London, 1849.
4 The development of railways is examined in M. J. T. Lewis *Early Wooden Railways*, London, 1970.
5 On the development of steam locomotion to 1830 see P. S. Bagwell *The Transport Revolution from 1770*, Batsford, 1974, pp. 90–2, H. J. Dyos and D. H. Aldcroft *British Transport*, Leicester University Press, 1969, pp. 111–18 and H. Perkin *The Age of the Railway*, Panther, 1970, pp. 70–2.
6 The central role of the Stephensons is explored in L. T. C. Rolt *George and Robert Stephenson: the Railway Revolution*, 1960 and in R. H. G. Thomas *The Liverpool and Manchester Railway*, Batsford, 1980. See also L. T. C. Rolt *Isambard Kingdom Brunel*, 1957.
7 Dyos and Aldcroft op. cit. pp. 118–26 gives a more detailed account of developments in the 1830s.
8 On the railway mania in the 1840s see ibid. pp. 126–32.
9 There are many studies of the regional history of railways and histories of individual railway companies. Many are listed in the bibliographies in P. S. Bagwell op. cit. and Dyos and Aldcroft op. cit.
10 On investment in railways see P. S. Bagwell op. cit. pp. 95–8 and Dyos and Aldcroft op. cit. pp. 189–94. T. R. Gourvish *Railways and the British Economy 1830–1914*, Macmillan, 1980, pp. 9–26 gives an up-to-date survey of the literature. More detailed studies can be found in S. Broadbridge *Studies in Railway Expansion and the Capital Market in England 1825–1873*, 1970 and M. C. Reed *Investment in Railways in Britain 1820–1844*, 1975. Several articles, cited in

T. R. Gourvish op. cit., are also of use especially T. R. Gourvish and M. C. Reed on financing Scottish lines, and G. R. Hawke and M. C. Reed's survey of financing throughout the nineteenth century. See also J. Lee 'The Provision of Capital for Early Irish Railways', *Irish Historical Journal*, 16, (1968).

11 W. T. Jackman *The Development of Transportation in Modern England*, new edn, edited by W. L. Chaloner, Cass, 1962, p. 584.

12 A. G. Kenwood 'Railway Investment in Britain 1825–1875', *Economica*, 32, (1965), B. R. Mitchell 'The Coming of the Railway and United Kingdom Economic Growth', *Journal of Economic History*, 24 (1964) and G. R. Hawke and M. C. Reed 'Railway Capital in the United Kingdom in the Nineteenth Century', *Economic History Review*, 22 (1969).

13 On the construction of railways and the role of navvies see T. Coleman *The Railway Navvies*, Penguin, 1968 and H. Perkin op. cit. pp. 77–95.

14 On the role of the state and the development of the railway see Dyos and Aldcroft op. cit. pp. 156–65 and P. Bagwell op. cit. pp. 169–98. H. Parris *Government and the Railways in Nineteenth Century Britain*, Routledge & Kegan Paul, 1965 is a more detailed study though his thesis on the role of government should be examined in relation to A. J. Taylor *Laissez-faire and State Intervention in Nineteenth Century Britain*, Macmillan, 1972.

15 The effects of railways are best approached through Dyos and Aldcroft op. cit. pp. 178–200, P. Bagwell op. cit. pp. 107–37 and H. Perkin op. cit. pp. 96–150. J. R. Kellett *Railways and Victorian Cities*, Routledge & Kegan Paul, 1969 looks at the effect of railways on urban development using five case studies.

16 G. R. Hawke *Railways and Economic Growth in England and Wales 1840–1870*, Oxford University Press, 1970, p. 245.

17 J. Clapham *The Economic History of Modern Britain*; Vol. I, *The Early Railway Age 1820–1850*, Cambridge University Press, 1926.

12 The economic revolutions – an overview

> The 'forces' operating in history cannot be defined or put in abstract terms, but one can behold them, observe them, and develop a sympathy for their existence.[1]

Between 1700 and 1850 major change occurred in people's experience and perception of the economic worlds in which they lived. These changes are often encapsulated in the concept of an 'industrial revolution'. The previous nine chapters have examined change from a much broader viewpoint, relating changes in population, communications, agriculture, trade, banking, finance and industrial organization to 'revolutionary' and 'non-revolutionary' industrial innovation. This chapter will attempt to draw together this discussion and raise questions about the historiography of industrial change. It will pose a series of questions which place the economic revolutions in a conceptual framework.

Harold Perkin wrote in 1969 that

> It was a revolution in men's access to the means of life, in control of their physical environment, it opened the road for men to complete mastery of their physical environment without the inescapable need to exploit each other . . . it was more than an industrial revolution.[2]

Perkin and many other historians have written much about the industrial revolution as the 'great discontinuity', the divide between what Peter Laslett called a 'world we have lost' and the modern world. In popular imagination it is supposed to have ended traditional society in England and initiated fundamental social change. It is supposed to have completely altered people's lives, liberating them from the constraints of Nature and, for the first time, giving them control over their environment. The cotton mill powered by steam epitomized both the promise and the exploitation of the 'new' economic order. How accurate a representation of the past are these perspectives and why have historians adopted them?

HISTORIOGRAPHY

The historiography of the industrial revolution can be traced back to the 1820s when the term was evidently coined in France.[3] It was given academic currency by Blanqui in the 1830s, translated into German by Marx and Engels in the 1840s and popularized in English by Arnold Toynbee in his *The Industrial Revolution*, published in 1884. For writers like this it has always served a polemic purpose and this tendency continues today. From the outset the notion of an 'industrial revolution' has been a forum of debate between groups of historians and polemicists who viewed it from different perspectives.[4] Two broad traditions of explanation for, and response towards, industrialization can be identified. One tradition, which was well developed by the 1830s involves a favourable evaluation of the effects of industrialization based primarily on materialistic criteria. Industrialization was seen as the epitome of individualism, a personal expression of the liberationist capitalist economic system. Thomas Carlyle, for example, wrote

> Were we required to characterise this age of ours by any single epithet, we should be tempted to call it, not an Heroical, Devotional, Philosophical, or Moral Age, but, above all others, the Mechanical Age. It is the Age of Machinery, in every outward and inward sense of that word. . . . What changes too, this addition of power is introducing into the Social System; how wealth has more and more increased. . . . Not the external and physical alone is now managed by machinery, but the internal and spiritual also. . . . [5]

A contradictory tradition emerged from the experience and observation of industrialization which challenged the basic assumptions of the materialistic approach. It evaluated both the causation and impact of the industrial revolution in terms of loss, exploitation and deprivation from a more humanistic perspective that went beyond the purely economic. William Blake wrote of more than just 'dark satanic mills' in his poem 'Jerusalem'

> And all the Arts of Life they chang'd into the Arts of Death in Albion.
> The hour-glass contemn'd because its simple workmanship
> Was like the workmanship of the plowman, & the water wheel
> That raises water into cisterns, broken & burn'd with fire
> Because its workmanship was like the workmanship of the shepherd;
> And in their stead, intricate wheels invented, wheel without wheel,
> To perplex youth in their outgoings & to bind to labours in Albion
> Of day & night the myriads of eternity: that they may grind
> And polish brass & iron hour after hour, laborious task,
> Kept ignorant of its use: that they might spend the days of wisdom
> In sorrowful drudgery to obtain a scanty pittance of bread,
> In ignorance to view a small portion & thinks that All,
> And call it Demonstration, blind to the simple rules of life.[6]

A 'social change' school

Within these two traditions four different, though overlapping, schools of thought about what really mattered during the industrial revolution can be distinguished. First, a 'social change' school, which owes its origins to Arnold Toynbee's belief that 'the essence of the Industrial Revolution is the substitution of competition for medieval regulation which had previously controlled the production and distribution of wealth'. To Toynbee, the industrial revolution was first and foremost a change in the way economic transactions occurred between people – the emergence of a market economy – and this led to fundamental changes in the way society was structured. There is a strong polemical element in this approach. To Toynbee and others some judgement on the value for people of the change to a market economy could be made. Simplistically 'pessimistic' and 'optimistic' perspectives have been put forward – perspectives which play an important role in 'the standard of living debates' – and which have political overtones since they highlight the value of the whole process of 'modernization'.

Organization

The second viewpoint places emphasis on industrial organization, on the structure and scale of firms and the rise of the factory system. This can be traced back to Marx's interpretation of the rise of 'Machinofactures' but has its classic exposition in Paul Mantoux's *The Industrial Revolution in the Eighteenth Century*, published in 1929. Related to this was the emphasis on the move from 'working' capital (raw materials for industry, seed for agriculture) to 'fixed' capital (machines, mines, structures).

Development economics

The third school of thought arose after 1945 in response to the emergence of development economic theory, particularly that of Simon Kuznets, which highlighted the question of economic growth. W. W. Rostow's *The Stages of Economic Growth*, published in 1960, is perhaps the most famous exemplar of this perspective. The emphasis is upon growth of national incomes, the rate of capital formation, investment ratios and growth in the labour force. It raised a question – why was Britain the first nation to industrialize? – which was directly applicable to underdeveloped countries. New Economic History, with its emphasis on trends, large collections of industries and individuals rather than single people, on the collective experience of growth and with hypothetical models, has its origins in this quantitative approach to change.

Technological change

The final school of thought places its emphasis on the impact of technology and the diffusion of new technical knowledge. This approach, found especially in David Landes' *The Unbound Prometheus*, published in 1969, was about more than just 'gadgets'. It emphasizes technology's impact on the organization of labour, consumer manipulation, marketing and distribution techniques.

Problems with these perspectives

Valuable insights have been achieved through these approaches to economic change. But they are all in some way partial. This is clearly demonstrated by the different chronologies of change each propounds. The social change school places its focus on the period between 1760 and 1850 between which two dates, it is maintained, there was a transition from a paternalist to a class ideology of social organization and structure. The industrial organization school also begins in 1760 but ends in 1840 by which time the factory system was firmly embedded as the dominant mode of industrial organization. The macroeconomic group pushes the starting point back to the 1740s, in the case of Deane and Cole, and forward to the 1780s for W. W. Rostow and ends in 1830 when the essential features of an industrialized economy based on growth mechanisms had been established. Finally, the technological school emphasizes the proliferation of invention and innovation between 1760 and 1800. These differing chronologies raise as many questions as they answer and many of the propositions on which they are based have been critically analysed in the previous chapters. For example, there certainly was a proliferation of inventions and innovations between 1760 and 1800 in certain sectors of the economy but not all and, as the application of the steam engine showed, invention did not mean diffusion. Many existing approaches to examining economic change in the eighteenth and early mid-nineteenth centuries place a quite justifiable emphasis on a particular aspect of change. However, they do not provide the overview necessary to integrate the various elements that existed into a coherent whole. The remainder of this chapter will examine four issues in an attempt to provide that coherent overview – the question of 'perspective', the question of 'time', the question of 'causation' and the question of whether the concept of an 'industrial revolution' still has relevance and value for historians – and will end with some consideration of the overall economic trends which can be identified between 1700 and 1850.

THE QUESTION OF 'PERSPECTIVE'

A 'total' experience

How far does looking at the industrial revolution from different perspectives alter how it can be perceived? The first issue is one of 'totality' – is it possible to see the industrial revolution in its 'total' setting? One criticism of quantitative economic history is that, as Georges Lefebvre ruefully commented, 'living, suffering man does not appear in it'. Statistics are one type of evidence historians can construct and use but they only provide trends or tendencies which need to be fleshed out. The industrial revolution did not just happen, it happened to people who acted, reacted, opposed and supported its events in different ways. This means that historians should, in Fogel's words,

> portray the entire range of human experience, to capture all of the essential features of the civilization they were studying and to do so in a way that would clearly have relevance to the present.[7]

But what is the 'entire range of human experience' and 'all of the essential features of the civilization'? The problem is that many historians of the industrial revolution have not really considered these problems and, where they have, there is little consensus on possible solutions. 'Total' history is unlikely to be practicable for a single country if all the sources are to be mastered and a full integration of the variety of experiences achieved. The geographical limits of the enquiry have to be drastically narrowed, which paradoxically often means that 'total' history turns out in practice to be local history. Le Roy Ladurie exemplified this approach in his study of rural Languedoc, writing that he examined

> the long-term movements of an economy and of a society – base and superstructure, material life and cultural life, sociological evolution and collective psychology, the whole within the framework of a rural world which remained very largely traditional in nature.[8]

Most writings on the industrial revolution at this level concentrate on a specific industry or town rather than a region. There is a powerful argument for looking at regional developments in Britain in a 'total' sense to create 'models' for change and continuity as a means of getting the 'total' experience of Britain into its proper perspective.

Historians have traditionally been suspicious, if not antagonistic, towards the notion of 'historical models'. What issues could be raised, for example, from a model based around 'people in society', their 'actions and interactions', 'beliefs and prejudices' and 'pasts and presents' as a means through which historians can mediate their discussion of change and continuity in the eighteenth and nineteenth centuries? Consider the issue of 'pasts and presents'. This necessitates an examination of individual and collective mentalities, the multi-dimensional private experiences within the context of multi-dimensional public spheres, the inherited experiences that underpinned existing cultural values and how these values were adapted and changed. This means the conscious drawing in of expertise, skills and concepts from other disciplines and the possible need for collaboration with other specialists. This attacks the essential individualism of much history writing and the autonomy of history as a discrete subject. The traditional approach, though it often works when historians examine events within a tight chronological framework using narrative techniques, is less valuable for considering long-term developments. If history is about re-creating and giving meaning as well as providing valid explanations and interpretations based on an objective analysis of evidence then any approach or technique which helps to illuminate this is perfectly valid. The 'total' approach using models to explicate the nature of development through time is necessary to achieve understanding of the industrial revolution.

A 'national' perspective – an approach through Britain

The second issue concerns the question of national perspectives. England, Wales, Scotland and Ireland had contrasting experiences between 1700 and 1850, a consequence of different resources, climate and histories. Most studies of the industrial revolution, however, have England and, to a lesser extent, Wales as their focal points. The general texts on British economic change between 1700 and 1850 almost without exception focus on England, drawing in examples from Scotland, Wales and Ireland to illustrate points rather than within the mainstream of discussion. The result of this has been that the English perspective has been accepted as the 'norm'. This process begins in schools where the periphery is examined only when it has an effect or impact on England. Did anything of any note happen in Ireland between 1801 and 1850 apart from the Great Famine? In Scotland, Wales and Ireland most pupils do courses on their own country as well as England, but rarely on the other two areas making up the United Kingdom. The effect of this can be seen in three ways. First, it reinforces ignorance which is carried into higher education and results in a failure to establish a dialogue between the English experience and the experiences of the other countries. Secondly, it perpetuates myths, and finally it means that British history actually means English history.

So how does looking at issues from a broader perspective help in understanding the process of historical development between 1700 and 1850? Take, for example, demographic growth. Why has English growth been considered the norm for demographic analysis? There is a problem with the available evidence, which may account for this. In England parish registers are available from almost all parishes but in Wales only about a third have survived and the figures are much lower for Scotland and

Ireland. Examination of the chronology of population change between 1700 and 1850 in the four areas shows marked differences. The populations of both Ireland and Scotland grew at faster rates than England between 1700 and 1750: 25 per cent, 21 per cent and 16 per cent respectively. England's rate of growth was less than Ireland's between 1750 and 1800, 0.7 per cent per annum compared to Ireland's 1 per cent per annum. Scotland's population revolution did not really begin until after 1800 when Ireland's had lost its momentum. The late eighteenth-century situation, when Ireland's rate of growth was three times Scotland's, was reversed. Differences in general trends are borne out by looking at particular reasons for growth. The introduction of the potato in Ireland, but also in Highland Scotland, arguably had an impact on birth rates. Did it remove constraints which had held population down? Why were prenuptially conceived births lower in Ireland than in England and Wales but highest in Scotland? With all these differences the impact of population growth needs to be evaluated much more carefully. The formula that 'population growth = growing demand = stimulus to economic growth' is an oversimplification. Ireland did not undergo dramatic industrial changes between 1750 and 1800 when its population was growing, while Scotland's burst of industrial activity in the 1770s predates population growth by twenty years.

The division of the British economy into its four national parts goes part of the way towards the approach put forward by Sidney Pollard in his *Peaceful Conquest: the Industrialisation of Europe 1760–1970*, Oxford University Press, 1981. He argues that the industrial revolution was an affair that took place in the context of national and regional economies. Regions frequently had distinct technological traditions and forms of industrial organization which affected their development. For example, in the Forest of Dean, the Derbyshire lead-mining district and the stannaries of Cornwall regional practices and styles were enshrined in distinctive laws. This approach allows historians to examine the 'total' experience of the different economies contemporaries could encounter and consider the comparative advantage of one form of industry over others. Britain did not have a unified economy in the eighteenth and early nineteenth centuries. Economic change was essentially a local or regional rather than national affair.

'Leading sectors' and change 'in slow motion'

There has been an understandable tendency to examine the industrial revolution in terms of the 'leading sectors' of cotton, iron, coal and steam – dramatic, promethean, revolutionary, apocalyptic, expansive. Does this emphasis misrepresent the reality of contemporary experience? Does it result in an unbalanced view of the productive sectors of the economy? Does it simply miss things out? Existing histories of the industrial revolution certainly present change 'writ large' but was rapid economic growth the experience of all regions of Britain? How can historians blend the cataclysmic vision of David Landes in his *Unbound Prometheus* which Maxine Berg sees as

> the bold sweep of technology's advance. It came like a republican army, confident in its principles and its moral precepts, and thus overcoming all economic, social and historical barriers. . . . Landes's Industrial Revolution, whose pre-ordained triumph was so obvious and so right, was based on the achievements of new machinery, new power sources and new raw materials.[9]

with the perspective of historians like A. E. Musson?

> in most industries there was no technical revolution in the century before 1850 . . . traditional handicrafts still predominated . . . there had been no widespread introduction of steam-power mechanisation and the factory system . . . the typical British worker in the mid-nineteenth century was not a factory operator in a factory but still a traditional craftsman or labourer or domestic servant.[10]

On the one hand the industrial revolution is seen in a revolutionary context while the alternative perspective is one of industrial revolution 'in slow motion'. Recently the idea of change in slow motion has gained currency and the views of Sir John Clapham have been revived and expanded by Nick Crafts and Maxine Berg. Both argue that it is essential to consider change in a longer perspective, beginning in the late seventeenth or early eighteenth century, and have reached certain broad conclusions. First, they argue that growth in the 'leading sectors' of the economy was atypical and that, in most industries, expansion was much slower and extended over a longer time-scale. This is combined, secondly, with the reassessment of Gregory King's and Joseph Massie's analyses of population. England and Wales were much more industrial and commercial in 1700 than King would have historians believe, which means that the extent of movement from agriculture to industry was not as great as originally thought. Thirdly, the move from traditional industries to factory-based, steam-powered industries was not as dramatic as contemporaries believed. Finally, Britain did not attain particularly high levels of industrial output per worker and the triumph of the industrial revolution lay in increasing the labour force rather than obtaining higher productivity from those already employed.

THE QUESTION OF 'TIME'

Two examples can be used to illustrate the less than revolutionary nature of change and the need for a more careful application of chronology to developments. Stationary steam engines have long been regarded as the single most important invention underlying the industrial revolution.[11]

They were the 'prime movers' supplying inexhaustible energy for working machines that produced consumer goods. Historians who have concentrated on the late eighteenth century emphasize the importance of James Watt and particularly his development of rotary motion. This view neglects two things: first, the importance of developments in steam before 1780 and, secondly, the improvements made in existing power sources. There is no doubt about the importance of Watt's improvements in the 1780s but just how dramatic were their effects?

A. E. Musson writes that

It is not generally appreciated that in 1800 steam power was still in its infancy, that in the vast majority of manufactures there had been little or no power-driven mechanization, and that where such mechanization had occurred water-power was still much more widespread and important than steam. And after 1800, the 'triumph of the factory system' took place much more slowly than had generally been realized; water-wheels long continued to be built and used, while most manufacturing operations remained largely unmechanized until after 1870.[12]

Concentration on large-scale industries like cotton led historians to overestimate the extent to which steam was applied to other industries. Not until the diffusion of high-pressure stationary engines after 1840 was there substantial reduction in fuel costs and an increase in the speed at which machines could run. The fullest application of steam power had to wait until accurate and reliably engineered machines had been developed.

Historians like antitheses, and central to people's image of the industrial revolution stands the 'dark satanic mill' and the contrasting domestic method of production.[13] This image, however, owes more to polemic than to the realities of the past. Engels and Marx may have used it in their radical critique of proletarian conditions and capitalist exploitation but closer examination demonstrates that the stark contrast is questionable and that there was continuity between the factory and pre-factory stages of development. Hand or outworking continued to play a major role in the British economy until after 1850. This essential continuity has been given increased credibility through the concept of 'proto-industrialization'. Industrial change, it is argued, could not have taken place without the previous development of forms of production which provided the key changes in the use of land, labour, capital and entrepreneurship. Revolutionary change may well have taken place in cotton and iron and steam power may have provided a more reliable source of energy but three-quarters of British manufacture was in diverse, dispersed and unspectacular industries.

The domestic system was a method of mass production, in which 'skill' played little part, no less than the factory system that emerged after the mid-eighteenth century. There was already a clear distinction between capitalists, who controlled and financed industries, and wage-earners.

There was continuity between both systems with firms active in setting up factories already active in the putting-out system. The chronology and character of change varied from region to region as the comparative advantage of one economic activity over another was realized. Some areas, like East Anglia and the Cotswolds, 'deindustrialized' because changes in other sectors of the economy resulted in different economic imperatives and opportunities emerging. Recent work has re-emphasized the distinction between the domestic system and the skilled urban artisan structure of small commodity production and the self-employed craftsman. Consumer preference in Britain was for differentiated hand-produced goods and the artisan trades suited this heterogeneity with the need for short production runs of unique items. Changes in the industrial organization were far more complex than merely a move from domestic to factory systems and the development of a domestic consumer market based entirely on machine-produced standardized goods was a product of the late not the early nineteenth century.

It is necessary therefore when considering the chronology of economic change between 1700 and 1850 to be quite clear what specific chronology is being examined. Change in some industries may have been rapid and revolutionary but historians should not assume that all industries followed this atypical pattern. J. C. D. Clark echoes A. E. Musson in writing that the

> very term 'Industrial Revolution' . . . vastly exaggerates eighteenth-century Englishmen's perceptions of the change they were living through. . . . Most sectors of the economy witnessed substantial growth before 1832, but only cotton increased exponentially. Not until the 1830s and 1840s, when the railway and the steamship arrived, did the output of iron and coal surge ahead. Not until then did mass-production and powered machine tools spread to many industries. Meanwhile the economy was dominated by its traditional sectors and by traditional technologies, slowly evolving. In 1832 Britain was still essentially horse-drawn and sail-driven.[14]

THE QUESTION OF 'CAUSATION'

The question of causation is generally approached through the question 'Why was there an Industrial Revolution?'.[15] This is then usually focused on why the textile, iron and coal industries expanded and what the impact of the diffusion of steam power was. Important though these questions are, they neglect the broader economic experiences of Britain between 1700 and 1850. The question 'Why did the industrial revolution occur in Britain rather than France or the Netherlands or Germany?' misses the crucial point that industrial change did not occur in Britain as a whole but in Lancashire or the Central Lowlands of Scotland or South Wales or round Belfast and that there was no necessary connection between development in one area and those in others. Trying to discover whether it was population growth or increased demand or agricultural change or any other thing which actually started economic change again seems to miss the point.

Accounting for the industrial revolution is an extremely difficult undertaking since economic changes had an effect – however small – on all aspects of society. Some circumstances which were present in Britain facilitated change and, in that sense, can be said to be causal. Others impeded progress but change occurred despite them. Historians have recently used counterfactual analysis – the 'what would have happened if' approach – to assess the indispensability of the different elements that existed particularly in the eighteenth century. Certain issues emerge from this. First, if change occurred over a much longer period than traditionally believed, this approach may prove valuable in assessing the long-term impact of, for example, agriculture, on other sectors of the economy. Secondly, given the nebulous nature of the industrial revolution, is it possible to identify causes at anything more than a superficial level? Historians have to be specific in terms of the sector, geographical area and time-span concerned. This can be expressed in the simple model shown in Figure 12.1.

THE PROBLEM OF 'MEANING'

Finally, the problem has been that historians have tended to explain the industrial revolution as a unidimensional phenomenon whereas for contemporaries change or continuity were mediated not in national terms but in terms of regional, local and individual experiences. It was the diversity of change and continuity that marked Britain out in the eighteenth and first half of the nineteenth centuries.

Is the concept of an 'industrial revolution' still of value to historians, given this diversity? A recent debate on this issue occurred between Michael Fores and A. E. Musson.[16] Fores is concerned with whether or not industrial societies have experienced a revolutionary break from the past with a change of attitudes, beliefs and new 'institutions'. He relates this to the notion of 'practical engineers' being responsible for all industrial development, regardless of science and technology, and concludes that, since there was no revolutionary change in techniques, practical craftsmen were still the same sort of people gradually developing new artefacts. In this argument there was no industrial revolution. Musson submits this to a penetrating critique, demonstrating the weakness of an argument that fails to place emphasis on the role of science and technology. Michael Fores does, however, provide a useful discussion of the four possible meanings of 'industry'/industrialization:

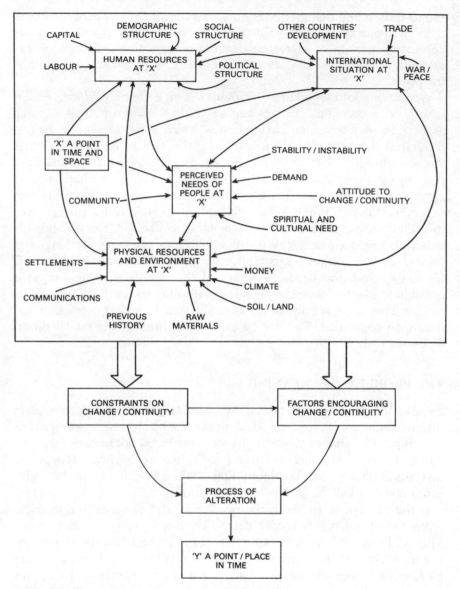

Figure 12.1 Economic development: a simple model

(i) 'industry' as a particular sector of economic life – the mining industry or agriculture;

(ii) 'industry' as a specifically manufacturing sector of an economy;

(iii) 'industrialization' as a process whereby a factory system is established;

(iv) 'industrialization' as a process by which a non-traditional 'modern' life is produced characterized by urban living and more 'rational' guidance and discipline for performance at work.

The extent to which there was 'discontinuity' in the chronology of change and the nature of growth in the economy in the eighteenth and first half of the nineteenth centuries depends which of these meanings historians emphasize. It is useful to regard Britain in this period as having a dual economy in which two economies coexisted. There were those areas which, though not stagnant, developed gradually along conventional lines with slow productivity growth (generally below 1 per cent per annum) and slowly rising ratios between capital and labour. This economy contained agriculture, construction, domestic industries and 'traditional' trades. A modern sector, containing cotton, iron, engineering, mining, transportation and some consumer goods like pottery and paper, characterized by higher productivity growth (up to 4 per cent per annum) coexisted with this traditional sector. J. Mokyr says that:

> Two-sector growth models imply that abrupt changes in the economy as a whole are a mathematical impossibility. Even if change in the modern sector itself were discontinuous, its share in the economy would grow only gradually, while the traditional sector would lose ground only slowly. In the long run the force of compound growth rates was such that the modern sector swallowed the entire economy.[17]

The value of the notion of an 'industrial revolution' remains, but viewed in the context of the economy as a whole not just cotton or iron or steam.

ECONOMIC FLUCTUATIONS

Economic change is not a steady process but one subject to fluctuation. Some fluctuations result from forces within the economic process itself, either internal to a particular economy or the result of forces operating in an international context. Other pressures are 'exogenous' or imposed on the economy from causes which are not part of the economic system.

Harvests

In the eighteenth and early nineteenth centuries, harvests and wars both had a profound exogenous impact on economic development. There was no regularity to either which could be built into any economic forward planning. Agriculture was the largest single component, either in the national income, capital and its labour force. T. S. Ashton rightly commented that 'What was happening at Westminster or in the City was of small account compared with what was happening in the heavens.'[18].

Harvests affected the economy as a whole in different ways. Their effect was most obvious on purchasing power. Poor harvests pushed the price of food up and depressed the purchasing power of most of the population for other goods. Farmers were the only people to benefit from higher food prices. Bad harvests also had an impact in the international economy through the need to import corn, a trend which increased after the 1760s. The corn trade was, however, still sporadic and dependent on the state of the British harvest. This created a sudden adverse balance of payments to be paid for largely in bullion. It also led to depressed home demand and poor harvests were often followed by slumps in manufacturing industries. This uneven rhythm of harvest crises can be traced throughout this period: 1710, 1725, 1767, 1773, 1783, 1792–3, 1795–6, 1799–1800, 1815–16, 1829, 1838, 1847.

War

War could kill, or create a foreign market. Capturing a French sugar island could make prices tumble, while losing it could push them up again. Control of the seas could allow merchants to obtain new markets as, for example, with the South American boom of 1807–8. Bad news or a defeat could result in a panic on the banks and the money market, as in 1745, 1793 and 1797. Internally, industries with a role to play in war expanded while some consumer industries were sapped by high wartime taxation. During the French Wars betwen 1793 and 1815 the iron industry expanded because of government demands for military and naval hardware. Peace in 1815 brought over-capacity and until 1820 there was a painful period of readjustment to normal conditions. This process was also evident in food production, where higher prices encouraged expansion using money borrowed at high rates of interest. Peace brought lower prices and depression on arable land for farmers saddled with higher mortgage repayments than their declining profits allowed.

Trade cycles

The cycle in both foreign and internal trade, of between four and seven years, is a much more regular indication of economic fluctuation. As the role of foreign trade in the national income expanded with the changes in the structure of the economy, the more the economy became exposed to its fluctuations. Poor harvests, war and political unrest could all affect the import of goods. Changed income conditions in Britain led quickly to modifications in demand for imports. Full warehouses meant that it would take time for stocks to be cleared. Potential customers could wait for prices to fall even lower and this fall in trading activity had a 'knock-on' effect on industries working for export markets, which similarly became depressed. Production could be cut or wages lowered, both of which had the effect of further depressing the purchasing power and spending of people working in those industries. Once stocks had run down the reverse sequence occurred. Demand and prices picked up, confidence and optimism returned and the economy revived.

This 'boom-slump' sequence can be seen clearly between 1815 and 1850. The French Wars led to a buoyant economy and prosperity mounted steadily from 1811 after Napoleon's continental blockade broke up. For over thirty years the British economy had been subject to a powerful growth stimulus. Industrial output increased rapidly. Agriculture and trade expanded. Between 1815 and 1820 there was a period of readjustment to peacetime conditions. A short post-war boom as exports of cotton goods, hardware and iron were rushed to starved markets ended in 1818 and the economy plunged into depression reaching its nadir in 1819. Agriculture did not have the benefit of this boom and prices fell disastrously for the already heavily mortgaged farmers. The response – the Corn Law of 1815 – did not resolve the farmers' dilemma of how to cope with being wedged between falling prices and fixed costs. Profitable outlets for investment almost ceased to exist and, despite long-term interest rates falling, there was insufficient incentive for businessmen to embark on new ventures.

By 1821 there were real signs of a general recovery which lasted until the mid-1830s. Industrial output accelerated and investment, both abroad and at home, went on continuously. Exports expanded. This growth was, however, not without its problems. Its tentative nature in the 1820s was clearly demonstrated in the financial crisis of 1825 and in the loss of economic confidence in 1829 and 1831, a result of poor harvests in 1828 and 1830. From 1832 to 1836 there was heavy investment at home in railway shares, and exports were boosted by loans to America which stimulated Anglo-American trade.

Between 1815 and 1836 it had become increasingly clear that continued expansion for British industry depended on stable foreign markets. Between 1836 and 1842 there was an intense depression which began in industry, was deepened after the severe financial crisis of 1839 and exacerbated by unpredictable harvests. Heavy grain imports were necessary, especially in 1838 and 1839, with the consequent loss of gold abroad and monetary stringency at home. Declining foreign investment, particularly in America, further depressed trade. Revival after 1842 was led by investment in transportation and by the removal of tariff control by Peel's government, creating conditions in which growth could occur.

The swings of the trade cycle took place within a rising long-term trend. Over-capacity was ultimately absorbed by a growing population and a growing demand coming from a rising national income. Short-term expansion was an unstable affair of boom and slump, inflation and deflation. Yet, as Peter Mathias argues 'At every point the problems of short-run economic fluctuations rested upon the fundamental forces operating for long-run economic expansion.'[19]

CONCLUSIONS

The traditional views of the industrial revolution have recently been re-examined and a picture of the economic changes of the eighteenth and early nineteenth centuries based on growth 'in slow motion' have been re-emphasized. Certain questions still need to be considered. How far did unequal development in England, Scotland, Wales and Ireland affect the 'revolutionary' nature of the changes in the industrial economy? Is an approach through interconnected studies of defined regions more valuable than through nation states? What was the balance between traditionally organized and forward-looking industries? Reinterpretation of a historical phenomenon of such importance as the industrial revolution will occur in each succeeding generation as new perspectives are examined, regional studies are produced and chronologies and causations adjusted. Economists may want to learn lessons from the past but they should reflect on the prognosis made by the Italian historian Croce that 'the only lesson that we learn from the past is that we learn no lessons from the past'.

NOTES

1 Leopold von Ranke 'The Great Powers', in G. G. Iggers and K. von Moltke (eds) *The Theory and Practice of History*, Indianapolis University Press, 1973, p. 100.
2 H. Perkin in *The Origins of Modern English Society 1780–1880*, Routledge, 1969, pp. 3–5.
3 The history of the expression 'industrial revolution' can be examined in Sir George Clark *The Idea of the Industrial Revolution*, Glasgow, 1953.
4 The voluminous historiography of the industrial revolution can be best approached through M. W. Flinn *Origins of the Industrial Revolution*, Longman, 1966, pp. 1–18, G. G. Iggers *New Directions in European Historiography*, Methuen, 1985, pp. 154–74 and J. Mokyr (ed.) *The Economics of the Industrial Revolution*, Allen and Unwin, 1985, pp. 1–52, especially 3–6. E. A. Wrigley *Continuity, Chance and Change. The Character of the Industrial Revolution in England*, Cambridge University Press, 1988, is a major revisionist study.
5 T. Carlyle 'Signs of the Times' (1829), in A. Shelston (ed.) *Thomas Carlyle – Selected Writings*, Penguin, 1971, pp. 64–5.
6 William Blake *Poems and Prophecies*, Dent, 1972, pp. 238–9.
7 R. W. Fogel and G. R. Elton *Which Road to the Past?*, Yale University Press, 1983, p. 19.
8 E. Le Roy Ladurie *The Peasants of Languedoc*, University of Illinois Press, 1966, p. 289.
9 M. Berg *The Age of Manufactures 1700–1820*, Fontana, 1985, p. 23.
10 A. E. Musson *The Growth of British Industry*, Batsford, 1978, pp. 252–3, 141.
11 This is examined in detail in chapter 5.
12 A. E. Musson 'Industrial Motive Power in the United Kingdom 1800–1870', *Economic History Review*, 2nd Series, 29 (1976), p. 416.
13 This is examined in detail in chapter 6.
14 J. C. D. Clark *English Society 1688–1832*, Cambridge University Press, 1985, p. 65.
15 On the question of causes see the editorial introduction to J. Mokyr (ed.) op.

cit., the essays in part two of R. M. Hartwell *The Industrial Revolution and Economic Growth*, Methuen, 1971 and the collection of essays by different authors in R. M. Hartwell (ed.) *The Causes of the Industrial Revolution in England*, Methuen, 1967.

16 Michael Fores 'The Myth of a British Industrial Revolution', *History*, 66 (1981); A. E. Musson 'The British Industrial Revolution', ibid., 69 (1982).

17 J. Mokyr (ed.) op. cit., p. 5.

18 T. S. Ashton *Economic Fluctuations in England 1700–1800*, Oxford University Press, 1955, p. 2.

19 P. Mathias *The First Industrial Nation*, Methuen, 2nd edn 1983, p. 216.

Addendum:
The following appeared too late to be considered but develop the general line outlined in this chapter: P. Mathias and J. A. Davis (eds) *The First Industrial Revolutions*, Blackwell, 1989 is an excellent summary of the current situation; A. Digby and C. Feinstein (ed.) *New Directions in Economic and Social History*, Macmillan, 1990 reprint articles from ReFRESH and R. Brown *Economic Revolutions 1750–1850*, Cambridge University Press, 1991 attempts a synthesis in the introduction.

13 Rent

Now, in every country of civilized men, acknowledging the rights of property, and by means of determined boundaries and common laws united into one people or nation, the two antagonist powers or opposite interests of the State, under which all other State interests are comprised, are those of permanence and of progression.[1]

Nothing is more certain than that our manners, our civilisation, and all the good things which are connected with manners and with civilisation, have, in this European world of ours, depended for ages upon two principles, and were, indeed, the result of both combined: I mean the spirit of a gentleman and the spirit of religion.[2]

David Ricardo divided society into three economic powers: rent, capital and wages. The next three chapters will sketch the major developments in British society between 1700 and 1850 through an examination of those groups which broadly corresponded to these three ways of living. They will be followed by a consideration of changing social ideologies in which 'paternalism' and 'class' will be evaluated. In the eighteenth and, to a lesser extent, in the nineteenth centuries a person's identity was characterized in relation to birth, property, occupation and rank in the social order. Women were generally defined through either their father's or husband's social status. Power, economic and political, lay in the possession and exploitation of land. Landowners either farmed their own land or rented it out to tenant farmers. It is with these social groups that this chapter is concerned.

LANDOWNERSHIP

In terms of rent the major distinction was between those who received rent (rentiers) and those who paid it (tenant farmers). In England there were major changes in landownership between the fifteenth and eighteenth centuries which consolidated the position of the great landowners and the gentry and made them into the dominant economic, political and social force in the country.

Table 13.1 Land ownership in England 1436–1873

Social group	Percentage of land held in			
	1436	*1690*	*1790*	*1873*
Great owners	15–20	15–20	20–25	24
Gentry	25	45–50	50	55
Yeoman freeholders	20	25–33	15	10
Church and Crown	25–35	5–10	10	10

Source: G. E. Mingay *The Gentry*, Longman, 1976, p. 59, table 3.1.

Up to 1700 there was an increase in the numerical importance of both gentry and yeomen at the expense of Church and Crown. The development of the gentry was the first stage in the monopolization of land by a rentier class. The eighteenth century saw the second stage with the concentration of land in the hands of great owners and gentry at the expense of the smaller freeholders. The 'agricultural revolution' consolidated capitalist relations of production in the countryside. Agriculture ceased, almost imperceptibly, to be simply a way of life and became an 'industry'. The distinction between 'landowner' and 'farmer' was sharpened. As Table 13.1 shows, great landowners and gentry increased their hold over land after 1690 as the smaller owners were forced to sell land with the failure of their incomes to meet rising expectations. The growth of the large estate in England was associated with the consolidation of tenancies into larger agricultural units. It is, however, important to put this in perspective. Though the economic and territorial dominance of the large farm was established by 1830, most farming was on a much smaller scale. The experience of Buckinghamshire was representative of most southern counties. In 1851 1,810 farms can be identified of which 872 were between 100 and 300 acres, only 229 with over 300 acres and an average size of 179 acres. In Yorkshire, by contrast, 70 per cent of farms were under 100 acres and in Lancashire and Cheshire the figure was 90 per cent. In 1851 there were only 7,771 English farms with over 1,000 acres while some 142,358 farms had under 100 acres.

Land ownership in England had, by 1700, a clearly defined legal basis. The concept of absolute and heritable private property had fully crystallized. Rights over land were transferable from one person to another and the contrast between 'ownership' and 'non-ownership' was central to an institutional mediation of power. Possession of land – in terms of legal ownership or 'practical' ownership through tenancy – gave power and social authority. Table 13.2 shows how it was possible to divide landowners in England and Wales in 1790.

Landlords, who had legal rights of ownership to units of land, may have directly controlled their use as capital or may have delegated this task.

Table 13.2 Landowners in England and Wales in 1790

	No. of families	Income (£ p.a.)	% non-common land
Magnates	400	5,000–50,000	20–25
Gentry			
Wealthy gentry	700–800	3,000–5,000	
Squires	3,000–4,000	1,000–3,000	50–60
Gentlemen	10,000–20,000	300–1,000	
Freeholders			
Wealthy	25,000	150–700	15–20
Lesser	75,000	30–300	

Source: based on G. E. Mingay *English Landed Society in the Eighteenth Century*, Routledge, London, 1963, p. 26.

This delegation or 'mediation of control' involved either employing managerial agents like estate managers, stewards and bailiffs or leasing out land to tenant farmers. In either case possession of landed capital was shared between rentiers, agents and tenants. Freeholders' farms had to be of sufficient size to generate a sustained marketable surplus over and above subsistence requirements. Where freeholders held insufficient land to do this then they either had to rent additional land or became landowning peasants differing from labourers only in having sufficient land to produce their own subsistence without having to sell their labour power to another person. Tenant farmers, numbering a further 100,000 families, like the owner-occupier lived on the actual profits of farming rather than from rentals from land. G. E. Mingay has commented that 'In discussing the life of the lowest ranks of landed society there is little point in distinguishing between owner-occupiers and tenant-farmers.'[3]

For both the owner-occupier and the tenant the primary significance of land lay in its function as a revenue-generating unit of production and this overrode the legal distinctions between them. It is important not to overstate the homogeneity of landed society above the level of owner-occupier. Although the peerage and the gentry had much in common, as Mingay says, 'between the main body of the peerage and the great majority of the gentry there yawned always a measurable social gulf'.[4]

THE ARISTOCRACY

An 'open' aristocracy?

Just how powerful was the English aristocracy in the eighteenth and early nineteenth centuries? Recent work has led to a re-examination of the position of the peerage at the centre of English social and political life and to their pre-eminence in the hierarchical social structure.[5] The traditional view, expressed in the contemporary setting by, among others, Voltaire, maintained that links between aristocracy and gentry and the sharing of power with commercial and mercantile groups produced a social mobility, even a social harmony which underpinned the peaceful constitutional and economic developments of the eighteenth and nineteenth centuries.[6] Intermarriage of peers and commoners had always been common, W. Lecky argued in the later part of the nineteenth century. In the mid-nineteenth century De Tocqueville distinguished the English aristocracy from its continental counterpart by the 'ease with which it has opened its ranks' and Perkin has made a strong case for an 'open dynamic aristocracy', which he sees as part of the explanation of England's industrial revolution.[7] But just how 'open' was the peerage? In 1700 there were 163 lords temporal and 26 lords spiritual and, throughout the eighteenth century, no more than 1,003 persons held peerages.[8] The 49 female peeresses in their own right were of some social significance and some may, through their roles as royal mistresses, have had political influence. There were perhaps a hundred non-noble families with great leverage through their possession of estates over 10,000 acres. Some, like Thomas Coke of Holkham in Norfolk, were later ennobled but the size of the House of Lords remained steady until Pitt's titles of the 1780s. Roy Porter puts it well: 'There was however no risk of Lilliput titles, or ennobling of small fry. The English peerage (unlike the Scottish) carried few passengers; the great landowners had a chance to breathe.'[9]

Of the 163 peers in 1700, 63 held titles which were less than twenty years old. With two exceptions (both of whom were lawyers) ennoblement occurred within the ruling elite: 28 were promotions within the peerage, 5 were foreign nobility, 14 were sons or grandsons of peers, the rest were sons of knights, had married illegitimate royal offspring or were political peerages. As John Cannon says: 'What is going on is not so much replenishment as re-cycling. We are dealing with a stage army.'[10]

In 1800 of the grand total of 257 peers, 113 had been granted titles since 1780. All of these, except seven, already had some connection with nobility. Of this seven four were lawyers and the remaining three men of substantial property.' Cannon again:

> It remains remarkably difficult to find new peers who had not already some connection with the nobility. . . . There is little evidence here to suggest that the social elite was expanding vigorously in the eighteenth century and finding room for large numbers of newcomers. On the contrary, it indicates a considerable narrowing of the commanding social heights.[11]

This notion of exclusiveness was reinforced by marriage patterns: 59 per cent of all marriages in eighteenth century England were to members of the close aristocracy.[12]

Gregory King's estimate of 160 temporal peers refers to the situation in 1688. Their average income of £2,800 gives a grand aristocratic income of £448,000 or about 1 per cent of the national income, which King puts at £44 million. His figures have been subjected to detailed analysis recently,[13] and their validity questioned. Certainly the average income of peers must have been substantially higher. Joseph Massie's analysis in 1760 did not suggest very marked changes but by Colquhoun's calculations in 1803, estimated family income had increased to £8,000. Their share of the national income remained about 1 per cent, though this did decline after 1820. They had maintained their share of the expanding national income, but other groups had done significantly better and were beginning to close the gap.

Economic strength

Economic conditions up to 1820 benefited the peerage. Landownership and agriculture were not always economically advantageous throughout this period but land values and rents were buoyant in the early eighteenth century and rose steeply from the 1760s. Between 1690 and 1790 land values almost doubled and this trend was exacerbated by the inflationary effects of the French Wars after 1793. H. J. Habakkuk argued in an influential article[14] published in 1940 that the general drift of property between 1690 and 1750 was in favour of large estates and great land-owners. He believed that the increasing use made of 'the strict settlement', which afforded the core of the family estate some protection against extravagant heirs, was of fundamental importance in this process. Under 'the strict settlement' or 'entail' the landowner was, in law, a life-tenant of the whole estate and had to submit to limitations on his rights to alienate or mortgage parts of the estate. This legal fiction did not create great estates but could help to preserve them. The problem with Habak-kuk's thesis is that it is based on only Bedfordshire and Northamptonshire and he admitted that land which changed hands between 1680 and 1740 usually went to families already with large estates in 1680. In that sense the process of consolidation seemed much less dramatic. There is little agreement on the prosperity of the peerage in the eighteenth and early nineteenth centuries. The economics of agrarian management and super-vision meant, in the first half of the eighteenth century, that there was geographical consolidation of estates and labour-saving management of home farms. This was necessitated by the exigencies of low grain prices between about 1710 and 1750 which squeezed the peerage, though less than smaller landowners who were often unable to obtain sufficient credit. Low interest rates after 1750 made borrowing money correspondingly easier. There may have been non-economic reasons for consolidation of estates. If land was to be translated into effective electoral and political power, there was much to be said for concentrating it. Thomas Coke of

Holkham represented his own county for forty years as a result of the consolidation of his agrarian base. John Cannon says rightly that 'In consolidating, good husbandry and good politics went hand in hand.'[15]

Peers did not rely totally upon landowning for their income. Diversification shielded them from the worst effects of falling arable prices, particularly in the early eighteenth century and after 1815. Many peers owned urban estates, especially in or near London. During the eighteenth century land values and rentals rose as peers laid out fashionable metropolitan sites. The Bedfords developed Bloomsbury and Covent Garden and their London properties netted £2,000 in 1700 but £8,000 in 1771. The dukes of Westminster developed Pimlico, Belgravia and Mayfair. In smaller cities and towns prominent landowners included the Duke of Norfolk and Earl Fitzwilliam in Sheffield; the Marquess of Salisbury and Earls of Sefton and Derby in Liverpool; the Marquess of Bute in Cardiff and the Calthorpes in Birmingham. By 1886 69 out of 261 provincial towns were largely owned by members of the peerage and a further 34 towns were owned by smaller landowners. F. M. L. Thompson says that

> Urban growth was another fertile source of wealth for landowners, either through the ground rents which many preferred in the south, or through the capital gains from outright sales of building land which was more characteristic of the north.[16]

Peers also invested deeply in government stock, the Bank of England and the great trading companies in the eighteenth century. They made substantial capital gains from land purchase and compensation money but until after the main lines had been built few invested in railway, except where, as in the case of the financing of the Furness Railway in the 1840s by the Duke of Buccleuch and Lord Burlington, it was for carrying their minerals. The Great Northern Railway may have missed Stamford because of the opposition of Lord Exeter, who wished to protect Burghley House against intrusion and no main line ever passed through Marlborough because of the intransigence of the Marquess of Ailesbury.

Exploitation of mineral deposits on their estates became increasingly important as industrial change occurred. Great estates yielded stone, slates, sand, brick-clay, timber and coal. It was the Duke of Bridgewater's desire to sell more of his Worsley coal in Manchester that precipitated the canal age. Other peers built harbours to facilitate the development of their mineral resources. In Cumberland, Whitehaven was virtually created by the Earl of Lonsdale and in 1839 the Marquess of Bute began to build his dock in Cardiff. Some peers involved themselves directly in industrial ventures but most drew their increasing incomes in the shape of royalties or rents and ceased to be an important source of mining capital simply because outside capital and managerial skill was becoming more plentiful. This rentier trend was particularly evident after 1820 and by 1869 no more than 5 per cent of the collieries in England were owned and managed by landowners. F. M. L. Thompson considers that non-agricultural incomes were of major importance and that the peerage benefited much more than the gentry from them. He maintains that

> a new line of division was being created by the progress of industrialisation between the great body of the mere gentry and the landed aristocracy plus a minority of the squirearchy. The economic distinction was certainly becoming more marked year by year between landowners who were purely agricultural, and landowners who were guaranteed a share in the wealth generated by industry and commerce.[17]

The peerage and public office

The peerage were also able to profit from the perquisites of high office. Peers monopolized the offices of state, their patronage and revenues. By 1720 a quarter of the peerage held government or Court offices. Many were sinecures – as Cannon notes 'Free parking has always been a great privilege.'[18] – or pensions. Horace Walpole, the Prime Minister's son, held three sinecures: Usher of the Exchequer, Comptroller of the Pipe and Clerk of the Estreat which brought in some £3,000 per annum. At the end of the eighteenth century George Rose had sinecures worth £11,602 a year. Many offices allowed the incumbent to take commission from contractors, gifts and use the public money as if it were their own. Through control of office peers could satisfy family, friends, neighbours and the strangers who clamoured for preferment, patronage and charity. It is possible to exaggerate the importance of office-holding as a source of income and few peers were able to base their economic position on their monopoly of office alone. Only the office of Paymaster-General seems to have consistently allowed holders to amass fortunes, as in the case of Marlborough, Walpole, Chandos, Henry Fox, Holland, James Brydges and others.

Life-style and power

In general terms the English peerage was extremely wealthy. This allowed them to dictate taste and fashion. Their country houses were designed or modernized by the leading architects, decorated by contemporary artists or with 'old masters' and peopled with the leading poets, playwrights and wits. The Great House was the symbol of economic power and political authority. Peers introduced tropical plants and new techniques in farming. They were conspicuous in their spending and consumption. Profit-seeking was a means rather than an end. As Perkin remarks,

> The pursuit of wealth was the pursuit of status, not merely for oneself but for one's family. In the last resort the ultimate motivation . . . was a dynastic one: to found a family, to endow them splendidly enough to

last for ever, and to enjoy a vicarious eternal life in the seed of one's loin.[19]

The peer's life-style was neither exclusively urban, nor purely rural. The estate and the country house, with its liveried servants, were at the heart of this life-style – they were tangible proof of the authority and status of hierarchy. The urban features of the life-style of the peerage centred on London 'society' and the associated 'season' of balls, dinners and race meetings where potential marriages could be discussed and arranged and when lawyers and bankers could be seen about estate affairs. The town house was an important arena for conspicuous spending. Unlike many continental monarchies the Court, though an important part of 'society', was not the sole arbiter of manners and acceptability.

During the eighteenth century the House of Lords was increasingly eclipsed by the Commons, as the focus of political power and influence and yet paradoxically the aristocracy continued to dominate politics. Mandeville wrote that 'dominion follows property'. Land gave the aristocracy control over many parliamentary seats and this was reinforced by their use of patronage to reward the loyalty of friends, family and clients and to buy off the disaffected. High positions at Court and in the Church, in the bureaucracy, diplomatic service and in the armed forces were used, openly and without moral scruple, to maintain their political dominance. Perkin writes that

> Patronage, however, was more than a device for filling jobs, fostering talent, and providing pensions for the deserving and undeserving. In the mesh of continuing loyalties of which appointments were the outward sign, patronage brings us very close to the inner structure of the old society. . . . 'Vertical friendship', a durable two-way relationship between patrons and clients permeating the whole of society, was a social nexus peculiar to the old society, less formal and inescapable than feudal homage, more personal and comprehensive than the contractual, employment relationships of capitalist 'Cash Payments'.[20]

This dominance was reflected in the ways that peers used the law to protect the economic basis of that domination. Unlike their continental counterparts, peers did not have widespread legal privileges and were not exempt from taxation. However, the instruments of mortgage, strict settlement and entail maintained the physical integrity of the estate, and parliamentary enclosure consolidated this position. The exclusiveness of their economic status was reinforced by the Game Laws which from 1671 to 1831 restricted the right to take game, even on one's own land, to owners of estates worth more than £100 per year. The early nineteenth century saw an increased viciousness in the laws against poaching – spring-guns were not prohibited until 1827, night poaching was punishable by transportation and attacks on gamekeepers could lead to hanging. Though the Game Laws may have protected estates their limited economic value was outweighed by the political capital which radicals made of their use. Control of the administration of localities and of the magistracy meant that property was fully protected. Arthur Young observed that 'Banishment alone will force the French to execute what the English do for pleasure – reside upon and adorn their estates.'[21]

From the 1780s there was a dramatic increase in the number of peers though promotions consistently exceeded creations. Under Pitt between 1784 and 1801 there were 51 creations and 66 promotions and between 1802 and 1837 a further 82 peerages were created compared to 121 promotions. Despite contemporary criticisms, this was hardly a dilution of the peerage. The bulk of the new creations came from traditional sources of the peerage: substantial landowners or high service in the navy, army, diplomacy and law. The French Wars from 1793 swelled the stream of service peerages but this was far less important a cause of expansion than the political need to find alternative forms of patronage. From the constitutional point of view the conferment of British peerages on holders of Scottish or Irish titles had the same effect as new creations since it increased the size of the House of Lords. Being advanced to a British title reflected the economic and political interests of Irish and Scottish peers. Irish peers were often substantial landowners in England and it was a matter of consequence for them to obtain a title which reflected that interest. By contrast fewer Scottish lords had major estates in England. Their motive for advancement lay in giving them membership of Parliament as individuals, saved them from the need to compete for a place among a limited number of Scottish representative peers and increased their status. This avenue to the House of Lords was not open to them until 1782 with the reversal of the rule of 1711 against the conferment of British titles on Scottish peers.

Roy Porter talks of the 'sly magic of authority' in explaining continuing aristocratic dominance.[22] Authority can only be upheld by consent or coercion. The aristocracy, lacking private armies, relied on the former. There was a unity of feeling, if not always action, between the aristocracy and the rest of society. The strength of the mystique of landed property is evident in the extent to which a social order based on land not only survived but flourished in an increasingly industrial environment. Agriculture may have declined relative to other sectors of the economy during the first half of the nineteenth century but the aristocratic tone of British society was still set by the great houses and the large landowners. But, as J. F. C. Harrison says,

> landed England did not survive unchanged. Had there not been flexibility in coming to terms with the economic realities of the industry state, and a willingness to retreat gradually and quietly from untenable positions of political privilege, landed society might not have outlived

the end of the century. In fact it displayed remarkable powers of tenacity and adaptation: it sought to engulf and change some of the new elements in society, though in the process it was itself changed.[23]

THE GENTRY

Beneath the large landowners stretched 'the gentry'.[24] The estates of the just under a thousand 'country gentry' were anything from 1,000 to 10,000 acres, with corresponding incomes of from £1,000 to £10,000 per annum. There were between 3,000 and 4,000 'squires' living on estates of between 1,000 and 3,000 acres. The third tier was made up of up to 20,000 'gentlemen' whose incomes ranged from £300 to £1,000 per year. Some of the gentry were knights or hereditary baronets but the majority had no title beyond that of gentleman. Apart from the home farm the gentry's chief source of income came from rents. The integrity of the estate was preserved through the strict settlement and entail for the same reasons as the aristocracy. Land gave status, economic security and political clout.

Image

The image of the squire, caricatured by Henry Fielding in *Tom Jones* as the booted, bloated, boorish and bigoted Squire Western, was not just a fictional one. But it can be counterbalanced by the astuteness of families like the Whitbreads. They were small Bedfordshire squires in 1700 and by 1800 they had £8,000 from their London brewery and £22,000 from land per year. The process of gentrification in northern England was through participation in the coal trade. Most of the gentry could not afford the conspicuous spending of the peerage and lived on their estates, occupying themselves with county and village matters. They controlled the localities through their close links with the parson, who could be a substantial landowner in his own right, as Justices of the Peace, as officers in the local yeomanry, poor law officials, churchwardens and as backbench MPs.

'Gentlemen'

There may have been differences between these levels of landed society in terms of income, status and power but all would have accepted the epithet of 'gentleman'. What was a 'gentleman'?[25] Between the mid-eighteenth and nineteenth centuries there was some attempt to clarify its meaning. The ideal of the gentleman underwrote and validated the model of a homogeneous, hierarchical society in which rank, order and degree had their place. The notion of a 'gentleman' expressed the solidarity of a culturally-defined elite that ranged across diverse economic conditions. Being a gentleman meant being 'recognized' as one. This recognition by either county or London 'society' guaranteed acceptance by other elite circles. Being a gentleman in the eighteenth century meant accepting a certain moral code in which 'honour' had the highest place, defended, if necessary, by the duel. Clark comments that

> The evidence suggests that duelling became more frequent at the end of the century; the pistol duel probably acted rather to promote the idea of equality of all gentlemen, the homogeneity of gentry and aristocracy. . . . [26]

The decline in duelling after 1815 reflects a change in the way a 'gentleman' was perceived. The man of honour was gradually replaced by the broader concept of the good Christian citizen. 'Gentlemanliness' became a recognizable characteristic of persons of no social position and probably no property but whose manners, bearing or achievements marked them out as uncommon and civilized. This broadening of the notion of a 'gentleman' may have had something to do with social mobility, but, as Geoffrey Best noted, not very much. The only way of knowing whether a person was a gentleman or not depended on whether he was treated as a gentleman and by whom. What occupation a person followed determined this, to a certain extent:

> If you were an officer in the army or navy, a lawyer, a civil servant, a doctor or a clergyman, and provided that you were neither too obviously 'self-made' nor socially unadaptable, you were eligible for acceptance.[27]

To the 'gentlemen of honour', people associated with factories, banks and warehouses – let alone shops – were generically suspect, the 'vulgar' masses. Gentlemen accepted that society should be ordered on hierarchical principles, consciously inegalitarian, but with the understanding that inequalities were and ought to be removable in the case of individual merit. This meant recognition and respect not just from inferiors but from the arbiters of their hierarchy's elite. Who your parents were mattered, though less to the self-made urban gentleman than to the country equivalent. Best writes that

> The old ruling class of peers and squires had been expected to exercise authority, and themselves expected to do so in order to maintain subordination. The new ruling class of gentleman had to work more tactfully in a quasi-democratic age and used gentler sounding words like 'responsibility' and 'leadership'. Nobility and gentry had commanded you to defer to their rank. Gentlemen persuaded you to defer to their quality.[28]

OWNER-OCCUPIERS TO TENANT FARMERS

Below the gentry, English landed society forked: there was a gradation of owner-occupiers with incomes ranging from £700 down to £30; and tenant farmers. During the eighteenth and early nineteenth centuries the position of small owner-occupiers changed relative to tenant farmers. Gregory King thought owner-occupiers better off than farmers but Patrick Colquhoun, a hundred years later, thought the reverse. Freeholders lacked the investable capital to compete in an increasingly capital-intensive agriculture[29] and except in boom conditions, during the French Wars for example, conditions for smaller landowners became more difficult. John Howlett said that

> The small farmer is forced to be laborious to an extreme degree; he works harder and fares harder than the common labourer; and yet with all his labour and with all his fatiguing incessant exertions, seldom can he at all improve his condition or even with any degree of regularity pay his rent and preserve his present condition. He is confined to perpetual drudgery. . . .

and Arthur Young

> I regard these small occupiers as a set of very miserable men. They fare extremely hard, work without intermission like a horse. . . .

By contrast, substantial tenant farmers prospered and by 1800 about three-quarters of England was cultivated by them. Roy Porter says that 'Farmers slip-streamed magnates along the turnpike road of improvement.'[30]

Large-scale commercial farming seems to have been abandoned by the large landowners in the late seventeenth and early eighteenth centuries. This may have been occasioned by the sharp fall in agricultural prices from the 1680s. By the 1730s the function of the landowner and that of the farmer had become distinctive. It was a distinction in which each made a contribution. The landowner provided the land, buildings, fences and other essential facilities. He normally paid the land tax, leaving the tenant with only the parish rate. Large capital investment – enclosure, drainage, improving communications, rebuilding farm buildings – was generally undertaken by the landlord, whose interests were protected by the farm steward or agent. The tenants, by contrast, provided the working capital for the farm – animals, implements, seeds – and paid the labourers. They held their land under leases which could, as in the case of those for the Holkham farms of Thomas Coke, specify certain aspects of the farming process like how often land should be marled and so on. Sir Joseph Banks summed up the position in the following way:

> A Landlord like a Monarch or a Father of his Tenants ought to Live among them delighted at their happiness and meeting their benefictions whenever he sees them. His care must be first not to destroy them by exhorbitant demands of Rent, and secondly not to suffer them to grow

rich enough to make their sons into Consumers of the Producers of the Earth as Lawyers, Parsons, Doctors, etc. . . .[31]

LANDLORD AND TENANT

The relationship between landowner and tenant was termed 'modern feudalism' in the 1850s and 1860s. This neglects the role that custom played in that relationship, particularly in the eighteenth century. In Cumbria, for example, tenants fought hard to maintain their rights. The issue of timber rights was brought to a head by a trial at the Carlisle assizes in 1757 between Sir John Pennington and the tenants of the manor of Waberthwaite in south-west Cumberland. The tenants accused the lord of the manor of abrogating their share of timber in the woods. The Penningtons had a long history of involvement in exploiting mineral and timber resources on their estates. The court, however, upheld the tenants' rights. Throughout the rest of the century tenants were able to sustain their use-rights against the landowners. Circumstances in Cumbria may have been different from the more arable areas of the country but this example does illustrate the importance of custom in determining landlord–tenant relationships. Economic conditions in the first half of the nineteenth century allowed tenants to drive hard bargains with landowners. Lord Monson wrote to his steward in 1850 that he had

> been in a dreadful taking about this farm on our hands and it has worried me much. He had promised to look out for someone to manage it, but he owned it would be a dreadful pull to take it in hand and stock it – however at the eleventh hour he got a Mr Coupland to make a proposition to take it but at a great diminution of rent, he only offers £550 per an. and he requires a certain quantity of land drained for which he offers to pay £4 per cent. The old rent was £760 . . . however rather than have the farm on my hands I have agreed. . . .

Tenants may have struggled with landlords over rents, or rights to game and timber, or over leases but throughout this period political deference was widespread. F. M. L. Thompson says that

> to the outside world it presented a united front, and it was more natural and even rational for an unsophisticated tenantry to trust the political wisdom and wishes of worldy-wise landowners than it is for modern mass electorates to trust a television image.[32]

and later:

> Politics were left to the landowners not simply because tenant farmers had no other choice, but also because they usually trusted the political opinions of their landlords. The tenant farmers were certainly aware that they depended on the goodwill of their landlords, just as they were

aware of loyalty to the estates as a social community. When the means of enforcing this dependence were weakened by the ballot, however, it made little difference to the nature of county politics.[33]

WOMEN AND THE LAND

Compared with men, historians know less about what women felt, thought and did.[34] Public life was men-only and women had little real influence over this. High public office, the universities, the professions and the Church were closed to women, though some, like Sarah Churchill and the Duchess of Devonshire exercised considerable power because of their breeding, high rank and force of personality. Intelligent women were treated with suspicion by both sexes. Elizabeth Montagu wrote in 1750 that 'Wit in women is apt to have bad consequences, like a sword without a scabbard it wounds the wearer and provokes assailants.'[35] Dr Johnson was clearly expressing contemporary opinion when he described a woman preacher as 'like a dog walking on his hind legs'. Generally the stereotyping of women created a kind of invisibility. They were viewed as an extension of men, their shadows.

Attitudes towards women were a result of long-held genetic assumptions legitimated through the legal system. Men and women were different in nature, capacity and so ought to play different and quite distinct social roles. Stereotypes proliferated. Men were decisive, active, excelling in reason, organized; women were passive, submissive, maternal, docile, virtuous. Anatomy had determined their respective destinies. Women, particularly among the landed elite and gentry, were dependent on men throughout their lives, first as daughters and then wives. Marriages were often arranged for them, though generally they had a veto. Women had no legal rights, particularly in marriage. Blackstone wrote that 'In marriage husband and wife are one person, and that person is the husband: the very being, the legal existence of the woman, is suspended during marriage.'

In common law a woman had no rights over her children or matrimonial property and could only make a will with her husband's consent, and even then after her death he could have it set aside. Women were judged by most men to be simply inferior, the 'weaker vessel'. There was already a double standard in male attitudes to sexual behaviour in 1700. Among landowners the fidelity of women was essential since, as Johnson wrote, 'all property depends on it'. A wife's adultery was ground enough for a husband to obtain a divorce, though these were rare since it required a private Act of Parliament, but a woman could not sue for divorce. In reality this submissive stereotype was not always borne out in practice, particularly among society ladies.

The process of socializing girls into the proper female role began with their education, or rather lack of it. Fewer were likely to be sent away to school and girls were generally educated at home by nurses, governesses, servants and aunts. Marriage was not about happiness, but was a matter of family policy concerned with security, title, family and land. Once married, women, whose husbands owned land, had four major functions. First was the duty of obedience to their husband: 'A husband has the right to beat his wife, ruled a judge, so long as the stick was no thicker than a man's thumb.'[36] Secondly, women were heir-producing machines. Regular pregnancies occurred because of under-use of what artificial contraception was available and of the need for several children to offset the high levels of infant mortality. Between 1696, when she was twenty, and 1716 Lady Bristol produced twenty children. The childbirth treadmill, though not usually as extreme as this, was an established and fearful aspect of women's lives throughout this period. The upbringing of children was often left to wet-nurses, maids and later governesses. Thirdly, women ran the household and finally, they had the duty to be 'ladylike', a characteristic defined by men.

During the eighteenth and early nineteenth centuries there were certain changes in the role of these women. They were still divorced from real power but attitudes towards marriage did begin to alter. Parental choice of marriage partners was, to a certain extent, curbed and women developed a more positive maternal role within the domestic family. But this did not alter male attitudes and as Mary Wollstonecraft, in her introduction to *A Vindication of the Rights of Women* (1792), who died in childbirth, wrote:

[Women] spend many of the first years of their lives in acquiring a smattering of accomplishments; meanwhile strength of body and mind are sacrificed to libertine notions of beauty, to the desire of establishing themselves – the only way women can rise in the world – by marriage. And this desire making mere animals of them, when they marry they act as such children may be expected to act, they dress, they paint and nickname God's creatures. Surely these weak beings are only fit for a seraglio! Can they be expected to govern a family with judgment, or take care of the poor babes whom they bring into the world?

WALES, SCOTLAND AND IRELAND

In Scotland, Wales and Ireland society was based upon land throughout this period to a far greater extent than in England.[37] How was the experience of those who lived by rent different in these areas from England and why? Part of the explanation can be found in two conditions. First, the spread of agricultural improvements into Scotland and Wales and, particularly, Ireland was much slower than in England which led to a more gradual increase in productivity and profits. Secondly, there was often a cultural gap between landowners, who were anglicanized and Anglican, and tenants, who were often native-speaking and either Nonconformist or Catholic. Unlike England, there was little or no community of feeling or interest between landlords and their tenants. Control was often expressed, not through paternalism, but through repression.

Wales

Wales had been legally assimilated into England since the 1530s and there were more parallels between its landowning society and England than was the case with Scotland and Ireland. Aristocratic landowners like the Earls of Worcester, created Dukes of Beaufort in 1682, and the Earls of Pembroke were both powerful and important but their estates in Wales were part of far larger estates in England. Welsh landowning society was dominated by the gentry. They were the main employers of labour and, in many counties, lay impropriation gave them a strong hold over the Church. Some families had owned land since the fifteenth century but by the eighteenth century ancestry was less important in a society with an obvious oligarchy of greater gentry, like the Bulkeleys of Anglesey, the Mostyns of Flint and the Wynns of Wynnstay, with incomes over £3,000 per annum. The number of families with incomes over £3,000 was, however, far fewer than of those with £1,000 per annum who formed the backbone of the squirearchy. As in England, the larger landowners increased their control over the land at the expense of those minor squires with incomes below £500 per annum. There was little to choose between many minor squires and yeomen except that the former were rentiers not farmers. Many old-established, but small, estates ceased to be independent units especially between 1720 and 1760, when there was a high failure of direct male heirs, and either devolved upon heiresses or passed to distant male heirs, often from England. Old family names disappeared except where new landowners believed they could derive advantage from them. For example, in marrying into the Tredegar family the Goulds adopted the name of Morgan, thus concealing the breach. Welsh gentry benefited from the increased number of peerages from the 1780s. The Rice family of Dinefwr received a peerage and a substantial fortune by marrying into a London banking family almost at the same time. By English standards spending on building programmes was small. However, many old houses like Powis and Chirk Castles were restored; Georgian-style houses, though not numerous, are fairly well distributed in Wales and landscaping of grounds was widespread.

Estates were run more professionally, especially with the appointment of stewards. As in England, the gentry exploited the resources on their estates. In Cardiganshire and Flintshire they were pioneers in the lead industry, in Glamorgan started ironworks and in Pembrokeshire worked coal. But few actually exploited resources personally and were content to receive royalties and rents which substantially increased their incomes.

The gulf between the greater gentry and the smaller freeholders and tenant farmers was immense and, as in England, the gulf grew wider during the eighteenth century. Demographic change and the increasingly commercial attitude of some larger gentry militated against the community leadership which they had previously commanded. Court records show that some landlords ruthlessly raised rents or used force to remove tenants who opposed the consolidation of estates. Literary sources indicate that landlords were seen as scheming and grasping. Traditional tenant attitudes and rights cut across new commercial attitudes and this increased tensions and widened the social gulf. Language and religion exacerbated this situation.

As in England, what was to transform the role of landowners, though it was a process not completed by 1850, was industrialization. It created great wealth, particularly in South Wales, which some landowners, like the Butes, the Morgans of Tredegar and the Penrhyn family in North Wales, were willing to exploit and others did not. However, in rural Wales a changing social structure was far less evident. The tenant farmer still dominated life in remarkably stable communities. There was no sizeable number of substantial freeholders in Wales equivalent to the English yeomen and the distinction between tenant farmers and their labourers was one of status rather than wealth. Population growth meant that demand for farm tenancies remained high and it was labourers, unable to get farms, who migrated to the towns.

Scotland

In Scotland the disintegration of the old landed social structure based on land began before the massive social changes caused by industrialization. This was most evident in the Highlands, where a conflict between two sets of ideas and customs emerged. Under the clan-system strategy rather than economy governed social relations. The binding obligation was kinship and the attachment of the Gael to the land. The ideology was one of a 'society at war'. By contrast, a new, primarily economic ideology emerged, acceptable in an industrial society but not one governed by custom. Landowners were concerned with the economic rather than the strategic value of their estates. This ideological clash alone was sufficient to rend Highland society, a process completed by the consequences of the 1745 Jacobite rebellion.

The Lowland landowners were less affected by the clash between ideologies based on custom and capitalism. They nonetheless possessed great power and, as in England, the larger landowners provided social and political leadership. Peers could sit in the House of Lords if elected as one of the sixteen representative Scottish peers or, after 1782, in their own right. Lesser landowners were represented in the House of Commons by thirty county members. Peers could, until the legislation of 1747, have heritable stewartries, sheriffdoms and regalities nor, after the Militia Act of 1797, could they be Lords Lieutenant. Some were also Commissioners of Supply, a post created in 1667. Smaller landowners were justices of the peace with powers which effectively increased as heritable jurisdiction declined. In 1700 Scottish landowners had the reputation of being the most absolute in Britain. Most of their tenants held land at will with no right to compensation for any improvements undertaken on their holdings. Their lord sat in judgement over them in the baron court, though its significance declined after 1750. Lord Gardenstone summed up the attitude of all substantial landowners in 1779 when he said 'The relationship between master and tenant, like prince and people, implies a reciprocal duty and mutual affection.'

From the mid-eighteenth century there was a lively land market and enhanced land prices as people were ambitious for estates. The impact of this on the structure of the landed elite was complex. It certainly prevented Scottish landowners from becoming an oligarchy of birth. However, it resulted in a marked division between the older aristocracy owning large estates, and the small or middling gentry, who were newcomers.

How many landowners were there? Sir John Sinclair produced the answer shown in Table 13.3.

Table 13.3 Scottish landowners in 1814

Number	Type of property	Valuation in £Scottish*
396	'large properties'	over £2,000
1,077	'middling properties'	£500–£2,000
6,181	'small properties'	under £500
Total 7,654 landed proprietors		

* £Scottish were based on the valuation of 1670.
Source: adapted from T. C. Smout *A History of the Scottish People*, Fontana, 1972, p. 265.

The first group contained the peers, some 100 families and the last group included 'bonnet-lairds' whose status was little better than any English owner-occupier. About 40 per cent of the small properties were in the five western counties (Lanarkshire, Ayrshire, Renfrew, Kircudbright and Dumfries). As in England and Wales, they were least able financially to adapt to the new economic conditions.

The peasant economy, where most people were subsistence producers, was replaced by an economy based on capitalist farmers and landless labourers who produced food for the growing towns filled with non-producing consumers. This change can be seen in the respective roles of the 'gudeman' and the 'farmer' in the eighteenth and nineteenth centuries. Lothian 'gudemen' were substantial tenants, holding perhaps 100 acres of fertile soil. They were not poor and their farming techniques were not

primitive. Their land may not have been enclosed, but was often consolidated. This relative economic sophistication should not hide the fact that
gudemen had little capital of their own, that they lived from hand to
mouth, lived with their farm servants and farmed in obedience to unwrit-
ten and only slowly changing tradition. Nineteenth-century farmers were
people with capital and resources who built stone houses to stress their
identification with the 'landed interest' and to separate themselves from
the wage-earning labourer. The change from 'gudeman' to farmer was
geographically and chronologically uneven. In the Lothians the process
was more rapid because of the diffusion of agricultural innovations than
in Dunbartonshire where farms were smaller.

As in England and Wales the changes in agricultural production altered
the relationship between those who owned or rented land and those who
worked it. Improvements were more readily carried out by landlords who
had greater capital resources and better access to bank credit. Tenant
farmers were regarded less favourably. Tension between landlord and
tenant can be seen in the Game Laws and the law of hypothec. The drift
of legislation in the eighteenth and nineteenth centuries was to preserve
game for the proprietor, which led to increased tenant resentment at the
resulting damage to crops. The right of 'hypothec', a peculiarly Scottish
legal doctrine, gave the landlord a general right over a tenant's moveable
property as security for the payment of rent. Opposition to hypothec
increased in the nineteenth century but it was not restricted until 1867,
and was abolished in 1880. The growing gulf between landlord and tenant
was also evident in the disapproval of landlords for their tenants who
joined the Free Church after the Disruption of 1843 and in the growth
of liberalism which questioned the established rights of property and
patronage.

Ireland

In Ireland there were major changes in landownership in the second half
of the seventeenth century and the growing resentment of the rents paid
to landowners and the leases which expressed them were a result of these
changes. Leases to Catholics were confined to 31 years under the penal
laws until 1778. This was quite a long time. The argument for longer
leases, regarded as a sign of improvement in the 1720s and 1730s, was
later in the century frowned upon. Tenants with long leases often secured
land on low rents which they then sublet. This was advantageous for
neither improver nor landowner, whose control over increasing rents was
considerably reduced. On the other hand, when prices rose, as they did
steadily in the fifty years after 1750, long leases were to the tenants'
advantage. Irish agriculture was dominated by farmers holding leases from
a landlord. In grazing areas farms were quite large but in grain-growing
areas they were much smaller. The possession of even small amounts of

capital marked off tenant farmers from labourers. Cottiers rented land at a nominal rent from farmers and discharged their rent in labour services. They, like some farmers and smallholders, had to supplement their farming incomes from textile activity.

Landlords played an active role in the economic life of the countryside. Their leasing policies changed after 1750 as the economic advantages of improvement became more obvious. Favourable leases were given to tenants who undertook to improve the land and landlords often took ground rent in the growing towns. Absentee landlords have been given a significance out of all proportion to their economic importance in the eighteenth century. Between 1720 and 1780 rents for absentees doubled while those of Irish landlords trebled and, as a proportion of the whole, absentee rents fell from about a fifth to an eighth in the same period. It was their political unpopularity which has been highlighted but the stereotype of the uncaring and exploiting landlord owes more to nationalist rhetoric than economic reality. During the eighteenth century there was little alienation between tenant and landlord. Demands for tenants' rights by name does not occur in agrarian grievances at all. The two main features of the nineteenth-century concept of tenants' rights – security of tenure and compensation for improvements – did not arise in a direct form. The composition of the countryside varied and there were sharp geographical contrasts but until 1815 farming, for those who collected or paid rent, was generally prosperous.

Census material allows historians to construct a far more accurate picture of Irish rural life, especially after 1830. In the 1831 census 100,000 farm occupiers employed hired labour, 564,000 employed no labour and there were 567,000 agricultural labourers. The 1841 census divided the population into four categories according to their means. The first category included property owners and farmers with more than 50 acres. The second included artisans and farmers with between 5 and 50 acres and the third category labourers and smallholders with up to 5 acres. The fourth category – 'means unspecified' – was not of numerical significance. For rural Ireland as a whole the first two categories accounted for 30 per cent of families but regionally there was a range from as high as 40 per cent in a number of eastern counties to as low as 15 per cent in Mayo. The nature of rural society differed markedly between and within regions. The eastern counties were generally more wealthy than the south-western and western counties and the contrast between the farmer and other rural classes was sharper there as a result.

Farmers may well have suffered in years of lowest prices but generally their conditions were not impoverished in pre-Famine Ireland. The more prosperous, especially those who concentrated on livestock, had the capacity to meet the changed conditions after 1815. Some landlords compensated for falling grain prices by reducing rents, but most did not. Leases were renewed with difficulty and tenancy-at-will became increasingly widespread. There was some consolidation of land and both the Ejectment Act of 1816 and the Subletting Act of 1826 testify to the desire of many landlords to hasten this process. Growing population and land hunger led to an expansion of tillage and increased subdivision of plots. Rents for subsistence plots were determined by this not by the fertility of the soil. The widespread adoption of the potato exacerbated this process since only a small plot was necessary for subsistence. In the 1820s and 1830s ejectments and forceful distraining of goods in lieu of arrears became more common. The relationship between landlord and tenant began to decline rapidly and agrarian secret societies, like the Rockites, Whiteboys and Terryalts, escalated the incidence of rural disorder. Failure of the potato crops in 1817, 1822 and throughout the 1830s in the western counties presaged the 'Great Famine' of the 1840s.

Land and its cultivation remained the major occupation throughout this period. Landowners and their tenants were still leading producers of wealth. Land gave economic security as well as political and social status. The early nineteenth century saw the gradual break-up of this ordered rural world. In Scotland, for example, the Clearances were a visible and physical expression of this process. In Ireland land hunger resulted in an increasing antagonism between landlord and tenant. In England industrialization provided alternative employment and the 'drift from the land' began, though it did not become a flood until after 1850. Britain was not an agrarian economy in 1850 as it had been in 1700. Farming had become capitalist in character on mainland Britain if not in Ireland. This move fractured the community of interest between those who received and those who paid rent. The development of the notion of tenants' rights demonstrated that the notion of reciprocal obligations implicit in paternalism were becoming increasingly inoperable. The future lay with capital not rent.

NOTES

1 S. T. Coleridge *On the Constitution of Church and State*, (1830), London, 4th edn, 1852, p. 26.
2 E. Burke *Reflections on the Revolution in France* in *The Works of the Right Honourable Edmund Burke*, London, 1887, Vol. III, p. 335.
3 G. E. Mingay *English Landed Society in the Eighteenth Century*, Routledge, 1963, p. 237.
4 G. E. Mingay *The Gentry*, Longman, 1976, p. 4.
5 See in particular J. C. D. Clark *English Society 1688–1832*, Cambridge University Press, 1985, pp. 93–118 and the more detailed works by J. Cannon *Aristocratic Century – the Peerage of Eighteenth-century England*, Cambridge University Press, 1984, L. Stone and J. C. Fawtier Stone *An Open Elite? England 1540–1880*, Oxford University Press, 1984 and J. V. Beckett *The Aristocracy in England 1660–1914*, Blackwell, 1986. A general comparative sweep of the issues can be found in J. Powis *Aristocracy*, Blackwell, 1984. E. Royle *Modern*

Britain. A Social History 1760–1985, Edward Arnold, 1987, provides a general overview.

6 A recent expression of this view can be found in R. Porter *English Society in the Eighteenth Century*, Penguin, 1982, pp. 64–7, though he does recognize that 'in some ways social fluidity was silting up'.

7 H. Perkin *The Origins of Modern English Society 1780–1880*, Routledge, 1969, especially pp. 56–63.

8 J. Cannon op. cit. p. 10.

9 R. Porter op. cit. p. 70.

10 J. Cannon op. cit. pp. 20–1.

11 ibid. pp. 23, 33.

12 ibid. pp. 71–92, especially p. 85, table 20.

13 G. Holmes 'Gregory King and the Social Structure of Pre-industrial England', *Transactions of the Royal Historical Society*, 5th Series, 27 (1977), pp. 41–68 and P. H. Linderts and J. G. Williams 'Revising England's Social Tables 1688–1812', *Explorations in Economic History*, 19 (1982), pp. 385–408. For Massie see the analysis in P. Mathias *The Transformation of England*, Methuen, 1979, pp. 171–89; for Colquhoun see P. Hollis *Class and Conflict in Nineteenth-Century England 1815–1850*, Routledge & Kegan Paul, 1973, pp. 5–8.

14 H. J. Habakkuk 'English Landownership 1680–1740', *Economic History Review*, 2nd Series, Vol. x, 1940.

15 J. Cannon op. cit. p. 139.

16 F. M. L. Thompson *English Landed Society in the Nineteenth Century*, Routledge, 1963, p. 267.

17 ibid. p. 268.

18 J. Cannon op. cit. p. 139.

19 H. Perkin op. cit. p. 85.

20 ibid. p. 19.

21 Arthur Young quoted in R. Porter op. cit. p. 68.

22 ibid. p. 81.

23 J. F. C. Harrison *The Early Victorians 1832–1851*, Weidenfeld, 1971, p. 115.

24 On the gentry see G. E. Mingay *The Gentry* op. cit.

25 On the notion of 'the gentleman' see J. C. D. Clark op. cit. and G. Best *Mid-Victorian Britain 1851–75*, Weidenfeld, 1971, pp. 268–78.

26 J. C. D. Clark op. cit. p. 114.

27 G. Best op. cit. p. 270.

28 ibid. p. 278.

29 On the debate about owner-occupiers see G. E. Mingay *Enclosures and the Small Farmer in the Age of the Industrial Revolution*, Macmillan, 1968.

30 R. Porter op. cit. p. 84.

31 Quoted more fully in G. E. Mingay *The Gentry*, op. cit. p. 85.

32 F. M. L. Thompson op. cit. p. 199.

33 ibid. p. 204.

34 The literature on women's history is growing but there is still no general study of women and land 1700–1850 above the level of the labourer. M. Prior (ed.) *Women in English Society 1500–1800*, Methuen, 1985 contains some useful papers but has little to say on the subject directly. On women and the family read L. Stone *The Family, Sex and Marriage*, Weidenfeld, 1977 and critiques of his conclusions in R. A. Houlbrooke *The English Family 1450–1700*, Longman, 1984 and M. Anderson *Approaches to the History of the Western Family 1500–1914*, Macmillan, 1980.

35 Quoted in R. Porter op. cit. p. 36.

36 ibid. p. 38.

37 The broad structure of Welsh, Scottish and Irish society is outlined in chapter

2. For the discussion on Wales, Scotland and Ireland general reference should be made to D. Williams *A History of Modern Wales*, 2nd edn, John Murray, 1977, G. E. Jones *Modern Wales: A Concise History c. 1485–1979*, Cambridge University Press, 1984, chapters 2 and 8 and D. W. Howell *Land and People in Nineteenth Century Wales*, Routledge, 1978; T. C. Smout *A History of the Scottish People 1560–1830*, Fontana, 1972, chapters 12–14 and R. H. Campbell *Scotland Since 1707*, 2nd edn, John Donald, 1985, chapters 2 and 9; L. M. Cullen *An Economic History of Ireland since 1660*, Batsford, 1972, F. S. L. Lyons *Ireland Since the Famine*, Fontana, 1971, E. M. Johnston *Ireland in the Eighteenth Century*, Gill & Macmillan, 1974, G. O'Tuathaigh *Ireland Before the Famine 1798–1848*, Gill & Macmillan, 1972 and J. Mokyr *Why Ireland Starved: A Quantitative and Analytical History of the Irish Economy 1800–1850*, Allen & Unwin, 1985, especially chapter 4. R. Foster *Modern Ireland 1600–1972*, Allen Lane, 1988 is both readable and illuminating.

14 Capital

> The middle state or what might be called the upper station of low life . . . was the best state in the world, the most suited to human happiness; not exposed to the miseries and hardships, the labour and sufferings of the mechanic part of mankind, and not embarrassed with the pride, ambition and envy of the upper part of mankind.[1]

> The bourgeoisie, whenever it got the upper hand, put an end to all feudal, patriarchal, idyllic relations, pitilessly tore asunder the motley feudal ties that bound man to his 'natural superiors' and left remaining no other bind between man and man than naked self-interest and callous cash payments.[2]

For both Defoe, in the 1720s, and Marx, writing over a hundred years later, the 'bourgeoisie', 'middling' or 'middle' class or classes was an established and important feature of British society. The Greek philosopher Aristotle saw it as preventing the very rich or the very poor from becoming dominant:

> It is manifest that the best political community is formed by citizens of the middle class and that those states are likely to be well-administered, in which the middle class is large and larger if possible than both the other classes.[3]

Historians have been divided over whether to blame the middle classes for accumulating wealth at the price of social misery or to praise them for creating a society with the potential for more freedom and abundance for all. Those who took or paid rent formed a clearly definable 'interest' in eighteenth- and early nineteenth-century British society. Those whose primary concern was with 'capital' did not. This chapter is concerned with those people for whom 'capital' was the major source of income or whose occupation was largely the result of the existence of 'capital'. To begin it is necessary to attempt a delineation of who we are talking about.

PROBLEMS OF DEFINITION

As will become obvious there is considerable difficulty in defining unam-
biguously those individuals for whom 'capital' was a central feature of life.
There are two major reasons for this. First, at least during much of the
eighteenth century, they did not form an 'interest' in the same way as
those concerned with rent. Secondly, and perhaps a reason for this, they
were characterized by considerable fluidity and high levels of social
mobility. What is clear is that in 1700 there were self-employed people, a
mercantile community, people with 'liquid' money to invest, entrepreneurs
who employed that money and emerging 'professions' which serviced these
individuals (though not them alone) and that these groups/occupations
were based largely in urban rather than rural centres. There is some truth
in the Marxist interpretation of the sixteenth and seventeenth century as
'the rise of the bourgeoisie' but it is equally true that the focal point of
political power had not altered and that, if successful, a merchant bought
land, not necessarily as an economic investment but as a symbol of status
– the ultimate sign of success in trade or business was the ability to leave
it. Roy Porter writes that

> In all ways 'the middle class of people in this country', as Chesterfield
> himself put it, were 'straining to imitate their betters'; to turn, if not
> into landed gentlemen, at least into a para-gentry who could put 'Esq'
> after their names without blushing. . . . English moneyed society
> wanted to cover its tracks; to show it was no vulgar 'shopocracy', but
> rather a rightful guest at the Quality Ball. . . . [4]

They were

> indeed chameleon-like . . . largely behind the scenes, operating a client
> economy servicing the Great. . . . Many middling men hated this being
> superior flunkeys, for clientage required sycophancy's mask. Economic
> dependence was humiliating and nerve-racking. . . . Yet imitation was
> also the sincerest form of flattery. What did envious bourgeois want
> more than to be welcomed into genteel society.[5]

This was a subtle form of 'parasitism', mutually beneficial even if, on
numerous occasions, relationships between client and patron were strain-
ed. Landed and mercantile and commercial elites may have been specialized and distanced by function but they were united in deferring to a
common code of manners and values: that of the landed elite. New men
were accepted but always on terms set by the aristocracy and gentry. For
J. C. D. Clark the divide that was to emerge in the eighteenth century
was not the marxist economic division between aristocracy and bourgeoisie
but

> a cultural one, between the patrician landowner, banker, lawyer, clergy-
> man or merchant on the one hand and the plebeian tradesman and

manufacturer on the other . . . and the challenge to the ancien regime, when it came, was from culturally defined groups, not from economically defined classes. 'Class' was more a consequence than a cause of that regime's collapse.[6]

Numbers?

The middle ranks were, according to Perkin.[7] distinguished from the gentry and nobility not so much by their lower incomes as by the necessity of earning a living, and at the bottom from the labouring population not by their higher incomes but by their property, however small, represented by stock in trade, tools or by the educational investment in skills or expertise. Until recently historians have accepted the evidence of Gregory King for 1688 and Patrick Colquhoun for 1803 that they made up about a third of the population of England and Wales.[8] There are, however, certain difficulties with their figures and terminology: for example, they included freeholders and farmers but excluded 'artisans' from their 'middle ranks' categorization. Some revision of both social tables is needed (see Table 14.1). Using these revised figures it is possible to produce the figures shown in Table 14.2. There was, on the basis of this, a dramatic increase between 1700 and 1800 in those families concerned with capital or receiving fees or salaries for their expertise or services.

A 'PROTEAN' STAGE OF DEVELOPMENT

The eighteenth century saw the middling ranks seek to emulate those who had established landed wealth. They were still at the 'protean' stage of development. They did not unite to form their own political ideology – though some historians would argue that they had absorbed Lockeian individualism – and political activism, as for example in the General Chamber of Manufacturers of 1785, was short-lived and directed at influencing decisions at Westminster. Those involved in trade and commerce rarely agreed with each other about war or foreign policy. Despite Wilkes and the radical movements after 1760, they couched their demands in the traditional rhetoric of a restoration of the ancient Constitution. The vocational aspirations of these middling ranks were similarly ill-formed. In medicine and the law there were no standards of training or responsibility. Few occupations were anxious to become formally chartered liberal professions, a quest which haunted them in the nineteenth century. Many 'service' employments, like nursing or schoolteaching, were poorly paid and low in status. As Porter says:

> White-collar professions did not tend to breed binding corporate professionalism: why should they? Their practitioners were content to be

Table 14.1 King and Colquhoun compared

	KING (1688)			COLQUHOUN (1803)		
	(a)	(b)	(c)	(d)	(e)	(f)
1. *Industry and commerce*						
Merchants (1)	2,000	400	800	2,000	2,600	5,200
Merchants (2)	8,000	200	1,600	13,000	800	10,400
Manufacturers	–	–	–	25,000	800	20,000
Warehousemen	–	–	–	500	800	400
Shipbuilders	–	–	–	300	700	210
Shipowners	–	–	–	5,000	500	2,500
Surveyors	–	–	–	5,000	200	1,000
Engineers	–	–	–	25,000	150	3,750
Tailors etc.						
Shopkeepers	40,000	45	1,800	74,500	150	11,175
Innkeepers	–	–	–	50,000	100	5,000
Clerks, shopmen	–	–	–	30,000	75	6,750
Artisans	60,000	40	2,400	445,726	55	24,515
2. *Professions*						
Civil offices (1)	5,000	240	1,200	2,000	800	1,600
Civil offices (2)	5,000	120	600	10,500	200	2,100
Law	10,000	140	1,400	11,000	350	3,850
Clergy (1)	2,000	60	120	1,000	500	500
Clergy (2)	8,000	45	360	10,000	120	1,200
Dissenting clergy	–	–	–	2,500	120	300
Arts, science	16,000	60	960	16,300	260	4,238
Education (1)	–	–	–	500	600	300
Education (2)	–	–	–	20,000	150	3,000
Naval officers	5,000	80	400	3,000	149	1,043
Army officers	4,000	60	240	5,000	139	1,816
Half-pay officers	–	–	–	2,000	45	181
Theatrical	–	–	–	500	200	100
Lunatic keepers	–	–	–	40	500	20
	165,000	–	11,880	760,366	–	111,148

Columns (a) and (d) are families, (b) and (e) income per family in £ and (c) and (f) aggregate income in £000.
Source: H. Perkin *The Origins of Modern English Society 1780–1880*, Routledge, London 1969, pp. 20–1.

men of business, guineas jingling in their purses, rather than public servants. Upward mobility was individual rather than collective.[9]

Businessmen and tradesmen did not have the same ambiguous identity as professionals and consequently were more identifiable. It was this group which took the greatest opportunity of the favourable economic conditions after 1700 to make money. What they lacked in formal education and political power was amply made up by their nose for business. To go 'into trade' did not have the social stigma attached to it that it did on the Continent. These merchant 'princes' invested in stock and in trade,

Table 14.2 Summary: percentage distribution

| | KING | | COLQUHOUN | |
	Family	Income	Family	Income
Rent	25.28	39.39	17.28	33.79
Capital	11.81	26.39	37.86	53.04
Wages	62.91	34.28	44.86	13.17

inter-married, pooled capital as partners and passed their businesses on. To quote Malthus:

> A bond of confidence in business was very commonly reinforced by kinship: marriage partners were chosen from the same charmed circle. . . . This could become self-reinforcing, particularly when the values protected in these enclaves encouraged a higher propensity to work and invest than in the echelons of society above these groups and below them in the social structure.[10]

Quaker families, for example, often 'visited' each other, families in one part of the country receiving members from elsewhere on short or longer visits. These would often lead to new business or kinship links and as a result a dense 'cousinhood' of Quaker families extended over much of Britain by 1800. Families like the Barclays, Lloyds, Trumans and Gurneys were involved in many overlapping ventures in iron, brewing, banking and other areas.

'SHOPOCRACY' – THE 'MIDDLING' OCCUPATIONS

Below the very rich, whom Porter calls the 'plutocrats', came a vast array of small traders, publicans, manufacturers and shopkeepers who took advantage of the market and changes in technologies to enhance their wealth. In transport, for example, William Chaplin's coaching service in the 1820s employed 2,000 men and used 1,800 horses, Pickfords ran ten canal boats and fifty waggons in the 1790s and Samuel Morton Peto was the largest contractor for railway construction in the 1840s and 1850s. In 1774 James Mackington began as a second-hand bookseller and by 1791 had modernized bookselling by standardizing prices, pioneering remainder-selling and issuing catalogues and was selling 100,000 volumes per year. Shops and small manufacturing businesses were everywhere. Cities like Edinburgh and Manchester had a great variety of 'middling' occupations (see Table 14.3), but so too did middling towns. (See Table 14.4).

The growing complexity of 'middling' occupational structure during the eighteenth century can be seen in the categories used by King and Colquhoun. 'Manufacturer' began to shed its traditional meaning of

Table 14.3 Edinburgh and Manchester in the 1770s compared

Edinburgh (1774)	Manchester (1772)
217 Merchants	140 Innkeepers
188 Advocates	75 Fustian manufacturers
171 Writers	58 Warehousemen
169 Grocers	49 Check manufacturers
141 Clerks to H.M. Signet	46 Hucksters
110 Vintners	44 Smallware manufacturers
94 Lords and Advocate Clerks	27 Shoemakers
86 Baxters	25 Tailors
80 Shipmasters	24 Grocers
79 Shoemakers	24 Clergy
64 Wrights	23 Carpenters/Joiners
61 Brewers	23 Hatters
56 Schoolmasters	
52 Tailors	23 Fustian cutters
46 Barbers	21 Lawyers
45 Smiths	17 Yarn merchants
45 Stablers	15 Linen drapers
45 Milliners	15 Butchers
39 Physicians	14 Fustian dyers
35 Clergy	14 Corn factors
33 Surgeons	13 Fustian callenders
30 Bankers	13 Toy/Hardware shops
24 Painters	12 Bakers
21 Booksellers	11 Cabinetmakers
21 Jewellers/Goldsmiths	11 Gardeners

Sources: Williamson's Directory of Edinburgh (1774); *Manchester Directory* (1772).

Table 14.4 Appleby and Cardigan compared (1793)

Appleby	Cardigan
11 Innkeepers	13 Innkeepers
7 Joiners/Carpenters	8 Shoemakers
6 Grocers	7 Shopkeepers
4 Shoemakers	5 Attorneys
4 Schoolmasters	5 Joiner/Carpenters
3 Lawyers	5 Tailors
3 Physicians	4 Shipwrights/Ropers
3 Spirit Merchants	4 Clergy
3 Weavers	3 Surgeons
3 Tailors	3 Merchants
	3 Butchers
	3 Hatters

Source: Universal British Directory (1739); all occupations with three or more representatives were included.

'craftsman' and came increasingly to mean large-scale owners of plant and employers of labour, less makers of goods than managers of resources and entrepreneurial expertise.

The 'middling orders' grew in both confidence and numbers in the eighteenth century and it is perhaps no coincidence that they should have been portrayed in literature. Some highly successful novelists – Defoe, Samuel Richardson, Henry Fielding and Laurence Sterne – rejected the knights and nobles of earlier romances, or caricatured them mercilessly, in favour of schoolmasters, clergymen, farmers, tradesmen and, in the case of *Robinson Crusoe*, mariners, and so encouraged further confidence. Economic and cultural hegemony went hand in hand.

Roy Porter[11] is perhaps right to maintain that the development of the 'middling orders' or 'petit bourgeoisie' antedated the industrial revolution but his conclusion that this occurred 'quite independently' is less certain. Pushing back the beginnings of major economic change to the early eighteenth century has the effect of synchronizing both chronological developments. Economic change had a formative influence on the emergence of the 'middling orders' in three important respects. First, it greatly increased their numbers. Secondly, it enhanced social fluidity, particularly after 1750, and greatly increased opportunities for upward social mobility. This was exemplified in the careers of James Watt and George Stephenson and by *John Halifax, Gentleman* (1856), a novel by Mrs Craik. Thirdly, economic change led to a substantial increase in the wealth and power of the emerging middle classes. Their power over clerks and workers was as great as that of landlords over tenants and labourers. But economic power was not political power.

AN IDEOLOGICAL FOUNDATION – TOWARDS THE MIDDLE CLASSES

The emergence of an evangelical approach to religion and utilitarian attitudes to 'practical' philosophy lay at the root of the middling orders' claims to political power as well as reinforcing their growing economic dominance. Ian Bradley maintains that

> evangelicanism was to do for the rising English middle classes of the early nineteenth century what Calvinism had done for the emerging bourgeoisie of Europe nearly three hundred years earlier. It gave them a creed, a confidence and a common consciousness and purpose.[12]

Evangelicalism

Evangelicalism, in both its Nonconformist and Anglican variants, was a reaction to the rationalism and loose morality of eighteenth-century aristocratic society. It was a 'call to seriousness' and many evangelical propagandists specifically aimed their tracts at the middling orders, emphasizing hard work, plain living, moral propriety, respectable family life and, above all, conscience – a life-style Bradley characterizes as 'eminently bourgeois'. It had two important effects on the emerging middle classes. It encouraged them to lose their sense of inferiority to those above them on the social scale. One of the themes running through many evangelical tracts was that society should take its values from the bourgeoisie rather than the aristocracy. Though Perkin is correct in pointing to the ultimate success of this 'entrepreneurial ideal' before 1850 this was limited, as the persistence of middle-class deferential attitudes illustrates. Secondly, evangelicalism converted middle-class careers into 'callings', providing rules which were useful in achieving success in them. Thomas Gisborne's *An Enquiry into the Duties of Men in the Higher Ranks and the Middle Classes of Society in Great Britain*, written in 1795, demonstrated this with chapters on politics, the civil service, business and commerce, the law, medicine, the Church and armed forces, showing their serious importance as 'callings' and the responsibilities that attached to them. Again an expression of 'seriousness' and 'conscience'.

Utilitarianism

The aristocratic conception of society was attacked not just for its moral laxity but for its inefficiency. Notions of tradition, restriction and 'influence' – values particular to landed society – were compared, generally unfavourably, with the bourgeois virtues of order, discipline and application. The growing number of capitalist employers and professional men were not only critical of the older values, but aggressive in their criticisms. This questioning tended to focus on a series of related topics concerned with the nature of the economy, the efficiency of public administration, the distribution of political power and the type of education most likely to produce the kind of citizen demanded by the shape of the new society. All these questions were loosely grouped together as being of general 'utility' and a basis on which solutions were being sought was in Benthamite terms of the greatest good for the greatest number. This intellectual debate, a reflection of the development of non-agricultural resources and non-manual occupations, was fought out in journals, with the *Edinburgh Review, Westminster Review* and later the *London Review* putting the radical case and the *Quarterly Review* defending the values of the past.

John Stuart Mill drew attention to the virtues of the middle class as

> those which conduce to getting rich – along with family affections, inoffensive conduct between man and man, and a disposition to assist one another, whenever no commercial rivalry intervenes.[13]

Through evangelicalism the middle classes were identified as the most respectable and moral elements in society, while utilitarianism created the idea of a link between middle-classness and intellectual capacity. The espousal of classical economics, through Adam Smith and particularly David Ricardo, with its notion of 'free trade' easily extendible into 'free trade in everything' completed the raising of middle-class consciousness. Spiritually, intellectually and economically they saw themselves as superior and yet they were excluded from political power. During the first half of the nineteenth century this new consciousness was focused on a series of struggles to gain emancipation from the strictures of aristocratic control. The repeal of the Test and Corporation Acts in 1828–9 gave them 'free trade in religion'. The Reform Act of 1832, though limited in its effects, recognized the right of the middle classes to a say in legislation. The Whig reforms from 1832 to 1841 brought 'utility' into public administration and the repeal of the Corn Laws in 1846 symbolized the 'moral', if not immediately political, victory of the middle classes.

G. Kitson Clark rightly counselled caution when he pointed out that:

> Of course, the general expression 'middle class' remains useful, as a name for a large section of society . . . [but] it is necessary to remember that a belief in the importance and significance of the middle class in the nineteenth century derives from contemporary opinion. . . . They do not always say clearly whom they have in mind, and since the possible variants are so great a modern writer should follow them with great caution. . . . [14]

This view is reflected by Richard Cobden who saw 'The insatiable love of caste that in England, as in Hindostan, devours all hearts, is confined to no walks of society, but pervades every degree from the highest to the lowest.'

THE MIDDLE CLASSES

The early nineteenth-century middle classes were an extremely hetero-geneous body embracing at one end city bankers and large industrialists with incomes from investment and profits of over £500 per year and at the other end small shopkeepers and clerks with annual earnings of only £50. At one extreme stood the 'haute bourgeoisie': the provincial elites, a small group of men and families controlling the growing industrial com-plexes with merchant bankers as their London counterpart. By 1850 the provincial elite's position was clearly evident and they had developed their entrepreneurial expertise in one of two ways. They had invested their capital in an enterprise in which either they took no interest other than receipt of profits, delegating responsibility to professional managers, or they took a direct part themselves. This elite, on familiar and sometimes marrying terms with the aristocracy, was not representative of the middle class as a whole – though they did highlight middle-class attitudes and values. A lower middle class emerged after 1800 composed of smaller manufacturers, shopkeepers, dealers, milliners, tailors, local brewers as well as the rapidly expanding ubiquitous 'clerk' in both business and government, schoolteachers, railway officials, an emergent managerial class, accountants, pharmacists and engineers. Aware of their 'caste' they maintained an important distinction between themselves as salaried or fee-earning employees and wage-earning manual workers. This 'petit bourgeoisie' was under continual pressure of being thrust down among the wage-earners. Improvements in technology causing economies of scale could oust the small producer – in textiles this was evident by the 1840s. But these improvements could also be beneficial raising the status, for example, of professional managers and those providing business expertise. Middle-class occupations in the 1851 Census are shown in Table 14.5.

Table 14.5 'Middle-class' occupations in 1851

| | England and Wales | | Scotland | | Ireland | |
	'000	%	'000	%	'000	%
Professions:						
Law	32	0.4	5	0.4	7	0.2
Medicine	60	0.7	7	0.5	7	0.2
Education	95	1.0	10	0.8	17	0.6
Religion	31	0.4	4	0.3	9	0.3
Art and amusement	25	0.3	3	0.2	3	0.1
Literature and science	2	–	–	–	–	–
Commerce:						
Clerks, accountants, bankers etc.	45	0.5	8	0.6	12	0.4
Administration: public	52	0.6	6	0.5	5	0.2
Trade, wholesale and retail	547	6.5	74	5.6	109	3.6
Totals	889	10.4	117	8.9	169	5.6

Source: G. Best *Mid-Victorian Britain 1851–1875*, Weidenfeld, 1971, pp. 105–6.

Dorothy Marshall writes that

> Some of these employments were lucrative, some poorly paid, but the men who engaged in them were united in the conviction that they were socially superior to the manual worker, however skilled. The struggling clerk, who earned less than the expert fine cotton spinner, underlined his superiority by his dress, his speech and his manners. These, and not his income, were what distinguished him from the working class.[15]

Little had changed when E. M. Forster wrote prosaically of England in 1910 in *Howard's End*, of Leonard Bast, a clerk:

The boy, Leonard Bast, stood at the extreme verge of gentility. He was not in the abyss, but he could see it, and at times people whom he knew had dropped in and counted no more. He knew that he was poor and would admit it: he would have died sooner than confess any inferiority to the rich. This may be splendid of him. But he was inferior to most rich people, there is not the least doubt of it.

MIDDLE-CLASS WOMEN

The emergence of the middle classes has been treated as male and the account of middle-class consciousness structured round public events in which women have generally been seen as playing little part. The place of women in conventional historiography lay at the centre of middle-class notions of family and home; their role was essentially domestic, dependent and private while the male role was having dependents and public. Catherine Hall rightly asks: 'Was "the separation of spheres" and the division between the public and the private a given or was it constructed as an integral part of middle-class culture and self-identity?'[16] and goes on to argue:

> But one of the ways in which the middle class was held together, despite many divisive factors, was by their ideas about masculinity and femininity. Men came to share a sense of what constituted masculinity and women a sense of what constituted femininity . . . masculinity meant having dependents, femininity meant being dependent . . . the idea of a universal womanhood is weak in comparison with the idea of certain types of sexual differentiation being a necessary part of class identity.

She argues, from the experience of Birmingham between 1780 and 1850, that women were increasingly defined as economically dependent during this period and that this dependence was an important influence for the way in which industrial capitalism developed, though she does not suggest that industrial capitalism would not have developed without sexual divisions.

Dependence and 'marginalization'

The centrality of the notion of dependence in marriage had been given a legal basis. Married women's property passed automatically to their husbands unless a settlement had been made in the courts of equity. Married women had no right to sue or be sued or to make contracts. Until the Infants' Custody Act of 1839 women could even be denied access to their children. There was no equivalent for middle-class families to the working-class idea of the 'family wages' which encapsulated the notion of economic dependence. The middle classes took on the aristocratic notion of patrilineal rights to property even though they broke with them at many other points. Certainly marriage settlements were used as a means of capital accumulation. Miss Weeton, tired of being a governess, married Aaron Stock, a small and ultimately successful Wigan factory owner, in 1814.[17] He probably married her for her money as she had saved and bought cottage property which brought in £75 per year. A daughter, Mary, was born in 1815 but the marriage was not successful. Mr Stock was violent, often expelled or threatened to expel her from the house or have her committed to the Lunatic Asylum and finally got her arrested on the grounds that she struck him. In 1819 she got a deed of separation, her husband allowing her £50 per year but she was not allowed to live within 2.5 miles of Wigan and could see her daughter only three times a year. The notion of economic dependence is made clear when she confessed that 'My principal ground of complaint is being kept so totally without money, at times when he is angry with me'.

In Birmingham Archibald Kenrick, a buckle-maker, married in 1790 and used his wife's marriage settlement to transfer his business from the declining buckle trade to become a more lucrative iron founder in 1791. Sometimes capital would come from a mother rather than a wife, since the wealthier bourgeoisie often protected a wife's settlement while the petit bourgeoisie, like Miss Weeton, did not.

The Birmingham Directories reveal middle-class women's involvement in small numbers in several, sometimes surprising, trades: there were women brass founders in the 1790s; a bedscrew-maker and coach-maker in 1803; several women involved in different aspects of the gun trade in 1812; an iron and steel merchant in 1821; plumbers and painters in the 1830s. Although the number of women involved in business increased after 1800, they were concentrated in specific trades. By the 1840s dressmaking, millinery, schoolteaching and the retail trades were the focus of women's trades. They were no longer engaged as employers in the central productive trades and had been marginalized into the servicing sector. Women increasingly did not have the necessary forms of knowledge and expertise to enter many businesses – jobs were being redefined as managerial or skilled and, therefore, masculine. Women could manage the home and the family but not the workshop or the factory.

A new 'public' world

Between 1750 and 1800 a whole new public world was created in which women had no part. As organizations became more formal women could be increasingly marginalized. They had either no role or a severely limited one in the formation of political organizations. The Birmingham Chamber of Commerce founded in 1785 brought only male manufacturers together to protect their interests. The Birmingham Political Union, the Complete Suffrage League, dissenting organizations fighting the established church and the Anti-Corn Law league were all male bodies. Middle-class women were not defined as 'political'. Their role was supportive, limited, as for example in the Anti-Corn Law League, to fund-raising. Their membership of new social organizations and institutions was also limited. They could not be full members of the libraries or reading rooms, or of the literary and philosophical societies. Women were used by philanthropical societies as visitors, subscribers, tract distributors or collectors of money, but they were given no formal powers of decision-making.[18] Jabez Bunting told the ladies at a meeting of the Methodist Missionary Society in Leeds in 1813 that women subscribers were preferable to women speakers. Men held all the positions of power and women were often excluded from meetings. They could not attend, for example, the annual general meeting of the Church Missionary Society until 1813 and the Bible Society until 1831. The Society for the Propagation of the Gospel admitted them in the 1820s but they had to be discreetly hidden from view. The Protestant Dissenting Charity School in Birmingham had a ladies' committee, responsible for the daily maintenance of the school, but membership could only be achieved through recommendation of the men's managing committee to which all important issues were referred.

Women and philanthropy

The contribution of women to institutional charity – whether under male control or not – began to rise markedly in the early nineteenth century. The reason lies partly in the piety and need for 'good works' implicit in evangelicalism but also in the decline of middle-class female occupations. Throughout this period much of their work was paternalistic and conservative in character, concerned with the perennial problems and vices – disease, lying-in and old age; drink and immorality. But some areas of concern, like anti-slavery and the cause of 'climbing boys' (young boys exploited by chimney sweeps) diminished in importance while other problems became more prominent. In the 1810s and 1820s women like Elizabeth Fry turned their attention to prison visiting only to find their influence decline in the 1830s as government inspectors moved in – a good example of formal institutionalizing of a problem leading to the marginalization of women's role.

A distinctive feature of women's philanthropic enterprise was the degree to which they applied their domestic experience and education, the concerns of the family and relations, to the world outside the home. Reformers like Hannah More argued that morality, self-denial and compassion – woman's domestic virtues – were just what was needed in English public life. It was a short step from the love of family to the love of the family of man, a step reinforced by the stress on charitable conduct by all denominations. The Evangelical concern with the importance of a proper home and family life can be seen as a move towards the more formal subordination of women that took place even in the more radical sects like the Quakers, who had already introduced separate seating for men and women by 1800. Service and duty were implicit in both philanthropy and family life.

'Separate spheres'

Definitions of masculinity and femininity certainly played an important part in marking off the middle classes from other social groups. The separation of the sexes existed at every level within society – in manufacturing, the professions and retail trades, in the churches and chapels, in public life of all kinds and in the home. Nonconformists, Anglicans, conservatives and radicals and the 'haute' and 'petite' bourgeoisie could agree on the subordinate position of women if nothing else and created a homogeneous ideology between the disparate groups within the middle classes.

WALES, SCOTLAND AND IRELAND

Wales

Wales did not develop a significant class of commercial or professional people until the eighteenth century and this was accompanied by a steady fall in the political status of the numerically strong lesser gentry. Gwyn Williams argues that

> Throughout the century there is a shuffling but increasingly visible rise in the numbers of artisans, craftsmen, professional agents of the service trades, many of them 'on tramp', and a notable increase in the strength of the professions . . . a surprising number of whom where of relatively humble origin; shopkeepers were colonizing whole reaches of society.[19]

With urban and industrial expansion shopkeepers, manufacturers and merchants became settled parts of the community, replacing the travelling packmen. Carmarthen with its river port and Wrexham and Dolgellau with their small industries became centres for merchant houses. Cattle dealers established banks at centres like Llandovery and Tregaron where they did most business. The Common Council of Cardiff had a significant commercial element in it in 1731 and this remained the case throughout the century. The growth of the iron trade in Merthyr involved a range of people in its commercial life and most of the members of its Court of Requests were shopkeepers. In rural and urban areas there was considerable variation in the wealth and influence of these emergent capitalists. At one extreme there were ironmasters like the Guests and Crawshays whose wealth and life-style put them on the same level as the landed gentry and who seem to have inherited the same autocratic and paternal attitudes towards the communities where their foundries were based. The life-style of the landed gentleman was as much the yardstick of social superiority in Wales as it was in England. Coal entrepreneurs similarly demonstrated middle-class attitudes. David Davies of Llandinam, a coal-owner, railway and dock builder, was a Nonconformist Welshman and he and his family took considerable interest in Welsh philanthropic activities in the mid-nineteenth century. Their social control was as great as that of the early ironmasters through being virtually sole employers in the mining valley towns and their public offices on boards of health and as JPs. Merchants with links, either commercial or in terms of partnerships, with Bristol or London could exploit their position far more extensively than the village shopkeepers and small traders and the variety of craftsmen and workers in wood, metal and leather, thatchers and later clockmakers who often combined their craft with work on the land.

The range of professional people increased in the eighteenth century. The clergy held second place in society to the squirearchy to which they were closely allied, in attitudes as well as family. As in England the squire often had the right to nominate to a living. The clergy were drawn from a wide social range and some livings which were very poor were run by poor curates who could have risen from the lower orders. Dissenting ministers often came from the ranks of the literate craftsmen and increasingly played an influential part in Welsh cultural life. The law was regarded as a respectable as well as lucrative profession and the Recordership of a corporation was often the door to a parliamentary seat. The number of lawyers, often in practices that were hereditary, increased in the eighteenth century since litigation over land and other kinds of property was important throughout this period and the growth of industry from 1750 created additional business. In related areas land agents and surveyors were required increasingly for surveying estates, and architects for designing new buildings. The Hopcyn family served the Margam estate as land agents for at least three generations and it was common for fathers to bring up their sons to their professions. Landlord absenteeism led to estate stewards becoming more common and acquiring considerable authority. Judges, lawyers and estate stewards were, perhaps, inevitably, unpopular in the community at large. They reflected what was increasingly seen as an alien and exploiting legal and economic system.

Doctors were few – in the late seventeenth century there were only three in the diocese of St David's – though their number grew in the eighteenth century. There were usually links with the gentry but medicine was not seen as a prestigious occupation until the mid-eighteenth century. By 1800 the Royal College of Physicians and Surgeons had laid down courses of study which took young Welshmen to Dublin if they lived close to the coast or to Edinburgh, which led in the field of medicine. The status and pay of teachers varied. Masters in grammar schools had some social standing and were well paid but there were few such schools in Wales and they were relatively poorly endowed.

The growth of the middle classes in Wales has to be counterbalanced by the successful maintenance of social and political control by the landed elite. Successful industrialists and merchants took on the attitudes of that elite and they, like the landowning slate-quarry proprietors of north-west Wales, were virtually omnipotent in their communities despite the existence of middle classes of some significance. The growth of the Welsh middle classes before 1850 was far less conducive to civic spirit and towards liberation from landed influence in towns than was the case in England.

Scotland

The Scottish middle classes in this period were vigorous and varied. At one extreme were those on the edge of the landed class like the judges of the Court of Session and the sons of lairds and noblemen who were put into the professions to make their money but who meant to return to the land. At the other extreme were those on the edge of the working class, especially those described in directories as 'mechanics' – artisans and craftsmen who were partly employers of journeymen and apprentices and partly workers in their own right. These great differences in wealth and status meant that, as in England, there was no homogeneous middle-class front against the landed elite.

From the 1750s, despite social heterogenity, almost all bourgeois groups prospered. Lawyers took the opportunities offered by increases in convey-ancing and from disputes about land. Merchants took advantage of the new trade with North America, the West Indies and Russia and to the export markets of France and Germany and finally, once they had broken the monopoly of the East India Company, with India and China. Business-men increased in old occupations and appeared in new ones. Tradesmen and mechanics seized the opportunities for increasing their trades. The professions increased in scale and office-holding became more important as a source of income.

Edinburgh and Glasgow – two streams of middle-class life

Edinburgh and Glasgow represented two streams of middle-class life: Edinburgh dominated by the professional classes and Glasgow by commer-cial and manufacturing interests. Other towns in Scotland were modelled to a lesser or greater extent on them: for example, Montrose, Dumfries and Ayr on Edinburgh; Greenock, Paisley, Galashiels and Dundee on Glasgow. Middle-class occupations seemed to flourish from the 1750s and centres of middle-class life appeared to flourish with them.

For most of the century people of all social classes lived in the tenements of the Old Town of Edinburgh, not segregated horizontally by fashionable and unfashionable streets but vertically according to the floor of the tenement on which they lived. The most respectable floors were generally the second and third, above the worst of the smell but without too many steps to climb. The most important development in Edinburgh in the late eighteenth century was the development of the New Town and the movement of the middle classes into it, a process of segregation not completed until the 1830s. This was not simply, however, a separation into a working-class and middle-class town, but into areas occupied by the more wealthy middle classes and those occupied by the working population and the petit bourgeoisie.

Edinburgh was not largely a business town, though businesses flourished there because of the growing affluence of its population. Traditional trades continued but with considerable loosening of the old guild rules. Major growth was in the consumer goods industry which lay outside the scope of the guilds. Edinburgh society was led not by merchants and tradesmen (despite their economic significance and control of the Town Council) but by professional men. Lawyers were pre-eminent in this field – the street directories for Edinburgh in the 1770s give evidence of this with their lists putting advocates first, then clerks and writers to the signet and their clerks, only then were the nobility and gentry with town houses included, and finally the rest of the middle class without distinction. The lawyers' closest links were not with the mercantile interest but with the country gentry of the Lothians. Success meant an estate in East Lothian or Midlothian both as an investment and for the political privilege and social prestige it gave one's family. Intermarriage between lawyers and gentry was common and they treated each other with equal respect. Urban lawyers and rural gentry formed a cultural and economic elite. After the lawyers, the profession which contributed most to the life of eighteenth- and early nineteenth-century Edinburgh was teaching. Education was a growth industry after 1720 and the University reached the height of its reputation between 1760 and 1820 with famous teachers like the historian William Robertson, William Cullen and, in chemistry, Joseph Black and Dugald Stewart and Adam Ferguson in moral philosophy. The Medical School, founded in 1726, had immense prestige due in no small measure to three generations of Alexander Munros who held the Chair of Anatomy unbroken between 1720 and 1846. Its excellence, a consequence of good teaching and a liberal curriculum, accounted for the dramatic increase in students, including many from England, Wales and Ireland: 400 in 1780 to over 2,000 by 1820. Edinburgh was also famous for educational establishments, for both sexes, other than the University. Hugo Arnot described it in 1779 as a city dependent for its support 'chiefly upon the college of justice, the seminaries of education and the inducement which as a capital it affords to genteel people to reside in it'.[20]

In late eighteenth-century Glasgow 30 per cent of occupations were classified as merchant and manufacturer while in Edinburgh it was only

12 per cent. The respective figures for professional men were 12 per cent and 29 per cent, for small tradesmen 42 per cent and 30 per cent and for nobles and gentry 1 per cent and 5 per cent. Glasgow's strength lay in the entrepreneurial skills of its business and manufacturing community and Glasgow rather than Edinburgh was the focal point for Scotland's industrial revolution.

Ireland

The middle classes developed far more slowly in Ireland than in the rest of the United Kingdom. Table 14.5 (p. 298) shows that in 1851 'middle-class' occupations accounted for 5.6 per cent of the total workforce compared to over 10 per cent in England and Wales and almost 9 per cent in Scotland. Lecky, the Victorian historian, argued that British repression before 1778 deliberately prevented the emergence of an Irish Catholic middle class and destroyed Irish trade and manufactures. The extent to which this was the case is difficult to determine but the growth of linen-cloth exports from 2 million yards in the 1710s to 25 million yards by the mid-1780s certainly calls this conclusion into question. It seems that during the second half of the eighteenth century a Catholic urban middle class emerged, largely unheralded, and by 1800 controlled a large share of Irish commerce.

There was some mobility between land, business and the professions in Ireland but on the whole it was not pronounced. This is confirmed by the stream of immigrants into business in the Irish cities. The influx of Scots into the wholesale trade and industry in the late eighteenth and early nineteenth centuries is an example of this. The range of families in foreign trade was comparatively narrow. Only in the south-east did a combination of social pressures and aspirations predispose even the lower classes to mobility on a scale unequalled elsewhere outside the ranks of Nonconformists and Presbyterians particularly in Ulster.

Ireland remained a gentry-based culture where, outside urban centres, the middle classes did not develop to any significant extent. A possible exception to this was the 'middlemen' who were perhaps the only group which constituted anything like a rural middle class. Middlemen leased land and lived off the profits between their head rents and the sub-rent paid by their tenants. Some adopted an entrepreneurial role in developing the rural economy in the eighteenth century. They helped to accelerate the spread of a stable market structure to remoter areas through their role in marketing produce, often received instead of cash rents. Middlemen were a function of the degree of backwardness of a region and were never a major facet of society in more developed areas like Kildare, Kilkenny or Meath and the spread of a cash economy after the 1750s made their position less economically viable. Middlemen stood between the small tenant farmers and the landowners and were important social brokers in the countryside, who, however archaic and conservative they were, contributed powerfully to the cohesion of social life. As they disappeared, the conflicting social interests of rural Ireland confronted each other much more directly.

THE 'PROFESSIONS'

One of the most distinctive features of the development of the 'middling ranks' was the expansion of 'the professions'.[21] Sociologists have defined a 'profession' as an occupation with the following characteristics: a collegial and hierarchical organization; control over recruitment policy; a self-imposed and self-regulated code of individual behaviour (within a framework of considerable individual autonomy) and group practice; a claim to monopoly in the particular area of expertise through their understanding and application of specialized knowledge; and finally, a sense of *esprit de corps* or professional solidarity. There are, however, certain problems with this sociological perspective. It has Whiggish implications – historians are being asked 'to measure the ancient professions against the yardstick of the modern'. It also implies an inevitable continuum, a route whereby groups achieved the goal of full professionalism. As Rosemary O'Day says: 'Rarely has there been a subject for study so elusive of satisfactory definition. For "profession" it not simply the equivalent of "occupation"; the word implies an ideology . . .'[22]

Why was there a growth in the 'professions' in the eighteenth century? Some historians, Geoffrey Holmes for example, see professionalization as a feature of urbanization if not industrialization. The existence of towns was certainly of major importance in the development of the professions but it does not provide a complete answer. The varieties of economic growth may.

The eighteenth century saw a growing and central importance of the notion of 'vocation' to the professional. A profession was not simply a specialized occupation but possessed status. Only the higher clergy, physicians and barristers were considered members of the 'liberal professions' and were recruited almost exclusively from the upper levels of society. Curates, surgeons, teachers, apothecaries and attorneys (as solicitors were called until 1874) were regarded as little higher than tradesmen. Status could be surrounded by mystique as in the case of physicians who wrote their prescriptions in Latin and left their dispensing to others. Apothecaries, because of their more limited education, wrote theirs in English and dispensed themselves. The practitioner, it was argued, possessed a calling from God. This was obvious when applied to professions like the clergy, but it was only gradually secularized and accepted that laymen and eventually laywomen also had callings. Out of the notion of vocation and the economic definition of a profession in terms of having 'cornered the market' institutionalized professions emerged during the first half of the nineteenth century.

Evangelicalism and the High Church Oxford Movement, as well as the reformation of Anglican church organizations in the 1830s re-established the Church as a serious professional vocation rather than just congenial sinecures for the younger sons of the gentry. In 1845 the first proper theological college was established at Cuddesdon to train ordinands for their new responsibilities. Teacher-training institutions date from the same decade. The Royal College of Surgeons was founded in 1800, the Institution of Civil Engineers in 1818 and the British Medical Council started life as the Provincial Medical and Surgical Association in 1832. The Law Society was set up in 1825 and in 1836 it supervised the first examinations held for any branch of the legal profession. The Inns of Court followed suit in 1851 when they set up the Council for Legal Education, though examinations for barristers was not compulsory until 1872.

By 1850 only the upper reaches of the armed services and the civil service were still 'unprofessionalized' in the sociological sense outlined above. Control over service commissions was not breached until the reforms of the early 1870s though the civil service was to be reformed, as a result of the government's Northcote-Trevelyan report in 1855 and pressure from the Administrative Reform Association. As John Bourne has recently argued,[23] historians should not neglect the importance of patronage in nineteenth-century England.

'MIDDLE CLASSNESS'

The concept of a middle-class standard of living was developed by the 1830s. It provides, despite the warnings of G. Kitson Clark in *The Making of Victorian England*, an objective set of standards against which membership of the middle class can be tested and a subjective set of goals which individuals strove for. This was a concept both of self and class consciousness and, as a result, the middle classes were much more conscious of their 'classness' than the labouring population. They possessed both organizational ability and ideological unity when the working population did not. The middle classes opposed many aspects of aristocratic society, especially what they perceived as its idleness and excess, and yet wished to emulate their 'betters'. Keeping up with the Joneses, and especially the Lord or Sir Jones, was an inherent part of the credo. They preached puritan values of sobriety and hard work, holding themselves up as a model for the working population – a moral imperative which succeeded in inculcating or developing a highly individualistic, upwardly-mobile attitude among a significant section of those workers. Contemporaries and modern historians both saw class relations as complex and, in the case of the working classes, downright confusing. But this was less the case for the middle classes. In terms of income and occupation, types of expenditure and pattern of family living the criteria used by contemporaries and today are very clear. Religious certainty, moral zeal and purity, respectability, the importance of 'appearance' were all essential to this self-definition. Growing economic strength and prosperity gave them exploitative power over the labouring population – economically as employers of the work force, but also socially and politically as a focus for emulation and sexually through the underworld of prostitution that existed behind the facade of family life. By 1850 a hegemony of middle-class social and economic values had been established. The emergence of the Liberal Party during the 1850s and early 1860s was to give these values national political power.

NOTES

1　D. Defoe *Robinson Crusoe* quoted in I. Bradley *The English Middle Classes are Alive and Kicking*, Collins, 1982, p. 63.
2　K. Marx, quoted in R. H. Tawney *Religion and the Rise of Capitalism*, Penguin, 1964 edn., p. 266.
3　Aristotle *The Politics*, Oxford University Press, 1947, Book IV, ix(8).
4　R. Porter *English Society in the Eighteenth Century*, Penguin, 1982, p. 88. P. Earle, *The Making of the English Middle Class*, Methuen, 1989 and P. Langford, *A Polite and Commercial People: England 1727–1783*, Oxford University Press, 1989 provide a much needed analysis of the eighteenth-century bourgeoisie.
5　ibid. pp. 86–7.
6　J. C. D. Clark *English Society 1688–1832*, Oxford University Press, 1985, p. 71.
7　H. Perkin, *The Origins of Modern English Society 1780–1880*, Routledge & Kegan Paul, 1969, p. 23.
8　King, Massie and Colquhoun have recently been scrutinized in a series of papers by P. H. Lindert and J. G. Williamson, conveniently summarized in N. Crafts *British Economic Growth during the Industrial Revolution*, Oxford University Press, 1985, pp. 11–17.
9　R. Porter op. cit. p. 92.
10　Quoted in J. Scott *The Upper Classes*, Macmillan, 1980, p. 70.
11　R. Porter op. cit. p. 97.
12　I. Bradley op. cit. p. 65.
13　J. S. Mill 'The State of Society in America', *Westminster Review*, January 1836.
14　G. Kitson Clark *The Making of Victorian England*, Methuen, 1965, p. 96.
15　D. Marshall, *Industrial England 1776–1851*, Routledge, 1973, p. 96.
16　C. Hall 'Gender Divisions and Class Formation in the Birmingham Middle Class 1780–1850', in R. Samuel (ed.) *People's History and Socialist Theory*, Routledge, 1981, p. 165. L. Davidoff and C. Hall *Family Fortunes*, Hutchinson, 1987 is now the definitive work on middle-class women.
17　Ellen Weeton *Miss Weeton: The Journal of a Governess*, ed. E. Hall, 1939 is very informative on the life and tribulations of middle-class women.
18　On women and philanthropy see F. K. Prochaska *Women and Philanthropy in 19th Century England*, Oxford University Press, 1980, and his more recent *The Voluntary Impulse: Philanthropy in Modern Britain*, Faber, 1988.
19　G. A. Williams *When Was Wales?*, Penguin, 1985, p. 146.
20　Quoted in T. C. Smout *A History of the Scottish People 1560–1830*, Fontana, 1972, p. 355.
21　For the development of the 'professions' see G. Holmes *Augustan England:*

Professions, State and Society 1680–1730, Allen & Unwin, 1982 and W. J. Reader *Professional Men: the Rise of the Professional Classes in Victorian England*, Weidenfeld, 1966. A useful summary can be found in the bibliographical essay by R. O'Day 'The Professions in Early Modern England', *History Today*, June 1986, pp. 52–5. F. M. L. Thompson, *The Rise of Respectable Society*, Fontana, 1988 offers a thematic approach from 1830.

22 R. O'Day op. cit. p. 52.

23 J. M. Bourne *Patronage and Society in Nineteenth-Century England*, Edward Arnold, 1986, especially chapters 1, 2 and 7.

15 Wages

All of you who are sixty years of age can recollect that bread and meat and not wretched potatoes, were the food of the labouring people; you can recollect that every industrious labouring man brewed his own beer and drank it by his own fireside. . . . You can recollect when the young men did not shirk about on a Sunday in ragged smock-frocks with unshaven faces, and a shirt not washed for a month, and with their toes pointing out from their shoes, and when a young man was pointed out if he had not, on a Sunday, a decent coat upon his back, a good hat on his head, a clean shirt with silk handkerchief around his neck, leather breeches without a spot, whole worsted stockings tied under the knee with a red garter. . . . There were always some exceptions to this; some lazy, some drunken, some improvident young men; but I appeal to you all, those of you who are sixty years of age, whether this be not a true description of the state of the labourers of England when they were boys?[1]

William Cobbett articulated deeply felt contemporary feelings when he lamented changes in the attitude of farm labourers between the 1760s and the 1820s. This sense of loss showed itself in nostalgia, a mourning for the passing of a richer life, not just materially but in terms of the quality of experience. While it is easy to demonstrate the empirical unsoundness of nostalgia, that each generation deceives itself in its old age, historians cannot escape the existence of a sense of loss. This chapter is concerned with those groups in society who worked with their hands and for whom wages, in one form or another, were the primary source of income. No matter how skilled they were, how high their earnings, their social status was determined by the kind of job they did. Labouring people lived in a world of their own, remote from the experience of their more prosperous and articulate contemporaries. They were both vulnerable to the changes that occurred in the British economy from the early eighteenth century and yet some were also able to exploit those changes to improve both their status and income. The working population was not a single entity, a homogeneous class. It was divided between town and country, manufacture and service, skilled and unskilled. Superimposed on these divisions was the deep separation of experience through gender and race. These distinctions were further overlaid by local and regional differences expressed in dialects, customs and loyalties. Poverty alone provided a unifying factor: the threat of poverty, the fear of poverty, the certainty of poverty. All I can hope to do in one chapter is to sketch the broad outline of developments and identify the major areas of concern for historians[2].

WAGES

A 'proletariat'?

The comprehensiveness of the Marxist formulation of a 'proletariat' as

> that class of society which procures its means of livelihood entirely and solely from the sale of its labour and not from the profit derived from any capital; whose weal and woe, whose life and death, whose whole existence depend on the demand for labour, hence, on the alternation of times of good and bad business, on the fluctuations resulting from unbridled competition.

is extremely appealing yet the way in which people were paid varied throughout the eighteenth and early nineteenth century. Increasingly wages were paid directly in cash, though this could be in the form of 'tokens' which could only be exchanged at the 'company store'. Wages were paid by the hour, day, week or at 'piece-rates'. In other cases wages were paid 'in kind'. Many farm servants 'lived in', receiving bed and board as well as small money wages. As late as the 1850s quarrymen of Swanage in Dorset received the equivalent money value of their wages in stone.

Wage labourers or the emergence of a 'cash' nexus

By 1800 wages accounted for about 45 per cent of the national income. Wage-labourers received a disproportionately small share of this. Probably around two-thirds of the population were living on wages[3] During the eighteenth century, though less in the nineteenth, it is sometimes difficult to determine whether a person was a wage-earner or not. Many people occupied small plots of land supplementing their incomes by working as wage-labourers for larger farmers or as outworkers in, for example, the cloth, straw or leather industries. It is also difficult to treat women and children working on family farms or workshops as employees working for wages. The emergence of fully fledged wage-labour as opposed to the ambiguous world of peasant labourers and family workers did not occur evenly over time. In areas where agricultural holdings were divided to accommodate an increasing number of people then the outcome was farms too small to support families by agriculture alone. Additional employment was necessary to supplement farm incomes and in the forest and upland regions of England and Wales and parts of Ireland this led to peasant manufacture which eventually became commercialized. Where systems of primogeniture were widespread, as in lowland England, growing population created an increasing body of landless labourers, who either worked for farmers possessing farms large enough to need wage-labour, or of moving to areas where work was available. Wage-labour was more an industrial than an agricultural phenomenon and was probably most widespread in the service sector, occupations requiring little skill which were easily available for people lacking land, capital or training. Wage-labour developed more slowly in agriculture. In 1831 there were only 2.5 farm-labouring families to every farm-occupying family. Farm servants frequently lived in farmers' houses, though the practice seems to have been in decline in England, if not Scotland and Wales, in the eighteenth century. At busy periods, such as harvest times, casual labour was employed including short-term migrants from Ireland. In two types of manufacturing industries wage-labour became more important. One was capital-intensive enterprises like metal-smelting and mining. The other was the more numerous category of wage-earners found in textiles, metal-working and leather-working, where wage-labour was combined with working capital to supply standardised goods of uniform quality and low prices to national and international markets. These wage-labourers had little chance of graduating to better things, unlike urban craft journeymen and apprentices, another group of wage-earners, who could achieve the status of small masters. Increasingly, however, the growth of metropolitan permanent journeymen who had little prospect of becoming masters was a feature of this period. As late as the censuses of 1841 and 1851 it remains difficult to distinguish between self-employed and wage-earners in craft occupations, though it is clear that such forms of employment declined in importance relative to wage-earners employed in capital-intensive enterprises.

The changing eighteenth-century labour market

One problem when discussing wage-labour in the eighteenth century is the nature of the labour market. In practice, before 1800 there were many rather than a single labour market. Institutions like guilds, municipal authorities and the state impaired their smooth operation while both employers and employees often restricted the free flow of labour. Poor communications, local traditions and customs, differentiation by skill and status combined to make labour one of the least immobile factors of production. Labour markets operated with fewest obstacles at the lowest levels of skill. By 1800 there was a considerable pool of unskilled labour which could be recruited to any manual occupation. Variations in the intensity of demand had a direct influence on wages. Incomes were generally higher in towns than in the countryside, because urban demand for labour was greater than its supply.

Changing social attitudes

There was a marked change in social attitudes to wage-earning in the eighteenth century. In the seventeenth century wage-labourers were generally despised, had no place in society, possessed no political rights and were accorded no consideration except as producers of wealth. Their wages were kept as low as possible to keep production costs down. Since they possessed no property, other than their labour, wage-earners were 'masterless men', out of harmony with a society in which the possession of property determined a person's place in the social hierarchy. Economic changes after 1700 reshaped relationships between employers and workers, widening the social gulf between them. This eventually resulted in a challenge to the rights of property with an articulation of the rights of men, the emergence of 'working-class consciousness'. Two intellectual developments strengthened arguments in favour of higher wages. The first was the refutation that labourers were lazy. Adam Smith argued that 'where wages are high . . . we shall always find the workman more active, diligent and expeditious than when they are low . . .'.[4]

Secondly, higher wages created a demand for consumable goods and so stimulated further economic growth. Smith argued that rising wages caused workers to copy the consumption patterns of their social superiors:

> it is but equity . . . that they who feed, clothe and lodge the whole body of the people, should have such a share of the produce of their own labour as to be themselves tolerably well fed, clothed and lodged.[5]

'STANDARDS OF LIVING'

There are major problems with the quantity of wages throughout this period and this is reflected in the vexed controversy over 'standards of living'[6]. 'What was the impact of economic change on standards of living for the labouring population?' is generally the question historians have asked. The conclusions reached range from those who point to the beneficial effects of industrialization upon wages to those who take a view of progressive immiseration. The popular conception of living standards in England between Peterloo and 'the hungry forties' is of a working population in a state of dire and unrelenting poverty. This view, expressed graphically if not always with historical accuracy, by Karl Marx in *The Communist Manifesto*, maintains that

> With the development of industry the proletariat not only increases in number; it becomes concentrated in greater masses, its strength grows,

and it feels that strength more. . . . Machinery obliterates all distinctions of labour and nearly everywhere reduces wages to the same low level.

Marx demonstrated the problem of making general statements and helps to explain why the best-known economic history controversy is distinguished by a low level of academic objectivity. Rigour needs to replace rhetoric.

'Real' wages

In attempting to ascertain living standards emphasis has been placed on the relationship between wages and prices: the question of 'real wages'.

So what was the course of 'real' wages between 1700 and 1850 and what methodological problems have historians encountered in attempting to determine this? Attention has focused on living standards in early industrial towns, especially cotton towns, for which there is ample evidence. The problem is whether their experience was representative of other areas of Britain and whether the contrast between these 'dark satanic mills' and 'merrie England' is a valid one or merely a construct of historians who have put ideological considerations before historical ones. Radical pessimists – some contemporary novelists, poets and social critics – had the better of the rhetorical debate and their stand was taken over by historians in the 1880s. Arnold Toynbee, the Webbs and the Hammonds were united in their condemnation of the long agony of the industrial revolution, characterizing it as 'history's blackest hour'. The counter-attack, led by Sir John Clapham, began in 1926 and, supported by Ashton and Hartwell, proved so powerful that E. P. Thompson could, in 1963, call it 'the new anti-catastrophe orthodoxy'. Recently, the optimists' advance has been checked.

The problem lies in the manner of compiling indices of real wages. By selecting appropriate starting and finishing points it is perfectly possible to construct any of a range of increases or decreases in real wages. For example, any index using 1800 as a base will, because high food prices depressed the value of real wages, show a marked upward bias. Tucker's index of real wages for London artisans shows a decline in real wages of 11 per cent between 1780 and 1840 but an increase of 25 per cent between 1790 and 1850. How wages were spent also creates problems. Most surviving series are for wholesale rather than retail prices and little is known of the weight that should be ascribed to different items or of the ways in which expenditure patterns responded to price changes or the introduction of new commodities. What, for example, was the impact on standards of living of the increased availability of potatoes? More difficulties arise from the need to adjust hourly or weekly earnings to compensate for periods of under- or unemployment. The best available statistics are those contained in customs and excise returns which include four items of importance in the diet of the labouring population – beer, tea, coffee and sugar. But interpretation is difficult. Beer returns end in 1830, while trends in tea and coffee often reflect not rising living standards but the fact that they were substitutes for each other. Supplies of bread, the main item of diet, were always dependent on harvest yields and increased potato consumption was seen as a sign of falling standards in the south but was welcomed in the north as a dietary variant. The main evidence for beef and mutton relates to the Smithfield indices but Smithfield may not have been representative as there were other meat markets, and these indices do not include pig prices, which made up an important part of the labouring population's diet.

Diversity of 'experience'

To the patchiness of this evidence and the difficulties inherent in its interpretation must be added the enormous diversity of working experience. Some workers experienced a rise in wages while others experienced a relative decline. Skilled workers in unmechanized occupations whose services were increasingly needed by a developing economy, like compositors, blacksmiths, building craftsmen, joiners etc. and new craftsmen like boilermakers, iron puddlers and railway engine drivers – conventionally labelled the 'labour aristocracy' – were prominent among the fortunate group. Factory cotton spinners, the majority of farm workers in the Scottish Lowlands, most domestic servants and perhaps building workers also experienced rising real wages. Workers hit by technological advance and who were unadaptable like handloom weavers, framework knitters and the nail-makers of the Black Country; a great many of the London workers mentioned by Henry Mayhew and the agricultural labourers of southern England, declined. Regional variations were imposed on these differences. If anything economic change markedly increased regional wage variations: by 1850 there were at least twelve distinct wage areas in Britain. In the early nineteenth century, for example, compositors earned 12s.–19s. in Scotland. 18s.–22s. in northern England, 18s.–24s. in the south-east and as much as 25s. in London. Emphasizing handloom weavers or agricultural labourers as opposed to factory workers, or one region rather than another, or 1790–1830 rather than 1800–50, would lead to different conclusions.

Conclusions?

Given all these qualifications can historians say anything about real wages with any degree of confidence? In the first half of the eighteenth century production of staple foodstuffs kept pace with population growth. Wheat prices were low and, after 1730, were falling, reaching their lowest point in 1755. By the 1760s the southern counties were largely on a wheat diet, though the northern counties, poorer than the south, continued longer on barley and rye and took to potatoes sooner. Lower prices increased the purchasing value of wages, allowing a greater proportion to be spent on manufactured goods and imports than previously. This increase in demand played an important role in stimulating economic growth and rising wages in the vicinity of industrial areas. However, the position of the labourer and cottager in southern England, where the opportunities for additional or alternative employment were limited, showed signs of deterioration. It was their low wages which were partly responsible for lower wheat prices down to 1755. Between the 1760s and 1790s corn prices began to rise faster than other prices and faster than wages. Average wages are estimated to have risen by 25 per cent between 1760 and 1795 and the cost of living by 30 per cent, though this obscures a definite rise in the industrial north and a distinct fall in London and the agricultural counties. From about 1790 until the end of the French Wars, M. W. Flinn estimated[7], real wages of most workers kept pace with rising prices. Between 1813 and the early 1820s prices fell sharply and to a greater extent than wages so that those who were in work (an important qualification) appear to have enjoyed an increase in living standards of up to a quarter. These gains seem to have been retained, though not increased, between 1820 and 1850 and with less unemployment a greater proportion of the labour force may have benefited from the earlier gains. There is nothing here to suggest that there was a general and sustained fall in real wages between 1790 and 1850. Lindert and Williamson, however, disagree with Flinn's analysis, arguing for a decline in real wages between 1815 and 1819 locating the real improvement between 1820 and 1850.[8]

Qualitative considerations

It is not enough to argue that because real wages rose for the bulk of the labouring population that there was an overall improvement in standards of living. Standards of living cover qualitative as well as quantitative conditions. When 'the quality of life' is considered the pessimists have a less assailable position. Exploitation, human misery, squalor are highly ambiguous and emotive concepts for historians to use. What validity is there in arguing, for example, that the change in the nature of work from the 'freedom' of the domestic system to the soul-destroying factory system marked a reduction in the quality of life? In what ways did the relationship between rich and poor change? How was the family affected? J. L. Hammond argued that there was a price to be paid for economic change, one that could not be measured in statistical terms, including 'the want of beauty, the same want of pageants or festivals . . . the ugliness of the new life, with its growing slums, its lack of beautiful buildings, its destruction of nature.'[9] But were conditions qualitatively worse for the labouring population in 1850 than in 1700? Again historians have problems with the 'general' and the 'specific'.

Much early industrialization took place in rural areas and manufacturers often provided housing and other social amenities for their workers. Jedidiah Strutt, the eighteenth-century mill-owner, for example provided houses, shops, schools, a library, a swimming pool with instructor and a room for dancing for his workers. The result was that conditions in industrial villages were often quite good though increasingly urban squalor and the proliferation of mills and mines were seen as synonymous. Overcrowding, jerry-building, impure water, street pollution and poor sanitation were the consequences. Many more people were exposed to the hazards of adulterated food. In 1819 alone, for example, there were nearly one hundred convictions of brewers and brewers' druggists for using a variety of substitutes for beer and hops. But Engels overstated the case when he wrote that 'Everything in this district that arouses our disgust and just indignation is of relatively recent origin and belongs to the industrial age. . . .'

Open sewers and adulterated foods were not the invention of the industrial age and neither was poor housing, though all were accentuated by the growth of manufacturing industries. Engels inherited a romanticized notion of pre-industrial rural cottages in which lived contented spinners and weavers. Urban death rates in 1700 or Hogarth's prints leave no doubt that squalor existed without modern industry[10]. The pessimist case relies too much on romanticized notions of pre-industrial England but the deterioration of the 'quality' of life may have offset any improvement in real wages.

The alleged loss of freedom when machines rather than traditional work rhythms dictated toil has been used by pessimists as a further example of qualitative decay. Great care must, however, be taken not unduly to exaggerate the degree of freedom and independence enjoyed by pre-industrial workers. In parts of Yorkshire woollen weavers seem to have purchased their own raw materials but this was not widespread as elsewhere weavers depended on entrepreneurs for their wool. The sense in which 'freedom' can be applied was limited to weavers' owning their own looms (though framework knitters generally rented theirs) and self-determination of daily work patterns. The 'loss of freedom' argument may fit the handloom weavers best, though even their independence was limited, but few other occupations. Agricultural labourers had long periods of underemployment punctuated by periods of intense labour at harvest and in the spring. Eighteenth-century miners frequently worked shorter shifts than became usual in the nineteenth century. Labour patterns had, in the words of E. P. Thompson[11], a 'characteristic irregularity', with alternate bouts of intense labour and idleness. The universality of irregular work patterns in pre-industrial England has been questioned. During the first half of the eighteenth century many trades developed a conception of a certain number of hours which made up a normal full working day. In most handicraft trades a 10-hour day was considered the norm by 1750, and weavers considered ten and a half hours a hard day.

Economic change merely increased the number of workers subjected to the growing regularity and intensity of work.

The spread of the factory system was slow and uneven and so was its impact on work patterns[12]. Freedom was replaced, according to Engels and others, by 'the tyranny of the factory bell'. For Wordsworth factories were 'an outrage against nature'. Discipline could be harsh and fines were imposed. The most publicized evils of the factory system were usually found in the older and smaller mills where machinery was so crowded together that passageways were not clearly defined and where accidents occurred most frequently from machinery not being boxed in. Ceilings were sometimes so low that it was difficult to stand upright, while lighting, ventilation and drainage were inadequate. The pessimists argue that, even if factory conditions were probably no worse than those in domestic industries, the transition to factory production still involved a major qualitative deterioration. The issue was one of the 'freedom' of capitalists to destroy the customs of a trade, whether by new machinery, by factories or by unrestricted competition which beat down wages and led to undercutting rivals and undermining standards of craftmanship. The notion that 'Time is Money', they argue, has its origins in this process. But even several contemporaries who were hostile to industrialization conceded the point that factory work required no more exertion than much other work. Labour was by waterwheel or steam engine, hours were no longer than in some non-factory occupations and after 1830, with progressive legislation curbing the working day, the cotton town gradually lost their reputation for excessive hours. Mills became safer, less crowded, better ventilated and less dependent on young children. Hightened social conscience and a determination to investigate and reform social evils have an important role in the optimists' case that the association of industrialization with a declining quality of life is founded on too rosy an interpretation of pre-industrial conditions. As E. H. Hunt says:

> Whether the people of industrial England were more or less contented than their rustic forebears cannot be determined – but the effects of industrialisation on their lives is less indeterminable than commonly supposed. The debate entails a comparison between England as it was and the non-industrial alternative.[13]

Families and children

The impact on the family of the economic changes was a cause of considerable pessimism among many contemporaries like Richard Oastler, Lord Shaftesbury and particularly Peter Gaskell[14]. The result of the transition from domestic to factory system was, for the textile workers' families, nothing less than catastrophic, 'a violation of the sacred nature of the home'. As with the 'standards of living' debate it is necessary to distinguish valid evidence from polemic. Two points are clear. First, the pessimistic critique stems from a contrast of the impact of factories with the presumed conditions of family life under the domestic system. Secondly, critics rarely went outside the textile industry in making comparisons. The domestic system was based on an integrated family unit of reproduction, production and consumption. Patriarchal control and moral guidance were exerted over both wives and children. Children often followed in their father's trade, a disadvantage in trades which were already overstocked. In this context the advent of the factory affected the 'independent' economic status of the family. Engels argued that it destroyed the pride and status of the breadwinner, now dependent on the factory earnings of his wife and children. Women were no longer able to carry out their domestic functions effectively and the family's dietary needs suffered. Daughters were not instructed in the domestic virtues and were exposed to a promiscuously early mixing with young men. The contrast was drawn, by Marx and others, between the artisan as an independent seller of his own labour and the slave-trader, selling his own and his wife and children's labour in the factory. William Cobbett wrote in 1821: 'You are for reducing the community into two classes: Masters and Slaves. . . . When master and man were the term everyone was in his place and all were free. Now, in fact, it is the affair of master and slaves . . .'.[15]

Neil Smelser challenged the consequences of the factory on the family in his *Social Change in the Industrial Revolution*, Routledge & Kegan Paul, 1959. In this influential book he argued, on the basis of the Lancashire cotton industry, that the separation of working children from their families did not really begin until after 1820 with the introduction of power-weaving. Technological change between 1820 and 1840 led to a redefinition of the economic functions of the textile family and sharply differentiated the roles of its members. Early cotton mills, he argued, relied on recruiting either 'unfree' pauper apprentices or 'free' families from farming rather than the domestic textile area. Mule-spinning was very much a family affair, with operative spinners hiring their own relatives as scavengers and piercers. This training relationship was codified in many early spinners' trade union rules which attempted to limit recruitment to the kinship unit (children, brothers, nephews etc.). As a result traditional family values and authority structures were perpetuated. Power-weaving did not reproduce this structure. It was overwhelmingly an occupation for young women assisted by child dressers recruited directly by factory masters. It was largely because of this development, which was outside parental instruction and supervision, Smelser argued, that factory reform became such an emotive issue in the 1830s. State intervention was necessary to safeguard conditions which had previously been regulated by the family.

Smelser has not been without his critics. First, demographic evidence contradicts his notion of the 'family in the factory'. Few mule-spinners would at any time in their working lives have had enough children of sufficient age to pierce for them, so they needed to employ people from outside the family. In 1816 only 12 per cent of people under eighteen in thirteen Preston mills and 25 per cent in eleven recorded cotton mills elsewhere were employed by parents, brothers or sisters. The remainder were often the children of handloom weavers whose wages were needed to supplement the contracting family budget. The proportion of children working with a parent was not as great as many contemporary polemicists believed. Secondly, the proportion of relatives working for mule-spinners remained at about 15 per cent between 1810 and 1840 and there was no significant or sudden change in the nature and extent of family-based employment in the mills between 1825 and 1830. Thirdly, it is difficult to generalize from the experience of this elite group to that of the proletariat as a whole. Skilled workers in areas other than cotton spinning – the skilled hewers in the Cornish tin mines for example – could give instruction to their male children who took not merely their fathers' workplace but also their fathers' positions in society. This was not the case with unskilled workers. The problem for any parent, whether skilled or unskilled, in the eighteenth and early nineteenth centuries was marrying the need simultaneously to bring children up and to exploit them economically. The degree of control which parents exerted over the latter was far more limited than polemicists would have historians believe.

WOMEN AND WORK

The extent to which the nature of work for labouring women changed has two dimensions which are historically and ideologically important. First, to what extent were changes in the nature of work, especially the development of the factory system, of significance in allowing women into the labour market as independent wage-earners? Secondly, how far did this employment alter women's role in the 'domestic sphere' and what impact did this have on the family?

Opportunities or marginalization?

Ivy Pinchbeck maintained, in her classic study of women workers, first published in 1930, that economic change after 1750 transformed female employment opportunities, increasing the availability of employment outside the home, improving women's status and conditions and being of vital importance in the destruction of the notion of the 'family wage'.[16] Valuable though Pinchbeck still is, several qualifications can be made to her basic thesis. The notion that the industrial revolution increased the participation of women in general outside the home is difficult to maintain. Eric Richards has shown that female participation rates in the productive economy declined after 1820. Female participation in cereal-producing areas probably declined from the mid-eighteenth century. This was largely the result of the replacement of the sickle by the scythe, never used by women, for cutting grain and resulted in women being reduced to the lower-status, lower-paid jobs of weeding or stone-picking – a process exacerbated by the 'depression' in cereal production after 1815. Only in East Anglia did the emergence of the 'gang' system reverse this process. By contrast, in pastoral areas women's participation did not decline and there may even have been an increase in real wages for women specializing in livestock, dairying and hay-making. On the north-eastern coalfields women ceased to work underground during the eighteenth century and none had worked below ground in Staffordshire, Shropshire, Leicestershire and Derbyshire for some time before they were forbidden to do so by the 1842 Mines Act. Levels of female participation varied according to area and occupation. The wives and daughters of migrant Scottish farmers astonished East Anglians in the 1880s by doing work which had been done exclusively by men there since before 1800. Few women found themselves emancipated by the economic changes in terms of having sufficient income to make them independent of either parents or husband. Contemporaries may have been impressed by the 'freedom' of the lasses of the mill towns who secured a reputation for flashy dressing and an undeserved one for sexual promiscuity. But they were not typical. In 1851 domestic service accounted for 37.3 per cent of female occupations (aged 15 and over), textiles 18.5, dressmaking 18 and agriculture 7.7 per cent. Most of these occurred in the home where constraints on emancipation were very real. Women's wages were at a level which was assumed to be supplementary.

Male attitudes

Male exclusiveness largely explains why changes in social attitudes to women's employment remained largely unaltered between 1700 and 1850. Traditionally, manufacturing skill had been associated with men and this had created a sense of male solidarity which extended beyond the workplace into community and home. Men's struggles to maintain their skilled priority in the workforce against machinery and against the encroachment of unskilled women was an important part of their effort to maintain their social status in the community and within their families. The sexual division of labour was a familial, customary and social construct rather than one largely determined by technical considerations. It was part of the social hierarchy established among activities – in male-dominated societies women's tasks are considered inferior simply because they are carried out by women. The division of labour is therefore an effect of the social hierarchy, not its cause.

This patriarchal ideology was used to justify keeping women away from new technology, as in a petition from the potters in 1845: 'To maidens, mothers, and wives we say machinery is your deadliest enemy. . . . It will destroy your natural claims to home and domestic duties . . .'.[17] It also limited their income, as cotton spinners pleaded in 1824: 'The women, in nine cases out of ten, have only themselves to support, while the men, generally, have families. . . . The women can afford their labour for less than the men . . .'.[18] And it kept them in their 'proper' place: 'Keep them at home to look after their families . . .'.[19]

These contemporary criticisms of working women were based on an ideological consideration of a proper women's sphere, not on a proper investigation of actual working conditions. With the exception of skilled artisans, whose status generally ensured an income sufficient to support a wife and family, most women among the labouring population worked not merely to 'top up' the family budget but to ensure basic levels of family subsistence.

THE LABOURING POPULATION – A CLASSIFICATION

Henry Mayhew in *London Labour and London Poor* in 1851 classified the social fabric of mid-nineteenth-century England into 'those who will work, those who cannot work, those who will not work and those who need not work'. The first three comprised the labouring population. It is possible to take this typology further when considering the diversity of labouring experience in England between 1700 and 1850.

'Those who will work'

At the top of the hierarchy of 'those who will work' were the highly skilled artisans, the so-called 'aristocracy of labour', who were well paid, enjoyed regular employment and superior working conditions. Many of them worked in traditional industries, had served long apprenticeships and were 'masters' of their craft. This 'aristocracy' was, however, far from homogeneous and a distinction was made between 'society' and 'non-society' men. The former were members of trade societies with conditions, wages etc. regulated by custom. The latter were less skilled, unorganized and, because of competition, forced to accept lower wages. In most trades 'society men' made up about a tenth of the whole. Among cabinetmakers in London, for example, there were between 600 and 700 society men producing high-quality work with a further 4,000 to 5,000 'non-society' men producing cheaper goods for the mass market. Economic changes led to new types of skilled workers emerging: fine cotton spinners, calico printers and dyers, locomotive engineers. There was no clear line between these skilled workers and the lower middle class. The economic position of skilled artisans was very similar to independent masters or small shopkeepers. At the lower level they shaded off into ordinary skilled workers, who may have had the attitudes and habits of artisans but lacked the same financial security.

Skilled and unskilled – the great divide

The great divide among the labouring population was between the skilled and the unskilled or semi-skilled. The divide was not merely one of skills and wages but of attitudes, education, life-style and aspirations. In Bradford skilled woolcombers did not drink in the same pubs as their less-skilled fellow workers. Trade societies maintained the privileged status of their members against the less skilled. It is difficult to differentiate between those non-artisans whose position changed during this period. Degrees of skill did not always correspond to earnings. Navvies were less skilled than handloom weavers but certainly earned more after 1810. Agricultural labourers earned more in northern England than in the south because of alternative employment in manufacturing. Regional, occupational and ethnic variations modified the general pattern of stratification.

Factory operatives were presented by many contemporaries as the heart of the new industrial civilization living, depending on the source used, in a state of continual misery or a life of comfort and respectability. Which of these contrasting views applied depends on which branch of which industry is being discussed. New technology and processes, the balance between male, female and child labourers, economic conditions, under- or unemployment all influenced the fortunes of different groups of workers.

Handloom weavers were one group of workers who were, initially, to benefit from industrial change and were ultimately destroyed by it.[20] Between 1810 and the 1830s their status was reduced from respectable artisan to workers on the edge of starvation – this represented perhaps the most important, certainly the most publicized, cultural shift within one of the largest sections of the labouring population. The handloom weaver was the victim of an outmoded technology but this valid explanation of their 'distress' obscures the impact which industrialization had on an immiserized section of the population. Until the 1840s handlooms continued to be used in the woollen industry, though less in cotton, taking up the slack in busy times and bearing the first brunt of depression. Their continued existence also acted as a check on the wages of powerloom operatives. Caught between the remains of the domestic system and the force of competitive industrial capitalism they could not, often would not because of their traditional 'independence', find other occupations. Trade societies prevented them from entering skilled handicrafts while they were unprotected by custom or by unions. Conditions and wages deteriorated as a result and by the 1840s they were amongst the lowest-paid workers in the country.

Other outworkers had similar experiences. Framework knitters also suffered a steady fall in earnings. This was largely the result of the system of frame letting and the growth of middlemen in the industry. The impact of the variable weekly cost of renting frames on earnings and the long periods of unemployment experienced by knitters were symptomatic of an industry overstocked with labour. Only in prosperous times was there sufficient work for everyone. Employers had a vested interest in renting out as many frames as possible and, with ease of entry into the trade, overcrowding was almost inevitable. The nailers of Worcestershire and the Black Country 'stuck to their trade' long after it ceased to provide a decent living. Andrew Ure in *The Philosophy of Manufactures*, 1835, believed that young women were prepared to sacrifice their health and comfort in lace-embroidery at home rather than enter the factory, which would have implied loss of status.

Until the late nineteenth century outworking still had an important role in the mass production of consumer goods.[21] It may have disappeared from some sectors where it had traditionally been important but it had taken a firmer root in others. By 1850 outworkers had virtually disappeared from northern England except in the mass-production clothing trade of the great provincial centres. In the Midlands and the south things were very different. Traditional nail-making and newer chain-making continued as outwork in the Birmingham area. But the principal provincial centres of outworking were found from Nottingham through Leicester, Coventry and Northampton down to Luton with footwear, dress-making, hosiery, silk, lace and straw-making located in and around these centres. London housed the other major concentration of outworkers in 1850. London industries were largely workshop-based and one of the effects of economic change was to accentuate the pre-industrial characteristics of the capital. The low pay of all these 'sweated trades' and prevailing social attitudes resulted in much of the work being done by women. Unorganized and incapable of resisting wage reductions, workers in these trades were among the most exploited in the country.

It is easy to overestimate the amount of work that was done using machines in 1850, and manual work supplied the motive power for innumerable operations that are today done by machine. Agricultural labourers were still the largest single category of worker in any industry in 1851, numbering over a million people. There were also 364,000 indoor farm servants and casual labourers (Irishmen, women and children and textile workers) who were generally called upon at harvest time. There was a subtle graduated hierarchy of farm workers – for example, ploughmen had higher status than the ordinary manual worker – but for the most part they were expected to turn their hands to whatever the season of the year required[22]. The navvy[23] was a product of economic change, digging and blasting the routes of roads and especially canals and railways – developments which provided employment opportunities for other workers like bricklayers and masons. Mining was still largely unmechanized by 1850 as was the work of many types of urban labourer: gasworkers, ironworkers, carters, draymen, porters, coalheavers, dockers, hodmen, sweepers. The army had 41,000 men at home and 90,000 abroad in 1841 and the navy and mercantile marine numbered over 200,000. All these workers had occupations which could be characterized as casual, were subject to fluctuations in the weather, their own health and strength and in the prevailing economic conditions.

Domestic service absorbed a large section of the labouring population. In 1851 it totalled more than a million workers. Though their work was less arduous than that of industrial or outdoor labourers it was often continual, tiring and poorly paid. The turnover rate among domestic servants was high because the majority were girls and young women who shortly left to get married. Recruits often came from the surrounding area or were daughters of respectable urban labouring families. The dramatic growth in domestic service was a nineteenth- rather than an eighteenth-century phenomenon, one of the early signs of growing middle-class prosperity but also of the growth in public institutions, hotels and eating houses.

Conclusions

It is possible to draw out certain broad conclusions from 'those who will work' in this period. First, the labouring population was subtly graduated with skills, education and training providing status, standing and social aspirations within communities. Secondly, this status can be seen most clearly in the distinction between occupations that were 'skilled' and those that were 'semi-' or 'unskilled'. Thirdly, economic changes led both to some employment becoming increasingly obsolete and to the creation of new opportunities and occupations. Skill remained important and generally led to higher wages, but the respective wages of handloom weavers and railways navvies in the 1830s illustrate the danger of generalization. Fourthly, gender played an important part in determining respective wage levels – women and girls were generally paid less than men and boys. Finally, the gap between relative prosperity and poverty was very narrow. Illness, old age, slump, an additional mouth to feed, falling real wages could all push members of the labouring population over the edge of subsistence.

'Those who cannot work'

Mayhew's second category was the generally involuntary 'those who cannot work'. Sickness, old age and unemployment were its major causes. The result in each case was the same: increased pressure on the family income, falling standards of living and growing poverty. Risks of injury at work were high and employers accepted no industrial liability, though serious accidents were often accompanied by token payments and rudimentary sickness funds operated in certain occupations. Hatters were 'mad', a paranoia symptomatic of mercury poisoning. Silicosis was an occupational hazard for miners. Grinders suffered from asthma, house painters and plumbers from lead poisoning, lace-workers from eye-strain and so on. Unfenced machinery could mutilate factory operatives. Sickness, particularly of the breadwinner, plunged the family into poverty unless other members of the family could find sufficient employment. Few members of the labouring population could make provision for their old age. Retirement was not something pleasantly anticipated.

Long-term unemployment was a condition in which many workers found themselves throughout this period. The resulting indigence was, to some extent, seen as an acceptable part of the lot of the working population and the concept of continuous employment was alien to contemporaries. How widespread national unemployment was between 1700 and 1850 is difficult to determine because of the lack of quantifiable evidence. Not until the 1830s did it become sufficiently acute to arouse alarm and investigation. Before then the 'laying off' of surplus labour during periods of slump, either generally or within specific trades, was seen as natural. Slumps in the economy in the 1810s and, to a lesser extent, in the 1820s were either short-lived or a consequence of the dislocation caused by the end of the French Wars. But the depression in the manufacturing economy from the mid-1830s until 1841–2 was more general and longer lasting and may have affected over a tenth of the total population.

In the 1850s Mayhew believed that only a third of the labouring population was fully employed, a third partially employed and the remainder unemployed at any given time. Underemployment was endemic for various reasons. First, poor weather could deprive bricklayers, painters, street sellers and navvies of wages. Secondly, there were brisk and slack periods of work in many trades. Agricultural labourers did little work in winter, coalwhippers little in summer. Tailors, shoemakers and milliners had a brisk period between February and July coinciding with the fashion season.

'Those who would not work'

The world of 'those who would not work' was also consciously hierarchical. Vagrants formed the bottom group, nomadic and 'rootless'. They were no new problem and estimates of their number in the early nineteenth century varied between 40,000 and 100,000 for England and Wales. Though suspected bv the 'respectable' throughout this period, clear explanations for their vagrancy did not really emerge until after 1780. 'Love of idleness' and the 'non-inculcation of the habit of industry' were two widely-used contemporary explanations. This was, however, not the only possible reason why people became vagrants. Some people became vagrants after failing to find work in the communities to which they had 'tramped'. Undoubtedly some chose to be beggars and, given the importance of conscience and being seen to be charitable, probably made quite a good living out of it. London and the larger towns were littered with people with varying degrees of physical and personal disabilities who solicited alms from passers-by.

Vagrancy was the nursery of crime, and habitual beggers, particularly the younger and more active ones, might well progress into the lower levels of crime. The criminal fraternity was as status-conscious as the labouring population. Housebreakers and burglars ('cracksmen'), high-waymen and high-class pickpockets formed a well-defined 'aristocracy'. Below them were the shoplifters, sneak-thieves, horse stealers, embezzlers and forgers. A system of 'fences' acted as a link between the worlds of legality and illegality. Crime, like work, had its own regulations and customs. There was a rough system of apprenticeship. Hours of work were determined by the nature of the job and criminals tended to congregate in certain areas of towns. Motivation for criminal actions, as today, varied considerably. In rural areas, for example, poaching was often as much a social protest against loss of customary rights or falling wages as a con-sciously criminal act. Growing towns, the inadequacy of preventive agen-cies and the possibility of 'rich pickings' made crime an attractive alterna-tive to the workhouse. Top criminals could probably live at a respectable level but prosperity could be short-lived with the likelihood of prison, transportation or death by hanging. The 'drop-out' rate among the crimi-nal population was therefore high.

Prostitutes were also a group with their own hierarchy of status and earnings, customs and aspirations. They ranged from the kept mistresses of wealthy businessmen and members of the aristocracy to those who solicited in the streets. High-class prostitutes, like Grace Dalrymple and Fanny Murray, won fame and respect, becoming high-prized models for leading painters. During the eighteenth century attitudes to casual sexual relationships were more liberal than in the nineteenth, though the efforts of the Society for the Reformation of Manners to outlaw prostitution from the streets received little general backing. Prostitutes did not form the outcast group, the Great Social Evil, that they became after 1850. Until recently historians, influenced generally by Victorian notions of morality, would have assigned prostitutes to Mayhew's category of 'those who would not work'. Some contemporaries did, however, recognize that prostitution was often a temporary phenomenon. For many young women who came to towns, isolation, low wages and vulnerability to under- and unemployment easily led to prostitution. It was often a strategy for survival until other work could be found or specific financial difficulties overcome.

TRADE UNIONISM

The Webbs' interpretation

Political reform was given high profile by contemporaries and by later historians but combinations of workers in trade unions to improve their economic conditions was also important, perhaps in retrospect more important.[22] The impression that trade unionism developed as a consequence of industrialization has, until recently, led to the neglect of the existence of unionism among many groups of skilled workers in the eighteenth century. This neglect owes much to the treatment which Sidney and Beatrice Webb adopted in their classic work, *The History of Trade Unionism,* London, 1920, and to the stark division historians have made between pre-industrial and industrial Britain.

The Webbs defined a trade union as 'a continuous association of wage-earners established for the purpose of maintaining or improving the conditions of their working lives.' This definition has important limitations and inclined them to belittle the evidence for early trade unionism, though they traced the movement's 'origins' back to the late seventeenth century. The emphasis on the idea of continuous existence – by implication they meant formal, institutionalized organizations – led the Webbs to deny the importance of informal, local combinations. It is, however, clear that men regularly brought together in the same workforce or area had unofficial leaders and developed their own customs and practices without embodying them in regular institutions. Formal organizations emerge only in times of particular crisis such as a strike but often, as in the case of the north-eastern sailors who struck twelve times between 1768 and 1825, there is little evidence for organizing committees. Informal collective pressures certainly existed, though again there is little specific evidence, and were used to exclude women and other 'outsiders'. Most of the disputes in the eighteenth century – C. R. Dobson lists 386 for the period 1715–1800 – do not seem to have involved formal continuous organizations, but there is little doubt that they involved wages, hours of work and control of the labour supply, which were 'trade union' issues. Some fell into the category of 'bargaining by riot' when workers attempted to secure their collective ends by violence and intimidation. The 1765 northern miners' strike was accompanied by so much violence and systematic destruction of winding gear that arson was specifically proscribed in an amended Malicious Injuries to Property Act in 1768. It is valid to see this sort of action as incipient trade unionism, even if not in the Webbs' sense.

A second major criticism of the Webbs' view of the eighteenth century lay in their efforts to prove that trade unionism was a relatively modern development, a characteristic of an industrialized society. Eighteenth-century Britain, however, was proto-industrial and was already characterized by significant separation of capital and labour. Workers no longer owned the materials on which they worked or sold the product to the consumer. Workers sold their 'labour power'.

Unionism before 1800

It is difficult to get much idea of the scope of trade unionism in the eighteenth century. Certainly by 1800 it involved a very small proportion of workers and it was still a minority movement in 1850. Trade unions were almost exclusively male. There were women in the Manchester small-ware weavers in 1747 and in 1788 as many as 18,500 females made up the Leicester Sisterhood of Female Handspinners. But these were exceptions. Despite evidence for the economic marginalizing of women workers, they had difficulty in organizing and it was not until the 1850s that unionism made much headway among them.

Trade unionism in the eighteenth century was predominantly the preserve of skilled workers who combined to protect their status and economic standing against attacks from employers who sought to cut wages and change customary ways of working.[23] They also combined to protect the 'closed shop' of their 'trade' against incursion from cheap labour and from women. Collective action was commonplace in eighteenth-century Britain among a wide range of workers and there is clear evidence for some continuity of organization through the workplace or village club. Industrial protest may have been sporadic, organization was not.

The degree of organization varied among different groups of artisans. London tailors, for example, had first come to the public's attention in 1720–1 when their actions led to an Act banning combinations in the tailoring trades of London and Westminster and fixed wages by statute. Wage disputes were renewed in 1744–5, 1752, 1764, 1768 and 1778. Similar evidence of what Francis Place called 'perpetual combination' existed for journeymen hatters and the effect of the union's strength was felt by master hatters in London, the Midlands, Bristol and Lancashire. Weavers and combers in the Devonshire serge industry developed effective unionism through town clubs from early in the century, culminating in an Act of 1726 prohibiting combinations among woollen workers. Weavers' combinations in Gloucestershire, Wiltshire and parts of Somerset also dated from the 1720s and in 1757 the employers secured parliamentary approval for ending the principle of wage regulation in this area of manufacture over fifty years before the general repeal of the wage-regulating clauses of the 1563 Statute of Artificers. Woolcombers' organizations existed in the south-west, Essex, Leicester and Yorkshire by the 1740s, among cotton weavers in Lancashire by 1750 and among papermakers, compositors, plumbers, painters, carpenters, shoemakers, bakers and metal workers by the end of the century.

There is widespread evidence for craft unions but the law was clearly on the employer's side and Adam Smith was not alone in dismissing unions' effectiveness. By 1799 there were already more than forty Acts on the statute book which could be used against trade unions, though many of these were confined to specific trades like those banning combinations among hatters in 1777 and papermakers in 1794. These Acts were passed by Parliament in response to pressure from employers for more effective ways of combating trade union organizations of journeymen in their trades. The presumption was that combinations were illegal. This was grounded in the concept of 'conspiracy', under which the fairness of the workers' case was not the issue, only the fact of conspiracy against the employers. It was not the refusal to work by an individual that was illegal but the collective action or conspiracy of the combination. Throughout the eighteenth century there were many occasions when conspiracy proceedings were taken against trade unions: for example, against seven Liverpool tailors in 1783, against Leicester hatters in 1777 and 1794. Though local court records have undoubtedly been lost, between 1710 and 1800 conspiracy proceedings as a weapon against trade unions were used in 29 cases. In Scotland, by contrast, judicial intervention was far more common than recourse to punitive action. Scottish judges regularly set wage rates and regulated hours during the eighteenth century and it was not until after the weavers' strike of 1812 that this legal regulation was swept away.

The law was not a particularly effective weapon against combinations in the eighteenth century. Proceedings could be very slow and costly, employers were disinclined to reopen old conflicts and had to face latent hostilities after their actions were over. Often the threat of legal action was sufficient to get people back to work. But legal action did not always correspond to economic advantage and workers who took action during an upturn in the economy often achieved their objectives as employers did not want to lose the advantages of a rising market. Combinations of employers were as much a part of the industrial scene as combinations of workers and could be just as secretive. Agreements between employers which resulted in wages cuts led to major disturbances in Somerset in 1738-9 and in 1764 a strike took place in the serge industry when weavers learnt that a meeting of masters was about to agree on lower prices. Employers were able to 'police' their own area, through refusing to employ workers who had no 'discharge certificate' from previous work, or by getting workers to sign agreements on wages and, under the threat from combinations, by locking workers out. In these circumstances the use of the legal process was superfluous.

How effective were workers in pressing their claims through combinations? Choosing the right moment for withdrawing labour was of central importance. Serge workers chose the spring when demand for lighter cloth was at its height. The death of Queen Charlotte in 1817 offered the Coventry weavers of black ribbon an ideal opportunity for pressing their wage demands. Part of the strategy of making strikes effective was building up a support fund and there is evidence for this among book-binders, printers, calico printers and others. Violence was frequently used as a means of intimidating employers and 'blackleg' workers, though many contemporaries saw it as an expression of desperation. It was used by skilled as well as unskilled workers and 'collective bargaining by riot' was as much a part of industrial action as the strike in the eighteenth century. It is difficult to estimate the effectiveness of trade union action in the eighteenth century. Skilled workers often saw themselves as protecting the tradition of their trades against interlopers and against their masters whose advantage lay in deregulation. Their effectiveness depended on local support, a sound financial basis, favourable economic conditions and, on occasions, the willingness of magistrates to act as arbiters between them and their employers. By 1800 there was a widespread, vibrant and not ineffective tradition of trade unionism in Britain.

Unionism under the Combination Act, 1799–1824

Trade unionism found itself under concerted attack in the first quarter of the nineteenth century.[24] The Combination Acts of 1799 and 1800 introduced legislative repression. The repeal of the apprenticeship clauses of the Statute of Artificers in 1814 threatened the exclusive 'property of skill' of the craft unions and the 'machinery question' their economic security. War, rising prices and the threat from political Jacobinism provided justification, though Ian Christie has recently maintained that the widespread existence of trade combinations acted as a safety-valve for discontent among the working population, confining revolutionary activity to a minority of the population.

The first quarter of the nineteenth century saw the Combination Acts in force. Passed in 1799 and modified in 1800, they have been represented in trade union mythology as the most outstanding example of the repression of the rights of the working population to combine in their own defence. The Webbs were correct in seeing them as a reflection of government fears of revolutionary ideas but their limited views of eighteenth-century unionism led them to the incorrect conclusion that the Acts marked a 'far reaching change of policy'. It was the general nature of the prohibition of combinations that was new, not prohibition itself.

The Acts were passed very quickly, with encouragement from both William Wilberforce and William Pitt, and took workers' organizations by surprise. They were certainly one-sided and did not treat combinations by employers as harshly as those by workers. The 1799 Act was intended to prevent dislocation of trade during wartime and was partly inspired by fears of revolution. It aimed to secure speedy settlement of disputes by summary proceedings before a single magistrate. Following protests against its unfairness it was modified in 1800 to bring employers' combinations under the law as well as workers' (though this proved inoperable), requiring two magistrates, who could not be masters in the trades concerned, and introducing arbitration clauses (though these never seem to have operated).

The effects of the Acts were exaggerated by contemporaries and subsequently by some historians. They were used infrequently and when used were often ineffective. Summary jurisdiction, their main intention, was largely defeated by appeals to the quarter sessions and convictions were frequently thrown out on technical points. The Combination Acts have been seen as a negligible instrument of oppression and employers continued to rely largely on the older legal controls provided by common law, existing statutes and the contractual law of master and servant. So why has a mythology been manufactured round the Combination Acts? M. D. George, as early as 1936, provided a convincing explanation. She argued that:

> these were the only Acts styled Combination Acts and therefore all the opprobrium attached to the mass of legislation repealed in 1824 was loosely and vaguely attached to the Act of 1800.[25]

Witnesses to the 1824 Committee were confused as to whether prosecution had been brought under the 1800 Act, or for conspiracy, riot, or for breach of contract. Though E. P. Thompson's statement that it did not matter to workers which law they were prosecuted under is undoubtedly true, it certainly does make a difference whether or not the Combination Acts marked a change of policy and whether they made legal repression more severe.

Combinations were certainly subjected to legal repression during this period and many individuals were prosecuted, fined and imprisoned. This seems to have been more widespread in areas of rapid technological growth and in the politically conscious textile areas of Lancashire and Nottinghamshire were outworking was widespread. Cotton spinners struck in 1810 and there were four separate strikes among cotton workers in 1818 by jenny spinners and powerloom weavers in Stockport, mule spinners in Manchester and handloom weavers. The intensity of opposition to the Combination Acts among handloom weavers and the repressive response from employers in Lancashire was a reflection of the struggle to maintain their livelihood; the tendency of modern historians to downgrade the effect of the Combination Acts gains little support from there.

Older skilled trade societies, though occasionally prosecuted, seem to have been more readily accepted by employers as legitimate channels of workers' grievances. Evidence to the 1824 Committee gives many examples of collective bargaining where employers did not choose to take legal action. Printing workers did not come into conflict with the law despite their spreading organization in London and the provinces. London artisans and artisans elsewhere emerged from the French wars more strongly organized than ever before with a new 'trade union consciousness' linking wages to organizational power. Intra-trade networks developed: in 1800 these existed in seventeen trades and by the mid-1820s in at least twenty-eight.

The effectiveness of trade unionism among skilled workers was threatened far more by the repeal, in 1814, of the statutory requirement that a seven-year apprenticeship should be served before a craft should be exercised than by the Combination Acts. The apprenticeship clauses of the Statute of Artificers had fallen into disuse in the eighteenth century, so why did this emerge as an issue in the early nineteenth century? The agitation against repeal was centred in London, but there was widespread support from the calico workers of Lancashire and in the frame-knitting district of the East Midlands. Skilled workers in these areas saw their control of work practices threatened by employers' use of unskilled and untrained labour and by new technology introduced to break the hold of the trade societies, according to Andrew Ure in *The Philosophy of Manufactures*, his defence of the factory system in the mid-1830s. Employers, by contrast, saw the apprenticeship clauses and the restrictive practices they ensured as a barrier to the further expansion of capitalist practices. In the case of apprenticeship and new machinery employers were successful in trades which were less protected and less well organized. The result was an influx of unskilled and cheaper labour into a trade undercutting the privileged status of skilled men. In trades where manual skills remained an essential feature of production and where well organized artisans could co-ordinate collective action apprenticeship, and with it the closed shop, survived.

By 1824 skilled workers had shown themselves capable of protecting their labour interests against the capitalist interests of employers as they had done in the eighteenth century. The 1814 appeal was in this respect more important for skilled workers than the Combination Acts because it legitimized the twin processes of deskilling and the introduction of cheap labour. But before 1824 there were few signs that unionism had crossed the boundary of skill between artisan and unskilled labour.

The repeal of the Combination Acts was achieved in 1824 as a result of a campaign led by Francis Place and supported by economists like Joseph Hume and J. R. McCulloch. His campaign, masterly in diplomacy, lobbying and argument, was aimed at a Parliament which already accepted the ineffectiveness and unfairness of the legislation. The 1824 Act swept away not only the Combination Acts but also excluded trade unions from prosecution for conspiracy. Many people had been convinced by Place's argument that repeal would bring trade unionism and strikes to an end. The events of 1824–5 quickly led them to rethink their position. Repeal coincided with a boom in trade releasing a flood of union activity with demands for wage increases accompanied by strikes and violence. Employers demanded the restoration of the Combination Acts and it took all Place's diplomacy to prevent this. The 1825 Act, the result of a report from a select committee, recognized the rights of combination and collective bargaining over wages and hours but restored union subjection to the law of conspiracy. It also made the law on picketing and intimidation more stringent. The Act was a compromise which gave unions the right to exist but limited their effectiveness to act with powerful legal sanctions.

A 'revolutionary decade' 1825–35

Historians have taken different views of trade union developments in the next ten years.[26] Left-wing historians like the Webbs, G. D. H. Cole and E. P. Thompson have characterized the period as one of growing political and class consciousness with the emergence of general unions. Other historians, like A. E. Musson, argue that the 'revolutionary ' nature of unionism in this period has been exaggerated and that much trade union-ism remained small, sectional and local. General unions may have been exciting to both contemporaries and to later historians but the organiz-ation, collective bargaining and friendly benefits for unemployment, sick-ness and death of the older trade societies and the superficiality of their response to Owenite and anti-capitalist ideology must be emphasized.

There were, however, two significant developments during these years. The first was organizational: the formation of district and national unions and attempts at general trades' unions or federations. The second was ideological: a broadening of union horizons to include political and social ideas and an anti-capitalist critique. These came together, though far from successfully, in the Grand National Consolidated Trades Union (GNCTU) of 1834. Owenite ideas had a limited impact on most workers, though they often expressed sympathy with Owen's aims and a few started small schemes of co-operative production. District and national unions in spec-ific trades proved to be more enduring than general unions and, though weakened by strikes and lock-outs, often survived to be resuscitated in the 1840s.

The movement towards regional and national unionism in specific trades was evident among cotton spinners. In 1824 Manchester spinners were involved in several local disputes and took up the object of forming a county union for Lancashire, trying to broaden their support by seeking federation with the Glasgow spinners who were also in dispute. Though this proved unsuccessful further strikes in 1825 and 1828 demonstrated the need for better organization. The result was the establishment of a Grand General Union of Operative Cotton Spinners (GGU) led by John Doherty in 1829. He wanted a stronger organization than those which had been attempted in 1810, 1818 and 1824 and, despite regional differences between cotton spinners, was able to achieve agreement on a national strike pay level of 10 shillings from a central fund and on the need for consent from other districts before industrial action could be taken. Expectations proved too high and in a series of strikes in Lancashire in late 1830 and early 1831 the GGU failed to deliver the goods: strike pay was only half that promised and there was poor support from other areas.

The GGU collapsed and further movement towards federation in Lancashire had to wait until 1842.

John Doherty, a practical trade unionist rather than a Owenite idealist, had already shifted his focus to the National Association for the Protection of Labour (NAPL). Formed in late 1829, its inaugural meeting was attended by workers from twenty trades from Lancashire. Although successful in spreading the movement into the Midlands and other northern industrial centres at its peak in the autumn of 1830 its 60–70,000 members came overwhelmingly from Lancashire and Cheshire. The NAPL gained support from declining handworkers like weavers and knitters as well as cotton mule-spinners but also from miners and potters. It lost both strength and momentum after the autumn of 1831, but it persisted in name until 1833. It failed to achieve any of its objectives and never attracted the most highly skilled workers like engineers and printers who kept to their craft unions, but had been successful in mobilizing much larger occupational groups.

Similar movement towards national unions was evident among building craftsmen. This began among carpenters and bricklayers in 1827 and soon led towards general unionism. Technology was not the problem in the building trade; innovation in organization was. The issue was one of 'general contracting'. The traditional system of architects employing master craftsmen in the various branches of the trade was being replaced by a tripartite system of architect, middlemen or employers of labour in crafts to which they did not belong, and master craftsmen. The claim was that these general contractors forced down rates and wished to change the working practices of the craftsmen. Demands for an ending of general contracting led to unsuccessful confrontation between the Builders Union and employers in 1833–4. The building industry, again split into its separate trades.

Robert Owen's Grand National Consolidated Trades Union (GNCTU) brought the ferment of trade unionism both to its zenieth and its end. It was in part a revival of Doherty's earlier general union and, although it has entered union mythology especially through the connected Tolpuddle Martyrs, it was even less successful than the NAPL, lasted less than a year and never became the vast organization into which it was later inflated by the Webbs. The GNCTU was not London's first attempt at general unionism: the campaign against repeal in 1814 had gone across trades and in 1818 John Gast, leader of the shipwrights, had organized London artisans in the 'Philanthropic Hercules', a formalization of existing inter-trade assistance. There had already been much interest by London artisans in co-operative production which predated Owen. The GNCTU was formed in a period of active unionism in London especially among the carpenters, shoemakers and tailors, who wanted to stop the drift from being skilled artisans towards being 'sweated' into a proletariat along with an expanding population of unskilled.

It is difficult to reconstruct the exact sequencing of events in London in 1833–4 but it is very clear that the formation of the GNCTU came at a time of existing and continuing union activity. The initiative was taken by the tailors and in mid-February 1831 the GNCTU was born. Its main aims represented artisan concerns: mutual support in strikes, provision of sickness benefits, employment of members who were on strike and of unemployed members. The Webbs' estimation of half a million members has been shown to have been ridiculously high. The total paid-up membership approached only 16,000 but there were attempts to broaden its appeal and certainly it had tacit support from many more workers. There was some movement towards the unorganized, including women workers, and it was this broadening of the movement which heightened government and employer hostility. The GNCTU failed to attract support from the majority of trade societies – London tailors, silk weavers and shoemakers formed a greater part of it. Though a few labourers, like those at Tolpuddle, briefly organized, it spread only to a limited extent beyond traditional craft trades. It had no real organization or financial basis and, when faced with employers' lock-outs and prosecutions, including that of the six Dorcester labourers for administering an illegal oath at Tolpuddle, it collapsed.

A. S. Musson has called the GNCTU 'a fascinating phenomenon, but sadly ephemeral' and it is true that movements for general unionism in the case of both the NAPL and GNCTU were very short-lived. Musson argues that historians have given the GNCTU attention out of all proportion to its significance and that the future lay with district and national federations within trades not with vast trades federations. Though his conclusion may be valid he has perhaps overstated his case and historians from different sides of the political divide, like Thompson and E. H. Hunt, agree that unionism between 1829 and 1834 did mark an important move in the direction of working-class consciousness. This was not a permanent, broad-based or continuous class consciousness out of which a working class was formed but a consciousness among skilled artisans and handworkers experiencing dilution into the 'unskilled'. The GNCTU was neither an aberration nor a radical departure for trade union development.

Developments after 1835

The inflation by the Webbs of both the numerical support for and the collapse of the GNCTU caused them, according to Musson, to produce a 'warped' interpretation of developments after 1834. This has led to two ways of looking at the subsequent period. For the Webbs there was an emphasis on a decline in confrontation and in overt class consciousness. Others stress the continuity of activity between the 1820s and the 1840s. Certainly, with the intense depression between 1836 and the early 1840s, trade unionism was under severe strain in the face of a sustained employer offensive. This led certain workers, like handloom weavers, to seek political rather than economic solutions to their problems. In Scotland the bitterness and defeat of the Glasgow spinners' strike in 1837 and the subsequent trial of union leaders set back the development of Scottish unionism for up to a decade.

How valid is the Webbs' claim? There is ample evidence that unions renounced the language of the class war, improved their organization and public image and concentrated on sectional, local and limited objectives. Violence in Glasgow, against blackleg labour during a cotton spinner strike in 1837, and in Cork and Dublin led to pressure for the government to reintroduce anti-union legislation. An enquiry in 1838 decided against this but the threat was taken very seriously and led to united action by London and provincial unions. The language of craft unions was moderated, at least in public, and the language of accommodation replaced the conflict rhetoric of the early 1830s. The potters displayed an approving interest in new technology and the printers distanced themselves further from the notion of general unionism for which they had always had little enthusiasm. Strikes were seen increasingly by craft unions as the final resort, though this did not mark a major alteration in how this strategy was perceived; flint glass workers declared them to have been the bane of the union movement and abolished strike pay.

Apprenticeship was, however, still a major issue between skilled trade unionists and their employers. It meant the closed shop crucial to union success was preserved in only two contexts: where a skill remained essential for production and could only be achieved through long apprenticeship or an effective closing of entry against unskilled men. New technology and the acceptance by a mass market of ready-made goods of often inferior quality led to changes in some trades but the preservation and survival of apprenticeship remained a key objective of many trades. The main weapon in the armoury of Sheffield cutlers and grinders, for example, lay in their restriction of the supply of labour. Tyneside shipwrights in 1841 still held the ratio of one apprentice to three craftsmen and it was firmly insisted on in the union rulebook in 1850.

There may have been much talk of the need for accommodation with employers and the prospect of achieving more by negotiation and conciliation than by strike action but the context in which this existed was fundamental. There was often little reciprocity on the part of employers, who were likely to respond to weakness by increased attempt to break unions. The Miners' Association, which was established in late 1842, had 60,000 members at its peak in 1844 from every major coalfield in the British Isles but was defeated by concerted action by coal-owners.

The Webbs' notion of accommodation should not be overemphasized. There were certainly continuities within skilled craft unions throughout the first half of the nineteenth century but what is important, for developments after 1850, was a shift in the meaning of 'elite' unionism. During the 1830s the leading craft unions were from the 'lower' trades, among weavers, tailors and shoemakers, but from the 1840s this primacy moved to the 'upper' trades. The 'aristocracy of labour' of the 1840s was fundamentally different from the traditional artisan 'aristocracy' of the 1820s. It was grounded in the new technology, new trades and in industrial change. It was necessary for capitalism to reach accommodation with these groups for its own survival and expansion. It is, however, important not to see this as a complete accommodation by all trade unions to the values of liberal capitalism. Struggles for 'workers' control' over the processes of labour and an insistence on apprenticeship remained points of conflict between capital and labour. Women were entirely excluded from accommodation by men, both employers and trade unionists. The unskilled, by far the majority of workers, remained outside and had no place in this *rapprochement*. In 1850 trade unions accounted for only a small proportion of all workers and many would have agreed with Sir Archibald Alison who dismissed them all as nothing more than 'a system of aristocracy of skilled labour against the mass of unskilled labour'.[27]

The interests of trade unions lay in maintaining differentials within the working population, not in promoting the interests of the unskilled from whom they were separated by a chasm of training, education and attitudes.

CONCLUSIONS

The labouring population was perhaps more diverse than the other sections of society. The reaction of workers to their social, economic and political environments was also diverse. Income, employment, locality, aspirations, economic changes all affected their perceptions. The difference between a skilled London craftsman and a Scottish crofter was, in many ways, as great as that between a member of the aristocracy and a prosperous shopkeeper. That difference was one of experience and outlook. Yet both could share a common sense of resentment and disillusion at the inequalities within society. Technical change both threatened and provided opportunities. For the craftsman it could spell insecurity and redundancy. The cropper threatened by the gig machine, the weaver menaced by the powerloom, the agricultural worker facing competition from threshing machines saw significant parts of their livelihood being swept away. For workers their capital was their skill which, unlike the resources of industrialists, could not easily be switched from one form of investment to another. People who live close to poverty do not have the same flexibility as those who possess regular and reliable incomes.

NOTES

1 W. Cobbett *Rural Rides*, quoted in T. Blackwell and J. Seabrook *A World Still to Win – The Reconstruction of the Post-War Working Class*, Faber, 1985, p. 34.

2 The literature on the working population is voluminous but can be approached in three accessible books: K. D. Brown *The English Labour Movement 1700–1951*, Gill & Macmillan, 1982, J. F. C. Harrison *The Common People*, Fontana, 1984 and J. Rule *The Labouring Classes in Early Industrial England 1750–1850*, Longman, 1986. E. Royle *Modern Britain*, Edward Arnold, 1987 provides a general overview.

3 The best introduction to wage-labour is L. A. Clarkson 'Wage-labour 1500–1800', in K. D. Brown op. cit. pp. 1–27.

4 Adam Smith *The Wealth of Nations*, Everyman edn, 1910, Vol. 1, p. 73.

5 ibid. p. 70.

6 A convenient summary of the 'state of the art' on standards of living can be found in J. Rule op. cit. pp. 27–45 and R. Floud 'A Tall Story? The Standard of Living Debate', *History Today*, May 1983. More detailed discussion can be found in A. J. Taylor (ed.) *The Standard of Living in the Industrial Revolution*, Methuen, 1975, IEA *The Long Debate on Poverty*, Institute of Economic Affairs, 1974, B. Inglis *Poverty and the Industrial Revolution*, Panther, 1972, P. K. O'Brien and S. L. Engerman 'Changes in Income and its Distribution during the Industrial Revolution', in R. Floud and D. McCloskey (eds) *The Economic History of Britain since 1700*, Vol. 1, Cambridge University Press, 1981, pp. 164–81, and papers by P. H. Lindert and J. G. Williamson and G. N. von Tunzelmann in J. Mokyr (ed.) *The Economics of the Industrial Revolution*, Allen & Unwin, 1985. On diet see J. Burnett *A History of the Cost of Living*, Penguin, 1969, pp. 128–281 and *Plenty and Want*, Scolar Press, 1969, pp. 15–122.

7 M. W. Flinn 'Trends in Real Wages 1750–1850', *Economic History Review*, 27 (1974).

8 Lindert and Williamson, op. cit.

9 J. L. Hammond 'The Industrial Revolution and Discontent', *Economic History Review*, (1929–30), pp. 224–5.

10 The 'urban question' is considered in more detail in chapter 18.

11 E. P. Thompson 'Time, Work-Discipline and Industrial Capitalism', *Past and Present*, 38, (1967), pp. 56–97. See also D. A. Reid 'The Decline of St. Monday 1776–1876', ibid., 71 (1976).

12 S. Pollard *The Genesis of Modern Management*, Penguin, 1968 clearly documents changing attitudes.

13 E. H. Hunt *British Labour History 1815–1914*, Weidenfeld, 1982.

14 On the question of the family see J. Rule op. cit. pp. 168–89 for a summary of recent developments.

15 *Political Register* 14 April 1824.

16 On working women the classic study is I. Pinchbeck *Women Workers and the Industrial Revolution* originally published in 1930, reprinted Virago, 1985 with an introduction by Kerry Hamilton. The emergence of women's history has supplemented and, on occasions, modified Pinchbeck's thesis. See in particular S. Alexander 'Women's Work in Nineteenth-century London: a Study of the Years 1820–1850', in J. Mitchell and A. Oakley (eds) *The Rights and Wrongs of Women,*' Penguin, 1976, M. Berg *The Age of Manufactures 1700–1820*, Fontana, 1985, especially pp. 129–78 and E. Richards 'Women in the British Economy since 1700: an Interpretation', *History*, 59 (1974). J. D. Young *Women and Popular Struggle*, Edinburgh, 1985 has much of value on Scottish and English working women. Two works published too late to be considered are: B. Hill *Women, Work and Sexual Politics in Eighteenth Century England*, Basil Blackwell, 1989 and D. Thompson *Women in the Nineteenth Century*, The Historical Association, 1990.

17 Quoted more fully in E. H. Hunt op. cit, p. 25.

18 ibid.
19 From the declaration of the Miners Association of Great Britain and Ireland in 1842, quoted ibid. p. 186.
20 D. Bythell *The Handloom Weavers*, Cambridge University Press, 1969 is the most detailed study but should be supplemented by the relevant parts of M. I. Thomis *The Town Labourer and the Industrial Revolution*, Batsford, 1974 and *Responses to Industrialisation*, David & Charles, 1976.
21 D. Bythell *The Sweated Trades*, Batsford, 1981.
22 For a more detailed discussion of the agricultural labourer see chapter 17.
23 On the navvy see chapter 11.
24 There is much on trade unionism in the general books especially E. H. Hunt op. cit., but see also J. Rule *The Labouring Classes in Early Industrial England 1750–1850*, Longman, 1986, pp. 253–349 and K. D. Brown *The English Labour Movement 1700–1951*, Gill & Macmillan, 1982, pp. 28–50. The following more detailed studies of unionism should be consulted: A. Fox *History and Heritage: The Social Origins of the British Industrial Relations System*, Allen & Unwin, 1985, H. Pelling *History of British Trade Unionism*, Penguin, 1963 and in various more recent editions and A. E. Musson *British Trade Unionism 1800–1875*, Macmillan, 1972. C. Wrigley 'The Webbs: Working on Trade Union History', *History Today*, May 1987 is a useful assessment of a classic study of trade unionism.
25 On eighteenth-century unionism see C. R. Dobson *Masters and Journeymen: A Pre-History of Industrial Relations 1717–1800*, Croom Helm, 1980 and J. Rule *The Experience of Labour in Eighteenth Century Industry*, Croom Helm, 1981. W. Hamish Fraser *Conflict and Class: Scottish Workers 1700–1838*, John Donald, 1988 is essential for the Scottish dimension. J. Rule (ed.) *Trade Unionism 1750–1850 The Formative Years*, Longman, 1988 contains important essays.
26 For unions under the Combination Acts see A. E. Musson op. cit. for the historiographical debate. E. P. Thompson *The Making of the English Working Class*, Gollancz, 1963 and M. D. George 'The Combination Laws', *Economic History Review*, 6, 1936 provide contrasting interpretations. A. Aspinall (ed.) *The Early English Trade Unions*, Batchworth, 1949 documents developments. M. Berg *The Machinery Question and the Making of Political Economy*, Cambridge University Press, 1980 is essential on responses to the new technology, and J. Rule op. cit on apprenticeship.
27 M. D. George op. cit., pp. 176–7.
28 For unionism after repeal see H. Browne *The Rise of British Trade Unions 1825–1914*, Longman, 1979, R. G. Kirby and A. E. Musson *The Voice of the People: John Doherty, 1798–1854, Trade Unionist, Radical and Factory Reformer*, Manchester University Press, 1975, W. H. Fraser 'Trade Unionism', in J. T. Ward (ed.) *Popular Movements 1830–1850*, Macmillan, 1970, pp. 95–115. On the GNCTU see W. H. Oliver 'The Consolidated Trades Unions of 1834', *Economic History Review*, 18 (1964), pp. 77–95 and J. Rule (ed.) op. cit. J. Marlow *The Tolpuddle Martyrs*, Deutsch, 1971 is a popular study.
29 Quoted in K. D. Brown op. cit., p. 50.

16 The impact of economic growth – a social revolution?

> The bond of attachment is broken, there is no longer the generous bounty which calls forth a grateful and honest and confiding dependence.[1]

> There is no community . . . there is aggregation . . . modern society acknowledges no neighbours.[2]

Both these nineteenth-century statements – the first by the poet Robert Southey, the second from a later Scottish source raise the question of how British society was organized and the ways in which it had changed as a result of economic and urban growth. In this chapter I want to consider whether a 'social' revolution took place between 1700 and 1850 and how people were differentiated within society.

PERSPECTIVES ON SOCIETY

What different perspectives can historians who want to examine society use and what do they tell us about the workings of society?[3] How applicable are they to British society between 1700 and 1850? Two approaches – from the 'top' and the 'bottom' – have been used to illuminate particular aspects of eighteenth- and nineteenth-century British Society. 'Minority history' traditionally concentrated on the activities of the powerful minority, those who held economic and political power. 'Minority historians' emphasize the importance of those who wield power in any society. They examine those who held power at a particular time, how this altered over time and how effective the various ruling groups were. These were the elites within society as a whole and within the localities. One major question which underlies this chapter is 'How far did economic change affect the entire nature of elites in Britain?' 'Majority historians', by contrast, are concerned with society beyond the boundaries of the elites and with the attempts of these 'outsider groups' to challenge the hegemony of the elites. They are concerned with the conditions of the mass of the people. It is the interface between 'high' and 'low' society where notions of radical change and consensual continuity can be most clearly seen.

It is important to have some notion of the 'wholeness' of society, whether nationally or within a given locality because it was the overall structure of society that people were reacting against or attempting to preserve. It is equally important, however, to establish the relationships between the different social elements. Individuals must be understood, given meaning and significance, not in isolation, but within their web of social relationships. Individual biographies can be explained only by reference to the whole of society – structuralists term this 'decentring the subject', pushing individuals away from the centre stage and explaining them within a larger, universal system.

ELITES

A theory of elites

The word 'elite' only entered the English language, according to the *Oxford English Dictionary* in 1823, but did not become widespread until the late nineteenth century.[4] What do we mean by an elite? 'Elite' applies to any who 'lead' in any social category of social activity: to actors and sportsmen as well as political or economic leaders. There are essentially three dimensions involved in the study of elites: the organization or structure of elite groups; the factors involved in recruitment to elite positions and the distribution of 'effective' power exercised by those in elite positions.

In analysing the structure of elites it is important to identify their level of both 'social' and 'moral' integration. 'Moral' integration concerns the degree to which those in elite positions shared common ideas and a common moral ethos and the extent to which they were conscious of their overall solidarity. 'Social' integration concerns the frequency and nature of the social contacts and relationships between elite groups. These may take various forms: marriage alliances between different elite families; the existence of personal ties of acquaintance and friendship between the different elite sectors; and the frequency of direct 'consultative' ties between them. During the eighteenth century there was considerable integration within elite groups based on a broad paternalistic ideology in which patronage played a central role.

Recruitment to elite positions depends on how far it is relatively 'open' to those drawn from varied socio-economic backgrounds or 'closed' in favour of those from privileged groups. It is not sufficient to distinguish degrees of 'openness' or 'closure; it is also important to examine the channels through which such recruitment takes place. It is possible to identify a 'sub-elite' which consists of two types of people who may or may not move up into the elite proper: a 'recruitment' stratum, and an 'administrative' stratum.

The notion of recruitment may be taken further and three types of

Figure 16.1 Elites and recruitment

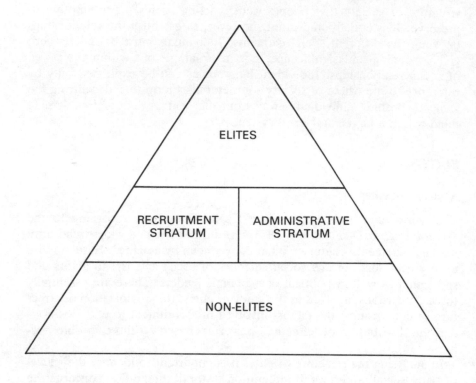

'circulation' can be distinguished. Within the elites themselves there is some circulation. Secondly, individuals from the sub-elite may succeed in entering existing elites. Economic change in the eighteenth century brought new social groups, like financiers, traders and manufacturers into this category, from which, like the Peels, Gladstones and Guests, they could enter the landed elite. Thirdly, individuals from the non-elites may form new elite groups which then engage in a struggle for power with the existing elites. It was not until the mid-nineteenth century that the economic and political power of the landed elite was effectively challenged.

In dealing with 'effective' power it is important to distinguish between how far power was 'diffused' throughout society and how far it was 'centralized'. In the eighteenth century 'effective' power, both economically and politically, lay with those who owned land, though increasingly 'control' over the land was vested in tenants. Landowners constituted a 'ruling class' making eighteenth-century society what some historians have seen as a 'one-class' society.

A landed elite

Between 1700 and 1800 the landed elite was dominant and received ideological support from the mercantile, financial and professional elites. The unified nature of those elite groups owed much to links either by family or by patronage. This elitist position has been called the 'Old Corruption', of which three main aspects can be emphasized. First, these elites possessed considerable strength and resilience and had sufficient confidence in their dominance not to be seriously challenged until the 1790s. Secondly, the social hierarchy was inegalitarian and privileged but not ossified or brittle. There was continual adaptation – money being seen as the key to entry, allowing the successful to buy landed property which alone gave status. Thirdly, the ruling order managed to achieve considerable consensus for their position in a restless society. Roy Porter sums this up:

> The hope was to win acquiescence and endorsement by influence and persuasion – bluster, grandeur, liberality, promises, show and swank, the open door left just ajar. Those in power and their media mouthpieces dangled before people's eyes ambition, self-respect, new enjoyments, polite values and fashionable life styles . . . [5]

Their hegemony was cultural, as well as economic.

This cultural hegemony was evident in the ritualized theatrical qualities of eighteenth- and nineteenth-century rule. The theatre of law was one part of this, as were the ritual of conspicuous consumption and the 'civilized' nature of the social life of the elite – elegant mansions with 'classical' façades and landscaped gardens, fenced-off parks, the hunt, the duel, reserved pews in church, coaches and footmen, the blending of rural and urban in the 'London season' – another. E. P. Thompson points to the reciprocity between this patrician society and the plebeian culture during this period.[6] The visibility of success and power, and the ritual of punishment, were crucial symbols of the legitimacy of the elite groups in society.

A hierarchical society

The underlying basis of this elitist society was one of mutual and reciprocal obligation within a hierarchical framework. Harold Perkin writes that

> The old society, then was a finely graded hierarchy of great subtlety and discrimination, in which men were acutely aware of their exact relation to those immediately above and below them, but only vaguely conscious except at the very top of their connections with those on their own level. . . . There was one horizontal cleavage of great import, that between the 'gentleman' and the 'common people', but it could scarcely be defined in economic terms. . . . [7]

Deferential attitudes were due to those above and paternalistic attitudes to those below. A Berkshire vicar wrote in 1795 that it is manifest that our laws consider all the inhabitants of a parish as forming one large family, the higher and richer part of which is bound to find employment and subsistence for the lower and labouring part.[8]

This was a form of social organization which, despite all its obvious inequalities and injustices, was acceptable to the vast majority of people in England and Scotland, where landlords were usually of the same nationality and culture. It was less the case in Wales and Ireland, where landlords were often 'Anglicized' and from both an alien culture and religion.

'Patriarchalism'

J. C. D. Clark argues that a dominant 'patriarchalism' survived and flourished in the eighteenth and early nineteenth centuries.[9] He points to the continued importance of the patriarchal writings of Sir Robert Filmer and contemporary neglect of the work of John Locke in the eighteenth century – a society based on patriarchal principals was more acceptable to contemporaries than one based on contractual principles. What mattered in the patriarchal ideology was not what was later parodied as 'forelock tugging' but sympathetic involvement by the elites in the lives of the rest of society, the expectations of reciprocity, the common outlook, identification of interests and, if necessary, sheer coercion to maintain the civil stability of a hierarchical social structure. Power, wealth, and, Clark argues, faith characterized this social system:

> Patriarchal doctrine, then, was sustained after 1688 not so much by the polemical needs of a dynastic regime as by the continued domination of society by the Anglican Church on the one hand, and, on the other, by the aristocracy and gentry.[10]

Symbolically and in fact English society in the eighteenth and early nineteenth centuries was hierarchical, authoritarian and confessional in character: 'A Christian faith and moral code was a common possession of all social strata: the realm of the communal, of what was later designated "public goods", was largely the realm of religion . . .'.[11] Rank, station, duty and decorum were central social values throughout this period and, until the evolution of 'class', hierarchical subordination was scarcely diluted:

> What destroyed the ancien regime in England . . . was not chiefly the widespread adoption of a democratic world view, but the advance of Dissent, Roman Catholicism and religious indifference. . . . The Confessional State had been partly undermined by 1828 not by its intellectual invalidity or some new awakening to it but by the erosion of the numerical position of the Church of England. . . .[12]

Patriarchalism governed relationships at all levels of society. Apprenticeship, for example, was more than induction into particular skills; it was an immersion in the social experience or common wisdom of the community. Practices, norms and attitudes were, as a result, reproduced through successive generations within an accepted framework of traditional customs and rights that has been called 'the moral economy'.

But was this a 'consensus' view of society? It was in so far as society was reciprocally organized – responsibilities were the obverse of duties. Many of the disturbances in the eighteenth and early nineteenth centuries were directed at perceived infringements of the 'moral economy' – low wages or high prices could provoke food riots, new technology a mob response. The appeal was to custom, to paternalistic Tudor and Stuart legislation, to established and traditional practice. The eventual breakdown of this consensus, which had not been fully accomplished by 1850, was the result of economic change, the expansion of towns which were broadly outside the paternal net, changing religious observance which broke the 'bond of dependency' between squire, parson and labourer, and what Thomas Carlyle called 'the abdication on the part of the governors', the dismantling of protective paternalistic legislation.

Paternalism

Patriarchal social ideology continued to have currency despite this breakdown in consensus and the emergence of the 'class' alternatives. David Roberts provides a useful model of paternalism in early Victorian society.[13] He argues that the paternalist saw society in the following way.[14] First, it should be authoritarian, though tempered by common law and ancient liberties. Secondly, it should be hierarchical. Thirdly, it should be 'organic' with people knowing their appointed place. Finally, it should be 'pluralistic', consisting of different hierarchical 'interests' making up an organic whole.

Within this structure paternalists had certain duties and held certain assumptions. First was the duty to rule, a direct consequence of wealth and power. J. B. Summner wrote in 1847:

> Charge them that are rich in this world, that they do good, that they be rich in good works, ready to distribute, willing to communicate. . . . There will always be many naked to be clothed, many hungry to be fed, many sick and afflicted to be relieved. . . . [15]

Parallel to this was the obligation to help the poor, not merely passively but with active assistance. Paternalists also believed in the duty of 'guidance', a firm moral superintendence. The Reverend Buller, vice-chairman of the Linton Guardians in Cambridgeshire wrote in 1836 that

> With respect to the behaviour of the poor [after the introduction of the workhouse] the farmers in general bear testimony to their improvement

in civility to their employers, their greater care to keep their place, and their endeavours to get their children into service. . . . [16]

In the Second Report of the Poor Law Commissioners the Earl of Hardwicke said

> I have no doubt that by a steady, and just administration of the law taking each case on its merits, we shall next year be able to give you a report that will show a greater saving, together with a large improvement in the moral state of the community.[17]

Poverty could be blunted but never removed. 'Just' prices and 'fair' wages and rent were not merely rhetorical devices for maintaining order but could be regulated by the magistracy, though increasingly they were not. Money was suspect, Roberts goes so far as saying hated, because it was 'rootless', free from obligation and without duties. Paternalists looked to the past, emphasizing its continuities, and David Roberts sums this up as those:

> who believe that society can be best managed and social evils mitigated by men of authority, property and rank performing their respective duties towards those in their community who are bound to them by personal ties of dependency.[18]

This idea of a 'moral' society was the ethos of an economic and cultural hegemony that looked with nostalgia to the past and with unease to the future. But it was osmotic, absorbing 'new' wealth and applied as much to industrialists like the Ashworths, Peels and Gregs as to landowners and clergymen.

Patronage

Central to the paternalistic ethic was patronage, recently shown to have retained its importance throughout the nineteenth century.[19] Samual Johnson, with typical spleen, defined a patron in his 1755 *Dictionary* as 'Commonly a wretch who supports with insolence, and is paid with flattery'. Patronage involved a 'lopsided' relationship between individuals – a patron and a client – of unequal status, wealth and influence; what has been called a 'package deal' of reciprocal advantage to the individuals involved. Bourne argues that the rationale behind patronage can be 'affective or instrumental, collaborative or exploitive, long-term or a single isolated transaction . . .'.[20] Perkin maintains that patronage was second in importance only to property and was 'the instrument by which property influenced recruitment to those positions in society which were not determined by property alone'.[21]

Government patronage was central to employment and advancement in the public services, armed forces and Royal Navy. Private patrons had in their gift church livings, local government offices, work for lawyers, estate agents, chaplains, secretaries, tutors, governesses, tenancies of farms and land. The East India Company was a major source of non-aristocratic patronage. Politics was dominated by patronage and, before the development of party discipline, it provided the only effective means for individuals to ensure political support. Patronage provided jobs for electors, employment for placemen and rewards for supporters. Crown patronage was essential if a minister was to secure a safe majority in the House of Commons but between 1780 to 1830 the 'influence of the Crown' declined. Wellington, even with the resources of the Crown behind him, could not avoid defeat in the 1830 general election.

'Politically useful' offices like sinecures were suppressed after 1780 and the 'influence of the Crown' declined but, Bourne argues, to assume that there was a general decline in patronage is to 'fundamentally misconceive' the issue:

> Far from being hostile to patronage many of the political, social and economic changes of the early nineteenth century greatly increased the amount of patronage which was available.[22]

The future lay with the increasing number of 'administratively necessary' offices. The prison, factory, health and schools inspectorate were all staffed through patronage. Local government paralleled this. 'Efficient' patronage was used by rival elites within communities as an extension of party politics. Offices may have been filled by personal nomination but the individuals chosen had to possess some basic competence – a notion of 'merit' which received a wider and fairer application after the Northcote-Trevelyan report of 1854, though patronage comfortably withstood much of the onslaught of merit until the 1870s.

Patronage was characteristic of an unequal face-to-face society. It crossed class barriers, bringing together potentially hostile groups, helping to stabilize and legitimize inequality. Pursuing patronage was not irrational but a recognition by individuals of their sense of belonging to a social system, engendering a sense of solidarity between patrons and clients. Only when the reciprocity of patronage broke down was there bitterness, recrimination and hostility. Patronage was fundamental to the emergent middle-class, providing real resources but also psychological and moral support. Only the urban industrial middle-class of the north was apathetic towards patronage. But the bulk of the middle class was located in the genteel world of the professions and propertyless independent incomes, far less entrepreneurial and competitive than their industrial equivalents. Patronage survived as an integral part of society until after 1850, increasing the sense of solidarity and co-operation of the like-minded. As long as a common area of shared values existed patronage continued to have broad application and utility.

Client relationships became less important as labour became more mobile and became centred in urban communities. Archdeacon Wilberforce said in 1840 that 'Where . . . are the old bonds of mutual affection and respect – of natural care of the one side and generous trust upon the other, by which the peasantry and gentry were united?'[23]

'CLASS'

Problems of theory

An alternative to the vertical relationships of a patriarchal hierarchical society lay in the horizontal solidarities of 'class'.[24]

Richard Dennis, in his study of nineteenth-century industrial cities, wrote that 'Evidently the road to class analysis crosses a minefield with a sniper behind every bush . . . it may not be possible to please all the people all of the time . . .'.[25]

The theoretical problems with the concept of 'class' in the early nine-teenth century are immense, leading many historians to use the term in a loose sense. What did contemporaries understand by the idea of 'class'? How many classes were there? What do historians understand by 'class consciousness' and how, if at all, does it differ from 'class perception'? Was there a 'working class' in 1800 or 1830 or 1850? R. S. Neale suggests that historians have used five main approaches to class. His classification ranges from those who use the conventional three-class model (aristocracy, middle class and working class), linked to an assumed, but generally undefined, notion of class consciousness, and based on contemporary perceptions, to those who use or have adapted Marxist or other sociologi-cal models where class consciousness is the central concept. In practice, Neale admits, most historians range, consciously or not, over all of these approaches, which leads to considerable methodological pluralism.

Putting people into 'classes'

Placing individuals in particular social classes is notoriously difficult. Occu-pation, status, perception, attitudes, location are variables which can all affect classification. Take occupations. They may be ranked by income, but where should historians draw the boundaries between different income groups? Navvies were, by early nineteenth-century standards, quite well paid, handloom weavers were not. Should navvies be put into a higher social grouping as a consequence? What about the 'skill factor' or the economic conditions? Does everybody necessarily belong to one class or another or, as Richard Dennis asks, 'do some people exist outside class structure or even belong to more than one class, depending upon the circumstances in which they find themselves?'

Does occupation create group solidarity and is this the same as 'class consciousness'? Class has been defined strictly in terms of the means of production, irrespective of attitudes or actions. But the attitudes of workers varied. Neale, for example, argues that it is possible to identify two working classes, one proletarian, the other deferential. Morris, by contrast, maintains that these two attitudes are merely different responses to the same objective class situation. Neale is also criticized because his deferential workers and his privatized, individualistic 'middling' class cannot be classes at all because they lack class consciousness. The years since the publication of E. P. Thompson's *The Making of the English Working Class* (1963) have done little to clarify the situation, and answers to the central questions of 'when?', 'how?' and 'why?' have been surprisingly inconclusive.

Before the early nineteenth century it is difficult to talk of 'classes' as such. Laslett described early modern England as a one-class society, on the grounds that the landed elite were conscious of their commonality of interest at a national level. Critics have argued that this was not the case because it takes two to play at class: class interest can only be defined through class conflict. This seems to neglect the fact that the landed elite were very conscious of their social position and responsibilities and that they clearly constituted an economic 'interest' in the same way that the 'cotton interest' and 'mining interest' did in the nineteenth century. Perkin argues that class was 'latent' and Thompson has maintained the paradoxical notion of 'class struggle without class' in the eighteenth century. Both identified a traditional popular culture that was rebellious and resisted inroads into the 'moral economy' from market forces and capitalist relationships within a hierarchical structure. Thompson suggests that changing landownership and land use began to fracture traditional rural social ties, a process assisted by urban growth and changing religious observance. The system of 'dependency' was beginning to break down.

'Two nations'?

It is not surprising that many contemporaries interpreted early Victorian society as a two-class society. Disraeli popularized the idea of 'two nations', the rich and the poor. Elizabeth Gaskell wrote of Manchester that she had 'never lived in a place before where there were two sets of people always running each other down'. Tory Radicals were not alone in using the two-class model. Engels referred to the working class in the singular and offered a model dominated by two classes, bourgeoisie and proletariat, in which other classes existed but were becoming increasingly less important. Recent Marxist historians, E. P. Thompson and John Foster, have also applied this model. For Thompson class experience was largely the result of the productive relations into which people entered. The essence of class lay not in income or work but in class consciousness, the product of contemporary perceptions of capital and labour, exploiter and exploited.

In the years between 1780 and 1832 most English working people came to feel an identity of interest as between themselves, and against their rulers and employers . . . the working class presence was, in 1832, the most significant factor in British political life.[27]

But this unified notion did not apply to all the working population. Iowerth Prothero has examined London artisans and found that, in those trades with traditional organization and practices, the workers were conscious of the value of their skills and the product of their labour. They did not generally perceive themselves as a class in conflict with their employers nor generally with the middle class. But they were opposed to the 'unacceptable face of capitalism' which they believed downgraded their skills and attacked their notions of respectability and independence. Foster, in his study of three industrial towns, maintains that 12,000 workers sold their labour to 70 capitalist families. The middle class of tradesmen, shopkeepers and small masters were deeply divided in their social and political behaviour, though politically aligned with the working class on many political issues. Attempting to explain away this petit bourgeoisie has been criticized by, for example, Neale, who interposes his 'middling' classes within both working and middle classes. Foster argues that the working population went through three stages in developing consciousness. They were, first, 'Labour conscious' where their major concern ceased to be consumer prices but improvements in their own wages; then 'class conscious', where industrial problems became politicized (as in the 1830s and 1840s) and where workers were inclined to revolutionary ideas and practices; and finally there was 'liberalized consciousness' by which the bourgeoisie, aided by growing economic prosperity, was able to attach important sections of the working population to its consensus ideology.

Three classes?

The majority of contemporary and modern analysts have adhered to the three-class model. Harold Perkin argues that, as a result of industrialization, urban growth and the midwifery of religion, a class society emerged between 1789 and 1833 or, more precisely, between 1815 and 1820. For Perkin class was characterized 'by class feeling, that is, by the existence of vertical antagonisms between a small number of horizontal groups, each based on a common source of income.'[28]

The paternalistic view of society was not, however, destroyed by these class antagonisms and the potential conflict of emergent class society was contained by modification of existing institutions. For Perkin, compromise was a central reason for the persistence of older social values and structures and only an 'immature' class society is characterized by violence. Each class developed its own 'ideal' and by 1850, Perkin argues, three can be identified: the entrepreneurial ideal of the middle class, a working class ideal and an aristocratic ideal based respectively on profits, wages and rent. The struggle between ideals was, Perkin maintains, 'not so much that the ruling class imposes its ideal upon the rest, but that the class which manages to impose its ideal upon the rest becomes the ruling class'.[29] In Perkin's model the mature class society that emerged by the 1850s, despite the differences that existed between classes, was not marked by overt conflict but by tacit agreement and coexistence under the successful entrepreneurial ideal.

A 'five-class' model

The three-class model may well be inadequate for explaining early Victorian society because it does not take account of the 'middling' group who were distinct from both the middle class and the bulk of the working class. This group was, by definition, transient – becoming or ceasing to be 'middle' – and demands a more dynamic view of society than the rigid models discussed above. R. S. Neale developed his 'five-class model' as a consequence. He argues that there are different forms of working-class consciousness: proletarian, deferential and privatized, which he identifies with Working Class A, Working Class B and Middling. The middle and upper classes he defines as in the three-class model. Working Class A was the industrial proletariat, urban, factory employees, politically and class conscious, seeking material improvement through class action. Working Class B was deferential and dependent on those with higher status – agricultural labourers, casual and non-factory urban labour, domestic servants and most working women (whatever their husbands' class). Its identity was expressed through social interaction, religious affiliation and acceptance of charity, not through political activity. Though non-deferential, the Middling class – skilled artisans, shopkeepers, aspiring professional men – pursued an 'individuated or privatized' way of life that developed into self-help as a means of social advancement. This model emphasizes less quantifiable criteria such as values, customs and language rather than objective and measurable economic criteria such as size of income, occupation or size of assets. It is deliberately dynamic and provides a fluidity of approach lacking in the more conventional models.

Organization often takes second place to consciousness and perception. Craig Calhoun uses the concept of 'community' as a means of identifying those social organizations which determined social action. He concludes that traditional communities were the foundation and unifying bond for collective radical action – he cites Luddism and the abortive Pentrich rising of 1817 as examples of this. In fact, these were examples of collective action within the framework of the 'moral economy' – not class but 'populist' action – with the nature of the action determined by the perception of the threat to the community. According to Calhoun, the working class that emerged was reformist rather than revolutionary, concerned more with modifying existing socio-economic structures than creating a new one.

A class society?

If it is legitimate to speak of a class only when a group is united in every conceivable way – socially, politically, economically, geographically, in terms of response – then the concept of class is rendered virtually meaningless. Classes are not and never were monolithic blocks of identical individuals. The critical question is whether working people in the first half of the nineteenth century consciously acted as members of a class or in other roles. Historians have interpreted early nineteenth-century society in different ways. At one extreme of the spectrum are those who argue that class and class action were abnormal and that individual interest was far more powerful than class loyalty. On the other there were historians who see social developments in terms of a scenario in which class conflict played an integral and inevitable role.

It is possible to reach certain broad conclusions from this tendentious debate. First, by 1850 there was a middle class with clearly defined 'consciousness' based upon notions of respectability and self-help and with a strong organizational base. That consciousness had percolated down and reinforced traditional artisan values. Secondly, there were important distinctions within the working population – rural/urban, agricultural/industrial, skilled/unskilled, technologically obsolete/innovative occupations – which helped to determine attitudes and perceptions. Thirdly, it is possible to identify different degrees of 'class consciousness' among the working population which found itself in a somewhat ambiguous relationship with the more homogeneous middle-class ideology. Its attempts to form national organizations lacked coherence and community, locality and region played a far more important role. Finally, consumer interests – prices of food, real and actual wages, levels of employment – largely determined the actions of the working population. The majority were unwilling to pursue actively a programme of social change outside the existing social, economic and political environment. The threat of revolution was a tactic in this process rather than a likely eventuality. The distinction between those working people who wanted change through evolution or revolution is central to explaining different 'class' attitudes.

During the first half of the nineteenth century there was complex interaction between three rather than two views of society and social change. On the one hand there was the paternalist view based upon traditional hierarchical principles with implicit inequalities but reciprocal obligations. On the other hand there were two class models. A 'revolutionary' model, based on horizontal social groupings, had co-operation between workers and a critique of industrial capitalism as its unifying characteristics and class conflict as its motive force. An 'evolutionary' model was also based

Figure 16.2 The nature of society: a tripartite model

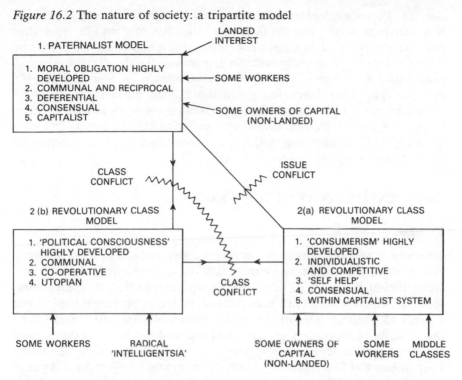

on horizontal groupings but these were individuated, competitive and operated within the existing urban and industrial environment. Change was the result of negotiating on specific issues to make the existing system fairer and consensual in character. These ideas can be seen in Figure 16.2.

A 'social revolution'?

The attitudes and values which underpinned British society changed between 1700 and 1850 but did that change constitute a 'social revolution'? If by 'social revolution' historians mean fundamental changes in the structure of power, a reduction in social inequality, the creation of an egalitarian society or the redistribution of wealth then changes of such importance did not occur in this period. But if historians mean that society changed in response to altering economic conditions then the case for a 'social revolution' may be stronger. Change in social attitudes and values was the result of dialogue between the older notion of 'paternalism' and the newer conceptions of 'class'. Whatever the pressures that drove people into classes it would be unwise to discount the impact of the appeal to individual, and not class, solutions to the problems created by an industrial and urban environment. In 1700 there was a clear differentiation between those in society who possessed visible landed wealth and those who did not. By 1850 society had become more complex with the growth of alternative sources of wealth and the dramatic expansion of a 'middle class' that had been very small in 1700. The 'labouring population' of 1700 had become more heterogeneous with the expansion in older occupations and the creation of new ones in response to economic change and demographic growth. This change occurred gradually, though not without dramatic effects on certain occupational groups. Historians have identified three further ways in which individuals were differentiated in society between 1700 and 1850 which transcend, but also contribute to, the 'paternalist-class' debate: religion, gender and race.

DIFFERENTIATION BY OTHER MEANS

Religion

Throughout society the language of religion was part of a common culture. For much of the eighteenth century this did not constitute a problem.[30] Until 1828–9 Britain was, in theory as well as practice, a 'confessional state' in which 'citizenship' was defined in terms of adherence to the Church of England. The strong squire–parson alliance, ideally suited to the majority of rural parishes, provided much of the moral underpinning for the paternalist dependency system. Though given legislative toleration, Catholicism and Dissent were clearly discriminated against by the penal legislation of the 1660s and 1670s which prevented individuals from holding public office and achieving 'real' social status. 'Occasional conformity' was one way of getting round these restrictions but, at least in England, Catholicism and Dissent had lost their social and cultural impetus and had become increasingly demoralized and introverted. After 1750, in response to internal dissatisfaction with the Church of England and its failure to respond to the newly created industrial and urban environment, an evangelical revival took place. Led by the Wesleys, Methodism developed outside the establishment. A movement for 'moral improvement' occurred within it.

The real problem after 1770 is to know what religion contemporaries were talking about and the depth to which Christianity was rooted beyond an outward conformity and the widespread evidence of religious feeling. Three aspects of religious life can be identified. At one level, religion is made up of a quest for individual truth and salvation. Many people throughout this period aspired sincerely to a rich interior life, an ardent piety which the evangelical movement exploited to full advantage. At a second level, that of organized religion, Christianity was an institution and religion a social and moral force providing a generally agreed framework for the 'Christian life'. Very few people denied all religious ties and did not belong, at least nominally, to a Church or sect. Finally, there was the level which transcended sectarian boundaries, an undenominational heritage of Christianity which influenced social and personal relationships. Churches, chapels and cathedrals provided visible symbolism of history, heresy and heritage. This period would be incomprehensible unless the power of the Bible and its constant presence in people's minds and hearts is taken into account – Bible quotations, Bible language and Bible pictures provided a common mental landscape.

It is the 'associational' dimension of religiosity that is of particular importance here. Was there a relationship between religious observance and an individual's social position? In broad terms the social appeal of the churches can be compared to a 'sandwich'. The Church of England corresponded to the top and bottom slices of society – the aristocratic elite and the 'lower orders' – while the interior of the sandwich consisted of middle-class Nonconformists. Roman Catholicism took up a similar position to the Church of England, with its small aristocratic fringe and proletarian support (a consequence largely of Irish immigration) being strong at the two extremities of the social hierarchy. In practice, however, social responses to religion were less clear-cut. Methodism penetrated into the working-class areas and both town and country and there was an extension of Anglican activity among the middle class, making the situation less clearcut in 1850 than it had been in 1750. Increasingly, only rural labourers remained in part loyal to the established Church, while the urban working class slid towards indifference. This was brought out clearly in the religious census of 1851 – there is clear evidence of the small number of churchgoers in London, as well as in Birmingham, Manchester and Newcastle.[31]

The degree to which religion prompted or restrained social change is a matter of disagreement among historians. Did Methodism prevent social and political revolution? In general terms Catholicism, Anglicanism and Nonconformity reinforced social inequalities, their Christianity was profoundly inegalitarian. They highlighted the importance of moral constraint and attacked 'popular' culture through their support for temperance and the role of Sunday, and the doctrine that 'sins of the flesh' were the supreme vice. Respectability and the Gospel became inseparable – by 1850 Christianity had become a thin veneer covering and defining 'proper' social relationships.

Gender

The most obvious means of differentiating between individuals within society was on the basis of gender.[32] Women were discriminated against legally, morally, economically and politically by men. Social attitudes were patriarchal and, if anything, those attitudes were reinforced between 1700 and 1850. Women were generally exploited – particularly economically and sexually – and denied the same social and political rights as men. These social attitudes went across the political spectrum – members of the landed aristocracy and agricultural labourers had a common attitude towards women, if nothing else. Society clearly differentiated between the worlds of men and women. Status and power lay in the former.

Changes in the economy after 1700 certainly adversely affected the wages of those women who had to work. They were generally excluded from the 'new' technology and increasingly were confined to the 'sweated' areas of domestic industry. Their wages, never equal, were further reduced with the support of both male employers and workers. The attempt by the Glasgow Spinners Association to negotiate equal rates of pay for men and women was exceptional, though it marked the recognition of a need for solidarity among the working population if it was to overcome the divisions capital had created between family and work, home and the factory, male and female. Women workers meant even more competition on the labour market. Legislation, like the 1842 Mines Act and various Factory Acts, either prohibited them from certain kinds of work or limited their hours. Most women did not organize into trade unions and their powers of resistance were correspondingly reduced. Rowbotham convincingly argues that:

> Work in the family was clearly separated from work in industry. The new capitalist organisation of labour was forming not only relations between classes but between the sexes . . . the old unity between work and home, where action over consumption was not distinct from action over production, was lost.[33]

There was some resistance to this patriarchal view of society. Daniel Defoe defended the right of women to education in 1697 and throughout the eighteenth century the right of women to education and opposition to marriage as an affair of property were frequent themes in pamphlets. In 1697 Mary Astell rejected the notion that women should merely be decorative and in 1739 'Sophia' took the attack on male privilege into the economic and financial sphere. But theirs was a minority position mocked, caricatured and satirized by contemporaries (female as well as male). Not until Mary Wollstonecraft produced her *Vindication of the Rights of Women* in 1792 was there a thorough critique of patriarchy. She countered the argument that women's subordination was inevitable and natural by maintaining that women should be free to decide what was in their best interests, rather than depending on men. She saw some relationship between the oppression of women and existing property relations and shared the faith, along with many male radicals, in education as a means of changing human consciousness. Only through 'reason' could inequalities be removed. Mary Wollstonecraft's notion of sexual equality was elitist in character, her ideas on education were limited to girls and women from her own level in society. She could not conceive of the daughters of the poor being taught to become rational beings. Neither could she imagine that women must organize themselves. Hers was, in many respects, a pseudo-feminist position which, while theoretically arguing that women should decide their own interests, she believed that in practice they must appeal to men to release them from dependence. The line from Mary Wollstonecraft to the gradual removal of legal disabilities for women is consequently quite clear.

A second strand of resistance to male oppression came through the early socialist movement.[34] The 1820s saw a widespread distribution of birth control information to working women. This was attacked by many male radicals, including William Cobbett, because the idea of limiting population was associated with the Malthusian notion of political economy – birth control was, for him, a device of the upper classes to put off social reform and an unnatural interference in the sexual rights of the poor. The case for and against birth control never freed itself from its original connection with Malthusian ideas and it had little or no effect on the birth rate. Abortion and infanticide remained the only effective alternatives to unwanted pregnancies, and birth control was not widely employed by the working population until the twentieth century.

Questioning the whole social and sexual position of women was only a strong minority interest in early nineteenth-century radicalism. Drawing on Mary Wollstonecraft and utopian socialism it emerged in opposition to middle-class radicalism which, rooted in evangelicalism, saw sexual inequality as part of the 'natural order' and as essential to effective capitalism. William Thompson, in his *Appeal of One Half of the Human Race, Women, Against the Pretensions of the Other Half, Men. . . .* (1825), and to a lesser extent Robert Owen argued that the whole basis of a competitive capitalist society kept women at a disadvantage, an inequality reinforced by crude cultural stereotypes. In a co-operative society, one organized to allow human beings to develop fully, they maintained, sexual discrimination was unnecessary. By the 1840s the connection between social revolution and women's liberation had been clearly established.

Demands for women's liberation were very much the minority position throughout the period 1700 to 1850. The strength of the patriarchal position, in which 'separate spheres' were clearly established and the position of women was subordinate, remained central to thinking across the social spectrum. Women's roles may have gradually altered, but male attitudes and values changed little if at all. British society was perhaps differentiated more clearly by gender than by any other thing.

Race

People could also be differentiated by race. To be 'successful' in the eighteenth and early nineteenth centuries meant being 'English', culturally if not by nationality. To become part of the ruling elite necessitated becoming 'Anglicized'. Adopting the cultural values and practices of the Establishment politically, socially, linguistically and religiously opened up a cultural gap between those who ruled and those who were governed. England ruled a largely docile Wales and Scotland though the co-operation of anglicized regional elites rather than by the direct intervention of the state. Ireland was less stable. Opposition to this cultural hegemony took the form of nationalistic cultural revivals, often repressed because they took a political stance opposed to that of the Establishment and the spread of the English state.

Michael Hechter argues that it is possible to examine the relationship between England, the national 'core' and its 'periphery', the Celtic fringe in terms of two alternative models of core–periphery relationships: a 'diffusion' model in which inter-group contact leads to ethnic homogeniz- ation and integration, and an 'internal colonial' model in which such contact may heighten ethnic conflict.[35] Politically the Celtic fringe was integrated into the English state by the early nineteenth century. Wales was annexed in 1536 when English land law, English courts and judges and the Church of England were imposed. The Welsh language was attacked by allowing only English-speaking Welshmen to hold administrat- ive offices in Wales. Union with Scotland was achieved by 'negotiation' in 1707 ending her political sovereignty, though the Scottish legal system and Presbyterian Church were allowed to continue. Union with Ireland came in 1801. Hechter argues that 'security' was the motive for incorpor- ation and that 'England desired to insure its territorial integrity at all costs, rather than suffer the threat of invasion by hostile Continental neighbours.'[36]

Whether or not Hechter's argument is valid, incorporation had impor- tant consequences. There was an insistence on English cultural superiority and a denigration of indigenous native cultures. The 1846 report on the state of Welsh education exemplifies this notion of cultural inferiority in its stinging indictment of the Welsh language, religion and national character:

> Because of their language, the mass of the Welsh people are inferior to the English in every branch of practical knowledge and skill. . . .
> The Welsh language distorts the truth, favours fraud and abets perjury . . . [it] is a vast drawback to Wales and a manifold barrier to the moral progress and commercial prosperity of the people.[37]

Speaking Gaelic and practising Roman Catholicism by the majority of people in Ireland were similarly attacked. Gaelic, like Welsh, was not considered conducive to rational discussion. Penal laws, which came to full fruition in 1727, denied Catholics any political or economic rights and remained in force until Catholic Emancipation in 1829. In Scotland alone the English had local allies in the process of cultural pacification. There were no comparable allies in either Wales or Ireland.

Anglicization was different in Scotland in two respects. First, the estab- lishment of the Presbyterian Kirk of Scotland allowed for far more cultural autonomy than in Wales and Ireland. Secondly, attempts at anglicization were carried out by native lowland Scots, already only marginally different from the English, rather than directly by the English government. Scotland was divided between the Presbyterian, English-speaking Lowland and the Catholic or Episcopalian and Gaelic-speaking Highlands. Dissent in the Highlands, always a problem, took on the Jacobite political dimension after 1689. Two Highland risings in 1715 and 1745, and abortive attempts at rebellion in 1708 and 1719 heightened both Lowland and English fears. Control was exerted in three ways. First, the potential solidarity of the Highlands was weakened by the aggrandizement of the Campbell clan, which seized smaller clans' territories. Secondly, a large standing army was maintained in the north with considerable mobility because of wide-spread road-building. Thirdly, the cultural identity of the Highlands was attacked. In 1709 the newly founded Scottish Society for the Propagation of Christian Knowledge decided that

> nothing can be more effectual for reducing these counties to order and making them more useful to the Commonwealth than teaching them their duty to God, their King and Country and rooting out their Irish language.

After 1745 Highland society was deliberately dismembered. Rebel chiefs lost their land, which was placed under the control of a committee dominated by Edinburgh lawyers. The kilt and bagpipes were banned and more roads brought further English influence, Internal peace was essential to Lowlanders if they were to attract English capital to Scotland for investment – anglicization can be seen, in this context, as part of the process of economic aggrandizement.

Language for hegemony

Accent was important. English may have been spoken in the Scottish Lowlands but with a distinctively regional flavour. 'Scottish' was a synonym for rudeness in England and the leading sectors of Scottish society hastened to educate their children in English schools. After the 1750s elocutionists visited Edinburgh to give lessons in English pronunciation. Being seen to be 'English' opened up career possibilities which being 'Scottish', 'Welsh' or 'Irish' did not.

English cultural hegemony had a firm economic base. It is clear that England exploited its resource base more effectively than the Celtic fringe. Economic growth was generally more dynamic in England and increasingly Scotland, Wales and Ireland were subject to comparative disadvantage in production. To call the economies of the Celtic fringe 'backward' in 1700 implies a value judgement of questionable validity but it is, I think, fair to argue that the dynamic for economic growth lay in England. Other economies were viewed as 'servicing' the 'mother country' rather than having an identity separate and autonomous. The mercantilist policies used during the eighteenth and early nineteenth centuries were 'racist' in the sense that they exploited Scotland, Wales and Ireland to the advantage of England without any real thought of their effects upon the indigenous population. This was, in many ways, as 'colonial' a policy as those used in English possessions outside the British Isles.

Politically, economically, socially, culturally and religiously Scotland, Wales and Ireland were systematically subordinated to the hegemony of England in the eighteenth and nineteenth centuries. Control was exerted through centrally appointed officials and through anglicized regional elites. Their indigenous populations were suspect: politically through support for the Jacobite cause, later through the republicanism of Jacobinism and the resurgence of nationalism, and religiously through adherence to Roman Catholicism or Dissent. Language was the symbol of both national identity and colonial oppression.[38]

Attitudes to 'foreigners' – the Celtic stereotype

English attitudes can best be seen in relation to Irish immigrants.[39] A trickle in the eighteenth century, Irish immigration increased after 1820, becoming a flood in the late 1840s. In the 1841 census there were 291,000 Irish-born individuals in England and Wales, 128,000 in Scotland; by 1851 there were 520,000 and 207,000 respectively. Most of these immigrants settled in the industrial towns of Lancashire and western Scotland, especially Liverpool and Glasgow. They stood out from and were suspected by the host population because of their poverty, nationality, race and religion. As Swift and Gilley say:

> The Irish Catholic immigrants look like the outcasts of Victorian society, outcast from British capitalism as the poorest of the poor, from mainstream British politics as separatist nationalists and republicans, from the 'Anglo-Saxon' race as 'Celts' and as Catholics from the dominant forms of British Protestantism. . . . [40]

The apartness of the Irish, often segregated by poverty, meant that the development of closer personal contacts and wider economic opportunities in the English Protestant-owned and run economy were denied. Suspicion resulted from the Irish immigrants being the largest unassimilated section of English society, largely rejected, generally despised and the butt, as in the Stockport riots of 1852, of xenophobic anti-papist Toryism. The anti-Irish stereotype was far more complex than *Punch*'s depiction of the Celt as a gorilla, on the lowest rung of the evolutionary ladder. Both antagonism and attitudes were ambiguous rather than simple.

Immigrants

There were other groups in British society who were distinguished by their race – immigrants.[41] A Jewish community had by 1808 consolidated its position largely as a result of European pogroms which drove Jews fleeing persecution to the relative security of Britain. Whatever their place of origin these immigrants were generally poor and placed an often unwelcome burden, so established English Jewry co-operated in trying to keep them out. By 1800 there were 15–20,000 Jews in London and a further 6,000 in provincial towns. A burden when poor, Jews were also condemned for being rich. There was a widespread anti-semitism in British society which periodically erupted in the eighteenth and early nineteenth centuries. When Dickens created Fagin he built on a popularly recognizable caricature.

French Huguenots fled to England following the Revocation of the Edict of Nantes in 1685. By 1718 there were 35 Huguenot churches in London alone. Many Huguenots became tutors and, though less well remembered, brought a tradition of gardening. It was, however, in silk weaving that the Huguenots made a contribution to economic development and their skills were grafted on to the older traditions of Spitalfields. This contribution was not without its tensions and there was a particular rivalry between Huguenot and Catholic Irish weavers, leading to riots in 1719 and 1736. Though London was the major centre of Huguenot settlement, many of the English southern and eastern coastal towns had Huguenot churches by 1700. Huguenots also played a central role in the expansion of the linen industry in the north of Ireland. Their Protestantism meant that, like immigrants from the Low Countries, they were more easily integrated into British society than the Jews and in, for example, Bristol and Ipswich, families of Huguenot descent were among the most successful and prosperous section of the population by the late eighteenth century.

A slave trade

Britain's involvement in the slave trade from the mid-seventeenth century meant that increasing numbers of blacks – often enslaved lived in England by 1700.[42] Though there was a great deal of confusion about the precise legal position, until 1772 black slavery was considered legal in England. By 1750 there was a sizeable black population in London, largely poor, working as domestics. Most were male and inevitably large numbers had liaisons with or married poor white women. There was fear and distrust of racial mixing and actual examples of racism are not difficult to find in this period. Attitudes towards blacks ranged across the whole spectrum from brutal slavery and degradation to friendship and intimacy.

Numbers of blacks in Britain declined in the last quarter of the eighteenth century and this process continued after 1800. Black slaves became too valuable in the Caribbean to be shipped to England. The campaign against slavery, which succeeded in 1807, had initially enhanced the value of slaves and then made their trade illegal. As James Walvin points out: 'the main and determining force behind black settlement up to the 1830s – the British slave trade and slavery – had exhausted itself'.[43]

A racism generated by slavery – the view that blacks were things, not people – had been pushed aside by the insistence of the abolitionists on black equality between 1787 and 1838. The abolitionists won the moral argument and in the 1820s and 1830s people of all social classes and from both sexes registered their opposition to slavery. Whether it was this or the less profitable position of the sugar trade that led to the end of slavery is difficult to ascertain but by 1850 there had been a revival of widespread public opposition to black humanity. Britain's economic and political problems in the 1840s led to a revived form of racism – in fact directed largely at the Irish – which characterized Victorian responses to non-white people for the rest of the century. Marx was unusual in turning to class rather than race as the key explanatory division between people. The world was increasingly seen in terms of racial ranks and orders, with white people at the top. Disraeli said in the Commons in 1849 'Race implies difference and difference implies superiority, and superiority leads to predominance.' Racism became scientifically respectable and was expressive of increasingly vigorous colonialism. The exploitation of the slave trade was replaced by the exploitation of 'civilizing' imperialism. The view expressed in *Blackwood's Magazine* in 1866 was, like all justifications for discrimination, based on accepted and unquestioned stereotypes.

> [is] the negro worth all the trouble, anxiety, bloodshed and misery which his wrongs and his rights have produced? . . . Did anyone ever hear of a negro mathematician, of a negro engineer, or a negro architect or a negro painter or a negro political economist . . . left to himself and without white control and guidance he forgets the lessons he had learnt, and slides rapidly back to his original barbarism.

CONCLUSIONS

British society between 1700 and 1850 was one in which inequality was the overriding characteristic.[44] People were unequal in terms of wealth and access to economic prosperity; legally in terms of political and 'human' rights; sexually and racially. The right to hold political offices and to be educated at a university was restricted in England and Wales to male members of the Church of England, with Dissenters, Catholics, Jews, atheists and women broadly discriminated against until after 1850. The right to vote, though extended after 1832, was confined to a minority of the male population until after 1850. The jury system, the strict independence of the judiciary from executive control and the application of the law to all irrespective of social status were different from the Continent, but the emphasis on protection for property meant that an even-handed system could be used to maintain an inegalitarian social system. What was important was status, respect for status and the widespread belief that individuals could improve their status.

For those with power and wealth and for those without, the realities of life changed little between 1700 and 1850. Attitudes remained paternalistic, masculine and suspicious of 'foreigners', those from the next county or village as much (perhaps more) than those from abroad. Industrialization did not create social inequalities but, because of the increasing focus of population in towns and cities, such inequalities became more visible and consequently less acceptable. The emergence of 'class' perspectives was largely a response to this, though as several historians have pointed out class can be identified in the pre-industrial period even if it was 'latent' or without 'class struggle'. Change in social attitudes was gradual, the result of dialogue between different, ambiguously interpreted social relationships and by 1850 it was by no means inevitable that class attitudes would replace paternalistic ones. Power numerically was with the former but authority still lay firmly with the latter.

NOTES

1 Robert Southey *Colloquies on the Progress and Prospects of Society*, 1829. p. 47.
2 J. H. Dawson *New Statistical Account of Scotland*, 1845, Vol. VII, p. 332.
3 On methodology see P. Burke *Sociology and History*, Allen & Unwin, 1980, P. Abrams *Historical Sociology*, Open Books, 1982 and C. Lloyd *Explanation in Social History*, Basil Blackwell, 1986.
4 T. B. Bottomore *Elites and Society*, Penguin, 1966, G. Parry *Political Elites*, Allen & Unwin, 1969 and P. Stanworth and A. Giddens (eds) *Elites and Power in British Society*, Cambridge University Press, 1974 provide theoretical perspectives.
5 R. Porter *English Society in the Eighteenth Century*, Penguin, 1982, pp. 360–1.
6 E. P. Thompson 'Patrician Society, Plebeian Culture', *Journal of Social History*, 7 (1974). See also P. Corrigan and D. Sayer *The Great Arch – English State Formation as Cultural Revolution*, Basil Blackwell, 1985, p. 87–113.
7 H. Perkin *The Origins of Modern English Society 1780–1880*, Routledge & Kegan Paul, 1969, p. 24.
8 Rev. David Davies *The Case of the Labourers in Husbandry*, 1795, p. 28.
9 J. C. D. Clark *English Society 1688–1832*, Cambridge University Press, 1985 especially pp. 69–93.
10 ibid. p. 82.
11 ibid. p. 87.
12 ibid. p. 89.
13 D. Roberts *Paternalism in Early Victorian England*, Croom Helm, 1979.
14 ibid. pp. 2–10.
15 J. B. Summner *Christian Charity, Its Obligations and Objects*, 1847, p. 22.

16 Printed more fully in Workers Educational Association *In and Out of the Workhouse*, EARO Resource and Technology Centre, 1978, pp. 34–5.

17 Earl of Hardwicke, Chairman of the Caxton and Arrington Union, Cambridgeshire, in *Second Annual Report of the Poor Law Commissioners*, Appendix B, pp. 233–5.

18 D. Roberts op.cit. p. 8.

19 What follows on patronage draws heavily on J. M. Bourne *Patronage and Society in Nineteenth-Century England*, Edward Arnold, 1986.

20 ibid. pp. 7–8.

21 H. Perkin op cit. p. 45.

22 J. M. Bourne op. cit. p. 22.

23 Quoted in K. D. Brown *The English Labour Movement 1700–1951*, Gill & Macmillan, 1982, p. 69.

24 The literature on 'class' is immense but the following will be found of particular value. Useful studies with a theoretical slant include P. Calvert *The Concept of Class*, Hutchinson, 1983, R. S. Neale *Class in English History 1680–1850*, Blackwell, 1983, the readings he edited entitled *History and Class: Essential Readings in Theory and Interpretation*, Blackwell, 1984 and A. Giddens *The Class Structure of the Advanced Societies*, Hutchinson, 1973. R. J. Morris has contributed a valuable bibliographical study *Class and Class Consciousness in the Industrial Revolution*, Macmillan, 1980 and also of interest is his 'Class and Common Interest', *History Today*, May 1983. The 'language' of class is best explored in A. Briggs' seminal paper 'The Language of Class in Early Nineteenth Century England', in A. Briggs and J. Saville (eds) *Essays in Labour History*, Macmillan, 1960, pp. 43–73 and G. Steadman Jones *Languages of Class*, Cambridge University Press, 1983. More detailed studies must start from E. P. Thompson *The Making of the English Working Class*, Gollancz, 1963 and go on to H. Perkin, op. cit., J. Foster *Class Struggle and the Industrial Revolution*, Weidenfeld, 1974, I. Prothero *Artisans and Politics in Early Nineteenth Century London*, Dawson, 1979 and C. Calhoun *The Question of Class Struggle*, Basil Blackwell, 1982. P. N. Furbank *Unholy Pleasure: the Idea of Social Class*, Oxford University Press, 1984 adds a note of sardonic caution. J. D. Young *The Rousing of the Scottish Working Class*, Croom Helm, 1979 surveys the eighteenth and nineteenth centuries.

25 R. Dennis *English Industrial Cities of the Nineteenth Century: A Social Geography*, Cambridge University Press, 1984, pp. 187–8.

26 ibid. p. 187.

27 E. P. Thompson *The Making of the English Working Class*, Gollancz, 1963, p. 3.

28 H. Perkin *The Origins of Modern English Society 1780–1880*, Routledge & Kegan Paul, 1980, p. 37.

29 ibid. pp. 218–70, for a discussion of the 'struggle between ideals'.

30 For what follows see A. D. Gilbert *Religion and Society in Industrial England*, Longman, 1976 and the statistical analysis in R. Currie, A. D. Gilbert and L. H. Horsey *Churches and Churchgoers – Patterns of Church Growth in the British Isles since 1700*, Oxford University Press, 1977.

31 On the religious census of 1851 see K. S. Inglis *Churches and the Working Class in Victorian England*, Routledge, 1963 and the shorter papers by B. I. Coleman 'Religion in the Victorian City', *History Today*, August 1980 and 'The Church of England in the Mid-Nineteenth Century: A Social Geography', The Historical Association, 1980.

32 The literature on women's history has increased dramatically in the last ten years but S. Rowbotham *Hidden from History*, Pluto, 1973 and *Women, Resist-*

ance and Revolution, Penguin, 1972 are still the most useful introductory studies.

33 S. Rowbotham op. cit., 1973, pp. 30–1.

34 Barbara Taylor *Eve and the New Jerusalem*, Virago, 1983 provides an excellent coverage of resistance through Owenite socialism and feminism.

35 M. Hechter *Internal Colonization: the Celtic Fringe in British National Development 1536–1966*, Routledge, 1975.

36 ibid. p. 69.

37 Quoted in ibid, p. 75.

38 For the issue of language in Wales see G. Williams *Religion, Language and Nationality in Wales*, University of Wales, 1979 and papers by Raymond Williams and O. Dudley Edwards in J. Osmond *The National Question Again – Welsh Political Identity in the 1980s*, Gomer, 1985.

39 On the Irish see R. Swift and S. Gilley (eds) *The Irish in the Victorian City*, Croom Helm, 1985 especially the essays by M. A. G. O. Tuathaigh, R. Samuel and the editors' introduction. R. Swift and S. Gilley (eds) *The Irish in Britain 1815–1939*, Manchester University Press, 1989, contains much of value.

40 ibid. p. 9.

41 For the discussion on immigrants see J. Walvin *Passages to Britain*, Penguin, 1984.

42 N. File and C. Power *British Settlers in Britain 1555–1958*, 1981 is the best introduction to a neglected subject.

43 J. Walvin op. cit. p. 37 and for the subsequent quotations pp. 40–1.

44 On the inegalitarian nature of society see H. Kaelbe *Industrialisation and Social Inequality in 19th-Century Europe*, Berg, 1986 and the more focused W. D. Rubenstein *Wealth and Inequality in Britain*, Faber, 1986.

Addendum:

Four recent books on Scotland should be noted:

T. M. Devine and R. Mitchison (eds) *People and Society* in Scotland, Vol. I, 1760–1830, John Donald, 1988; W. H. Fraser and R. J. Morris (eds) *People and Society in Scotland*, Vol. II, 1830–1914, John Donald, 1990; T. C. Smout *A Century of the Scottish People 1830–1950*, Collins, 1986; T. C. Smout and S. Wood *Scottish Voices 1745–1960*, Collins, 1990.

17 The impact of economic growth – change in the countryside 1700–1850

Unbounded freedom ruled the wandering scene;
No fence of ownership crept in between
To hide the prospect from the gazing eye;
Its only bondage was the circling sky. . . .
Enclosure came, and trampled on the grave
Of labour's rights, and left the poor a slave. . . .
Fence meeting fence in owner's little bounds
Of field and meadow, large as garden-grounds,
In little parcels little minds to please,
With men and flocks imprisoned, ill at ease. . . .[1]

John Clare, the nineteenth-century Northamptonshire poet made a distinction between rural society before and after enclosure in terms of a loss of freedom. How valid was his observation? This chapter explores, through a series of case studies, the impact of economic change on the countryside between 1700 and 1850 and examines the nature of change, its effects and people's reactions to it.

INTRODUCTION

Some aspects of change in the countryside have already been examined.[2] First, the variety of agricultural experience, the importance of the countryside in 'proto-industrialization', the different chronologies of change and the persistence of older techniques, both between localities and between England, Wales, Scotland and Ireland, have been highlighted. Secondly, despite the rationalization of land usage and the emergence of the large estate, most agricultural production occurred on farms of under 100 acres and the significance of large-scale farming should not be overestimated. Similarly, the importance of enclosure after 1750 must be seen in the context of earlier developments and in terms of its regional incidence. Thirdly, the continued importance of paternalistic social attitudes, particularly their 'moral imperative' has been discussed. Finally, the importance of land, as evidence of both economic and social status, throughout this period has been emphasized. Only in terms of the economy as a whole did the importance of agriculture diminish; in its own terms, British farming generally became more productive and more efficient between 1700 and 1850. However, it was unable to feed the burgeoning population after the 1760s and, increasingly, Britain relied on grain imports. The revolution in agriculture was perhaps more limited, in this sense, than historians have previously believed.

CHANGE IN THE COUNTRYSIDE – CASE STUDIES

How far did the nature of rural communities and their priorities change between 1700 and 1850? Certain questions arise from the following discussion of the representativeness or otherwise of Myddle, Cardington, Houghton Regis, Ashwell and Risby.[3] These communities raise a series of important issues about rural society which can be applied, to a lesser or greater extent, to other parts of Britain.

Myddle

The History of Myddle, in Shropshire, was written by Richard Gough around 1700.[4] His study provides a useful base from which to consider the question of changing priorities. Myddle was a remote community in one of the most thinly populated parts of England. Just how parochial was Myddle? Though 160 miles from London it was not as cut off from the mainstream of national life as might be supposed. Richard Gough had visited London in his youth, meeting a fellow parishioner there, and his frequent mention of London implies that it was common for his neighbours to have been there. People from all sections of the community went to London and information about events in the broader world filtered through to Myddle in their letters. People were certainly familiar with their immediate surroundings, centred on the market towns of Shrewsbury, Ellesmere and Wem. While North Shropshire may have been their 'county', there was a sense of belonging not only to this particular place but to a wider region. Their mental horizons were far from parochial, though events were refracted through the medium of the parish community.

North Shropshire was a woodland area and people did not live in hamlets or isolated dwellings rather than nucleated villages. Gough structured his history round the arrangement of the pews in the parish church, the focus of the community. This formalized the social structure of the parish, with the gentry at the front, yeomen and husbandmen in the middle and the cottagers at the rear. Gough felt deeply about the proper order of society – a consequence of his legal education, his Anglicanism and his belief in monarchy – and reflected more general opinion when he wrote: 'it was held a thing unseemly and undecent that a company of young boyes, and those persons that paid noe [church-rates], should sitt . . . above those of the best of the parish'.[5]

Gough wrote of a society in which duty and obedience were central features and this was reflected in his own unpaid work on behalf of his parish and county. He served on the Shropshire Grand Jury, which examined indictments at the assizes and quarter sessions. In Myddle he helped with settlement cases, acted as churchwarden, drew up a glebe terrier for the archdeacon's visitation, witnessed wills and appraised probate inventories. He supported the political and religious settlements of 1660 and 1689 but his Christianity was concerned with charitable works and he was quick to condemn those who failed to live up to that ideal. He was critical of Robert Wilkinson, bailiff of the manors of Wem and Loppington who 'tooke more care to gett money among the tenants, than to gaine theire love or preserve his owne credit'.[6] And of Richard Wicherley, a wealthy parishioner, who was never 'commended either for his charity to the poore, his hospitality to his neighbours, nor his plentifull housekeeping for his servants.'[7]

Gough stood for a reciprocally ordered society in which 'place' was important. The owners of the largest farms provided leadership in Myddle, as well as employment for farm servants. There were twelve farms between 100 and 650 acres but, though often described as gentlemen, no individual farmer was powerful enough to fill the role of squire. The experience of the leading families in Myddle shows that they had only a 50:50 chance of retaining their property over two or three generations. Historians have generalized about the gentry, and Gough's account of successive owners of Balderton Hall shows how misleading this can be.[8] William Nicholas built the hall but went bankrupt after speculating in the timber trade in the 1570s and 1580s. Michael Chambre, his successor, frittered his fortune away and ended in prison. Each of the two Shrewsbury drapers who followed had to sell when their London connections went bankrupt. The hall was then bought, in his retirement, by the rector of Hodnet. It was then purchased by Matthew Lath, a farmer with humble beginnings but was lost by his son-in-law Thomas Hall and was bought by Richard Hayward, a neighbouring yeoman, around 1700.

These 'parish gentry' were not sharply divided from the rest of society and it was quite common for one family to contain people of different occupations and social standing. Gough did, however, differentiate between the twelve farms and the 48 'tenements', which varied between 10 and 90 acres depending on the quality of the land. About a quarter were freehold and the rest were held on leases for three lives, the normal Shropshire method of tenure, from the lord of the manor. The occupants of these family farms, who earned extra income from tailoring, weaving and other crafts, saw themselves as yeomen and were less vulnerable to poor economic conditions than husbandmen. Both yeomen and husbandmen in Myddle were economically more secure than their counterparts in corn-growing areas. Farming in Myddle was pastoral and prices were more stable than on arable farms. It was geared to dairying, the rearing of beef and, particularly in the late seventeenth century, the 'Cheshire cheese' trade. The little land in Myddle devoted to corn was already enclosed by 1700 and over 1,000 acres of former woods were converted into meadows and pasture by the early seventeenth century.

The existence of spacious commons and woodlands in Shropshire led to squatters taking over land. One squatter erected a cottage in Myddle-wood by 1581 and by 1701 there were fourteen cottages in this area. Some squatters were very poor and Gough was annoyed that the poverty of families like the Davieses and Beddows led to the higher poor rate than earlier in the seventeenth century. Others, however, seized the opportunities provided by day-labour, cloth-making and their right to keep animals on the commons to improve their position. Despite Gough's criticisms, Shropshire was able to absorb squatters without the tensions produced by the increase in the poor in the more crowded villages of other parts of England.

The parish described by Richard Gough was socially graduated on the basis of land. The lords of Myddle were remote figures who played no direct role in the community. Power – economic and social, even if not political – lay with the owners of the larger farms. Below them lay the yeomen and husbandmen, different in degree rather than kind. Finally, there were the squatters, a fluid group, who looked upwards for promotion into the ranks of the 'parish gentry' and who provided additional day labour. More specialist services were provided by craftsmen – Gough specifically mentions a carpenter and a shoemaker.

Cardington

Cardington, in Bedfordshire, is the second community to be examined.[9] The survey of the parish compiled by James Lilbourne, a local schoolmaster, in 1782 and the 1851 census allow historians to assess change over time. The Parish of Cardington lies on the southern slope of the Ouse valley, an area of good clay and gravel soil, adjacent to Bedford, the county town, to the north-west.

The 1782 listing (Table 17.1) was determined, not by social hierarchy, but by the grouping of multiple tenement cottages and may, because of the lack of detail for the higher social levels, have been compiled to ascertain how much public and private provision was needed for maintaining the parish poor. The detail given in the listing allows an analysis of social structure according to the occupational status of the household head.

The domestic textile industry is prominent in the list of occupations. Category 3(a) is entirely female and so is much of 8. Thomas Batchelor's *General View of the Agriculture of the County of Bedford* (1808) described

Table 17.1 Distribution of occupation in Cardington in 1782

Occupational Category	Household heads No.	%	Others No.	%
1. Gentry:				
(a) Esq, Mr, Mrs	8	3.8	1	0.4
(b) Clergy	2	1.0	–	–
2. Agriculture:				
(a) Farmers	24	11.4	1	0.4
(b) Labourers	91	43.1	4	1.5
3. Manufacture (incl. apprentices):				
(a) textiles: makes lace	9	4.3	94	34.9
spins linen	7	3.3	32	11.9
spins jersey	3	1.4	30	11.1
(b) clothing: taylor	1	0.5	3	1.1
seamstress	–	–	1	0.4
mantua-maker	–	–	2	0.7
(c) food: miller	1	0.5	2	0.7
maltmaker	1	0.5	–	–
butcher	1	0.5	1	0.4
baker	1	0.5	–	–
(d) wood products carpenter	6	2.8	2	0.7
sawyer	1	0.5	–	–
(e) leather products: shoemaker	2	1.0	1	0.4
(f) metal products: blacksmith	3	1.4	2	0.7
(g) equipment: wheelwright	2	1.0	–	–
4. Building:				
(a) bricklayer	3	1.4	–	–
5. Distribution and trade:				
shopkeeper	5	2.4	–	–
innkeeper	2	1.0	–	–
hawker	1	0.5	–	–
ragman	1	0.5	–	–
6. Service:				
servant	–	–	20	7.4
works for	–	–	2	0.7
7. Pauper	18	8.5	21	7.8
8. Others:				
laundress	1	0.5	–	–
nurses	1	0.5	–	–
housekeeper	1	0.5	–	–
*Town Howard	1	0.5	–	–
Bailiff	1	0.5	–	–
Workhouse governor	1	0.5	1	0.4
Sexton	1	0.5	–	–
Parish Clerk	1	0.5	–	–
At school	–	–	49	17.5
Schoolmaster	1	0.5	1	0.4
Midwife	–	–	1	0.4
9. Unknown	9	4.3		
TOTAL	211	100.0	269	100.0

This is a table of occupations, not of persons. Dual occupations have been counted twice on eight occasions.
* The Town Howard was the village hayward responsible for the hedges and the uses of parish common land.
Source: *The Inhabitants of Cardington in 1782*, ed. D. Baker, Bedfordshire Historical Record Society, 1973, p. 25.

how lace-making employed three-quarters of the non-domestic servant population, creating a shortage of maidservants. The range of occupations far exceeds that for Myddle.

Cardington, like Myddle, had a pyramidal social structure. Labourers accounted for 45.7 per cent of households and 49.4 per cent of the population and with craftsmen/tradesmen they made up 68 per cent and 73.7 per cent respectively. While there was a significant difference at the extremes between gentry and non-gentry in Cardington there were many subtle gradations in between and the dividing line was by no means clear. The Land Tax assessment of 1783 distinguished between those who owned land, tenants and, by implication, those who had none at all. Status could be indicated by liability for jury service, applicable to men with land worth over £10 per annum; being a parish office-holder; appointment as a JP; the possession of sufficient property to require the making of a will; the appointment as a trustee of a will, particularly if there was no blood relationship with the maker of the will. Three 'county gentry' – individuals with status outside the community – lived in Cardington: John Howard, the prison reformer, Samuel Whitbread, senior and John Nesbitt. Below them was a subtly graduated parish elite who owned or rented land and whose status was largely limited to Cardington itself. There were twenty one households which Baker terms as 'local gentry' and thirty two households of the 'parish elite'. The difference between these two groups is evident in the higher property valuation of the former in the 1783 assessment. John Adams (died 1809) and Thomas Estwick are examples of members of the local gentry. Adams was assessed at £56 for his Cardington land in 1783 and had been a churchwarden (1778–9, 1779–80, 1780–1), overseer (1778–9) and member of the Vestry (1778–9). Estwick was assessed at £26 14s. in 1783 and had been Constable (1777–8, 1778–9), overseer (1776–7) and member of the Vestry (1779–80) and had been on jury service in 1781. William Brown (1744–1823) is a good example of a member of the parish elite. He was a shoemaker and Parish Clerk, occupying land assessed at £0. 17s. in 1783. His status can be demonstrated in his witnessing of wills (John Brown's in 1787) and acting as a trustee (Ann Preston, in the same year).

One hundred and forty-four family heads were labourers, craftsmen or tradesmen. Again the subtleties of the social hierarchy are evident. Compare for example, Joshua Crockford, a Dissenter, who occupied land in Cardington assessed at £0. 12s. in 1783 and who left an inventory of goods for probate on his death in 1823, and Thomas Willamot (1726–86), a labourer who had received relief from the poor rates. Finally seventeen family heads were classified as 'paupers'. There was an exceptional, and probably untypical, degree of commitment in Cardington to the poor, largely the result of the philanthropic attitudes of Howard and Whitbread, who in 1787 built four houses for 'deserving poor'. John Aikin commented in 1792 that there are few Counties in England which afford less employment to a numerous poor than that of Bedford; of course wages are low and much distress would prevail, were it not for the humanity of gentlemen who reside on their estates.

The flexibility that existed in Myddle for absorbing squatters and the poor did not exist in Cardington.

Between 1782 and 1851 the population of the parish increased from around 800 to 1,451. Despite this the socio-occupational structure remained largely unchanged (Table 17.2).

Table 17.2 Cardington households by social and occupational status

Description of household	No. of households	%	No. of people	%
Farmer	32	11.3	204	14.1
Tradesman	26	9.2	155	10.7
Craftsman	28	9.9	131	9.0
Labourer	187	65.7	920	63.4
Others	11	3.9	41	2.8
TOTAL	284	100.0	1,451	100.0

Source: N. L. Tranter 'The Social Structure of a Bedfordshire Parish in the Mid-nineteenth Century', *International Review of Social History*, 18 (1973), p. 90.

'Farmers', the wealthier and more substantial members of the community, made up only a small proportion of the total population while agricultural day labourers and people involved in the usual trading and craft activities characteristic of rural parishes made up the large majority of the population. As in 1782 the overwhelming proportion of resident females aged over five was occupied in domestic handicraft trades of various kinds, though principally lace-making. As Tranter says: 'If the social structure of Cardington changed in any respect during the first half of the nineteenth century, it did so against a background of economic continuity.'[10]

Risby and Houghton Regis

There were important similarities and differences between Risby (population 355), in Suffolk, and Houghton Regis (population 2,196), in southern Bedfordshire, and Cardington in 1851.[11] All three parishes had the same basic social structure – leading landowners, a 'parish elite' and a labouring population. Most of the population in each parish was either born there or in close proximity. Less than one in ten came from outside either Suffolk or Bedfordshire. Parishes, at least in southern England, were distinctly parochial. Risby was an overwhelmingly agricultural parish: agricultural labourers made up 80 per cent of its total population. In Cardington and Houghton Regis rural industries were of more importance: for example, only 14 per cent were specified as 'Ag Labs' in Houghton Regis. The reason lay in the proximity of the hat-making trade in Luton and Dunstable leading to the growth of a domestic-based straw-plaiting industry in Houghton Regis absorbing up to 40 per cent of the population.

INDUSTRY IN THE VILLAGE

What was the significance of industry in villages?[12] First, it enabled population to have a better standard of living than would have been possible by relying on agriculture alone. Secondly, it had important socio-economic implications within the village community. In areas where a craft or industry was well developed, another significant social group was added to landless labourers, farmers, landowners and tradesmen. Industrial groups were, however, closely integrated with the rest of the community through the existence of dual occupations. This could – though in the cases of Cardington and Houghton Regis, where industry was essentially done by women and children, it did not – lead to a challenge to the hegemony of the landed elite. In the south Yorkshire parish of Ecclesfield, for example, nail-making was important in the north and cutlery on the southern Sheffield side. Workers in both these occupations farmed as well and, in the early eighteenth century, one household in eight contained a smithy. Many of the nailers and cutlers were better off than those who made a living entirely from farming and some were able to rank with the yeoman. Rural industries were still expanding in 1800 but by 1850 several important industrial processes – e.g. brick-making, framework knitting, handloom weaving – had begun to use coal and/or steam power. At the same time the railways became an effective system and the country craftsmen found their livelihoods threatened by cheaper, mass-manufactured products.

'OPEN' AND 'CLOSED' VILLAGES

Risby, Cardington and Houghton Regis were all 'open', as opposed to 'closed' villages.[13] In broad terms an 'open' village was controlled by its freeholders while a 'closed' village was controlled solely by large landowner(s). In 1832 there were 308 rural townships in Leicestershire with a density of owners ranging from only 5 acres per owner in industrialized Mountsorrel to 2,273 acres per owner at Stapleford, an estate village where the Earl of Harborough was sole proprietor. Of the 134 villages which were closed, 39 were classified as estate villages while the remaining 95 had absentee landlords. The 174 open villages were even more varied than the closed villages. The number of owners varied from barely 10 to well over 100 and from an average of 5 acres per owner to over 200. Mills argues that

> it is possible to consider two situations which are conceptually distinct – one in which a large number of owners, including owner-occupiers, form the basis of a well developed 'peasant' community, the other where the land is merely divided between so many owners that no one of them, or even a caucus of two or three, can be said to have a controlling interest.[14]

What implications do these divisions have for change in the countryside? The characteristics of open and closed villages are summarized in Table 17.3.

Table 17.3 Open and closed villages: a typology

Open	Closed
Large populations	Small populations
High population density	Low population density
Rapid population increases	Slow population increases
Many small proprietors	Large estates
Peasant families	Gentlemen's residences
Small farms	Large farms
High poor rates	Low poor rates
Rural industries and craftsmen	Little industry and few craftsmen
Plentiful shops/public houses	Few shops/public houses
Housing poor but plentiful	Housing good but in short supply
Nonconformity common	Strong Anglican control
Radical and independent	Deference strong in politics and social organizations
Poachers	Gamekeepers

Source: D. R. Mills *Lord and Peasant in Nineteenth Century Britain*, Croom Helm, 1980, p. 117, table 6.1.

Population density and population growth was much lower in closed than open parishes. In Bedfordshire, for example, the 25 closed parishes had one person per 5.61 acres, while in the 90 open parishes the figure was one person per 3.34 acres. One important consequence of this was that open villages often provided labour for farms in closed villages. Specialist workers, like stockmen and gamekeepers, were found cottages in the closed village but day labourers would be drawn in from the neighbouring open villages, particularly at harvest time. In this way some integration occurred between open and closed communities. The use of gangs, especially in eastern England, was partly a result of the shortage of harvest labour in closed villages and of unemployment in open villages.

The latter was also a reason why labourers walked to work in neighbouring towns.

The estate system of large farms was found particularly in the arable areas of lowland England. Smaller family holdings, except in areas like the Fens, Kent and the Vale of Evesham, were found mainly in pastoral areas, especially in northern and western England, and in the areas of wood pasture in south-east England, like the Weald and the Chilterns. Pastoral farming favoured a peasantry and provided a basis for industrial growth because it was less demanding on capital, was less prone to drastic economic fluctuations, could be made profitable on a smaller scale than arable farming and it made widespread use of cheaper female labour. Pastoral farming was less labour-intensive and could consequently be combined with domestic production more easily than arable farming more easily. The early stockingers in the east Midlands, where there was no scope for absorbing surplus labour in farming, were often substantial tradesmen or open-village farmers who had capital available for the purchase of stocking frames. Comparative economic advantage led areas in southern England and East Anglia away from industry into more innovative arable farming, which absorbed most of the available capital and labour. The occupational structures of arable and pastoral areas developed distinctive features.

There were important differences between open and closed parishes in terms of the quality of housing.[15] The poor housing standards of the large, often overcrowded, open villages contrasted with the formally planned estate village. Demand for housing resulted in higher rents than in closed villages and sanitation and water supplies were frequently inadequate. The control over housing which the landlord commanded in closed villages was part of the process of social control, an expression of patriarchal influence in the same way that control was exerted through religion. The squire and parson wielded considerable influence in closed parishes – they have been called 'miniature welfare states' – and there was little possibility of Nonconformity or independent thinking developing. The estate system made tenants and labourers dependent on squire and parson and was only challenged where there were substantial peasant holdings and freeholdings or where there was a distinct artisan grouping. Contemporaries may have emphasized that non-attendance at church was the root cause of lack of deference in open parishes but this neglects the pervasiveness of control of the closed parishes. Vertical social control of closed villages took several forms. Control through housing was one expression of this. Tenancy agreements often specified attendance at church. When the Earl of Radnor built the Berkshire village of Coleshill, to replace dispersed cottages, he gave as his reasons

First   To put the inhabitants under the influence of public opinion
Second To put them near the Church

Third   To put them near the School
Fourth To put them near the Post Office
Fifth   To put them near the shop by which the labourer saves 15 per
            cent of his wages.

The closed village, in theory and frequently in practice, was a controlled society, deferential, dependent, compliant.

Open villages and dispersed settlements were often more politically radical than closed, nucleated villages. Rights tended to be based on custom rather than law and were vigorously defended. This can be seen in reactions to the Black Act of 1723 which turned many forms of rural protest and crime, such as deer-stalking, 'blacking' (poaching in disguise), cutting trees and maiming cattle, into capital offences.[16] Crown property in Windsor had long been used by squatters to relieve population pressure. The forests also provided important additional employment and resources – charcoal-making, lime-burning, brick-making, obtaining sand and gravel, making articles out of wood – for small freeholders in hamlets and dispersed settlements. Lax forest administration had led to the emergence of customary practices which supported a local economy that was traditional rather than capitalistic and market-oriented. The introduction of Whig gentry, who obtained the forest offices which they exploited with callous disregard for traditional customs, led to conflict. The Black Act can be seen as a piece of legislation designed to reinforce Whig economic hegemony which was threatened by lack of social deference from the inhabitants of open parishes. Recent research has, however, suggested a narrowly political motive, namely the Jacobite attitude of the foresters. The resurgence of 'blacking' in an organized form was the response. Deer was poached, less for its food value than as a symbol of Whig authority which threatened traditional economy, crops and agrarian rights. In Ireland turnip crops were destroyed for the same reason in the early nineteenth century. Protest could also occur because traditional economic elites prevented capitalist practices being introduced. In the early nineteenth century, for example, smuggling was carried out by the rising class of tradesmen resentful of the domination of the landed elite in the Blaxhall district of Suffolk.

The early nineteenth century saw a growth of rural protest as population growth outstripped rural demands for labour – in both farming and industry – and where the poor laws demoralized the labouring population. It may not have been organized and systematic but it was certainly not ephemeral.[17] Hobsbawm and Rudé found that the open–closed dichotomy was less clear-cut than presented by contemporary writers. Tradesmen and Nonconformist preachers, whose mere presence was a challenge to the authority of the landed elite, were frequently in the forefront of protests. They may have had a direct grievance about farm wage levels – relevant in terms of the purchasing power of labourers – but it was more a question of their social identification with the labouring population and their general position as community leaders, the result of superior education and 'knowledge of the world'. Open villages contained a higher proportion of tradesmen, artisans and small family cultivators who were economically, socially and ideologically independent of the landed elite and who had less to lose by protesting than the labourers in closed villages. Open villages contained more pauperism and unemployment than closed villages, particularly in southern England with its highly fluctuating demand for labour. Loyalty in open villages was to self and family rather than to the estate and in this situation protest was more likely to occur.

ASHWELL – A VILLAGE IN DEPTH

Ashwell, in northern Hertfordshire, was described by Arthur Young in 1804 as 'a poor, open parish'.[18] It had about 750 inhabitants in the early years of the nineteenth century and the problems they encountered were paralleled, to a lesser or greater extent, by villagers all over southern England. The larger houses, inns and one or two shops were found in the High Street but the most important feature was the dozen farmhouses scattered along its length, each with barns and other buildings round a central yard with a 'home close' of pasture land behind. In Back Street, which ran parallel to High Street, were the workshops and homes of the craftsmen and tradesmen of the village. There was also a village church (St Mary's), a mill, a Merchant Taylors' School and the Old Workhouse (Figure 17.1). Young noted the poor nature of roads to Ashwell and Davey is undoubtedly correct in writing

> Isolated by its position, unnoticed and unnoticing, Ashwell depended almost entirely on its own resources, and was mainly concerned with the day-to-day struggle to ensure that those resources could meet its needs.[19]

A village economy

The village economy was based on farming 4,000 acres of chalk soil. Within the parish, largely farmed under an open system until 1863, there was a heavy dependence on grain crops with barley as the most productive. The late enclosure of all but 300 acres in the western part of the parish was largely because two-thirds of the land was in the hands of several absentee landlords and there was consequently a lack of drive to enclose – B. G. Snow of London owned 600 acres, C. S. Tinling of Devon over 1,000 plus several other private and institutional estates such as those of St John's College, Cambridge and of the Bishop of London. In the 1841 census, of the 21 men who classified themselves as 'farmers', two-thirds were almost exclusively tenant farmers and of the seven owner-occupiers only four (John and Thomas Chapman, 231 and 306 acres respectively,

Figure 17.1 Ashwell in the 1840s

Farms and homesteads

1 Westbury Farm (B. Christy)
2 Farrows Farm (J. Sale)
3 (T. Chapman)
4 (J. Westrope)
5 (A. Hart)
6 (W. Bacon)
7 (T. Westrope)
8 (J. Chapman)
9 (J. Bowman)
10 (J. Kirbyshire)
11 The Bury (E. Fordham's
   Farm and brewery)

Other buildings

C St Mary's Church
M Mill
S Merchant Tailors' School
V Vicarage
W Old Workhouse

Source: B. J. Davey *Ashwell 1830–1914: The decline of a village community,* Leicester University Press, 1980, p. 10.

Richard Westrope 255 acres and Edward Fordham 147 acres) had substantial acreages. Ashwell showed considerable continuity of tenant farmers – the Tinling estate changed hands three times between 1830 and 1914 but two of its most important farms remained in the hands of the Sale and Christy families throughout. The dominant pattern of agriculture in Ashwell lay in several large farms – the average size of farm in the 1840s was 163 acres and ten farms were between 200 and 300 acres.

Ashwell may not have been enclosed but some farmers appear to have consolidated their strips into more compact units. In 1840 Farrows Farm, for example, had its 330 acres divided up as follows: 62 acres in 18 lots of enclosed land, 56 acres in 55 strips in North Field, 59 acres in 69 strips in Redland Field, 80 acres in 73 strips in Claybush Fields and 70 acres in 56 strips in Quarry Field. The Sale family acquired land in the west of the parish to consolidate their holdings but it was a slow process and by 1840 little real progress had been made. There were only 23 acres of common pasture in the parish and grazing rights were strictly controlled by the Vestry and the pinder, who collected animals from the farms, returned them at the end of the day and ensured that no one abused their common rights. The large farmers kept sheep which were systematically folded over their own strips to manure the soil. The poor seem to have had few common rights other than crossing the open fields on the maze of footpaths.

Grain was the major crop of all the farms. In the 1810s Farrows Farm grew on average 80 acres of wheat, 70–80 acres of barley and 25–30 acres of oats (largely for home consumption by eight horses). Higher wheat prices, as for example between 1813 and 1818, led to wheat being sown at the expense of barley. Farmers used the new methods of farming, as far as their small plots of land would allow. Production at Farrows Farm shows evidence of convertible husbandry, cultivation of clover and turnips (over 100 acres in total), beans, peas, potatoes and coleseed. This enabled the Sale family to maintain 150 sheep (for meat and wool as well as manure), cows (largely for the dairy products and meat for home consumption) and pigs. Farming in Ashwell has been described as 'not prosperous [but] it is clear that it might be described as thriving'.[20]

Arthur Young was wrong to see Ashwell as poor and backward simply because it had open fields.

A diverse community

Agriculture was the foundation of Ashwell's life but entries in nineteenth-century directories which stated that the inhabitants were 'wholly engaged in agricultural pursuits' are misleading. Rural communities, depending on their location, were more or less self-supporting. In 1841, for example, Ashwell contain 14 individuals who classed themselves as carpenters, 9 bricklayers, 5 blacksmiths, 7 shoemakers, 4 millers, 2 bakers, 6 publicans,

3 thatchers, 3 saddlers, 2 carriers, 3 grocers, a brewer, a barber, a rope-maker, a painter and glazier and a well-established family of rat-catchers. Though some of these individuals were employed by others, there were master-craftsmen in each of the major occupations and, including unskilled labourers and apprentices, almost a hundred men (about 25 per cent of the male adult population) were involved in crafts and trade. Davey[21] argues that they were 'wholly' involved but this is unlikely and many could have combined crafts and trade with work in agriculture at critical times in the farming year. These men were, however, a distinct social group with greater status and security than the mass of agricultural labourers, and their work frequently took them outside the parish. For example, Abraham Thorne, a master-wheelwright, plied his trade in a number of villages within a 10-mile radius of Ashwell and often arranged business on his regular visits to Royston market.

Agricultural labourers formed the largest occupational group in the village – about 50 per cent of adult males in 1841, 54 per cent in 1851 and 57 per cent in 1861. They formed a definable rural proletariat with only five owning any land in 1840 (only 10 acres in total). The farm servant, hired for the year, was uncommon in Ashwell and most labourers were employed on a weekly or daily basis. Their position became increasingly insecure after 1810. In the 1810s the 330 acres of Farrows Farm were worked by eight men and four or five boys. The men earned between 1s. 8d. and 2s. 3d. per day. It was extremely rare for them to be laid off and wet weather often meant higher wages since they were then used for threshing. In addition a shepherd and housekeeper were employed at a basic rate of 10s. per week, a lower weekly rate than for general labourers but they were slightly more secure in their jobs. From this one example it can be seen that there was considerable variety in the employment and pay of labourers, depending on their work, their ability and their age. The low level of Ashwell's poor rates between 1800 and 1820 can be explained by the existence of weaving, bonnet-making and some lace-making and by the growth of the more lucrative straw-plaiting. Women and children did most of the straw-plaiting and until the 1840s when several factors began collecting the plaits, sold their products at Hitchin market on Saturday mornings. This could bring an income of up to £1 a week in the first half of the nineteenth century and played a major part in the family budget. As Davey says, 'It remained a vital factor in the Ashwell labourer's economy, and seems to have rescued him from that grinding poverty which was the lot of so many of his fellows elsewhere.'[22]

Education

The standard of education in Ashwell was potentially high. The 1841 census identified four schools. There was a free school for boys adminis-tered by the Worshipful Company of Merchant Taylors but most children went to 'plait schools' where basic literacy and numeracy were taught in addition to straw-plaiting. Most children appear to have attended school at some time in their lives though many 'lost the habit' once they were employed in jobs which did not use reading, writing or arithmetic. An emphasis on boys' education can be seen among tradesmen and among the farmers who sent their sons to small private schools in the east coast towns.

Housing

By contrast the standard of labourers' housing and sanitation was low. The thatch and chalk clunch buildings were infested with vermin, and open cesspits, polluted water and filthy streets bred infection. Improvements were made only after larger and more powerful local government agencies took an active role. Throughout this period the village was self-governing. There was no squire and the burden of government fell on the Vestry, a body which officially included all the ratepayers and owners in the parish, but in practice only the vicar and between 10 and 20 people attended. It had wide-ranging powers including administering local charities, controlling parish land and property, maintaining roads and bridges, settling open-field disputes and sometimes offering village opinion on national political issues. It appointed two unpaid overseers and a Surveyor of the Highways, who tended to be farmers, and a constable, who was usually one of the craftsmen, frequently the blacksmith in Ashwell. Davey comments: 'In a truly representative, if not fully democratic way, it [the Vestry] was the government of the community, by and for the community. . . .'[23]

This may be an over-optimistic viewpoint because whatever community of interest and economic independence there was in Ashwell was to be shattered by economic change after 1830.

Change and continuity

What were the issues which affected Ashwell in the first half of the nineteenth century? The most obvious was a dramatic expansion of population, which doubled between 1801 and 1851 from 715 to 1,425 inhabitants. There is no evidence to suggest that this was any more than a natural increase of the indigenous population with immigration playing no significant role. The major effect of this was the need to find work in the village for these increased numbers. Farmers could not afford to employ more men and plaiting was more widely adopted in the 1830s and 1840s. Plaiting was, however, almost exclusively women's work and dependent on an external market for its produce. Men increasingly looked to the crafts and trades for employment, to the extent that a third of all adult men were employed in them in 1851. Ashwell was a barley-growing area and beer-making became increasingly important as an employer of labour. By 1851 the brewing trade employed at least 30 men and probably gave part-time work to many more.

These new opportunities were insufficient to absorb all the surplus labour and high levels of unemployment, particularly among farm workers, were evident from the early 1830s. Davey estimates that 15 per cent of labouring men were unemployed in this period.[24] This put increasing pressure on the system of poor relief operating in the parish. Ashwell had established a workhouse in 1727 and had six cottages which it rented out to old people at nominal rents. Most of the unemployed were given 'outdoor relief', doles in money or in kind given on personal application to the overseers. Ashwell had no fixed 'Speenhamland'-type system and each application was treated on its merit. This required considerable judgement on the part of the overseers and became expensive as unemployment began to rise. In 1815 poor relief cost the parish £250 per annum; by 1821 this had risen to over £300 and by 1830–4 it amounted to £500 per annum.

The Vestry approached this problem by using two strategies, motivated perhaps by the Swing Riots, rural disturbances affecting large areas of southern England in 1830 which, though they did not touch Ashwell, came perilously close. First, it provided work. In late 1831 14 major farmers agreed to employ one man for every 40 acres they farmed for a year and in June 1835 some surplus labourers were employed digging stones at the quarries. Secondly, the Vestry encouraged emigration. In 1836 a contribution of £60 was made to defray the expense of poor people wishing to emigrate to Canada. Nine young men – the group most hit by unemployment – left the village in late May 1836 for this purpose. This was repeated in 1854, though only £15 was provided.

The poor and the police

Ashwell's attitude to the poor was broadly paternalistic. Those more wealthy inhabitants had a moral duty to mitigate the effects of unemployment and economic depression for the less well-off. This protection, however, only extended to individuals from the parish and 'strangers' and vagrants were generally 'encouraged' to leave as quickly as possible. The relative autonomy which the parish had in dealing with its poor is generally thought to have ended after 1834 with the implementation of the Poor Law Amendment Act.

Responsibility for the poor passed to the Royston Union, with Ashwell represented on the Board of Guardians by one elected member though Mr T. Westrope, one of the major owner-occupiers, sat as an ex officio member because he was a JP. A new workhouse, opened in 1837, was built just outside Royston and this generated considerable hostility here as in other localities. Opposition round Royston was mobilized by two local clergymen but did not lead, as elsewhere, to the violent destruction of the workhouse. Ashwell was declared an 'outdoor area', like many parishes in large rural Poor Law Unions and the new workhouse seems to have had a similar role to the parish workhouse. It was the last resort for the utterly destitute, the severely sick, abandoned children and some of the aged. But the stigma of the workhouse threw a long shadow and outdoor relief after 1834 was far less benevolent than before. The new relieving officers, often from outside the parish, tended to be less sympathetic than the locally appointed overseers.

The most obvious impact of the 1834 Act was a substantial reduction in the poor rates: they were roughly halved and remained at between £250 and £300 per annum until the 1870s. The Vestry continued to take some interest in the plight of the poor though its decision to sell the six old people's cottages in 1851 reflected the effective transfer of responsibility. But the parish still looked after its own and from 1835 onwards a large number of Friendly Societies and Benefit Clubs were established in the village with some financial support from the Vestry. Most labourers were members of some sort of club by 1850 and few could not support themselves during temporary unemployment due to illness.

The independence of the village was also affected by the establishment of the County Police Force in 1842 replacing the local constable elected by the Vestry with full-time professionals, the new PCs. They had more time than the local constable to enforce the law and many people saw this as interference with established custom, even when the custom was technically illegal. Petty poaching, long a feature of village life, was now prosecuted more vigorously and after 1842 a constant stream of Ashwell men appeared before the courts.

Migration from the parish increased after 1830 with some 150 men leaving between the 1841 and 1851 censuses. This reflected the inability of Ashwell to absorb the growing population, which became increasingly dependent on external markets for the products of straw-plaiting and brewing and a depressed agricultural sector. It was not only poor relief and policing that were now outside parish control. Economically Ashwell was far more obviously dependent on the market in 1850 than it had been in 1800. Paternalist relations were being replaced by more stridently capitalist ones. The crisis for Ashwell came after 1850 in the period that historians have called 'the Golden Age' for farming.

From the specific to the general

How representative was the experience of the inhabitants of Ashwell of other villagers in England? In two important respects it was not. First, Ashwell did not undergo the, often traumatic, experience of enclosure. Secondly, though there is evidence for the increasing importance of domestic production it never replaced agriculture as the main occupation in

Ashwell unlike villages in other areas where manufacturing production expanded.

In other respects, however, the problems and tensions in this community had parallels throughout England. First, it had to cope with major environmental problems – poor housing for the bulk of the population, low levels of sanitation and deficient drinking water and widespread ill-health. Secondly, Ashwell experienced a reduction in the control which it had over its own affairs, particularly over dealing with the poor and with law enforcement, though the Vestry continued to adopt paternalist strategies for mitigating, if not eliminating, problems. Thirdly, customs, which had previously legitimized actions and been the arbiter of village affairs, were diluted by an increasingly strict application of 'legal' as opposed to 'moral' rights. This led, fourthly, to a questioning of the paternalist system of social organization.[25] In Ashwell this was an implicit rather than explicit process, a case of gradual modification of attitudes rather than dramatic change. There is no evidence of food riots or disturbances in Ashwell itself but the labouring population would undoubtedly have been aware of events outside the parish and this may have influenced both their attitudes and those of the major employers. Finally, Ashwell was a community in which the effects of changing emphases in the economy were having some impact. Within fifty years it went from having sufficient labour to being in surplus. This surplus could not be absorbed in agriculture without dramatically reducing farmers' profits. The results – an increase in poor rates and the move towards domestic production – were evidence of falling profit margins in arable farming after 1815. Ashwell, to a certain degree, mirrored the impact of change in agrarian communities throughout England.

SCOTLAND

In 1700 most parts of Scotland had a largely subsistence economy, though the Highlands and Islands were least developed. The clan system which dominated these areas was based on military service and kinship. The main type of settlement in early eighteenth-century rural Scotland was a hamlet of multiple tenants know as a 'ferm-toun' in the Lowlands and sometimes as a 'bailie' in the Highlands. Payment of rent was mainly in kind and in labour until feudal tenure was abolished in 1746. During the eighteenth century the Scottish landscape underwent a process of rapid change – this was far more 'revolutionary' than in England. The result, according to Dennis Mills, was that

Wales approximated to the English peasant system, being a more developed form of peasant society, while Scotland exhibited most of the characteristics of the estate system . . . [so that] Not only in the highland zone, but throughout Scotland the lasting impression is of a landed class which carried all before it on a journey to full-blooded capitalism and outdid the English in speed and thoroughness.[26]

The old clusters of small farms typical of the ferm-touns disappeared and were replaced by large, modern farms with sleeping quarters for single servants and cottages for married men. The subsistence economy of common fields (run-rigs), peasant holding and common pasture were swept away and replaced by estates owned by capitalist farmers and worked by a landless proletariat. In crofting areas, the old clustered settlements were replaced by separate and dispersed crofts. The speed and thoroughness of change was made possible by four things. First, there was no equivalent to the English yeoman or class of small owner-occupier, which could have acted as a barrier to the creation of consolidated estates. Secondly, there was a general absence of long-standing customary rights in arable land. Thirdly, Scottish landowners were given a far freer hand than their English counterparts in enclosing land by Acts in 1661, 1685, 1695 and 1770. Finally, the failure of the Jacobite rebellions led to widespread confiscation of land, particularly in the Highlands. There was no effective challenge to the dominant position of large landowners in the Scottish rural economy.

This dominance was reflected in the planned village movement, the Scottish parallel to the English estate system. However, the rationale behind the planned villages rose out of landlord need for local consumption and servicing points in an emergent commercial economy. As a result many planned villages started out as industrial and commercial centres concerned with simple processing activities, and only later diversified into textile production. Scottish landowners supported this movement for two main reasons. First, this absorbed labour made surplus by enclosure and 'improvement'. Secondly, they supported industrial growth because it increased their rents and allowed continuation of social control over industrial workers. Planned villages let them do this and if a successful industrial village evolved into a town they tended to withdraw.

There is some disagreement over how many planned villages were founded in the eighteenth and early nineteenth centuries: estimates vary between 130 and 268. T. C. Smout's analysis omits landlord villages not physically replanned from his total of 130.[27] He distinguishes eight main groupings of planned villages: group I in north-east Scotland in which crofters were rehoused as a result of Highland clearances; group II near Aberdeen were largely agrarian but often included fishing and weaving; group III in the central Highlands were planned to achieve social control over the clans; group IV on the western coast were mainly fishing and harbour settlements; group V was a linen group based on yarn sent out from Perth and Dundee; group VI were factory villages round Glasgow and Paisley; and groups VII and VIII in the Southern Uplands had origins in farming, industry and trade.

The control which Scottish landowners had over the economy was reflected in the operation of the Scottish Poor Law. Landlords were able to develop sectors of the economy, which in England were often controlled by the emergent bourgeoisie, and consequently absorb unemployed farm servants. They were aided in this by the nature of the Scottish Poor Law which gave no relief to the able-bodied, only the destitute and kept the level of relief to the bare minimum; only one in ten parishes were assessed, with funds provided in the others by voluntary church collection. In terms of poor relief, at least until all parishes were assessed after 1846, there was no sharp contrast between neighbouring parishes as there was in England.

The degree to which the clan system was in decay in the early eighteenth century is a matter of disagreement among historians. Certainly by 1700 the Highlands provided important supplies of labour, wool, sheep, cattle and kelp for the Lowland towns. Culloden and its aftermath may be seen as a dramatic continuation of trends already evident. The Highlands were becoming increasingly commercialized and by the first half of the nineteenth century most Highland landowners had either to embark on clearances or sell out to Lowlander or even English capitalists. The unity of interest and language that existed in the Highlands in 1700 was replaced by lack of understanding between nineteenth-century proprietors and their crofting tenants.

Crofting arose out of the collapse of the clan system and complete reliance on a subsistence economy. In addition to arable farming it relied on the sale of animals and wood and additional employment in fishing and weaving. It replaced the hierarchical clan system with co-operation between independent households particularly for certain agricultural operations like 'souming' (control of the common pastures) and 'fanks' (round-ups of animals). The boundary between bare subsistence and profit for crofters was a narrow one and clearances were one method employed to remove the impoverished. They were replaced by capitalized tenant farmers who used the same land for large-scale sheep and cattle farming. Crofters did not have any security of tenure and landlords were able to proceed without too much opposition. This modernization of the Highland economy resulted in widespread emigration from Scotland. Some of the dispossessed crofters migrated to the Lowlands, firstly seasonally and then permanently, while others were allocated inferior land, often on the coast where fishing and kelp-burning were important occupations. Landlords encouraged this until technical changes in glass manufacture led to the decline of kelping in the 1820s. Landlords then brought sheep into the coastal areas, promoting emigration to reduce unemployment.

Landlord and crofter had different priorities during this period. Landlords and large tenant farmers were concerned with maximizing profits on the basis of substantial capital expenditure. The crofter, by contrast, lacked the capital to engage in large-scale farming and was concerned to maximize social solidarity. Potato-growing, which required minimum capital outlay, gave good return on a small acreage and used family labour, was widely adopted in the late eighteenth and early nineteenth centuries as a way of countering landlord pressure. Even so, eviction was a constant threat.

Landlord and crofter differed linguistically, politically and religiously. Crofters clung to Gaelic long after it had been abandoned by the gentry and town dwellers. The Free Church which, like the Primitive Methodists in England, was sympathetic to the problems of the labouring population, was able to make significant advances in crofting areas. Crofters appear to have been radical or Liberal in political persuasion, following the lead of the Scottish urban population, rather than Tory like their landlords. But as Mills says: 'So the landed classes in Scotland produced a rural landscape of large dispersed farmsteads and planned villages having greater freedom of action than their counterparts in England.'

WALES

Kinship played an important role in the development of rural Wales though the dilution of its tribal system predated the end of the Scottish clans by 200 years. As in Scotland by 1700 larger farms were associated with dispersed settlements, though in general the typical Welsh farm remained small, a process exacerbated by enclosure. The Welsh gentry was anglicized before their Scottish counterparts and their authority was reinforced by the adoption of primogeniture, which allowed the accumulation of estates. Smaller farmers still clung to the traditional 'gavelkind', a form of partible inheritance which divided rather than consolidated land.

Sixty per cent of land in Wales was in the form of estates over 1,000 acres compared to only 53 per cent in England. Only 13 per cent of land was, however, in estates over 10,000 acres compared to 25 per cent in England. This reflected a weakness of estate management and the lower productivity of Welsh land. The Welsh gentry did not rent land to well-capitalized tenants, who could act as agrarian improvers, as in England and Scotland. Husbandry techniques remained largely unimproved – drainage, the key to good farming, was poor; green crops and roots were sparsely grown; there was little attention to livestock breeding and implements were crude. Tenurial relations did to some extent hinder change and fear of rent increases was often a crucial obstacle to improvement. For many – landowner and tenant – land was not regarded as a commercial speculation but simply a means of providing a livelihood. Even the railways, while altering the system of marketing, did not provide the vital injection of enterprise and capital into Welsh agriculture after 1835.

Welsh rural society was relatively classless below the gentry. The rising commercial and professional middle class belonged to urban rather than

rural Wales. Kin not class provided social cohesion, a consequence, perhaps, of the poverty of a semi-subsistence economy. Land hunger was
also a problem and many men worked as labourers for part of their lives
before taking a holding of their own. It is, however, possible to distinguish
between different types of small farmer: those labourers and cottagers
who farmed up to 20 acres and who often supplemented their earnings
from farming as quarrymen, gardeners, coal miners and craftsmen;
medium-sized farmers with 20 to 80 acres relying on sons and close relatives or who employed more than two labourers for manpower, and large
farms with over 80 acres.

Is it sufficient to argue that the lack of change in Welsh rural society
was the result of under-capitalization by both the large landowners and
the smaller gentry? Why did landlords not play a constructive role in
providing fixed capital in generous amounts? The traditional argument is
that many landlords were non-resident and took little interest in their
estates apart from the collection of rents, that there was insecurity of
tenure and lack of tenant compensation for improvements and that the
employment of English and Scottish agents created tensions between
tenant and owner. David Howell has challenged this view in his study of
Welsh landownership in the nineteenth century.[28] He suggests that

> Hereditary Welsh owners, large and small alike, far from being wholly
> out of sympathy with their tenants, possessed an inborn sense of respon-
> sibility for their welfare. . . . Tenants felt no strong sense of insecurity.
> They were charged fair and often lenient rents, competition for holdings
> being the decisive factor in determining rents.[29]

and that

> the 'Welsh Land Question' – the agrarian indictment against the land-
> owners – was largely the invention of Welsh Nonconformist Radicalism
> towards achieving political democracy and national fulfilment, and
> that . . . Radical leaders . . . often pressed anti-landlord allegations
> which had no basis in fact.

If anything, Howell argues, it was the dramatic growth of Nonconformity
in early nineteenth-century Wales which challenged the traditional political and social hegemony of landlords by introducing a different set of
values:

> The landowners were disappointed and affronted at what they con-
> sidered to be the ungrateful behaviour of people whose welfare they
> had always sought to promote. They undoubtedly felt 'betrayed' and
> strongly resented the perfidy of the meddling preachers. . . . The
> 'chapel screw' was a power which landlords could not hope to meet; in
> fact spiritual influence replaced economic sanction as a subtle form of
> coercion.[30]

There are two problems with Howell's argument. First, much of his evidence comes from the records of a relatively few large estates, partly because they have survived while those of smaller estates have not. Secondly, where smaller estate papers have survived they strongly support traditional views of Welsh landowners and their attitude towards their tenants. What Howell has done is to provide a case more balanced than that presented through the vast political propaganda associated with 'The Land Question' but this does not alter either the case for under-capitalization of Welsh farming generally or the major contrasts between English and Welsh experience.

IRELAND

Population growth was the dominant feature of Irish rural change between 1700 and 1850. From less than 2.5 million in 1750, Ireland's population rose to 4.4 million in 1791, reached 6.8 million in 1821 and 8.2 million in 1841. The impact of this on the shape of the agrarian social structure is not in doubt.[31] The number of labourers and cottiers increased markedly. By 1845 cottiers (who held less than 5 acres) and wage-labourers outnumbered small and large farmers by two to one. If small farmers (who held land between 5 and 15 acres) are ranked with cottiers and labourers, the people in these three categories were four times as numerous as the elite of larger farmers (holders of over 15 acres).

There was constant tension over the mismatch between needs and resources in Ireland. Increases in food production, oats as well as potatoes, were achieved by the forcible conversion of pasture to arable. This tactic was usually accompanied by efforts to regulate the price of 'conacre' (land rented seasonally by labourers to grow their potatoes). Parallel to this were attempts to make Irish farming more commercial, a process stimulated by Britain's swelling food requirements. This led to an extension of the area devoted to corn crops in Ireland. These two processes, however, had divergent effects. Population growth led to the increased subdivision of Irish holdings while commercial farming necessitated larger estates. The shift away from pastoral farming exacerbated existing cultural tensions within Irish society particularly over the payment of clerical taxes or tithes. Between 1735 and 1823 livestock and livestock products were largely exempt from tithes and the burden of supporting the clergy of the Protestant Church of Ireland fell on those engaged in arable farming. The shift to tillage resulted in religious and particularly economically motivated opposition. In Munster and parts of Leinster potatoes were tithable, unlike the rest of Ireland, and there was a clear relationship in these areas between demographic growth, increased potato cultivation and unrest because of tithes.

The transformation of the agrarian social structure, the commercialization of agriculture and its almost exclusive dependence on the, sometimes depressed, British grain market together produced increasing tension between the large farmers and the rural poor. Though land was owned by a small elite, fewer than 10,000 aristocrats and gentry, their estates were sub-let to such an extent that for the majority of the rural poor their landlord was not the owner of the soil but a large farmer. These farmers were mostly leaseholders, with extended tenure at a fixed rent for the term of the lease. Before 1790 terms of three lives or thirty-one years, whichever lasted longer, were quite common, though shorter terms probably dominated after then. Small farmers and especially cottiers were usually tenants-at-will. As a result large farmers could adjust the rents their tenants paid while being themselves protected by the fixed lease. Labourers and cottiers often became victims of the narrowing margin between what they had to pay for food and land and the means they possessed for doing so. They were economically squeezed by rising rents, falling real wages and tithes.

CONCLUSIONS

British rural society exhibited both continuity and change between 1700 and 1850. A contrast is often drawn between the English rural social structure of large landlords, tenant farmers and hired labourers and the peasant economies of Scotland, Wales and Ireland. But rural society was far more complex. Scotland, particularly the Lowlands, exhibited many of the characteristics of the English estate system. Elements of a peasant economy can be identified in England.[32] The dangers of oversimplification have been brought out by Mick Reed:

> Capitalist producers do not all have identical material interests. Industrialists and farmers, landlords and tenants, have different interests in some respects, and make up different fractions of the capitalist class. Similarly peasant producers with land will have different interests, to a degree, from those without land, just as subsistence producers will have, again to a degree, differing concerns from simple commodity producers . . . the social formation of the English countryside was a complex one, rather than the simple polarisation favoured by historians generally, with capitalists (large or small), on the one hand, and labour on the other being the only classes of significance. . . . [33]

NOTES

1 John Clare 'Enclosure', in *John Clare: Selected Poems*, ed. J. Reeves, Heinemann, 1954, pp. 22–3.
2 Chapter 4 examines the revolutions on the land, chapter 13 those for whom paying or receiving rent was central to their lives and chapter 16 discusses the notion of paternalism..

3 M. Stanford *The Nature of Historical Knowledge*, Basil Blackwell, 1986, pp. 56–75 contains a useful methodological discussion of evidence.

4 R. Gough *The History of Myddle*, ed. D. Hey, Penguin, 1981 and a more modern analysis by D. Hey *An English Rural Community: Myddle under the Tudors and Stuarts*, Leicester University Press, 1974. K. Wrightson *English Society 1580–1680*, Hutchinson, 1982, also contains much of value.

5 R. Gough op. cit. p. 117.

6 ibid. p. 224.

7 ibid. pp. 138–9.

8 ibid. pp. 217–21.

9 David Baker has edited the 1782 census with an introduction which explains its problems as a source: *The Inhabitants of Cardington in 1782*, Bedfordshire Historical Record Society, Vol. 52, 1973. N. L. Tranter has written two articles on Cardington: 'Population and Social Structure in a Bedfordshire Parish: the Cardington List of Inhabitants, 1782', *Population Studies*, 21, 1967, pp. 261–82 and 'The Social Structure of a Bedfordshire Parish in the mid-Nineteenth Century', *International Review of Social History*, 18 (1973), pp. 90–106.

10 N. L. Tranter, 1973, op. cit. p. 91.

11 The brief analysis of Risby and Houghton Regis is based on census enumerators' returns and on a pamphlet *Victorian Risby* produced by pupils of King Edward VI Upper School, Bury St Edmunds in 1975.

12 On rural industry see G. E. Mingay (ed.) *The Victorian Countryside*, Routledge & Kegan Paul, 1981 and G. E. Mingay *Rural Life in Victorian England*, Heinemann, 1977, pp. 107–25, 169–83.

13 See D. R. Mills *Lords and Peasants in Nineteenth Century Britain*, Croom Helm, 1980, pp. 64–97 for a useful discussion of 'open' and 'closed' villages. See also D. R. Mills (ed.) *English Rural Communities*, Macmillan, 1973 and D. Spring *The English Landed Estate in the Nineteenth Century: Its Administration*, Baltimore, 1963. K. D. M. Snell *Annals of the Labouring Poor*, Cambridge University Press, 1985 and A. Armstrong *Farmworkers*, Batsford, 1988 are essential. P. Horn *Life and Labour in Rural England 1760–1850*, Macmillan, 1987 contains documents.

14 Mills, 1980, op. cit. p. 76.

15 See J. Burnett *A Social History of Housing 1815–1985*, 2nd edn, Methuen, 1986 for the question of rural housing.

16 E. P. Thompson *Whigs and Hunters: The Origins of the Black Act*, Allen Lane, 1975 is indispensable on this issue as well as being an excellent read. On poaching generally see H. Hopkins *The Long Affray – The Poaching Wars in Britain 1760–1914*, Secker & Warburg, 1985 and P. B. Munsche *Gentlemen and Poachers: The English Game Laws 1671–1831*, Cambridge University Press, 1981.

17 The most valuable studies of rural radicalism in the early nineteenth century are J. P. Dunbabin *Rural Discontent in Nineteenth Century Britain*, Faber, 1974, A. J. Peacock *Bread or Blood*, Gollancz, 1965, on the 1816 disturbances, and E. J. Hobsbawm and G. Rudé *Captain Swing*, Penguin, 1973 edn. See also R. Wells 'Rural Rebels in Southern England in the 1830s', in C. Emsley and J. Walvin (eds) *Artisans, Peasants and Proletarians 1760–1860*, Croom Helm, 1985, pp. 124–65.

18 I have drawn very heavily on B. J. Davey *Ashwell 1830–1914: the Decline of a Village Community*, Leicester University Press, 1980.

19 ibid. p. 9.

20 ibid. p. 15.

21 ibid.

22 ibid. p. 18.

23 ibid. pp. 21–2.
24 ibid. p. 26.
25 See above, chapter 16.
26 Mills, 1980, op. cit. pp. 145, 147.
27 T. C. Smout 'The Landowner and the Planned Village in Scotland 1730–1830', in N. T. Phillipson and R. Mitchison (eds) *Scotland in the Age of Improvement: Essays in Scottish History in the Eighteenth Century*, Edinburgh University Press, 1970.
28 D. W. Howell *Land and People in Nineteenth-Century Wales*, Routledge & Kegan Paul, 1977.
29 ibid. p. 149.
30 ibid. pp. 151–2.
31 S. Clark and J. S. Donnelly (eds) *Irish Peasants: Violence and Political Unrest 1780–1914*, University of Wisconsin Press, 1983 contains a useful discussion of peasantry in Ireland.
32 M. Reed 'The Peasantry of Nineteenth Century England: a Neglected Class?', *History Workshop*, 18 (1984), pp. 53–76.
33 ibid. p. 71.

18 The impact of economic growth – the urban explosion 1700–1850

No, Sir, when a man is tired of London, he is tired of life, for there is in London all that life can afford.[1]

Towns are not like villages, subject it may be, to the oversight and guidance of a single family, or a single clergyman.[2]

The notions of the 'country' and the 'town' have always roused strong feelings, evoked powerful images and created fundamental contrasts.[3] Round the 'country' have gathered either the idea of a natural way of life, of peace, innocence and simple virtue or the belief that the countryside was a place of ignorance, backwardness and limitation. Round the 'town' clustered either the idea of it as a centre of achievement, of learning and communication or as a place of worldliness, noise, ambition and corruption. Like all stereotypes these polarities contain some truth. The previous chapter considered the persistence and varied modification of rural communities during a period of economic and demographic change. This chapter will examine those changes from the viewpoint of expanding urban centres.

TOWN AND CITY – A PROBLEM OF DEFINITION

What do historians understand by a 'town' or 'urban area'?[4] There is no real agreement on what constitutes either a town or a city. Is it a physical collection of streets or houses, or is it a centre for exchange and trade? Is it a particular kind of society or the more nebulous notion of a 'frame of mind'? Has it a certain size or specific density? Using 'size' as the criterion illustrates the problem of definition very clearly. Some countries have adopted a simply numerical value. A town or city is bigger than a village community. There is no real problem with this if historians are dealing with very large settlements. But the boundary between a village and a town at the lower end of the scale is far less precise. In Denmark, for example, a settlement of 200 people constitutes a town today while in Greece the figure is 1,000 and in the United States, 2,500. There are circumstances when a numerically small settlement may have urban characteristics, like density, markets, administrative functions and others in which a numerically large settlement may still obviously be a village because of its agrarian occupational structure. 'Size' cannot, on its own, be used as a clear indicator of urban settlements.

The same problem of definition applies to the distinction between a town and a city. Saying that a city is a town which has been 'designated' a city tends to confuse perhaps more than it enlightens. Historically, in Britain cities have been associated with cathedrals. However justified this may have been it is difficult to think of St Asaph or Ely as cities in the same way as Manchester or Birmingham. The difficulty of definition stems from a desire for clarity which historically simply did not exist. While it is possible to identify those settlements in 1700 which had charters designating them towns and giving them certain rights many were little different from larger village communities in terms either of social structure or economic emphases. Rural and urban merged, in many cases almost imperceptibly. 'Urban-ness' or 'rural-ness' was a matter of degree.

Functions

Definitions, whether in economic or legal terms, or merely in terms of size, may not help historians seeking to understand the nature of urbanism, but it is still important to understand what the functions of towns and cities were in Britain in the early eighteenth century. Three major functions can be identified. First, towns reflected the economies of their surrounding areas and in a complementary way the region was dependent on the town or city for all those specialist functions which hinge on exchange and manufacture and service. Economic functions fell into several categories. Towns were important as 'marketing' centres especially for foodstuff coming from the surrounding rural area, though increasingly from a broader area, into the urban area. This was a central economic function since towns had a higher proportion of non-food producers. Towns also acted as marketing centres for goods produced in rural proto-industries and for manufactured goods produced in the towns themselves. Broadly, towns were centres of commerce and increasingly of the services associated with trade – banking, communications and finance generally. The rural and urban economies complemented each other. Secondly, towns acted as a social focus either as centres of intellectual and cultural life – universities and theatres, for example, were in towns – or as a focus of 'opportunity' for individuals who wanted upward social mobility. The latter is a reflection of the medieval notion that 'town air is free air' and the belief that the streets of towns were 'paved with gold'. Given early eighteenth-century sanitary arrangements, nothing could have been further from the truth. The vast majority of those who sought wealth and fortune in towns and cities found that they had only replaced the poverty of the countryside for the poverty of the town. Thirdly, towns and cities were administrative centres for the courts of law, bishops' palaces, local and central government and the expanding bureaucracy of the modern state.

Social and economic heterogeneity

Towns and cities were characterized by both social and economic heterogeneity. Though many of the smaller British towns maintained the same face-to-face characteristics as a villages and hamlets, demographic growth contributed to a loss of personal contact and to the substitution of different forms of communication, to diversity and specialization and to anonymity. During the eighteenth and first half of the nineteenth centuries the old urban social structure was modified by a loss of face-to-face contact, decline in the importance of kinship and a weakening of family ties. Urban instability became the norm and social mobility took on an increased significance. Towns and cities ceased to be communities in the same way that villages were.

THE EIGHTEENTH-CENTURY URBAN SETTING

How does the study of British towns between 1500 and 1700 fit into this general framework?[5] Using the typology of G. Sjoberg,[6] Clark and Slack argue that:

> there are five basic and readily recognizable characteristics of English pre-industrial towns: first, an unusual concentration of population; second, a specialist economic function; third, a complex social structure, fourth, a sophisticated political order; and fifth, a distinctive influence beyond their immediate boundaries.[7]

As we have already seen, there are problems with trying to set any precise lower level to the size of a town or to quantify when it ceased to be a village. In 1696 Gregory King included all places with between 150 and 200 houses, implying a population as low as 600 people. But this has to be related to specialized economic functions. The larger the town the greater the economic diversity. The other three characteristics were common to the majority of towns, though they were not all shared by smaller centres. The town was characterized by a more overtly stratified social pyramid than was found in the countryside. There were sharp and visible differences in wealth and status, the latter underlying much of the institutional fabric of urban life. But urban elites experienced a far higher turnover rate than their rural counterparts, more a reflection of higher levels of migration than social mobility. Towns had often secured political privileges: from the grants of markets, freedom from tolls and the jurisdiction of hundred or manorial courts to chartered status as boroughs. This led to the development of councils and courts, municipal officials and guilds to regulate the political and economic life of the community. Size determined the degree of social and political complexity and the extent to which the town had extra-urban influence. Clark and Slack admit that five elements of their urban definition 'are inevitably rather rough tools for social analysis. But it is reassuring to find them reflected in contemporary views of the town, imprecise through these were'.[8]

In 1700 Britain had a large number of towns in relation to its size and its total population, but they were almost all quite small.[9] There were up to 500 market centres with mainly local spheres of influence with populations of between 400 and 2,000. There were about fifty towns of between 2,000 and 5,000 people with regional importance. Less than thirty towns had a population of over 5,000 people and only ten had more than 10,000 people. These were the major provincial centres. London was the exception.

Country towns

The small English country towns were marketing centres and had grown in importance in the seventeenth century with the expansion of internal trade. They acted as centres of trade between local producers and consumers and as collecting and distributing points for a wider regional trade. Although the majority of their inhabitants did not work on the land, their livelihoods were directly related to farming. Many of the occupations of tradesmen and craftsmen – tailors, blacksmiths, millers, shoemakers – were found in the countryside and others were directly concerned with either processing agricultural products or making farming implements. Some of these small towns were specialist centres. Burford in Oxfordshire was a posting station and because of this was full of inns and specialized in harness-making. Shoreham in Sussex was dependent on shipbuilding. In industrial areas such as the textile regions of the West Riding or south Lancashire, most towns were service centres, a link between the area and much of the rest of the country. Populations tended to be denser and less dependent on farming. The townsmen worked up or distributed raw materials like wool, yarn or bar metal, storing and dispatching finished products outside the area. In general these towns were far less self-sufficient and relied on corn and other foodstuffs imported into the area. Historians have asked several questions about these smaller towns in the eighteenth century: how far was the earlier period of prosperity followed by decay and eclipse as the direction of internal trade tended to move in favour of the larger country towns with their better communication? Was there a limited revival in the course of the eighteenth century with the renewal of agricultural expansion?

Regional centres

English towns with populations of between 2,000 and 5,000 inhabitants were generally regional commercial centres, whose hinterlands included several market towns and were often county towns. The market might be well known outside the area for the sale of specialized goods produced in the region, besides handling larger quantities of goods than the smaller towns. They had a wider range of distributive, manufacturing and service functions, were local social centres, attracted the gentry and their families to the assizes and quarter sessions or to the diocesan centres.

Of the English towns with between 5,000 and 10,000 inhabitants about half were regional centres similar to those described above, though only Bury (Lancashire) and Bury St Edmunds (Suffolk) relied mainly on this role. Seven other regional centres in agricultural areas – Canterbury, Ipswich, Leicester, Nottingham, Salisbury, Worcester and Shrewsbury – were supported by industry in the town or in its hinterland. C. W. Chalklin argues that there seems to have been a limit to the size of regional centres in farming areas unless they provided additional employment for their growing populations. Eight towns relied almost entirely on industry. The economies of Birmingham, Coventry, Leeds, Manchester and perhaps Tiverton (Devon) were based on their own manufacture and the services provided for a largely industrial hinterland. Chatham, Portsmouth and Plymouth depended on naval shipbuilding. Finally there were three ports: Liverpool, Hull and Sunderland. They were not county towns or diocesan centres and their chief role lay in the countrywide waterborne distribution of a range of important products. The number and population of towns dependent on industry swelled in three major ways. First, they were distributing and collecting centres for the industry of their hinterlands. Secondly, because of the increased population supported by industrial areas outside the towns, there was more work for urban shopkeepers and craftsmen. Thirdly, manufacturing processes were done in most of these towns especially the finishing processes.

Provincial centres

Apart from London, there were six or seven towns with over 10,000 inhabitants which served as provincial centres – York, Exeter, Newcastle, Bristol and Norwich, plus Colchester and Yarmouth. The place of London, with its population of a quarter of a million in 1700, was paramount. It was important as the economic and social centre of the kingdom. It was the hub of overseas and internal trade and has been characterized by F. J. Fisher as 'an Engine of Economic Growth.'

The Scottish, Welsh and Irish urban experience

In Scotland the leading city in 1700 was Edinburgh with a population of about 45,000. Its importance rested on a wide range of commercial, industrial, political and cultural functions. The ordinary royal burghs were the rough equivalent of the English boroughs but were usually substantially smaller. In the sixteenth and seventeenth centuries they had suffered increasing economic competition from the aggressive merchants of Edinburgh and from the smaller baronial burghs established by local landowners to curtail the trading privileges of the larger towns. By 1700 some of the royal burghs had recovered their vitality, helped by expanding trade with England and the colonies and by the ending of their more restrictive commercial practices. The baronial burghs became the market towns of Scotland, closely integrated with the local agrarian economy, but their position was threatened after 1700 by the growth of long-distance trade.

Scottish and Welsh country towns followed the same pattern as their English equivalents. In Wales the old fortified boroughs lost their medieval military and political functions after the 1536 Act of Union. Urban growth moved away to more open towns which either, as in the case of Denbigh, grew up outside the walls of the decaying fortified centres or, like Dolgellau or Presteigne, developed as market centres which had close ties with the surrounding countryside. As in England, the smaller towns expanded in the seventeenth century but by 1700 the main growth points were larger towns and ports such as Swansea and Cardiff, which benefited from the expansion of the coal trade with England while the smaller towns fell under the increasing domination of local landowners.

In Ireland Dublin was the major urban centre with a population of about 60,000 by 1700. It was the country's leading port and presided over a network of internal trade as well as being a major textile-producing centre. Historians know most about the country towns planted in Ulster in the seventeenth century. Prior to this the only towns of any significance were Carrickfergus and Newry. Expansion was retarded by political instability and the Irish rebellion of the 1640s and Belfast had a population of only 4,000 in 1700. However, the growth of trade with England and the spread of the linen trade, both evident by 1700, led to a marked upswing in urban fortunes during the first half of the eighteenth century.

URBAN GROWTH 1700–1800

Between 1500 and 1700 urban growth throughout the British Isles had been centred on the small market towns and for many larger urban centres this had been a period of difficulty. During the eighteenth century the pendulum swung towards the larger centres. London and the main regional centres flourished as did many country towns. Most striking was the prosperity of the major ports and centres of manufacturing production.

Changing distribution of population

The change in the distribution of population in towns and cities between 1700 and 1800 can be seen in Tables 18.1 and 18.2.

Table 18.1 Population of England and Wales living in towns of 2,500+ inhabitants in 1700 and 1801

Size of town	No. of towns		Urban population	
	1700	1801	1700	1801
100,000+	1	1	575,000	948,040
20,000–100,000	2	15	52,000	702,473
10,000–20,000	4	33	55,000	428,040
5,000–10,000	24	45	168,000	313,759
2,500–5,000	37	94	120,000	332,859
Total	68	188	970,000	2,725,171

Source: P. J. Corfield *The Impact of English Towns*, Oxford University Press, 1982, p. 8.

Table 18.2 Percentage of population of England and Wales in towns of 2,500+ inhabitants in 1700 and 1801

Size of town	1700	1801
Over 100,000	11.1	10.7
20,000–100,000	1.0	7.9
10,000–20,000	1.1	4.8
5,000–10,000	3.2	3.5
2,500–5,000	2.3	3.7
All towns	18.7	30.6

Source: ibid. p. 9.

Between 1700 and 1801 the number of people living in towns in Britain increased from under a fifth of the total population to almost a third. London played a major role but the most significant growth was in the large provincial centres particularly those with expanding industries and trade. Agricultural and manufactured production and colonial imports were expanding. Town and village retail shops were spreading. Merchants, wholesalers and other middlemen increased in number and specialization. Urban professions grew and the increased wealth of the middle class helped the development of a small leisured class which congregated in urban centres. Towns expanded their role as centres for processing, manufacture and distribution. Regional centres, by contrast, appear to have expanded to their optimal size.

Pattern of growth

The pattern of growth, however, was not even among these larger centres. Both Bristol and Liverpool prospered but one more so than the other. This can be seen in Table 18.3.

Table 18.3 The changing urban hierarchy 1700–1801

Rank in 1801	1700	1750	1801
1. London	550,000	657,000	960,000
2. Manchester	10,000	18,000	84,020
3. Liverpool	6,000	22,000	78,000
4. Birmingham	7,000	23,700	74,000
5. Bristol	20,000	50,000	64,000
6. Leeds	6,000	16,000	53,000
7. Plymouth	6,500	14,000	43,194
8. Norwich	30,000	36,196	36,832
15. Exeter	14,000	16,000	17,000
17. York	11,000	11,400	16,145

Source: R. Pawson *The Early Industrial Revolution*, Batsford, 1978, pp. 213–4.

The reasons for this are complex. Liverpool had a rapidly expanding hinterland, not merely in south Lancashire but, through the canal system, in the Midlands. By 1795 it had overtaken London as the major cotton importer. Bristol did not have such a valuable hinterland and its harbour was less convenient and accessible than Liverpool's deep-sea port. Bristol also lagged behind Liverpool in dock improvements and this complacency was symptomatic of the different attitudes of the two communities. Bristol had a well established trade with Ireland by 1700 and was the leading port of the slave trade. Liverpool had no difficulty breaking into this trading system and was second to London in the Anglo-American trade by 1750. Liverpool's more northerly trading routes were safer from French privateers in the long wars after 1793 than either London or Bristol.

The importance of the hinterland is reflected in the growth of the east coast ports. In 1700 Hull and King's Lynn both had about 6,000 inhabitants. Yarmouth, the great herring fishing centre and outport of Norwich, was bigger, with about 10,000. All had extensive agricultural hinterlands and yet by 1801 Hull had outstripped the other two, 27,000 compared to Lynn's 10,000 and Yarmouth's 15,000. Unlike King's Lynn and Yarmouth. Hull's hinterland consisted of the West Riding textile area, the Sheffield cutlers but also the Nottingham hosiers and Manchester cotton manufacturers.

Figure 18.1 Towns with 2,500+ inhabitants in England and Wales, 1700

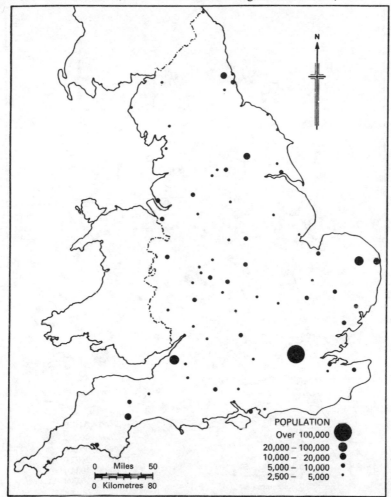

POPULATION
Over 100,000
20,000 – 100,000
10,000 – 20,000
5,000 – 10,000
2,500 – 5,000

0   Miles   50

0   Kilometres   80

Source: P. J. Corfield *The Impact of English Towns, 1700–1800*, Oxford University Press, 1982, p. 12.

Urban growth and industrial development

The development of industry was the most important influence in English provincial urban growth. By contrast in East Anglia, southern England and the West Country, stagnating or declining textile manufacture retarded the expansion of the towns which it served. The largest town was Norwich whose industry declined relative to that of Lancashire and particularly the West Riding. Norwich's population was at best stagnant after 1750 and may have declined in the 1780s and 1790s as competition intensified. Regional roles contracted in the textile centres of Worcester, Shrewsbury, Salisbury and Exeter but these towns did have alternative

Figure 18.2 Towns with 2,500+ inhabitants in England and Wales, 1801

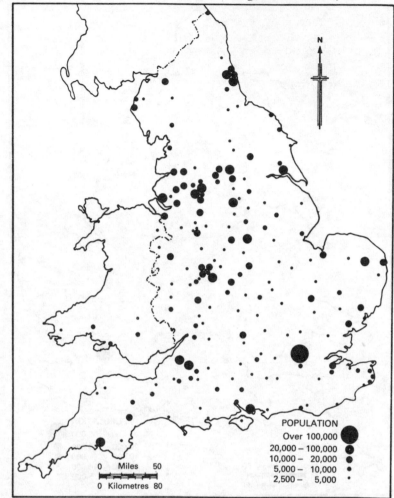

Source: P. J. Corfield *The Impact of English Towns 1700–1800*, Oxford University Press, 1982, p. 14

functions. Smaller textile centres which did not have any alternatives were very badly hit. Tiverton lost inhabitants and not until 1821 did numbers recover to those of a century before. Urban growth tended to be concentrated in the more prosperous textile-producing areas especially after 1750. This was most marked in Lancashire, particularly Manchester. Its population (including that of Salford) rose from less than 20,000 in the 1750s to over 84,000 in 1801. In view of its nodal position in south Lancashire and its historical development as a regional centre, it is understandable that cotton merchanting should have concentrated in Manchester. Because it controlled the market and manufacture of cloth, Manchester played a major role in cloth bleaching and printing and became the main supplier of certain specialized services to the industry. Finally, Manchester's importance lay in the general services it provided as the regional capital of south-east Lancashire.

In the other developing textile areas, urban growth was also impressive. The expansion of the woollen and worsted industries was the main cause of expansion in the West Riding textile areas. Unlike Manchester, Leeds did not have as complete a dominance over its hinterland. Although the population of Leeds grew about five times in the eighteenth century and reached over 48,000 by 1821, Wakefield rivalled it as an importer of food and raw materials into the region; much of the worsted trade passed through the piece halls of Halifax and Bradford and, because of the lack of interest from long-established Leeds merchants, large-scale manufacturing did not take the hold in the vicinity of Leeds that it did at Huddersfield, Bradford and Halifax after 1780. Despite this, Leeds was still larger than these other towns in 1801. The reasons lay in its position as a major communication and trading centre. The creation of the Aire and Calder Navigation in 1699 placed Leeds at its western end and the turnpike system that developed in the 1740s and 1750s had strengthened its links with other centres. These transport developments enhanced Leeds' role as the main cloth market of the region and were accompanied by its development as the main food market, wholesale distributor and entertainment centre of the region.

Nottingham and Leicester were also areas where rapid expansion took place from the 1750s. Leicester's population doubled to almost 17,000 between 1750 and 1801 while Nottingham's expanded quickly from the 1740s, reaching 17,771 in 1779 and 28,861 by 1801. Both were county towns and therefore social centres and their market function was important. This rapid expansion was, however, largely the result of the growing prosperity of the hosiery industry. While part of the knitting work was put out into neighbouring villages and smaller market towns like Hinckley and Mansfield, the number of knitters using small workshops or house rooms in both Leicester and Nottingham rose with the general growth of the industry.

The production of metal goods was also an important stimulus to urban development. In the Black Country Birmingham consolidated its metropolitan role in the later eighteenth century, becoming the hub for production and distribution in the area. This role was enhanced by its position in the canal network, which linked it with other Black Country towns like Dudley, Wolverhampton and Walsall and more distant centres like Nottingham, Coventry, Oxford and Liverpool. Several factors contributed to the multiplication of small workshops making guns, buttons, metal toys and jewellery in Birmingham itself: the availability of cheap coal after the Birmingham canal was opened in 1770, the general reputation of the town among retailers outside the area and the existence of marketing services. Between 1780 and 1820 the other towns in the Black Country were completely overshadowed by Birmingham, though all were local marketing centres as well as sites for metal workshops.

In the metalware-producing area of the West Riding, the population of Sheffield almost trebled in the later eighteenth century: 12,983 inhabitants in 1755, 26,538 in 1788 and 35,344 (including the suburb of Brightside Bierlow) in 1801. Unlike Birmingham, Sheffield's hinterland was small and it remained geographically isolated with no canal reaching the city until 1819. The skilled and specialized nature of cutlery production and tool-making and the proximity of water power helps to explain urban concentration, though similar manufacturing existed in the hamlets and villages of the area.

The organization of the shipbuilding industry, with the various trades concentrated in the yards, gave a special economic structure to the dock-yard towns. Unlike the manufacturing areas of Lancashire, Yorkshire and the Midlands, the service trades and general crafts relied specifically on the people in these towns and minimally on the population outside. The Channel dockyard towns of Plymouth and Portsmouth grew fastest, though intermittently, throughout this period, stimulated particularly by the American and French Wars after 1775. The long peace after 1815 brought this rapid expansion to an end.

Merthyr Tydfil was the only Welsh town of more than 10,000 people in 1821 which depended on manufacturing or mining. It was an isolated village in the mountains of Glamorgan until ironworks were established there in 1757. Ironstone, water power, timber and coal were all on hand though rapid expansion had to wait until the puddling and rolling process of the 1780s which allowed all the stages of ironmaking to be concentrated in one place. By 1801 Merthyr was the largest town in Wales, with a population of 7,705 and by 1821 had reached 17,704. Elsewhere industrial production was not large enough to produce towns of more than 5,000 people. Amlwch in Anglesey, a centre for mining and smelting copper ore from the Parys Mountain after 1770, appeared to be growing as quickly as Merthyr Tydfil. Its fortunes after 1800 were in marked contrast to Merthyr and revealed the effects of dependence on a single industry. While Merthyr prospered during the war years, there was a decline in employment in the Amlwch copper industry and its population fell.

Locating urban growth

In general, the larger of the rapidly growing industrial towns were in four main areas – south-east Lancashire, the West Riding, the Black Country and the east Midland counties of Nottinghamshire and Leicestershire – and even in these areas there were only six centres with more than 25,000 inhabitants in 1821, and thirteen with more than 15,000. What was new was the rate of growth rather than the creation of new towns or the transformation of primarily agricultural centres. Merthyr was the biggest exception to the general tendency that the industrial towns grew out of long-established roots. Although each town had its own distinctive social and economic characteristics, certain general factors explain the rapid growth of the larger centres. First, several types of manufacture, not all exclusively urban, were the basis of their economic prosperity. Secondly, some of these industries were highly specialized and this necessitated a pool of skilled artisans and some geographical concentration of workshops. Thirdly, finishing trades, especially textiles, were largely urban. The volume of goods being handled encouraged trades involved to group themselves around places of transfer (inns, markets, warehouses). Fourthly, production in factories was increasingly urban, especially after 1800. This can be explained by access to a growing urban labour force, but also the effect of encouraging labour from the surrounding countryside into the urban centres. Finally, towns provided general services for all the inhabitants of their hinterland and this attracted specialized crafts, trades and markets for the service of the whole region. This was aided by the role of the towns as centres for communication (turnpike roads, canals and later railways). As C. W. Chalklin says, 'big manufacturers and small independent artisans alike had an incentive to migrate to metropolitan centres such as Birmingham and Manchester'.[10]

Spas and seaside resorts

The development of spas and seaside resorts was perhaps the only original urban development of eighteenth-century England. The expansion of inland spas and the emergence of seaside resorts was, as Chalklin says,

> the result of the growing wealth and numbers in the middle and upper classes . . . the number of people able to make a summer visit or to live permanently at a resort was increasing fast . . . the opportunity to drink or bathe in the medicinal waters . . . was [often] a pretext cloaking the real motive, the lure of the entertainments provided by parades, assembly rooms and card rooms and theatres.[11]

Bath remained the undisputed leader of the inland spas and its population continued to grow. By 1801 it had 34,160 inhabitants and an influx in the second decade of the nineteenth century pushed this up to 46,588 in 1821. Why was Bath so successful? First, it was accessible. Improvements to the River Avon in the early eighteenth century assisted in the carriage of goods. Bath also rapidly established coach services and the need for good roads attracted some of the earliest investment in turnpikes. Accessibility alone was, however, insufficient to promote a spa and a second reason for Bath's success lay in its provision of suitable amenities. The eighteenth century saw the building of Georgian Bath to satisfy the need for good-quality accommodation. Rebuilding in the old lower town near the Abbey was complemented by the growth of an upper town to the north and west.

John Wood, architect and developer, was the central figure in this process starting with Queen's Square (built between 1728 and 1735) and ending with the Royal Crescent (of 1767–75). Visual unity was achieved through the widespread use of local stone, much of it from quarries on Combe Down owned by Ralph Allen, an entrepreneur and powerful local figure. Domestic developments were paralleled by the growth of public buildings: theatres, pump rooms, assembly rooms, baths. Aesthetic unity was accompanied by an archiecture of manners, of codes of etiquette.

The third reason for Bath's success lay in the nature of its patronage. Initial social prestige was achieved by the summer visits of Queen Anne in 1702 and 1703 and throughout the eighteenth century Bath drew strongly on aristocratic and fashionable London society. But its clientele was not exclusive. There was awareness of social rank here, as elsewhere in this period, but not segregation. Bath had relative social openness, an openness that became more obvious with the emergence of the middle classes in the late eighteenth century. Its size increased and with it some loss of exclusiveness and fashion occurred. Cheltenham, Tunbridge Wells, Leamington Spa and Harrogate provided alternative places to 'take the waters'. Lastly Bath depended for its success on the promotion of an attractive image which was fostered by Beau Nash in the early eighteenth century. He established, during his long period as Master of Ceremonies from 1705 to 1761, the image of the city as the natural home for elegant leisure and a code of proper behaviour and routine for all, irrespective of social origin.

The growth of the seaside resort reflected the growing scale and diversification of the leisure industry and provided increasing competition for the inland spas. Sea-bathing had been advocated on medicinal grounds since the mid-seventeenth century and bathing-machines were in use in Scarborough by the 1730s. In 1749 Dr Richard Russell wrote an influential tract advocating drinking and bathing in seawater for the treatment of glandular complaints and in 1754 he settled in Brighton, beginning an extensive promotion of the resort. Brighton's population grew rapidly after 1750: in 1761 about 2,000 people; 1783, 3,500; 1794, 5,669; 7,339 by 1801 and 24,429 by 1821. It did not overtake Bath as the premier leisure resort until 1851. Like Bath, Brighton gained social prestige from royal patronage, with the Prince of Wales visiting regularly from 1783 onwards, and it developed its own social code and routine. There were other settlements on the east and south coast which attracted leisure classes from the 1750s onwards: Margate, a cheaper version of Brighton; Weymouth, visited by George III in 1789 and 1805; Eastbourne, Scarborough, Worthing and Littlehampton. Their population was generally small and in the eighteenth century, except for Bath and Brighton, the contribution made by resorts to the overall growth of towns was small. After 1800, however, the English spas and resorts showed a faster rate of growth (in aggregate) than the great manufacturing towns and ports.

URBAN GROWTH AFTER 1800

The process of urban growth that began in the eighteenth century continued unabated after 1800.[12] Urban populations increased much faster than that of Britain as a whole. The major difference between eighteenth- and nineteenth-century urban growth was qualitative rather than quantitative – the development of 'urbanization as a way of life':

Furthermore this phenomenon was not only quantitative, in the demographic and economic order of things, but also qualitative, socially and culturally, turning British mentalities and conditions of life upside down.

. . . in the course of this urbanisation a new visual scheme emerged together with a new system of social relations and a new life style – in brief a new civilisation came into being.[13]

What has been called 'galloping urbanization' occurred in the first half of the nineteenth century. The urban population grew by an average of 27 per cent every decade between 1801 and 1851, a movement which accelerated after 1820 and reached its peak between 1841 and 1851 when it was accentuated by the influx of Irish immigrants. Towns with populations of more than 2,500 absorbed 67 per cent of the total increase of England's population between 1801 and 1841. Rural regions had a large excess of births over deaths, a result of migration from country areas towards urban centres and of the transfer of labour from agriculture to industry and services.

Industrial concentration and urban growth

Industry was increasingly concentrated in towns which before 1800 often had been more commercial than industrial. This concentration was due to the expansion of large-scale industry, the increasing use of steam power, railway building which improved the supply of foodstuffs and raw materials to larger centres, external economies resulting from the development of industries and services ancillary to the staple industries in each centre as well as the existence of a ready labour force. Growth was cumulative once industrial activities had taken root in a town and conditions developed favourable to a new growth. In some cases industrial and communication developments created specialist new towns. Railway towns like Crewe, Swindon, Rugby and Doncaster developed at the site of important junctions or railway workshops. There were also towns, like Barrow-in-Furness and Middlesbrough, resulting from the working of new ore deposits and the ironworks which were set up near them. But these were exceptional cases; it was usually existing towns which developed and there was little change in the urban hierarchy between 1800 and 1850.

Rural–urban migration

Rural–urban migration gathered momentum in the 1830s and 1840s but the extent to which urban growth was primarily the result of this varied from one place to another. In 1851 more than half the adult populations of Leeds, Sheffield and Norwich were born in the town but the percentage fell to a quarter in Manchester, Bradford and Glasgow and was even smaller in Liverpool. In London immigration seems to have been responsible for about half of the total increase between 1800 and 1850 and this gave rise to serious problems of integration and assimilation for the many newcomers, particularly in the Irish colonies, who lived in defined areas. Apart from the Irish, the nature of migration to towns was not one of long-distance moves. Within England there was no large-scale inter-regional migration, but a complex of small local movements. In particular there was no significant movement from the agricultural south to the industrial north. The northern industrial towns recruited their immigrants from the surrounding country areas and 'they also had a strong natural increase due to high fertility. Industrial regions produced their own labour-force . . . which became an essential factor in the change of demographic balance between north and south.'[14]

Rates of growth depended on the type of town. Small market towns without significant industrial resources grew more slowly than the total urban population. Towns of between 2,500 and 20,000 inhabitants accounted for 14.5 per cent of the total population of England and Wales in 1801 and only 15.3 per cent in 1841. On the other hand rapid progress was registered by both the many medium-sized industrial centres such as the cotton towns of Lancashire, mining towns like Wigan, ironmaking or processing towns like Wolverhampton and seaside resorts and inland spas. The most dramatic urban growth, however, occurred in the large and very large towns. In 1801 there were 16 towns with between 20,000 and 100,000 inhabitants and only one over 100,000 but by 1841 there were 48 and 7 respectively. With the exception of London – these were the large provincial and particularly regional capitals like Manchester, Birmingham, Liverpool, Sheffield and Leeds.

Engels argued in 1845 that 'What is true of London, is true of Manchester, Birmingham, Leeds, is true of all great towns. . . . Everywhere barbarous indifference, hard egotism on one hand, and nameless misery on the other. . . .'[15] and J. G. Kohl, a German visitor to Britain a year earlier commented:

> The manufacturing cities of England are none of them very attractive or pleasing in appearance, but Leeds is, perhaps, the ugliest and least attractive town in all England. In Birmingham, Manchester and other such cities, among the mass of chimneys and factories, are scattered, here and there, splendid newsrooms, or clubs, and interesting

exchanges, banks, railway stations, or Wellington and Nelson monuments. Leeds has none of these.[16]

What characterized England's urban development after 1700 was the diversity of experience it created. Urban growth was neither as uniform as Engels intimated nor as monotonous and uninviting as Kohl believed.

A DIVERSITY OF URBAN GROWTH

What created this diversity? Kohl attributed Birmingham's lack of distinctive architecture to its industrial structure of small workshops compared to Manchester's large factories. Alexis de Tocqueville visited both cities in 1835, commenting

> At Manchester a few great capitalists, thousands of poor workmen and little middle class. At Birmingham, few large industries, many small industrialists. At Manchester workmen are counted by the thousand, two or three thousand in the factories. At Birmingham the workers work in their own houses or in little workshops in the company of the master himself. . . . Separation of classes, much greater at Manchester than at Birmingham.[17]

Certainly, housing in Manchester and Birmingham was very different. In Birmingham few houses were divided into flats, cellars were little utilized and the quality of street cleansing and drainage was better than in Manchester and other Lancashire towns. Birmingham's better housing was attributed by contemporaries to its social structure as much as to better natural drainage. As Richard Dennis says:

> It is tempting to arrange England's industrial cities along a continuum of social and spatial structure from Manchester at one extreme, by way of Leeds where factories in the woollen industry were smaller than in Lancashire cotton, to Sheffield and Birmingham, the principal examples of workshop industry. But such a continuum ignores the major seaports . . . and it suggests, falsely, that the satellites of each of the major cities could also be ranged along a continuum paralleling that of the regional capitals.[18]

Engels may have described Manchester as 'the classic type of a modern manufacturing town' but how typical was it, or Birmingham, of England's urban growth and problems? Contemporaries reflected the obsessions of the age, the cultural and political prejudices of observers and the expectations of their readers more than any discussion of an 'objective' reality. There is the danger of caricature in the search for literary effect as, for example, in Dickens' description of the monotony of Coketown in *Hard Times*. It was important to writers like Engels that all towns should be alike, a viewpoint motivated by the need to convince readers of the universality of the class struggle, of unscrupulous landlords and of exploitation in the market-place and in work. Official reports in the 1840s also stressed the 'sameness' of problems to justify central government intervention and national legislation. The reality was one of intense diversity rather than 'sameness' – this is evident even in Dickens' *Hard Times* – and nineteenth-century towns and cities do not fit easily into any Manchester–Birmingham continuum, useful though this model is for historians. The first effect of industrialization may have been to differentiate communities but contemporaries maintained that all towns experienced, or thought they experienced, the same problems. Historians have identified various dimensions by which towns and cities differed: socio-political structure, the strength and diversity of religious adherence, the significance of migrant populations and a variety of demographic characteristics, as well as by economic function and size.

Socio-political structures

Two dimensions – socio-political structure and religious affiliation – illustrate the diversity of urban growth. John Foster shows the diversity of social and political response in medium-sized industrial towns.[19] He argues that difference in class formation between Oldham, South Shields and Northampton initially followed the Manchester–Birmingham continuum. There was a clear distinction between employed and employer in Oldham while Northampton had a self-employed or small master petit bourgeoisie. It was in the impersonal factory character of the former, Foster argues, that a strong sense of working-class consciousness developed and where there was considerable potential for working-class political control. Foster's conflict model has, however, not gone unchallenged. Oldham factories were on a smaller scale, averaging only 79 workers per cotton mill in 1841 compared to 281 in Blackburn. Working-class control in Oldham was achieved, D. S. Gadian maintains,[20] not by conflict but by inter-class collaboration and that control was lost in the 1840s when the interests of employers and workers diverged. Gadian argues that Oldham was not the place to illustrate Foster's thesis:

> In such communities as Stockport, Blackburn, Manchester, Bolton and Ashton-under-Lyne, where large-scale factory industry had developed furthest, working and middle class reformers were unable or unwilling to achieve the effective level of class collaboration that was managed in Oldham and Rochdale.[21]

In the West Riding woollen industry mechanization occurred later, units of production were smaller and employers showed less interest in the conditions of the working population. The result was a heightened sense of political activism rather than trade unionism. In Lancashire, by contrast, ownership of production lay with large and often paternalistic owners and here it was trade unions that were important in an attempt to control production through negotiating better working conditions and wages. This accounts for the less politicized nature of working-class action in urban Lancashire.

Religious affiliations

It was possible to distinguish between towns in terms of the political party and religious denomination associated with the dominant groups. Mill-owners and ironmasters were not all liberal Nonconformists. Many originated in local landed society or in the ranks of commerce and often subscribed to a form of radical Tory Anglicanism. This was reflected in their paternalistic attitudes to workers. The effect of this can be illustrated by comparing Burnley with Blackburn, Preston and Bolton. Burnley was the last cotton district to develop in the first half of the nineteenth century. Employers were more often new arrivals than from local families and were neither rich enough nor sufficiently confident to provide the paternalism offered by long-established employers in the other towns. Wages were lower, working conditions poorer, continuity of employment less assured in Burnley and consequently politicized working-class action was more common. In Blackburn, Bolton and Preston conditions were better and there was a closer correlation between the political and religious affiliations of employers and workers.

The religious profile of towns can be ascertained from the 1851 Religious Census. K. S. Inglis has developed an index of attendance which simply divides total attendances in an area (including double attendances) by total population.[22] Though there are problems with this approach some interesting patterns emerge. The index of attendance for the whole of England and Wales was 61 but, with the exception of York and Wakefield, the only towns to exceed this were south of the River Trent. All the major textile towns of north-west England, the principal towns of north-east England and Liverpool, Manchester, Birmingham and Leeds recorded an index of below 49.7 (the average of all towns of more than 10,000 inhabitants). The pattern becomes more complicated when the denominational structure of each town is considered. Liverpool, Preston, Manchester, Bolton and Blackburn all shared high attendance at Catholic churches and relatively low attendance at Nonconformist chapels, but other Lancashire towns – Oldham and Bury, for example – deviated from this pattern. Salford and Macclesfield had equal proportions of all three religious groups and shared this profile with Newcastle, Walsall and Coventry.

URBAN GROWTH IN WALES, SCOTLAND AND IRELAND

Wales

Urban growth in Wales, Scotland and Ireland was, with notable exceptions, far less dramatic than in England. In 1700 Welsh towns were small in size. Towns of military origin like Caernarfon had evolved as administrative centres and the county towns were the sites for the Court of Great Sessions which met twice annually and for the quarter sessions. Both these types of town became centres for lawyers and professional men whose services were in increasing demand as economic activity accelerated.

During the eighteenth century Welsh towns were undergoing change though architecturally and from the standpoint of town planning they did not compare favourably with some English or even Irish towns that were developing at this time. There is Georgian architecture in Wales but it is fairly well distributed. Georgian houses can be found in Beaumaris, Brecon, Ruthin, Haverfordwest, Aberystwyth, Chepstow and Monmouth. Two trends in urban life became apparent by the early nineteenth century: first, the desire for economic expansion and second, the growth of civic pride. Increased resources resulted in a growth of public buildings: the development of Nonconformity led to the building of considerable numbers of chapels; town and guild halls were built using corporation money and private subscriptions.

Improved communications between towns and especially with London played a central role in urban development. By 1765 Brecon was connected to London by post-coach and by 1800 Cardiff had daily coach services to London. This encouraged the opening of inns along the routes which acted as post-offices. Much transport was seaborne and river ports as well as small coastal towns owed their prosperity to this. The expansion of agriculture, seasonal fishing and the development of industry in their hinterland contributed to their prosperity. Aberystwyth, for example, profited from mining developments and by 1800 the town was largely under the control of mining speculators. It procured a Harbour Act in 1780 which increased trade and led to a growth in the number of merchants who opened businesses in the town.

As in England, spas became very popular in Wales after 1700. Theophilus Evans is credited with discovering wells at Llanwrytd and Builth. By 1740 Llandrindod Wells was the 'Welsh Bath' and Trefriw became the spa of North Wales, though was never as popular as the spas of Brecknockshire and Radnorshire. The inland spas, unlike their English counterparts, were less able to compete with the rise of seaside resorts. Some parish authorities paid the expenses of invalids to go to the seaside for a cure, Lampeter, for example, as early as 1779. Swansea, already developing as an industrial centre by 1800, also wanted to be regarded as a fashionable resort. The laying of a horse tramway in 1804 to convey visitors to Mumbles was the world's first passenger railway. Resorts in north-east Wales were slower to develop but Abergele was described in 1797 as a much-frequented place and Colwyn and Llandudno had already begun to develop by the 1830s.

Industrial development played the most important part in Welsh urban development. Towns which were not incorporated were often centres of various trades because they were free from guild control. Dolgellau became a centre for cloth finishing and Bala for the stocking and hat trade; Wrexham, with a variety of small artisan workshops, became a centre for cloth dealers from Yorkshire as well as a banking centre for a growing industrial area. The Severn valley towns of Welshpool, Newtown and Llanidloes were the only places, with the exception of the lower Teifi valley, where a factory-based industry was successfully established. The effect of industrial growth on urban development was most apparent in South Wales and by 1801 Merthyr Tydfil had a population of over 7,000 people, increasing by half every decade between 1801 and 1851. Developments at Aberdare were comparable with those at Merthyr but at the heads of the Monmouthshire valleys industrialization caused more diffuse settlement. Settlement around Ebbw Vale was dispersed along the Ebbw Fawr and Ebbw Fach valleys and the town grew out of a collection of industrial villages. Pontypool, a centre of ironworking and tinplate manufacture, was also a settlement strung out in a linear pattern along the river. Tredegar was probably the nearest to a nucleated town in this area. In the early nineteenth century industrial South Wales saw a dramatic increase in population, largely through immigration. The Welsh-speaking population gathered at the top of the valleys especially round Beaufort, with the English and Irish further down. Racial, linguistic and religious differences as well as geography retarded their assimilation with important consequences for public order as the 'Scotch Cattle' violence demonstrated in the 1820s and 1830s.

Scotland

The balance of Scotland's population did not alter radically until the 1780s, and in this predominantly rural society towns were small. Edinburgh was the exception, with a population of over 47,000 in the early eighteenth century. It had the reputation for the worst tenement housing in Europe where people's social status depended on the layer of the tenement in which they lived. The better-off sections of society were sandwiched between the less well-off. Edinburgh built upwards rather than outwards because of defensive and geographical limitations. Large-scale expansion was, however, made possible by the building of the New Town from the 1760s. This partly political decision was designed to attract Scottish gentry back from London by turning Edinburgh into a modern social and economic metropolitan centre. James Craig's plan, accepted in 1767, aimed at preventing some of the old difficulties and defects and a 1771 Act limited the height of houses to three storeys on the main streets and two on intermediate streets. His plan was based on a gridiron pattern with a square at each end connected by three parallel avenues (Princes, George and Queen Streets). Initial enthusiasm for the project waned after the collapse of the Ayr Bank in 1772 and vigorous house construction did not restart until the mid-1780s. After 1800, when the streets in Craig's plan were practically all built up, the New Town was extended to both north and west with the addition of many new squares (Charlotte Square designed by Robert Adam after 1800 for example), circuses and avenues, and building enjoyed a considerable boom until 1830. Though the City Council regulated the design of houses in a very general fashion, there was no attempt to impose architectural uniformity until the Adams family became involved in the 1790s. Consequently the overall effect lacked the homogeneity of Bath and the new houses provided accommodation for only a fraction of the Scottish people. The building of the New Town led to a social segregation which the tenements did not. The wealthy, urban gentry, merchants and professional people moved to the New Town leaving the traders, shopkeepers, artisans and poor in the Old Town.

Glasgow's growth from a modest cathedral and college town to a major trading and industrial centre relied on the Clyde estuary to the west and deposits of coal and iron to the east. Unlike Edinburgh, Glasgow did not suffer from geographical restrictions. It developed along the Clyde valley, which explains why Glasgow grew faster, particularly after 1780. Clustered round the Clyde were industrial centres for which Glasgow was the focus: Paisley, Kilmarnock, Motherwell, Airdrie, Coatbridge. The experience of these satellite towns had much in common with the industrial metropolis of Glasgow. Textiles initially set the tenor of life but during the first half of the nineteenth century heavy industry, iron and mining became more important. Some towns remained largely agrarian, continuing to service farming regions and providing marketing points. The market towns of Perth, Inverness and Dumfries, like their English and Welsh counterparts, expanded but not on the same scale as the industrial centres. What industries they had tended to be closely related to agriculture.

Like Edinburgh and Glasgow, the two remaining principal Scottish cities – Aberdeen and Dundee – had long histories. Aberdeen did not grow at a comparable rate to the cities of the Lowlands largely because of its northern location. As a result it did not have the same environmental or social problems as Glasgow and Edinburgh. Neither did it suffer from excessive economic specialization or narrow market dependence. Whereas Glasgow attracted the Irish and the Highlanders on a large scale, migration into Aberdeen was highly regional. Aberdonians were to a very large degree north-eastern stock. By 1850 Aberdeen had certain striking characteristics. First, it possessed economic resilience based on the adaptability of business leaders who found new means of investment and employment when old ones faded. The railways, linked to the improved port facilities, stimulated and focused trade. Secondly, its population grew slowly and was absorbed into the economic structure without the political problems experienced in Glasgow and its satellite towns. Even when Aberdeen's cotton industry was at its height there was no large industrial proletariat. Thirdly, Aberdeen did not adopt either the heavy industrial development associated with Glasgow or Edinburgh's combination of the professions, landed wealth and small-scale enterprise. In the eighteenth and early nineteenth centuries it traded with the Baltic, had a fishery industry and was the marketing and cultural centre for the agrarian north-east. Improvements to farming in its hinterland after 1770 brought increasing prosperity to Aberdeen, which acted as the collecting centre for shipping farm produce south. In 1832 a new process for polishing granite added to the city's exports. But textiles supplied most employment and throughout this period Aberdeen was the regional centre for the putting-out system of linen and woollen spinning and weaving, sustaining employment and incomes in the crofts and village cottages. The development of the factory system threatened the small-scale subsistence farming of the area and crofters had already moved to the city in considerable numbers by 1800. By 1845 a quarter of Aberdeen's population was employed in factories along the River Don. By 1850 Aberdeen, unlike Glasgow or Dundee, had a diversified textile sector, shared by cotton, wool and linen. But distance from southern markets and lack of coal were both severe handicaps and after the collapse of the railway boom in 1847 local manufacturers experienced considerable difficulty. Only two textile factories survived the 1850s. The collapse of an industry from 81,000 bales of textiles leaving Aberdeen harbour in 1845 to only 9,000 ten years later brought widespread unemployment and it was not until after 1860 that a changed and more specialized textile manufacture revived.

Dundee developed a mixture of small industries, including textiles, during the eighteenth century. But from the 1820s jute challenged flax as Dundee's staple textile. Mills, together with working-class tenements, defined the town and flax and jute dominated everything. Dundee was a polarized city, economically and socially. It lacked a substantial middle class and, largely as a result, was highly proletarianized with clear and generally antagonistic relations between the jute masters and their factory workers. Though Dundee had other industries, by 1850 jute dominated the life of the city which depended on a fairly narrow set of markets. To this was added the social imbalance that stemmed from the jute labour force in which women predominated. This created a low-wage industry and led to increasing congestion of labour round the mills in industrial slums. In many families the women were the wage-earners and there was often a reversal of sex roles: masterful women dominated husbands who 'boiled the kettle'. There was also a fierce class distinction among women between the aristocratic weavers and the more lowly spinners.

By 1850 Scotland had four principal city regions and four distinctive modes of urban life. In many senses Scotland had two national capitals – Edinburgh and Glasgow – which, though only 40 miles apart and sharing a common heritage, were distinctive geologically, climatically, racially and spiritually. Dundee and Aberdeen were outlying urban cores. Glasgow, the giant among Scottish cities, had developed a pattern of heavy industry based upon world markets. Edinburgh enjoyed the advantages of a metropolitan centre and its service industries, though its growth had been limited to half that of Glasgow. Aberdeen showed the ability to adapt to changing circumstances and markets. Dundee, by contrast, became a city dominated by a single product and the low-wage female labour it had generated.

Ireland

Ireland was also a predominantly rural country and in 1725 under 10 per cent of the population lived in the eight largest towns. Most towns were small, apart from Dublin and Cork. Dublin was the largest town in Ireland and its population was already growing rapidly in the 1720s and 1730s while the national population grew only slowly, a reflection of changes in economic organization which enhanced its importance. The proportion of the customs revenue from imports and exports collected in Dublin rose from 40 per cent in the second half of the seventeenth century to over 50 per cent by the 1750s. The city also handled most of Ireland's foreign banking needs, except those of Cork. Capital was provided for the development of the linen industry in Ulster and the bulk of the linen produced was, at least initially, exported through Dublin. The development of inland transport focused on Dublin with the first stage-coaches radiating from the city. By 1800 Dublin's population was almost 200,000. Cork, with a population of between 70,000 and 80,000 by 1800 (plus some 20,000 in adjacent rural districts), was the only Irish town to bear comparison with Dublin in the eighteenth century. Cork had an extensive trade in butter, beef and yarn and, apart from Dublin, was the only extensive banking centre in the country. It was Ireland's most cosmopolitan port, one of the major ports of the entire Atlantic economy, and supplied provisions to every country in Europe. Dublin, by contrast, focused its trade on mainland Britain.

In 1725 eight of the ten major towns were ports. Kilkenny, the only large inland town, ranked next in importance to Dublin, Cork and Limerick. Of the 23 major towns and cities in 1798 six were inland towns: in rank order, Kilkenny, Clonmel, Bandon, Cashel, Lisburn and Armagh. Existing towns grew significantly after 1750 and many unimportant villages also grew rapidly, expanding round a market for livestock, produce or cloth. Although towns were neither more numerous nor larger in the north. Towns with an active linen market, like Dungannon, Armagh and Strabane, were brought prosperity by commerce rather than the manufacture of cloth.

Towns could not have expanded without the growth of inland and foreign trade. All the major towns were deeply involved in trade, especially as seaports. They were connected with the interior by road or waterways and improved transport facilities and internal markets grew up as part of an internal network of communications serving the ports.

Villages and small towns flourished around markets and these subsidiary centres grew rapidly in the second half of the eighteenth century.

The first half of the nineteenth century, particularly between 1815 and 1841, saw towns as a whole failing to keep pace as they had earlier with rural population growth and few major towns, apart from Dublin and Belfast, expanded during this period. Many medium and smaller centres stagnated and some even declined. Maritime centres like Kinsale and Cobh, tied up with naval requirements, are examples of this. Estate towns and villages, and textile centres outside the north, also stagnated. This did not apply to all towns. The rapid increase in communications resulted in some towns expanding their economic importance and this was reflected in growing populations. Location was the key reason for this. For example, Youghal, Middleton, Mallow, Kanturk and Tralee grew while ports like Dingle, Cobh and Kinsale and industrial centres like Bandon declined or stagnated. In Galway, Gort, Tuam and Ballinaslow – market centres – grew while Loughrea, a textile centre, declined. As the main centre of the import–export trade, Dublin continued to grow, reaching 232,726 by 1841, even if its textile industries were in decline. The linen towns in counties Cavan, Monagham and Longford ceased to expand but Derry, Dungannon and Coleraine and the linen market towns of Armagh, Down and Antrim grew, even if only modestly. Belfast and some of its satellite towns grew. Belfast, in particularly, saw rapid growth: 18,320 in 1791, 37,277 in 1821 and 75,308 in 1841. Newtownards and Bangor also grew rapidly in the same period. The three were, with their spinning mills and urban cotton weavers, the first industrial towns of Ireland.

Urban growth in Wales, Scotland and Ireland occurred at different rates and for different reasons between 1700 and 1850. While in Ireland growth was concentrated largely in the eighteenth century, the expansion in South Wales was largely after 1780. In each of these countries, unlike England, urbanization began from a much smaller base, though the social and environmental problems thrown up were common to all the United Kingdom.

LONDON

London was the exception among British towns throughout this period.[23] Its size and dominance made it a model for any aspiring provincial town. It was a very complex place, not falling into any one specialist category. London was the capital city, the locus of both court and government, an international port and finance centre, focus of a growing overseas empire, an immense market and centre for internal trade, a communication centre, the location of a number of substantial manufacturing industries and a social resort. By comparison with other European capitals, London was outstanding for its size and economic and social diversity.

In 1700 London and its environs had a population of 575,000 people, rising to 900,000 by 1801. During the eighteenth century London showed signs of structural change and its population did not increase much more rapidly than the population of the country as a whole. London retained immense powers of attraction, and demographic growth was fuelled by immigration from rural Britain. Urban mortality rates were high, particularly in the first half of the century, and the London conurbation needed a minimum annual recruitment rate of 8,000 people to maintain its growth. Up to three-quarters of those living in London during the eighteenth century may have been born outside the capital. It was a magnet for considerable Welsh, Scottish and Irish migration in the course of the century. By the 1780s there were some 14,000 Catholic households, mainly Irish in origin and centred in St Giles and Holborn. There were fewer Protestant Scots and their residences were more dispersed. Foreign communities settled in the eighteenth-century capital: some 20,000 Jews largely in the East End, French Huguenots in Spitalfields and small numbers of Negroes from North American shipping. London's 'pull' over migrants became more geographically constricted after 1700 and rural migrants from the north and Midlands were more likely to turn to more local growth points.

London's own economy showed signs of change in the eighteenth century. It remained a huge and demanding market for food and raw materials – in the 1720s Defoe vividly described the impact of the economic tentacles of the capital on local economies. This trade grew after 1700 and became better organized though by the 1790s all the major wholesale produce markets – Billingsgate, Bear Key and Queenhithe, Smithfield and Covent Garden – were experiencing severe congestion. Trade in grain and meat became increasingly concentrated. The London grain market was in the hands of fourteen major dealers by 1800 and so was Smithfield. In other wholesale trades control was less marked and markets were organized more diversely.

A large proportion of all English imports and exports was conveyed through London. In 1700 a quarter of the capital's workforce may have been employed on trades connected with the port. An increase in the size of ships after 1700 produced major problems from congestion and delays and in 1796 a parliamentary committee was set up to investigate remedies. This led to a spate of dock-building in the first decade of the nineteenth century: the West India Dock opened in 1802, the London Dock at Wapping in 1805, the East India Dock in 1806 and the Surrey Docks on the south bank the following year. Most of London's trade lay with mainland Europe and in the East and West Indies trades, resulting in its growing role as a centre for the lucrative re-exporting trade. London became a great entrepôt, a clearing house. By contrast it played little part in Anglo-Irish trade and the bulky coal-export business. As a result London's overall proportion of England's overseas trade fell gradually from 75.8 per cent in 1699–1701, to 69.8 per cent in 1752–3 and 63.4 per cent by 1790.

London's role as the major English trading centre was, however, confirmed by its growing specialization as an international banking and financial centre. Marine insurance was institutionalized round Lloyd's coffeehouse. Stockbrokers met in the Exchange coffee-house. A central banking clearing house was established in Lombard Street in 1775. These institutions, with the Bank of England, provided specialist services for provincial and manufacturing business communities and during the eighteenth century London superseded Amsterdam as Europe's premier money market.

Increasing specialization also occurred among London's heterogenous industries. Most permanent were those associated with London's role as port and entrepôt. Colonial raw materials were refined and processed. London specialized in the construction of large ocean-going ships, particularly for the East India trade. Commerce-linked industries expanded after 1700 with the growth of foreign and internal trade. London was the only mass market in 1700 and, despite the growth of other centres, largely retained that position throughout the eighteenth century, if not to 1850.

Commercial and industrial growth resulted in a greatly strengthened service economy. The central position of the law courts encouraged the growth of the legal profession. London was also a major educational centre, though it did not have a university until after 1828. The medical profession was to be found in large numbers in the capital either in private practice or attached to the large London hospitals. It was a social centre, attracting the polite to Court for the winter season, for 'culture' in the clubs, salons, galleries and theatres and for the semi-licit market in sexual services.

In 1700 London was a fairly compact urban area hugging the great bend of the River Thames from Westminster to Wapping. By 1800 it had, however, begun to extend northwards away from the river. Two further bridges were built in the eighteenth century, Westminster Bridge in 1750 and Blackfriars in 1769, giving three access points to the south. In 1801 about 15 per cent of the population of this 'greater London' lived south of the river. Within this growing urban area different sections of the town catered for different specialisms and these distinctions were evident in housing and economic and social structures. Fashionable society focused on the West End of London, itself expanding north and west. Most of the great estate developments of the eighteenth century were concentrated here. This fashionable society was serviced by large amounts of labour and the West End was not as monolithic as its architectural image might suggest. Close to the respectable West End was Seven Dials in the parish of St Giles, one of the most populous, poverty-stricken and notorious areas of eighteenth-century London. It contained a third of the capital's beggars and was considered one of London's most dangerous criminal 'rookeries'. The old centre in the City of London was much less fashionable and its population fell from an estimated 87,000 in 1750 to 78,000 by 1801. What new building there was tended to confirm the City's increasing importance as a financial and business centre: the Mansion House between 1739 and 1753, the repair of London Bridge in 1757–9 when it lost the last of its shops and the gothic refronting of the Guildhall in 1789.

A large and fast-expanding industrial and commercial zone spread out to the north, east and south from the old city centre. As many of the trades were domestic these were among London's most densely populated residential areas. The metropolitan complex was surrounded by a loosely organized outer ring of suburban villages, where City merchants and West End grandees retreated to escape the crowds, smog and smell of town. Hampstead, Highgate, Epping and Stratford attracted the affluent City gentry.

London's population continued to grow in the first half of the nineteenth century, reaching 2,362,236 by 1851. Concentrated urban development south of the river was still limited, principally to Lambeth, Southwark and Bermondsey, though Kennington, Newington, Walworth and Camberwell were being rapidly filled in, a process aided by more bridges being built across the Thames. To the north suburbs extended no further than Camden Town or Islington and to the west Kensington Gardens marked the boundary. On the east, although the marshes of the River Lea were a limitation on expansion, the city still fell considerably short of them. Railways opened up further expansion. In many ways London remained a pre-industrial city but this was in the process of changing. Gas lighting made streets safer at night: Pall Mall was illuminated as early as 1807. The establishment of the Metropolitan Police in 1829 led to the introduction of a system of official regulation and restraint; this reinforced changes in people's behaviour, which Dorothy George saw beginning in the second half of the eighteenth century.

London's importance as a centre of manufacturing industry in the nineteenth century is frequently overlooked by historians. London was, and remained throughout the nineteenth century, the country's principal centre of production. London was a centre for many craft industries and several were highly localized: silk, in decline after 1800, in Spitalfields; leather in Bermondsey; hatting in Southwark; clock and watch-making in Clerkenwell; coach-making round Long Acre and sugar-refining in Whitechapel. This intense concentration of some industries in small, separated areas together with its opposite, the dispersal of many industries throughout London, helps to explain why many contemporary observers, and historians who use their work, give the impression that London was not the capital of manufacturing industry.

In London the typical unit of production and distribution in the first half of the nineteenth century was small. In 1851 about 20,700 masters employed less than six men, only 217 masters employed more than 50

Figure 18.3 The growth of London 1700–1831

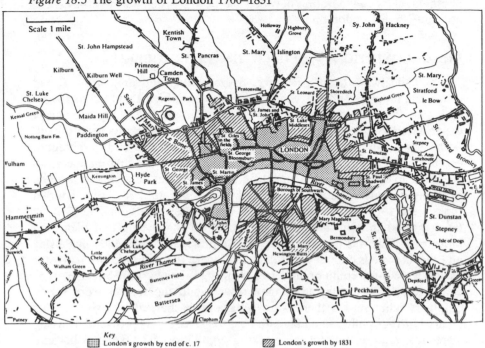

Key

▦ London's growth by end of c. 17   ▨ London's growth by 1831

Source: M. Reed *The Georgian Triumph 1700–1830*, Routledge & Kegan Paul, 1983, p. 152.

men, and 80 masters over a hundred. By the 1840s many workers believed that the number of large employers had increased and were continuing to emerge out of the shoals of small masters. Though London had a large number of independent artisans and many workers were hand craftsmen often working at piece rates, there is little doubt that the second quarter of the nineteenth century saw the emergence of a metropolitan proletariat. In the 1851 census 80 per cent of the total active population can be assigned to the 'working class'.

London was also a centre of a luxury market serving not only its more permanent residents but the wealthy of the whole nation. This ensured the continuance of quality production and highly skilled craftsmen, even if they increasingly worked within a capitalist structure. On the other hand there was a vast mass market to be satisfied. This was achieved not by using steampower mechanization or factory production but by expanding the workforce, lowering wages (particularly for women) and as a result manufacturing low-priced goods. The development of capitalist practices and 'sweated' trades ran parallel. By these means metropolitan craftsmen too were proletarianized and their 'independence' successfully attacked. Despite superficial socio-economic similarities between Birmingham and

Sheffield, class collaboration between the bourgeoisie and the artisans did not flourish in London.

URBAN CONDITIONS – A PUBLIC HEALTH PROBLEM

Towns had always been insanitary, overcrowded and unhealthy. Rapid urban and industrial growth exacerbated these problems and led to awareness that the social hazards being created far exceeded any previously experienced.[24] There were enormous technical problems to be resolved. Some towns already had piped water supplies in the early eighteenth century and George Sorocold of Derby was one of the first engineers to specialize in this branch of engineering. But water was delivered in wooden or lead pipes and was totally untreated. It was not until 1817 that wooden pipes were forbidden in London. By 1800 water was being purified by being passed through filter beds first used in the dyeing and bleaching industries. This was not extended to drinking water until 1804 in Paisley and the filter beds built at Chelsea in 1827 were the first in London. Water closets were quite common in better-quality houses by 1800 but they were connected to cesspools rather than sewers and the former were rarely emptied. What sewers there were generally discharged into rivers. This created further pollution and health hazards since rivers provided drinking water for large sections of the working population. The Thames became so heavily polluted that the smell from 'the Great Stink' compelled Parliament to abandon its sittings on several occasions.

There were several reasons why urban conditions were not improved until after 1850. First, there was a total ignorance of the existence of water-borne bacteria throughout this period. The relationship between filthy conditions and poor health was not established conclusively until the 1830s and 1840s. Despite local surveys dealing with the relationship between conditions and disease like those for London and Chester in 1774, Manchester in 1795, Dublin in 1806 and James Kay's survey of Manchester in 1832, it was not until the publication of Edwin Chadwick's *Report on the Sanitary Condition of the Labouring Population of Great Britain* in 1842, the Royal Commission on the Health of Towns 1844–5, which had been set up to validate Chadwick's personal finding, and the establishment of a relationship between infected water supplies and the incidence of cholera by John Snow that 'official' opinion recognized the extent of the problem.

Secondly, what efforts were made between 1700 and 1830 tended to be on a purely local and ad hoc basis. This was done by applying to Parliament for a local act to set up a body of improvement commissioners. By 1830 there were over 300 such bodies, nearly a hundred of which were in London. They were run by groups of men, appointed for life by the act, filling vacancies by co-option, with specific functions (for example, paving, cleansing or lighting streets). They could either hire labour or contract the work out and could levy a rate to meet the expense. The quality of the 'improvements' achieved varied but even the most efficient commissions tended to confine their attention to the central streets. Side streets, alleys, courts and lanes largely remained untouched. Improvement commissions may have had 'good intentions' but their efforts were hampered by lack of technical knowledge, disputes over their jurisdiction and legal powers and by the refusal of householders to fund what they considered unnecessary improvements.

Thirdly, existing urban government did not have the necessary administrative organizations to provide effective control over building and town planning for removing sewage and piping purified water. Some of the older towns had corporations but these were often self-elected and corrupt and lacked powers to exercise real local control over the environment. Newer cities, like Birmingham and Manchester, without corporations, were still governed under the parochial arrangements that pre-dated expansion. The Municipal Corporation Act of 1835 reformed the variegated nature of urban government opening it to a significant degree of middle-class control but, with notable exceptions, this made little real difference to urban conditions. Improvement still relied largely on local efforts. In the 1840s the largest cities obtained local acts to cope with their own circumstances: Leeds in 1842 and 1848; Manchester in 1848; and, the Liverpool Sanitary Act of 1846 which made the Corporation in effect a health authority, empowering it to appoint an engineer, an Inspector of Nuisances and, above all, a Medical Officer of Health.

Fourthly, these local acts were partially a reaction against growing pressure for national action on public health and the belief that local communities knew best how to cope with their problems. Pressure for state action tended to increase only when there was a sudden and tragic visitation of an epidemic. A short-lived Board of Health was set up in 1805–6 under the threat of yellow fever. But it was the cholera outbreaks of 1831–2 and 1848–9, a disease which did not discriminate by social class, that struck fear into the hearts of local and national governors and led to some state control. The possibility of state intervention raised a series of important questions in the 1830s and 1840s. First, how were improvements to be financed? Local resources for social utilities were always scarce and, except during epidemics, sewerage was not a popular issue. If localities were unable or unwilling to finance 'improvements' where should the money come from? Central government? If so, should it be raised by national taxation? Secondly was it right that local powers should be taken over by national bodies? This question was at the heart of the problem of public health throughout the first sixty years of the nineteenth century. Increasing central government powers attacked individual liberty and property rights. For Chadwick local control meant inaction, the result of either demarcation disputes between competing inefficient commissions or deference to interested parties among electors and elected. For urban communities central control meant fear of impersonal, impartial and powerful administrators. Support for the Public Health Act of 1848, initially accepted because of the return of cholera, vaporized in 1849–50 and the demise of the General Board of Health and the retirement of Chadwick in 1854 were largely unmourned.

By 1850 the 'sanitary idea' had not been achieved. This was a result of the immensity of the task and the weight of local opposition to central control. It was also the result of Chadwick's personality. His dogmatism, arrogance and impatience, which marred his ability to implement supported change, limited the effectiveness of reform. It was easy for anti-centralizers like Joshua Toulmin Smith to attack centralization as an attack on people's 'liberties' and on the principle of representation, and *The Times* could focus the issue round a caricature of Chadwick's personality.

CONCLUSIONS

The vitality of urban life betwen 1700 and 1850 was a compound of many diverse experiences. There is no simple index of urban economic and social structure or performance. The difference between the reality of development in individual towns and the more generalized evaluations by historians needs to be considered. Urban society was just as diverse as its rural counterpart. Given this stricture, is it possible to make any generalized statements about the role of towns in the expanding economy between 1700 and 1850?

Urban economic life was both flexible and adaptable. Towns were vast reservoirs of skilled and unskilled labour. Jobs were generated within towns by the simple economic interaction of a sheer mass of people. The productivity of towns was matched by wages generally higher than those in the surrounding countryside. In the north, where towns offered alternative employment, this had the effect of pushing up rural wages, while in the south lack of urban and industrial opportunities kept them depressed. The expanding urban population had a stimulating effect on the commercialization and development of the agrarian economy, though foreign imports played an increasingly important role after 1760. Towns were crucial nodal centres for exchange and distribution, generating pressure for improvements in the systems of transport and communications. Urban growth was often a stimulus to river, road and later rail improvements and docks and canals were often built to facilitate movement of raw materials and finished products. Towns increasingly played an important role in the development of industry. From being marketing and finishing centres, some towns developed as major centres of production in their own right. They were the locations of an extensive and broadening range of service industries: banking, insurance, law, medicine, education, government, and were accumulators and circulators of investment capital. Finally, towns had a society that was relatively open, fluid, competitive and acquisitive and which propagated a new market-oriented consumer ethos. It was this which many contemporaries criticized as leading to worldliness, emulation and the desire for luxury.

Whether there was a causal relationship between 'new', 'free' towns and growth and 'old' incorporated towns and stagnation is a matter of debate among historians.[25] Economic regulation, which existed in non-incorporated centres though in different forms from the older guilds, mattered less than location, resources, natural or 'improved' communication, labour supply and business enterprise. Urbanization is not the ever-elusive 'first cause' of Britain's industrial revolution but it represented and fostered structural transformation.

The responses of contemporaries to urban growth were ambivalent. Voltaire saw the pursuit of industry and urbane pleasures as the marks of the city and therefore of civilization. Adam Smith argued that the city secured and extended the industry of the country, and was a centre of freedom and order while recognizing that as a market and manufacturing centre it was liable to breed a volatile and insecure people. There was a new urbanity in the writings of Swift, Pope and Johnson. Yet for Hogarth, Fielding, Gay and Defoe there was a darker reality. Hogarth's 'Gin Alley', Gay's *Beggar's Opera* and Defoe's *Moll Flanders* represent urban development as being opposed to the idea of civilized order. This ambivalence continued after 1800. For William Cobett London was the 'Great Wen', monstrous and diseased. To Charles Dickens cities were fearful, unnatural, anonymous places. Towns were no longer face-to-face communities with close and obvious links to their rural hinterlands. The pre-industrial sense of community of interest and balance between urban and rural had been lost by 1850.

NOTES

1 Samuel Johnson in 1777, quoted in E. Pawson *The Early Industrial Revolution*, Batsford, 1978, p. 192.
2 R. Vaughan *The Age of Great Cities*, London, 1843, p. 153.
3 This issue is explored in more detail in R. Williams' seminal *The Country and the City*, Chatto & Windus, 1973 and some of its implications for an industrialized society in M. Weiner *English Culture and the Decline of the Industrial Spirit 1850–1950*, Cambridge University Press, 1982.
4 E. Jones *Towns & Cities*, Oxford University Press, 1966 provides a useful and accessible, if somewhat dated, introduction to the nature of urban expansion and life.
5 On the development of the early modern town see the reader edited by P. Clark *The Early Modern Town*, Longman, 1976 and P. Clark and P. Slack *English Towns in Transition 1500–1700*, Oxford University Press, 1976. H. J. Dyos (ed.) *The Study of Urban History*, Edward Arnold, 1968 is the central work on 'setting the agenda' for urban historians. D. Fraser and A. Sutcliffe (eds) *The Pursuit of Urban History*, Edward Arnold, 1983 takes the 'Dyos agenda' forward into the 1980s.
6 G. Sjoberg *The Preindustrial City: Past and Present*, 1960 is the starting-

point for anyone wanting to theorize about the pre-industrial city. Though not without its critics and flaws, it is still a valuable book to read.

7 Clark and Slack op. cit. pp. 4–5.

8 ibid. p. 6.

9 On the town in the eighteenth century see C. W. Chalklin *The Provincial Towns of Georgian England*, Edward Arnold, 1974, especially chapters 1 and 2 and P. J. Corfield *The Impact of English Towns 1700–1800*, Oxford University Press, 1982. A. McInnes *The English Town 1660–1760*, The Historical Association, 1978 provides a brief overview. For Wales see H. Carter *The Towns of Wales*, London, 1965 and for Scotland H. Hamilton *An Economic History of Scotland in the Eighteenth Century*, 1963 and I. H. Adams *The Making of Urban Scotland*, 1978.

10 Chalklin op. cit. p. 47.

11 ibid. p. 51.

12 On the town after 1800 see A. Briggs *Victorian Cities*, Penguin, 1968, R. Dennis *English Industrial Cities of the Nineteenth Century*, Cambridge University Press, 1984, H. J. Dyos and M. Wolff (eds) *The Victorian City: Images and Realities*, Routledge, 1973 and D. Fraser *Power and Authority in the Victorian City*, Blackwell, 1979. J. Walvin *Urban Life 1776–1851*, Hutchinson, 1984 is excellent on urban society, D. and A. Shelton, *The Industrial City 1820–1870*, Macmillan, 1990, combines literary with specifically historical sources.

13 F. Crouzet *The Victorian Economy*, Methuen, 1982, p. 89; F. Bedarida *A Social History of England 1851–1975*, Methuen, 1981, p. 17.

14 Crouzet op. cit. p. 95.

15 F. Engels *The Condition of the Working Class in England*, 1969 edn, p. 58.

16 J. G. Kohl *Ireland, Scotland and England, Book 3*, London, 1844, p. 103.

17 A. de Tocqueville *Journeys to England and Ireland*, London, 1958, pp. 104–5.

18 R. Dennis op. cit. p. 18.

19 J. Foster *Class Struggle and the Industrial Revolution*, Weidenfeld, 1974.

20 D. S. Gadian 'Class Consciousness in Oldham and other north west industrial towns', *Historical Journal*, 21 (1978).

21 ibid. p. 171.

22 The pioneering work on the 1851 Religious Census was done by K. S. Inglis 'Patterns of Religious Worship in 1851', *Journal of Ecclesiastical History*, 11 (1960), pp. 74–86. See also D. M. Thompson, 'The 1851 Religious Census: Problems and Possibilities', *Victorian Studies*, 11 (1967) pp. 87–97 and B. I. Coleman 'Religion in the Victorian City', *History Today*, August 1980.

23 On the development of London begin with M. D. George *London Life in the Eighteenth Century*, Penguin various editions, first published in 1925. G. Rudé *Hanoverian London 1714–1808*, London, 1971 is an excellent, more recent survey and should be supplemented with M. Byrd *London Transformed: Images of the City in the Eighteenth Century*, Yale University Press, 1978 and J. Summerson *Georgian London*, London, 1945. On the nineteenth century see S. Humphries and J. Taylor *The Making of Modern London*, 3 vols, 1983–6 and two works by D. J. Olsen *The Growth of Victorian London*, Batsford, 1976 and his comparative *The City as a Work of Art: London, Paris, Vienna*, Yale University Press, 1986.

24 On the environment of the town P. J. Corfield op. cit. pp. 168–85 provides a convenient survey for the eighteenth century. On housing see S. D. Chapman (ed.) *The History of Working Class Housing: A Symposium*, David & Charles, 1971, E. Gauldie *Cruel Habitations*, Allen & Unwin, 1978 and J. Burnett *A Social History of Housing 1815–1985*, Methuen, 1986. A. Wohl *Endangered Lives: Public Health in Victorian Britain*, Methuen, 1985 is an excellent intro-

duction to the problems of urban conditions. R. Rodger *Housing in Urban Britain 1780–1914*, Macmillan, 1989 provides a brief bibliographical study.
25 See M. J. Daunton 'Towns and Economic Growth in Eighteenth Century England', in P. Abrams and E. A. Wrigley (eds) *Towns in Society: Essays in Economic History and Historical Sociology*, Cambridge University Press, 1978, pp. 245–77.

Addendum:
Four studies on urban growth now need to be considered:
J. G. Williamson *Coping with City Growth during the British Industrial Revolution*, Cambridge University Press, 1990; T. Koditschek *Class Formation and Urban Industrial Society: Bradford 1750–1850*, Cambridge University Press, 1990, and two readers, P. Borsay (ed.) *The Eighteenth Century Town*, Longman, 1990 and R. J. Morris and R. Rodger (eds) *The Victorian City*, Longman, forthcoming.

19 Culture, economic and social change 1700–1850

So far as studies of cultural history are concerned, the concept of 'revolution' has been somewhat peripheral, employed for the most part as little more than a synonym for 'watershed' or 'turning point'.[1]

The character and functions of certain social institutions and attitudes have been examined in earlier chapters of this book. This chapter examines the problems of reaching a working definition of 'culture', considers how historians have studied culture in the eighteenth and early nineteenth centuries and will describe certain aspects of that culture.

'CULTURE'

Definitions

Raymond Williams suggested in 1976 that 'culture' is one of the most difficult words in the English language, partly because it has a history of shifting meanings, and partly because the word is now used to cover important concepts in several distinct disciplines.[2] Two types of culture tend to be identified: first, 'high' or minority taste culture – in particular certain kinds of music, literature, language and art – which are associated with a 'cultivated' elite; secondly, 'popular' or mass culture, often perceived as crude and 'vulgar'. This stark contrast, though it has its uses, does reflect value-judgements about what is considered 'important' and 'worthwhile' and often leads to a downgrading of popular culture. For sociologists and anthropologists culture means everything that is man-made in a society: tools and technology, language and literature, music and art, science and mathematics, values and attitudes – in effect, the whole way of life. Should historians see culture as the observable features of the pattern of life within a community – a concrete definition? Or should culture be restricted to the organized system of knowledge and belief through which people structure and give meaning to their experiences – a view emphasizing ideas rather than things?

It is possible to distinguish culture as an all-embracing concept covering all social processes in their historical and intellectual setting from the more limited sense of the culture surrounding certain kinds of social interaction. In this approach, political culture, for example, becomes the culture surrounding political interaction, providing the setting for the style, tone and colouring of that interaction. This distinction allows historians to focus on the relationship between the total culture of society and its various subcultures which colour a limited section of activity.

Hegemony

The application of the concept of 'hegemony', with its emphasis on consent and negotiation as crucial elements in creating a legitimated culture, has helped in explaining the relationship between these two views of culture.[3] Antonio Gramsci developed the notion of hegemony in the 1920s and 1930s and used it to describe and analyse how modern capitalist societies were organized.[4] Hegemony, in the sense of cultural and moral leadership, was exercised by civil society and by the state. Power is exerted over individuals in several ways: coercive power in the form of the police and armed forces of the state; work discipline through the economy, wages and monetary control; and moral leadership through civil society. Gramsci came to see the central importance of educational and legal institutions in the exercise of hegemony.

Hegemony is important for historians because it helps to explain why the economic and political 'domination' of particular social groups is acceptable to society as a whole. Coercion, through control of the state apparatus, is one way of retaining domination but it is prone to violent opposition. Hegemony provides moral and intellectual 'leadership'. This means at times pursuing policies which are in the interest of the whole people rather than a narrow class interest – willingness to compromise. But this is always in the economic interest of the dominant group in the state. Hegemonic leadership involves producing a world-view, a moral and cultural outlook which subordinate groups in society accept. Hegemony is leadership resulting in consent for action rather than domination by force.

Cultural systems – structures

'Culture' can be defined as the way of life of a society and 'hegemony' as one strategy employed by dominant economic and political groups to maintain their position. Cultural systems can be subdivided into the following eight structures which interact and influence each other. First, the social structure or social system defines relationships within society as a whole. This can be explained by using concepts like kinship, family, status, role, duty, obligation and class. Second, the economic system deals with the problem of scarce resources, their distribution and exchange. Third, the technology system concerns attempts if not to control the environment at least to lessen domination by it. The communication system is the fourth structure and deals with the ways in which people communicate with each other: speech, non-verbal communication, the written word. Fifth, the rationality system defines what a society considers to be 'reasonable' and what counts as an explanation in terms of cause and effect. What is accepted as rational will vary between societies and across time: for example, the persecution of witches declined as a result of changed notions explaining behaviour in the eighteenth century. Sixth, all societies have some kind of code of ethics that distinguishes between right and wrong behaviour. This morality system may be unitary and taken for granted, or pluralistic, experiencing difficulty in transmitting rules of behaviour because total agreement is lacking. Closely connected with the morality system is the dominant belief system. In some cultures the moral code will be backed up by, or closely related to, religious belief. Finally, people have aesthetic drives and needs. Societies produce art and entertainment for their members even when they live close to subsistence level. After 1700 these cultural systems began to alter. Was this the result of economic and social change? Can historians profitably discuss the notion of a 'cultural revolution' between 1700 and 1850?

Marxist emphases

The emphasis for Marxist historians like Raymond Williams and E. P. Thompson is upon 'experience', 'tradition' and 'structures of feeling'. Williams saw culture as a particular way of life expressing certain meanings and values not just in aesthetic terms but also in institutional and ordinary behaviour. Thompson argues that the reactions of the labouring population to economic and political pressures after 1790 was not an automatic one but was shaped by 'a moral culture', a 'popular tradition'. Responses to change – food riots, poaching and its repression and threatening letters – were 'moral' responses, a reflection of the growing conflict between the customs of traditional communities and the rise of capitalism. This 'plebeian culture', in Thompson's view proto-working class, is contrasted with a 'patrician culture'. He suggests that ruling-class control in eighteenth-century England was located primarily in a cultural hegemony but that the plebs, though not revolutionary, were far from deferential, much given to ritualistic protest and acting out 'a theatre of threat and sedition'.

Cultural conflict and control

Cultural conflict, confrontation and control are central to the approach of certain historians. At one extreme was ranged the growing middle classes, concerned with the taming of popular festivals – diagnosed as disorderly and irrational – in the name of 'discipline' and 'rational recreation' together with the police presented as the allies of the bourgeoisie or even as 'missionaries' of their values. However, the working population defended their traditions, resisted change and defined themselves through their opposition to middle-class values. An emphasis on control allows historians to place local struggles in a much wider context, to link them to processes of social change such as urbanization, through competition for the use of open space and the rise of capitalism and the need for discipline at work and a regular work rhythm. But historians need also to take account of a series of distinctions.

First, the aims of those who wished to control popular culture were far from homogenous. Municipal authorities were concerned with public order, control of alcohol and temperance while dissenting groups focused on public morality and entrepreneurs promoted 'rational recreation'. They were respectively aiming at 'discipline', 'conversion' and 'improvement'. These may have been incompatible; for example, encouraging people to learn to read or think for themselves could make them less obedient to the authority of Church, state or workplace. Secondly, the reactions of the working population to the modification or suppression of traditional pastimes and culture was also far from uniform. Elements of the working population assimilated and reinterpreted some of the new values, such as temperance and 'respectability'. The conflict model needs to be modified to take into account instances of negotiated hegemony as opposed to coercion. Thirdly, aspects of popular culture had already been commercialized by 1800 and consumer spending by the working population – when they could afford it as well as when they could not – had established a more harmonious relationship with capitalism than the conflict model allows. Popular culture did not change either quickly or completely between 1700 and 1850 as some historians have argued. Some traditional cultural forms, like the Lancashire wakes, were resilient enough to survive both urbanization and industrialization while others had already begun to change by the early 1700s. Cultural change must be seen in a long-term perspective if it is going to be meaningful. But, as Peter Burke says:

> The pace of cultural change is far from steady, but even in the case of periods of accelerated change like the nineteenth century the term 'revolution' seems too strong. The movement was too protracted. Looking back at it, Raymond Williams saw what he described . . . as a 'Long Revolution'. But if we are going to use the concept with any degree of precision, a long 'revolution' is a contradiction in terms.[5]

Diverse cultures

Eighteenth-century popular culture, at least in England and Lowland Scotland, was neither 'traditional' nor the culture of peasant societies.[6] It was variegated culture, different between and within regions, between areas of Catholicism and Protestantism, between upland and lowland and country. Peter Burke has argued that Europe had a substantially intact peasant culture in 1500 but that by 1800 it had been eroded by the repression of religious reformers, the withdrawal of the upper sections of society and by the development of printing which had modified cultural expression making it more secular and political.[7] The degree to which English popular culture fitted into this peasant model is a matter of considerable debate. Was England different? Alan Macfarlane maintains that England followed a different path from the thirteenth century.[8] What distinguished England from Europe was its lack of peasantry and a legal system which emphasized individual rights and ownership of land. If Macfarlane is correct – and by the eighteenth century, if not earlier, he probably is – then the notion of peasant culture is of little value. English popular culture was significantly different from that found elsewhere in Europe. It was more commercial, more individualistic, less corporate and more secular. It was the culture of a society where an increasing proportion of the workforce was no longer directly engaged in agriculture.

There remained many features of popular culture which were traditional and exhibited continuity with the past and had parallels in other European societies. There was a close association of leisure with work, especially farming. The holidays, festivals and fairs which punctuated the year rose naturally out of work and continued to make sense because they remained attuned to work patterns. Secondly, recreation and leisure, like work, occurred in the context of small communities. Thirdly, sports and pastimes were violent, crude, usually involving betting and blood. These activities were tolerated by those in authority because they were traditional – and the squires and magistrates still regarded themselves as part of the community – and because they acted as a safety valve releasing tensions which could otherwise have been exhibited in more subversive ways. But there were significant differences. The need to neutralize the importance of Catholic festivals had already led to a significant decline in the religious character of popular culture by 1700. Culture had become secular. England was much more socially mobile than much of Europe, resulting in village communities not based exclusively on notions of kinship but upon more self-conscious association where work and leisure created strong bonds and collective identity could be acquired. Economically and socially England was qualitatively different from Europe. It was more commercialized and the market played a far more significant role. The case made by R. W. Malcolmson that there was a decline in popular recreations in the late eighteenth and early nineteenth centuries associated with the gradual breakdown of a traditional society is only convincing if there was a traditional society to break down.[9]

Despite Puritan attacks in the seventeenth century, much traditional popular culture survived in 1700 fiercely defended by the labouring population as their right by custom. It was not vital simply in rural areas, and in London and the major provincial centres leisure and recreation shared many of its characteristics. The cultural division of town and country came later.

Models?

The two-tier model of high and popular culture works best for societies which have only a small middle stratum. The two traditions coexisted though it was only the elite which participated in both cultures. Cultural adaptation was, however, a two-way process. The notion of 'the dance' originally developed in popular culture was taken up and modified by the elite. Architectural styles and fashions, by contrast, descended the social structure. Increasingly after 1700 English society became more status conscious and graded, and cultural attitudes became more complex. A move to a three-tier model with the worldly and pleasure-loving aspects of high culture, the godly and rational culture of the middle orders and the lewd and fleshly pursuits of the poor would certainly be tidy but such a clear-cut division neglects the diversity and overlapping of cultural experiences. The significance of the emergence of a third cultural perspective did, however 'accelerate the process of cultural transmission, to modify or adapt aspects of high culture and, most fittingly, to commercialize culture into a marketable commodity'.[10]

CULTURAL CHANGE 1700–1850

The eighteenth century saw two major modifications in the cultural experience of English society. First, there was erosion of the older popular culture as a result of the withdrawal of patronage by the governing elite, the gradual dismantling of the agrarian social and economic framework which gave it justification by widespread industrialization, and the attacks on its public expression by a combination of religious evangelicalism and a secular desire to promote work discipline. Secondly, and by contrast, a more commercialized culture developed, entrepreneurial, marketable and, if J. H. Plumb is correct, largely urban and bourgeois.[11] This involved modification of both the content and transmission of high culture in the interests of polite society and, later in the century, the promotion of popular cultural products like circuses, prize and cock-fights for profit. Cultural experiences, like economic and social ones, were adaptable. Change was, in most cases, gradual.

Popular culture under attack

In what ways was popular culture attacked in the eighteenth century and why? It was part of the assault on the life-styles and recreations of the labouring population that had been gathering impetus since the sixteenth century. It had two interconnected thrusts: a religious concern that popular culture was profane, irreligious and immoral, and a secular belief that it was detrimental to economic efficiency and social order. The desire to turn people into sober, godly citizens motivated by an interest in work and social discipline had maximum political leverage and was a dominant intellectual stance from the early nineteenth century, receiving its fullest, though highly ambiguous, expression in the notion of 'Victorian values'.[12] Religiosity, sexual repression and patriarchal authoritarianism, in both family and economic life, were its major characteristics. Its motivation was a sense of cultural crisis, a challenge to hegemony which called for moral regeneration and stricter disciplining of the lives of the labouring population. In that sense the attacks on popular culture in the eighteenth as well as early nineteenth century can be seen as a response to pressures on existing forms of social control, of demographic and urban growth and the consequent erosion of paternalism.

Anglican Evangelicalism played a central role in this critique of popular culture. In many ways its greatest success was in obtaining some agreement from a broad section of the governing elite to its central moral tenets through groups like the Society for the Reformation of Manners and the Society for the Suppression of Vice. Its views had their greatest success with mercantile, commercial and professional groups, who looked with both economic and social distaste at the irrational and sinful nature of much popular leisure and were appalled by the amount of gratuitous cruelty to animals this involved. Methodism had greater impact on the working population and on artisans and small shopkeepers through its incessant attack on the worldliness and sensuality of popular culture. Distaste for present pleasures was also a characteristic of secular radicalism. For articulate radicals popular culture was too closely linked with the paternalistic social order. It offended their emphasis on reason and they stressed moral and intellectual self-improvement. Books, education, debating not bear-baiting, races or circuses. This ideological position was at variance with the populist and reactionary beliefs and emotions of those who argued for a 'moral' economy. Secular radicals, no less than evangelicals, sought to redeem the labouring population but through reason rather than Christ even if it meant a division between their respectable, independent, non-deferential culture and a crude, callous, irrational popular culture.

This ideological attack was combined with what Thomas Carlyle called an 'abdication on the part of the governors' in his essay 'Chartism' published in 1839. The aristocracy and gentry gradually withdrew from participation in popular culture and no longer championed it against reformers. The extent of this participation during the eighteenth century has often been overdrawn by historians but there was a gradual modification in the life-styles of aristocracy and gentry. Society became less face-to-face, except on special occasions, with each social group confined to its own world. The layout of country houses and gardens demonstrated a move towards domestic privacy. This was more than just symbolic and reflected a much broader 'cutting-off' of the lives of the aristocracy and gentry from the lives of the labouring population. Rural sports, customary holidays, apprenticeship rituals came to be seen not as socially desirable but as wasteful distractions from work and threats to social order.

Changes in popular culture occurred slowly and drew on older cultural traditions. There was no revolution, rather a change of emphasis consequent on greater individual autonomy, the growth of a wider market and the prospect of higher profits. Neither, despite the work of reformers, was there great haste in imposing curbs on popular behaviour. Had government wished to legislate against brutal pastimes it would have had to provide effective policing and, given contemporary opposition to this as incompatible with the Englishman's freedom, this it was not prepared to do.

Characteristics of popular culture

The major characteristics of popular culture at the end of the eighteenth century were that it was a public, robust, gregarious culture, largely masculine, and involving spectacle and gambling with an undercurrent of disorder and physical violence. The distinction between high and popular culture, between opera and drama on the one hand and spectacle, circus and showmanship on the other had broken down:

> Shakespeare, melodramas and performing animals not merely coexisted but intermingled. . . . The relationship between high and popular art forms is to a considerable extent one of interdependence, and the one is continually reinforced by the other.[13]

Pleasure fairs played a major role in this process with many major actors starting their careers in their theatrical booths. English theatre and opera was produced not for cultivated and informed but for mass audiences for whom melodrama, lavish stage sets and performing animals were essential and managers and actors bored them at their peril. Expanding audiences funded the extensive rebuilding of Covent Garden, Drury Lane and Sadler's Wells as well as theatres outside the West End, and entrepreneurs gave melodrama a legitimate place on the stage as well as developing the modern pantomime. The London theatre was highly innovative and fiercely commercial. Actors and actresses became increasingly professional and conscious of stardom and salary. Provincial theatres followed the example of London and by the 1820s there had been some decline in theatre-going by the provincial bourgeoisie, a result as much of the rougher audiences frightening them away as the impact of evangelicalism.

Sport

Developments in sport showed the same commercialism and capacity to survive in the face of the hostility of authority. Shooting and hunting were the only sports to remain exclusively elitist. Until 1831 shooting was legally restricted to owners of land worth at least £100 and the Game Laws ensured that poaching was severely punished. While shooting demonstrated a horizontal cleavage in rural society, fox-hunting had a far greater community interest. Though dominated by the landed aristocracy and country gentlemen, it was open to urban gentry and professionals and the poorer sections of the community followed the spectacle on foot. Some hunts were the property of single great landowners but were expensive to maintain and subscription hunts became more common: there were 69 packs of hounds in Britain in 1812 and 91 by 1825.

Horse-racing was, however, the sport of both the rich and the labouring population. It could not maintain its exclusiveness though different prices charged for the stands, the paddocks and the ordinary enclosures were as much an expression of social hierarchy as different class carriages on trains. Horse-racing combined two obsessions, love of horses and gambling. Professional bookmakers appeared around 1800; by 1815 the 'classic' races – the Derby, the Oaks, the One Thousand and Two Thousand Guineas, the St Leger and Ascot Gold Cup – were all established and by 1837 there were 150 places in Britain where race meetings were held. By 1850 off-course betting had been established, further broadening participation.

Pugilism began as a sport of the labouring population and attracted aristocratic patronage in the late eighteenth and early nineteenth centuries. It was very popular with working men and the great champions of the day – Tom Spring, Tom Crib and Dutch Sam – were popular heroes who aroused fierce regional loyalties. Like horse-racing it was increasingly commercialized and its heroes were full-time professionals. Both flourished as industries with their own specialist newspapers yet they were also evocative of an older, probably imaginary, culture where sporting squires and labourers rubbed shoulders in a common appreciation of animal or physical prowess. Upper-class support for prize-fighting waned after the 1820s but it retained its popularity among the working population and its real decline did not occur until after 1860.

Other sports like cricket, rowing and pedestrianism, had similar characteristics to horse-racing and prize-fighting. They all became more organized and professional, more dependent on attracting spectators and were accompanied by extensive betting. Cricket originated as an activity of the labouring population in southern England and was then taken up by the aristocratic elite. The game took on much of its modern character after 1787, when the MCC was founded at Lord's in Marylebone. Pedestrianism and rowing also began as popular sports before moving up the social scale later in the nineteenth century.

Continuity of cultural experience 1700–1850

Many traditional customs continued until well after 1850. There is evidence for largely unchanged New Year's mumming festivals in northern England until the 1870s. Guy Fawkes Night was still celebrated despite attempts by various authorities to suppress fires and the burning of effigies.[14] Changes to traditional customs were not easily enforced even in areas, like industrial Lancashire, where factory discipline was most firmly established. The Lancashire Wakes Weeks,[15] traditionally the most important event of the recreational year, were forced on mill-owners rather than freely given. It was not simply employers who attacked wakes and fairs. Moral reformers, the magistracy and later the police recognized that these acted as a focus for criminal activity, could potentially lead to violence and threatened public order. That they continued until the late nineteenth century was due not to lack of opposition to them but to disagreement about what action to take.

Spectacle

Spectacle, and senses of justice and morality came together in the carnival atmosphere that surrounded public executions. They symbolized the macabre, callous and sensational nature of early nineteenth-century leisure activities. Hangings were public theatre, a dialogue between Life and Death, Good and Evil. There was considerable interest in the careers of famous villains, a mini-industry producing ballads, broadsheets and pamphlets giving accounts of murders and murderers' confessions. The upper classes shared as avidly the interest in executions as the mass of the population for whom, ostensibly, the spectacle was provided but from the 1840s there was a controversy which finally led to the abolition of public executions in 1868.[16]

CULTURAL REFORM

By the 1820s a clear contrast was apparent between the nature of much popular recreation and evangelicalism and rational liberalism, the dominant intellectual movements of the day, with their argument for a self-conscious and moralistic cultivation of respectability. This produced much of the impetus for reform. From the formation of the Proclamation Society in 1787, the campaign for reform gained momentum. By the 1830s there were societies for preventing cruelty to animals, the Lord's Day Observance Society founded in 1831 and the British and Foreign Temperance Society. Parliamentary reform in 1832 gave such societies slightly more influence over Parliament and as the police force was extended they gained the means to enforce legislation. Betting was an early and obvious target for reform but lotteries were not made illegal until 1823 and 1825 and further measures to discourage gambling had to wait until the 1840s and 1850s. Reform was not achieved easily, quickly or completely. Neither was it the prerogative, nor was it dictated by the interests, of any one social group. It traversed class boundaries, dividing all groups, especially the labouring population, internally.

CHANGING ATTITUDES – THREE CASE STUDIES

Cruelty to animals

The problems of changing people's attitudes can be seen in the cases of cruelty to animals, temperance and the growing problem of drug addiction. English travellers on the Continent in the eighteenth century were shocked by how foreigners treated their domestic animals, hunted and used animals in recreational activities.[17] But the staging of contests between animals was still one of the most common and popular forms of recreation in England. Bulls and bears were 'baited' by being tethered to a stake and attacked by dogs. At Stamford and Tutbury there was an annual 'bull-run'. Badgers, apes, mules and even horses might all be baited in a similar way. Cock-fighting was a normal feature of fairs and race meetings by 1700. It involved a mingling of all social groups, though only men, and was accompanied by heavy betting and often local and regional rivalries. Hunting and hawking were widespread. In addition to stylized and formal methods of tormenting animals, there was an infinity of informal ones. Small boys were notorious for amusing themselves in torturing living creatures but they merely reflected the standards of the adult world. A distinction has been made between the cruelty of indifference and the cruelty of vindictiveness and, as Keith Thomas says,

> what was normally displayed in the early modern period was the cruelty of indifference. For most persons, the beasts were outside the terms of moral reference. . . . It was a world in which much of what would later be regarded as 'cruelty' had not yet been defined as such.[18]

During the eighteenth century the feelings of animals became a matter of very great concern and led to agitation in the early nineteenth century, culminating in the formation in 1824 of the Society (later Royal Society) for the Prevention of Cruelty to Animals and the passage of legislation against cruelty to horses and cattle in 1822, cruelty to dogs in 1839 and 1854 and against baiting and cock-fighting in 1835 and 1849.

Why did this change occur? There had long been a tradition that unnecessary cruelty to animals was wrong but rather because of its brutalizing effects on human character than as a reflection of any moral concern with animals. It did not go unnoticed that the poisoner William Palmer, executed in 1856, had conducted cruel experiments on animals as a boy. There was, however, a move away from this strictly anthropocentric point of view to one which regarded cruelty to animals as morally wrong regardless of whether it had human consequences or not. It is important to see this moral change in relation to the association of animal sports with noise, gambling and disorder. Bull-baiting was prohibited at Birmingham in 1773 and was in retreat elsewhere by 1800, though it was not finally banned until 1835. Cock-fighting was more resilient. Hunting also proved a more difficult issue, because of its aristocratic support, and there is something in the contemporary argument that 'It is often pointed out that in the long war against blood sports it was the most plebeian activities . . . and that those sports with gentry and upper class support [that] survived.'[19]

Temperance reform

Alcohol gave stimulus, release, oblivion.[20] In a period when water supplies were often contaminated, ale, wine and spirits were cheap, and these were drunk in large quantities. In the early eighteenth century 11.2 million gallons, or about 7 gallons per person of spirits were drunk in London each year. Gin was very popular and legislative control over it in the 1750s was once believed by historians to have played an important role in the decline of the death rate. There were many outlets for alcohol. In the early eighteenth century London had 207 inns, 5,875 ale-houses and 5,659 brandy shops and Northampton (population 5,000 in 1750) had 60 inns and 100 ale-houses.

The expansion of towns did little to alter social attitudes to alcohol, though improvements in the sobriety of the labouring population began in the 1750s. With the dangers of disease from untreated water it was natural for town-dwellers to rely increasingly on alcohol and on water that had been boiled with beverages. People did not believe that local water would ever be safe to drink, as Chadwick's inspectors found out from London slum-dwellers in the 1840s. The scarcity of drinking water even created the profession of water-carrier. There were alternatives to alcohol: milk, though this was considered a dangerous drink even when fresh; soda-water was not made commercially until 1790 and ginger-beer was not sold in London until 1822; tea had become a virtual necessity among the labouring population by the 1830s and per capita coffee consumption increased faster than tea between 1820 and 1850. But alcohol was more than just a thirst-quencher, it was thought to impart physical stamina, extra energy and confidence. Agricultural labourers, for example, believed that it was impossible to get in the harvest without their 'harvest beer'. Alcohol was regarded as a pain-killer: it assisted dentists and surgeons before the use of anaesthetics, quietened crying babies and gave protection against infection, although it created diseases like gout. It also relieved psychological strain, moderating the sense of social isolation and gloom, and enhanced festivity; drinking places provided a focus for the community. Many of the major political movements of the eighteenth and early nineteenth centuries met in public houses.

In the eighteenth century drinking was not rigidly segregated by rank. Squires, for example, often drank with their social inferiors. However, by the early nineteenth century a measure of social segregation had developed and by the 1850s no respectable urban Englishman entered an ordinary public house. Private as opposed to public drinking was becoming the mark of 'respectability':

> A social gulf was not imposed between those responsible for licensing regulation and those affected by it: indeed, statutory legislation after the 1830s was partly a substitute for the personal supervision of lower-class drinking which magistrates had exercised hitherto.[21]

Drinking was also a predominantly male preserve and encouraged men to enjoy better living standards than their wives. On pay days drinking houses were often besieged by wives anxious to get money to feed and clothe their children before it was drunk away. There was a direct correlation between levels of violence to women and drinking throughout society.

The drink trade comprised a large complex of different interests. Of particular importance was the powerful landed interest, which helps to explain the regional variations in support for the temperance movement. The barley crop was most important to farmers and without the distillers' demand for poor-quality grain, lighter lands in Scotland and Ireland might never have been cultivated. Politically the drink trade drew its prestige from the reliance government placed on drink taxes for national revenue. In 1822 Brougham had denounced tea-drinking because it did not lead to the cultivation of any British land. Beer, however, raised strong patriotic sentiments, a view expressed by Sydney Smith in 1823: 'what two ideas are more inseparable than Beer and Britannia!'

Attitudes to alcohol were deeply ingrained throughout British society. Abandoning drinking was, for the labouring population, more than simply not going to drinking places. It isolated workers from much popular culture, from a whole complex of recreational activities. No total abstinence movement appeared in the eighteenth century. The Reformation Societies that emerged after 1700 were enthusiastic about temperance but the main platform of their movement was the legislative suppression of vice. The temperance movement that emerged in the 1830s differed from them in their concentration on the single issue of spirits, their belief in total abstinence and their repudiation until after 1850 of legislative support.

Why did an anti-spirits movement develop in the early 1830s? First, it was not a planned movement, at least initially, and arose independently at the same time in several places. Secondly, it was one of several attempts to propagate a middle-class style of life. Thirdly, it arose at a time when drunkenness was already becoming unfashionable. Sobriety received the support of groups: medical opinion from the 1790s increasingly attacked the effects, both physical and psychological, of excessive alcohol; coffee traders wished to popularize their produce; evangelicals saw excessive drinking as a sin; radicals attacked alcohol for its effect on the standard of living of the labouring population. Finally, the movement would not have made such an impact in the 1830s without the techniques of agitation used by evangelical humanitarians, especially the anti-slavery movement which matured into an organized propagandist campaign after its rather timid start in the 1780s.

Though any clear link between industrialization and temperance is diffi-cult to establish, the earliest anti-spirit societies originated in textile manu-facturing areas of Ulster and Glasgow and spread through England from the textile centres of Preston, Leeds and Bradford. Some employers wel-comed the more reliable workforce that temperance encouraged but others did not stand by teetotal employees. Money not spent to drink could, of course, be spent on home-produced consumer goods and some industrial-ists welcomed a movement which would accelerate economic growth and educate people on where to spend the proceeds. As Brian Harrison says:

> Industrialisation also lent self-confidence to new groups in British society with new attitudes. It enabled moral initiative to be displayed independently of Westminster – and to some extent in criticism of it – by individuals for whom state intervention meant class domination.[22]

Throughout the 1830s and 1840s a debate within the temperance move-ment raged between those whose attack was focused on spirits while advocating moderation elsewhere and those who believed in total absti-nence. But while these approaches gained support among those sections of the working population for whom respectability was an objective, the appeal of temperance and abstinence from alcohol was of more limited appeal for the poor, for whom it still provided temporary escape.

Drug-taking – 'the opium eaters'

The importance and impact of drug-taking across social boundaries throughout the eighteenth and nineteenth centuries has only recently become a subject of serious historical study.[23] Opium or opium compounds were most widely used and, though the main features of addiction and withdrawal had been known since the 1750s, in 1800 doctors and others still thought of opium not as dangerous or threatening but as central to medicine. Until 1868 opium was on open sale and could be bought in any grocer's or druggist's shop. Regular 'opium eaters' were acceptable in their communities and rarely the subject of medical attention. They were certainly not seen as 'sick', deviant or diseased as they were to be by 1900.

In the first half of the nineteenth century opiate use was not generally defined as a 'problem'. Lack of access to orthodox medical care, the suspicion of the medical profession and positive hostility to professional medical treatment ensured the position opium held in popular culture as a major form of self-medication. In reality throughout early nineteenth-century society the medical use of opium for sleeplessness, headache or depression shaded imperceptibly into non-medical or 'recreational' uses.

Opium consumption was particularly high in the Fens in the nineteenth century and, according to an analysis made in 1862, more opium was sold in Cambridgeshire, Lincolnshire and Manchester than in other parts of the country. The Fens were an unhealthy, marshy area, where medical assistance, especially for the poor, was severely limited and where many of the labouring population were prone to ague, rheumatism and neural-gia. The habit was geographically limited to the low-lying areas centring on the Isle of Ely and south Lincolnshire. To some extent high opium consumption may have characterized areas like this: there is evidence, for example, of similar practices in Kent's Romney Marshes. The largest consumers were the labourers who came in from the outlying fens rather than villagers or urban dwellers. It is difficult to say whether there was expanded use of opium and opium preparations after 1800 but the death rate from opium poisoning did increase in rural Lincolnshire from the 1820s and the high general death rate of 22 per thousand living in Spalding in the 1840s was as high as industrial areas like Huddersfield and Keighley.

Why was opium of such importance in the Fens? First, there was a tradition of self-medication with opium being used for animals as well as people. Secondly, the introduction of new methods of exploiting the land resulted in declining standards of child care and an increase in the doping of young babies with opiates. Infant mortality in Wisbech was 206 per thousand in the 1850s, higher than urban centres like Sheffield. The drainage of unpopulated parts of the Fens led to the use of itinerant 'gangs' of both women and children employed by a gang master. Doping young babies was essential as women could be away from home for long periods. Opiates may also have been used to dispose of unwanted children, though this was not peculiar to the Fens. Thirdly, opium was used as an escape from the perceived reduction of status for the agricultural labourer which resulted from enclosure and drainage. Certainly use for euphoric effect was a possibility in the Fens; as Dr. Rayliegh Vicars wrote later in the century: 'their colourless lives are temporarily brightened by the passing dreamland vision afforded them by the baneful poppy'.[24]

Reactions to opium eating in the Fens, with its population apparently able to control and moderate its consumption, was markedly different from the concern expressed about the urban problem. The 'stimulant' use of drugs by the urban labouring population was perceived as a threat to public order in a way which opium eating in the Fens was not. This was indicative of the way in which views of opiate use were coloured by social and class settings. The use of opium for child-doping and the belief in the stimulant use of the drug were both attacked from the 1830s. Behind the campaign against child-doping lay a desire to remould popular culture into a more acceptable form and a critique of the basic pattern of child-rearing by the labouring population. Using opium as a scapegoat led to criticism of its use being diverted from the realities of the social and cultural environment to the individual failings of working mothers. There was also a belief that working people were turning to opium as an alternative stimulant to alcohol: in Elizabeth Gaskell's *Mary Barton*, published in 1848, John Barton falls victim to the drug. A writer in the *Lancet*, which consistently publicized the dangers of opium for the labouring population, wrote in 1815 that

> For those unfortunate creatures who daily resort to this baneful drug as a cheap species of intoxication, I have but little sympathy or commiseration. Their weakness entails a severe punishment even in this world.[25]

The uses of opium by adults and for children in the rest of society went unremarked or were viewed more tolerantly. The use of opium in the early part of the nineteenth century by writers like Thomas De Quincey and Samuel Taylor Coleridge attracted a great deal of attention but popular usage was far more widespread. Though these authors drew attention to the habit and this possibly led to a gradual change towards a harsher, more restrictive response, opium was, for large sections of society, simply part of life, neither exclusively medical nor entirely social.

Conclusions

These three examples of changes in attitudes to popular culture illustrate the importance of pressure, either voluntary or through legislation, to control and modify aspects of popular creation. To those, from all sections of society, who argued for change the issue was one of improving the quality of economic and social life, enhancing 'respectable' attitudes and removing potential tension and disorder. To those affected, improvement attacked what they maintained was their traditional right to enjoy themselves and to escape – if momentarily – from their social conditions.

CULTURAL CHANGE OUTSIDE ENGLAND

Language: cultural and nationalist expression

Finally I intend to examine two examples of the impact of cultural change during the eighteenth and early nineteenth centuries in Wales, Scotland

and Ireland. The first focuses on language as a means both of cultural and nationalist expression, particularly in Wales.[26] Peter Burke argues that

> It was in the late eighteenth and early nineteenth centuries when traditional popular culture was just beginning to disappear, that the 'people' or the 'folk' became a subject of interest to European intellectuals.[27]

Samuel Johnson and James Boswell toured the Western Isles of Scotland, 'to speculate upon the remains of pastoral life . . . [to look for] primitive customs'.

This rediscovery of the past and its culture was, in Wales, an important expression of 'nation'.[28] The eighteenth century witnessed major upsurges in education, religion and culture in Wales in addition to the impact of economic changes. In 1700 Welsh culture was at a low ebb. The seventeenth century had seen the virtual extinction of the bardic order which had nurtured Welsh language, poetry and collective memory. Poetry did not completely disappear but its volume, quality and professionalism was depressingly small. The partial anglicization of many of the country gentry was also a damaging blow to 'Welshness'. Though Defoe commented favourably on their hospitality and willingness to tell him their genealogies, the gentry's concern for language and literature had largely evaporated.

The initiative for cultural revival came mainly from those of 'middling' and educated status. Some were members of the lesser gentry, such as Edward Lhuyd and Rhys Jones, editor of an important collection of medieval Welsh poetry in 1773. Some were in the professions. This applied to all the Morris brothers: Lewis was an agent of the Crown in Wales, Richard a clerk in the Navy Office in London and William a customs officer at Holyhead. Goronwy Owen, perhaps the finest poet of the century, and Moses Williams were clergymen and Iolo Morganwg and William Owen-Pughe were artisans. They did not operate within an intellectual void and had close links with London and, to a lesser extent, Dublin. Whether Gwyn Williams is correct in seeing the new Welsh nation as 'manufactured' in London, it is certain that the first bardic *gorsedd* was held on Primrose Hill and much enthusiasm for antiquarianism was focused on the Welsh societies founded in London – the Cymmrodorion in 1751; Gwyneddigion in 1771 and the Cymreigyddion in 1794. The revival in the early eighteenth century was influenced by the Augustan poets, with their emphasis on neo-classical forms of verse, and led to an urge to seek out early examples of Welsh poetry and classical models drawn from Welsh verse. Later in the century there was a potent infusion of romanticism, an unbounded admiration for the 'primitive' in culture and nationality.

The boundary between myth and fabrication was indistinct in the eighteenth century. Iolo Morganwg wove his own fabrications into genuine discoveries to clinch his argument; he invented Welsh traditions the Welsh had never known. Some of the poems he credited to Dafydd ap Gwilym are as good as any written by the poet himself. As Williams says:

> His very forgeries convey a perception which no one else seems to have been capable of. . . . He had an intuitive grasp of the historical function of Welsh traditions and of their functional utility to the half-starved and often self-despising Welsh of his own day. Welsh poets . . . had been the rib-cage of the body politic, remembrancers, a collective memory honed for historic action. So he invented a gorsedd, a guild of those 'bards' . . . deploying a usable past in order to build an attainable future. . . . [29]

This was particularly evident in the 1760s with the Scot James Macpherson's 'translations' of the reputedly third-century poet Ossian, described by contemporaries as the 'Celtic Homer'. Such was the controversy over whether these were forgeries that in 1797 the Highland Society of Scotland set up a committee to investigate their authenticity; it concluded that Macpherson

> was in use to supply chasms, and to give connection, by inserting passages which he did not find, and to add what he conceived to be dignity and delicacy to the original composition, by striking out passages, by softening incidents, by refining the language . . .

The boundary between reassembling fragments of oral traditions and manuscripts of an early epic and creative editing was difficult to define.

Parallel to the revival in Welshness offered by scholars and mythologists was a vigorous, though narrow, moralistic and serious, alternative culture associated with religion, particularly Dissent and Methodism. It too was in Welsh and used the language more freely and less self-consciously than scholars and nationalists. Its appeal was broader and went across the social spectrum, while the Welsh revival tended to have a more direct appeal to the educated and literate. By the 1830s and 1840s it had produced a culture more vigorous than that of the cultural revival. It was a culture for action where the recovery of the past had been connected with raising the status of the Welsh language, literature and history and only rarely with direct social and political action. The Welsh way of life changed its meaning between 1840 and 1860 away from the notion of 'Wild Wales', primitive, reactionary and rural, to one identified with Nonconformity, radicalism and progress. The ancient past remained but only as a prelude to what really mattered: the risk of Nonconformity and of the common people. Myth was still important and romantic failures like Dic Penderyn, hanged after the Merthyr Rising of 1831, quickly attained mythic status.

Cultural growth in Scotland – an 'enlightenment'

The eighteenth century saw an expansion of cultural activity in Scotland.[30] This 'Scottish Enlightenment' drew upon many different aspects of human knowledge and experience: from philosophy to science, politics to history, literature, art and architecture. Architecture was the one art in the eighteenth century in which Scots provided the most creative minds. Robert Adam and his brothers were the leading exponents of neo-classicism, building elaborately decorated country houses in Derbyshire and Middlesex and urban architecture in London. Civil engineering was dominated by Thomas Telford, son of an Eskdale shepherd, and by the Scottish John Rennie, John Smeaton and Robert and Alan Stevenson.

Scottish imaginative literature achieved its apogee in the poetry of Robert Burns and the novels of Sir Walter Scott but appeared to lead into a cul-de-sac. In poetry the problem was a linguistic one, a consequence of the modification and dilution of Scottish by English. By 1700 Scottish was seen as the language of the poor, the uncouth and the humorous while the landed and professional sections of society used English. Speaking with a Scottish dialect betrayed one's provincial origins and by the 1750s classes on the proper pronunciation of English were widespread. By 1800 there was a triple crisis in Scottish poetry. First, Burns had pushed the use of Scottish dialect to perhaps its most imaginative extreme and it was difficult for other poets to follow him. Secondly, the older Scottish tongue had ceased to develop as a language and was largely incapable of expressing a wide range of both philosophical and emotional ideas. Even Burns seemed to agree with the eighteenth-century conviction that Scottish was unsuitable for serious work and he used English if he wanted to write solemnly. Thirdly, Scottish poets could not yet use English properly. By contrast Gaelic poets like Alexander Macdonald, Duncan ban MacIntyre and Rob Donn were among the finest poets Scotland had produced. In the development of the novel the question of a breakdown in linguistic tradition did not occur on the same scale as with poetry. The novel came to Scotland via England but in the twenty-two novels Scott wrote between 1814 and 1826, particularly those set in the late seventeenth and eighteenth centuries, a nostalgia for Scotland's past was established. He established the historical novel but his contemporaries and successors lacked his qualities and their attempts to write novels about the rural past became more and more irrelevant to industrializing Scotland. That they did not break out of the 'Scott mould' was because historical novels were popular but, as T. C. Smout says,

> Scott deliberately and Burns unwittingly, thus provided the public with the nostalgic stability and sense of nationhood in the past that it sensed it was losing in the present. The result, however, was catastrophic to literature, as it twisted its head back to front – its poetry looking always to Burns and a dead language, in prose to Scott and a past society.[31]

Why was there this cultural Enlightenment in Scotland after 1740? The majority of the major figures were Lowlanders and from the emerging professional and middle classes. The Highlands contributed little to this cultural revival. English was an alien tongue, educational provision was inadequate in that area and social and economic changes after 1770 shattered whatever limited common culture they had. There was considerable patronage from the landed interest. David Hume and Adam Ferguson lived for a time with families of English peers; Adam Smith gave up his chair at Glasgow to become tutor and travelling companion to the Duke of Buccleuch. The character of Scottish education also played a major role. Very few of the cultural pathfinders were self-taught, attending the parish schools and often going on to the grammar school. The universities were innovative in terms of curriculum and teaching; for example, lecturing in Latin ceased in Glasgow in 1730. Finally, the influence of the Presbyterian Kirk was moderate. If it did not always encourage changes at least it did not obstruct them. Cultural development in Scotland was then a consequence of the combination of aspiring and gifted individuals supported by widespread aristocratic patronage and an innovative education system.

CONCLUSIONS

There is much cultural achievement between 1700 and 1850 which has not been considered in this chapter: developments in Ireland; the nature and achievements of Augustan and Romantic poetry; the rise of the novel; the development of drama; artistic and architectural change and British music; the impact of the Enlightenment on British thought and the impact of political philosophy; the development of moral philosophy, utilitarianism and classical economics; and the emergence of historical writing. Cultural change was diverse and its impact often limited to particular sections of society or geographical areas. It was often gradual, building on previous work but, over the decades between 1700 and 1850, this change took on a far more dramatic and potentially 'revolutionary' form.

NOTES

1 Peter Burke 'Revolution in Popular Culture', in R. Porter and M. Teich (eds) *Revolution in History*, Cambridge University Press, 1986, p. 206.
2 R. Williams *Keywords: A Vocabulary of Culture and Society*, Fontana, 1976 pp. 76–7 but see the whole of his discussion pp. 76–82 and his later critique *Culture*, Fontana, 1981. M. Shiach *Discourse on Popular Culture*, Polity, 1989 is illuminating in theoretical terms and in its case studies.
3 B. Bocock *Hegemony*, Tavistock, 1986 provides a useful discussion of the development of the concept.
4 On Gramsci see the brief book by James Joll *Gramsci*, Fontana, 1977 and R. Simon *Gramsci's Political Thought*, Lawrence & Wishart, 1982.

5 Peter Burke op. cit. p. 221.
6 On popular culture in the eighteenth century see R. Porter *English Society in the Eighteenth Century*, Penguin, 1982 especially chapters 4, 6 and 7 for a general discussion. More detailed studies can be found in P. Burke *Popular Culture in Early Modern Europe*, Temple Smith, 1978, J. M. Golby and A. W. Purdue *The Civilization of the Crowd*, Batsford, 1984 and R. W. Malcolmson *Popular Recreation in English Society 1700–1850*, Cambridge University Press, 1973. B. Bushaway *By Rite: Custom, Ceremony and Community in England 1700–1880*, Junction Books, 1982 is excellent on the rural dimension. H. Cunningham *Leisure in the Industrial Revolution*, 1980, questions Malcolmson's thesis that many traditional practices and pastimes disappeared after 1780. For the commercialization of leisure in the eighteenth century see N. McKendrick, J. Brewer and J. H. Plumb *The Birth of a Consumer Society*, Hutchinson, 1982, especially pp. 265–85 and for the nineteenth century P. Bailey *Leisure and Class in Victorian England*, Routledge & Kegan Paul, 1978.
7 P. Burke op. cit.
8 A. Macfarlane *The Origins of English Individualism*, Basil Blackwell, 1978.
9 R. W. Malcolmson op. cit.
10 J. M. Golby and A. W. Purdue op. cit. p. 30.
11 N. McKendrick, J. Brewer and J. H. Plumb op. cit.
12 For a recent discussion see J. Walvin *Victorian Values*, Deutsch, 1987 and the series of articles in *History Today*, February–May 1987, now published, edited by G. Marsden, Longman, 1990. See also E. M. Sigsworth (ed.) *In Search of Victorian Values*, Manchester University Press, 1988 for a valuable collection of papers on what Victorians themselves valued.
13 J. M. Golby and A. W. Purdue op. cit. pp. 68–69.
14 See R. Swift 'Guy Fawkes Celebrations in Victorian Exeter', *History Today*, November 1981.
15 R. Poole 'Lancashire Wakes Week', *History Today*, August 1984.
16 On the debate about public executions and the abolition of capital punishment see D. D. Cooper *The Lesson of the Scaffold*, Allen Lane, 1974.
17 On cruelty to animals see K. Thomas *Man and the Natural World: Changing Attitudes in England 1500–1800*, Penguin, 1984 especially pp. 143–91, M. Ritvo *The Animal Estate*, Penguin, 1990 and B. Harrison 'Animals and the State in Nineteenth-Century England', in his *Peaceable Kingdom: Stability and Change in Modern Britain*, Oxford University Press, 1982, pp. 82–122.
18 K. Thomas op. cit. p. 148.
19 J. M. Golby and A. W. Purdue op. cit. p. 55.
20 The most detailed study is B. Harrison *Drink and the Victorians: The Temperance Question in England 1815–1872*, Faber, 1971.
21 ibid. p. 46.
22 ibid. p. 98.
23 V. Berridge and G. Edwards *Opium and the People: Opiate Use in Nineteenth-Century England*, Yale University Press, 1987, especially chapters 3–9, should be read for what it has to say about the problem now as well as in the past.
24 Quoted ibid. p. 45.
25 ibid. p. 107.
26 On language in this period generally see P. J. Corfield 'From Rank to Class: Innovations in Georgian England', *History Today*, February 1987 and her more detailed paper 'Class by Name and Number in Eighteenth Century Britain', *History Today*, February 1987 and her more detailed paper 'Class by Name and Number in Eighteenth Century Britain', *History* 72 (1987) in which she explored the ways in which people's views of society were reflected in different language use. O. Smith *The Politics of Language 1791–1819*, Oxford University

Press, 1984 examines how ideas about language were used to maintain repression and class division. G. Crossick 'Classes and the Masses in Victorian England', *History Today*, March 1987 takes the argument forward into the nineteenth century.

27 P. Burke op. cit. p. 3.
28 On the relationship between language and nationality see G. Williams *Religion, Language and Nationality in Wales*, University of Wales Press, 1979 and P. Morgan *The Eighteenth Century Renaissance*, Christopher Davies, 1981.
29 G. A. Williams *When Was Wales?*, Penguin, 1985, p. 165.
30 On the Scottish Enlightenment see T. C. Smout *A History of the Scottish People 1560–1830*, Fontana, 1972, pp. 451–83 and B. Lenman *Integration, Enlightenment and Industrialization: Scotland 1746–1832*, Edward Arnold, 1981 for general comments. More detail can be found in A. C. Chitnis *The Scottish Enlightenment: A Social History*, 1976 and J. Rendall *The Origins of the Scottish Enlightenment 1707–1776*, 1979.
31 T. C. Smout op. cit. p. 469.

Index